ANNUAL REVIEW OF ANTHROPOLOGY

VOLUME 12, 1983

BERNARD J. SIEGEL, *Editor*
Stanford University

ALAN R. BEALS, *Associate Editor*
University of California, Riverside

STEPHEN A. TYLER, *Associate Editor*
Rice University

ANNUAL REVIEWS INC.   4139 EL CAMINO WAY   PALO ALTO, CALIFORNIA 94306 USA

ANNUAL REVIEWS INC.
Palo Alto, California, USA

International Standard Serial Number: 0084-6570
International Standard Book Number: 0-8243-1912-5
Library of Congress Catalog Card Number: 72-82136

Typesetting by Kachina Typesetting Inc., Tempe, Arizona; John Olson, President
This volume coordinated by Janis Hoffman

PRINTED AND BOUND IN THE UNITED STATES OF AMERICA

PREFACE

The editors of the *Annual Review of Anthropology* aim to provide a more or less consistent set of chapters in each subfield of anthropology each year, relative to the body of published research, but they are not always able to do so. As an example, for reasons beyond the control of the editors, Volume 11 (1982) was very lean in biological anthropology and archaeology and contained no chapters in anthropological linguistics. Volume 12 not only redresses this imbalance and keeps abreast of specialists' current concerns, but, we trust, will also be of broad interest to nonspecialists as well.

For several years we have sought to persuade George and Louise Spindler to prepare a review of the literature on American culture that we felt could evolve from the very successful course at Stanford which they developed in recent years. Although the Spindlers found it a very time-consuming task, the results are happily in this volume. Given the ever-growing interest among anthropologists in studying American society, we expect to continue publishing reviews in this domain periodically. Obviously there are alternative orientations and theoretical approaches of a problem-defining nature for which the present chapter should be viewed as a useful point of departure.

At the same time, we have sought to extend our coverage of European anthropology, with a chapter on Eastern Europe to complement a general review on Europe as a whole and specialized ones on northern and Mediterranean areas.

Finally, we call attention to our continuing commitment to reviews in various facets of applied anthropology, with another chapter this year in the medical field. To date we have also invited reviews in the anthropology of industry, administration and public policy, education, nutrition, and community development. We intend to keep abreast of continuing work in these areas, and would appreciate hearing from our readers about other felt needs in applied anthropology to which we should attend in the future.

THE EDITORS

Annual Review of Anthropology
Volume 12, 1983

CONTENTS

ARTICLES IN OTHER *ANNUAL REVIEWS* OF INTEREST TO ANTHROPOLOGISTS

(Continued)

S. L. Washburn

Ann. Rev. Anthropol. 1983. 12:1–24

EVOLUTION OF A TEACHER

Sherwood L. Washburn

Department of Anthropology, University of California, Berkeley, California 94720

Anthropology dawned on me as a pleasant surprise. I had never heard of it before going to college, and I only took an introductory course because it was taught by Professor Tozzer. He was my freshman adviser and an old friend of my family. Here was a mixture of biological evolution, archaeology, and cultural anthropology which appealed to me. At that time I had been considering majoring in zoology and, possibly, going to medical school, but I quickly changed the plan to a major in anthropology with the idea of choosing a career later on. I never went back to the earlier plans.

During vacations from school I had done volunteer work in the Harvard Museum of Comparative Zoology for which eventually I was paid 25 cents an hour. This was the depth of the Great Depression, and any pay was appreciated. Although my major was anthropology, friends in the MCZ were very important in my life. Glover Allen, then Curator of Mammals, not only supervised my first job and advised me over many years, but finally served on my oral examinations. I took his course on mammals and wrote my undergraduate honors thesis in his department. Barbara Lawrence, Allen's assistant and later successor, was a great help, guiding me through the problems of classification. The Director of the MCZ, Thomas Barbour, was an encouraging friend, and Harold Coolidge helped me and later included me in his research plans. I stress this network of old friends in the Museum because over a number of years they provided guidance and escape from a number of anthropological errors which were common at that time.

The late E. A. Hooton was my principal professor and his teaching strongly influenced my interests. *Up From the Ape* was the bible for physical anthropologists for a number of years, and that, plus the one-year laboratory course, formed the basis of the physical anthropology program. People have often asked me about Hooton and about the reasons for his success as a teacher. Hooton was enthusiastic, imaginative, and helpful. These qualities, plus his sense of humor, came across very clearly in the introductory course. The

1

advanced laboratory course had only 10 to 12 people, so we got to know Hooton very well. He was an impressive person. I think his students were lucky people. They could not have received a better education in physical anthropology at that time, the 1930s. The great breadth of his interests can be seen in his popular books, or even by just glancing at the table of contents in *Up From the Ape*.

But the 1930s were a time of great change in the study of evolution. Genetics had begun to exert a profound influence on the way scientists looked at evolution, and problems and methods changed radically with the events which led to the synthetic theory. Hooton's research methods, unfortunately, were not compatible with genetics. All of Hooton's major studies depended on the statistical validation of typologies and his advanced teaching was simply incorrect. Hooton thought that he was right and that it was bias, particularly in social science, which led people to reject his views. He stated that his popular books and articles were designed to skip the professionals and reach the intelligent layman. Naturally, he was particularly upset when some of his own students disagreed with his conclusions and the methods on which they were based. Hooton believed that the world's problems were fundamentally biological, and that improvement would only come when the breeding of the biologically inferior was controlled. He considered the environment, but minimized its importance. These views, coupled with the concept of pure races (Nordic, for example) in the 1930s and 40s led to severe criticism, and it was very difficult for many to see that a Hooton student might appreciate his undergraduate teaching, his support of evolutionary studies, and his interest in behavior, but repudiate his concept of race, research methods, and his applications of physical anthropology.

I have always been grateful that my background in the Museum of Comparative Zoology helped me to appreciate the best of Hooton but stay removed from his research methods and some conclusions. The complications of being a Hooton student are well illustrated by my first meeting with Theodosius Dobzhansky. When I dropped in on him at Columbia he asked me if I was not a Hooton student. "Yes," I replied. He then said, "I do not understand the method of finding several racial types in one population." I answered that "I do not believe in types and think that it is populations which should be compared." He beamed, shook my hand, and there began a very pleasant friendship.

My first graduate year was highlighted by courses in comparative anatomy and paleontology with A. S. Romer. The efficiency with which he managed human evolution without biometry impressed me and reinforced an uneasy feeling that there was very little communication among anthropology, paleontology, and zoology. Starting in the summer of 1936, a series of events ensued which laid the background for my scientific career. Harold Coolidge had planned an expedition to Thailand to make collections for the Museum of Comparative Zoology. Several people were involved, but as far as I was concerned, the principals were A. H. Schultz to collect primates and C. R. Carpenter to study primate behavior. In both cases gibbons were the main objectives, and Coolidge invited me to assist Schultz and Carpenter. Needless to say, I was eager to go and a Sheldon Traveling Fellowship made it possible to accept. But the participants were not meeting until 1937 in Singapore, and I had six months in the summer and fall which were spent studying human anatomy at Michigan and Oxford. As it worked out, the plan could not have been better.

At Michigan the medical anatomy class met at 8 in the morning for a lecture and then worked in the laboratory until 5 in the afternoon. The work was traditional and intensive with excellent laboratory assistants. One of them, W. T. Dempster, was very interested in locomotion and the work of some of the German anatomists. He explained to me how the body works, and showed me how it was necessary to combine an understanding of the joints with the lengths of the bones to produce the functional system. Here was the key to the limitations of biometry—no joints—but also the way to relate it to a vastly broader functional anatomy. Laboratory teaching basically gives the time for what amounts to individual tutorials, and Dempster checked the dissections and then showed how the meaning of what was seen depended on a broad understanding, a philosophy of anatomy.

After the summer at Michigan I went to Oxford as a special student for the fall quarter. LeGros Clark's lectures were superb. He combined the information usually taught in several different courses and gave elegant lectures which were polished essays. He liked to take long walks on weekends, discussing whatever was on his mind. He asked me to accompany him on some, and we had many discussions on these and over tea. He saw evolution as changes in patterns, and he believed that much of the confusion in the study of human evolution came from reliance on isolated "facts." The patterns came from experience and intuition, and Clark never made it clear how one knows where a pattern begins and ends. It was the intuitive element that left Clark's evolutionary conclusions open to Zuckerman's attacks. A medical student and I helped in one of Zuckerman's endocrine projects, and Zuckerman gave me monkey material to dissect. This enabled me to make comparisons with the humans in the laboratory, but overwhelmingly the most important part of my few weeks at Oxford was becoming acquainted with the personality and lectures of LeGros Clark.

After Oxford I spent a month in Ceylon making a small collection for the MCZ, then on to Singapore where Coolidge's expedition was gathering. In a few weeks we were all camped on a mountain in northern Thailand. Coolidge's plans were excellent and the hunters he had hired and local people brought in gibbons almost daily. Schultz would measure and record any point of special interest. My job, preparation of the skeletons, enabled me to spend almost every day dissecting, and gave me the great opportunity of having unlimited, unembalmed material to study. Every day was a seminar with Schultz, supplemented by applying Dempster's ideas and LeGros Clark's notion on the importance of patterns. I worked very rapidly, stressing one part on one gibbon and a different area on another. Monkeys were not at all common in the vicinity, but a few were collected, and I could compare them with the gibbons. How human the gibbons appeared! In point after point human and gibbons were basically the same and very different from the monkeys. My experience was essentially the same as that of Sir Arthur Keith, and the conclusions were the same.

Carpenter found that it was impossible to study behavior from the same camp used for the collecting. He moved to an area some miles away where gibbons were even more abundant. I spent a few weeks making observations for Carpenter. The gibbons, hanging-feeding, walking bipedally on big limbs and swinging under smaller ones, and diving from one tree to the next gave a vivid view of their anatomy in action. It also contrasted with the quadrupedal monkeys progressing through the same tree. The social behavior of the gibbons, each group consisting of a female-male pair and their young, contrasted with the much larger groups of langurs and macaques in the same area. In a very short time Carpenter had collected the information for his monograph on gibbon behavior. Excellent visibility at the end of the dry season, the number of gibbons, and the simplicity of the social group all worked together so that the information for a major work could be collected in a short period of time.

Collections for the MCZ were completed in May and Coolidge, Schultz and I headed back to Singapore and then on to Borneo. It took a week from Singapore to Borneo, and the freight boat stopped nearly every day. The weather was beautiful and I spent my time on the deck reading Conrad's *Victory*. We stopped at many of the ports described in the book, and I found, much to my surprise, that the descriptions which I had assumed to be imaginative were almost photographic. British North Borneo was the last of the chartered companies, and one could still buy stock in it (although we were strongly advised not to do so). Coolidge had made arrangements for transportation to Abai on the Kinabatangan River. We brought materials with us and a small house was constructed in three days. The area was rich in primates. Every morning two or three hunters would leave at sunrise and return with three or four specimens by midmorning. Then Schultz would measure them and make notes. The notes were illustrated with pen and ink drawings of remarkable quality. He drew rapidly and beautifully, many of the figures in the notes being suitable for publication without alteration.

The work at Abai was much more intense than the earlier collecting in

Thailand. Most of the time Schultz and I were the only scientists there, and we worked all day every day. I skinned and dissected specimens and supervised the local helpers who cleaned skeletons. The routine in the camp was always the same, but the hunters brought in proboscis monkeys, orangutans, two kinds of macaques and three kinds of leaf monkeys. The opportunities for study were amazing, far more than I could fully utilize. We talked about almost nothing but anthropology. Adolph informed me on the problems of the field, and urged me to stick to problems of biometry, growth, and variation. I soon found that he had little interest in muscles, joints, or behavior. The remarkable variety of specimens gave me the opportunity of seeing what a master did superlatively well. It also made vivid the limitations of anthropometry.

Most unfortunately, Harold Coolidge had been ill, and so he could not take part in the Borneo collecting as he had planned. He did come to the Abai camp briefly and approved the collections soon to be headed for the MCZ. His approval was a relief to me because I thought that he might have wanted more general collecting rather than the emphasis on primates.

Schultz was very considerate of me, suggesting that there were plenty of problems with the small monkeys for a thesis for me while he wrote on the gibbons, orangutans, and proboscis monkeys. He was never critical, even when I grew a beard. Only when I shaved it off he remarked, "It is a great improvement." Adolph left camp a few weeks before I did. This had been planned all along, but it did come shortly after we had run out of gin. I'll never forget Adolph raising a glass of warm coconut milk and the last of the gin and saying, "Sherry, the best drink in the world is Drambuie!"

On arrival back in the USA I received a telegram asking me to be the teaching assistant in Professor Tozzer's introductory course. I was delighted, even though there were seven sections and a short quiz every week. One hundred and forty papers to correct! The teaching convinced me that that was what I wanted to do, and I found I learned far more teaching than I had as a student. One session I took the class to see the exhibits in the Museum of Comparative Zoology. I knew every one of those stuffed primates, and ended my demonstration saying that they did not have to remember them all but should get an idea of the variation. I heard a Radcliffe woman comment, "They all look just the same to me!" No truer words were ever spoken.

Finally the crates with all the Asiatic Primate Expedition specimens arrived. Each skeleton had to be cleaned. After a few tests Gabriel Lasker and I set up an assembly line for the macerations. At one time we had over 90 skeletons in various stages of preparation. The cleaning was routine and Lasker and I discussed anthropology constantly. He helped me to understand why the genetics of populations replaced typology, and the nature of Boas's contributions to biometry.

Lasker's experiences in China and his interests in genetics and migration ideally supplemented my background, and he clearly saw the social importance of anthropology. Our long discussions were an important part of my education, and helped later on in planning the Viking Fund summer seminars on physical anthropology.

In the fall of 1938, Dr. Hooton asked me to teach a course on primates. It was to be a joint course, but Hooton was very busy and turned the whole course over to me. Hooton and Coolidge came to all the lectures, and we used specimens from the MCZ. I stressed that all the major families of primates could be seen as adaptive radiations, but Hooton was sure that the families should be defined by nonadaptive characters. This was an issue we never settled. It has been reopened by the neutral theory and by evidence that changes at the molecular level occur at surprisingly constant rates.

S. R. Detwiler offered me a job in anatomy in his department at Columbia. It sounded fascinating, especially when Dr. Detwiler said the job would pay $2400. "Are you married?" he asked. "Yes." "Then I'll make it 25." What a contrast with all the searches and mechanics of hiring today! A recommendation from Dr. Wislocki of the Harvard Medical School, a word from Dr. Hooton, and Detwiler was free to act as he chose.

The Harvard years had been fun and useful, but I had a feeling that what I had been taught was already out of date. Surely anthropometry was much too limited a technique for functional or evolutionary problems. In thinking back (always a risky business), I discovered that the three books which influenced me most were Bridgman's *Logic of Modern Physics,* Ogden and Richards' *The Meaning of Meaning,* and Malinowski's *Argonauts of the Western Pacific."* Bridgman's operationalism gave clear guides to the relations of technique to analysis. Ogden and Richards helped one to see the nature of words and avoid at least some of the most common errors. Malinowski read like a great novel, after courses in which little was stressed beyond descriptions and distribution.

Today none of these have the impact they did many years ago. Times have changed but the basic issues have not. Biometry was designed to describe bones and its exclusive use brings the limitations of death to the study of the living. Words must stand for clearly defined referents. Human behavior cannot be reduced to trait lists.

The Columbia Medical School was a complete change from anything I had known before. The research on all sides convinced me that what I had learned was mostly out of date. The head of the anatomy department, Dr. Detwiler, was doing fascinating experiments on amphibian embryos. I asked him about the relation of the orbit and the eye. He replied, "Let's find out." So he put the eye of a large form into the developing orbit of a much smaller form. The eye displaced the orbital structures, making an orbit 140% of normal. What was to become hard bone was greatly influenced by the soft tissue, and I remembered LeGros Clark's remark that bone was, next to the blood, the most plastic tissue in the body. I wrote a paper, applying the results of the experiment to anthropological problems. Of course, it was turned down by the American Journal of Physical Anthropology. After some correspondence and considerable revision, it was accepted—but I had learned my lesson. Anyone trying to use experimental methods in anthropology was going to have a hard time.

At the time I thought that the basic issue was simple. I still think it is! The form of the traditional question in comparative anatomy or physical anthropology is: describe with words and measurement, compare and draw conclusions. Little attention is paid to what is being compared or to a discussion of the conclusions. While there was no doubt in Detwiler's study that the large species of salamanders had larger orbits, one could not tell how much this was the result of the form of the skull or how much the form of the skull was adapting to the size of the eyes. The experiments showed that the developing eyes were very important in determining the form of the orbit. Generalizing from this one case, the traditional form of comparisons was: describe, compare, and speculate. The modified form is: choose what is to be compared on the basis of some clearly defined important problem; compare; speculate; then devise experiments to determine the probability of the speculations. The main research effort should be in the experimental analysis.

Over the next few years at Columbia, I devised a series of experiments designed to help in understanding the factors which influence the form of the mammalian skull. Newborn rats are exceedingly immature and are readily available and inexpensive to maintain. I learned to operate through very small incisions using a dissecting microscope. The role of individual muscles, nerves, and bones was investigated, and it soon became apparent that the experiments revealed anatomical patterns. For example, removal of the temporal muscle altered the mandible, occlusion, temporal line, and nuchal crest. But these were described in different chapters of the standard anatomy textbooks. The results did not lend themselves to description, either bone by bone or area by area. The growth in a suture was not characteristic of a bone, but depended on the particular suture as well as on the adjacent bones and muscles. Early closure of the sagittal suture in human beings makes the skull grow long and changes the length, breadth, and height of the skull. In cases which cause extreme deformation, the neurosurgeon opens the suture by operation and the skull then returns to normal form.

The diagram gives a first approximation of the relatively independent areas of the jaw (Figure 1). It can be seen at once that the chin is the result of the core bone projecting farther forward than the tooth-supporting bone. This condition is characteristic of modern humans.

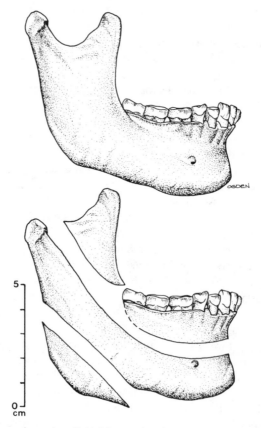

Figure 1 The human lower jaw divided into some of its principal parts. These may vary remarkably independently. The basis for defining the parts depends on: experiments, growth, comparisons, and pathology.

In people living on soft foods that do not cause wear on the teeth, the upper incisors bite over the lower ones and act like an orthodontist's band. This makes the chin more prominent. Male hormone stimulates the growth of the basic core bone and so accentuates the chin. The chin then is the result of a number of factors, including culture through the preparation of food. For the purposes of research, one must study the nature of face and jaw, not the chin.

Changes in form and function during growth frequently provide information closely paralleling what is obtained from experiments. Figure 2 shows the skull of a young baboon compared to that of an adult. Note that not only has the face grown larger, but it has changed in fundamental ways. The buttress of bone between the cheek bone and the tooth-supporting bone is above the first molar tooth in the juvenile and behind the third molar in the adult. As the face grows

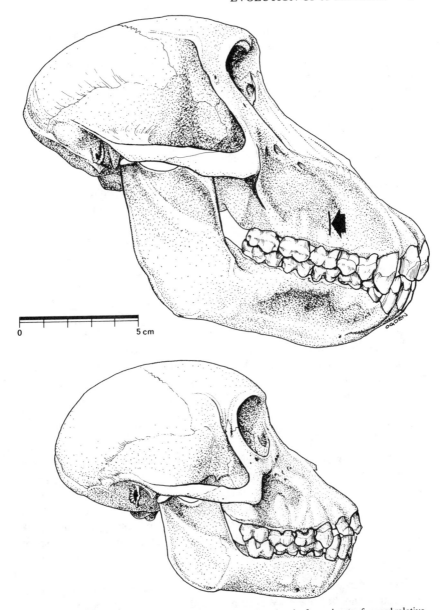

0   5 cm

Figure 2   Skulls of adult female and juvenile baboons. Note that the face migrates forward relative to the cheek bones. The cheek bone is over the first permanent molar in the juvenile and behind the third in the adult. The line and arrow mark where the cheek bone was when the adult was a juvenile. The canine fossa is full of developing teeth in the juvenile and becomes large in the adult. The same is the case for the mandibular fossa which is not present at all in the juvenile. There are no fixed points but only patterns of changing relations.

the relation of cheek bone and teeth changes from before first molar to after third molar, a distance of more than 5 centimeters.

In growth one sees not only the changing relations but sees that they are related to changes in the face. In classification or the study of fossils, the relation of the buttress to a tooth is often taken as a "fact," something to use in classification, not as a symptom, something to be understood in terms of the pattern of growth of the face.

Also, the juvenile has a very small canine fossa, while the adult has a very large one, as shown in the figure. The fossa is caused by an area of very thin bone being surrounded by the buttress, alveolar bone, and thick bone, as noted in the figure. Presence or absence of a fossa is not an independent fact but the result of the relations of the main parts of the face. In the juvenile the developing teeth fill the area which will become thin bone later on.

The same principle may be seen in the lower jaw. In the juvenile the developing teeth fill the mandible. As they erupt and the tooth-supporting bone is separated from the core bone along the base of the mandible, the outer table of bone is resorbed and a fossa appears.

To generalize the situation, almost all the traditional anthropological measurements and observations are composite. Biometry is a science of symptoms, not of the biological factors that lie behind the symptoms and cause them.

All the measurements are composite, suitable for description but not analysis. For example, reduction in the size of the canine tooth may change the shape of the palate, of the jaw, of the nose, of muscles and their bony origins. If the reduction of the tooth is the result of aggressive behavior being based on tools rather than teeth, then much of the evolution of the human face is the result of culture.

This may seem obvious and it was not new, but the implications are profound. The words and measurements used in the study of human evolution are useful for preliminary description but not for analysis. The logic of traditional physical anthropology is: describe with words and measurements, compare, and draw conclusions. The operations are so simple that anyone can learn them in a few hours, and no knowledge of modern biology is required. A different way of looking at the situation is that the descriptions result in a set of problems and the problems must be analyzed before the conclusions are very useful.

These issues are so obvious today that the reader may have difficulty seeing how important they were. Weidenreich's descriptions of Peking man, for example, have been recognized as probably the most useful descriptions of fossil humans. This is fortunate because the originals are lost. Yet the lower jaws, teeth, and skull were described in different monographs. This not only leads to a very large amount of repetition, but makes it difficult to determine the morphological patterns. Weidenreich was exceedingly generous with the fossils in his possession. I remember visiting him at the American Museum. The skull of Java man was on the table and Weidenreich said, "Pick it up. Pick it up. It is the original!" I will never forget Weidenreich at the Physical Anthropology annual meeting receiving the first Viking Fund medal for physical anthropology. Krogman was president at the time and he towered over Weidenreich as he presented the medal and check. With tears pouring down his cheeks, Weidenreich said, "It is not the medal. It is not the money. It is that you have made me welcome."

I saw Weidenreich a number of times at the American Museum of Natural History, and he was always eager to discuss the fossils. He asked about what I was doing, and I explained the experimental work. "But," he said, "what have rats to do with anthropology?" It seemed obvious to me that they play the same role they do in medical research. They help in solving problems, and the solutions help human beings. Just as fruit flies helped in laying a basis for human genetics, so experimental anatomy can lay a basis for understanding human form.

During the war years the Army sent groups of surgeons for special training. The anatomy department gave quick reviews to plastic and orthopedic, neuro- and maxillo-facial surgeons. The courses were intensive, and the content was adjusted to each group of specialists. In addition, the Army sent the first-year medical students to Columbia at the beginning of the summer, although the regular medical courses did not start until fall. Anatomy was offered in the summer, and this gave me the opportunity of altering the course. One of the main problems with anatomy as taught at Michigan or Oxford was that one area was dissected in detail before its functions could be appreciated. For example, the plexus of nerves that go from the spinal cord to the arms was studied in detail before the arms were studied. In the summer, when changes were possible, arms and legs were dissected at the same time, one side superficially and the other in depth. Then the orthopedic anatomy of the whole being was demonstrated and discussed.

New York is a remarkable city because of its range of resources. For someone like myself, employed in an anatomy department, there was also the American Museum and evening meetings of the Ethnological Society and the anthropology section of the New York Academy of Sciences. Even more important, from my point of view, was the Viking Fund (later the Wenner-Gren Foundation for Anthropological Research). Paul Fejos, an M.D., was the founder and director. He asked me to come to his office and explain my research. I brought the skull of a rat whose parietal bone had been removed on day 2 and had then lived for some two months. I showed the skull to Dr. Fejos, explained the operation and the reasons for some experiments in anthropology. His immediate reaction was, "It is magic. How much will it cost to finish the experiment?" "Eighteen hundred dollars," I replied. "Ask for it, ask for it," he said.

Paul Fejos was a dramatic person. He enjoyed the new. When he heard of Carbon 14 he flew to Chicago, discussed the technique with Willard Libby, and arranged for a grant of $25,000. That was the way he enjoyed operating. He saw the importance of encouraging the new in physical anthropology and partially supported the summer seminars in physical anthropology. He encouraged me, on many occasions invited me to the Foundation, and sent me on my first trip to Africa.

Fejos was very interested in international anthropology and took advantage of the Foundation's tenth anniversary to promote a major conference. The 52 papers were published in a volume nearly 1000 pages long. This conference was a major success, giving the Foundation an assured position in the world of anthropology. Fejos, typically, was not satisfied with the conference; he had hoped it might lead to more suggestions of change. Alfred Kroeber, who was president of the congress, pointed out that anthropology was small enough so that most of the major parts could be represented at the meeting. Today the profession is some ten times as large and much more diversified. The conference marked the end of an era, a time in which anthropologists could know most other anthropologists. Kroeber asked me to chair the final dinner, and I remember looking over the room and seeing that I knew the majority of people who were there. Many were friends who had helped me with my career.

In the summers of 1946, '47, and '48, seminars for physical anthropologists were held at the New York headquarters of the Viking Fund. As secretary of the American Association of Physical Anthropologists, it seemed to me that the profession was handicapped by being too small, too restricted in interests, and too conservative. Also, it had been greatly disrupted by the war. Fejos aided the seminars and courses were arranged at Columbia to help in the financing. Gabriel Lasker founded the *Yearbook* to expand the possibilities of publication, and the *Yearbook* carried accounts of the seminars. The second seminar had 34 participants, and 69 people attended at least some of the sessions. I think the seminars performed a very useful function in accelerating progress in physical anthropology. With the aid of the *Yearbook,* the seminars certainly provided a greatly expanded vision of the scope of the field and of the diversity of problems and techniques.

For some years Fejos planned dinners at the Foundation for groups of anthropologists. There was a talk and discussion, and this enabled him and the staff of the Foundation to sample anthropology in an effective, first-hand way. Most of the dinners centered around an anthropological specialty, and the guests too were specialists in the same area. Fejos invited me to many of the dinners, and this was a major factor in my keeping up to date in anthropology although employed in anatomy.

The American Anthropological Association had no requirements for membership except the dues. There were many interested members who were not trained, and Julian Steward thought that the AAA should be reorganized with the professional business being managed by a new class of fellows who were to have professional qualifications. The rapid expansion of anthropology after the war made some changes necessary, but there were strong differences of opinion as to what they should be. Ralph Linton, then president of the Association, appointed a committee of nine to draw up a plan for change and present it to the Association at the annual meeting at Chicago in 1946. It was a very interesting committee, and, as the youngest member, I was fascinated to hear the views of Julian Steward, Ralph Linton, Pete Murdock, Dunc Strong, and many others.

It was lucky that I had paid very close attention to the discussions because less than an hour before the business meeting was to start Murdock came to me and said that the committee had decided that I was to present their recommendations. After recovering from my surprise, I asked for the report. Murdock replied, "Actually there isn't one—but you have a way of putting things." So I made a few notes and then addressed the business meeting, stating the main arguments for change. Fortunately, the motion passed, but I have rarely felt so on the spot as I did presenting a nonexistent report to a highly critical audience.

Later the same day Sol Tax told me that Bill Krogman was leaving Chicago and going to Pennsylvania and that I was being considered as a possible replacement. I had very mixed feelings because the experiments I had under way at Columbia needed about two years for completion, but good jobs in physical anthropology were rare and the Chicago department was one of the best. The formal offer included the promise of space in the anatomy department, and this made it ideal from my point of view.

The anthropology department at Chicago was a powerful institution. Fred Eggan, Bob Redfield, and Sol Tax formed the core, old friends who had been highly influenced by A. R. Radcliffe-Brown. The British tradition of social anthropology was reinforced by visitors such as I. A. Schapera, Raymond Firth, Meyer Fortes, E. E. Evans-Pritchard and others. Departmental meetings were held in a small room at the faculty club. They were mostly general discussion; business was disposed of quickly. Particularly when a visitor was present, the business lunches were more like seminars than business meetings. Shortly before I went to Chicago the curriculum had been revised. It then consisted of a three-quarter introduction to ethnology, organized by Eggan, a three-quarter introduction to social anthropology, organized by Tax, and a three-quarter introduction to human evolution and archeology, organized by Bob Braidwood. Much of the teaching was joint and there were frequent visitors. I think that the department functioned as smoothly as it did because there was a very high level of understanding among the members.

Redfield inspired many students. As one student remarked, "It was not just the way he said it, it was what he said too." Redfield thought in typologies, ideal types. These were clear and were used to make important general points.

But the link between the type and the ethnological fact was a subjective leap. Exciting as this mode of thought was, it provided no guide for research, and this, in my opinion, is why so few students finished graduate programs under Redfield's guidance. Eggan not only commanded a remarkable number of ethnological facts, but illustrated how data and theory are interrelated and how this guides research. Tax always had students involved in some project, frequently close to the university. His desire to involve native Americans in applied projects led students to understand the practical problems from the native point of view. The combination of ideal type, action anthropology, and Philippine ethnology, plus the heritage of Radcliffe-Brown and the social anthropology visitors, made a rich and challenging program.

The most interesting part of Braidwood's course was on the origins of agriculture and the Near East. The origins of civilization was treated with the aid of visitors from the Oriental Institute. In retrospect, the most important aspect of the course was the joint teaching, discussion, and having visitors. Almost inevitably, the content of the course was modified from year to year far more than if it had been taught by any one person. The biases of Robert Maynard Hutchins' educational reforms exerted a strong influence on the anthropology program and courses. It was quite impossible to be a physical anthropologist in the traditional sense. As the years went by, my part of the course stressed behavior more and structure less.

The department and teaching were very satisfactory, but the anatomy department had withdrawn its offer of space for research, and the space finally assigned to physical anthropology was most unsatisfactory. Over the years, several students made heroic efforts to maintain our experimental animals. The principal research was on the growth of the skull as shown by intravital dyes.

In the spring of 1948 I went to South Africa and Uganda, a trip planned with Dr. Fejos and supported by the Viking Fund. In Johannesburg I called on Professor Raymond Dart. He was most cordial, welcoming me to his laboratory and showing me his specimens. A paper was on his desk and he complained bitterly that it had just been turned down. He reminisced about how he had always had problems getting his ideas published. I urged him to send the paper to the *American Journal of Physical Anthropology*. Dale Stewart had recently become editor, and I know that he was short of papers. Dart's paper was accepted, and this started a long series of papers, not only from Dart, but from other South African scientists.

Dart drove me over to Pretoria on the occasion when Robert Broom was to receive his Commemorative Volume. Typically, Broom gave the major speech himself. He remarked, after mentioning many of the troubles he had had, that "God was on my side, or at least I was on the side of God." Days later, I visited Broom's laboratory and saw the remarkable specimens. The pelvis and vertebrae of *Australopithecus* were still largely in the rock. On the shelves were numerous specimens, the best collection of the man-apes at that time.

Broom took great pleasure in showing the specimens and discussing his problems. A geologist walked past the door of the lab, and Broom's voice boomed out, "There goes my worst enemy. Do you have enemies like that?" He showed me a skull bone which was indented, probably by a blow, and added, "That wouldn't surprise you coming from Chicago, would it?" Broom was a remarkable old man, energetic, difficult, and a great collector. He revived the search for fossil man in South Africa which had been stalled for some years.

In South Africa I spent my time in museums in Johannesburg, Kimberley, and Cape Town. Then I flew to Uganda. In Kampala I stayed with Alexander Galloway, Dean of the Makerere Medical School. Galloway was interested in my research on monkeys and helped in obtaining animals, assistants, and working space. I collected data on the relations of muscle size to behavior and skull form, and devised a method of preparing the skeletons which took less than half of the time spent on previous collections.

At that time Uganda was a beautiful peaceful country. In the game reserves one got images of what it must have been like before the expansion of human populations. We went from Butiaba to Murchison Falls by boat. For hours hippos were constantly in sight and there were great crocodiles on the banks. At the falls we disembarked and walked around to the top. There the whole Nile dashed through a gap only 14 feet wide. In the trees watered by the spray were black and white colobus. Elephants browsed leisurely a few hundred yards away. One could see the great importance of big game for human hunters.

The time in Africa had been varied, rich, and rewarding. I had seen australopithecine fossils, studied Bush and Bantu skeletons, collected monkeys, and met fascinating people. But on my way back to Chicago, as I pondered the diversified experiences, I realized that I needed a much more explicitly stated point of view to bring it all together. At the time I looked to the biological sciences and Malinowski's social anthropology for a synthetic theory. I now see, following Misia Landau's ideas, that what I was really doing was trying to assemble information for making a consistent story of human evolution and supporting it with facts wherever possible.

The factual side of the story of human evolution was brought together in a major symposium, organized by Th. Dobzhansky with some help from me. The Cold Spring Harbor Symposium of 1950 was designed to bring genetics into a working relationship with physical anthropology. At that time physical anthropology was still such a small field that most of the major American scientists were participants.

Of the 18 anthropologists presenting papers, 11 were students of the late E. A. Hooton. This gives a measure of his influence, and although one of the main purposes of the conference was to stress the importance of thinking in terms of populations, typology continued to be used by a number of the participants. Population vs type was probably too fundamental an issue to be discussed usefully in a public meeting. Three of the contributors—Dobzhansky, Ernst Mayr, and George Simpson—made, and have continued to make, contributions which have exerted major influences on the study of human evolution.

A Pan African Congress was held in Livingstone in 1955. This was organized by J. Desmond Clark, and the papers and discussions showed that he was the leader in the study of African prehistory. Raymond Dart exhibited a collection of bones, illustrating the osteo-donto-keratic culture. Louis Leakey remarked of them, "Just ordinary veldt bone." One of the reasons for regarding the bones as the product of hunters was that the distribution of the kinds of bones was not random. A few weeks later I collected bones in the Wankie Game Reserve and found that the kinds of bones on the surface were not randomly preserved, but the frequencies agreed with the ones exhibited by Dart. Some bones are preserved much more frequently than others, and for middle-size game, preservation appeared to be a function of edibility. Ribs and other easily eaten parts go first, jaws and teeth last. Here was an explanation of the preservation of fossil primates. It is not just that teeth are hard; teeth and jaws are the least edible parts of the animal.

After the Congress, with Desmond Clark's help, I arranged for a small collection of baboons. But much more importantly, as it turned out, there were troops of baboons close to the Victoria Falls Hotel where I was staying.

The supply of baboons was irregular, and I spent any extra time watching the local troops. This was so much more rewarding that I closed out the collecting and spent my time watching the tame baboons. The troop next to the hotel must have been the tamest in Africa; one could walk between the animals. The next troop would let one come·close, but not between troop members. The third troop out would not permit a close approach. Almost at once the animals ceased to be just baboons; they became personalities. There was only one large dominant male. He got the best of everything. Later he was displaced by a much younger male from the next troop. I did not see the fight, but the wounds were apparent the next day, and the new dominant male was constantly making the old one move. There was no doubt of the change of power. The local people threw rocks at the baboons, and the animals could judge the necessary escape distance precisely. I never saw one get hit, even when stealing mangoes from the hotel garden.

In order to see baboons under much more natural conditions, I made a trip to the Wankie Game Reserve. Along with marvelous views of buffalo, eland, and lions, there were numerous troops of baboons. I was impressed by how each troop seemed to be an independent social system. One day I was watching a mixed group of impala and baboons when three cheetahs came along. The impala and baboons looked at the cheetahs as they approached, but showed no signs of fear. Suddenly one big male baboon started toward the cheetahs and gave a warning bark. The cheetahs turned and trotted off. This demonstrated that one function of the troop was protection, and the ease with which one baboon drove off three large carnivores, and the fact that the impala knew they were in no danger as long as they were with the baboons, was very impressive. The functions of the troop could be observed, and Malinowski's functional theory probably works more usefully for monkey than for human beings. Language adds a new dimension and complicates everything. Radcliffe-Brown's analogies are quite unnecessary when studying nonhuman primates.

The 1955 trip had been most rewarding in learning about prehistory, distributions of bones, baboon anatomy, and behavior. Thinking over the experiences, I realized that a much more behavioral approach to human evolution would be useful. Emphasis on behavior was a necessary consequence of the synthetic theory of evolution. The opportunity for considering a fundamental change in emphasis in my thinking came in 1956–57 at the Center for Advanced Study in the Behavioral Sciences. During that year we ran a seminar which interested about half of the Fellows, a little more than 20 people, who represented numerous social sciences and biology. Uniquely, at least in my experience, everyone seemed interested in new ideas, and everyone was free from the normal pressures of academic life. The seminar was the kind of activity the director, Ralph Tyler, had hoped might take place, and it certainly marked a high point in my academic experiences.

In January, David Hamburg arrived at the Center and became a major contributor to the seminar. Hamburg was interested in evolution and the primates and eventually was an important spokesman in explaining these topics to the medical profession. He contributed his strong interest in learning and emotions.

Theodore McCown invited me to lunch at Berkeley, and there we discussed evolution and the problems of teaching physical anthropology. After a time McCown said that the department at Berkeley was considering adding a second physical anthropologist and asked me whom I recommended. I said, "Me." He said, "Will you come if we make the offer?" "Yes." In retrospect, I think that there was a variety of reasons for wanting to leave Chicago. The decision could be explained in terms of climate, the chance to keep monkeys, the opportunity of having my own introductory course (after being in other people's courses for 19 years). But I think the main reason was just that I had been at Chicago for 11 years and the time at the Center had made me see the need for change.

Irven DeVore and his family spent the year 1958–59 studying baboons as a part of our Ford Foundation-financed project on primate behavior and human evolution. I, together with my wife Henrietta and younger son Stanley, joined them in the summer. Irv had been studying the baboons in the Nairobi Park and introduced us to the tamest troop and showed us the social system. After the animals had been studied for some months, Irv used small amounts of food to work out the hierarchy. If a bit of food was tossed between two or three animals, one would take it. With careful application this simple method let one see which animal was dominant. My bias is that after several months in which the animals are disturbed as little as possible, experiments are necessary to make sure the social system is analyzed correctly. We saw baboons catch and eat hares, but found that meat formed a very small part of their diet. The compact nature of the troop was an especially interesting feature. A year was not an adequate amount of time to understand the baboon troop. In the short run it seemed independent and inbred, but longer studies have shown that males generally leave the troop when three or four years old.

After a few weeks in Nairobi, we went to the Amboseli Game reserve. Here were much larger troops of baboons than in the Nairobi Park, and they had been far less disturbed. These troops varied in size from a little over a dozen to nearly 200. Animals with broken limbs or animals carrying dead infants were not rare. Injured animals made every effort to keep up with the troop, and this reinforced our feelings from Victoria Falls and Nairobi that baboons are very social; fearing the dangers of separation, they make every effort to stay with the troop.

Amboseli, with its elephants, rhinos, and numerous ungulates, was an exciting place. On an average day, watching baboons mostly near waterholes, we would see some 1500 head of game. It was not unusual to see gazelle, impala, giraffe, zebra, elephant, rhino, warthog, and baboons all at the same time. The animals usually paid no attention to each other or to us. The human idea of "wild" is the result of hunting disturbing the animals. It is likely that until our ancestors became hunters, they were of as little interest to other animals as those around the waterholes.

We paid particular attention to kills, both to see the distribution of the bones and to see how much might be left over for a primate. Scavenging has been much discussed in the literature as a possible stage in human evolution, but actually the carnivores eat most of the animal, and the kill is a dangerous place until they have left. While carnivores can and do scavenge, scavenging is an unpredictable source of food. A minimum of hunting would provide an early human with more food than could be obtained by scavenging. The primary killers (lions, leopards, cheetahs, hyenas) are rare compared to the primates. It was estimated that there were some 40 lions and 400 baboons in Nairobi Park. Except under most unusual circumstances, most groups of primates will only rarely be near a kill.

We returned to Nairobi, and DeVore directed some motion pictures on baboon behavior. Later the movie won a prize, and it has been available for more than 20 years.

The 1960s were a very busy time. There was great scientific progress and political turmoil. I was elected president of the American Anthropological Association, and it is hard to believe now how calm the academic scene was in 1962. The executive board looked for indications of needed changes but found no discontent. At one meeting a resolution on race was discussed. In an effort to make the resolution accurate, it became more and more qualified until Steve Boggs, the executive secretary, said, "If that is the board's resolution, I resign as of now." This shocked the board and there was keen discussion, but it was not heading for a solution. Joe Casagrande suddenly turned to me and said, "Sherry, you can get us out of this." "How?" "If you give your presidential address on race, we will accept that as the board's position." So that is how I happened to talk on race rather than on primate behavior.

Field studies on primate behavior expanded rapidly in the late 1950s and 1960s. In marked contrast to a decade earlier, there were plenty of studies, so an assessment seemed in order. Dave Hamburg and I, with the aid of Ralph Tyler and Preston Cutler, organized a meeting and a year-long study group for the Center for Advanced Study in the Behavioral Sciences. The purpose of this project was to produce a book. The result was *Primate Behavior,* edited by Irven DeVore, published in 1965. The 18 chapters included papers on the behaviors of monkeys, apes, and the implications of the field studies. The group at the Center was enthusiastic, and there was a strong feeling that a useful first step had been taken and the next few years would see the establishment of a science of primatology. In reality, the expansion in terms of scientists, societies, and journals has been far greater than any at the Center expected.

Paul Fejos regarded American anthropology as being much too provincial. To overcome this difficulty, he thought that the Foundation should have an international center where conferences could be held. With this in mind, he purchased a castle, Burg Wartenstein, located a few miles south of Vienna. Fejos asked me to help in the organization of a conference on the "Social Life of Early Man," and in 1961 the results were published in a volume of the same name. Primate studies were included, especially through the contributions of Ernest Caspari, DeVore, and Hamburg. A much more integrated conference followed on "Classification and Human Evolution," and this was published in 1963. Evolution was treated as the guiding principle, uniting classification, structure, behavior, and psychology. At the conference there was enough agreement for useful discussion and enough disagreement to keep the session lively. No conference with Louis Leakey and Bill Straus could be dull! Before the end, Leakey had challenged Mayr's views on classification, and Anne Roe and George Simpson had stationed themselves one on each side of Straus to limit his contributions. The main unresolved conflict was between Morris Goodman and Emile Zuckerkandl, stressing the importance of molecular anthropology, and the more traditional but no less important views of Simpson and Mayr.

Paul Fejos died in 1963. As director of the Wenner-Gren Foundation, he had been remarkably successful, supporting many new developments such as Carbon 14. He was one of the most imaginative and creative people I have ever known, and his death brought a great sense of personal loss. His wife, Lita Osmundsen, succeeded him as director, and she has continued many of his policies down to the present.

One of the first conferences at Burg Wartenstein under Osmundsen's direction was on primate behavior. This was organized by Phyllis Jay (now Dolhinow) and the results published in 1968. The 19 papers formed a useful introduction to what was then known about primate behavior and its implications for the understanding of human evolution. Primate studies were now moving so rapidly that Dolhinow published a second edited volume in 1972. The influence of the 1962–63 year at the Center for Advanced Study of the Behavioral Sciences remained strong.

In the fall of 1964 many Berkeley students refused to obey the university regulations controlling activities both on and off the campus. Students occupied the administration building and were arrested. Many students struck, and there was a long series of demonstrations. That fall there were some 1200 students in the introductory physical anthropology course, and all of the teaching assistants in that course went on strike. There was confusion at every level. The university was not prepared for violent action, and a small part of the student body eagerly promoted violence at every opportunity. I spent a considerable amount of time listening to the speeches and watching the riots. I learned two things almost at once. The university had been trying to treat the situation as local, but the issues were national—the civil rights movement and the threat of the draft. The issues could not be settled locally, so the efforts of both students and administration were largely beside the point. The apparent chaos of the riots was actually highly structured.

In Berkeley most students live away from campus. They will assemble at noon and listen to speeches. If enough is going on, a march may then take place. But if the crowd loses interest, there will be no riot. At Stanford, by contrast, students mostly live on campus and the activity is after dinner, a time of peace at Berkeley.

During those Berkeley riots, when the police were called on to control the students as they advanced, most students would retreat. But there were some who seized tear gas canisters and threw them back at the police. Other students would shake their hands or clap them on the back, and they received immediate public acclaim for their actions. In this way the crowd has a life of its own with great rewards which have nothing to do with the reasons for the strike. Burton Benedict and I watched several of the student-police confrontations. It was clear what the reward was—the crowd's recognition of personal risk and aggressive courage. In almost no time the protection of free speech became a very rough game which intensified feelings but did nothing to solve the issues.

The first phase of the strike ended with students going back to classes. Jane Lancaster told me that the teaching assistants and other students were expecting me to discuss the situation, not just continue with the course. I tried to give a speech showing the interrelations of biology and social science in understanding the situation on the Berkeley campus. It was the most difficult talk I ever gave and it was greeted with a standing ovation. Lancaster, my liaison with the teaching assistants throughout the strike, reported success. For my own part, I realized the possibility of a much more useful relationship between behavior, bones, and baboons. The strike had shaken me out of my academic rut, and my introductions to human evolution were never quite the same again.

In spite of the political unrest, the anthropology department at Berkeley expanded rapidly in the 1960s. Frank Beach had started a center for the study of animal behavior, so when Phyllis Dolhinow joined the department in 1966, she had a place to keep live monkeys. The animals constituted the basis for the teaching and research. When her students went to the field they were trained in methods of observation and were familiar with monkeys. It was a great improvement over what I had been able to do before.

Since the Wenner-Gren conference on classification in 1962, I had been looking for someone in molecular anthropology. The main contributors to the field were not anthropologists, but we were fortunate to be able to employ Vincent Sarich, an anthropologist who had trained in Allan Wilson's biochemical laboratory at Berkeley.

Ted McCown died in 1969. For many years he had done all the teaching in physical anthropology. He had strongly supported the expansion and diversification of the program. After a careful search, Clark Howell was appointed to continue the work in paleoanthropology. But the program in human evolution depended on much more than physical anthropology. We received strong support from other departments, and from Desmond Clark and Glynn Isaac in archeology. I note that my most frequent luncheon companions have been Burton Benedict, Elizabeth Colson, and George Foster—all social anthropologists. I audited the graduate introduction to social anthropology on several occasions, and Benedict and I have done considerable joint teaching. He has been a great help in evaluating the possible contributions of the primate studies to social science.

In looking back over this manuscript, I see that I have omitted the best organized symposium I ever attended—*Behavior and Evolution,* the volume edited by Anne Roe and George Simpson, 1958. Also, the Ciba Foundation conference on aggression and my Huxley lecture might be mentioned. But these events which influenced me so much were only important because they led to constant modifications in teaching. Over the years I supervised some 40 doctoral programs, and the students did their research in a wide variety of techniques. I think that all of the thesis committees had members from other departments. There were no fixed course requirements for the advanced work; everyone got some exposure to anatomy, paleontology, genetics, and some behavioral science. Much of the best education came from the discussions among the students. My role was to open up the subject of human evolution at an elementary level and then encourage students to pursue their own kinds of anthropology.

After all, physical anthropology is not defined by a technique as it once was, but is given cohesion by its goals, the understanding of human evolution. At an elementary level such understanding might well be a part of everyone's education. But the evidence for human evolution has become much more complex. This means that there are many different kinds of anthropologies and this trend to increasing specialization will itself increase. This situation is by no means confined to anthropology; it is a fundamental problem in modern science. It is intensified in anthropology because the technical aspects of human evolution relate differently to archeology, linguistics, and social anthropology.

I retired in 1979. Looking back over 50 years of studying human evolution I have a feeling of satisfaction. The number of physical anthropologists has increased tenfold, from a little over 100 scientists to well over 1000. Fifty years ago few departments had one physical anthropologist. Now many departments have several, allowing for diversification in problems and techniques.

Over the last few years there have been major changes in biology. In general these have been resisted in anthropology. As I see the matter, the relations between the contemporary mammals may be more accurately assessed by molecular methods (analysis of DNA, order of amino acids in proteins, immunology, electrophoresis) than by the traditional anatomical methods. After 100 years of study, scientists could not agree whether humans were closely related to the African apes, or even if there had been an ape-like form in human ancestry.

Molecular biology settles this problem (Figure 3). Humans are very closely related to the African apes and much less closely related to the Asiatic apes. Paleontology and comparative anatomy tell about the events of the past (when humans evolved large brains, for example), but these methods were unable to produce agreement among scientists.

The usual course on human evolution starts with the events of time long past. But that is where knowledge is least certain. Molecular biology has not only brought new techniques, but also the interest and competence of far more scientists than are directly involved in the study of human evolution. If I were offering a course on human evolution today, I would start with now, what is

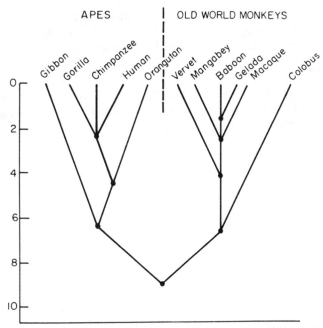

Figure 3   A single set of determinations of relationships by the method of DNA hybridization effectively settles the debates over the position of humans among the primates. The conclusions are supported by immunology and other molecular methods. The whole history of human evolution would have been very different if modern methods had been available. Today we should be going with the new and not repeating the errors of the past. [From Raoul Benveniste and George J. Todaro, "Evolution of Type C Viral Genes: Evidence for an Asian Origin of Man," *Nature* 261 (1976).]

known of the molecular biology, behavior, and experimental biology of contemporary forms. Then I would go back to the fossils, seeing the variety and the order of events of the past.

Suggesting a course of this nature is just a teacher's way of saying that the balance of methods and conclusions which give meaning to the study of evolution have changed, and changed radically. The techniques which give the basis for the study of evolution now include the molecular methods as well as the traditional ones. The synthetic theory of the 1940s is now being modified by the discovery of vast amounts of variation, stochastic factors, and the neutral theory. The view of evolution as necessarily gradual is being modified to an unknown extent by the theory of the punctate origin of species.

Teachers of human evolution have been immersed in the past. The problems, methods, and theories have all been continuations of the nineteenth century. But starting in the 1960s, a new approach to human evolution became possible.

Time and relationships could both be accurately measured. This combination offers a new setting for the interpretation of the fossils, for the study of behavior, and for a new attempt to understand the meaning of human evolution.

ACKNOWLEDGEMENTS

The writing of this article was supported by the University of California faculty research funds. I wish to thank Mrs. Alice Davis for editorial assistance on this and many other manuscripts.

Ann. Rev. Anthropol. 1983. 12:25-48

THE STONE AGE PREHISTORY OF SOUTHERN AFRICA

Richard G. Klein

Department of Anthropology, University of Chicago, Chicago, Illinois 60637

INTRODUCTION

For more than three decades, between 1924 and 1959, our knowledge of the australopithecine phase of human evolution came entirely from southern Africa. In addition, southern Africa has a longer tradition of stone age studies than any other part of the continent. It was in fact on southern African materials that A. J. H. Goodwin based his now classic definition of Early, Middle, and Late Stone Age culture-stratigraphic stages (29).

However, in recent years, both specialists and lay persons have looked increasingly to East Africa for basic insights into human origins and subsequent evolution. The reason is that, beginning at Olduvai Gorge in 1959, East Africa has been the scene of repeated and often spectacular discoveries of australopithecine and other early hominid fossils, and also of very early traces of human behavior. Unlike southern African sites, East African ones often contain volcanic extrusives from which the absolute ages of associated fossils and archeological finds may be estimated. As much or more than the actual discoveries, this has placed East Africa centerstage, while moving southern Africa to the sidelines.

Yet paleoanthropological research has continued vigorously in southern Africa, and even today the southern African australopithecine sample remains larger than that from East Africa. Equally important, beginning in the mid-1960s, intensive, multidisciplinary research on the later phases of human evolution in southern Africa has led to some unique discoveries of potential global significance. Perhaps chief among these is the possibility that anatomically modern people (*Homo sapiens sapiens*) appeared in southern Africa earlier than anywhere else in the world. In addition, there is some unparalleled evidence for Stone Age human ecology, including evidence for evolution in

25

0084–6570/83/1015-0025$02.00

human ability to exploit animal resources. The purpose of this paper is to outline the Stone Age prehistory of southern Africa, with special emphasis on those aspects that are of more than local interest.

THE EARLIEST EVIDENCE FOR CULTURAL BEHAVIOR

In East Africa, Olduvai Gorge, Omo (Shungura), Koobi Fora, Melka Kunturé, Chesowanja, and Gadeb have provided stone artifacts that are almost certainly between 2.1 and 1.6 million years old (36). Often lumped in the Oldowan Industrial Complex, the artifact assemblages consist variously of crude flakes or of flakes and elementary core tools on pebbles or angular fragments. The appearance of the Oldowan Complex coincides closely with the appearance in the fossil record of the robust australopithecine, *A. boisei,* and of the earliest human species, *Homo habilis,* both about 2 million years ago. It is generally assumed that *H. habilis* was the tool maker, though only theory excludes *A. boisei* from this role. The fact that Oldowan tools occur in distinct concentrations, along with fragmentary animal bones that probably represent food debris, shows that by two million years ago, *H. habilis* and possibly *A. boisei* had developed the typically human habit of accumulating refuse at repeatedly visited camp sites.

Still earlier stone tools, perhaps only slightly younger than 2.9–2.7 million years, have recently been reported from Kada Gona in the Hadar region of Ethiopia (75, 91). There are no hominid fossils in stratigraphic association, but if the age of the tools has been correctly assessed, they were probably made by an australopithecine, perhaps one descended from *Australopithiecus afarensis* and directly ancestral to *Homo habilis.* Whatever the case, with the well-documented Oldowan assemblages dated to between 2.1 and 1.6 million years ago, the Kada Gona artifacts mark the beginning of the Early Stone Age in Africa.

In southern Africa, the principal sites at which evidence for early artifact manufacture could be expected are the five South African australopithecine caves—Taung in the northern Cape Province; Sterkfontein, Swartkrans, and Kromdraai in the central Transvaal; and Makapansgat in the northern Transvaal (Figure 1). Taung unfortunately was destroyed before it could be investigated systematically for traces of early hominid behavior, but there is a long history of paleoanthropological research at the Transvaal caves.

Recent research has shown that the Transvaal caves are stratigraphically more complex than was originally thought (3, 6, 8, 63, 64, 89). Faunal studies, aided by geomagnetic polarity determinations, now permit reasonably secure correlations between the various stratigraphic units and radiometrically dated units in East Africa (59, 88, 94).

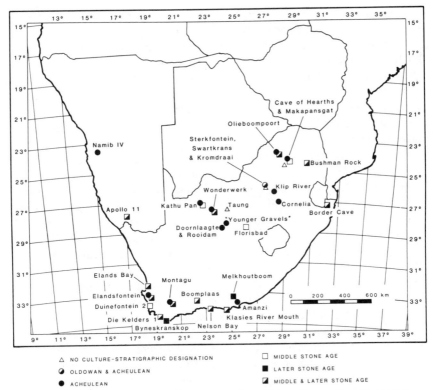

Figure 1 Approximate locations of important southern African sites mentioned in the text.

It is now clear that the deposits that contain *Australopithecus africanus* at Makapansgat and Sterkfontein are between 2 and 3 million years old, that is, broadly contemporaneous with the deposits that provided the very ancient Kada Gona artifacts. Yet there are no unequivocal stone artifacts in association with *A. africanus* at either Transvaal site. Additionally, Raymond Dart's now famous claim that the Makapansgat australopithecines manufactured bone, tooth, and horn ("osteodontokeratic") tools is far from compelling (3).

Sterkfontein, Swartkrans, and Kromdraai all contain substantial deposits that are probably between 1.5 and 2 million years old, when Oldowan artifacts were being widely manufactured in East Africa. At Kromdraai, these deposits have provided remains of *Australopithecus robustus,* but no certain artifacts. However, stone artifacts have been found at both Sterkfontein and Swartkrans, where they are associated stratigraphically with early *Homo* (at both sites) and *A. robustus* (at Swartkrans). The total number of implements involved is small, and some may be derived from yet younger deposits present at both sites.

Typologically, the artifacts are broadly comparable to ones found at like-aged Oldowan sites in East Africa (87).

Microscopic examination of some Oldowan tools from Koobi Fora in northern Kenya has revealed that they were variously used for cutting meat and grass stems or reeds and for scraping and sawing wood (39). Marks made by Oldowan stone tools have also been found on animal bones at Koobi Fora and Olduvai (4, 66). It therefore seems certain that Oldowan people in East Africa ate meat, though its importance in their diet remains undetermined and perhaps indeterminate. It is also unknown whether meat was obtained mainly by hunting or by scavenging. Some scavenging is probably implied by bones on which stone tool cut marks overlie carnivore tooth marks.

With the exception of stone tool marks on a single antelope bone from Sterkfontein (3), there is still no evidence that Oldowan people ate meat in southern Africa. Additional evidence may be very slow to come forth, insofar as the bones at the two putative Oldowan sites (Swartkrans and Sterkfontein) were probably accumulated primarily by carnivores rather than by people. Bone accumulation mainly by carnivores might also explain the rarity of artifacts in the 2–1.5 million year old deposits of Sterkfontein and Swartkrans and their absence in like-aged deposits at Kromdraai and in the pre-2 million year old deposits of Sterkfontein and Makapansgat (3, 53).

More generally, there is the problem that Makapansgat, Sterkfontein, Swartkrans, and Kromdraai were all deep underground caverns into which bones and other objects either fell or were washed. The objects were then commonly cemented into a hard limey rock ("breccia") which cannot be excavated by the fastidious archeological techniques that have been used to document very early hominid behavior in East Africa. In sum, barring the discovery of new sites in more favorable geomorphic circumstances, it seems likely that southern Africa will always trail East Africa as a source of information about the earliest tool makers.

THE ACHEULEAN INDUSTRIAL COMPLEX

The kinds of bifacial stone artifacts that archeologists conventionally call handaxes and cleavers first appeared in East Africa about 1.6–1.5 million years ago (35). By definition they mark the emergence of the Acheulean Industrial Complex, undoubtedly out of the preceding Oldowan Complex. Together, the Oldowan and Acheulean Complexes comprise the Early Stone Age.

There is broad correspondence between the appearance of Acheulean artifact assemblages and the emergence of *Homo erectus* in East Africa, also about 1.5 million years ago. Although the robust australopithecine *A. boisei* probably lingered on, perhaps to as recently as one million years ago, *Homo erectus* was almost certainly the maker of the earliest Acheulean tools.

It is uncertain how long the Acheulean persisted in East Africa, but potassium/argon dates from Gademotta in Ethiopia indicate that the succeeding Middle Stone Age was in place by 180,000 years ago (92). Assuming that the latest Acheulean is only slightly older than this, the Acheulean as a whole spanned much more than one million years. The rate of artifactual change during this long time span appears to have been remarkably slow (35). However, there is a tendency for later handaxes to be more refined than earlier ones, as well as a tendency for later assemblages to contain a greater variety of recognizable tool types.

There are relatively few hominid fossils associated with Acheulean artifacts in East Africa. Earlier Acheulean assemblages apparently were made by *Homo erectus*, represented mainly by various fossils from Beds II and IV at Olduvai Gorge (71). Later Acheulean assemblages were manufactured by archaic *Homo sapiens*, represented by the Bodo skull from Ethiopia (17, 38) and the Lake Ndutu skull from northern Tanzania (16, 61). The morphology of the archaic *H. sapiens* skulls points to derivation from *H. erectus*, but the timing (?500,000–400,000 B.P.) and nature of the speciation event remain unestablished (73). If speciation occurred rapidly, following the punctuationalist model, there is no evidence yet that it was accompanied by a quantum change in artifact manufacture or in any other aspect of human behavior. There is a similar lack of evidence for significant cultural change accompanying the emergence of *Homo sapiens* in Europe.

Both *Homo erectus* and the Acheulean Industrial Complex may have appeared in southern Africa as early as they did in East Africa. The same deposits that have provided abundant remains of *A. robustus* at Swartkrans have provided an incomplete cranium and other fragmentary fossils that may derive from 1.5 million year old *H. erectus*. Alternatively, they may come from *Homo habilis*. (74). Some fragmentary hominid fossils from Sterkfontein, probably dating to between 2.0 and 1.5 million years ago, are similarly problematic from a taxonomic point of view.

Acheulean artifacts definitely occur at both Swartkrans and Sterkfontein, and some may be as old as 1.5 million years. However, those whose stratigraphic provenience or faunal associations are well documented are probably much younger than this (3). On typological grounds, Acheulean assemblages from the 10 m terrace of the Klip River [a tributary of the Vaal (57)] may be as old as any in Africa, but there is no independent geologic/paleontologic evidence to support this. At other Acheulean sites in southern Africa, the geologic/paleontologic context either suggests a relatively recent date or permits no age estimate at all.

As in East Africa, the Acheulean in southern Africa seems to have ended more than 180,000 years ago (8, 9, 82; see also below). Although direct evidence is lacking, on analogy with East Africa, it seems likely that *Homo erectus* manufactured earlier Acheulean artifacts in southern Africa. Later ones were made by archaic *Homo sapiens*, represented particularly clearly by the "Saldanha skull" associated with later Acheulean artifacts at Elandsfontein (= Saldanha = Hopefield) in the southwestern Cape Province of South Africa (67, 74, 79, 80).

The Saldanha skull is similar to the archaic *H. sapiens* skulls from Bodo and Lake Ndutu in East Africa and especially to the remarkably complete cranium of "Rhodesian Man" from Broken Hill (Kabwe) in Zambia. The artifactual associations of the Broken Hill cranium are uncertain (15), but associated faunal remains suggest a geologic age comparable to that of the Elandsfontein skull and far in excess of the 40,000 B.P. date that has often been assumed (e.g. 19). There is a good possibility that the Broken Hill skull belonged to a person who made late Acheulean artifacts.

Most Acheulean sites in southern Africa are surface occurrences that are impossible to date. Even important sealed sites such as those at Amanzi Springs (21) and Doornlaagte (5, 58) are almost impossible to place in time, except on potentially circular typological grounds. The problem is that most sites lack faunal remains and materials suitable for radiometric dating. The only radiometrically dated Acheulean occurrence is at Rooidam, where uranium series dates on lacustrine limestones indicate that a typologically very late Acheulean is somewhat older than 174,000 years (82).

At Montagu Cave (40), Wonderwerk Cave (54; P. B. Beaumont, unpublished), the Cave of Hearths (57), Olieboompoort Cave (57), Kathu Pan (P. B. Beaumont, unpublished), and Kalambo Falls (14), Acheulean artifacts are stratified directly below those from the Middle Stone Age. In each case, this may be taken to imply a very late age for the Acheulean, but caution is advisable, because there is the possibility of a substantial hiatus between the Acheulean and Middle Stone Age occupations at each site.

Bones have not been preserved at most southern African Acheulean sites. Faunal remains that are sufficient to aid in age determination are known only from the Vaal "Younger Gravels" (18, 32, 33), Elandsfontein (34, 44, 81), Cornelia (11), Kathu Pan (P. B. Beaumont and R. G. Klein, unpublished), and Namib IV (78). The faunas may be used to "date" the Acheulean occurrences with respect to Olduvai Bed IV with an assumed age of 0.8–0.6 million years (31).

There has never been a carefully controlled excavation of a fossiliferous Acheulean site on the Vaal. The composite faunal assemblage which is presently available from the "Younger Gravels" implies that some Acheulean occurrences may be older, some younger, and some equivalent in age to Bed IV. At Cornelia, a fauna essentially similar to that of Bed IV overlies Acheulean artifacts. At Elandsfontein, Acheulean tools are probably mainly coeval with a somewhat later fauna, largely postdating Bed IV. The clearest faunal evidence for a post-Bed IV Acheulean comes from Kathu Pan and Namib IV where the artifacts are associated with a very advanced form of *Elephas recki*.

As a group, southern African Acheulean assemblages are remarkably similar to those from East Africa, or for that matter to ones from North Africa and Europe. As in East Africa, Acheulean assemblages in southern Africa changed through time—later ones tend to contain more refined handaxes and a wider variety of recognizable tool types—but the pace of change appears to have been agonizingly slow. Overall, the Acheulean seems to have been characterized by remarkable cultural homogeneity and conservatism through space and time.

Besides artifactual changes, it appears there were also changes through time in the numbers and locations of Acheulean sites in southern Africa. Later sites are much more numerous than earlier ones, while only later sites occur in the drier, western half of the subcontinent (22). This implies both population increase and the development of means to cope with more arid environments.

To date, very little is known about Acheulean settlement and subsistence systems in southern Africa. Acheulean sites appear to be more closely tied to water sources than are later sites [particularly those from the Later Stone Age (22)]. This may indicate that unlike later people, Acheuleans did not possess impermeable water containers.

It is generally assumed that Acheulean populations obtained a significant portion of their food from hunting. Traditionally, the bones associated with Acheulean artifacts at sites such as Elandsfontein and Kathu Pan have been interpreted as Acheulean butchering debris. If this is so, southern African Acheuleans were formidable hunters, because the most common animals at Elandsfontein and Kathu Pan are elephants, rhinoceroses, buffalos, and other large ungulates.

However, at both sites there is a problem common to perhaps all other open-air Acheulean sites, not just in southern Africa, but also in East Africa, North Africa, and Europe. Acheulean artifacts clearly imply the presence of Acheulean people, while bones apparently bashed or cut by stone tools demonstrate some degree of human involvement with the large ungulates, or at least with their bones. However, bones with tooth marks indicate that large carnivores were also involved to some extent. The problem is perhaps particularly acute at Elandsfontein where carnivore-gnawed bones and hyena coprolites substantially outnumber cut bones and stone artifacts. The possibility arises that most of the animals represented at open-air sites like Elandsfontein and Kathu Pan were killed by carnivores or died naturally near ancient water sources. The concentration of artifacts at such sites may simply reflect the fact that people were also attracted to the water sources, without demonstrating that they regularly killed or even scavenged large ungulates there.

In order to evaluate Acheulean hunting proficiency, a minimal requirement is a site where it is reasonably certain that people were the primary bone accumulators. Some of the caves that Acheulean people occupied in southern Africa might qualify, but none of them have provided enough bones for meaningful analysis. No Acheulean cave sites are known in East Africa, while faunal remains from pertinent European caves have not been analyzed from this perspective. For the moment, perhaps the most secure basis for assessing Acheulean hunting effectiveness derives from the study of their Middle Stone Age successors, discussed below. If it is fair to project backwards from the Middle Stone Age, Acheulean people were probably very ineffective hunters.

The animal bones at Acheulean sites in both southern and East Africa commonly belong to species such as Reck's elephant (*Elephas recki*), a giant gelada baboon (*Theropithecus oswaldi*), a large roan-like antelope (*Hippotragus gigas*), and a large bushpig-like suid (*Kolpochoerus olduvaiensis*) that are unknown in faunas from Middle Stone Age and later sites (49). This raises the possibility that their extinction resulted from Acheulean "overkill," as suggested by Martin (55, 56). This interesting hypothesis would be easier to evaluate if it were possible to obtain secure information on Acheulean hunting abilities, and if it could be shown that the extinct species disappeared more or less simultaneously at the end of the Acheulean. For now, difficulties in dating Acheulean sites in both southern and East Africa allow for the possibility that the species disappeared gradually during the long Acheulean time span as environments changed and competitors evolved and flourished.

THE MIDDLE STONE AGE

The time when the Middle Stone Age began is difficult to determine. The limited number of radiocarbon dates that were available in Africa prior to 1970 suggested that the Acheulean had persisted until 60–40,000 years ago and that the Middle Stone Age then spanned the interval between 40,000–30,000 and 10,000 B. P. (13). It is now realized that the Acheulean radiocarbon dates were simply minimum values, while the large number of radiocarbon dates that became available in the 1970s show that even the youngest Middle Stone Age is probably older than 40–30,000 B.P. This is true in both southern Africa (2, 12, 24, 42, 62, 81, 86, 90, 93) and in East Africa (60, 85).

In southern Africa there are several Middle Stone Age sites that clearly date from the earlier part of the Last Glacial or from the Last Interglacial. The most important of these sites are the Klasies River Mouth Caves (81), where a combination of geologic, geochemical, and faunal evidence shows that the Middle Stone Age was firmly installed from the very beginning of the Last Interglacial (= deep-sea oxygen-isotope stage 5), approximately 127,000 years ago. Geomorphic/sedimentologic studies at Duinefontein 2 (K. W. Butzer, unpublished), Elands Bay Cave (7), and especially at Bushman Rock Shelter and Border Cave (9) suggest the Middle Stone Age was already in place during the span of deep-sea oxygen-isotope stage 6, between 195,000 and 127,000 years ago.

An age of 195,000 years (or more) for the earliest Middle Stone Age in southern Africa is consistent with the previously cited potassium/argon dates from Gademotta (Ethiopia), indicating that the Middle Stone Age there began more than 180,000 years ago. There are also Middle Stone Age artifacts from Laetoli in northern Tanzania where the geological context implies an age of up to 150,000 years (20).

In sum, evidence from both southern and eastern Africa indicates the Middle Stone Age spanned the interval between perhaps 200,000–180,000 years ago and 40,000–30,000 years ago. The exact dates may ultimately turn out to depend on the place.

In both southern and eastern Africa, the principal factor that differentiates Middle Stone Age assemblages from preceding late Acheulean ones is the absence of large bifacial tools (handaxes and cleavers). Although this difference from the Acheulean is striking, its behavioral significance is obscure, in large part because we know so little about how ancient stone artifacts were used. On-going studies designed to infer use from wear traces may one day tell us what Acheuleans did with handaxes that Middle Stone Age people did with other tools or didn't do at all.

Middle Stone Age assemblages are dominated by flakes and blades that tend to be well made and that are sometimes retouched into sidescrapers, points, denticulates, notches, backed elements, and other formal tool types. Typologically, the assemblages vary more in time and space than do Acheulean ones, but it is still true that assemblages separated by thousands of kilometers or thousands of years tend to differ not so much in the presence or absence of specific types as in their relative abundance (87). In many instances, the differences are probably caused by variation in the extent to which the same activities were carried on at different sites or to differences in the quality of rock types available for working. Overall, Middle Stone Age artifact assemblages suggest relatively little cultural differentiation in either time or space.

Lumps of baked clay associated with Oldowan artifacts at Chesowanja, Kenya, may reflect human control of fire more than 1.4 million years ago (30, 37). Elsewhere, secure evidence for fire is much younger, the oldest site perhaps being Choukoutien (north China) with a putative age of 0.5 million years. Except for Chesowanja, the oldest unequivocal evidence for use of fire in Africa comes from the Middle Stone Age. Fossil hearths, in the form of lenses of ash and charcoal, have been found at virtually every well-excavated Middle Stone Age site.

There is considerable uncertainty about the physical identity of Middle Stone Age people, mainly because very few human remains have been recovered in Middle Stone Age contexts. This contrasts strikingly with the relative abundance of Neanderthal remains from contemporaneous Mousterian sites in Europe. Undoubtedly the difference partly reflects the greater number of Mousterian sites that have been excavated, which in turn partly reflects the greater number of professional archeologists in Europe. However, it is also important that the Neanderthals sometimes buried their dead in the limestone caves they occupied. The graves helped to protect the skeletons from disarticulation and destruction by scavengers, such as hyenas and wolves, while the limey matrix preserved the bones from chemical dissolution. Frost-fracturing of cave ceilings and walls during glacial intervals insured a rapid buildup of deposit into which relatively deep graves could be dug.

In Africa, frost-fracturing was limited or absent in most caves occupied by Middle Stone Age people, and in general, the rate of sediment accumulation was very slow. As a result, Middle Stone Age graves may often have been very shallow, so that buried bodies were easily exhumed by hyenas and other scavengers. Additionally, most Middle Stone Age caves are in rock types other than limestone that do not favor the preservation of bones. At most sites, not only human remains, but bones of any kind are lacking.

These facts may help to explain why to date not a single well-documented Middle Stone Age burial has been found. At most Middle Stone Age sites where bone is preserved, such as the Klasies River Mouth Caves (81) and Die Kelders Cave 1 (43, 76) in the southern Cape Province of South Africa, human bones are either absent or highly fragmentary. Such sites obviously tell us little about the physical type of Middle Stone Age people.

At those sites where relatively complete human fossils have been found, there is the problem of demonstrating genuine Middle Stone Age associations. Perhaps the most prominent site in this category is Border Cave in northern Natal Province, South Africa (1, 2, 9). Fossils of four different individuals from this site suggest that its Middle Stone Age occupants were completely modern in appearance, more than 90,000 years ago, perhaps making them the oldest known representatives of *Homo sapiens sapiens* in the world (70, 72). However, two of the critical fossils were excavated by "guano" diggers who did not record their stratigraphic associations, while the remaining two may come from post-Middle Stone Age graves that were intrusive into the Middle Stone Age layers. This is suggested by a strong contrast in state of preservation between the human bones and animal bones that occur in the same levels. Unlike the animal bones which are poorly preserved and highly fragmented as a result of substantial postdepositional leaching and profile compaction, the human bones are relatively well preserved and complete.

The Border Cave evidence that at least some Middle Stone Age people were anatomically modern is perhaps supported by the handful of human fossils from the Middle Stone Age layers of the Klasies River Mouth Caves. None of the fossils possesses clearly archaic features (72). Particularly notable is a fragment of modern-looking frontal bone with a geologically inferred age of greater than 95,000 years. The Klasies evidence would be more compelling if the fossils were more complete and more numerous.

A much more complete fossil suggesting anatomical modernity for Middle Stone Age people is the anatomically modern skull known as Omo I from the Kibish Formation in the Lower Omo River Valley of southwestern Ethiopia (51). Middle Stone Age artifacts were associated (10), while geologic context and associated radiocarbon dates indicate Omo I is much older than 35,000 years. An age between 150,000 and 100,000 years ago is probable.

An unresolved problem in assessing the significance of the Omo I skull is the Omo II skull, believed to come from the same geological horizon and with the same probable age and cultural associations. Unlike the Omo I skull, it exhibits numerous archaic features, and there is general agreement that it represents an archaic (vs modern) variety of *Homo sapiens*. It seems unlikely that Omo I and Omo II could have belonged to the same population, and their apparent contemporaneity remains a paleoanthropological enigma.

Probable Middle Stone Age human remains from elsewhere are more uniformly archaic in appearance. This applies to a fragmentary skull from the Florisbad spring mound in the Orange Free State of South Africa, which resembles Omo II in important respects (69, 72). The Florisbad skull came from poorly controlled excavations, but was probably associated with Middle Stone Age artifacts. Recently obtained radiocarbon dates indicate it is older than 42,000 years, while its geologic context suggests an age in excess of 150,000 years (8). A much more complete skull recently found in the Ngaloba Beds at Laetoli in Tanzania clearly represents a distinct variety of *Homo sapiens* (20). Artifacts of "Middle Stone Age affinity" were found nearby, and the deposits have an estimated age of 120,000 ± 30,000 years. A broadly similar archaic *H. sapiens* skull is known from the Jebel Irhoud cave site in Atlantic Morocco (27, 28). No artifacts were found with it, but a fragment of a second, apparently similar skull from the same site was associated with artifacts that have been called Mousterian and that could as well have been called Middle Stone Age.

The archaic *H. sapiens* populations represented by the Florisbad, Ngaloba, and Jebel Irhoud skulls probably evolved from yet earlier *H. sapiens* populations represented by skulls like those from Saldanha, Broken Hill, Bodo, and Lake Ndutu. Neither Florisbad, Ngaloba, nor Jebel Irhoud closely resembles the broadly contemporaneous Neanderthals (*Homo sapiens neanderthalensis*) of Europe and the Near East (84), and it seems increasingly unlikely that Neanderthals in the narrow sense ever lived in Africa. It is possible that one or more of the populations represented by Florisbad, Ngaloba, and Jebel Irhoud evolved into modern *H. sapiens sapiens,* perhaps through the population represented by the Omo skulls, and that this happened while Neanderthals still occupied both Europe and the Near East. However, such a thesis is far from established.

In sum, from the limited evidence that is available, it can be argued that Middle Stone Age people were anatomically archaic or perhaps both archaic and modern, depending upon the time and place. Many new fossil discoveries from well-controlled and well-dated contexts will be necessary to determine which alternative is more likely.

THE LATER STONE AGE

The artifact assemblages that succeed Middle Stone Age assemblages in Africa are commonly grouped as Later Stone Age. Radiocarbon dates from both eastern and southern Africa indicate that the Later Stone Age began 40–30,000 years ago, the precise time perhaps depending upon the place. Thus, dates from Border Cave in Natal indicate the Later Stone Age was underway there at least 38,000 years ago (2), while dates from Boomplaas Cave in the southern Cape Province of South Africa suggest a more recent beginning of perhaps 30,000 years (24). The antiquity of the earliest Later Stone Age may prove difficult to fix in many parts of southern Africa because sites were often abandoned at or before the end of the Middle Stone Age and only reoccupied many thousands or even tens of thousands of years later. The probable reason is that over much of southern Africa, the period between 50–40,000 and 15–12,000 years ago was hyperarid, so that human settlement was probably very sparse.

The upper limit of the Later Stone Age is relatively easy to establish. People making Later Stone Age artifacts still lived in parts of southern Africa at time of European contact, beginning just a few hundred years ago. Elsewhere they had been displaced by Iron Age pastoralists and agriculturists, beginning perhaps 2500 years ago in East Africa and about 2000 years ago in southern Africa (26, 52, 65).

From an artifactual point of view, the Later Stone Age is difficult to characterize succinctly, in part because its earliest phases, antedating 20–15,000 years ago, are known from very few sites, where the artifact assemblages are small, largely undescribed, or both. There is also the problem that Later Stone Age artifact assemblages tend to vary far more in time and space than preceding Middle Stone Age ones. Later Stone Age assemblages do share some highly distinctive features, however. Most striking is the widespread use of bone to produce standardized artifact types known as "points," "awls," "hide-polishers," and so forth (26). Bone artifacts have been found in Middle Stone Age and earlier sites, but besides being rare, they tend to be very casually made and do not exhibit the repetitive, formal, patterned shaping that characterizes Later Stone Age bone tools.

In further distinction from Middle Stone Age and earlier peoples, Later

Stone Age peoples commonly manufactured art objects and ornaments, especially beads and pendants made in bone and shell. A hallmark of most Later Stone Age sites that preserve bone or shell is the occurrence of small ostrich eggshell beads, whose use in necklaces, armbands, belts, and so forth was recorded ethnohistorically. On the evidence from Border Cave, such beads were manufactured from the very beginning of the Later Stone Age, at least 38,000 years ago.

Later Stone Age people also produced wall art, but it is restricted to relatively exposed rock surfaces, where most of it is probably no more than a few thousand years old. On such surfaces, most older art would have weathered away, and deep caves such as those that perserve Upper Paleolithic wall art in Europe are very rare in Africa. However, rock slabs on which animals were painted have been found in levels dated to more than 19,500 years ago at Apollo 11 Cave in Namibia (93), and rock fragments on which animal figures or stylized designs are engraved were recently found in Later Stone Age deposits spanning the last 10,000 years at Wonderwerk Cave in the northern Cape Province of South Africa (83). Yet older paintings and engravings may be awaiting excavation at these or other sites.

With regard to stone artifacts, many Later Stone Age assemblages may be distinguished from Middle Stone Age and earlier ones by an abundance of "microlithic" tools (26). These include pieces called scrapers, partly because of their presumed function and partly because they resemble the much larger pieces known as scrapers from Middle Stone Age and earlier sites. They also include small flakes and blades on which one edge was deliberately dulled or "backed." Ethnohistoric observations indicate that microlithic tools were usually inserted or attached to wooden or bone handles or shafts where they functioned as scrapers, projectile tips, and so forth. Microliths found at some Later Stone Age sites, such as Melkhoutboom and Boomplaas Caves in the southern Cape Province of South Africa (25), still preserve traces of the vegetal mastic that was used to fasten them to shafts or handles.

The physical type of Later Stone Age people who lived before 18–15,000 years ago remains unknown, but it seems reasonable to suppose they were anatomically modern. Numerous skeletons are known from Later Stone Age graves that postdate 12–11,000 years. Such graves are particularly abundant in shell midden sites in the southern Cape Province of South Africa. The people involved closely resembled the historic San aborigines of southern Africa to whom they were probably ancestral (68, 74).

MIDDLE AND LATER STONE AGE SUBSISTENCE

Southern Africa is particularly rich in evidence bearing on the subsistence of Middle and Later Stone Age people. Some relatively late Later Stone Age sites contain abundant plant remains (23), documenting the importance of plants in prehistoric human diets. Their importance can only be assumed for earlier sites where plant remains are rarely preserved.

Middle and Later Stone Age sites also include some caves where there are numerous animal bones that were introduced primarily, if not exclusively by people. This provides an opportunity to evaluate Middle and Later Stone Age hunting proficiency in a way that is so far not possible for earlier cultures.

The ages at death of the animals represented in Middle and Later Stone Age caves provide particularly interesting insights into stone age hunting capabilities. In order to understand how this is so, it is first necessary to understand something about the age structure of a typical population of large mammals. Generally speaking, unless the overall size of the population is changing rapidly, successively older age classes will contain progressively fewer individuals. In paleobiology, an age profile of this kind is usually referred to as "catastrophic," because it could become fixed in the fossil record if a live population were suddenly wiped out by a great catastrophe, such as a volcanic eruption, an epidemic disease, or a flash flood.

In contrast to a catastrophic age profile is the one that can be constructed from the numbers of individuals that die between successively older age classes. Paleobiologists frequently call such a profile "attritional," because it results from routine, attritional mortality due to endemic disease, accidents, predation, and so forth. Attritional profiles are dominated by the very young (in roughly the the first 10% of potential lifespan) and the old (beyond 40–50% of potential lifespan), because these are the individuals who are most likely to die from attritional causes. Prime-age (reproductively active) adults (between roughly 10% and 40–50% of lifespan) are rare, particularly compared to their abundance in live populations.

The relationship between catastrophic and attritional profiles is illustrated graphically in Figure 2. The precise form of the catastrophic and attritional profiles that characterize a population will depend upon its biology and upon the attritional mortality factors that affect it at any given time. However, the general shape of the catastrophic profile, resembling a flight of stairs, holds for all populations. Corresponding attritional profiles may be either U-shaped (with a large peak in the first 10% of lifespan and a second, smaller one after 40–50% or so) or L-shaped [with a large peak in the first 10% of lifespan and no obvious peaks thereafter (48)].

Figure 2 also shows age profiles for two of the large ungulate species represented in the Middle Stone Age layers of Klasies River Mouth Cave 1 and in the Later Stone Age layers of nearby Nelson Bay Cave. The profiles were derived by estimating age from dental crown height, utilizing a quadratic formula which assumes that the rate of dental wear slows with age. This formula has been shown to provide reasonably accurate ages from the crown heights of known-age animals in various species like the ones considered here (50). The calculated ages are certainly adequate for establishing the shape of an age profile, particularly when they are grouped into relatively broad age classes, as they have been here. The constants that enter into the quadratic formula vary from species to species, depending upon initial (unworn) crown height, the timing of dental eruption, and the potential lifespan of individuals.

The profiles in Figure 2 probably contain fewer young individuals (in the first 10% of potential lifespan) than were in the sites initially, because the relatively fragile teeth and jaws of very young animals were probably differentially removed by leaching, compaction of the sediments, and other postdepositional destructive factors. With this fact in mind, the eland profile from Klasies 1 is clearly "catastrophic," while the buffalo profiles from both Klasies 1 and Nelson Bay are "attritional." The eland profile from Nelson Bay contains too few individuals for adequate characterization. It has been included precisely because it shows the relative rarity of eland at the site, a point whose significance will become clearer below.

The difference between the Klasies eland profile on the one hand and the two buffalo profiles on the other is explicable in terms of the behavior and ecology of the two species. The eland is a large (700–900 kg) antelope, which was very widespread in Africa historically, but nowhere very numerous. It is relatively docile and easy to drive into corrals or other traps where hunters can obtain individuals of various ages in proportion to their live abundance. Middle Stone Age awareness of the ease with which eland may be driven into traps probably accounts for the catastrophic age profile at Klasies 1.

The Cape buffalo is similar in size to the eland and is also gregarious. Historically, its range in Africa was more restricted than that of the eland, but where the two species overlapped, buffalo tended to be much more numerous. The buffalo is known for its aggressiveness, and both individuals and groups often respond to potential predators by charging. Unlike eland, buffalo are difficult to drive, and the attritional profiles in Figure 2 suggest that both Middle and Later Stone Age people were forced to stalk individuals, whereupon they obtained mainly the most vulnerable ones—the very young and the old.

The buffalo age profiles are in fact very similar to the age (mortality) profiles that have been observed recently for buffalo dead of natural causes in East African national parks. It is therefore even conceivable that the Klasies and Nelson Bay people did not kill most of the buffalo represented in their sites, but simply scavenged individuals whose carcasses they found in veldt. However, recent observations show that lions and hyenas are much better at locating carcasses than people are, and they rapidly consume whole carcasses of young individuals even from large species like buffalo. Carnivore feeding probably explains the rarity of young individuals in attritional profiles that characterize large ungulates at some nonarcheological, open-air fossil sites in South Africa.

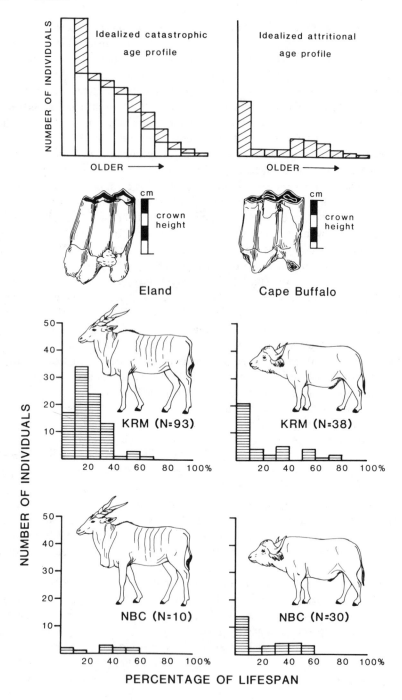

Idealized catastrophic age profile

Idealized attritional age profile

OLDER →

OLDER →

Eland

Cape Buffalo

KRM (N=93)

KRM (N=38)

NBC (N=10)

NBC (N=30)

PERCENTAGE OF LIFESPAN

Together, the historic observations and the fossil data suggest that the Klasies people would probably have found very few young buffalo to scavenge, so that the high proportion of very young individuals in their sites most likely reflects active hunting (47).

The age profiles presented in Figure 2 can be augmented with profiles for these and other species at other Middle and Later Stone Age sites, particularly Die Kelders Cave 1, Byneskranskop Cave 1, and Elands Bay Cave (45, 46). Overall, the profiles suggest that in both Middle and Later Stone Age sites, species that were especially amenable to driving or snaring tend to exhibit catastrophic profiles, while species that were probably hunted individually with hand-held weapons tend to exhibit attritional ones. By themselves, therefore, the age profiles suggest no difference between Middle and Later Stone Age hunting abilities.

Such a difference is indicated, however, when the age profiles are considered in combination with the relative abundance of species in Middle and Later Stone Age sites occupied under similar environmental conditions. Klasies Cave 1 and Nelson Bay Cave provide excellent cases in point. Middle Stone Age occupation at Klasies 1 occurred primarily during the earlier part of the Last Interglacial, between approximately 127,000 and 95,000 years ago, while Later Stone Age occupation at Nelson Bay occurred primarily during the Present Interglacial, after 12–10,000 years ago. At both sites, those few occupation levels that probably or certainly accumulated under glacial conditions (between 75,000 and 12–10,000 years ago) have been excluded from consideration. Only teeth from "interglacial" levels were used to construct the age profiles in Figure 2.

Geologic and geochemical studies indicate that Last and Present Interglacial

◄───

Figure 2 Top left: the numbers of individuals in successive age classes in an idealized, schematic catastrophic age (mortality) profile (blank bars), and the number of individuals who die between successive age classes (hatched bars). Top right: an idealized, schematic attritional age (mortality) profile, comprising a separate display of the hatched bars in the profile immediately to the left. Although the basic shapes of catastrophic and attritional profiles will be the same for all ungulate populations that are approximately stable in size and age structure, the precise shapes will vary from population to population, depending upon species biology and upon the mortality factors that affect the populations.

Center: Lower third molars (M3s) of eland *(Taurotragus oryx)* and Cape buffalo *(Syncerus caffer)* showing the crown height dimension the author measures.

Bottom: Mortality profiles based on the crown heights of eland and Cape buffalo teeth from the Middle Stone Age layers of Klasies River Mouth Cave 1 (KRM) and The Later Stone Age layers of Nelson Bay Cave (NBC). It is probable that postdepositional leaching, profile compaction, and other destructive factors have selectively destroyed teeth of very young eland and buffalo at both sites. Keeping this in mind, the eland profile from Klasies is clearly catastrophic while the buffalo profiles from both sites are attritional. The eland profile from Nelson Bay contains too few individuals for assignment to profile type.

conditions near both sites were broadly comparable to historic ones, while historically both sites enjoyed basically the same environment. Thus, the historic abundance of eland and buffalo is at least a rough guide to their relative abundance near each site when the teeth providing the age profiles in Figure 2 accumulated. Historically, buffalo probably far outnumbered eland. A glance at Figure 2 will show that the historic situation is reflected at Nelson Bay but not at Klasies 1.

Eland not only outnumbers buffalo at Klasies, but also all other ungulate species found in the site, though like buffalo, the other ungulates were probably all more common than eland in the ancient environment. One possible explanation for the abundance of eland at Klasies is that Middle Stone Age people were especially good at hunting them. However, the Klasies people could not have killed eland very often or their hunting method, permitting the capture of prime-age adults in proportion to their live abundance, would have seriously reduced eland numbers, perhaps even driving the species to extinction. The species obviously did not become extinct, nor is there evidence it declined in numbers during or following the many thousands of years that Middle Stone Age people occupied Klasies 1.

Historically, eland were very widespread in Africa, but eland groups tended to be widely dispersed and difficult to find, especially ones in a position suitable for driving into a trap. It was probably this characteristic that preserved the species in the face of the hunting strategy employed by the Klasies people. Whatever the case, the important point is that since the people obtained virtually all the prime-age adults in the eland groups they captured, they could not have captured very many groups compared to the total number available. In more prosaic terms, the Klasies people could not have been very good at hunting eland.

If eland were not especially abundant near Klasies and the people were not especially good at hunting them, the most plausible explanation for the abundance of eland in the deposit is that the people were even worse at hunting other ungulates, all of which were either more dangerous to approach than eland or more difficult to drive. By extension, the relatively small number of eland at Nelson Bay need not mean that the Nelson Bay people killed eland less frequently than the Klasies people did, but rather that they killed other, more dangerous or elusive species more often. It is important to remember that these other species were probably much more common than eland in the environment and thus that the Nelson Bay people would have benefited very considerably from an enhanced ability to hunt them.

The principal advantage that the Nelson Bay people and other Later Stone Age hunters probably had was the bow and arrow and perhaps other weapons that allowed them to attack from a distance. Historic Later Stone Age peoples all knew the bow and arrow, while its use for a few thousand years before historic contact is suggested in rock paintings and more securely by fragmentary bow staves and arrow shafts preserved in some relatively recent Later Stone Age sites.

Where preservational conditions are less favorable, as they are at virtually all sites older than a few thousand years, use of the bow and arrow can be inferred from bone and stone artifacts that are essentially indistinguishable from pieces known to have been parts of arrows in later times (26). These artifacts include bone objects that could have been linkshafts or arrow points and backed and nonbacked microliths that could have been arrow points or barbs. On the basis of such finds, it seems highly probable that the bow and arrow was known in southern Africa during the entire 12,000 year period providing the Nelson Bay faunal remains discussed here, and it is possible to argue for its presence from the very beginning of the Later Stone Age, at least 38,000 years ago at Border Cave. There is little or no evidence, direct or indirect, for the presence of the bow and arrow during the Middle Stone Age.

Additional evidence that Later Stone Age people exploited animal resources more effectively than their predecessors comes from coastal sites. Sites like Klasies Cave 1 that were occupied by Middle Stone Age people during the Last Interglacial, when sea levels and coast lines approximated historic ones, provide some of the earliest evidence in the world for the systematic use of coastal resources. This consists of numerous shells of limpets and other intertidal mollusks and of the bones of seals and penguins, still found on South African coasts. Curiously, however, the Middle Stone Age sites contain very few bones of flying shore birds and especially of fish, which are abundant nearby today and which are well represented in Later Stone Age sites occupied under comparable climatic and environmental conditions during the Present Interglacial. Pertinent Later Stone Age sites include Nelson Bay (41), Byneskranskop Cave 1 (77), Elands Bay Cave (62), and many others.

The conclusion is inescapable that Later Stone Age people possessed an ability to fish and fowl which their Middle Stone Age predecessors did not. Consistent with this conclusion is the fact that artifacts reasonably interpreted as fishing and fowling gear have been found only in Later Stone Age sites. These artifacts include grooved stones that were probably used as line or net sinkers, as well as bone "gorges" that were probably baited to catch either fish or flying sea birds (26).

A final indication that Middle and Later Stone Age people differed in exploitative ability comes from studies of limpet shells and tortoise bones in their sites. Both limpets and tortoises tend to be much smaller on average in Later Stone Age sites than in Middle Stone Age ones occupied under broadly similar environmental conditions (45; R. G. Klein, in preparation.) Unlike mammals, limpets and tortoises grow continuously throughout their lives, and smaller average size at a site suggests greater human predation pressure.

Greater predation pressure in the Later Stone Age probably reflects higher population densities promoted by advances in hunting-gathering technology.

In sum, the composite archeological and paleoecological evidence suggests that the Later Stone Age represented a quantum advance over the preceding Middle Stone Age. One interesting phenomenon that this quantum advance may help to explain is the extinction of the giant, long-horned buffalo (*Pelorovis antiquus*), giant hartebeest (*Megalotragus priscus*), southern springbok (*Antidorcas australis*), Bond's springbok (*Antidorcas bondi*), and giant "Cape horse" (*Equus capensis*), all of which seem to have made their last appearance in southern Africa at or shortly before the beginning of the Present Interglacial 12–10,000 years ago (49).

All five species survived the similar change from glacial to interglacial conditions at the beginning of the Last Interglacial, 127,000 years ago. This suggests that climatic/environmental change by itself is insufficient to explain their final disappearance, though it probably reduced their numbers and ranges. The principal new factor at the beginning of the Present Interglacial was the presence of more effective hunter-gatherers. It is possible that their attempts to maintain their accustomed way of life perturbed the rapidly changing ecosystem sufficiently to cause the disappearance of large ungulate species that would otherwise have survived.

SUMMARY AND CONCLUSIONS

From an archeological or behavioral point of view, southern Africa is far less informative than East Africa on the earliest phases of human evolution, antedating 2–1.5 million years ago. Hominids were present in southern Africa from perhaps 3 million years ago and they were making stone tools from perhaps 2 million years ago, but there is little direct evidence of what they were doing with the tools or how they were making a living.

For the succeeding Acheulean phase, between approximately 1.5 million and perhaps 200,000 years ago, southern and East Africa are more nearly equal in the information they have provided. Neither area has told us very much about human settlement patterns or subsistence activities, nor has much information on these topics been forthcoming from other parts of the world that were occupied during this time interval. Most of what we "know" concerns trends in artifact technology and typology, and even that is not very secure, due in large part to problems in dating many Acheulean sites. However, insofar as can be established, artifactual change through time was very slow, in keeping with what may prove to have been the equally slow pace of evolutionary change in the human organism.

Although much remains to be learned, far more is known about the Middle Stone Age, which succeeded the Acheulean in southern and East Africa perhaps 200,000 years ago, and about the Later Stone Age, which succeeded the Middle 40–30,000 years ago. For the Middle and Later Stone Ages, southern Africa has proved particularly informative. The Later Stone Age is particularly interesting as a phase of innovation without parallel earlier on. It was in the Later Stone Age that people first made widespread use of bone to manufacture formal tool types, and also of bone, shell, and other materials to produce art objects and ornaments. Later Stone Age artifact assemblages were far more variable in time and space than earlier ones, probably reflecting an enhanced human ability to innovate in the face of environmental change. The intellectual/behavioral advances this ability implies were probably also responsible for the fact that Later Stone Age people exploited animal resources more effectively than their predecessors.

Overall, the southern African evidence indicates that the Later Stone Age represented a kind of quantum advance over the Middle Stone Age, analogous to the kind of advance that the like-aged European Upper Paleolithic may represent over the preceding Mousterian. In Europe there is a broad coincidence between the appearance of the Upper Paleolithic and the appearance or spread of *Homo sapiens sapiens*. It is possible that the appearance of the Later Stone Age was also closely correlated with the spread of anatomically modern people in Africa, but the evidence on this is equivocal, even contradictory. On present evidence, it is possible that anatomically modern people appeared in southern Africa long before the advent of the Later Stone Age.

One feature of the Later Stone Age that bears emphasis is that it appeared during a period, 40–30,000 years ago or before, when much of Africa appears to have been hyperarid. The possibility thus arises that the cultural advances involved, as well as any biological advances that may have accompanied or preceded them, represent evolutionary responses to the extraordinary pressures that hyperaridity imposed on human populations. This hypothesis will be difficult to test, but a less speculative statement may eventually be possible if archeological and related research continue at their present pace, aided and stimulated by technological advances that may place the basic cultural and biological events entirely within the reliable range of radiocarbon dating.

ACKNOWLEDGMENTS

My thanks to K. W. Butzer, K. Cruz-Uribe, G. P. Rightmire, and T. P. Volman, who provided helpful comments on a preliminary draft. My research is supported by the National Science Foundation.

Literature Cited

1. Beaumont, P. B. 1980. On the age of Border Cave hominids 1–5. *Palaeontol. Afr.* 23:21–23
2. Beaumont, P. B., de Villiers, H., Vogel, J. C. 1978. Modern man in sub-Saharan Africa prior to 49,000 years B.P.: a review and evaluation with particular reference to Border Cave. *S. Afr. J. Sci.* 74: 409–19
3. Brain, C. K. 1981. *The Hunters or the Hunted.* Chicago: Univ. Chicago Press. 365 pp.
4. Bunn, H. T. 1981. Archaeological evidence for meat-eating by Plio-Pleistocene hominids from Koobi Fora and Olduvai Gorge. *Nature* 291:574–77
5. Butzer, K. W. 1974. Geo-archaeological interpretation of Acheulian calc-pan sites at Doornlaagte and Rooidam (Kimberley, South Africa). *J. Archaeol. Sci.* 1: 1–25
6. Butzer, K. W. 1976. Lithostratigraphy of the Swartkrans Formation. *S. Afr. J. Sci.* 72:136–41
7. Butzer, K. W. 1979. Geomorphology and geo-archeology at Elandsbaai, Western Cape, South Africa. *Catena* 6:157–66
8. Butzer, K. W. 1983. Archeogeology and Quaternary environment in the interior of southern Africa. In *Southern African Prehistory and Palaeoenvironments,* ed. R. G. Klein. Rotterdam: Balkema. In press.
9. Butzer, K. W., Beaumont, P. B., Vogel, J. C. 1978. Lithostratigraphy of Border Cave, Kwazulu, South Africa: a Middle Stone Age sequence beginning c. 195,000 B.P. *J. Archaeol. Sci.* 5:317–41
10. Butzer, K. W., Brown, F. H., Thurber, D. L. 1969. Horizontal sediments of the lower Omo Valley: the Kibish Formation. *Quaternaria* 11:15–30
11. Butzer, K. W., Clark, J. D., Cooke, H. B. S. 1974. The geology, archaeology, and fossil mammals of the Cornelia Beds, O. F. S. *Mem. Nas. Mus.* (Bloemfontein) 9:1–84
12. Carter, P. L., Vogel, J. C. 1974. The dating of industrial assemblages from stratified sites in Eastern Lesotho. *Man* 9:557–70
13. Clark, J. D. 1970. *The Prehistory of Africa.* London: Thames & Hudson. 302 pp.
14. Clark, J. D. 1974. *Kalambo Falls Prehistoric Site II: The Later Prehistoric Cultures.* Cambridge: Cambridge Univ. Press. 420 pp.
15. Clark, J. D., Oakley, K. P., Wells, L. H., McClelland, J. A. C. 1950. New studies on Rhodesian Man. *J. R. Anthropol. Inst.* 77:7–32
16. Clarke, R. J. 1976. New cranium of *Homo erectus* from Lake Ndutu, Tanzania. *Nature* 262:485–87
17. Conroy, G. C., Jolly, C. J., Cramer, D., Kalb, J. E. 1978. Newly discovered fossil hominid skull from the Afar Depression, Ethiopia. *Nature* 275:67–70
18. Cooke. H. B. S. 1949. Fossil mammals of the Vaal River Deposits. *Mem. Geol. Surv. S. Afr.* 35(3):1–117
19. Coon, C. S. 1962, *The Origin of Races.* New York: Knopf. 724 pp.
20. Day, M. J., Leakey, M. D., Magori, C. 1980. A new fossil skull (L. H. 18) from the Ngaloba Beds, Laetoli, northern Tanzania. *Nature* 284:55–66
21. Deacon, H. J. 1970. The Acheulian occupation at Amanzi Springs, Uitenhage District, Cape Province. *Ann. Cape Prov. Mus.* 8:89–189
22. Deacon, H. J. 1975. Demography, subsistence and culture during the Acheulean in southern Africa. In *After the Australopithecines,* ed. K. W. Butzer, G. Ll. Isaac, pp. 543–69. The Hague: Mouton. 911 pp.
23. Deacon, H. J. 1976. Where hunters gathered. *S. Afr. Archaeol. Soc. Monogr. Ser.* 1:1–231
24. Deacon, H. J. 1979. Excavations at Boomplaas Cave—a sequence through the Upper Pleistocene and Holocene in South Africa. *World Archaeol.* 10:241–57
25. Deacon, H. J., Deacon, J. 1980. The hafting, function and distribution of small convex scrapers with an example from Boomplaas Cave. *S. Afr. Archaeol. Bull.* 35:31–37
26. Deacon, J. 1983. Later Stone Age people and their descendants in southern Africa. See. Ref. 8
27. Ennouchi, E. 1963. Les Néanderthaliens du Jebel Irhoud (Maroc). *C. R. Acad. Sci. Paris Ser. D* 256:2459–60
28. Ennouchi, E. 1968. Le deuxième crâne de l'homme d'Irhoud. *Ann. Paleontol.* 54:117–28
29. Goodwin, A. J. H., van Riet Lowe, C. 1919. The Stone Age Cultures of South Africa. *Ann. S. Afr. Mus.* 27:1–289
30. Gowlett, J. A. J., Harris, J. W. K., Walton, D., Wood, B. A. 1981. Early archaeological sites, hominid remains and traces of fire from Chesowanja, Kenya. *Nature* 294:125–29
31. Hay, R. L. 1976. *Geology of the Olduvai Gorge.* Berkeley: Univ. Calif. Press. 203 pp.
32. Helgren, D. M. 1977. Geological context of the Vaal River faunas. *S. Afr. J. Sci.* 73:303–7

33. Helgren, D. M. 1978. Acheulian settlement along the Lower Vaal River, South Africa. *J. Archaeol. Sci.* 5:39–60
34. Hendey, Q. B. 1974. The Late Cenozoic Carnivora of the South-Western Cape Province. *Ann. S. Afr. Mus.* 63:1–369
35. Isaac, G. Ll. 1975. Stratigraphy and cultural patterns in East Africa during the middle ranges of Pleistocene time. See Ref. 22, pp. 495–542
36. Isaac, G. Ll. 1981. Emergence of human behaviour patterns. *Philos. Trans. R. Soc. London Ser. B* 292:177–88
37. Isaac, G. Ll., 1982. Early hominids and fire at Chesowanja, Kenya. *Nature* 296: 870
38. Kalb, J. E., Oswald, E. B., Tebedge, S., Mebrate, A., Tola, E., Peak, D. 1982. Geology and stratigraphy of Neogene deposits, Middle Awash Valley, Ethiopia. *Nature* 298:17–25
39. Keeley, L. H., Toth, N. 1981. Microwear polishes on early stone tools from Koobi Fora, Kenya. *Nature* 293:464–65
40. Keller, C. M. 1973. Montagu Cave in prehistory. *Univ. Calif. Anthropol. Rec.* 28:1–150
41. Klein, R. G. 1972. Preliminary report on the July through September 1970 excavations at Nelson Bay Cave, Plettenberg Bay (Cape Province, South Africa). *Palaeoecol. Afr.* 6:177–208
42. Klein, R. G. 1974. Environment and subsistence of prehistoric man in the Southern Cape Province, South Africa. *World Archaeol.* 5:249–89
43. Klein, R. G. 1975. Middle Stone Age man-animal relationships in southern Africa: evidence from Die Kelders and Klasies River Mouth. *Science* 190:265–67
44. Klein, R. G. 1978. The fauna and overall interpretation of the "Cutting 10" Acheulean Site at Elandsfontein (Hopefield), southwestern Cape Province, South Africa. *Quat. Res.* 10:69–83
45. Klein, R. G. 1979. Stone age exploitation of animals in southern Africa. *Am. Sci.* 67:151–60
46. Klein, R. G. 1981. Stone age predation on small African bovids. *S. Afr. Archaeol. Bull.* 36:55–65
47. Klein, R. G. 1982. Age (mortality) profiles as a means of distinguishing hunted species from scavenged ones in stone age archeological sites. *Paleobiology* 8:151–58
48. Klein, R. G. 1982. Patterns of ungulate mortality and ungulate mortality profiles from Langebaanweg (early Pliocene) and Elandsfontein (Middle Pleistocene), southwestern Cape Province, South Africa. *Ann. S. Afr. Mus.* 90:49–94
49. Klein, R. G. 1984. Mammalian extinctions and stone age people in Africa.

In *Quaternary Extinctions.* ed. P. S. Martin, R. G. Klein. Tucson: Univ. Ariz. Press. In Press.
50. Klein, R. G., Allwarden, K., Wolf, C. A. 1983. The calculation and interpretation of ungulate age profiles from dental crown heights. In *Hunter-Gatherer Economy in Prehistory,* ed. G. A. Bailey, pp. 47–57. Cambridge: Univ. Cambridge Press
51. Leakey, R. E. F., Butzer, K. W., Day, M. H. 1969. Early *Homo sapiens* remains from the Omo River region of south-west Ethiopia. *Nature* 220:1132–38
52. Maggs, T. 1983. The Iron Age south of the Zambezi. See Ref. 8
53. Maguire, J. M., Pemberton, D., Collett, M. H. 1980. The Makapansgat Limeworks grey breccia: hominids, hyaenas, hystricids or hillwash? *Palaeontol. Afr.* 23:75–98
54. Malan, B. D., Well, L. H. 1943. A further report on the Wonderwerk Cave, Kuruman. *S. Afr. J. Sci.* 40:258–70
55. Martin, P. S. 1967. Prehistoric overkill. In *Pleistocene Extinctions,* ed. P. S. Martin, H. E. Wright, pp. 75–120. New Haven: Yale Univ. Press. 453 pp.
56. Martin, P. S. 1983. Late Pleistocene extinctions: the model of Blitzkrieg and overkill. See Ref. 49
57. Mason, R. J. 1962. *Prehistory of the Transvaal.* Johannesburg: Witwatersrand Univ. Press. 498 pp.
58. Mason, R. J. 1967. Prehistory as a science of change—new research in the South African Interior. *Occas. Pap. Archaeol. Res. Unit Univ. Witwatersrand* 1:1–19
59. McFadden, P. L., Brock, A., Partridge, T. C. 1979. Palaeomagnetism and the age of the Makapansgat hominid site. *Earth Planet. Sci. Lett.* 44:373–82
60. Miller, S. F. 1979. Lukenya Hill, GvJm 46, excavation report. *Nyame Akuma* 14: 31–34
61. Mturi, A. A. 1976. New hominid from Lake Ndutu, Tanzania. *Nature* 262:484–85
62. Parkington, J. E. 1978. *Follow the San.* PhD thesis. Univ. Cambridge, Cambridge, England. 500 pp.
63. Partridge, T. C. 1978. Re-appraisal of lithostratigraphy of Sterkfontein hominid site. *Nature* 275:282–87
64. Partridge, T. C. 1979. Re-appraisal of lithostratigraphy of Makapansgat Limeworks hominid site. *Nature* 279:484–88
65. Phillipson, D. W. 1977. *The Later Prehistory of Eastern and Southern Africa.* New York: Holmes & Meier. 323 pp.
66. Potts, R., Shipman, P. 1981. Cutmarks made by stone tools on bones from Olduvai Gorge, Tanzania. *Nature* 291:577–80

67. Rightmire, G. P. 1976. Relationships of Middle and Upper Pleistocene hominids from sub-Saharan Africa. *Nature* 260: 238–40
68. Rightmire, G. P. 1978. Human skeletal remains from the southern Cape Province and their bearing on the stone age prehistory of South Africa. *Quat. Res.* 9:219–30
69. Rightmire, G. P. 1978. Florisbad and human population succession in southern Africa. *Am. J. Phys. Anthrop.* 48:475–86
70. Rightmire, G. P. 1979. Implications of Border Cave skeletal remains for later Pleistocene human evolution. *Curr. Anthropol.* 20:23–35
71. Rightmire, G. P. 1980. Middle Pleistocene hominids from Olduvai Gorge, northern Tanzania. *Am. J. Phys. Anthropol.* 53:225–41
72. Rightmire, G. P. 1981. Later Pleistocene hominids of Eastern and Southern Africa. *Anthropologie* (Brno) 19:15–26
73. Rightmire, G. P. 1981. Patterns in the evolution of *Homo erectus. Paleobiology* 7:241–46
74. Rightmire, G. P. 1983. The fossil evidence for hominid evolution in southern Africa. See. Ref. 8
75. Roche, H., Tiercelin, J. J. 1977. Découverte d'une industrie lithique ancienne in situ dans la formation d'Hadar. *C. R. Acad. Sci. Paris Ser. D* 284:1871–74
76. Schweitzer, F. R. 1970. A preliminary report of excavations of a cave at Die Kelders. *S. Afr. Archaeol. Bull.* 25:136–38
77. Schweitzer, F. R., Wilson, M. L. 1981. Byneskranskop 1, a late Quaternary living site in the southern Cape Province, South Africa. *Ann. S. Afr. Mus.* 88:1–203
78. Shackley, M. 1982. Namib IV and the Acheulean technocomplex in the central Namib Desert (South West Africa). *Palaeocol. Afr.* 14:151–58
79. Singer, R. 1954. The Saldanha Skull from Hopefield, South Africa. *Am. J. Phys. Anthropol.* 12:345–62
80. Singer, R., Wymer, J. J. 1968. Archaeological investigations at the Saldanha Skull site in South Africa. *S. Afr. Archaeol. Bull.* 23:63–74
81. Singer, R., Wymer, J. J. 1982. *The Middle Stone Age at Klasies River Mouth in South Africa.* Chicago: Univ. Chicago Press. 234 pp.
82. Szabo, B. J., Butzer, K. W. 1979. Uranium-series dating of lacustrine limestones from pan deposits with Final Acheulian assemblages at Rooidam, Kimberley District, South Africa. *Quat. Res.* 11:257–60
83. Thackeray, A. I., Thackeray, J. F., Beaumont, P. B., Vogel, J. C. 1981. Dated rock engravings from Wonderwerk Cave, South Africa. *Science* 214: 64–67
84. Trinkaus, E. 1983. Evolutionary continuity among archaic *Homo sapiens.* In *The Transition from Lower to Middle Palaeolithic,* ed. A. Ronen. Haifa: Univ. Haifa Press. In Press
85. Van Noten, F. 1977. Excavations at Matupi Cave. *Antiquity* 51:35–40
86. Vogel, J. C., Beaumont, P. B. 1972. Revised radiocarbon chronology for the Stone Age in South Africa. *Nature* 237:50–51
87. Volman, T. P. 1983. Early prehistory of Southern Africa. See. Ref. 8
88. Vrba, E. S. 1976. The fossil Bovidae of Sterkfontein, Swartkrans and Kromdraai. *Transvaal Mus. Mem.* 21:1–166
89. Vrba, E. S. 1981. The Kromdraai Australopithecine site revisited in 1980: recent investigation and results. *Ann. Transvaal Mus.* 33:17–60
90. Walker, N. J 1980. Later Stone Age research in the Matopos. *S. Afr. Archaeol. Bull.* 35:19–24
91. Walter, R. C., Aronson, J. L. 1982. Revisions of K/Ar ages for the Hadar hominid site, Ethiopia. *Nature* 296:122–27
92. Wendorf, F., Laury, R. L., Albritton, C. C., Schild, R., Haynes, C. F., et al. 1975. Dates for the Middle Stone Age of East Africa. *Science* 187:740–42
93. Wendt, W. E. 1976. "Art mobilier" from the Apollo 11 Cave, South West Africa: Africa's oldest dated works of art. *S. Afr. Archaeol. Bull.* 31:5–11
94. White, T. D., Johanson, D. C. Kimbel, W. H. 1981. *Australopithecus africanus:* its phyletic position reconsidered. *S. Afr. J. Sci.* 77:445–70

Ann. Rev. Anthropol. 1983. 12:49–78

ANTHROPOLOGISTS VIEW AMERICAN CULTURE

George D. Spindler[1] and Louise Spindler

Department of Anthropology, Stanford University, Stanford, California 94305

INTRODUCTION

Anthropologists, including Franz Boas (7), have written about American culture since the beginning of the discipline. The 1940s witnessed an explosion of interest, expressed well in the popular books by Margaret Mead (80) and Clyde Kluckhohn (60). An early issue of the *American Anthropologist* (2) was devoted entirely to American culture, and the works of Lloyd Warner (150, 151), John Dollard (20), Allison Davis (16), James West (152), and the Lynds (73, 74) stand today as solid examples of how anthropological concepts and methods of research can be applied to the study of communities in our own complex society. The works cited above were all published before the mid-1950s. Various shifts in conceptual ordering and to a minor extent in the methods of research employed by anthropologists in studies both at home and abroad occurred at that time. These shifts include a movement away from the notion of community as a bounded, isolated, and self-sufficient place toward a concept of community as a dependent part of a larger system (59). Vidich and Bensman, for instance, clearly represent this move in their benchmark *Small Town in Mass Society* (145). A loss of interest in national character and related concepts and a turning to particularistic analyses of single contexts also occurred. Spradley and Mann's *Cocktail Waitress* is a good example (131).

The longevity and discontinuity of anthropological approaches, as well as of certain continuities, make this review particularly difficult to write. An adequate analysis would require an in-depth sociology of knowledge approach. Social scientists in general, and anthropologists more than most, seem to project the special disciplinary and intellectual dogmas of their times in their

---

[1]Also in the School of Education, Stanford University.

49

0084–6570/83/1015–0049$02.00

writings, and especially when they write about their own culture. An adequate analysis would relate what anthropologists have written about American culture to not only the unfolding history of anthropology but also to the changing character of American society and culture. When we write about our own culture we are ourselves expressions of what we are writing about.

This embeddedness has recently become a special issue to anthropologists who have rediscovered the study of their own culture as they have been rebuffed abroad or have become convinced that there is a moral imperative to "study up," as Nader (88) has phrased it. These themes are particularly well developed in *Anthropologists at Home in North America* (82). Various contributions to this volume highlight the problems of credibility, preconception, social status and role, relativism, and objectivity that are inherent in working at home.

In this chapter we will cite works that in our opinion represent major trends or characteristics of anthropological studies of American culture—by which we mean in this instance the United States. No attempt will be made to cite exhaustively, though we will confine ourselves, with a few necessary exceptions, to works by anthropologists. We will not cover certain topics some would consider essential, such as kinship, socioreligious movements, and ethnicity, although we will refer to such studies as relevant to other problems. The literature of kinship, of ethnicity, and of movements in America cannot be reviewed adequately in the context of a review of works on American culture. We have chosen to write an essay in which we try to think through on paper what appear to us to be some of the important problems posed by our own work as well as that of our colleagues. We want to express our gratitude to Mariko Fujita and Karen Field, who prepared annotated bibliographies and working papers for their PhD exams, and to Barbara Nay, who did her senior honors thesis on the topic (89) under our direction at Stanford University.

WHAT ANTHROPOLOGISTS STUDY AT HOME

It is sometimes difficult to decide what anthropologists are studying when they study American culture. The anthropologists of the early period studied cultural values, themes, symbols, configurations, postulates, social character, national character, social class, and communities. Anthropologists of the later period are still studying some of the same phenomena but with different labels and different emphases. They are also paying much more attention to language, both as a model for the organization of cultural knowledge and as social discourse.

Varenne's *Americans Together* (142) is a good example. He studies a midwestern community in which he established residence, gained access to peer groups, family life, and institutions, and did what anthropologists always do in the field—watched, listened, inquired, and learned as people went about being themselves in customary contexts. But Varenne's analysis is quite different from that of a Lloyd Warner or Allison Davis. Where Warner and his contemporaries attempted to delineate structures such as social classes that apparently had boundaries and membership as well as community symbols, values, rituals, and ideology, Varenne describes exchanges among persons that define transient nodules in the flow of social interaction and communication. He pays a great deal of attention to how and when things are said by whom in what context. Both Warner and Varenne use what people say about themselves and others, as well as direct observation of their behavior, and collected indices of their behavior as data. Both attend to symbols and rituals, though Warner et al (151) attend to them more formally. But the analysis of one leads to a delineation of bounded, defined social entities and the other leads to the description of a loosely bounded, almost nonsystem of social interaction. Though the people in Varenne's midwestern community are subject to cultural imperatives of which they are only dimly or not at all aware, just as people are in Warner's Yankee City, they seem to express these imperatives in social dramas and contexts that are more fluid and unbounded than in Yankee City.

One is left wondering: are the communities described by Varenne and by Warner and his associates so different, or are the anthropologists? It seems reasonable that midwestern American communities have changed significantly in the nearly 50 years between the two studies, and in the direction of loosening boundaries between social classes, statuses and roles, sexes, families, and identities. It can be argued that in the American cultural system as a whole, boundaries have become so permeable as to create problems in communication and order. The oppsitions between parts that make social structure possible are so weak that the structure itself may be dissolving. Richard Merelman, a political scientist using models of analysis drawn from the anthropological structuralists, develops this interpretation tellingly (81).

Is Varenne simply recording and interpreting phenomena that Warner, Davis, Dollard, or the Lynds would have described in similar fashion? Or is Varenne really a different kind of anthropologist, influenced by a Lévi-Struss, a Saussure, a Turner, and a Schneider who did not influence Warner and his co-workers? It seems clear that Varenne is a different kind of anthropologist but that the phenomena he studies are also different. The relative weight of these two factors is precisely what an adequate sociology of knowledge analysis might illuminate. It is a kind of question that a review can raise but not answer.

We do know that the earlier workers as well as most contemporary workers have acted like anthropologists are supposed to act as they have worked their field sites. They participated, observed, conversed, collected census and other quantifiable data, and interviewed. They elicited and explored the cultural knowledge of their informants; they took the view of the native as important; they attended to symbols and rituals. In these respects there is a high degree of continuity in anthropological work in American communities, however different the end results of the work may be.

There is another genre of anthropological writing on American culture inherited from the earlier period. The writings of Mead (80), Kluckhohn (61), Hsu (45), Gorer (31), and others, including early work by Bateson (109), were not studies of single communities or limited sectors of American society. They were studies of the whole. They were attempts to extract and expand upon the central themes and ethos of American culture. It is not that they lacked specific data or that their writings did not use direct experience and observation, but their interest was in the culture as a whole system, or at least in those essences of the system as represented in values, themes, or national character.

Though one rarely hears talk of cultural values, themes, or national character today, some anthropologists are still trying to capture the essence of the whole (28). In *America Now,* Harris (34) attempts to explain technological breakdown from errant toasters to space capsules, as well as uncivil help, the shrinking dollar, women's liberation, gay liberation, rising crime rates, and religious movements in the phrasings of material determinism. As he says, "In the holistic tradition of anthropology, this book provides a general framework for understanding the bewildering changes taking place in America today."

No matter that Harris's form of material determinism seems to slip occasionally into psychological determinism in the use of such concepts as alienation, depersonalization, and apathy as intermediate interpretive concepts, his is a brave attempt to produce a coherent explanation for diverse and perplexing phenomena.

It is clear that Harris is studying American culture holistically and it seems clear at first that Varenne is studying a community. It is not true, however, that Varenne is confining his interpretations to his midwestern community. He studies in Appleton but in a sense is not studying Appleton at all. He studies in Appleton, just as he studies later in Sheffield High School (144), in order to understand how American culture works. His discussions in *Structured Diversity* are surprisingly unbound by Appleton. In fact, one never knows what Appleton is like. One does find what some Americans are like as they try to make sense to one another in Appleton.

Varenne discovers that the Americans he knows who happen to live in Appleton are *individuals*. They believe they are individuals, that individuals are important, and that as individuals they must act in certain ways. They are not only free to make personal choices from a variety of possibilities but they *must* make them, even when the choices turn out to be destructive. In their valued individual freedom they are subject to uncontestable cultural imperatives.

But Varenne also discovers community. Not community in the sense of a bounded Newburyport (Yankee City), but community in the sense of voluntary associations and of communitas. Love, in the sense that Schneider uses it in his writings on kinship and community (113–115)—as a symbol of enduring solidarity—is what pulls and holds individuals together, and at times separates them. It must be love that does this because there is little else that could do so in the very loosely bounded "community" that Varenne discovers in Appleton. Individual and community are then complementary though in opposition. They are never entirely separable. They are in a fluid relationship to each other, like everything else in Appleton.

Warner and Varenne are both trying to understand American culture through a place called a community, but their conceptions of the relationship between the part and the whole are different. Warner sees the community as a replication, at least in significant parts, of the structure of other communities equally separate and equally bounded. Varenne sees his community as a place through which individuals pass, making sense to each other in cultural terms, using cultural symbols and meanings. They are making sense to each other even when their actions sadden and confuse, particularly as the generations confront one another on a stage set for the enactment of cultural scenes over which they seem to exert little control even as they exercise their rights as individuals to make free choices.

A quite different kind of community study is represented by the social history of Starkey, a small rural town in central California, by Elvin Hatch (35). The author is not concerned with understanding American culture so much as understanding the deterioration of small-town life in America. Of course, such an understanding could not be irrelevant to the larger whole. Hatch traces early settlement, land grants to homesteaders, the emergence and stabilization of farming patterns, and the development of Starkey as a service town. He describes the loss of morale about rural life after World War II, a process he believes to be widespread if not universal in the United States. He points out that although there is an enormous literature on community deterioration, our understanding of the process is primitive.

His analysis centers on Starkey as a place where people were sufficiently important in one another's social universe that their assessments of social position counted very much. This did not result in the development of sharp social class or status lines. Social merit was awarded for individual personal achievement but the achievement was linked with, in fact partly expressed in, community service and leadership. "Boosterism," widely ascribed to leadership in small towns in the literature, is not motivated in Starkey by the prospect of individual material self-gain but by the desire for recognition—a positive assessment by the members of one's reference group.

The deterioration of Starkey as a community occurred because of a growing emphasis on individual economic achievement rather than on achievement as social merit. This in turn is linked with the capitalization of agriculture and the emergence of the middle-class businessman farmer-rancher. The validity of social merit in Starkey is further eroded by the difference between ideas and styles from outside, diffused to Starkey by the mass media, and those that had governed life and the award of social merit inside Starkey.

In contrast to either the Warner school or a modern study in but not of a community, Hatch has produced a biography, a social history of a small town. By attention to a sequence of related events within Starkey and between Starkey and the outside world, he provides dimension that makes both Warner's and Varenne's analyses look dimensionally flat. There is an implication of timelessness in both approaches that is, of course, unrealistic. The historical dimension, when coupled with anthropological analysis, produces a valuable kind of understanding that is lacking in either the functional model of the earlier school or the contemporary communication-in-context model.

Anthony Wallace's recent book *Rockdale* (148), reconstructs the growth of an American Village in Pennsylvania in the early industrial revolution. This surprising volume does everything, and more, that a good ethnography based on 2 years of fieldwork could do for a village of 2000. It is a reconstruction of a way of life and the effect of industrialization upon it over time, the emergence of Christian capitalism, machines and human adaptations to them, the human costs of work under the conditions imposed by the cotton mills, the forms of family, sex roles, life careers, values, evangelicism, antimasonry, personalities, the Civil War, voluntary association, and good works. All of these diverse but interrelated elements are woven together into a compelling social history that is as lively as any lively ethnography of a contemporary community. And it was all done with data gleaned from a wide variety of public and personal documents, a little oral history, and the author's personal exploration and observation of surviving mill and hamlet sites and the remaining mansions in and around Rockdale.

It seems probable that the kinds of ethnographic social history represented by Hatch's and Wallace's volumes will constitute one of the major productive approaches to the study of American culture by anthropologists. Without the time depth this kind of study can give us, we will not understand the processes of change and will be led to the false conclusion that whatever is now is somehow permanent.

Thurnstrom, the historian, points out that the Yankee City " . . . whose social superstructure . . . remained very much what it had been at the end of the War of 1812, was largely a creation of Lloyd Warner's imagination" (139). Its inhabitants were not descended from Yankee ancestors of the eighteenth and early nineteenth centuries, as Warner posited. Migration of old residents from the community and the immigration of newcomers had, by 1885, already created a city that was not mainly descended from old Newburyport families. Warner's synchronic, ahistorical functionalistic commitment prevented him from exploiting the great historical resources available to him and led him to a false construct. It is not that the structures and styles Warner described were wrong, but they were not necessarily the permutations of old yankee structures and styles that he thought them to be.

Varenne's model of community is equally time-bound. He may be so biased toward flowing interaction, voluntary community, and immediate context that he overlooks elements of stability, boundedness, and structure that would make Appleton a different place than the one it seems to be through his eyes. History can function as a corrective for observations made in evanescent contexts. What he discovers may not be American culture but rather the communicative exchanges of transients. The ideal analysis of our culture must sample both the diversity contained within any single research site and the changes that occur through time. The futures of our ancestors are our own present and past.

SPECIAL CONTEXTS

Another way of approaching what there is to study as anthropologists look at American culture is represented by publications that in various ways examine specific institutions, cultural settings, and contexts rather than American culture as a whole or a community as a window to a larger cultural whole. Schools and schooling have probably received as much attention as any other special setting, together with hospitals, health services, and medical schools. Two recent collections of original research papers, *Doing the Ethnography of Schooling* (125) and *Children In and Out of School* (30), include chapters on resistance to change in educational practice, differing ethnic styles of communication and learning, the special languages of schooling, the social organization of schools and classrooms, play as a learning context, children's folklore, value systems in inner-city schools, and other topics that utilize data collected by anthropologists in schools and related settings using standard ethnographic techniques. It is probably correct to say that some of the best ethnographic studies of special contexts in our own society have been done in schools.

It is paradoxical that these studies seem to tell us relatively little about American culture, since most of them are explicitly studies of cultural transmission. They tell us about ethnicity and pariah statuses in classrooms and the effects of these statuses upon learning and teaching. They tell us about styles of communication that vary by ethnic group and social class. They tell us about the selection and transmission of working-class attributes as against managerial and professional class attributes. But they do not, by and large, tell us about the broader articulation of our cultural system, and they tell us little about mainstream culture. It may be that the preoccupation with ethnicity and social class status differences in the schools makes it unlikely that we will find out much about anything else.

Some exceptions include G. Spindler's *The Transmission of American Culture,* in which the specific cultural orientations of a mainstream teacher are analyzed as influences on classroom behavior (123); Ogbu's *Minority Education and Caste* (91); McDermott & Aron's attention to the cultural compulsion to test, grade, and sort children in order to teach them "more effectively"—with precisely the opposite effect (77); Henry's analysis of punishment and reward in "Golden Rule Days" in the elementary school classroom (36); Peshkin's *Growing Up American,* in which he shows how a small community in the rich Illinois-Iowa farm belt depends upon the school for survival and how the school is shaped so that it functions to support the community (94, 95); and a collection edited by Sieber & Gordon (116), which includes attention to not only school but to the 4H organization, summer camp for girls, Boy Scout camp, and combat training in the U.S. Army. Varenne's *Structured Diversity* also qualifies. But even these works tell us more about their special settings than about American culture.

Another kind of special setting study, well represented by Spradley & Mann's ethnography of a college bar (131), provides a more direct look into the wider culture. In contrast to a community, a college bar is a relatively manageable context in which to study behavior. One can be fairly sure, after a sufficient period of participant observation and interviewing, that one knows what is going on. Excepting for this relative manageability, however, limited context studies of this sort seem to have some of the same problems, as points of access to the wider culture, that community studies do.

In Brady's bar, even though it is a college bar, women are viewed as passive, low in status, as peripheral to male social life, and as persons who serve others. A woman gains if she does a man's work—so the waitresses are eager to get behind the bar—but bartenders never cross over to clean up tables. Brady's bar is thus seen as a microcosm of the relationships between the sexes in the wider cultural framework.

The meanings of the bar in American culture and of this bar in the local culture, however, are not probed. Lacking information of this kind, we do not know the extent to which sex roles and relationships may be exaggerated or in some way reshaped in the setting. No matter how excellent the study of Brady's bar may be, we are left in the dark about the significance of sex roles in this bar for the understanding of sex roles in American culture (25). Anthropologists seem to display a tendency to study contexts as self-contained whether communities, schools, classrooms, drug abuse program centers (137), hospitals (138), or college bars. The open model implicit in Varenne's work in Appleton and in Sheffield High School is a useful alternative. Nevertheless, the virtue of working in relatively restricted settings such as Brady's Bar or a single classroom is not to be gainsaid.

Quite a different approach to the study of our culture is taken by Perin in *Everything in its Place: Social Order and Land Use in America* (93). She studies neither a community nor a limited context but a process, though she terms this process an institution. Her purpose is to avoid psychological reductionism and explain social matters in terms of collective, not individual, behavior. "By postulating that ideas, beliefs, premises, assumptions, and definitions (and the signs and symbols standing for them) are independent data and that they are evident in the collective consequences of individuals' behavior, then social practices (not the attitudes and behavior of an imaginery actor) can be subjects of inquiry" (p. 25). She is very concerned with shifting the vocabulary away from psychological concepts toward cultural concepts and a semiotic analysis. She wants to unearth the conceptual framework for the activities of Americans engaged in buying, selling, planning, talking about, and living on real estate. She wants to avoid prefiguring categories of belief, sentiment, value, etc and instead to discover them. In this she sees the major difference between anthropology and the other social sciences. With these principles firmly in hand, she explores various aspects of land use such as home owning, zoning, and planning, and arrives at principles of social order through a semiotic analysis of interview material and other statements by participants. She shows how cultural conceptions invest newcomers, ethnicity, density, tenure, ownership, etc with meaning that influences land use behavior.

Perin's work is satisfying and convincing and yet one wonders why she is able to state her conclusions with such certainty. Semiotic analysis seems no less tenuous than in-depth psychoanalysis, though the former is possibly burdened with fewer preconceptions. Her analysis does provide an approach to the study of American culture that seems at least as direct as through the study of behavior in limited contexts, and it is more comprehensive. Again, however, the lack of historical depth may vitiate the validity of what her analysis reveals as a statement about American culture. Her analysis centers on a time (the mid-1970s) when expansion in home ownership was at its peak and everyone was being urged to invest in real estate. It was a period of low interest rates and high profit. Conditions will never be precisely the same again and they were not that way before then.

This review has so far concentrated on what anthropologists study when they turn their attention to American society and culture. We have discussed several kinds of study that use the community as a point of departure but end with very different constructions. We have discussed special contexts as windows into a wider cultural landscape, and we have made an argument for expanding synchronic analysis with a time dimension, an argument for history. Our next step will be to consider the possibility that there are features of American culture that are characteristic of the whole and about which there is consensus on the part of those who have studied it. And we will examine the possibility that these features are of long standing.

CONSENSUS AND CONTINUITY

An analysis of all of the global earlier works on American culture, such as those by Mead (80), Kluckhohn (60), Gorer (31), Ruesch & Bateson (109), Hsu (45), Spindler (120, 121), and Gillin (29)—and there are others—reveals certain commonalities in their characterizations. Though each author phrases the qualities of the culture being analyzed somewhat differently, these observations converge into a fairly coherent list of features. The precise nature of these features, as concepts, is more difficult to define than their content. We will furnish them as descriptive statements of belief and value in presumably pivotal areas of American culture. They are a kind of statement of cultural ideology. They include:

Individualism   The individual is the basic unit of society. Individuals are self-reliant and compete with other individuals for success.

Achievement orientation   Everyone is concerned with achievement. Achievement, when recognized as success, is a measure of one's intrinsic worth.

Equality   Though born with different attributes and abilities, everyone stands equal before the law and should have equal opportunity to achieve, utilizing one's individual ability and energy in a self-reliant manner.

Conformity   Everyone is expected to conform to the norms of the community or group. Conformity and equality are closely related in that equal can be translated as "the same as."

Sociability   Friendliness and the ability to get along well with others, to make friends easily, to be open to others are desirable qualities.

Honesty   Keeping contracts is moral. It is also good for business. It is the "best policy."

Competence   One should be able to do things well in order to succeed, but one should also be able to take care of oneself and those dependent upon one . . . to be independent.

Optimism   The future is hopeful. Things will work out for the best. Improvement is possible, even inevitable if one works hard and is competent.

Work   Work is good, not just a necessary evil. Idleness is bad and leads to dissolute behavior. Working hard is the key to success, even more than ability.

Authority   Authority, from within a hierarchy or as represented by external power or even expertise, has negative value excepting under special conditions.

In 1952 we began administering a simple open-ended sentence "values test" to Stanford students in our classes that was organized around these points of consensus. We have continued to do so intermittently since that time and have published interpretive summaries of the results in 1955 and 1974 (122, 124). We regard the responses from our now rather large sample as expressions of cultural ideology. Over the now 30-year period for which we have data, certain response modalities have exhibited a high degree of consistency. Others have exhibited significant shifts.

Those features exhibiting the most continuity through time are: equality; honesty (as the best policy); the value of work coupled with clear goals; the significance of the self-reliant individual; and sociability—getting along well with others and being sensitive to their needs and appraisals. Those features exhibiting the greatest shifts in meaning and value are: optimism about the future; tolerance of nonconformity; and the value of material success.

The changes in response modalities over time exhibit a trend that can be described as progressively less traditional, if we take the statement of cultural ideology furnished above as our starting point. More tolerance for nonconformity, more interest in self-development than rugged individualism, more concern for other people and their needs, a more relativistic conception of order and morality, less certainty that the time-honored formula of work to get ahead will indeed work at all, more suspicion of authority—the changes have been consistently in these directions. That is, they were until the late 1970s and early 1980s. Now there is a swing back to the traditional formulas. Work, success, achievement, and individualism are stated in the 1979–1982 sample in ways very similar to the 1952 sample.

That the modalities of responses we have collected from Stanford students are not as biased by that provenience as one might expect is indicated by large samples from elsewhere in California and the east coast, and selective samples of minority groups. It is interesting that the latter in general, both at Stanford and elsewhere, express a more traditional profile than do mainstream students. The results of a survey of 200,000 freshmen at 350 colleges by the American Council of Education support our Stanford data (124). Though the eliciting device is not the same, many of the categories of belief and value overlap.

The Stanford data appear to tell us something about American culture, or at least its ideology. We may hypothesize that the core features of this profile are those that have exhibited the greatest continuity. But even the changes that have occurred over this 30-year period have occurred around pivotal areas defined by the list of consensi furnished above. This is not surprising, since the eliciting frames were set up around them, but we also asked respondents to describe in one paragraph their ideal person. Their responses in this sector are also phrased around the cultural pivots of the consensus list. The results of this research (originally intended as a teaching device, not a research) appear to correlate well with the insights of the earlier anthropological workers. For whatever reason, these anthropological observers and interpreters of the American scene seem to not only to have agreed with each other but to have hit upon some significant features.

Our next step in the search for global cultural continuities will be to examine some of the observations made by both foreign and native interpreters of the American scene well before there was an anthropology. We will not be able to linger over their very interesting observations and the wonderful prose they were expressed in, but will summarize briefly the essence of some of their interpretations.

The best known of these observers is undoubtedly Alexis de Toqueville, who wrote about the Americans in 1831 (139a) when we were 24 states and 13 million people. He saw our ancestors as independent, resistive of authority, dedicated to justice, preoccupied with material success, and worried about being different than one's neighbors. Though de Toqueville admired much of what he saw in Americans, he was uncompromisingly critical of what he interpreted as our need to conform and believed that it was so pervasive that it threatened two other values that Americans held dear—individuality and freedom.

An earlier observer, M. G. St. Jean de Crevecoeur, wrote about America before there were states, when the colonies were at the point of revolution (12, 13). His observations were made during his tenure as a farmer in Orange county, New York, from 1765 to the outbreak of the war against domination by the British crown. He described the Americans of that time as deeply egalitarian, patriotic and very identified with being American, freedom-loving and independent, industrious, valuing competence, and agrarian.

Harriet Martineau, an English reformer, traveled in the United States for 2 years beginning in 1834. She, like de Tocqueville, perceived elements of both individualism and conformity, though she saw them less as universal American attributes and more as regional, the easterners being more the conformists. She saw "the workings of opinion" as the "established religion" of the United States, taking precedence over even the pursuit of wealth and overshadowing even the love of freedom and the regard for the individual (76a).

We cannot leave the historical dimension behind us without a glance into Frederick Jackson Turner's famous frontier hypothesis (141). The hypothesis, somewhat simplied, is that the opportunities and imperatives of the frontier, constant to the time of his writings (beginning in 1893), were the cause of individualism, intolerance of restraints, inquisitiveness, masterful grasp of material things, buoyancy and exuberance marking the American character. Among the factors most important was the availability of free land, which supported incessant expansion and constant movement. This "hypothesis," at least the characterizations of the American character it was purported to explain, relates well to the profile of attributes delineated, though it emphasizes individualism, optimism, and materialism (and material success) and de-emphasizes conformity.

There were other earlier observers that one would cite in a more extended sampling of interpretations, including Thomas Jefferson, who saw America as a country of farmers and wanted to keep it that way (54), and Baron J. A. Graf von Hübner, who saw our individualism as a not unqualified success (147). The three summarized are sufficient for our purposes. It is clear that what they describe for the America they knew, now 100 to more than 200 years past, does not sound unfamiliar in the framework of pivotal attributes that anthropologists writing in the 1940s and 1950s produced, or that we were able to delineate with our Stanford and related samples.

INDIVIDUALISM AND CONFORMITY: A KEY OPPOSITION

A key concept which emerges from the writings of both the anthropologists of the earlier period and historical observers such as de Toqueville is that of individualism. Turner was only one of the last of the historical observers to focus upon this attribute. In one way or another, individualism figures largely in the formulations of Crevecoeur and Martineau as well as de Toqueville and is never absent from the interpretations of any of these historical observers.

Individualism is still a major focus in many current writings. Hsu, both in his earlier publications (45) and in his chapter in the Smithsonian volume, *Kin and Communities* (48), as well as in his extensively rewritten and expanded third edition of *Americans and Chinese* (49), makes individualism a key factor in American life, past and present (46, 47). In fact, he sees most of our major problems such as juvenile delinquency and corruption in government, racial tensions, prejudice, and preoccupation with sex as consequences, of "rugged individualism." The American version of individualism stresses "militant" self-reliance, competition, and rejection of authority. The individual becomes isolated and, as a consequence, insecure. This insecurity in turn leads to preoccupation with sex, because sexual contact is at least some form of communication and involves some cooperation. Insecurity also leads to con-formity, for the isolated individual can only be reassured by being like others, even though this may not lead to meaningful communication.

Hsu's analyses are notable both for their extensive and complex interweav-ing of seemingly unrelated patterns of behavior and belief and also for the fact that they are comparative. He contrasts American and traditional Chinese cultural foci. American culture is individual-centered while the Chinese culture is situation-centered. Individual achievement, with consequent isolation, is valued in the first, whereas mutual dependence that produces collective achievement is valued in the latter. It is a lesson in integrative analysis to read Hsu's works and observe how he weaves these key constructs into interpretations of art, sex, homelife, school, social class, marriage, heroes, government, religion, old age, crime, violence, economics, and industry.

Hsu's comparative stance is productive, whether or not one accepts all of his interpretations and particularly his single-mindedness with respect to "rugged individualism" as the root of all evil. Much of the literature by anthropologists, in fact, suffers from a lack of comparison to any other culture or situation. This is true in all sectors of the anthropological attempt to make sense of our culture, from the global interpretive essays on American culture or national character to the limited context studies of the "new" anthropology. There are exceptions, to be sure (121, 140, 143, 146), and the social histories such as Hatch's and Wallace's suffer less because a historical analysis is inherently comparative through time.

The opposition between individualism and conformity in American culture and character has been a preoccupation with many writers other than anthropologists. We have declared this review to be limited to anthropological writings, but we cannot consider individualism and conformity without mentioning David Riesman. His constructs of inner- and outer-directed character types are the most complete single "theory" of individualism and conformity (104, 105). His analysis, cast as it is in character types, is likely to be rejected by most contemporary anthropologists who want to limit their analyses to cultural phenomena in the form of symbols and signs and social meaning, largely through analysis of language, as in the work of Varenne, Perin, and in a somewhat different way, Spradley. The material determinism of a Marvin Harris will also eschew characterological approaches. Nevertheless, there is probably no single work by a contemporary social scientist on American culture that has been so influential as Riesman et al's *The Lonely Crowd,* first published in 1950 (105). Riesman, however, was not solely character-oriented, for he was also much concerned with the kind of society and institutional settings that called for these kinds of characterological attributes. *Individualism and Conformity in the American Character,* edited by Rapson (103), is particularly valuable as an integrative collection and interpretation of major writings on the topic up to the publication date, 1967. David Potter, the historian, Francis Hsu, and the sociologists Seymour Lipset and David Riesman, as well as the early observers of the American scene that we have mentioned, are included.

In the first analysis of the data from Stanford students in the mid-1950s (122), a movement in American culture from "traditional" to "emergent" value orientations was posited. Traditional orientations centered upon hard work, success, individual achievement, future orientation, and absolute morality. Emergent orientations centered upon conformity to the group, sociability, hedonistic present orientation, sensitivity to others, and relativistic, situation-centered morality. These clusters were not unlike Reisman's constructs but centered more on social contexts.

Over the years of continuing data collection and reflection, however, it has seemed more likely that the "traditional" and "emergent" constructs are not so much a statement of change as a statement of strain within the American cultural system. The same can be said of Riesman's constructs and in fact of the whole individualism/conformity dialogue. If our culture is as loosely bounded as Merelman suggests (81), furnishing no firmly bounded contexts in which roles can be played, membership had, and stable identities formed, we would expect individualism to become a creed and conformity to immediate social pressure to be its companion. There would not be much else with which people might do their social work and character building. When we examine carefully what the observers said in the early .period of our history, we are led to the conclusion that America has always been loosely bounded. The traditional boundaries of European society were what people coming to America were trying to escape from, and the expanding society (not necessarily simply the frontier society) in which they found themselves never recreated the bounded societies from which they originated.

The most recent anthropological analysis of the individual/conformity duality is contained within Varenne's discussion of Appleton (142). Varenne does not directly discuss conformity, but rather community—symbolized and reaffirmed in governmental and administrative activities and meaningful to individuals as a relationship created by love. Individuals are, however, rarely committed to community, and when individual satisfaction, free choice, or particularly "happiness" is threatened by commitment or membership, the individual withdraws to find new alignments. The emic concept of individualism is the ability to make free choices. There is, therefore, a constant opposition between individual and community, even though the existence of one depends upon the other. Both the individual and the community are considered from the native's viewpoint. In this sense, neither may exist in structural terms with which Lloyd Warner would be comfortable. On the other hand, Warner, believing himself that social classes existed and had clear boundaries, may have in part created them.

G. Spindler found essentially the same individual vs community (broadly interpreted) relationship in a controlled comparison of German and American GIs as they responded to the hierarchical structures of the Wehrmacht and the U.S. Army respecitvely in World War II (120, 121). The American G.I. persistently asserted his individualism and resisted submersion in the hierarchical order by rejecting authority and engaging in activities that were declared court-martial offenses. German soldiers were much more incorporated in the structure and resisted authority less. American G.I.s also withdrew their love of the group more quickly under combat conditions than did the Germans when the survival of ego was threatened.

However phrased, it appears that individualism, and the opposition (and complementarity) of the individualism/conformity duality, is a central feature of American culture. The recognition of it has been surprisingly constant for about two centuries. Although modes of interpretation have changed, there is considerable continuity. If we did not have the writings of the early historical observers and the analyses of a few anthropologists whose natal culture was not American (Gorer, Hsu, Varenne), we might question whether this emphasis was not a projection of our own "imbeddedness" in our culture, since American analysts, it is said, tend to reduce all social phenomena to individual psychology (110). We need both history and cultural variety on the part of observers to make social interpretation work.

DIVERSITY, CONFLICT, AND ACCOMMODATION

So far in this review we have used broad and undifferentiated terms, such as "American culture" to refer to what we are discussing and what anthropologists have addressed themselves to, even when they were working in limited contexts or communities. The only diversity we have encountered is the diversity of individual choices. But the United States of America is considered to be diverse regionally, structurally, and culturally. Yet as one crosses the country by auto and stops in small towns, uses roadside conveniences, and samples local affairs via newspaper and radio, one is impressed with the uniformity of the American scene.

Diversity in the USA may be less ethnic or regionally cultural, although to be sure there is some significant variation, than it is interactional. That is, various groups conflict with and make various accommodations to the "establishment," or "mainstream," or the "power structure," or "the man," or "the white man," or their parents, and in so doing create a certain shallow, often transient diversity.

There is ample evidence to support the perception of diversity in American culture. Strickon and Lewis, for example, in their work on ethnicity in rural populations in Wisconsin, establish a convincing thesis that ethnicity in this state at least has depth (71, 135, 136). Ethnicity is expressed in trust relationships, intermarriage, celebrations, and in economic activity, and has played a significant role in the development of the region up to the present. Meyerhoff (87) tells poignantly how a California coast community of Jewish retirees celebrates its culture. Yinger (159) reviews and interprets countercultures as confrontations with established norms. Yanagisako (158a) shows how Japanese-American Nisei preserve certain aspects of Japanese kinship and combine them with mainstream American elements so that the cultural structure of Japanese-American kinship "is pervaded at all levels by people's conceptions of their social (ethnic) identity." Her analysis is presented as a challenge to Schneider's assertion (114) that at one level of analysis, that is, in the system of distinct features that define a person as a relative, the cultural order, there is uniformity (he acknowledges variation at other levels).

Similar analyses of differences in the ordering of kin at the cultural level for other ethnic groups in America might well show significant variation. Ethnicity, however, much less this kind of study of ethnic variation, has not been the major focus of anthropological work in this country. Examination of a current, seemingly well-balanced textbook on American ethnicity shows the anthropological contribution to be relatively small compared to that of other social scientists (5).

The interpretation of American kinship and culture by Schneider (113–115) sheds light on both diversity and uniformity. He early characterized American kinship as diverse but centering on basic unity, and he has enlarged upon this core position in a succession of papers and books. No review of his comprehensive writings can be attempted here. While other analysts have produced interesting works on American kinship, they have relatively infrequently attended to the larger cultural arena of which kinship is a part. Schneider's works, in contrast, have been much involved with the larger problem. Particularly interesting is his delineation of cultural "galaxies," such as kinship, nationality, ethnicity, and religion, defined by a common cultural code for conduct—in this instance diffuse, enduring solidarity. The variability is in the "substance" for each unit in the galaxy, so kinship is distinguished by blood, community by locality, etc. This galaxy in turn is contrasted to one constituted of work, commerce, and industry, with a cultural code of enlightened self-interest, personal advantage, and dominant rationality. Schneider's model of kinship in American culture has not gone unchallenged, as Scheffler's (112) and Yanagisako's (158a) arguments demonstrate.

It is interesting that the individual/conformity-community poles we discussed previously can fit within the structural opposition of these two galaxies. Some interpretive orientation of this general type appears to be cast up in attempts to analyze the core features of American culture. The uniformity of American culture may extend well beyond the surface features one so easily observes, and in fact may even pervade the dialogue of diversity. It is interesting that Henry produced a similar interpretation when he distinguished a cluster of features centering around "drive," such as achievement, competition, profit, mobility, and expansion, and another cluster centering on "love," such as kindness, quietness, simplicity, etc (37). The continuity of interpretations, in variable terminology and with different analytic models, is impressive.

The problem of greatest interest is not whether there is diversity or uniformity in American culture. Surely there are both. There are discernible variations in behavior and symbol for each of the approximately 30 ethnic groups in the USA. There are also variations, often of more significance, in region and social class and age group despite impressive uniformity at the level of commercial and pop culture, mass media, clothing, highway strip culture, and possibly even core values. Religious cults, sexual habits and preferences, and family culture add to the diversity.

The problem is, to what are variations attributable, and how deep do they go? No single factor explanation will suffice because most of the core problems of sociocultural dynamics are involved. However, there are at least two seemingly useful models that we term the residual and interactional. The first assumes that cultural patterns, including phenomena that range from highly specific behaviors to very diffuse symbols such as "love" and solidarity, are simply inherited from a past when the differentiation was greater, whatever it is. The other deals with variation, particularly in ethnic, religious, and social class components, as produced and reinforced as various elements in society interact with each other.

The two processes are apparent in our analysis of contemporary Menomini Indian culture, as they are in other studies of Indian-white confrontation and adaptation (8, 33, 39, 40, 53, 117, 160). Our data, collected over a period of some years, show that there are several major adaptive components among the Menomini (126–128). These components have psychocultural as well as sociocultural depth. Each of these components is a product of long-term interaction with the mainstream American power structure, economy, churches and religious orders, the education establishment, world view, and prejudice. The underlying processes of contemporary Menomini adaptation may be described as reaffirmative, compensatory, syncretic, anomic, marginally constructive, segmentalized, and so forth. These processes are stabilized in the form of actual groups such as a native-oriented enclave, a peyote cult, etc. Similar adaptive responses appear in various contexts, not only in studies of American Indians, but in studies of other ethnic groups (18, 19, 155, 157). The same general line of interpretation can also be applied to religious movements, sects and cults (14, 56, 66, 101, 154, 161), and to the flux and flow of political behavior (81).

Taken from this point of view, diversity in American culture is a product of confrontation, conflict, and accommodation between populations such as ethnic and mainstream elements initially marked off by historically derived distinctions. Though some groups or movements such as hippie communes, Moonies, Jonestown, the Birch Society, etc have little specific historic depth, they do have historical antecedents in American society. Conflicts and accommodations appear, and then are stabilized in various institutional and cultural forms. The processes of interaction reinforce initial differences selectively, and then add new ones. There is, in fact, the possibility that the long-term and continuing process of conflict and accommodation is necessary to the maintenance of the American cultural system. Only by a contrast to diversity and cultural "disorder" can American order and unanimity be recognized and defended.

When ethnic discourse is examined, as Ruskin and Varenne have done for Puerto Rican Americans (110), the focus on interaction may be taken yet further. They acknowledge ethnicity in the USA as a factor contributing to diversity and point out that immigration is continuing and that ethnic enclaves are being replenished. What they are interested in, however, is the possibility that the experience of ethnicity "particularly as it is mediated by the structural discourse people must use to express it," is in fact a "fully melted" American experience. The American ethnic discourse is similar to discourses Americans will use in other contexts such as religion and politics. It will center on individualization, psychologization, the need for unanimity, and conformity. Ruskin and Varenne take off in their analysis from the seminal work of Schneider (114), who points to the possibility that such homologies would be found between cultural content domains. Their results so far have been inconclusive, but the model is congruent with what we have termed an interactionist explanation of American cultural diversity. If ethnicity is indeed mediated by a structural discourse that is culturally American, the experience of ethnicity itself is decidedly American even though differences are recognized, and in fact exist.

THE PROBLEM OF WOMEN

Though the literature on sex roles in the USA is now extensive, there are few interpretive analyses and even fewer empirical studies by anthropologists. There are some studies of minority women, but not even the most recent and major collected volumes or texts include serious attention to mainstream American culture, although suggestions for the improvement of women's status in this country and elsewhere are not lacking. The task of anthropologists working with sex roles is apparently self-defined as cross-cultural. Naomi Quinn has provided a knowledgeable review of such studies (102). The *Wilson Quarterly* provides a useful though nonprofessional review essay on some of the research on "Men and Women" (86). Though research in other cultures by anthropologists is cited, there is no identifiable piece by anthropologists cited on any part of the USA. In the influential Rosaldo-Lamphere collection (106), there is only one of 16 chapters devoted to an American population.

How does Woman, the "other" or the "second" sex, fit into American culture (17)? The "problem" of women may be considered a subset of the problem of diversity in American culture. Anthropologists have until recently neglected women in their research (106). Because the majority of anthropologists have been males, it is not surprising that they have attended to the highly visible public roles played by males in most societies (107). And in classic analyses of American culture by sociologists and historians, it has been assumed that since American men have been dominant status-wise, the characteristics of American men were the characteristics of the American people, including women (100). In his frontier hypothesis, Turner (141) was referring only to male values. Riesman's concept of a shift from inner to outer orientation (105) is quite inapplicable to women, who have always been "outer-oriented" to children and family. At best, the woman's world is difficult for a male to research. Now that female anthropologists are focusing on women in cross-cultural studies and are therefore calling attention to the infrastructures of society instrumented mainly by women, we can expect eventually to reexamine role relationships in American society from a cross-cultural viewpoint. Jane Collier, for example, views women as political strategists who use resources available to them in support of interests often opposed to those of men (11). Women's strategies, she claims, are important components of the processes by which social life proceeds. This kind of approach could well be the focus of some anthropological work on American women, particularly because they have, in part, moved out of infrastructural roles.

Florence Kluckhohn, a sociologist with strong anthropological leanings, has presented one of the few organized macromodels of differences in male and female roles in mainstream American culture (62). Using her "Values Orientation" schema, she showed that women's roles historically have expressed "variant" rather than "dominant" values in American culture. She posited that individualism—with man as autonomous free agent—was a dominant male value, while women as wives and mothers were oriented toward group goals. Where the valued personality type for males was the "Person of Action," the "Doing Personality," for women it was the philanthropist type, dedicated to community improvement and family morality. And while the time orientation for males has been the future, for practical reasons for women it has been the present. Some such form of cultural analysis, with appropriate modifications, might be applicable to the contemporary scene.

Some of the best work by anthropologists on women's roles in American society has been done on black women. Carol Stack's *All Our Kin* presents a vivid, cutting analysis of urban black domestic relationships (134). Stack suggests that the characterization of urban black families as matrifocal is static and misleading. She views black women as strategists, coping with problems of poverty, unemployment, and oppression in a resilient manner. She illustrates with personal histories the ways women form alliances, relying on an enduring network of kin among whom goods and services are exchanged. Other studies also illustrate the resiliency and creative aspects of the strategies used by black women in rural as well as urban settings (4, 21). American Indian women as members of a minority group have also received a share of anthropological attention (78, 128, 129). Estelle Smith's study of Portugese-Americans (118, 119) and Agnes Aamodt's study of neighboring among Norwegian-American women (1) extend our knowledge of ethnicity and women's roles. Sylvia Yanagisako's analysis of women-centered kin networks shows that Japanese-American centrality of women in kinship is similar to that of other middle-class Americans (158).

Women's adaptations to culture change have occupied some attention. A published symposium chaired by Ann McElroy and Carolyn Mathiassen (78) includes chapters on changing sex roles among the Oglala Sioux, Native American women in the city, Mexican-American women in the midwest, the Eskimo, and on the Iroquois as well as on women in Africa, Sri Lanka, and Iran. In our own research, starting with the Blood, Menomini, and Cree Indians, and in our recent studies on urbanizing villages in southern Germany, we have been careful to include matched samples of both sexes in our research design and data collection. Females are less tradition-oriented, less reserve- or village-oriented, and more outside- and urban-oriented than are males in all four samples (129). Sex was the single most significant antecedent variable in our quantified data analysis. Some parallel results might be expected were the same research design applied to other American minorities and to selected mainstream groups. The two sexes apparently do respond to culture change, urbanization, and modernization differently, and some features of their differ-ence may well be generalizable transculturally. Such generalization would have practical as well as theoretical significance.

Elizabeth Moen and co-workers (84), in their study of women and economic development in two Colorado mining towns, show that the social and ultimate-ly economic costs of ignoring women in development planning are substantial. As the two case studies reveal, the parallels between the effect of economic development on women in the Third World and in these two western American towns are striking. Most development planning has been conceptualized and applied as though women did not exist, or were like men (52).

A community study of southwestern Saskatchewan women by Seena Kohl (63) offers a useful model for studies needed on American women. Kohl provides the rich historical background of the community and traces the key roles women have played in its formation and maintenance. She describes three generations of development. Kohl regards the view taken of women in agri-cultural enterprises as "crypto-servants" as misleading. She found that women were full participants in the developments which laid the base for contemporary agriculture in the area. Women were the most important components of the developing social order and were highly valued as such. They were and are, as household managers, the "gatekeepers" for consumption wants. The situation among agrarian communities in the western United States seems similar enough to warrant some generalization.

Beyond empirical studies of ethnic and particularly mainstream sex roles there is a strong need for an ethnography of the feminist movement itself in the United States. This study should be done by researchers with both the traditional social science perspective and by those involved in feminist studies, where a sense of oppression and a deep concern for change are integral to their work (58). A more interactive and sharing pattern than is usually the case might be required in the research role in a change-oriented feminist setting, as Light and Kleiber's study of women's health collective suggests (72).

In such an ethnography of the movement there would also have to be attention to working-class and minority women who tend to identify more strongly along class and race lines than on the basis of sex. Many feel little in common with affluent housewives and professional women and students in the liberation movement. They feel that their men need rights as much as the "already privileged feminists" (50). Working-class women often feel that men are put down as much as women, and black women insist that their own emancipation cannot be separated from that of their men.

Studies of women's roles and especially their roles in change in the USA may lead to some surprises. Most anthropologists who dared to predict the course of sex role changes in the future of the USA have predicted more identity, or sameness, in sex roles for men and women, more public roles for women, and more domestic engagement for men (76). As Spiro's revisit to the Kibbutzim of Israel shows (130), a return, in some unpredictable degree, to more traditional sex roles may occur when some as yet undifferentiated point is reached in liberation. Our own most recent work in Germany shows something of the kind occurring there as well. The current conservative swing in the USA already seems to be carrying sex roles along with it to some extent. One thing is clear, the differences between men and women go deep in culture and social contextualization, however deep they may or may not be in biology. How these major forces comingle and separate in sex-linked behavior will continue to be a major focus of study by all the disciplines for a long time to come.

LANGUAGES IN THE USA

The title of this brief section is taken from a recent collection edited by Ferguson & Heath (24). We offer the following comments as a reminder that language is an integral part of culture and can be treated as a significant dimension of American culture. Of five recent edited collections on American culture discussed in the next section, however, only two include explicit attention to language. Possibly this is the case because the greater part of the work on language in the USA has been done by nonanthropological linguists.

American English appears to be an expression of a loosely bounded or open culture. Tendencies to eliminate the past tense in conversation, disregard distinctions between adjectives and adverbs, adsorb words and phrases from Black English, Italian, Jewish, etc, use exaggerated terms, abbreviate extensively in both writing and speaking, compound parts of words into new words, and use contact words extensively characterize current mainstream language use (81).

There is, however, little solid evidence of language homogenization in the USA. In fact, variety in social dialects may be on the increase as special groups and life styles have developed in urban contexts. Though regional and social class distinctions in language are much less than in Great Britain, dialectic diversification is continuing (24, 81).

In addition to life styles and interest groups, ethnicity is a major source of diversification. Much more work has been done on the speech usages of ethnic minorities; this is appropriate, since some 28 million Americans have a language other than English as a mother tongue or live in households where some other language is spoken. Ethnic diversity is currently being renewed with the influx of refugees and migrant workers as well as the many thousands from Great Britain and Europe seeking improvements in material well-being. Only a small portion of this study had been carried out, however, by anthropological linguists. Black English has received the most attention (9, 67, 68, 83, 149, 153).

Anthropological linguists have long been interested in the classification of and relationships among American Indian languages, but few have been concerned with the social signficance of contemporary Native American language use (70). Some work, however, has been done recently on the social contexts of speech acts (10, 96, 97).

Some recent studies in the special languages of occupational groups suggests that this is a rich field that can profitably be worked further and will contribute to our understanding of increasing diversification (90, 98).

It seems apparent that all dimensions of the study of language should be studied as a part of a larger concern with American culture. Some of the questions raised in this review concerning uniformity and diversity can be pursued profitably in studies of language usage.

COLLECTIONS AND CASE STUDIES

Courses on American culture, devised and taught by anthropologists, have apparently proliferated on American campuses, to judge from the appearance of several major collected volumes and texts for class use, starting with Jorgenson & Truzzi's *Anthropology and American Life* in 1974 (55), the first to appear since the special issue of the AAA in 1955 (2). Montague & Arens' *The American Dimension* (85) has already appeared in two editions (1976 and 1981). Others include Spradley & Rynkiewich's *The Nacirema* (133). Holmes' *The American Tribe* (42), and most recently Kottak's *Researching American Culture* (64). Each of these volumes except the latter contains a sample of published articles and some original pieces. Several include material researched and written by undergraduate students. This trend was pioneered by Spradley and McCurdy with a 1972 text (132) that outlines an approach to ethnographic research employing an ethnoscientific model and includes twelve mini ethnographies·by undergraduate students.

The range of topics and approaches subsumed by the collected volumes prohibits coherent review in short compass. Though many of the pieces included in each of the collected volumes are of first class qualtiy, some lack enough depth to be taken seriously by undergraduate users. There is a tendency at times to produce scintillating observations without much hard evidence to support them. Anthropologists still seem prone to take American culture less seriously than they do those of others. Doubtless some of this can be traced to an attempt to titillate and stimulate student interest and probably some of it is successful in so doing. In our experience in a course at Stanford on American culture that we initiated in 1973 and that has enjoyed a growing undergraduate enrollment, the more in-depth analyses with substantial evidence to support them are the most effective. We find also, with other instructors, that students thrive on instruction in and application of ethnographic methods to their own surroundings in field studies they can carry out themselves.

The other major indication of a growing interest in anthropology at home for instructional use is the appearance of case studies on various segments of American culture. The most recent include Applebaum's study of construction workers (3), Gamst's on locomotive engineers (26), Williams' of a black urban neighborhood (155), and Wong's of the New York Chinatown (157). The first American culture case study in the series edited by the Spindlers appeared in 1969 with Keiser's first edition of *Vice Lords* (57). The first studies of a segment of the mainstream appeared in 1972, with the publication of Pilcher on longshoremen (99) and Partridge on a hippie ghetto (92). Other widely used case studies on segments of American culture include Madsen & Guerrero on Mexican Americans in South Texas (75), Hostetler & Huntington on the Hutterites (44) and on the Amish (43), Hicks on an Appalachian community (38), Daner on the Hare Krsna (14), Jacob's on a retirement community (51), Rosenfeld on a slum school (108), Wolcott on an elementary school principal (156), Davidson on Chicano prisoners (15), Aschenbrenner on black families in Chicago (4), Dougherty on rural black women (21), Kunkel on a rural black community (65), Safa on the poor of Puerto Rico (111), and Sugarman on a drug therapy center (137).

A number of the case studies published on American Indians are explicitly oriented to interaction with the mainstream American culture, including Garbarino on the Seminole (27), McFee on the Blackfeet (79), Hoebel on the Cheyennes (41), Spindlers on the Menomini (126), Downs on the Washo (22) and the Navajo (23), and most recently Grobsmith on the Lakota Sioux (32).

Thirty case studies on segments of American culture appeared in the series between 1969 and 1983. Though their publication by a major commercial publisher is evidence that academic concern with American culture by anthropologists has been taken seriously, it is noteworthy that the sales of these studies have never approximated the volume of sales of other studies in the series devoted to remote non-Western cultures. The wisdom of their publication from a profit-oriented point of view has always been questionable, however useful they may have been to instructors in the emerging curricula of anthropological American studies. Because of their marginality in this framework, many of these studies will shortly become unavailable for multiple class use. In our experience, case studies are essential instructional materials. They provide a relatively in-depth look into the phenomenal variety of American culture(s). They exemplify the cross-cultural view, but within the boundaries of American culture and society, that anthropologists have claimed as their special advantage in examining behavior elsewhere.

CLOSING REMARKS

We have not attempted in this review to cover everything written on American culture by anthropologists and have touched on very little written by others. Nevertheless, 161 references have been cited. American anthropologists have made a significant effort to study their own culture. The pace of such efforts has increased of late and will probably continue to accelerate. The boundaries between "foreign," "overseas," "exotic," or even "primitive" or "nonliterate" and "at home" or "in our own culture" are disappearing as the world culture becomes more uniform at one level and more diverse at another. Within the USA the diversification is particularly impressive. All of the skills and insights gained by anthropologists in cultures away from home can be used to good advantage at home. Anthropologists attend to symbols, ceremonies, rituals, communities, language and thought, beliefs, dialects, sex roles and sexuality, subsistence and ecology, kinship, and a multitude of other topics in ways that historians, sociologists, political scientists, and psychologists will not, because of the heritage of experience with "other" cultures from primitive to peasant to urban away from home.

Literature Cited

1. Aamodt, A. 1981. Neighboring: discovering support systems among Norwegian American women. See Ref. 82, pp. 133–49
2. *American Anthropologist.* 1955. The U.S.A. as anthropologists see it. See Ref. 69
3. Applebaum, H. 1981. *Royal Blue: The Culture of Construction Workers.* New York: Holt, Rinehart & Winston
4. Aschenbrenner, J. 1975. *Lifelines: Black Families in Chicago.* New York: Holt, Rinehart & Winston
5. Bahr, H. B., Chadwick, J., Stauss, R. 1979. *American Ethnicity.* Lexington, Mass: Heath
6. Deleted in proof
7. Boas, F. 1928. *Anthropology and Modern Life.* New York: Morton
8. Braroe, N. 1975. *Indian and White: Self-Image and Interaction in a Canadian Plains Community.* Stanford, Calif: Stanford Univ. Press
9. Burling, R. 1973. *English in Black and White.* New York: Holt, Rinehart & Winston
10. Cazden, C., John, V., Hymes, D., eds. 1972. *The Functions of Language in the Classroom.* New York: Teachers Coll. Press
11. Collier, J. 1974. Women in politics. See Ref. 106, pp. 89–96
12. Crevecoeur, M. G. St. Jean de. 1904. *Letters from an American Farmer.* New York: Fox, Duffield
13. Crevecoeur, M. G. St. Jean de. 1967. The American, this new man. See Ref. 103, pp. 15–18
14. Daner, F. 1976. *The American Children of Krsna.* New York: Holt, Rinehart & Winston
15. Davidson, R. T. 1974. *Chicano Prisoners: The Key to San Quentin.* New York: Holt, Rinehart & Winston
16. Davis, A., Gardner, B., Gardner, M. 1941. *Deep South: A Social Anthropological Study of Caste and Class.* Chicago: Univ. Chicago Press
17. de Beauvoir, S. 1953. *The Second Sex.* New York: Knopf
18. DeVos, G. 1980. Ethnic adaptation and minority status. *J. Cross-Cult. Psychol.* 11:101–24
19. DeVos, G. 1981. Adaptive strategies in American minorities. In *Ethnicity and Mental Health,* ed. E. E. Jones, S. Korchin
20. Dollard, J. 1937. *Caste and Class in a Southern Town.* New Haven: Yale Univ. Press
21. Dougherty, M. 1978. *Becoming a Woman in Rural Black Culture.* New York: Holt, Rinehart & Winston
22. Downs, J. 1966. *The Two Worlds of the Washo: An Indian Tribe of California and Nevada.* New York: Holt, Rinehart & Winston
23. Downs, J. 1972. *The Navajo.* New York: Holt, Rinehart & Winston
24. Ferguson, C., Heath, S. 1981. *Language in the U.S.A.* New York: Cambridge Univ. Press
25. Fujita, M. 1979. *A Review Essay on Community Studies in America.* Stanford Univ: Unpublished manuscript
26. Gamst, F. 1980. *The Hoghead: An Industrial Ethnology of the Locomotive Engineer.* New York: Holt, Rinehart & Winston
27. Garbarino, M. C. 1972. *Big Cypress: A Changing Seminole Community.* New York: Holt, Rinehart & Winston
28. Garretson, L. R. 1976. *American Culture: An Anthropological Perspective.* Dubuque, Iowa: Brown
29. Gillin, J. 1955. National and regional cultural values in the United States. *Soc. Forces* 34:107–13
30. Gilmore, P., Glatthorn, A., eds. 1982. *Children in and out of School: Ethnography and Education.* Washington DC: Language & Ethnography Ser.
31. Gorer, G. 1948. *The American People: A Study in American Character.* New York: Norton
32. Grobsmith, E. 1981. *Lakota of the Rosebud: A Contemporary Ethnography.* New York: Holt, Rinehart & Winston
33. Hallowell, A. I. 1957. The backwash of the frontier: the impact of the Indian on American culture. In *The Frontier in Perspective,* ed. W. Wyman, C. Kroeber, pp. 229–58. Madison: Univ. Wis. Press
34. Harris, M. 1981. *America Now: The Anthropology of a Changing Culture,* p. 10. New York: Simon & Schuster
35. Hatch, E. 1979. *Biography of a Small Town.* New York: Columbia Univ. Press
36. Henry, J. 1963. *Culture Against Man,* pp. 283–322. New York: Random House
37. Henry, J. 1966. A theory for an anthropological analyses of American culture. *Anthropol. Q.* 39:90–109
38. Hicks, G. L. 1976. *Appalachian Valley.* New York: Holt, Rinehart & Winston
39. Hodge, W. 1975. Ethnicity as a factor in modern American Indian migration: A Winnebago case study with references to other Indian situations. In *Migration and Development,* ed. H. Safa, B. Dutoit. The Hague: Mouton

40. Hodge, W. 1981. The first Americans in the larger contemporary society: the parts and the whole. In *The First Americans, Then and Now*, ed. W. Hodge, pp. 503–33. New York: Holt, Rinehart & Winston

41. Hoebel, E. A. 1977. *The Cheyennes: Indians of the Great Plains*. New York: Holt, Rinehart & Winston. 2nd ed.

42. Holmes, L. 1978. *The American Tribe*. Lexington, Mass: Xerox Publ. program

43. Hostetler, J. A., Huntington, G. E. 1971. *Children in Amish Society: Socialization and Community Education*. New York: Holt, Rinehart & Winston

44. Hostetler, J. A., Huntington, G. E. 1980. *The Hutterites in North America*. New York: Holt, Rinehart & Winston. Fieldwork ed.

45. Hsu, F. 1953. *Americans and Chinese: Two Ways of Life*. New York: Schuman

46. Hsu, F. 1972. American core values and national character. In *Psychological Anthropology*, ed. F. Hsu. Cambridge, Mass: Schenkman

47. Hsu, F. 1973. Rugged individualism reconsidered. *Colo. Q.* 9:145–62

48. Hsu, F. 1979. Roots of the American family from Noah to now. In *Kin and Communities: Families in America*, ed. A. Lichtman, J. Challinor. Washington DC: Smithsonian Inst. Press

49. Hsu, F. 1981. *Americans and Chinese: Passage to Differences*. Honolulu: Univ. Hawaii Press

50. Hymowitz, C., Weissman, M. 1978. *A History of Women in America*, p. 361. New York: Bantam Books

51. Jacobs, J. 1974. *Fun City: An Ethnographic Study of a Retirement Community*. New York: Holt, Rinehart & Winston

52. Jacobs, S. 1982. Women in development programs. *Am. Anthropol.* 84:366–71

53. James, H. 1976. The Plains gourd dance as a revitalization movement. *Am. Ethnol.* 3:243–59

54. Jefferson, T. 1781. The moral independence of the cultivators of the earth. See Ref. 103, pp. 18–19

55. Jorgensen, J., Truzzi, M., eds. 1974. *Anthropology and American Life*. Englewood Cliffs, NJ: Prentice-Hall

56. Kane, S. 1974. Ritual possession in a Southern Appalachian religious sect. *J. Am. Folklore* 87:293–302

57. Keiser, R. L. 1979. *The Vice Lords: Warriors of the Streets*. New York: Holt, Rinehart & Winston. Fieldwork ed. 1st ed. 1969

58. Kennedy, E. L. 1979. A perspective of feminist studies. *Occas. Pap. Anthropol.* No. 1, pp. 189–93. Buffalo: State Univ. New York

59. Kimball, S. 1955. Problem of studying American culture. *Am. Anthropol.* 57:1131–41

60. Kluckhohn, C. 1949. *Mirror for Man*. New York: McGraw-Hill

61. Kluckhohn, C. 1951. Values and value-orientation. In *Toward a General Theory of Action*, ed. T. Parsons, E. Shils, pp. 388–433. Cambridge: Harvard Univ. Press

62. Kluckhohn, F. 1950. Dominant and substitute profiles of cultural orientation. *Soc. Forces* 28:376–93

63. Kohl, S. B. 1976. *Working Together: Woman and Family in Southwestern Saskatchewan*. Toronto: Holt, Rinehart & Winston

64. Kottak, C., ed. 1982. *Researching American Culture: A Guide for Student Anthropologists*. Ann Arbor: Univ. Michigan Press

65. Kunkel, P., Kennard, S. 1971. *Spout Spring: A Black Community in the Ozarks*. New York: Holt, Rinehart & Winston

66. LaBarre, W. 1962. *They Shall Take Up Serpents*. Minneapolis: Univ. Minn. Press

67. Labov, W. 1966. *The Social Stratification of Non-standard English*. Washington DC: Center of Applied Linguistics

68. Labov, W. 1970. *The Study of Non-standard English*. Champaign, Ill: Natl. Counc. Teachers of English

69. Lantis, M., ed. 1955. The U.S.A. as anthropologists see it. *Am. Anthropol.* 57:1113–80. Special issue

70. Leap, W. 1981. American Indian languages. See Ref. 24, pp. 116–45

71. Lewis, H. 1978. European ethnicity in Wisconsin: an exploratory formulation. *Ethnicity* 8:174–88

72. Light, L., Kleiber, N. 1981. Interactive research in a feminist setting: The Vancouver women's health collective. See Ref. 82, pp. 167–84

73. Lynd, R., Lynd, H. 1929. *Middletown*. New York: Harcourt Brace

74. Lynd, R., Lynd, H. 1937. *Middletown in Transition*. New York: Harcourt Brace

75. Madsen, W., Guerrero, A. 1974. *Mexican-Americans of South Texas*. New York: Holt, Rinehart & Winston. 2nd ed.

76. Martin, M., Voorhies, B. 1975. *Female of the Species*, pp. 383–409. New York: Columbia Univ. Press

76a. Martineau, H. 1837. *Society in America*, Vol. 3. London: Saunders & Otley. See also Ref. 103, pp. 19–24

77. McDermott, R., Aron, J. 1978. Pirandello in the classroom: on the possibility of equal educational opportunity in American culture. In *Futures of Education for Exceptional Children: Emerging Struc-*

tures, ed. M. Reynolds, pp. 41–63. New York: Counc. Except. Child.

78. McElroy, A., Matthiasson, C., eds. 1979. Sex roles in changing cultures. *Occas. Pap. Anthropol.* No. 1, Buffalo: State Univ. New York

79. McFee, M. 1972. *Modern Blackfeet: Montanans on a Reservation.* New York: Holt, Rinehart & Winston

80. Mead, M. 1943. *And Keep Your Powder Dry.* New York: Morrow

81. Merelman, R. 1983. *Making Something of Ourselves.* Berkeley: Univ. Calif. Press

82. Messerschmidt, D., ed. 1981. *Anthropologists at Home in North America: Methods and Issues in the Study of One's Own Society.* New York: Cambridge Univ. Press

83. Mitchell-Kernan, C. 1972. Signifying and marking: two Afro-American speech acts. In *Directions in Sociolinguistics: The Ethnography of Communication,* ed. J. Gumperz, D. Hymes. New York: Holt, Rinehart & Winston

84. Moen, E., Boulding, E., Lillydahl, J., Palmer, R. 1981. *Women and the Social Costs of Economic Development: Two Colorado Case Studies.* Social Impact Assessment Ser. No. 5. Boulder: Westview

85. Montague, S., Arens, W. 1981. *The American Dimension: Cultural Myths and Social Realities.* Sherman Oaks, Calif: Alfred Publ.

86. Murphy, C. 1982. A survey of research. In *The Wilson Quarterly,* special issue on "Men and Women," 6:63–80

87. Myerhoff, B. 1978. *Number Our Days.* New York: Simon & Schuster, Touchstone Book

88. Nader, L. 1974. Up the Anthropologist: perspectives gained from studying up. In *Reinventing Anthropology,* ed. D. Hymes, pp. 284–311. New York: Random House, Vintage Books

89. Nay, B. 1974. *American Values: An Anthropological Analysis.* Senior Honors project, Dep. Anthropol., Stanford Univ. Unpublished manuscript

90. O'Barr, M. 1981. The language of the law. See Ref. 24, pp. 386–406

91. Ogbu, J. 1978. *Minority Education and Caste: The American System in Cross-Cultural Perspective.* New York: Academic

92. Partridge, W. L. 1972. *The Hippie Ghetto: The Natural History of a Subculture.* New York: Holt, Rinehart & Winston

93. Perin, C. 1977. *Everything in its Place. Social Order and Land Use in America.* Princeton: Princeton Univ. Press

94. Peshkin, A. 1978. *Growing Up American: Schooling and the Survival of Community.* Chicago: Univ. Chicago Press

95. Peshkin, A. 1982. The researcher and subjectivity: reflections on an ethnography of school and community. See Ref. 125, pp. 48–67

96. Philips, S. 1972. Participant studies and communicative competence: Warm Springs children in community and classroom. See Ref. 10, pp. 370–94

97. Philips, S. 1972. Acquisition of rules for appropriate speech usage. See Ref. 10

98. Philips, S. 1982. The language socialization of lawyers: acquiring the "cant." See Ref. 125, pp. 176–210

99. Pilcher, W. W. 1972. *The Portland Longshoremen: A Dispersed Urban Community.* New York: Holt, Rinehart & Winston

100. Potter, D. M. 1964. American women and the American character. In *American Character and Culture: Some Twentieth Century Perspectives,* ed. J. A. Hague, Ch. 8. Deland, Fla: Everett/Edwards

101. Prince, H. 1974. Cocoon work: an interpretation of the concern of contemporary youth with the mystical. See Ref. 160, pp. 255–74

102. Quinn, N. 1977. Anthropological studies on women's status. *Ann. Rev. Anthropol.* 6:181–225

103. Rapson, R., ed. 1967. *Individualism and Conformity in the American Character.* Boston: Heath

104. Riesman, D. 1955. *Individualism Reconsidered.* Garden City, NY: Doubleday

105. Riesman, D., Denny, R., Glazer, N. 1950. *The Lonely Crowd: A Study of the Changing American Character.* New Haven: Yale Univ. Press

106. Rosaldo, M. Lamphere, L., eds. 1974. *Women, Culture and Society.* Stanford, Calif: Stanford Univ. Press

107. Rosaldo, M., Lamphere, L. 1974. Preface. See Ref. 106, pp. v, vi

108. Rosenfeld, G. 1971. *"Shut Those Thick Lips": A study of Slum School Failure.* New York: Holt, Rinehart & Winston

109. Ruesch, J., Bateson, G. 1951. *Communication: The Social Matrix of Psychiatry.* New York: Norton

110. Ruskin, G., Varenne, H. 1982. The production of kinds of ethnic discourse in the United States: American and Puerto Rican patterns. In *The Sociogenesis of Language and Human Conduct: A Multidisciplinary Book of Readings,* ed. B. Bain, pp. 1–32. New York: Plenum

111. Safa, H. I. 1974. *The Urban Poor of Puerto Rico: A Study in Development and Inequality.* New York: Holt, Rinehart & Winston

112. Scheffler, H. 1976. The meaning of kinship in American culture: another view. In *Meaning in Anthropology*, ed. K. Basso, H. Selby. Albuquerque: Univ. New Mexico Press

113. Schneider, D. 1968. *American Kinship: A Cultural Account*. Englewood Cliffs, NJ: Prentice-Hall

114. Schneider, D. 1969. Kinship, nationality and religion in American culture: toward a definition of kinship. In *Forms of Symbolic Action*, ed. V. Turner, pp. 73–81. Proc. Am. Ethnol. Assoc., pp. 116–25

115. Schneider, D. 1977. Kinship, community, and locality in American culture. In *Kin and Communities*, ed. A. Lichtman, J. Challinor, pp. 155–74. Washington DC: Smithsonian Inst. Press

116. Sieber, T., Gordon, A. 1981. *Children and Their Organizations: Investigations in American Culture*. Boston: Hall

117. Smith, J. F., Kvasnicka, R., eds. 1981. *Indian-White Relations: A Persistent Paradox*. Washington DC: Howard Univ. Press

118. Smith, M. E. 1974. Portuguese enclaves: the invisible minority. In *Social and Cultural Identity*, ed. T. Fitzgerald. S.A.S. Proc. No. 8. Atlanta: Univ. Georgia Press

119. Smith, M. E. 1976. Networks and migration resettlement: cherchez la femme. *Anthropol. Q*. 49:20–27

120. Spindler, G. 1948. The military: A systematic analysis. *Soc. Forces* 29:305–10

121. Spindler, G. 1948. American character as revealed by the military. *Psychiatry: J. Oper. Statement Interpers. Relat*. 11: 275–81

122. Spindler, G. 1955. Education in a transforming American culture. *Harvard Educ. Rev*. 25:145–56

123. Spindler, G. 1959. *The Transmissions of American Culture*. Cambridge: Harvard Univ. Press

124. Spindler, G. 1977. Change and continuity in American core cultural values: an anthropological perspective. In *We the People: American Character and Social Change*, ed. G. D. De Renzo, pp. 20–40. Westport: Greenwood

125. Spindler, G., ed. 1982. *Doing the Ethnography of Schooling: Educational Anthropology in Action*. New York: Holt, Rinehart & Winston

126. Spindler, G., Spindler, L. 1971. *Dreamers Without Power, the Menomini Indians*. New York: Holt, Rinehart & Winston

127. Spindler, G., Spindler, L. 1978. Identity, militancy, and cultural congruence: The Menominee and Kainai. See Ref. 159, pp. 73–85

128. Spindler, L., Spindler, G. 1958. Male and female adaptations in culture change. *Am. Anthropol*. 60:217–33

129. Spindler, L., Spindler, G. 1979. Changing women in men's worlds. *Occas. Pap. Anthropol*. No. 1, pp. 35–48. Buffalo: State Univ. New York

130. Spiro, M. 1979. *Gender and Culture: Kibbutz Women Revisited*. Durham: Duke Univ. Press

131. Spradley, J. P., Mann, B. 1975. *The Cocktail Waitress: Women's Work in Man's World*. New York: Wiley

132. Spradley, J. P., McCurdy, D. 1972. *The Cultural Experience: Ethnography in Complex Society*. Chicago: Sci. Res. Assoc.

133. Spradley, J. P., Rynkiewich, M. 1975. *The Nacirema: Readings on American Culture*. Boston: Little, Brown

134. Stack, C. B. 1974. *All Our Kin: Strategies for Survival in a Black Community*. New York: Harper & Row

135. Strickon, A. 1975. Ethnicity and entrepreneurship in rural Wisconsin. In *Entrepreneurs in Cultural Context*, ed. S. Greenfield, A. Strickon, R. Aubey, pp. 159–90. Albuquerque: Univ. New Mexico Press

136. Strickon, A., Ibarra, R. n.d. *Norwegians and Tobacco in Wisconsin: The Changing Dynamics of Ethnicity*. Unpublished manuscript

137. Sugarman, G. 1974. *Daytop Village: A Therapeutic Community*. New York: Holt, Rinehart & Winston

138. Taylor, C. 1974. *In Horizontal Orbit*. New York: Holt, Rinehart & Winston

139. Thurnstrom, S. 1964. *Poverty or Progress? Social Mobility in a Nineteenth Century City*, p. 195. Cambridge: Harvard Univ. Press

139a. Toqueville, A. de. 1901. *Democracy in America*, transl. H. Reeve. New York: Appleton

140. Townsend, J. 1979. *Cultural Conceptions and Mental Illness: A Comparison of Germany and America*. Chicago: Univ. Chicago Press

141. Turner, F. J. 1921. *The Frontier in American History*. New York: Holt. See also Ref. 103, pp. 25–27

142. Varenne, H. 1977. *Americans Together: Structured Diversity in a Midwestern Town*. New York: Teachers Coll. Press

143. Varenne, H. 1978. Is Dedham American? The diagnosis of things American. *Anthropol. Q*. 51:231–45

144. Varenne, H. 1982. Jocks and freaks: the symbolic structure of the expression of social interaction among American senior high school students. See Ref. 125, pp. 210–35

145. Vidich, A., Bensman, J. 1958. *Small Town in Mass Society: Class, Power, and Religion in a Rural Community*. Princeton: Princeton Univ. Press

146. Vogt, E. Z., Albert, E., eds. 1966. *People of Rimrock: A Study of Values in Five Cultures*. Cambridge: Harvard Univ. Press

147. von Hübner, G. 1874. *A Ramble Around the World*. London: Macmillan. 2 vols. See also Ref. 103, pp. 22–25

148. Wallace, A. 1980. *Rockdale: The Growth of an American Village in the Early Industrial Revolution*. New York: Knopf

149. Ward, M. 1971. *Them Children: A Study in Language Learning*. New York: Holt, Rinehart & Winston

150. Warner, W. L. 1941. *The Social Life of a Modern Community*. Yankee City Ser. 1. New Haven: Yale Univ. Press

151. Warner, W. L., Meeker, M., Eels, K. 1949. *Social Class in America*. Chicago: Sci. Res. Assoc.

152. West, J. 1945. *Plainville, U.S.A.* New York: Columbia Univ. Press

153. Whately, E. 1981. Language among Black Americans. See Ref. 24, pp. 92–110

154. Whitehead, H. 1974. Reasonably fantastic: Some perspectives on Scientology, science fiction, and occultism. See Ref. 161, pp. 147–90

155. Williams, M. D. 1981. *On the Street Where I Lived: A Black Anthropologist Examines Lifestyles and Ethos in an Urban Afro-American Neighborhood*. New York: Holt, Rinehart & Winston

156. Wolcott, H. F. 1973. *The Man in the Principal's Office: An Ethnography*. New York: Holt, Rinehart & Winston

157. Wong, B. 1982. *Chinatown: Economic Adaptation and Ethnic Identity of the Chinese*. New York: Holt, Rinehart & Winston

158. Yanagisako, S. 1977. Women-centered kin networks in urban bilateral kinship. *Am. Ethnol.* 4:207–26

158a. Yanagisako, S. 1978. Variations in American kinship: Implications for cultural analysis. *Am. Ethnol.* 5:15–29. Special section: American Kinship

159. Yinger, J. M. 1982. *Countercultures: The Promise and the Peril of a World Turned Upside Down*. New York: Free Press

160. Yinger, J. M., Simpson, G., eds. 1978. Special Issue: American Indians today. *Ann. Am. Acad. Polit. Soc. Sci.* 436:1–212

161. Zaretsky, I., Leone, M., eds. 1974. *Religious Movements in Contemporary America*. Princeton: Princeton Univ. Press

Ann. Rev. Anthropol. 1983. 12:79–103

VARIATION IN PREHISTORIC AGRICULTURAL SYSTEMS OF THE NEW WORLD

Ray T. Matheny and Deanne L. Gurr

Department of Anthropology, Brigham Young University, Provo, Utah 84602

INTRODUCTION

In this paper we present a brief summary of prehistoric agricultural developments as they are presently understood in the New World. Constraints prevent detailed evaluation of all of the cultural areas defined in the New World. Emphasis is placed, therefore, on Mesoamerica and the Central Andes, where aboriginal high cultures were found. The American Southwest, Midwest, Southeast, and Eastern Woodlands are not treated even though agriculture was an important part of cultural development in those areas. The fact that many important cultigens now shared by the world came from the Mesoamerican and Central Andean areas places a priority on understanding something about food production of the American past.

Within these cultural areas we attempt to show research trends that have occurred over the past two decades. Since more intensive work has been done in Mesoamerica, it receives the greatest attention. The central question for Mesoamerica and the Central Andes has been the relationship of food production to the rise and fall of the state (15, 57, 73, 108, 117). Over the past decade the question has been redefined in terms of a significant increase in information obtained from an extensive amount of fieldwork.

MESOAMERICAN HIGHLANDS

Central Mexico

Intensive agriculture in a number of forms was a regular practice in most highland communities in prehistoric times. This statement stands without

79

0084–6570/83/1015–0079$02.00

challenge and is supported by observations by many field-workers of numerous terraces, dikes, dams, and irrigation channels from the Valley of Mexico (105, p. 6; 37) through the highlands of Guatemala (25, pp. 17–58). That the agricultural systems of the past supported dense populations in some of the highland areas is undeniable, but the standard of living in the past may have been lower in many areas than it is today (105).

In central Mexico, the basin of Mexico is bounded by volcanic mountains that form a large interior drainage with several tributary valleys and minor depressions, and it is classified as semiarid land. In this dry land, soil and water were conserved by building agricultural terraces set up without mortar in walls 0.5 m to 1.5 m high. Soil accumulated behind the wall or in some cases soils might have been carried in. Abandoned terraces are found particularly on high ground, but they are also found elsewhere. There seems to be a terrace type for each part of the varied landscape: steep hillslopes, gentle sloping hills, gullies, and soil-filled channels.

The system of farming the terraces is poorly understood. Investigation tends to be descriptive, which is a necessary early step. Within descriptions are included classifications of agricultural features. Donkin (25, p. 42) notes that "east of Texcoco there are (1) broad, irrigated terraces on the lower piedmont; and (2) irrigated and (3) dry contour benches in the foothills." Added to these are high terrace walls, some 2 m in height, located on gentle sloping ground; cross-channel terraces in steep-sloping ground are up to 6 m high; bench terraces that are closedly spaced appearing as flights of stairs on steep slopes; and broad, nonirrigated terraced fields and sod terraces.

Presumably the primary purpose of terrace construction was to create agricultural land that could be used intensively. The terrace impedes the loss of soil and moisture, and in many cases it accumulates valuable soil in areas where otherwise it would be lost. The landscape in which the terraces are found is extremely varied, as are many microenvironmental factors. Each econiche exploited required special treatment of the soil, appropriate terrace construction, vegetation control, upland manipulation for water catchment, proper crop choice, and timing for the season.

Sanders (105, p. 41) thinks that the deep-soil plains of the Teotihuacan Valley where irrigation water was available was the area of concentrated agricultural activities. Millon (71, 72) favors plains in both the Teotihuacan Valley and the Valley of Mexico as areas of agricultural concentration. However, the presence of canals, a dam, and numerous terraces upland (107) indicate that concentrated effort may have been invested elsewhere as well. The Basin of Mexico has a rich history of terracing and land manipulation. Donkin (25) has carefully reported locations of terraces and has described their different construction in varied landscapes.

Some of the agricultural features reported for the Valley of Mexico include stone terraces at: Zacatenco, 1150–650 B.C. (120, p. 310); Ticoman, 560–300 B.C.; Ixtapalapa-Texcoco, 650–300 B.C.; and Tezoyuca 300–100 B.C. Canals are noted at Cuicuilco, 750 B.C.; Santa Clara Xalostoc (109) and Santa Clara Coatitlan (80), possibly 920–650 B.C.; and Otumba, 300–100 B.C. (107, p. 267). Numerous canals are reported near Teotihuacan (109, p. 2), possibly dating as early as 300–100 B.C. or earlier. All of these features are evidence of intensive agricultural practices associated with Formative cultures. The early dates are surprising and suggest significant experience in land manipulation for agricultural purposes. The canals in the Valley of Teotihuacan serviced approximately 5000 ha of land and may have required highly organized labor for their construction and maintenance. Channelized raised fields at Teotihuacan covered more than 100 ha and also may have involved organized activity. Both constructions suggest systems of intensive agriculture with considerable investments in labor.

In the Christian era the same constructions are known with the addition of chinampas. Chinampas may have been in use as early as 200 B.C. near Tlatilco but the evidence is tentative. The extensiveness of chinampa gardening in the Valley of Mexico clearly points to an elaborate system of high production (4). Coe (9) has stressed the high production of food available to the Aztecs, who used the chinampa system in the Valley of Mexico. He points out that chinampas now produce up to seven harvests a year of different crops from a single plot. This same rate of productivity is thought to have been achieved by the Aztecs, and it may have contributed to their wealth and power. Though the chinampas are best known as a system practiced in more recent times, the idea that they had earlier origins is supported by the fact that they are oriented 15–17° east of true north. This is the same orientation as the streets of Teotihuacan which date to Formative times. Other chinampa towns seem to have favored the same orientation.

MacNeish (63, pp. 314–15) notes that in the Tehuacan Valley of Puebla, "truly effective food production" occurred for the first time in the Santa Maria phase, 850–150 B.C., as a result of the introduction of irrigation. In the subsequent Palo Blanco and Venta Salada phases, 150 B.C. to A.D. 1500, there was a development from villages with temples to much more complex settlements. This development was based on the success of intensive agriculture, mainly irrigation, in a land that receives only 400–900 mm of rain a year.

It is evident that several systems of food production had been worked out successfully in the Central Mexican Highlands during Formative times. The systems assisted ancient farmers in coping with the problems of little rainfall, few adequate perennial streams, land subject to serious, rapid erosion once disturbed, swampy ground, shallow lakes, and an increasing population.

There are a number of trends represented in current studies in the area of Central Mexico. Sanders & Santley (109) have examined modern cultivation practices by small producers in the Tehuacan Valley. Their study begins with an analysis of ecological zones that shows considerable variability of environment. Items such as soil fertility, texture, depth, susceptibility to erosion, frost cycle, rainfall, drainage, and other special problems are taken into consideration. The techniques of modern farmers are examined to see how each econiche is handled for preplanting irrigation, planting schedule, tool assemblages and techniques required, crop selection, percentage of dependence upon each crop for total food consumption and that which is marketed. Sanders and co-workers also consulted ethnohistorical sources and considered the relationships of modern farming to ancient agricultural features.

Other studies are supplemented by investigations of the type represented by Gonzales-Jacome (39), who has shown the importance of home gardens in Central Mexico. Ethnolinguistic interpretations are presented from Aztec sources that precisely describe gardening practices of the sixteenth century. The level of sophistication of Aztec gardening technology is revealed in terms of manuring, fertilizing by water and mud, irrigating, planting trees, pruning, grafting, and other arboricultural techniques. The sources specify plots located next to the house, orchard gardens, vegetable gardens planted with seeds, including flowers, home gardens surrounded by walls, home gardens for pleasure, land with fruit trees or with grafted trees, land cultiviated with avocados, and a garden or place with lilies.

Gonzales-Jacome sees historic evidence for the conversion by Spanish edict of the native intensive labor agricultural systems to small-scale local systems, dependence upon seasonal rainfall crops, and self-supply oriented agriculture. This is followed by a study of five agrosystems currently in use in the Puebla-Tlaxcala Valley. These systems include seasonal rainfall plots, terraces, irrigation plots, drained fields, and home gardens. Although these same kinds of plots existed in the past, the social system that maintained them in their past configurations no longer exists. The agricultural zones have been transformed to support the European economies that lead to abandonment of terraces and other agricultural plots. Therefore, ethnographic comparisons and analogies will not provide the level of understanding of past agricultural systems that might be hoped for. The modern plots include many native American cultigens, but European cultigens are also present to support a cattle industry. The different plot systems no longer complement each other to the same degree as in the past because there is a modern tendency toward monocropping, and ecological management of resources on a large scale is no longer carried out. The collective labor that maintained the agrosystems of the past has been dispersed with the redirection of society.

Another trend is represented by an attempt to bridge the gap between the ethnohistorical sources and the physical remains of the Aztec occupation (106).

Spanish tax data from the sixteenth century are used as a control of archaeologically determined population estimates in the Basin of Mexico. Elaborate classifications of settlements from rural sites to "supra-regional centers" follow with assignments of periodization and population estimates of sites. Explanation of ecological adaptation and technologies to accomplish the adaptations over time that are developed in this study has provided us with the best understanding to date of social history of a past civilization of the New World.

Central Valley of Oaxaca

The highland central Valley of Oaxaca has a semiarid climate similar to that of Central Mexico. It includes an area of approximately 3400 km^2 and lies about 1550 m above sea level. The valley bottom covers about 700 km^2 where alluvial soils are found. Rainfall is limited to between 500 and 700 mm annually, and the surrounding mountains receive up to 1000 mm (35, p. 449).

The water table in the floodplain of the river is about 3 m below the surface. Soil and moisture available in the western part of the valley allow for dry farming. Flannery et al (35) suggest that large-scale irrigation is not practical within the valley because water sources are not adequate. Shallow well irrigation techniques, called "pot irrigation," where water was taken from wells 1.5 to 3 m deep and was poured on individual plants, were developed as early as 700 B.C. Up to three harvests a year could be obtained using "pot irrigation." This method required no organization beyond the household level within the high water table area. Dry farming and pot irrigation account for much of the success of early villages. Small-scale irrigation is noted later on upland streams and may be associated with the development of towns and ceremonial centers from 1000 B.C. to 350 B.C. (35, 36). Larger "master canals" are known that directed water to small channels within the piedmont zone. Neely (79) reports a hot water spring where fossilization by precipitated travertine took place, preserving the entire physical layout of the canal system. His 41 test excavations within the complex of canals and dry-laid stone terraces revealed ceramics dating from 500 B.C. to A.D. 1350.

The early villages and towns were supported by four agricultural systems (35, p. 452): dry farming, pot irrigation, small canal irrigation, and less intensive fallowing systems in the piedmont. These systems apparently were adequate to permit considerable population growth.

During Monte Alban II times (A.D. 1–250), extensive rock terraces were constructed on the lower slopes of mountains. These terraces received only rainfall. The terraces, soil, and moisture-retaining features extended the amount of land under cultivation and added another system to food production. Blanton & Kowalewski (5, pp. 98–100) discuss the administrative structure that was required to feed the dense population at Monte Alban at 300–200 B.C.

Once it had reached a threshold population of city proportions, a central institution and administrative hierarchy governing surplus food production and distribution became necessary.

Going beyond description of agricultural features, Lees (57) and Downing (27) have studied contemporary small-scale Oaxacan irrigation systems. Their investigations have shown that a complicated social order is associated with the use of water. Plants have specific water requirements during growing phases in order to survive and to realize maximum production. Once a canal system is instituted from a common water source, controls over the water are necessary for impoundment, flooding ground during periods of plant stress, and for maintenance of the system that calls for cooperative effort depending on the variables present.

An interesting aspect of the small-scale irrigation system at Diaz Ordaz, a town in the Valley of Oaxaca, is its relationship with the village of San Miguel del Valle, which is located high on the watershed (27). The upper villagers practice swidden agriculture, principally growing beans and potatoes. The vegetable debris and soil displaced by swidden farming upstream provides the nutrients for the small-scale irrigation plots of Diaz Ordaz below. The discovery of the interconnectedness of food production activities gives insight into the complications of a single agricultural system.

Central Mountain Chain

This area includes the Meseta Central of San Cristobal, the Comitan Plain, and the Sierra Madre of Guatemala. Ancient agricultural terraces have been noted on high ground (1500–2000 m) from San Cristobal de las Casas, Chiapas, Mexico, to Guatemala City. Although the elevation drops slightly below 2000 m at about 50 km south of San Cristobal, it rises again in the Cuchumatanes Mountains and the high ground runs southeast to San Salvador.

In Chiapas Donkin (25, p. 73) illustrates stone terraces constructed across small tributaries and outwash fans between Chamula and Saklamanton. Also, terraces are numerous on the slopes of dry valleys in the basin of Amatenango. This land is mountainous and where slopes are not steep and adequate soil is present, coinfers abound. The high, shallow valleys often are covered with grass or trees. Terrace constructions are also found at Aguacatenango, San Francisco, Comitan, and between Ocosingo and Comitan. The limestone hills are covered with oak, cypress, and pine, and now suffer from severe erosion because of deforestation. The ancient terraces are contour benches 1 to 2 m high faced with cut stone. At Hunchavin, just northwest of Comitan, hill slopes are almost entirely sculpted in rock terraces. The lower terraces are used on occasion for milpa. Adams (2), in his transect survey of the area, describes numerous small terraces associated with archaeological sites.

Numerous developed springs and wells exist in the Chiapas Highland tract (67, pp. 170–71). The well at San Francisco is a walk-in type that may be an ancient well refurbished in recent times or may have been constructed according to an ancient model. Water has been a precious item, especially drinking water, in the highlands. Some springs are guarded by Tzotzil Maya today (122, p. 14), and ceremonies and rituals are held at water holes (121).

Below Comitan, on the southwestern edge of the Comitan plain, are sharply rising limestone mountains. Within these mountains are many ancient terrace constructions. Most notable is the Late Classic (A.D. 600–900) site of Tenam Puente (6, pp. 425–28). There are no springs or running streams at the site, but there are hundreds of terraces. The terracing is continuous and 174 have been counted on an aerial photograph in 1 km^2 (68). Many of the terraces are of the contour type following slopes horizontally, creating a series of narrow parallel fields. Weir-type terraces closely spaced were built across gulleys. Even today there is no appreciable erosion despite abandonment for nine or ten centuries. Modern farmers do clean off and use some of the old terraces and there are a few places where they have been repaired. The carefully arranged layout at Tenam Puente, which has afforded considerable environmental control, included at least terracing, public buildings, and residences. The terms "mountain garden town" has been suggested for this type of settlement (67, p. 171). Considerable engineering skill in conceptualization, execution, and maintenance is expressed in placing the soil and water resources under such careful control.

Within the Central Depression of Chiapas, below the mountainous country around San Cristobal de las Casas, Lowe & Mason (61, p. 227) report extensive agricultural terracing including walls laid up across drainages, check dams across arroyos, "accompanied by vast zones of stone house foundations and intermittent ceremonial precincts." Lowe (58) further reports agricultural terracing along the Grijalva River drainages. Perhaps the most ubiquitous ancient agricultural feature of the upper Grijalva drainages are the lineal-sloping dry fields where stones have been set in long rows perpendicular to slopes. These lineal alignments of stones have not been investigated by excavation nor studied to reveal how they functioned. The alignments of stone are continuous at some sites, effectively tying together large parcels of land. There was no attempt to build the stepped rock terrace commonly found in the mountains. The linkages of lineal-sloping dry fields with their stones set in patterns may have served to disperse water rather evenly over the ground (114). These fields extend up into the gentle hills that rise from the ancient upper Grijalva river terraces at the foot of the Cuchumatanes Mountains of Guatemala at Quen Santo (110, pp. 84, 97).

In addition to lineal dry fields, "fossilized" canal systems and other agricultural features have been reported from the upper Grijalva tributaries area

(68). Fossilization of the canals at sites such as Lagartero and Rancho Berlin was caused by the precipitation of travertine. These canal systems have yet to be explored and excavated.

In the highlands of western Guatemala the presence of ancient agricultural features is less well documented. There is a lack of stone in these volcanic lands and many terraces are built of soil. Historical records suggest a dense population in the sixteenth century which may have necessitated the practice of intensive agriculture. No agricultural features have been reported from the important site of Zaculeu, but terraces are reported at Todos Santos, Jacaltenango, and Quetzaltenango. Terraces made of river cobbles are found in the valley of the Rio Samala southwest of the basin of Quetzaltenango. Terraces are found in the basin of San Marcos, and extensive and elaborate terraces are found in the basins of Lake Atitlan and Amatitlan. Dating of the Guatemalan terraces is problematical, and McBryde (69) suggests that the soil terraces and some rock terraces were constructed in historic times to raise European vegetables such as onions.

Maya Lowlands

Perhaps it was Cowgill's (12) response to the results of agronomic studies in the Maya lowlands (32, 47–49, 102, 115) that stimulated the wealth of current studies in the Maya area. The surveys of Emerson & Kempton (32) brought into focus the problem of diminishing production in milpa agriculture, while Kempton (51) determined that diminishing yield in successive use of a piece of ground was due to loss of soil fertility, and that the ground does not receive fertilizer in the form of ashes. Steggerda's (115) study focused on experimental agricultural plots providing controlled data. Dubious interpretation of Steggerda's experiments did not help to settle the question of nutrient loss from the soil. Hester (47–49) experimented with cutting down trees using stone tools versus cutting them down with steel tools. This had a bearing on the time and labor it took to clear forest cover for swidden agriculture. Cowgill's (12) approach was to gather empirical evidence through observing and interviewing milperos in the Peten, Guatemala. Information on corn consumption was gathered to relate to productivity per farmer and the total crop required to support a community. Cowgill determined that mineral loss was more important than weed competition in swidden agriculture. This study was the most significant of the time in presenting excellent data on yield, decline in yield year by year, nutrient content of the soil, household size, and consumption of corn on a comparative basis. These data show that in the central Peten forest four crops of corn a year were possible, most of the land is usable for corn planting, a population density of 100 to 200 people per square mile was possible, one milpero could produce enough corn for two households, two successive plantings of cultigens caused a decrease in all minerals and organic materials measured, and more than two successive plantings would yield adequate results. The bottom line in the study was that loss of soil fertility was not significant in the collapse of Classic Maya civilization.

Wilken (123, p. 432) proposed that swidden agriculture did not have to be defended as the sole means whereby Maya civilization survived. He argued that intensive agricultural systems required considerable control over environmental aspects of soil and water. This control further required cooperation or administrative enforcement, and intensive "agriculture may be quite sensititve to social or political change" (123, p. 433). He suggested that the knowledge of intensive food-producing systems spread rapidly from area to area. Terraces, tablones, irrigation, chinampas, drained fields, gardens, tree culture, and high-performance milpa were shown to be alternative intensive agricultural systems available to the ancient Maya. There have been many specialized studies of these alternative systems, and notions that the urban developments in the Maya area preceded the advent of intensive cultivation (30) were challenged. Bronson's (8) suggestion of root crops as an alternative to corn was challenged by Cowgill (13), who postulated that the Maya found a grassland at ca 2000 B.C. instead of a forest. She suggests that root crops such as manioc would not thrive in a grassland environment and that tropical forest development was a result of human modification. Lowe (60), on the other hand, proposed a dependency on manioc on the west coast of Chiapas during the Barra and Ocos horizons (just prior to 1600 B.C.) and suggests that forest products were very important (59, p. 236).

Puleston & Puleston (94) stress the rich environment of plant and animal resources available to the Maya and include the ramon nut as an alternative to corn for carbohydrates in the diet. Puleston & Doyle (95) analyze the diet of modern Maya groups located in both highland and lowland areas. Their quantification of diet provides a model that may be applied to the ancient Maya, showing that adequate protein could be obtained from plants.

Siemens & Puleston (111) made the discovery of many ancient ridged fields and canals along the Candelaria River in Campeche. Excavations confirmed the artificial nature of the ridges and a piece of wood provided a radiocarbon date of A.D. 229 ± 50 years. This discovery cast doubt on the viability of the swidden system to support the Classic Maya civilization. Harris (43, p. 257) provided the article of faith when he said that if the Maya had achieved civilization exclusively on swidden cultivation then they did what

'no other swidden society has achieved: namely, to overcome all the ecological and social limitations inherent in the system and to generate mechanisms of centralized authority sufficiently powerful to control land rights and regulate shifts in cultivation over such an extensive area that swidden could continue for many centuries without getting out of equilibrium with the environment.'

Eaton's (31) discovery of hundreds of ridged fields and hillside terraces associated with ancient farmsteads in the Rio Bec area was a further confirmation of intensive agricultural activities dated to Classic Maya times. Turner (116) brought together numerous published references of terraces and raised fields in the Maya Mountains of Belize, Guatemala, Campeche, and Quintana Roo. He notes that despite the fact that these relics have been known for some time in an area not far from Tikal, they were not considered seriously when discussing the subsistence of the ancient Maya. The Rio Bec farmsteads discovery led to a survey extending to Becan, Xpujil, Chicanna, and other Classic Maya sites in the Rio Bec area. Turner (116, p. 119) reports that "tens of thousands of relic terraces crisscross the hillsides of southern Campeche and Quintana Roo, encompassing an area exceeding 10,000 square kilometers." These terraces are mostly classified as the linear sloping dry field type that have no artificial water and depend upon natural precipitation. Other features that were found includes: checkdams and weir terraces made of cut limestone walls; terraces occurring on slopes of 4° to 47°; linear ridges running up and down slopes built up of parallel limestone walls filled with rubble; and the connection of these to terraces or to form walkways.

The purpose of the terraces was to capture soil and prevent it from dispersing along with the precious water. The soil in the Rio Bec area is only 5–45 cm deep, and the soil and water retention terraces conserved these precious resources for agriculture. The walkways acted to control runoff water, preventing damage to the network of terraces and serving as transportation paths.

Hammond (40, p. 328) sees terracing as corporate activity requiring the labor of an organized workforce. He suggests that intensive agriculture was more labor-effective than extensive milpa. Raised fields could be viewed in the same way as terraces in this context. When Turner (116) became aware of raised fields in bajos, or areas where seasonal innundation occurs, he realized the great potential for the agricultural use of these areas traditionally viewed as badlands. The artificially raised portions of ground increased the agricultural land available to the ancient Maya by reclaiming marginal land. When Puleston (91, p. 452) reported a date of 1110 ± 230 B.C. from a post that had been driven into sediments of an ancient canal in an area of raised fields in Belize, he stimulated great interest in the antiquity of intensive agriculture in the lowlands. Also, because of the question of the antiquity of agriculture in the lowlands, Puleston's discovery made the discovery of *Zea mays* pollen and burnt grass from the bottom of Laguna de Petenxil in the Peten dating to 2000 B.C. seem more believable (14). Extensive evidence was found for Middle Preclassic occupation in the Lake Yaxha and Lake Sacnab areas (98, p. 442) that was presumably based on swidden agriculture. *Zea mays* was being grown at 2000 B.C. (uncorrected) at Cuello, Belize, in a forest setting (42, 70). Puleston's discovery is the only evidence for the lowlands that intensive agricultural techniques were practiced as early as the Middle Preclassic period.

Coe & Diehl (10), in working with the Middle Preclassic Olmec culture on the Gulf Coast point out that a study of microenvironments is required to understand agricultural potential. They used aerial photography in 1:5000 and 1:2500 scales with machine mapping to produce a 4 m contour map of the study area. Their approach was to do a kind of ethnography of the environment as it now appears, and they produced detailed descriptions of plants, soils, animals, climate, and technologies used to extract a living from the environment. The techniques used provided no direct information on past agricultural practices but did set parameters of probable practices necessary for success within the area.

Others have picked up the trend of environmental studies. Archaeologists are turning to specialized studies of subjects such as: soil conditions and problems of tropical soils (104); soil mapping, analysis, and potential crop productivity of soils near Maya sites (81); and analysis of lake deposits that tell of past ecological changes (19, 21). An important problem is that interpretation of lake sediment data about past environment and cultural use of the land is difficult because dating the material cannot confidently be done (E. S. Deevey, personal communication).

Two recent publications incorporate articles representative of many of the current trends in the study of ancient Maya agricultural systems. These publications are *Pre-Hispanic Maya Agriculture,* edited by Harrison & Turner (45), and *Maya Subsistence,* edited by Flannery (34). That two such volumes should appear within such a short time is indicative of the interest that the topic currently holds for Mayanists. Examples from many parts of the Maya area point out the many known subsistence alternatives available to the ancient Maya. *Pre-Hispanic Maya Agriculture* provides the "official burial of the swidden hypothesis" (55, p. 663), and in an excellent review article concerning ancient Maya agronomies, Drucker & Fox (28) praise the volume as a pioneering effort in breaking the bonds that have inhibited past studies. *Maya Subsistence* has a greater scope in that while it too presents descriptions of evidences of ancient agricultural systems, it also includes ethnohistorical, ethnographic, and experimental agricultural approaches. While their contents are not specifically reviewed here, both volumes are very significant, and several articles from them will be discussed as they relate to current trends.

A recent study by Deevey et al (20) has investigated the impact of Maya urbanism on the area of Lake Yaxha and Lake Sacnab in the Peten. They indicate that by Classic times the forest had been cleared for building and agricultural purposes and that sediments in the adjoining lake area contained masses of soil loaded with phosphorus and other minerals. They label the riparian soils as anthrosols. Their thesis of deforestation on a local basis is no longer a hypothesis based on meager facts but is established by quantitative physical and chemical analyses. Much of Maya prehistory may be recounted from the accumulated detritis from similar lakes and swamps. The "flush" of phosphorus in Lake Sacnab within the Late Preclassic zone of occupation is evidence for use of the land without much control (20, p. 305). Also, the fact that Rice & Rice (99–101) found no terraces, ridged fields, canals, or other evidence of environmental control within the survey area of Lake Yaxha and Lake Sacnab may suggest a lack of population pressure in the area over time or perhaps a misuse of soil and vegetation resources. Other parts of the Maya area did have highly developed controls of soil and water resources.

The concept of agricultural expansion in the Maya lowlands promulgated by Hammond (41) provides a model that appears to be useful. Agricultural expansion includes intensification defined by Hammond as the frequency with which a plot of land was cultivated in comparison to the use of the plot under a swidden system. Expansion refers to the amount of labor that is absorbed by the plots calculated on the total labor time available within the society. Hammond suggests that lateral and vertical expansion occurred in bringing new land under cultivation across the landscape in valleys and uphill slopes and ridges. When hill slopes are put under intensive cultivation, then terracing is necessary to impede erosion and loss of moisture. A similar case is found in bringing waterlogged bottom lands under control. Raised fields, canals for drainage or irrigation, or specialized, repeatedly used plots come under the concept of intensification and expansion. Hammond (41, pp. 26–27) suggests that intensification and expansion constitute a case for highly organized activity.

The number of intensive food-producing systems available to the lowland Maya is amazing and suggests long-term experience in varied microenvironments (44, 123). How the various systems functioned in antiquity is a subject that was investigated by the late Dennis Puleston (91), who began experiments along the Candelaria River in Campeche and the Hondo River in northern Belize. He attempted to duplicate ancient practices by planting raised fields with corn, beans, and other cultigens. Other studies were designed to gather operational data from modern farmers, such as that of Cowgill (12), who obtained from the milperos of the Peten details on agricultural practices, production and consumption of food. Reina (97) provides an informative study of modern milperos in the Peten, describing milpa cycles, distribution of tasks, sociology of milpa activities, economics of milpa, and implications for the study of Classic Maya practices. An older study in Tabasco by Drucker & Heizer (29) provides details of milpa practices in the Olmec Gulf Coast area. That data presentation, comparable to Reina's, makes an interesting contrast. Other studies focus on second growth species in Guatemalan milpa plots (113), the hydrological cycle of plants and soil (26), the morphology of agricultural terraces (3, 114), and raised field agricultural technology and its distribution (24). These studies give considerable detail on the technical aspects of intensive agriculture, demonstrating the specialities involved in each system, and the widespread use of this knowledge. Denevan (24, pp. 188–93) quantifies data on raised fields for southern Campeche, southern Quintana Roo, and northern Belize, where he has accounted for 28,000 ha of raised fields.

Following this trend of discovery and quantification, Adams et al (1) conducted an experiment using synthetic aperture radar for mapping of the Peten, parts of Belize, and Quintana Roo. They have calculated that there is "a theoretical maximum of 12,425 km^2 of canal-drained land" (1, p. 1462) in the survey area. Since the method used will not render an image of an object under 15–20 m in size, only the largest canals and sets of raised fields can be discerned. Calculating that only 20 percent of the alignments would be canals, a maximum of 2475 km^2 would represent drained fields. A minimum estimate is 1285 km^2. Ground truth of the features has not been estabished directly except in a few places, and a major effort will have to be made to confirm the interpretation of the radar imagery.

Ground confirmation of raised fields and canals has been taking place at Pulltrouser Swamp in Belize. Turner & Harrison (118) report that the swamp covers about 8.5 km^2. Water flows into the swamp from ridge land to the west and some water remains within the swamp all year. Approximately 311 ha of patterned land shows raised fields, and there are 357 ha elsewhere that are not as clearly defined. The size of the fields averages 500 m^2. A complicated network of canals, some large enough to support canoe traffic, feeds water throughout the system. A radiocarbon sample and ceramics provide tentative dating for the fields from the Middle Preclassic period (1000 to 400 B.C.) through the Lake Classic period (A.D. 600–850). The radiocarbon sample came from 75 cm below the surface and gave an age of A.D. 150 ± 150 years. Pollens of corn, amaranthus, and possibly cotton, along with a corncob fragment and a few pieces of cacao wood, were identified.

A canal network, possibly with raised field, and associated with a Late Preclassic period occupation, has been reported at Cerros on the coast of Belice (38, pp. 135–39, 148). It does not seem unreasonable to credit the Preclassic Maya with hydraulic engineering skills. The extensive and intricately constructed canal system at Edzna, Campeche (65, 66), built in Late Preclassic times, suggests the presence of a powerful political system and knowledgeable engineers. The canals may have been used to drain waterlogged land and for dry season pot irrigation. Hydraulic works are known from Classic times at Tikal, Uxmal (7), and in the Copan Valley in Honduras (119), presumably constructed at least in part for agricultural purposes. Relating the numerous raised fields to the obsession with aquatic symbolism in various art forms produced by the Maya (90, 93), it may be possible to consider the ancient Maya as a hydraulic society as early as the Late Preclassic period (66, p. 210).

Recovery of pollens, seeds, and other kinds of macro plant remains that identify species and/or varieties of cultigens is rare in archaeological contexts. A recent trend involves doing ethnohistorical research from documents that reveal information on farming and gardening practices, identification through dictionaries and linguistic means of plants and animals raised and consumed, and special uses of these products. Hellmuth (46) presents excerpts from sixteenth and seventeenth century documents recently discovered in Spain and Guatemala that provide much information on daily events of lowland Maya life, including food production systems. Instead of dependency on the triad of corn, beans, and squash, the "real Maya ate: *camote* (sweet potato), *jicama* (rootcrop), probably macal (yautia, *Xanthosoma yucatense*), and definitely *yuca* (manioc), hearts of palm, various zapote fruits, plums, *guayaba*, grapes, cacao, and a variety of other fruits and nuts (*ramon* was not eaten though, except rarely), chiles of several varieties, tomatoes, and other vegetables" (46, pp. 427–32). To these foods may be added generous quantities of corn, beans, and calabashes. The vegetable diet was supplemented by "two species of monkey, at least one species of peccary, aguti, rabbit, tapir, iguana, faisan, turkey, and more than six kinds of smaller birds, lake fish, river fish of several species, crayfish, freshwater shrimp, several species of freshwater shellfish, land snail, and most likely river turtles, and eels" (46, p. 432). The written sources also speak of monkeys and birds in cages, dogs penned, use of eggs, domestic turkeys, use of wild cabbage, vanilla, *achiote,* maguey plant to make "water, wine, oil, vinegar, honey, 'jarabes,' string or thread, needles, beams and roofing for their houses and other things" (46, p. 435). Many other products of the land are mentioned and provide a new persepective in which to view archaeological evidence for intensive agriculture.

Marcus (64) has engaged in similar research, presenting food items eaten in the sixteenth and seventeenth centuries, including famine foods. She points out that the idea of monocropping is a European notion of farming and that the ancient Maya practiced a vegeculture. Marcus increases the list of foods by including fruit-bearing trees in Yucatan, root crops, and plants of ritual and economic importance. Sanders et al (107, pp. 233–36) present information on crops and when they appear in the archaeological record of the Mexican highlands. They also give data on meat consumption, noting that the prehispanic population focused on white-tailed deer, cottontail rabbit, domestic dog, domestic turkey and migratory ducks. It is evident that the ancient Maya, Mexicans, and other peoples had considerable variation in their diet, and that the practice of monocropping was forced upon them by Spanish rule. The variety of environments and econiches supported a vast trade network. Freidel (38) calls agricultural intensification, on the scale noted by recent studies, commercial agriculture linked with trade centers.

The view presented for Mesoamerica of ancient agriculture and food production is consonant with the idea that there were complex civilizations in prehistoric times but they were not based on swidden agriculture. Many of the intensive agricultural techniques seem to have been shared throughout Mesoamerica, perhaps from the Preclassic period, but these were systems that took time to develop in each area according to the uniqueness of the econiches involved.

THE CENTRAL ANDES

Our consideration of prehispanic agricultural variation in South America will necessarily be brief and selective. Much of the continent remains unexplored for the evidences of intensive agriculture. Major studies and interest have focused on the Central Andes where some forms of intensive agriculture have long been known to have been practiced by highly advanced prehispanic cultures. Included within the Central Andes, which will be considered in this section, are the highlands and coast of Peru and the highlands of Bolivia. This has long been recognized as a culture area in that it represents the spread of basically homogenous cultures throughout the area during prehispanic times (62, p. 7). Relatively little of the extensive archaeological research in the area has been directed toward agriculture, and the studies which have been done are more numerous for the coast than for the highlands. In comparison with the extensive amount of material concerning prehispanic intensive agriculture now available from Mesoamerica, the Andean data are rather limited. Many of the studies are merely descriptive and do not seek to explore the relationship between agriculture and other aspects of society. In this review, four general types of intensive agriculture will be considered. These include irrigation, terracing, sunken fields, and drained fields.

Irrigation

Archaeologists have long emphasized the importance of prehistoric irrigation in the Central Andes, but there have been no detailed investigations of it for the entire area. Price (89) summarized much of the data available at that time, but new information has since become available. According to Farrington (33, p. 83), many of the published materials have tended to be valley-by-valley descriptive surveys, studies of specific valleys based on projecting modern hydrological data into the past rather than considering the hydrology and importance of the ancient system, studies in which irrigation is seen as the prime mover in the development of civilization, and studies involving settlement patterns in which irrigation was studied as an interpretive aid. Most of the studies of ancient irrigation involve coastal valleys, and the models that have been developed to explain the beginnings of irrigation and its expansion and decline reflect this bias. It should be noted that most of the coastal valley irrigation systems have yet to be investigated intensively. One is the huge system in the Lambayeque region where five valleys were once connected by canals. Kosok (54, p. 147) estimates that this area included almost one-third of the cultivated area and almost one-third of the population of the coast.

At present there is no good date for the beginning of irrigation in the highlands. On the coast the first canals surviving in the archaeological record date no earlier than 400 B.C. (75, p. 77). The earliest canals and fields are assumed to have been destroyed by later developments. Based on studies of settlement and subsistence patterns in the Ancon-Chillon-Rimac region of the central coast, Moseley (75) suggests that irrigation began ca 1750 B.C. in that region. The model proposed for the development of irrigation focuses on events occurring between 1800 and 1600 B.C. It is proposed that by ca 2500 B.C. hunting and gathering was abandoned as a lifeway on the coast, and the subsistence base became large nucleated settlements. The largest known site, El Paraiso, covers more than 50 ha and is located near the mouth of the Rio Chillon, where both fishing and flood water farming could be carried out on the river plain. Flood water farming may be a forerunner of irrigation because it involves some control of the collection, transfer, and distribution of water resources (33, p. 83). Evidence from midden deposits seems to indicate that agriculture at that time did not include any staple crops and was a secondary subsistence activity. There is evidence of corporate labor projects at most of the larger sites, including residential and nonresidential construction. At El Paraiso extensive masonry residential structures were erected. At other sites projects included the construction of residential terraces and artificial mounds. At about 1750 B.C. many of the known maritime sites were abandoned, including El Paraiso and another of the four known sites of the Ancon-Chillon-Rimac region. It is postulated that population growth at these sites exceeded the maritime support capacity and the capacity of flood water farming for which there was only a limited amount of land available. This may have been a major factor in the shift of settlement to valley interiors where irrigation seems to have been developed, likely in areas where the gradient was steep and canals constructed to channel water from rivers could be quite short and require less labor investment (124, p. 392). Moseley (75, 76) suggests that irrigation technology developed and spread quickly down the valleys to the desert lands. He also postulates that populations at the larger maritime sites were preadapted to irrigation agriculture in that they had already been carrying out corporate labor projects. This combined with population growth and the introduction of agricultural staples into an already well-developed agricultural system are some of the variables involved with the development of irrigation. Most of the basic features of this model had been stated earlier by others (11, 52, 56), but Moseley has added the Ancon-Chillon-Rimac data, the notion of irrigation preadaptation, and attempted to create a more processual model.

Based on data from the coast, Moseley (76) has proposed that Andean civilization had a maritime rather than an agricultural base. The question of the relationship between agriculture and the rise of civilization has been of general interest to scholars in the Central Andes and in Mesoamerica (125, p. 231). Moseley sees the corporate labor projects, mortuary practices, and large nucleated maritime settlements as evidence of the existence of a corporate authority in late Preceramic times (prior to 1750 B.C.). It is suggested that a level of complex social organization had been reached at that time. Two published articles (96, 126) have questioned a number of the elements of the maritime model, including the proposed level of sociopolitical organization achieved by the inhabitants of the maritime settlements, the continuous availability of ample amounts of marine resources, the secondary position of agriculture in subsistence, and the lack of agricultural staples at maritime settlements. Also, as Willey & Sabloff (125, p. 234) have mentioned, full states did not come into being in Peru until a level of fully effective agriculture had been achieved.

As irrigation developed it grew from small local systems to systems encompassing whole valleys. Eventually, in some areas, multivalley complexes of canals were constructed. The best evidence for these developments comes from the north coast of Peru, where it has been documented for the Viru Valley (124) and the Moche Valley (77). The Moche Valley has been of particular interest to scholars because even though it is not a large valley, it was the location of important prehispanic sites, including Chan Chan, and was a major center of political power. In a recent volume (77) a synthesis of the work of the Chan Chan-Moche Valley Project is presented. Day (17) expressed the goal of the study as follows: "analysis of the architecture and patterns of environmental exploitation for the purpose of reconstruction of the development of social, economic, and political organization of the North Coast of Peru."

Contributing to this general goal, Moseley & Deeds (78) describe the irrigation system associated with Chan Chan. They discuss its development in terms of a model of canal conduct applying to areas of elevated terrain and related to the expansion, reform, and collapse of the agricultural system. One set of canals was constructed on the south side of the lower Moche Valley and another set on the north side. There are three principal canals in each subsystem. There is evidence that some intakes and intial sections of canals were built in Salinar (ca 500 B.C.) times or earlier. Land reclamation continued through succeeding phases as existing canals were extended or new canals were constructed. Most of the canals were extended beyond the area of modern cultivation during the Moche Phase. The Chimu brought irrigation to its peak of development in the Moche Valley, reclaiming several pampa areas that had not been previously irrigated. It was also during the Chimu occupation at about A.D. 1200 that the canal known as La Cumbre, more than 70 km long, was constructed to bring water from the Chicama Valley to the fields near Chan

Chan. There is an ancient road going from Chan Chan to the junction of the canal (16, p. 183). This intervalley canal was never completed and thus never delivered water from the Chicama Valley. One study considers the cause of the abandonment to be problems of tectonic movement but suggests that the Chimu possessed a high level of surveying skill (82). However, Pozorski & Pozorski (88) contend that the canal effort failed because of uphill slope errors by the Chimu engineers. They suggest that the canal should be considered as an expression of the impressive power of Chimu rulers rather than an example of great engineering skill.

There is evidence for two instances of agrarian collapse before Inca conquest of the Chimu (78, pp. 47–49). The first collapse was caused by dune formation on the south side of the valley. It was localized, involved some permanent loss of agricultural land, and seems to have occurred during Moche IV times. The second collapse was caused by massive flooding that washed out large areas of the Chimu irrigation system, probably attributable to a particularly severe occurrence of the El Nino. The Chimu rebuilt their irrigation system, but some areas were not cultivated again. Chan Chan seems to have been abandoned after the Inca conquest, about A.D. 1465, along with many of the canals and fields associated with it.

In considering the relationship between irrigation and sociopolitical organizations, Moseley & Deeds (78, pp. 34, 50–51) present a model to account for the rise to preeminence of the Moche Valley inhabitants over those of neighboring valleys. Conditions in the Moche Valley, when combined with irrigation, are thought to have stimulated the development of a single valley inclusive political entity. Water limitations seem to have acted to prevent the development of independent canal systems. Additional water from a large river in the Chicama Valley perhaps allowed for a number of independent canal systems and polities. In the Viru Valley, river water is limited but groundwater seeps are available which also seem to have encouraged the development of independent systems of canals. The Chicama and Viru Valleys with their multiple independent canal systems also have multiple large sites as foci of multiple political entities. The Moche Valley, from the Early Horizon and after, has one very large site during most phases which is much larger than all others and likely was the center of political power in the valley. The key to power in the Moche Valley is postulated to have been control over the major canal.

As Price (89) has said "few general hypotheses have stirred such controversy as that which postulates a causal link between the phenomenon of irrigation agriculture and the origins of the state." Her investigation is the most comprehensive review of the topic in recent times and treats Mesoamerica and the Central Andes. Irrigation is not seen as a prime mover in the development of the state but as one aspect of a total adaptive system which may, depending on the circumstances, have certain effects upon the system as a whole.

Sunken Fields

Sunken fields, also called sunken gardens, pukios, mahames, hoyas, and wachaques, are found near prehistoric sites along the coast of Peru and Northern Chile (74, 86, 87, 103, 124). The fields were created by excavating surface soils to tap ground water, and they are often located near the ocean where the water table is high. The antiquity of sunken fields is unknown. Parsons (86) suggests that they may be an early type of agriculture, but in the Moche Valley those sunken fields that have been investigated are no earlier than the Late Intermediate Period or ca 1000 A.D. (50). There are several views concerning the functioning of sunken fields in the agricultural systems of the coastal valleys. Moseley (74) suggests that they were supplemental to the irrigation system. The extensive irrigation system at Chan Chan is postulated by Day (16) to have raised the water table enough to supply water for the walk-in wells at the site. Sunken fields are located at the southern edge of Chan Chan (18), and the raised water table probably made their construction less laborious.

There has been no censensus about what was grown in the sunken gardens. However, macro and microanalysis of materials from a well-preserved midden at Medanos la Joyada indicates that a range of agricultural products was present. The amount of corn pollen indicates that it was probably being grown at the site along with other food plants and industrial plants.

Sunken fields were not the only alternative to irrigation on the coast, as Knapp (53) indicates that landforms on the coast at Chilca, Peru, previously assumed to be sunken fields, are actually embanked fields. They were situated to take advantage of combinations of floodwater and watertable farming.

Terracing

Donkin (25) has produced the most complete summary of prehispanic terracing and the following information is derived it. Terracing occurs as extensive systems in the highlands of Peru and Bolivia. There are a number of excellent Spanish colonial accounts of terraces, called andenes, in highland Peru. The antiquity of terracing is unknown, but it may have begun by 500 B.C., continuing to the time of the conquest and beyond. Though it was practiced by many other groups, terracing reached its greatest development among the Incas. At a number of highland sites, terracing and irrigation were combined, pushing cultivation into agriculturally marginal areas. It is not known what crops were grown on terraces in ancient times, but crops grown on them in modern times provide some clues. On the Lake Titicaca terraces, quinoa, barley, and the local tubers, oca, ullucu, and potatoes are grown (25, p. 120). Much of the terrace building in the highlands, especially that associated with irrigation, is assumed to have been associated with the cultivation of maize. In high valleys, above where maize can be grown, terraces were probably used to grow root crops and local grains.

Most of the published works concerning terraces are descriptive. More exploration and excavation needs to be done to elucidate the chronological position of the terraces and their association with settlements.

Raised Fields

The importance of irrigation has been so emphasized that little attention has been paid to drainage as a land reclamation technique. Raised fields were constructed to achieve drainage, and remains of them have been found in Surinam, Venezuela, Columbia, Equador, Peru, and Bolivia (22, 23, 83–85, 112). The antiquity of raised fields in South America is not known, nor is it known what crops were grown on them. Parsons & Bowen (84, pp. 336–37) suggest that yuca (sweet manioc) was the most likely crop to have been grown on the ridged fields of the San Jorge River floodplain of Colombia. This interpretation is based on early Spanish accounts which document the presence of many fields of yuca, sweet potatoes, and other tubers. Extensive gardens are mentioned, and one source comments on the absence of maize in the area.

The existence of the lowland raised fields was most surprising as it indicates a fairly dense population in some areas where it was not previously suspected. Much of what has been written about raised fields is descriptive, and a number of different kinds of raised fields have been described (23, pp. 649–50), but their functional significance is imperfectly understood. Many sites need extensive ground exploration, and their chronological and cultural affiliations are unknown. One of the most interesting studies of highland raised fields is that carried out in the Lake Titicaca region in Peru and Bolivia (112). The area of known ancient fields and ditches is 82,056 ha. These are thought to be pre-Inca and are on ground level between 3800 m to 3890 m. In the Titicaca area there is a correlation between raised fields and terracing. Regions in which raised fields are very abundant are those where hillside terracing is most complete. Crops such as potatoes and other tubers were probably grown as well as native grains such as quinoa and canihua.

The most recent research on raised fields in all areas of Latin America has been summarized by Denevan (24). In the same article he compares the basic measurement of raised fields at nine sites in the highlands and lowlands of South America and Mesoamerica to assess their importance as compared to that of swidden agriculture. Few scholars have yet tried to make comparisons between raised fields in the two areas. Puleston (92) argues for the unitary origin of raised fields in South America, Mesoamerica, and the Caribbean based on a cognized model of the environment which he believes they shared.

CONCLUSIONS

In both the Central Andes and Mesoamerica, complex civilizations developed out of similar backgrounds. During the past two decades, research concerning the agricultural alternatives that were developed in these areas in prehispanic times has burgeoned, especially in the Maya area. The research continues and its preliminary results are only beginning to be examined, but several points can be made. It is clear that we have been incredibly naive in our previous assessments of agricultural systems of the past. Descriptions of ancient irrigation, raised fields, terracing, sunken fields, and other systems show that there was a wide range of complex systems in operation in many areas during various time periods. Several different systems were sometimes used in this area, such as terracing and irrigation or terracing and raised fields. These systems were practiced on various levels of complexity requiring corporate organization of varying types. Since the presence of intensive techniques is a phenomenon of a time/space continuum, the degree of corporateness is difficult to assess, but at times it must have been at the state level, especially in the Central Andes, the Mexican Highlands, and the Maya lowlands.

Though research on agricultural systems has been intense, particularly during the last 10 years, the major work has scarely begun. Many areas that contain intriguing relics of ancient agricultural systems remain unexplored. Much fieldwork is still required to gain a better understanding of the functioning and chronology of the various systems and their relationship with settlement pattern. We also expect to see more developments in the areas of ethnohistorical and ethnographic research, as well as environmental research and agricultural experimentation with ancient techniques.

Literature Cited

1. Adams, R. E. W., Brown, W. E. Jr., Culbert, T. P. 1981. Radar mapping, archaeology, and ancient Maya land use. *Science* 213:1457–63
2. Adams, R. M. 1959. Report on an archaeological reconnaissance in the central highlands of Chiapas, Mexico. *Rep. "Man-in-Nature" Proj. in the Tzeltal-Tzotil-speaking region, State of Chiapas, Mexico,* Part 2: The Data, pp. 1–58. Chicago: Univ. Chicago Dep. Anthropol.
3. Andress, J. M. 1972. The morphology of agricultural terraces in the Kumaon Himalayas. *Assoc. Pac. Coast Geogr. Yearb.* 34:7–20
4. Armillas, P. 1971. Gardens on swamps. *Science* 174:653–61
5. Blanton, R. E., Kowalewski, S. A. 1981.

Monte Alban and after in the valley of Oaxaca. In *Supplement to the Handbook of Middle American Indians,* ed. J. A. Sabloff, 1:94–116
6. Blom, F., LaFarge, O. 1926–27. Tribes and temples, 1 & 2. *Tulane Univ. Middle Am. Res. Inst.,* Publ. 1. 536 pp.
7. Brasseur de Bourbourg, C. 1865. *Rapport sur les ruines de Mayapan et d'Uxmal au Yucatan (Mexique), addresse a Son Excellence M. Le Ministre de L'Instruction Publique.* Paris: Impr. Imp.
8. Bronson, B. 1966. Roots and the subsistence of the ancient Maya. *Southwest. J. Anthropol.* 22:251–79
9. Coe, M. D. 1964. The chinampas of Mexico. *Sci. Am.* 211:90–98
10. Coe, M. D., Diehl, R. A. 1980. *The*

Land of the Olmec: The People of the River, Vol. 2. Austin: Univ. Texas Press. 198 pp.

11. Collier, D. 1955. Development of civilization of the coast of Peru. In *Irrigation Civilization: A Comparative Study*, ed. J. H. Steward. *Wash. Soc. Sci. Sec. Dep. Cult. Aff.*, Pan American Union

12. Cowgill, U. M. 1961. Soil fertility and the ancient Maya. *Trans. Conn. Acad. Arts Sci.* 42:1–56

13. Cowgill, U. M. 1971. Some comments on manihot subsistence and the ancient Maya. *Southwest. J. Anthropol.* 27:51–63

14. Cowgill, U. M., Hutchinson, G. E. 1966. The chemical history of Laguna de Petenxil, El Peten, Guatemala. *Conn. Acad. Arts Sci. Mem.* 17

15. Culbert, T. P. 1973. Introduction: A prologue to classic Maya culture and the problem of its collapse. In *The Classic Maya Collapse*, ed. T. P. Culbert, pp. 3–19. Albuquerque: Univ. New Mexico Press. 549 pp.

16. Day, K. C. 1974. Walk-in wells and water management at Chan Chan, Peru. In *The Rise and Fall of Civilizations: Modern Archaeological Approaches to Ancient Cultures*, ed. C. C. Lamberg-Karlovsky, J. A. Sabloff. Menlo Park: Cummings

17. Day, K. C. 1982. Preface. See Ref. 77, pp. viii-xx

18. Day, K. C. 1982. Ciudadelas: Their forms and functions. See Ref. 77, pp. 55–66

19. Deevey, E. S. Jr. 1978. Holocene forests and Maya disturbance near Quexil Lake, Peten, Guatemala. *Pol. Arch. Hydrobiol.* 25:117–29

20. Deevey, E. S., Rice, D. S., Rice, P. M., Vaughan, H. H., Brenner, M., Flannery, M. S. 1979. Mayan urbanism: Impact on a tropical Karst environment. *Science* 206:298–306

21. Deevey, E. S. Jr., Brenner, M., Flannery, M. S., Yezdani, G. H. 1980. Lakes Yaxha and Sacnab, Peten, Guatemala: Liminology and hydrology. *Arch. Hydrobiol. Suppl.* 57:419–60

22. Denevan, W. M. 1963. Additional comments on the earthworks of Mojos in northeastern Bolivia. *Am. Antiq.* 28:540–45

23. Denevan, W. M. 1970. Aboriginal drained-field cultivation in the Americas. *Science* 169:647–54

24. Denevan, W. M. 1982. Hydraulic agriculture in the American tropics: Forms, measures, and recent research. See Ref. 34, pp. 181–203

25. Donkin, R. A. 1979. Agricultural terracing in the aboriginal New World. *Viking Fund Publ. Anthropol.* 56. Univ. Ariz. Press

26. Dooge, J. C. I. 1973. The nature and components of the hydrological cycle. In *Man's Influence on the Hydrological Cycle*. Irrigation and drainage paper, Spec. Issue 17, Food and Agric. Organ. United Nations

27. Downing, T. E. 1974. Irrigation and moisture-sensitive periods: A Zapotec case. In *Irrigation's Impact on Society*, ed. T. E. Downing, McG. Gibson. *Anthropol. Pap. Univ. Ariz.* 25:113–22

28. Drucker, P., Fox, J. W. 1982. Swidden didn' make all that midden: The search for ancient Mayan agronomies. *J. Anthropol. Res.* 38:179–93

29. Drucker, P., Heizer, R. F. 1960. A study of the Milpa system of La Venta Island and its archaeological implications. *Southwest. J. Anthropol.* 16:36–45

30. Dumond, D. E. 1961. Swidden agriculture and the rise of Maya civilization. *Southwest. J. Anthropol.* 17:301–16

31. Eaton, J. D. 1973. Ancient agricultural farmsteads in the Rio Bec region of Yucatan. Unpublished paper

32. Emerson, R. A., Kempton, J. H. 1935. Agronomic investigation in Yucatan. *Carnegie Inst. Washington Yearb.* 34:138–42

33. Farrington, I. 1974. Irrigation and settlement pattern: Preliminary research results from the north coast of Peru. See Ref. 27, pp. 83–94

34. Flannery, K. V., ed. 1982. *Maya Subsistence: Studies in Memory of Dennis E. Puleston*. New York: Academic. 368 pp.

35. Flannery, K. V., Kirkby, A. V. T., Kirkby, M. J. 1967. Farming systems and political growth in ancient Oaxaca. *Science* 158:445–58

36. Flannery, K. V., Marcus, J., Kowalewski, S. A. 1981. The Preceramic and Formative of the valley of Oaxaca, see Ref. 5, pp. 48–93

37. Fowler, M. L. 1969. A Preclassic water distribution system in Amalucan, Mexico. *Archaeology* 22:208–15

38. Freidel, D. A. 1982. Subsistence, trade, and development of the coastal Maya. See Ref. 34, pp. 131–55

39. Gonzales-Jacome, A. 1981. *Home gardens in Central Mexico, their relationship with water control, and their articulation to major society through productivity, labor and market*. Presented at Aust. Natl. Univ., Canberra, Conf. Prehist. Intenstive Agric. in Tropics

40. Hammond, N. 1976. Agricultural intensification in the Maya Lowlands. *Actes 17th Congr. Int. Americanistis, Congr. Centenaire, Paris*, 8:329–33

41. Hammond, N. 1978. The myth of the Milpa: Agricultural expansion in the Maya Lowlands. See Ref. 45, pp. 23–34

42. Hammond, N., Miksicek, C. H. 1981. Ecology and economy of a Formative Maya site at Cuello, Belize. *J. Field Archaeol*. 8:259–69

43. Harris, D. R. 1972. Swidden system and settlement. In *Man Settlement and Urbanism*, ed. P. J. Uko, R. Tringham, G. W. Dimbleby, pp. 1–18. London: Duckworth

44. Harrison, P. D. 1978. So the seeds shall grow: Some introductory comments. See Ref. 41, pp. 1–11

45. Harrison, P. D., Turner, B. L. II, eds. 1978. *Pre-Hispanic Maya Agriculture*. Albuquerque: Univ. New Mexico Press. 414 pp.

46. Hellmuth, N. 1977. Cholti-Lacandon (Chiapas) and Peten-Ytza agriculture, settlement pattern and population. In *Social Process in Maya Prehistory: Studies in Honor of Sir Eric Thompson*, ed. N. Hammond, pp. 421–48. London: Academic. 609 pp.

47. Hester, J. A. Jr. 1951. Agriculture, economy and population densities of the Maya. *Carnegie Inst. Washington Yearb*. 51:266–71

48. Hester, J. A. Jr. 1952. Agriculture, economy and population densities of the Maya. *Carnegie Inst. Washington Yearb*. 52:288–92

49. Hester, J. A. Jr. 1953. Maya agriculture. *Carnegie Inst. Washington Yearb*. 53:297–98

50. Kautz, R. R., Keatinge, R. W. 1977. Determining site function: A North Peruvian coastal example. *Am. Antiq*. 42:86–97

51. Kempton, J. H. 1935. Report on agricultural survey. *Carnegie Inst. Washington Rep. Gov. Mexico, 12th Year Chichen Itza Proj. Allied Invest*.

52. Kidder, A. II. 1964. South American high cultures. In *Prehistoric Man in the New World*, ed. J. D. Jennings, E. Norbeck, pp. 451–86. Chicago: Univ. Chicago Press. 633 pp.

53. Knapp, G. 1982. Prehistoric flood management on the Peruvian coast: Reinterpreting the "Sunken Fields" of Chilca. *Am. Antiq*. 47:144–54

54. Kosok, P. 1965. *Life, Land and Water in Ancient Peru*. New York: Long Island Univ. Press. 264 pp.

55. Kowalewski, S. A. 1981. Review of *Pre-Hispanic Agriculture*, ed. P. D. Harrison, B. L. Turner, II. *Am. Anthropol*. 83:663–64

56. Lanning, E. P. 1967. *Peru Before the Incas*. Englewood Cliffs: Prentice-Hall

57. Lees, S. H. 1974. The state's use of irrigation in changing peasant society. See Ref. 27, pp. 123–27

58. Lowe, G. W. 1959. Archaeological exploration of the Upper Grijalva River, Chiapas, Mexico. *Pap. New World Archaeol. Found*.

59. Lowe, G. W. 1971. The civilizational consequences of varying degrees of agricultural and ceramic dependency with the basic ecosystems of Mesoamerica. In *Observations on the Emergence of Civilization in America*, ed. R. F. Heizer, J. A. Graham. *Contrib. Univ. Calif. Archaeol. Res. Facil*. 11:212–48

60. Lowe, G. W. 1975. The Early Preclassic Barra Phase of Altamira, Chiapas: A review with new data. *Pap. New World Archaeol. Found*. 38

61. Lowe, G. W., Mason, J. A. 1965. Archaeological survey of the Chiapas coast, Highlands and Upper Grijalva basin. In *Handbook of Middle American Indians*, ed. G. R. Willey, 2:195–236. Austin: Univ. Texas Press. 560 pp.

62. Lumbreras, L. G. 1974. *The Peoples and Cultures of Ancient Peru*. Washington: Smithsonian Inst. Press. 248 pp.

63. MacNeish, R. S. 1971. Speculation about how and why food production and village life developed in the Tehuacan Valley, Mexico. *Archaeology* 24:307–15

64. Marcus, J. 1982. The plant world of the sixteenth- and seventeenth -century Lowland Maya. See Ref. 24, pp. 239–73

65. Matheny, R. T. 1976. Maya Lowland hydraulic systems. *Science* 193:639–46

66. Matheny, R. T. 1978. Northern Maya Lowland water-control systems. See Ref. 45, pp. 185–210

67. Matheny, R. T. 1982. Ancient Lowland and Highland Maya water and soil conservation strategies. See Ref. 24, pp. 157–78

68. Matheny, R. T., Gurr, D. L. 1979. Ancient hydraulic techniques in the Chiapas Highlands. *Am. Sci*. 67:441–49

69. McBryde, F. W. 1945. Cultural and historical geography of southwest Guatemala. *Smithsonian Inst., Inst. Soc. Anthropol., Publ*. 4

70. Miksicek, C. H., Bird, R. McK., Pickersgill, B., Donaghey, S., Cartwright, J., Hammond, N. 1981. Preclassic Lowland maize from Cuello, Belize. *Nature* 289:56–59

71. Millon, R. F. 1954. Irrigation at Teotihuacan. *Am. Antiq*. 20:176–80

72. Millon, R. F. 1957. Irrigation systems in the valley of Teotihuacan. *Am. Antiq*. 23:160–66

73. Morley, S. G. 1958. *The Ancient Maya*, rev. G. W. Brainerd. Stanford: Stanford Univ. Press. 507 pp. 3rd ed.

74. Moseley, M. E. 1969. Assessing the archaeological significance of Mahamaes. *Am. Antiq.* 35:485–87

75. Moseley, M. E. 1974. Organizational preadaptation to irrigation: The evolution of early water-management systems in coastal Peru. See Ref. 27, pp. 77–82

76. Moseley, M. E. 1975. *The Maritime Foundations of Andean Civilization*. Menlo Park: Cummings. 131 pp.

77. Moseley, M. E., Day, K. C., eds. 1982. *Chan Chan: Andean Desert City*. Albuquerque: Univ. New Mexico Press. 373 pp.

78. Moseley, M. E., Deeds, E. E. 1982. The land in front of Chan Chan: Agrarian expansion, reform, and collapse in the Moche Valley. See Ref. 77, pp. 25–53

79. Neely, J. A. 1967. Organizacion hidraulica y sistemas de irrigacion prehistoricos en el Valle de Oaxaca. *Bol. Inst. Nac. Antropol. Hist.* 27:15–17

80. Nichols, D. L. 1982. A Middle Formative irrigation system near Santa Clara Coatitlan in the basin of Mexico. *Am. Antiq.* 47:133–44

81. Olson, G. W. 1978. Algunas Observaciones Pedologicas de los Suelos del Area en Relacion con la Arquelogia. *Bol. Escuela Ciencias Antropol. Univ. Yucatan* 32:14–23

82. Ortloff, C. R., Moseley, M. E., Feldman, R. A. 1982. Hydraulic engineering aspects of the Chimu Chicama-Moche Intervalley Canal. *Am. Antiq.* 47:572–95

83. Parsons, J. J. 1969. Ridged fields in the Rio Guayas Valley, Ecuador. *Am. Antiq.* 34:76–80

84. Parsons, J. J., Bowen, W. A. 1966. Ancient ridged fields of the San Jorge River floodplain, Colombia. *Geogr. Rev.* 66:317–43

85. Parsons, J. J., Denevan, W. M. 1967. Pre-Columbian ridged fields. *Sci. Am.* 217:93–100

86. Parsons, J. R. 1968. The archaeological significance of Mahamaes cultivation on the coast of Peru. *Am. Antiq.* 33:80–85

87. Parsons, J. R., Psuty, N. 1975. Sunken fields and prehispanic subsistence on the Peruvian coast. *Am. Antiq.* 40:259–82

88. Pozorski, T., Pozorski, S. 1982. Reassessing the Chicama-Moche Intervalley Canal: Comments on "Hydraulic Engineering Aspects of the Chimu Chicama-Moche Intervalley Canal." *Am. Antiq.* 47:851–68

89. Price, B. J. 1971. Prehispanic irrigation agriculture in nuclear America. *Lat. Am. Res. Rev.* 6:3–61

90. Puleston, D. E. 1976. The people of the cayman crocodile: Riparian agriculture and the origins of aquatic motifs in ancient Maya iconography. In *Aspects of Ancient Maya Civilization*, ed. D. de Montequin, pp. 1–25

91. Puleston, D. E. 1977. Experiments in prehistoric raised field agriculture: Learning from the past. *J. Belizean Aff.* 5:36–43

92. Puleston, D. E. 1977. *Raised fields in Mesoamerica and South America: Colonization or independent invention?* Presented at 42nd Ann. Meet. Soc. Am. Archaeol.

93. Puleston, D. E. 1977. The art and archaeology of hydraulic agriculture in the Maya Lowlands. See Ref. 46, pp. 449–67

94. Puleston, D. E., Puleston, O. S. 1971. An ecological approach to the origins of Maya civilization. *Archaeol.* 24:330–37

95. Puleston, O. S., Doyle, M. D. 1971. *The use of model diets for the study of ancient Maya food patterns*. Presented at 70th Ann. Meet. Am. Anthropol. Assoc.

96. Raymond, J. S. 1981. The maritime foundations of Andean civilization: A reconsideration of the evidence. *Am. Antiq.* 46:806–21

97. Reina, R. E. 1967. Milpas and Milperos: Implications for prehistoric times. *Am. Anthropol.* 69:1–20

98. Rice, D. S. 1976. Middle Preclassic Maya settlement in the Central Maya Lowlands. *J. Field Archaeol.* 3:425–45

99. Rice, D. S., Rice, P. M. 1980. Second Preliminary Report, Proyecto Lacustre. Natl. Sci. Found. Rep.

100. Rice, D. S., Rice, P. M. 1980. The northeast Peten revisited. *Am. Antiq.* 45: 432–54

101. Rice, D. S., Rice, P. M. 1981. Third Preliminary Report, Proyecto Lacustre. Nat. Sci. Found. Rep.

102. Ricketson, O. G., Ricketson, E. B. 1937. Uaxactun, Guatemala, Group E, 1926–31. *Carnegie Inst. Washington* Publ. 477

103. Rowe, J. H. 1969. The sunken gardens of the Peruvian coast. *Am. Antiq.* 34:320–35

104. Sanchez, P. A., Cochrane, T. T. 1980. Soil constraints in relation to major farming systems of tropical America. In *Priorities for Alleviating Soil-Related Constraints to Food Production in the Tropics*. Int. Rice Res. Inst. Manila. 107 pp.

105. Sanders, W. T. 1971. Settlement patterns in Central Mexico. See Ref. 61, 10 (1):3–44

106. Sanders, W. T. 1981. Ecological adaptation in the basin of Mexico: 23,000 B.C.. to the present. See Ref. 5, pp. 147–97

107. Sanders, W. T., Parsons, J. R., Santley, R. S. 1979. *The Basin of Mexico: Ecolo-*

gical Processes in the Evolution of a Civilization. New York: Academic. 561 pp.
108. Sanders, W. T., Price, B. J. 1968. Mesoamerica: The Evolution of a Civilization. New York: Random House. 264 pp.
109. Sanders, W. T., Santley, R. S. 1977. A prehispanic irrigation system near Santa Clara Xalostoc in the basin of Mexico. Am. Antiq. 42:582–88
110. Seler, E. 1901. Die alten Ansiedelungen van Chacula: Im Distrikte Nenton des Departements Huehuetenango de Republik Guatemala. Berlin: Reimer (Vohsen). 223 pp.
111. Siemens, A. H., Puleston, D. E. 1972. Ridged fields and associated features in southern Campeche: New perspectives on the Lowland Maya. Am. Antiq. 37: 228–39
112. Smith, C. T., Denevan, W. M., Hamilton, P. 1968. Geogr. J. 134:353–67
113. Snedaker, S. C., Gamble, J. F. 1969. Compositional analysis of selected second-growth species from Lowland Guatemala and Panama. BioScience 19: 536–38
114. Spencer, J., Hale, G. 1961. The origin, nature, and distribution of agricultural terracing. Pac. Viewpoint 2:1–40
115. Steggerda, M. 1941. Maya Indians of Yucatan. Carnegie Inst. Washington Publ. 531
116. Turner, B. L. II. 1974. Prehistoric intensive agriculture in the Mayan Lowlands. Science 185:118–23

117. Turner, B. L. II. 1979. Agriculture and state developments in the Maya Lowlands. Presented at Symp. Mexican Agro-Systems: Past and Present, 43rd Meet. Int. Congr. Americanists
118. Turner, B. L. II, Harrison, P. D. 1981. Prehistoric raised-field agriculture in the Maya Lowlands. Science 213:399–405
119. Turner, B. L. II, Johnson, W. C. 1979. A Maya dam in the Copan Valley, Honduras. Am. Antiq. 44:299–305
120. Vallant, G. C. 1930. Excavations at Zacatenco. Am. Mus. Nat. Hist. Anthropol. Pap. 32: Pt. 1
121. Vogt, E. Z. 1969. Zinacantan: A Maya Community in the Highlands of Chiapas. Cambridge: Belknap (Harvard Univ. Press). 733 pp.
122. Wagner, P. L. 1959. Chiapas: The habitat. See Ref. 2, pp. 1–21
123. Wilken, G. C. 1971. Food-producing systems available to the ancient Maya. Am. Antiq. 36:432–48
124. Willey, G. R. 1953. Prehistoric settlement patterns in the Viru Valley, Peru. Bur. Am. Ethnol. Bull. 155
125. Willey, G. R., Sabloff, J. A. 1980. A History of American Archaeology. San Francisco: Freeman. 313 pp. 2nd ed.
126. Wilson, D. J. 1981. Maize and men: A critique of the maritime hypothesis of state origins on the coast of Peru. Am. Anthropol. 83:95–120

Ann. Rev. Anthropol. 1983. 12:105-24

REMOTE SENSING

Michael Parrington

136 Hartford Road, Mount Laurel, New Jersey 08054

INTRODUCTION

Man has an insatiable curiosity about his past, and whatever intellectual or practical value this interest has, it remains a fact that a fair amount of money is expended in indulging it. One of the tools used to help man find the archaeological sites where he can exercise his curiosity is remote sensing. Conventional archaeological sites are usually buried in the earth, and often no knowledge exists as to their precise location. In remote sensing a variety of techniques (usually borrowed from other disciplines) are used to locate archaeological remains. Although an interpretation of the site located is sometimes possible, excavation is the only real way to test the truth of what remote sensing instruments are detecting.

HISTORY OF REMOTE SENSING

The history of remote sensing extends back several centuries. The English antiquarian William Camden, writing in the sixteenth century, noted of a Roman city: "But now age has eras'd the very tracks of it; and to teach us that Cities dye as well as men, it is at this day a corn-field, wherein when the corn is grown up, one may observe the draughts of streets crossing one another (for where they have gone the corn is thinner) and such *crossings* they commonly call *St. Augustine's cross*" (quoted in 18, p. 37). What Camden was observing was differential growth in a crop that was reflecting the street grid pattern beneath. Other English antiquarians noted this phenomenon, and one of them (William Stukely) is credited with the first archaeological plan of a cropmark, a Roman temple, which he apparently saw from the window of an ale house in the early eighteenth century (4, p. 51). Until the invention of powered flight, observations of cropmarks by archaeologists were mainly confined to areas where suitable circumstances existed such as high ground overlooking an

0084-6570/83/1015-0105$02.00

archaeological site. Such circumstances can sometimes reveal a wealth of detail (Figure 1) but are obviously rather limited in their scope. With the widespread use of aircraft from the period of World War I onward, the potential of aerial photography as an instrument for recording cropmarks and other evidence of archaeological sites has come into its own.

Aerial archaeology is perhaps the earliest remote sensing technique, and it remained the only one used by archaeologists until 1946, when a resistivity survey was carried out on a site in Dorchester, England (5, p. 20). The circumstances under which this survey was made were almost ideal, and its success led to widespread use of the method on other sites where field conditions were not as good (13, p. 695). The next instrument to join the spectrum of remote sensing techniques available to the archaeologist was the magnetometer, which was first used on an archaeological site in 1958 (3, p. 189). This device went through a number of "improvements" culminating in the lightweight, transistorized versions available today. Experimental use of a radar system was made in 1974 at Chaco Canyon, New Mexico, with successful results (53), and since then radar has been used with varying success on a number of archaeological sites. Aerial photography, resistivity survey, magnetometry, and radar are now standard techniques for archaeological remote sensing and are constantly being revised and improved.

Figure 1   Low-level oblique photograph of a prehistoric site in southern England. Photographed from a highway embankment during the summer of 1975. The circular feature is the cropmark of a ditch around a plowed out burial mound; the markings inside the circle may be burials. Photograph by the author.

In the United States the growth of cultural resource management and contract archaeology which has resulted from recent federal legislation has stimulated the development and use of remote sensing. Federal and sometimes state legislation requires that archaeological surveys be carried out before any potentially destructive projects funded from government sources can begin. Conventional methods of locating sites such as surface collection or shovel testing are expensive. In contrast, remote sensing techniques can sometimes pinpoint the precise location of a site more easily and at less expense. The more usual way in which remote sensing is used, however, is in precisely locating the focus and boundaries of an archaeological site in a finite area so that excavations can be carried out on the site in the most economical way. This was the reason for carrying out the first archaeological resistivity survey at Dorchester in England, where the approximate position of the archaeological features was known from aerial photographs. For archaeological purposes it was desirable to locate specifically the center of the site, and the survey was successful in doing this to an accuracy of 2 feet (5, p. 20).

A number of organizations in different countries have carried out research into various methods of remote sensing for archaeology, including, most notably, the Research Laboratory for Archaeology and the History of Art at Oxford, England, under the direction of Martin Aitken; the Rheinisches Landesmuseum in Bonn, Germany, under the direction of Irwin Scollar; and (until 1978) the Museum Applied Science Center for Archaeology (MASCA) in Philadelphia, USA, under the direction of Elizabeth Ralph. These three groups have done much to refine and improve the techniques used in remote sensing. Modern magnetometers are now much more sophisticated and accurate than their predecessors and are also much lighter, an important factor for the person carrying the device. The National Park Service has also inspired much research into remote sensing and has published a series of valuable reports on the subject through their remote sensing division. Research units attached to universities, such as the Nebraska Center for Archaeophysical Research (NEBCAR) of the University of Nebraska, have also generated much research. NEBCAR, for example, carried out surveys or processed information from surveys from 17 states and France and Japan between 1973 and 1981, and the total area covered by these surveys was over 36 hectares (personal communication from John Weymouth, 1982).

AERIAL REMOTE SENSING

As is noted above, the phenomenon of cropmarks has been recognized for several centuries. The pioneer of aerial photography for recording these features was the English archaeologist O. G. S. Crawford, who recorded his attempts to utilize aerial photographs for archaeology after the 1914–18 War

(17, pp. 46–50). Crawford and his contemporaries photographed sites in southern England, and in 1928, together with Alexander Keiller, Crawford published the pioneering work *Wessex from the Air,* which illustrated and interpreted the aerial discoveries they had made. In America, Charles Lindbergh was an early exponent of archaeological aerial photography. In 1929 he and his wife photographed Pueblo sites from the air in the American Southwest and later in the same year photographed Mayan sites in Central America (19, pp. 189–209). After these pioneering efforts, aerial archaeology came to be recognized as a valuable tool for locating and recording sites. England has been preeminent in exploiting the technique, as demonstrated by a recent estimate of the numbers of aerial photographs of England as 2,000,000, in contrast to estimates of 100,000 in France and 40,000 in Germany (48). In America comparatively little use appears to have been made of this remote sensing technique until the late 1960s (26, p. 16).

The types of archaeological remains which can be recorded by aerial remote sensing can be classified as cropmarks, soilmarks, shadowmarks and snowmarks. Cropmarks are created by differential growth over an archaeological feature; they may result in more luxuriant growth over a buried ditch which has more nutrients or retains more moisture than the surrounding subsoil, or they may result in stunted growth over a buried wall. Soilmarks show up in newly plowed fields when the differential fill of archaeological features may stand out against the surrounding plow soil. Shadowmarks are evident in the early morning and late evening when the sun is low on the horizon and slight earthworks which may not be visible from ground level cast exaggerated shadows. This effect may also show up in cropmarks which are photographed in the early morning or late evening. Snowmarks appear when a light fall of snow has drifted against slight earthworks of the type which create shadowmarks. Differential melting of the snow because of the greater thickness against the earthwork will effectively outline the earthwork for a short period. These types of features are of course extremely ephemeral as a rule, and researchers have found a great deal of variability from year to year and day to day in the consistency with which archaeological features show up on the same site.

There has been some research into the precise factors which are responsible for the formation of cropmarks. The major factor appears to be potential soil moisture deficit, or PSMD. This occurs when the rainfall rate is less than the transpiration rate of a crop in a particular area, which forces the crop to utilize the moisture in the soil. Most of the soil nutrients and the roots of crops are in the upper 30–40 cm, so when the soil moisture is used up to this depth, growth will cease (31, p. 3). On sites where there are subsurface archaeological features and shallow soils, the roots of crops will penetrate more deeply into the archaeological features where more moisture will be stored and where more soluble nutrients will be present. The nature of the soil is also important: in sandy soils the moisture in the soil is readily released, whereas in clayey soils water is released more gradually. Consequently, crops on sandy soils will quickly use up the available moisture and wilt, but on clay soils the water will be used up more slowly and growth will be slower and wilting less likely (31, p. 3). By using rainfall records and data on the soils of two sites in the United Kingdom, it was possible to show a correlation between rainfall and periods when cropmarks showed at the two sites. At one site where soils were shallower than at the other, cropmarks appeared when the PSMD was 30 mm; at the other site cropmarks were observed when the PSMD was 80 mm (22, p. 74). The same study also found that a PSMD 40 mm greater than that needed for the formation of cropmarks was required before marks showed up in grassland (22, p. 63). By calculating the rainfall needs of crops in a given area and subtracting the monthly rainfall, it should be possible with due allowance made for soil types to calculate when an imbalance or PSMD will occur and when conditions for the development of cropmarks are most likely. A method of doing this in the United Kingdom was described by Jones (30, pp. 656–68), and his methods should be applicable to the USA. The application of computerized data manipulation in a study of this kind should make it possible to predict where and when cropmarks are likely to occur over a wide area. One important factor to program into the computer would be a predictive model of the location of sites in the study area which would enable the subsequent flights to be concentrated in areas where growing crops can be found on probable site locations.

Extensive aerial photographic surveys have been carried out in many countries for mapping purposes, and these photographs have then subsequently been used for archaeological purposes. These photographs are invariably taken from high altitudes and may not be entirely satisfactory for archaeological purposes. If they are taken at the right time of year, as in the illustrated examples (Figures 2 and 3), they may contain a vast amount of information. Figure 2 is a vertical photograph of Valley Forge National Historical Park, Pennsylvania, taken on May 13, 1965. This photograph was taken a year after a Boy Scout jamboree was held at the Park. For this jamboree underground water, electrical and telephone lines were installed; 3900 latrine pits, each 1 foot in diameter and 4 to 5 feet deep were dug; 90 water stations, each of which required two holes 1 foot 2 inches by 4 to 5 feet deep, were dug; and 30 showers were installed, each of which required excavation of a hole 4 feet wide by 4 feet deep and 12 feet long (45, p. 18).

The result of all this activity is still visible a year later on the aerial photograph as cropmarks in the grass. The small white rectangles visible in the bottom left-hand corner of the photograph are presumably the showers and the paired white dots the water stations. Individual white dots are probably the latrines and the many linear features the service lines. In Figure 3, a later vertical photograph of the same area taken on March 13, 1973, many of these

Figure 2 Vertical aerial photograph of Valley Forge National Historical Park taken on May 13, 1965. The white markings are the cropmarks resulting from the Boy Scout jamboree held at the park in 1964. Photograph courtesy of MASCA.

Figure 3   Vertical aerial photograph of Valley Forge National Historical Park taken on March 13, 1973. The cropmarks from the Boy Scout jamboree are still readily apparent. Photograph courtesy of MASCA.

features are still visible despite the fact that the photograph was taken in mid-March, hardly an optimum time for the cropmarks to show. The most noticeable features are the service lines which show up well because of their linearity.

The two photographs show rather dramatically the changing nature of the landscape around Valley Forge and illustrate the problems of carrying out a remote sensing survey at such a site. The photographs were acquired during a survey of Valley Forge carried out by MASCA of The University Museum, University of Pennsylvania, in 1977–78, which was designed to locate traces of the Revolutionary War encampment (40, pp. 193–201; 44). The Boy Scout jamboree at Valley Forge was the last of three held there, each one of which had similar effects on the site (45, pp. 15–18). The conclusion of the aerial remote sensing arm of the survey was that the combination of the three jamborees had created such a plethora of surface marking that little evidence of the Revolutionary War encampment could be discerned on aerial photographs (29, p. 79). Aerial remote sensing at Valley Forge may have been more successful before the jamborees, as suggested by the reconstruction of Fort Greene (Fort John Moore). This was based on the evidence of aerial photographs taken on May 24, 1948, before the first of the jamborees, and on subsequent archaeological excavations (45, p. 26). Of interest to the history of remote sensing is the fact that mine detectors were employed to search for the fort earlier in the year (45, p. 26), which is one of the earliest instances of the use of remote sensing in the service of archaeology, other than aerial photography, in America.

Vertical aerial photographs have tended to be the type favored in the United States because distortion in mapping archaeological features is very slight. Oblique aerial photographs, in which the camera axis is at an angle to the earth, create mapping problems, but the technique in used widely in Europe and various ways of overcoming the distortions created by the method have been devised. These are described by Scollar (47) and Palmer (39), and involve the use of various trigonometric and computer techniques to achieve an accurate plot. The main problems associated with these methods are created by changes in slope on the site being investigated, or a lack of control points from which accurate measurements can be made. Recent research has improved the technique and an accuracy of one to two meters may be possible with it (27). While this degree of accuracy may not be as precise as that of a vertical photograph, it is sufficiently detailed to allow a site to be located on the ground, to enable relationships between various aspects of a site to be discerned, and to allow an interpretation of the relationships between adjacent sites to be made.

Various surveys have been made which rely on information from aerial photographs to interpret the landscape. The earliest and most famous is *Wessex from the Air* (19, pp. 52–53). More recently, surveys have been published that plot sites onto maps which can then be used as planning documents and which also allow much of the prehistoric and later occupation of a region to be identified and interpreted (7). This type of survey has been carried out at Chaco Canyon, New Mexico, where intensive aerial survey has enabled the detailed plotting of a prehistoric road system (35, pp. 111–34; 54, pp.135–67). Individual sites such as Valley Forge (40) and Chalmette National Historical Park, Louisiana (36), have been the subject of detailed aerial surveys. Some of the results of the Valley Forge survey are described above, where it was concluded that later activities obscured the Revolutionary War component of the site. At Chalmette National Historical Park, imagery included black-and-white prints and color infrared film. Three kinds of anomaly were recorded, and although possible explanations were offered for two types, no archaeological testing was carried out (36, pp. 75, 86).

At both these sites, however, aerial photographic techniques were successful in recording anomalies, some of which are likely to be of archaeological interest. Given that both these sites are predominantly wooded or grassland, it is remarkable that so much showed up at all in these unsuitable mediums. It would be interesting to see similar surveys carried out in adjacent areas under crops and see how the results compare. Archaeological testing after such surveys is also highly desirable. When looking at archaeological features on an aerial photograph it is sometimes possible to infer a relationship between individual anomalies, as for example when a linear feature obviously deviates to avoid another feature. What is most often seen, however, is a palimpsest of archaeological features in which there are obviously several periods of activity represented. In cases like this some excavation of crucial areas to establish relationships is needed before any kind of coherent interpretation of a site can be offered. The very minimum of archaeological attention such as field reconnaissance can often eliminate features seen on aerial photographs from further consideration. For example, some features noted on aerial photographs of Valley Forge were found after field inspection to be outwash from road drainage ditches. There is also the famous story of the archaeologist who noted five circular features on an aerial photograph which he interpreted as the remains of burial mounds. Field examination of the features, however, revealed that five tethered goats, each cropping the grass at the end of its tether, were responsible for the pattern (19, pp. 45–46).

RESISTIVITY, EM, MAGNETOMETER, AND RADAR SURVEY

Resistivity is one of the simplest and cheapest methods of remote sensing. In practice, electrodes are placed in the ground and the resistance of the ground to a charge of electricity is measured. The presence of archaeological features in the ground is shown by changes in the resistance of the earth to the electrical charge. The method works best in damp ground and is most successful in locating walls. The disadvantages of resistivity are the time involved in moving the probes and its unsuitability for use in dry ground. Recently, however, its use as a tool to examine larger geographical areas rather than as a device for locating individual structures has been suggested (11). In another paper, the value of resistivity in carrying out a detailed examination of a single structure is demonstrated (34). A variation on resistivity is electromagnetic (EM) survey. The EM survey instrument measures the earth's resistance to electricity, but in contrast to resistivity survey, no contact with the ground is necessary and a continuous display of the measurements received is shown on the device. A field trial of the method in Cyprus in 1980 produced indifferent results (24, p. 47), but more recent results have been comparable to those of resistivity survey. For a description of the theory behind this technique, which is similar to that of a metal detector, see Aitken (3, pp. 191–98).

A comprehensive book on resistivity surveying has recently been published and provides a current account of the state of the art of this branch of remote sensing (12). The simplicity of the technique and the relative cheapness of the equipment required has made resistivity surveying one of the most widely used methods of remote sensing. The development of the EM meter, which enables a survey to be carried out with a speed comparable to that of a magnetometer, is an important advance in this area of remote sensing. The EM meter also gives good results in dry soils and is best suited for locating ditches or the remains of earthen mounds. Unlike a conventional resistivity survey which requires several people, an EM survey can be carried out successfully by one person. The EM device is more sophisticated than the equipment required for a resistivity survey and consequently is much more expensive to buy. The savings in personnel time in carrying out a survey with this instrument and its ability to operate in dry soils, however, more than compensate for the greater initial cost of the device, and it seems likely that the EM meter will become a widely used remote sensing technique in the near future.

The magnetometer is probably the most widely used remote sensing device. One of the chief exponents of the technique until the late 1970s was MASCA of the University of Pennsylvania. This group carried out surveys in the Old and New Worlds, including an extensive survey of the site of Sybaris, Italy. Throughout this period a great deal of research and field trials of magnetometers were carried out, resulting in instruments that are lighter, quicker to operate, and more sensitive to subsurface remains. A discussion of the technical merits of the different varieties of magnetometers is beyond the scope of this article, and the interested reader is referred to the following sources (2, 10, 42, 43). While various research groups still attempt to improve the scope and efficiency of magnetometers, one of the more interesting developments in recent years is the manipulation of magnetometer data by computer. A great deal of data is generated by even a small survey, and recording this in the field and then converting it into a meaningful pattern in the laboratory is very time consuming.

Computers are now being used to both record the field data and to manipulate them into a display on a TV screen or computer printout. Extensive use of computers to record data was first made in Germany in 1966 (49, p. 62). Early methods of plotting these data used simple dot density diagrams. With the application of more sophisticated computer software it became possible to screen out such undesirables as nonarchaeological variations in soil magnetism or surface iron (46, p. 75). Color graphic displays on a TV screen produced from computer data can give a very dramatic picture of the nature and distribution of features on an archaeological site. For economy in publishing results, a black-and-white photograph of the color monitor (Figure 4) can also provide a good graphic display. To survey one hectare of an archaeological site at a one-meter spacing requires at least 10,000 readings, and the computerized recording and manipulation of this volume of data represents an obvious saving in time in completing a survey and in flexibility in interpreting the results.

The magnetometer works by measuring the slight differences in magnetism which might be present in culturally disturbed soil. It can also detect walls and stone structures, but it works best at locating iron or burnt features in which the temperature of the feature has been raised above the Curie point. The system works very well in large clear areas where there is no magnetic disturbance from, for example, motor vehicles, trains, power lines, or buried service pipes. As was demonstrated at Valley Forge, these factors can produce so much "background noise" that signals from the cultural features of interest are masked (40). This basic problem of the magnetometer is unlikely to be resolved, so sites where the technique is to be used should be chosen with care.

The use of radar in archaeological prospecting is comparatively new. The first experiments were made with the device at Chaco Canyon, New Mexico, in 1974 (53). Since that date the technique has been applied to a number of sites with a good success rate (23, 24, 33, 40). In principle the technique is the same as aerial radar. In use on a site (Figure 5) the signal from a radar antenna mounted on a cart is transmitted into the ground, and discontinuities in the earth will be shown on a receiver. One of the advantages of the system is the immediate results received, although some interpretation of the data is required. Unlike the magnetometer, radar is unaffected by magnetic disturbance and can be used in areas where the magnetometer cannot. Radar has depth limitations in some kinds of soil, but an electrical resistivity test of the ground can indicate its suitability for the use of the method.

Because the radar antenna is mounted on a cart, it is difficult to use in thickly wooded or rough terrain. In operation the antenna is pulled across the survey area in regular traverses, the spacing of which is determined by factors such as the time available to carry out the survey and the size of the features it is

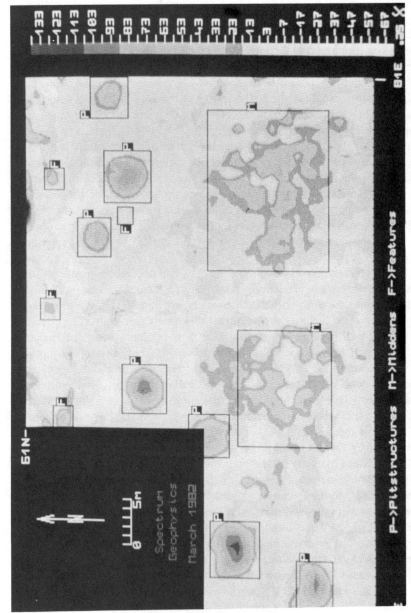

Figure 4   Black-and-white photograph of color coded, computer-generated magnetic data from an Anasazi site in the Southwest. Definition is of course much better in color. Photograph courtesy of Robert Huggins, Spectrum Geophysics, Fort Worth, Texas.

Figure 5 The archaeological radar antenna in use at Valley Forge National Historical Park. In this instance the device is being used to test alongside an excavation trench. Photograph courtesy of Nicholas Hartmann, MASCA.

anticipated may be located. The readings from the antenna are transmitted to the receiver which prints out the stratigraphic patterns of the earth that have been recorded during each traverse. These printouts can show great detail, including stratigraphic layers and other discontinuities in the ground caused by man-made features (Figure 6). Figure 6 shows the radar profile of a Revolutionary War trash pit at Valley Forge. This feature was located during a magnetometer survey and subsequently half-sectioned, the profile recorded, and then back-filled. The radar antenna was then pulled over the unexcavated part and the back-filled portion of the pit, and the printout shows the amount of detail that was recorded. The dark area in the center of the picture between the dashed lines is the unexcavated portion of the pit which gives a strong echo. The back-filled portion of the pit shows up as a lighter, much weaker echo to the right of the unexcavated portion of the pit. The natural strata of the site are shown by the horizontal bands each side of the pit feature.

Of all the remote sensing techniques available, radar is perhaps the one that

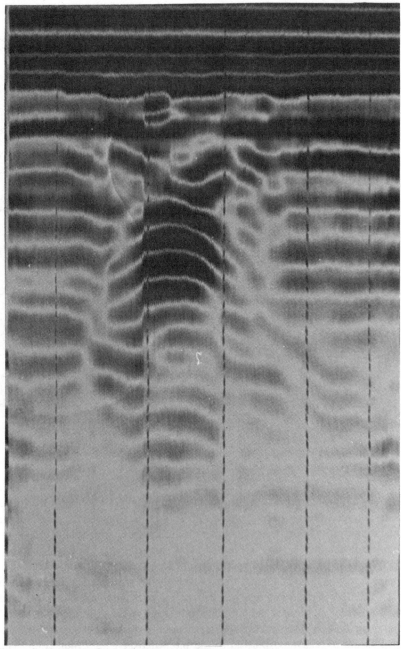

Figure 6 Photograph of a radar printout from a Revolutionary War trash pit at Valley Forge which was partially excavated in 1978. The dark central area represents the unexcavated half of the pit. The area to the right is the backfilled portion of the pit which gives a much weaker signal. Photograph courtesy of Bruce Bevan, Geosight, Pitman, New Jersey.

gives the archaeologist information most comparable to that obtainable from excavation. Under the right conditions the radar printout may show the stratigraphic layers in an archaeological feature in the same way they would be seen in an archaeological cross-section of the feature. The technique is good for locating walls and earth-filled features such as the pit discussed above, as well as linear features such as ditches. The equipment needed for a radar survey is very expensive, and this is probably the major reason why the technique has been used less than it might have been.

The four techniques described above are probably the geophysical detecting methods most widely used today in the United States. There is a great deal of literature, much of it highly technical, which is available for those interested in pursuing an understanding of the scientific principles behind these techniques, and the references cited in this section should lead to it. All of these techniques will work well under the right circumstances and on the right kind of site. The choice of the technique to be used on a site will depend on a number of factors such as soil type, terrain, the type of site being investigated and the amount of time and funding available to do the survey. An evaluation of these factors should be made before a geophysical survey is carried out, and then a technique can be chosen which is appropriate to the site.

In practice a grid is usually superimposed on the area being surveyed by these techniques and measurements are taken at fixed points on the grid. The spacing at which the measurements are made depends on the size of the feature it is hoped will be located. If small features such as refuse pits are anticipated, then measurements will be required at smaller intervals than would be needed to locate large linear features such as ditches. There is also a correlation between the volume of an archaeological feature and the ease with which it can be detected, so that in general the larger the feature, the more easily it can be located by these techniques. The contrast between the soil fill of a feature and the surrounding subsoil is also important, and usually the greater the contrast the more easily the feature can be detected. Under some conditions a combination of several different techniques may give the most comprehensive picture of the archaeological remains of a site. Subsurface testing during the survey is often useful in assessing the efficiency of the technique being used and may indicate that a different instrument would give better results. These generalized statements will hold true for most surveys, but each site is of course unique with its own particular requirements, and ideally a geophysical survey should be tailored to fit the needs of each individual site.

OTHER TECHNIQUES

The remote sensing techniques discussed so far are now used conventionally in most countries of the world. Acoustic sensing is a new technique that is being pioneered in Japan, where it has been used successfully to locate a stone coffin buried at a depth of 2 meters (38, p. 87). In operation, a sound generator sends a low-frequency acoustic signal into the earth and the echo is measured in a receiver. Another experimental technique is thermal prospecting, in which instruments are used to measure differences in surface temperature of the earth. This has been attempted successfully from aircraft in France, where a scanner radiometer was used to measure soil temperature differences (41, 52). The technique has had some success in the United States, where it has been tried on a small-scale experimental basis by using a portable infrared thermometer to detect objects buried at various depths (6). Good results were also reported from an aerial thermographic survey carried out in Arizona (8, pp. 588–600).

Another type of survey that has been attempted on an experimental basis is radioactivity detection. Depth penetration is poor with this method and measurements take a relatively long time, but some success has been reported (3, pp. 198–99). This method was attempted at Valley Forge where readings taken by a gamma-ray spectrometer showed an anomaly in the potassium and thorium counts in an area where a stone structure was subsequently excavated (9, pp. 147–50). The new techniques described here have not been used to any great extent in archaeological research, but it may become clearer with more experimental work if they can be usefully applied to remote sensing procedures on a large scale.

The field of remote sensing has seen a great deal of expansion since the first use of geophysical detecting devices on archaeological sites in the 1940s. Besides the remote sensing techniques described here, many other devices have been used with varying degrees of success including metal detectors, sonar, side-looking aerial radar, and LANDSAT (1, 20, 24, 28). Another technique which appears not to have been used on an archaeological site as yet has been developed by Barringer Research of Toronto and Denver for geological research. This technique with the trade mark name of Surtrace samples the surface microlayer of the ground either from a helicopter or at ground level. Elemental material in the microlayer reflects the underlying geology in the area sampled, and there seems to be no reason why material of archaeological interest should not also be present in the microlayer which could indicate the presence of an archaeological site.

PHOSPHATE TESTING

All the methods of detecting sites described above can be defined as remote sensing in the strictest sense of the term as they involve taking various kinds of measurements from the ground without actually removing anything from the ground. Phosphate testing is not, strictly speaking, a remote sensing technique as it involves taking samples of earth for subsequent testing in the lab. The technique, however, is being used more and more with conventional remote sensing methods, and some discussion of it here seems justified.

The principle behind phosphate testing is based on the fact that certain kinds of material associated with human activity contain compounds such as phosphorus, calcium, and nitrogen. These compounds are present in human and animal excreta and also in bones and some types of refuse. Phosphorus as a phosphate is the most stable of these compounds, and its presence in above-normal quantities in a soil sample is strong evidence for human activity on a site (21, p. 206). Testing for bone phosphate is frequently carried out on cemetery sites where acid soils may have destroyed the bones and the only surviving evidence for the actual burial may be an abnormally high phosphate level (51, pp. 254–56).

The technique has also been used on occupation sites with good results, especially in Europe (50, pp. 447–54), and some work has been carried out in American sites (25, pp. 52–55; 32). Recently soil phosphate analysis has been used with remote sensing techniques to compare the efficiency of the two techniques. The results of one survey which compared phosphate data with magnetometer data showed that the two techniques provided similar distributional information about the location of features (14, p. 191). More detailed work was carried out at a number of sites in eastern England, where good correlation was found between archaeological features detected by aerial photographs and magnetometer surveys (15, 16). The sampling methods used in this work indicated that phosphate levels in plow soil reliably reflected the level of phosphate in subsurface features, and also that the plow zone's archaeological usefulness was not destroyed because valid archaeological data could be obtained from it (16). Good results were obtained during surveys in Illinois which combined magnetometry with soil testing on the sites of Fort Kaskaskia and Fort De Chartres Number 1 (55). In these surveys chemical tests and the magnetometer results were successful in locating the boundaries of the forts and in identifying internal structures (55, pp. 13–14). The success of these various surveys in England and the United States shows that phosphate testing has good potential as a remote sensing technique. The significance of these studies is not only relevant to the field of remote sensing, however, and should be noted by all exponents of the theory that the plow zone of all sites is archaeologically sterile (37, p. 145).

SUMMARY

Virtually all of the techniques described above were originally developed for purposes other than archaeology and were then adapted into a form suitable for archaeological remote sensing. Another factor they share is that they all rely on "hard science" to produce the information that the discipline of archaeology requires. The archaeologist's ultimate dream is a remote sensing instrument which will provide reliable, detailed information on the vertical and horizontal distribution of the features on an archaeological site. None of the techniques currently available comes close to meeting these specifications. What is available can provide information on the presence or absence of features on a site and sometimes, as in the case of aerial photography, an interpretation of the site is possible, but archaeological excavations are always needed to verify the information. Remote sensing, however, is a valuable tool for the archaeologist, a tool which can be used to locate sites at a fraction of the cost of conventional subsurface testing if the right technique is chosen. Choosing the right technique or combination of techniques requires some specialized knowledge, and hopefully this review of the techniques currently available will prove helpful in making that choice.

ACKNOWLEDGMENTS

I would like to acknowledge the help, advice, and encouragement of the following people: Bruce Bevan, Robert Brodkey, Paul Craddock, John Haigh, Nicholas Hartmann, Robert Huggins, Helen Schenck, and John Weymouth.

Literature Cited

1. Adams, R. E. W., Brown, W. E. Jr., Culbert, T. P. 1981. Radar mapping, archaeology, and ancient Maya land use. *Science* 213(4515):1457–63
2. Aitken, M. J. 1971. Magnetic location. See Ref. 13, pp. 681–94
3. Aitken, M. J. 1974. *Physics and Archaeology*. Oxford: Oxford Univ. Press. 291 pp. 2nd ed.
4. Ashbee, P. 1972. Field archaeology: Its origins and development. In *Archaeology and the Landscape*, ed. P. J. Fowler, pp. 38–74. London: Baker. 263 pp.
5. Atkinson, R. J. C., Piggott, C. M., Sandars, N. K. 1951. *Excavations at Dorchester, Oxon*. Oxford: Ashmolean Museum. 151 pp.
6. Benner, S. M., Brodkey, R. S. 1981. *Underground detection using differential heat analysis*. Presented at Symp. Archaeom., 21st, Brookhaven, NY
7. Benson, D., Miles, D., Balkwill, C. J., Clayton, N. 1974. *The Upper Thames Valley: An Archaeological Survey of the River Gravels*. Oxford: Oxfordshire Archaeol. Unit. 113 pp.
8. Berlin, G. L., Ambler, J. R., Herly, R. H., Schaber, G. G. 1977. Identification of a Sinagua agricultural field by aerial thermography, soil chemistry, pollen/plant analysis, and archaeology. *Am. Antiq.* 42(4):588–600
9. Bermingham, D., Bevan, B., Hartmann, N. 1979. Case studies of geophysical anomalies. See Ref. 44, pp. 139–50
10. Breiner, S. 1973. *Applications Manual for Portable Magnetometers*. Sunnyvale, Calif: Geometrics. 58 pp.
11. Carr, C. 1977. A new role and analytical design for the use of resistivity surveying in archaeology. *Mid-Cont. J. Archaeol.* 2(2):161–93
12. Carr, C. 1982. *Handbook on Soil Resistivity Surveying*. Evanston, Ill: Cent. Am. Archaeol. Press. 704 pp.
13. Clark, A. J. 1971. Resistivity surveying. In *Science in Archaeology*, ed. D. Brothwell, E. Higgs, pp. 695–707. Great Britain: Thames & Hudson. 720 pp. 2nd ed.
14. Clark, A. J. 1977. Geophysical and chemical assessment of air photograph sites. *Archaeol. J.* 134:187–93
15. Craddock, P. 1982. Quand les archéologues analysent les phosphates. *La Rech.* 133(May):666–67
16. Craddock, P., Gurney, D., Pryor, F., Hughes, M. 1983. The application of phosphate analysis to the location and interpretation of archaeological sites. *J. Archaeol. Sci.* In press
17. Crawford, O. G. S. 1970. *Archaeology in the Field*. London: Dent. 280 pp.
18. Daniel, G. 1967. *The Origins and Growth of Archaeology*. Harmonds-

worth, England: Penguin Books. 304 pp.
19. Duel, L. 1973. *Flights into Yesterday: The Story of Aerial Archaeology.* Harmondsworth, England: Penguin Books. 330 pp.
20. Edgerton, H. E. 1976. Underwater archaeological search with sonar. *Hist. Archaeol.* 10:46–53
21. Eidt, R. C. 1973. A rapid chemical field test for archaeological site surveying. *Am. Antiq.* 38(2):206–10
22. Evans, R., Jones, R. J. A. 1977. Crop marks and soils at two archaeological sites in Britain. *J. Archaeol. Sci.* 4:63–76
23. Faulkner, A. 1981. Pentagoet: A First Look at Seventeenth Century Acadian Maine. *Northeast Hist. Archaeol.* 10: 51–57
24. Fischer, P. M. 1980. Applications of technical devices in archaeology: The use of X-rays, microscope, electrical and electro-magnetic devices and subsurface interface radar. *Stud. Mediterr. Archaeol.* 63:1–64
25. Grubb, T. C. 1979. Experience with the phosphate test to locate ancient habitation sites. *Ohio Archaeol.* 29(2):52–55
26. Gumerman, G. J., Kruckman, L. D. 1977. The unrealized potential of remote sensing in archaeology. See Ref. 35, pp. 15–33
27. Haigh, J. G. B. 1982. *Practical methods for the rectification of oblique aerial photographs.* Presented at Symp. Archaeom., 22nd , Bradford, England
28. Hamlin, C. L. 1977. Machine processing of LANDSAT data: An introduction for anthropologists and archaeologists. *MASCA Newsl.* 13(1/2):1–11
29. Hartmann, N. 1979. Aerial photography. See Ref. 44, pp. 58–85
30. Jones, R. J. A. 1979. Crop marks induced by soil moisture stress at an Iron Age site in Midland, England, UK. *Proc. 18th Int. Symp. Archaeom. Archaeol. Prospection, Bonn, 14–17 March, 1978:*656–68
31. Jones, R. J. A., Evans, R. 1975. Soil and crop marks in the recognition of archaeological sites by air photography. In *Aerial Reconnaissance for Archaeology,* ed. D. R. Wilson, pp. 1–11. London:Counc. British Archaeol. 158 pp.
32. Keeler, R. W. 1977. *An earthy view of life on a seventeenth-century farm.* Presented at Ann. Meet. Soc. Hist. Archaeol., 10th, Ottawa
33. Kenyon, J. L., Bevan, B. 1977. Ground-penetrating radar and its application to a historical archaeological site. *Hist. Archaeol.* 11:48–55
34. Klasner, J. S., Calengas, P. 1981. Electrical resistivity and soil studies at Oren-

dorf archaeological site, Illinois: A case study. *J. Field Archaeol.* 8:167–74
35. Lyons, T. R., Hitchcock, R. K. 1977. Remote sensing interpretation of an Anasazi land route system. In *Aerial Remote Sensing Techniques in Archaeology,* ed. T. R. Lyons, R. K. Hitchcock, pp. 111–34. Albuquerque: Natl. Park Serv., Univ. N. Mex. 201 pp.
36. Mathien, F. J. 1981. Chalmette National Historical Park: A remote sensing project. *Hist. Archaeol.* 15(2):69–86
37. Noël Hume, I. 1982. *Martin's Hundred.* New York: Knopf. 343 pp.
38. Ozowa, K., Matsuda, M. 1979. Computer assisted techniques for detecting underground remains based on acoustic measurement. *Archaeometry* 21(1):87–100
39. Palmer, R. 1977. A computer method for transcribing information graphically from oblique aerial photographs to maps. *J. Archaeol. Sci.* 4:283–90
40. Parrington, M. 1979. Geophysical and aerial prospecting techniques at Valley Forge National Historical Park, Pennsylvania. *J. Field Archaeol.* 6(2):193–201
41. Perisset, M. C., Tabbagh, A. 1981. Interpretation of thermal prospection on bare soils. *Archaeometry* 23(2):169–87
42. Ralph, E. K. 1965. Comparison of a proton and a rubidium magnetometer for archaeological prospecting. *Archaeometry* 7:20–27
43. Ralph, E. K., Morrison, F., O'Brien, P. 1968. Archaeological surveying utilizing a high-sensitivity difference magnetometer. *Geoexploration* 6:109–22
44. Ralph, E. K., Parrington, M., eds. 1979. *Patterns of the Past: Geophysical and Aerial Reconnaissance at Valley Forge.* Philadelphia: MASCA, Univ. Penn. 166 pp.
45. Schenck, H. R. 1979. Nineteenth and twentieth century history of Valley Forge. See Ref. 44, pp. 10–19
46. Scollar, I. 1974. Interactive processing of geophysical data from archaeological sites. *Computer Appl. Archaeol.* 1974: 75–80
47. Scollar, I. 1975. Transformation of extreme oblique aerial photographs to maps or plans by conventional means or by computer. See Ref. 31, pp. 52–59
48. Scollar, I. 1982. *Geophysical prospecting and remote sensing: Natural and technical limits for archaeology.* Presented at Ann. Meet. Soc. Archaeol. Sci. 4th, Minneapolis
49. Scollar, I., Kruckeberg, F. 1966. Computer treatment of magnetic measurements from archaeological sites. *Archaeometry* 9:61–71

50. Sjöberg, A. 1976. Phosphate analysis of anthropic soils. *J. Field Archaeol.* 3:447–54
51. Solecki, R. S. 1951. Notes on soil analysis and archaeology. *Am. Antiq.* 16:254–56
52. Tabbagh, A. 1979. Thermal airborne prospection of the Lion En Beace Township (Loiret, France). See Ref. 30, pp. 700–9
53. Vickers, R. S., Dolphin, L. T. 1975. A communication on an archaeological radar experiment at Chaco Canyon, New Mexico. *MASCA Newsl.* 11(1):n.p.
54. Ware, J. A., Gumerman, G. J. 1977. Remote sensing methodology and the Chaco Canyon prehistoric road system. See Ref. 35, pp. 135–67
55. Weymouth, J. W. 1982. *Final Report on Magnetic Surveys over the Sites of Fort Kaskaskia and Fort De Chartres Number 1, Illinois*. Lincoln: Nebraska Cent. Archaeophys. Res. Univ. Nebraska.

Ann. Rev. Anthropol. 1983. 12:125–42
Copyright © 1983 by Annual Reviews Inc. All rights reserved

ANALYSIS OF STYLE IN ARTIFACTS

Stephen Plog

Department of Anthropology, University of Virginia, Charlottesville, Virginia 22903

An immense amount of information on patterns of stylistic variation in prehistoric artifacts has been produced by studies done throughout the history of archaeological research. The construction of space-time frameworks for most regions on the basis of such patterns has produced detailed information on stylistic sequences through time and stylistic distributions across space. Much of that critical information is encoded in complex sets of artifact types which have been developed. When questions concerning stylistic variation move beyond general patterns of variation across space and through time, however, the available information decreases drastically despite the decades of research on stylistic variation. However, significant improvements have been made during the last 20 years. Beginning at least as early as the innovative ceramic sociology studies of the 1960s (11, 27, 41–43, 65), when initial attempts were made to examine the relationship between stylistic variation and aspects of social organization, many new questions about stylistic variation began to be addressed. Can spatial clusters of stylistic attributes smaller than the previously defined culture areas be isolated that might be the result of residence groups, lineages, marriage networks, or clusters of communities cooperating in economic activities? Can studies of stylistic variation lead to more accurate and precise estimates of site occupation dates? Why do rates of stylistic change and degrees of stylistic variation fluctuate so much through time or across space?

As the questions about the causes and nature of stylistic variation have increased, so have the number and types of studies. Within the last five years, for example, at least a dozen doctoral dissertations have been written that have focused almost exclusively on issues concerning stylistic variation. In addition, an increasing number of ethnographic studies of patterns of stylistic variation

125

have been initiated (20, 22, 30, 32, 33, 44) to complement the information which can be obtained from analyses of prehistoric artifacts.

While it might be expected that the increasing number of studies would have resulted in some generally accepted answers to the kinds of questions listed above, such has not been the case. Nowhere is this clearer than in the ethnographic or "ethnoarchaeological" studies noted above, studies which some believed would provide many of those answers because of the possibility of talking to and observing the makers of the artifacts and obtaining clear-cut information about variables such as marriage patterns. One need only compare studies of the Kalinga in the Phillipines (22, 44) and of several populations in Africa (30, 32, 33) to see that some of the conclusions reached are contradictory. If there is any inference that is common to most, if not all, recent studies, it is the important but nevertheless somewhat unfulfilling conclusion that the causes of stylistic variation are complex. There is, therefore, considerable difference of opinion concerning the degree of support or lack of support for various theories which have been developed to explain stylistic variation. These theories will be described briefly in the following section, and I will then discuss some of the types of studies which have been suggested as necessary to resolve some of the current differences of opinion.

THEORIES OF STYLISTIC VARIATION

As noted above, many recent studies of stylistic variation have led to differing conclusions concerning the reasons similarities or differences in style occur or do not occur among different individuals, social groups, villages, or regions. One theory which continues to be advocated is the fundamental tenet of the ceramic sociology studies: the degree of stylistic similarity between individuals, residence groups, or villages is directly related to the amount of social interaction between those individuals, groups, or villages. As Flannery (19) has noted, this argument is an extension to smaller social groups of some of the basic assumptions which archaeologists always have used in defining culture areas. The isolation of culture areas was based on the assumption that stylistic distributions would be marked by spatial discontinuities with homogeneous distributions within individual areas. Thus, stylistic similarities or differences could be used to identify membership in regional social groups but not directly to estimate levels of interaction intensity. In contrast, many of the studies based on the social interaction theory explicitly assumed that levels of stylistic similarity or agreement could be used as direct estimates of interaction intensities. This is exemplified by the following statement: "It is assumed that if a pair of contemporaneous sites share a higher coefficient of agreement than another contemporaneous pair, there has been greater contact between the former pair" (16).

In addition to the social interaction theory, it also has been suggested that one of the major sources of variation in some stylistic characteristics is differences among individuals in motor habits (28, 29). It has been proposed that this variation in the execution of particular stylistic attributes is subconscious and thus unrelated to levels of social interaction.

In contrast to the above theories which view aspects of stylistic variation simply as a by-product or passive reflection of culture systems or individual motor habits, others have proposed that style may play a very active role. Several individuals (2, 3, 8, 9, 51, 68, 69) have argued that stylistic variation may be used in certain contexts to signal or communicate information "not only about the identity of the maker or user, but also potentially about his social group membership, status, wealth, religious beliefs, and political ideology (2, p. 118). Wobst (69, p. 323) suggests, however, that the utility of stylistic messages decreases with increasing social distance between the sender and receiver, inasmuch as there would be fewer messages that could not be transmitted more cheaply using another mode of communication. Thus, stylistic variation would be expected to be used in information exchange only under certain social conditions which have been outlined by several archaeologists (2–4, 26, 51, 62).

Hodder (32, 33) also has emphasized an active, symbolic role for stylistic variation, stating (33, p. 36) that "material symbols can actively justify the actions and intentions of human groups." He argues, however, that the manner in which material culture relates to society depends on factors such as ideological structures and symbolic codes (33, p. 210). Thus, "styles may well express and justify ethnic differentiation, but the manner in which they do this can only be understood by examining structures of symbolic meaning" (33, p. 205).

Unfortunately, attempts to test these theories have not always led to consistent conclusions. On the one hand, for example, a variety of evidence has been presented in several studies (2, 3, 30, 33, 49–52) suggesting that the relationship between stylistic variation and social interaction proposed by some of the ceramic sociologists is not supported. On the other hand, a number of individuals (22, 62–64) have defended the validity of that relationship. There are a variety of reasons for these differences of opinion. One problem has been that critical concepts often have been ambiguously defined. Rubertone (58, p. 100) has noted that the use of "the term 'interaction' indiscriminately as a concept to describe the sum of all interaction between units masks the variability in social relations that is essential to understanding complex societies, e.g. the nature of class affiliations, the existence of ethnic groups, and neighborhoods." In addition, tests of the different theories are far from complete and frequently lack the methodological rigor that ideally we would like to see. While some of my own research (51) has been regarded as supporting the information exchange theory, I have noted that, for a number of different reasons, including the lack of adequate stylistic analyses of broad areas, my evaluations of the theories had to be based on a synthesis of the subjective impressions of a number of archaeologists, rather than on an objective analysis of a large set of stylistic data. Many analyses, including some of the early ceramic sociology studies as well as some very recent research, also have been based on inadequate stylistic classifications and have failed to control a number of basic factors which can affect variation in the distributions of stylistic attributes (51). Finally, views concerning the complexity of the relationship between stylistic variation and social, religious, economic, and demographic factors often have been overly simplistic.

It is significant, however, that an increasing number of studies of style are being conducted and many have been directed toward solving some of the above problems. While some have attempted to develop a synthetic view of style which integrates some of the alternative theories (22, 62), for example, others have attempted to expand upon aspects of the theories (1–3, 26, 31–33, 66, 67). Thus, despite some of the differences of opinion that exist, I am optimistic about the results that may be achieved in the future. Archaeologists too often have been willing to accept proposals concerning stylistic variation that had not been adequately tested and had minimal empirical support. The current debates over various issues that are characteristic of a number of recent studies are not without their problems, but they are a good sign that more rigorous testing of ideas is being demanded and ultimately they should lead to some definite progress in our understanding of stylistic variation. Also, while there may not be widespread agreement concerning the factors that cause similarities and differences in stylistic distributions, many studies have reached similar conclusions concerning some of the steps that must be taken if future analyses are to increase our understanding of style. These steps include more adequate consideration of artifact production and exchange, expansion of studies to focus on stylistic variation on more than one type of material or artifact, better studies of variation over large geographical areas rather than concentration on a few sites or a small valley, and recognition that variation in different structural or hierarchical levels of style or different types of stylistic attributes may be caused by different factors. These are the steps on which I will concentrate in this paper.

CLASSIFICATION AND LEVELS OF STYLISTIC VARIATION

One of the most important changes in stylistic analyses that has occurred has been greater emphasis on classification methods. Classifications used in many of the ceramic sociology studies, as well as some developed during earlier decades (7, pp. 47–48), suffered from a number of different problems including lack of replicability (51, p. 42; 60) and a lack of equivalency of the analytical units such as design elements (51, 54). However, it should be noted that these problems occurred primarily with studies of materials on which stylistic elaboration was complex, such as ceramic vessels with painted designs or textiles, as opposed to analyses of other materials such as stone tools. The deficiencies were a result to a large degree of the inexplicit, intuitive criteria for isolating the analytical units (cf 27, p. 23). In recent years, however, the issue of classifying more complex types of stylistic elaboration has received considerable discussion (2, 3, 20, 22, 51, 54, 55, 62).

While questions concerning classification procedures still remain and adequate tests to demonstrate the degree of replicability of suggested approaches must still be conducted, progress is being made. One important example is the increasing recognition that stylistic elaboration is not a single, indivisible entity but can be described in terms of a number of different attributes ranging from the symmetry patterns of designs to the width of individual painted lines or the location of notches on projectile points. This point was made 15 years ago by Whallon (65, p. 223), who noted that "style has many aspects and levels of behavior which may be analytically distinguished and measured," and was underscored by Friedrich's (20) study of Tarascan potters and vessels. It has not had a significant impact on analyses of complex stylistic elaborations until recently, however.

In addition to the multidimensional nature of style, it also has been emphasized that stylistic attributes may be regarded as having a hierarchically organized structure (20). In discussing the structure of designs on ceramic vessels from the Tarascan village of San José, for example, Friedrich (20, p. 333) distinguished three hierarchical levels: spatial divisions, design configurations, and design elements. The highest hierarchical level was the system of spatial divisions. Within those divisions were placed designs which had two levels of organization: design elements and configurations. Design elements were "defined as the smallest self-contained unit," while design configurations were "defined as arrangements of design elements that are of sufficient complexity to fill a spatial division" (20, p. 335).

Recent studies have argued that the recognition of the multiple attribute, hierarchical nature of complex stylistic forms is important in evaluating theories of stylistic variation because variation in specific aspects, levels, or attributes of style may be explained by different factors (20, 22, 51, 62). In one of the most comprehensive studies done, for example, using sherds from the neolithic period in northwestern Europe, Voss (62) argued that variation in some stylistic attributes is likely to be the result of variation in levels of social interaction, while other design attributes are more likely to have been used for the type of information exchange discussed by Wobst. These proposals were to a large extent based on conclusions reached in the study by Friedrich noted above. Voss (62) suggested that determination of which attributes would be affected by different factors cannot be determined *a priori* (62, p. 112), but he suggests that it is likely that studies of interaction intensity should focus on design "features which involve the relative use of space and those which deal with variability within design configurations, particularly continuous or interval scale measurements such as design element repetitions and the width of particular lines" (62, p. 105). Such attributes may be good measures of interaction because they are not recognized as components of the formal design structure and thus are not regarded as part of the design by other potters (62, p. 106). Thus, "the nuances of style, those design attributes which are often identified with individual variability, appear to be reflective of interaction" (62, p. 106). In contrast, Voss (62, p. 112, 205) suggests that common, discrete or nominal scale design attributes which are highly visible and part of the formal design structure are more likely to be used for information exchange. Thus, "it would be expected that stylistic variability should incorporate at least one dimension related to social group affiliation and group linkages, and one dimension related to the specifics of social group interaction" (62, p. 274).

Although Voss suggests the patterns of stylistic variation on neolithic ceramic assemblages from northwestern Europe are consistent with his proposals, consideration of other data provides only mixed support for his specific arguments. Friedrich's (20, p. 338) analysis of Tarascan potters, for example, suggested three possible indicators of communication intensity. Two of the three are attributes at lower hierarchical levels of the design structure, but none of the indicators are the continuous or interval scale attributes which would be expected from Voss's proposal, although some are characteristics which vary within design configurations. Rather, they are structural characteristics of the designs, such as the organization of spatial divisions, or discrete characteristics, such as the shapes of areas that may be filled with particular design characteristics. Also, as noted above, Hill (28, 29) has argued on the basis of his studies that variation in a number of continuous stylistic attributes would not be affected by the intensity of interaction between individuals. In support of Voss's proposal, however, Newton's (47) analysis of differences in hammocks between two Brazilian tribes indicated that two discrete attributes of the twining were statistically significant indicators of tribal boundaries while several continuous twining measures were not. Also, analysis of design attributes on ceramic vessels from a small region of the American Southwest has shown that factors such as exchange, stylistic change through time, and vessel forms tend to have a more significant impact on continuous attributes than on nominal or discrete attributes. Seventy percent of tests involving continuous attributes revealed statistically significant differences while only 27 percent of the tests with nominal attributes produced statistically significant results (51, p.

113). This pattern may be related to Graves' (22, p. 296) proposal that "The lower the level of decoration in the design hierarchy and in motor performance, the greater the likelihood of design variation or change."

In addition to Voss's proposals, other studies also have suggested relationships between specific design characteristics or hierarchical levels and factors which would be expected to cause variation in those characteristics. Similarities and differences in the frequency of symmetry classes have been argued to be a result of variation in interaction intensities (63, 64). Analysis of Kalinga ceramic design suggested that "easily substituted design attributes," attributes that can be interchanged without affecting the coherence of the entire design system, "least reflect kin group affiliation" (22, p. 293). In contrast, structural classes of design tend to be associated with individual settlements or a community made up of a group of settlements (22, p. 297). None of these proposals should be regarded as established facts, but all of them are important steps toward increasing our understanding of stylistic variation.

Whether or not these specific proposals prove to be correct, it is clear that certain types of attributes do vary in a different manner than other attribute types and thus may be affected by different factors. This simple conclusion has several important implications. First, factor, regression, or other multivariate analyses of large sets of stylistic attributes are unlikely to produce any clear-cut spatial patterns since variation in the different attributes may have been produced by a variety of different factors. Thus, it is not surprising that reanalysis of the long design element lists used in some of the early ceramic sociology studies (27, 43) has failed to reveal any spatial clusters of stylistic attributes that could correspond to residence groups (50).

Second, not only our attempts to understand patterns of stylistic variation but also our use of such variation to understand the archaeological record will be improved by focusing on individual attributes or at least small sets of similar types of attributes. One such improvement is exemplified by several recent studies which were conducted in an attempt to improve dating accuracy in different areas. As noted above, artifact types overwhelmingly have been the analytical unit which archaeologists employ in most areas to date sites. While in part based on technological attributes, types also are defined to a large extent by a variety of stylistic attributes of different hierarchical or structural levels. Although the use of types to date sites undoubtedly has been successful in most cases, the recent studies referred to above suggest that further refinements in dating accuracy can be achieved by focusing on individual attributes rather than artifact types (14, 24, 40, 53).

This can best be illustrated by considering a study in the American Southwest, an area where ceramic types have been studied and redefined for over 50 years and have been dated almost throughout that period through associations with tree-ring samples (5). Types in the area are defined by a number of different technological and stylistic characteristics, including both nominal and interval scale stylistic attributes of different hierarchical levels, but are largely distinguished from each other by a variety of decorative characteristics (45, p. 252). For example, one ceramic type, Kana-a Black-on-white has been characterized as having the following design features: thin lines, zigzag lines, secondary ticks as opposed to dots, irregular lines, equilateral triangles with appended flags, and overlapping lines. Some have argued that prehistoric sites in the American Southwest can be dated to periods as short as 25 years by considering the relative frequencies of ceramic types. However, a recent multiple regression analysis of tree-ring dates and ceramic type frequencies from sites on Black Mesa in northeastern Arizona indicated that the standard error of the dates estimated from the type frequencies was ±44 years (39).

In a subsequent study, a similar analysis was done by using frequencies of individual stylistic attributes rather than the frequency of types (53). The attributes considered, however, were those used to define ceramic types in the area. Of the 52 attributes considered, the frequencies of only 26 (50 percent) were correlated with the tree-ring dates at higher than the 0.50 level. Thus, less than 25 percent of the variation in the frequency of half the attributes used to define the traditional ceramic types could be accounted for by factors causing stylistic change through time. More importantly, when multiple regression analysis was used to measure the extent to which the tree-ring dates could be estimated from the attribute frequencies, it was found that estimated dates with a standard error of ±19 years could be generated using an equation based on the frequencies of only three attributes. All three of the attributes selected by the step-wise multiple regression analysis were characteristics at lower hierarchical levels in the design structure, a finding that is consistent with Graves' (22) conclusion that there is a greater likelihood of change or design variation as the level of decoration in the design hierarchy or in motor performance decreases. A subsequent study using data from other areas of the American Southwest has produced results similar to the Black Mesa study (24). These analyses thus support the argument that some stylistic attributes vary in a different manner from other attributes. It also demonstrates that important improvements can be made in areas such as dating accuracy by focusing on individual attribute frequencies, as Rowe (57) suggested, rather than by using analytical units such as types or analyzing stylistic units such as the design elements (27, 44, 60) that are defined by similarities and differences in a number of different stylistic attributes. Although the reliability of style as an indicator of chronology has sometimes been questioned (10), the problem is not that style is unreliable, but that some dating studies have focused on the wrong aspects of style or have emphasized polythetic analytical units such as types. Because variation in the multiple attributes used to define types may be caused by different factors, variation in type frequencies also will be caused by a number of factors rather than simply those that cause stylistic change through time. Polythetic type definitions thus in some cases may obscure the dating value of individual stylistic attributes.

Archaeological studies such as those noted above and ethnoarchaeological analyses such as Graves' (22) examination of the relationship of stylistic variation and birth cohorts are likely to increase our ability to date sites accurately using stylistic attribute frequencies. The selection of attributes for different types of archaeological studies often has been intuitive (65, p. 224). As our understanding of the factors that cause variation in different attributes increases, however, more explicit selections can be made based on the topic of interest. As a result, our ability to describe and understand the archaeological record should improve.

EXCHANGE AND STYLISTIC VARIATION

The relationship between spatial patterns in style distributions and the production, exchange, and consumption of material items is another topic upon which future studies should concentrate. Studies of stylistic variation too often have been based on the assumption that the artifacts analyzed were locally produced (26). As more and more studies of exchange patterns have been conducted using mineralogical or chemical characterization, however, it has become clear that exchange was much more common prehistorically than many studies, particularly those focusing on stylistic analysis, have recognized. Thus, the extent to which patterns of spatial varation in stylistic attributes can be explained by the spatial distribution of exchange networks must be considered more frequently in future studies.

While this point is a simple one, its importance cannot be underemphasized because without an understanding of artifact production and consumption, the conclusions of many analyses of stylistic variation must be questioned. In one recent study of ceramic vessels, for example, Crown (10) drew several conclusions about the nature and causes of decorative variation on the vessels, conclusions that were based on the assumption that the vessels were all locally produced. However, although some mineralogical and chemical tests were made in an effort to determine whether or not the vessels studied had been locally produced, the results of those analyses were ambiguous. If, in fact, some of the vessels were not produced locally as assumed, many of the conclusions which were drawn concerning the causes and patterns of stylistic variation would not be supported. Thus, the absence of adequate answers to questions concerning the location of artifact production leaves the conclusions of many stylistic analyses questionable.

Beyond the simple point that exchange networks can affect patterns of stylistic variation, there are other issues concerning the relationship between exchange and stylistic variation that have been raised by recent studies. First, the nature of artifact production and consumption has implications for the extent to which conclusions derived from ethnographic or ethnoarchaeological studies are relevant to any prehistoric time period or geographical area or the extent to which the patterns of stylistic variation discovered in ethnographic studies will coincide. Longacre (44), for example, chose the Kalinga area for his ethnoarchaeological study because it provided a context in which "variability in ceramics and other cultural materials as well as aspects of behavior and organization that they might reflect" could be controlled. For example, pottery was produced by each household, for the use of that household (44, p. 51). Longacre notes (44, pp. 50–51) that if the ceramics had been produced by specialists for distribution in a market, then different "selective pressures" would influence the manufacture of the vessels. Thus, while the Kalinga provided an excellent context for Longacre's study, the extent to which the conclusions of that study are relevant to other situations will depend on several factors including the degree to which the production and consumption of artifacts is comparable to the Kalinga.

Second, too often it is assumed that there is a simple relationship between stylistic patterns, the nature of craft production, and the degree of exchange. Two examples can be used to illustrate this problem. Hodder (33) has noted that we often take it for granted that the extent of centralized production can be inferred from the spatial distribution of stylistic characteristics. That is, we assume that local production results in localized style distributions and that centralized production and abundant exchange will produce widespread, homogeneous style distributions. His ethnoarchaeological study in Africa did not support that assumption, however, and Van der Leeuw (61, p. 400) has noted other studies which revealed similar problems. Some archaeological studies of the distribution of stylistic attributes also suggest that artifact production actually may have been more localized during periods of widespread style zones than during periods of localized style zones (26, 51).

In addition to the fact that stylistic distributions across space cannot be used to infer production characteristics, patterns of stylistic change through time cannot be tied to particular modes of production. Similar patterns of stylistic change over time may be a result of different modes of production. Braun's (3) analysis of Woodland period ceramics from Illinois, for example, demonstrated a decrease in both stylistic variation and vessel wall thickness on locally produced pots during a portion of the period studied. These changes were shown to be a result of related changes in social networks and subsistence. A similar trend of decreasing decorative diversity and vessel wall thickness was discovered by Irwin (35, pp. 300, 315;36) in a study of ceramics from the Mailu area of southeast coastal Papua New Guinea. In that case, however, it was argued that both trends were a result of increasing specialization and centralization in the production of pottery, a conclusion that was reached after mineralogical and chemical analyses of sherds and clays. Thus, Braun's and Irwin's studies, as well as a somewhat similar case discussed by Krause & Thorne (38, p. 253), illustrate the possibility of similar stylistic trends resulting from different modes of artifact production.

This lack of a simple relationship between stylistic patterns, craft production, and exchange suggests that the frequent attempts to infer exchange patterns from stylistic distributions are often likely to result in incorrect inferences (26) and may lead to circular reasoning. For example, in her symmetry analysis of ceramic designs on a group of prehistoric vessels, Washburn (63, p. 172) assumed that a high degree of structural similarity in designs within sites indicated local production of the pottery. No mineralogical or chemical characterization was done to test that assumption, and the possibility that the structural similarity could be the result of the importation of large numbers of vessels, a phenomenon that has been demonstrated for regions near Washburn's study area as well as in many other regions of the world, was not tested adequately. Also, while Washburn argues on the one hand that the vessels were produced locally because the designs have a high degree of structural similarity, on the other hand she explains the structural similarity by the proposal that the vessels were produced locally by a group of interacting potters (63, pp. 172–82). Escape from such circular reasoning can only be achieved if style and exchange are measured independently, rather than assuming that exchange can be inferred from patterns of stylistic variation.

Such studies must not, however, oversimplify the complex dimensions of craft production. Hantman and I (26) have noted that "too often the extremes of household production or regional specialization are assumed to be the dominant modes of production in an area, although considerable variation exists between these extremes." The production and distribution of craft items can vary along a number of different dimensions, and it would be surprising if such variation did not seriously affect spatial and temporal variation in stylistic patterns in many areas. Also, Rubertone (58) has argued that patterns of consumption must be understood as well as patterns of production. Thus, in order to understand prehistoric patterns of stylistic variation, it is important that we direct greater attention to the relationship of style and aspects of production, exchange, and consumption. Several recent studies (e.g. 12, 13, 17, 56) indicate many analyses of this type are beginning to be conducted in several areas.

THE SIZE OF STUDY AREAS

One of the major types of stylistic data that is currently lacking in most areas is detailed information on the frequencies of individual stylistic attributes over broad areas. This type of information is necessary for a variety of reasons.

First, it has been noted that different models of stylistic variation lead to somewhat different expectations concerning the distributions of stylistic attributes. Because of the lack of detailed regional stylistic information, it is difficult to evaluate these expectations. Second, it is clear from the minimal amount of data available that different stylistic attributes have somewhat different spatial distributions and any comprehensive theory of style must account for those differential distributions (48, p. 18). Third, many studies in the last few decades have stressed that prehistoric populations participated in widespread social networks. If the organizational and demographic characteristics of those networks are likely to influence aspects of stylistic variation and, in turn, if information on stylistic variation is useful in making inferences about social networks as some have argued (4, 26, 52), it is important that analyses of stylistic variation begin to encompass such broad geographical areas.

Although some stylistic analyses traditionally have considered regional style distributions in order to construct space-time frameworks, much of that information is encoded in type descriptions, as noted above. In addition to the fact that such units are polythetic and mix stylistic attributes of different hierarchical levels, they also suffer from another serious weakness. Because of a variety of factors, such as the inexplicit nature of some type descriptions and the subjectivity involved in the identification of types, it appears that many differences exist among archaeologists in their definitions of types and, as a result, in their classification of artifacts (53). Fish (18), for example, has found discrepancies in type identifications as high as 30 percent among archaeologists trained at one university by a single individual. In another experiment, the ability of several archaeologists who work in the American Southwest to agree on the ceramic types represented by 27 whole vessels from the Cibola area of east-central Arizona and west-central New Mexico was tested (59a). The 20 archaeologists were selected for their knowledge of Cibola ceramics. The experiment indicated that the average agreement on type identifications was below 50 percent, and in one case as many as 13 different type names were suggested for one vessel. Type identifications thus may suffer from a strong lack of replicability. Therefore, despite the excavation of numerous sites within many regions and the publication of the information from that research, it is questionable whether or not reliable information on stylistic distributions across broad areas can be extracted from such reports.

Archaeological and ethnoarchaeological studies are needed in order to collect information on frequencies of stylistic attributes across space and some research of this type already has been completed (e.g. 3, 66, 67). Although published analyses of data from previous excavations or surveys may often be inadequate, in many instances reanalysis of the collections from such fieldwork may be an efficient means of obtaining the necessary geographic coverage while minimizing costs.

COVARIATION OF STYLISTIC PATTERNS

In addition to studying the distribution of stylistic characteristics over larger areas, other changes in stylistic analyses are also needed. One of the consistent characteristics of many studies of patterns of stylistic attributes is that they are limited to attributes on only one type of material or artifact or even subset of an artifact type, such as ceramic bowls. Ceramic vessels, in particular, have been emphasized in such analyses. There are at least two reasons for this limitation. First, some materials such as ceramics are abundant in the archaeological record of many regions and time periods, while many other materials are scarce. Second, Green (23) has noted that there are basic differences in the processes by which different artifacts are manufactured. For example, she characterizes the manufacture of ceramic vessels and stone tools as additive and subtractive processes, respectively. That is, ceramic vessels are produced by combining a number of different materials, while the majority of stone tools found by archaeologists were manufactured by the removal of parts of a single type of material. In addition to the implications this difference has for determining the area of production for tools made through subtractive versus additive processes, it is also likely that such differences can account in part for dissimilarities in the degree of stylistic variation present on different types of artifacts, and thus the extent such artifacts are useful in developing space-time frameworks for different regions.

Some archaeologists have argued that stylistic analyses conducted to test proposals such as the social interaction theory should be limited to ceramic vessels and to painted designs on those vessels in particular. I suggest, however, that it is important that future studies should begin to examine when possible the degree of covariation of stylistic patterns on different materials, different types of artifacts, or different forms of an artifact type if an adequate understanding of the complex causes of stylistic variation is to be achieved. First, in addition to the suggestion noted above that basic characteristics of the manufacture of different artifacts may affect degrees of stylistic variation, it also has been proposed that very specific aspects of the manufacture or decoration of artifacts such as ceramic vessels must be considered. In discussing Mississippian ceramics from the eastern United States, Brown (6, p. 128–29) states that "a distinction must be made between two independent systems—a ceramic decorative technology restricted to wet-paste manipulation (as exhibited in modeling, incising, punctating, etc) and dry-paste decoration best known through engraving and painting." He argues that it is not accidental that there are clear differences in the form and distribution of styles executed in the two technologies, as wet-paste decoration must be completed during the manufacture of the vessel, and thus must be done by the potter, while dry-paste decoration is free from such restrictions. Brown (6, p. 129) suggests that "from that simple difference ensue important potential differences in the sociology of ceramic decorative production."

In addition to their relevance to Brown's study of Mississippian ceramics, such factors could be important, for example, in accounting for some of the very different degrees of stylistic variation presented on corrugated (wet-paste technology) and black-on-white (dry-paste technology) painted vessels in the American Southwest, differences that are difficult to explain using any of the theories of style discussed above (51, p. 138).

Second, Saitta (59) has suggested that if stylistic variation is viewed as a means of communicating information such as social affiliation, it would be expected that such messages "should be associated with artifacts requiring little post-production maintenance or artifacts which have low turnover rates, so that message integrity and longevity is maximized." This proposal, for example, also could help account in part for the very different levels of stylistic variation in banded or corrugated and painted ceramic vessels from the American Southwest. Banded or corrugated vessels from the Southwest appear to be containers used for cooking food (51, pp. 82–96) and, from ethnographic studies (21, 44), would likely have relatively short use-lives. Painted vessels, however, were probably used as serving bowls and for storage, activities which result in longer use-lives for vessels (21, 44). Given Saitta's proposal, the longer use-lives of painted vessels could increase their utility for carrying social messages, and this could account in part for the greater degree of decorative elaboration on such vessels as opposed to banded and corrugated pottery from the Southwest.

Third, as noted above, one expectation of the information exchange theory is that items of differing visibility will vary in utility as mediums for stylistic messages. As a result, they would be expected to have dissimilar patterns of stylistic variation. For example, it has been suggested that domestic utensils are unlikely to be useful for carrying stylistic messages owing to their low visibility (69). In particular, it has been proposed that artifacts such as ceramic vessels would not be used in efforts to communicate information such as social group affiliation (22, pp. 309, 314; 59). A variety of ethnographic data, however, indicates that the cultural identity of individuals may be encoded on visible items or features such as lip plugs, earrings, and hair and beard styles, as well as much less visible items or features such as stools, pottery, the manicure of dogs, butchering methods or hearth location or other subtle physical arrangements (33, 34, 37, 46). Present evidence thus suggests that patterns of stylistic variation on different materials may be dissimilar for several reasons. In addition, patterns of stylistic variation on items with differing degrees of visibility are not, in all cases, consistent with some of the expectations derived from the information exchange theory.

If the latter conclusion is correct, it has important implications for the validity of components of the information exchange theory. Wobst has emphasized the visibility of items in part because of his proposal that stylistic messages are more likely "if the potential receivers have little opportunity to receive the message otherwise, but nevertheless are likely to encounter it and are able to encode it" (69, p. 322). As a result, the utility of stylistic messages decreases with decreasing social distance between the sender and the receiver inasmuch as there would be fewer messages that could not be sent more cheaply using another mode of communication (69, p. 323). Visible artifacts or features thus are emphasized because it is those artifacts which are more likely to be seen by socially distant individuals. However, if patterns of stylistic variation on artifacts of different visibility are similar, these proposals would not be supported and it might be more reasonable to propose that stylistic variation on many items, including pottery, functions "as a symbol of social group identity for members of a community" (22, p. 309). Such an interpretation would be consistent with Voss's (62, p. 111) suggestion that style should be viewed as an identity function, and with some of the proposals of Hodder (33) and Rubertone (58, p. 91).

CONCLUSIONS

The above discussion of recent research on stylistic analyses and the types of studies that are needed in the future indicates some of the areas where advances have been or should be made in our understanding of stylistic variation. It should be emphasized, however, that we are still a long way from adequately testing ideas concerning the causes of stylistic variation or developing a comprehensive theory of style. More appropriate and more rigorous tests of different hypotheses will move us in that direction, but we also must begin to focus more extensively on at least one area where efforts are only beginning to be made: the interaction between stylistic variation, and not only social but also economic, political, demographic, religious, and ideological variables. Wiessner (66, 67), for example, has conducted ethnographic studies of the relationship between spatial patterns of stylistic variation and alternative social and economic strategies for reducing risks in social and natural resources. Somewhat similar studies have been carried out using archaeological data (2–4, 51, 52, 62). Economic factors also have been stressed in some of the studies of Hodder (31, 33). Possible relationships among stylistic variation, population density, marriage systems, and the development of discrete communications networks have been considered in another series of studies (4, 26, 51), while aspects of social stratification, ideology, and age and sex differences in relationship to style have been discussed by Hodder (33). Continued efforts in these directions are needed, however. Additional ethnoarchaeological studies, particularly analyses such as Wiessner's (66, 67) which consider broad regions, should be an important part of such an effort. Ethnoarchaeological studies will not provide all of the answers, however. Archaeological studies which focus on the development of stylistic patterns over long periods of time should and will make an important contribution. Analyses of stylistic variation have a long history in archaeology and they also have a promising future.

Literature Cited

1. Bradley, R., Hodder, I. 1979. British prehistory: an integrated view. *Man* 14:93–104
2. Braun, D. P. 1977. *Middle Woodland-(Early) Late Woodland social change in the prehistoric central midwestern U.S.* PhD thesis. Univ. Mich., Ann Arbor. 456 pp.
3. Braun, D. P. 1984. Ceramic decorative diversity and Illinois Woodland regional integration. In *Measurement and explanation of ceramic variation: some current examples,* ed. B. A. Nelson. Carbondale: South. Ill. Univ. Press. In press
4. Braun, D. P., Plog, S. 1982. Evolution of "tribal" social networks: theory and prehistoric North American evidence. *Am. Antiq.* 47:504–25
5. Breternitz, D. A. 1966. An appraisal of tree-ring dated pottery in the Southwest. *Anthropol. Pap. Univ. Ariz. No. 10*
6. Brown, J. A. 1976. The southern cult reconsidered. *Midcont. J. Archaeol.* 1: 115–35
7. Colton, H. S. 1953. *Potsherds.* Flagstaff: North. Ariz. Soc. Sci. Art. 86 pp.
8. Conkey, M. W. 1978. Style and information in cultural evolution: toward a predictive model for the Paleolithic. In *Social Archaeology: Beyond Subsistence and Dating,* ed. C. L. Redman, M. J. Berman, E. V. Curtin, W. T. Langhorne, N. M. Versaggi, J. F. Wanser, pp. 61–85. New York: Academic. 471 pp.
9. Conkey, M. W. 1980. Context, structure, and efficacy in Paleolithic art and design. In *Symbols as Sense,* ed. M. L. Foster, S. H. Brandes, pp. 225–48. New York: Academic. 432 pp.
10. Crown, P. L. 1981. *Variability in ceramic manufacture at the Chodistaas site, east-central Arizona.* PhD thesis. Univ. Ariz., Tucson
11. Deetz, J. 1965. The dynamics of stylistic change in Arikara ceramics. *Ill. Stud. Anthropol. No. 4*
12. Deutchman, H. L. 1979. *Intraregional interaction on Black Mesa and among* the Kayenta Anasazi: The chemical evidence for ceramic exchange. PhD thesis. South. Ill. Univ., Carbondale. 288 pp.
13. Deutchman, H. L. 1980. Chemical evidence of ceramic exchange on Black Mesa. In *Models and Methods in Regional Exchange,* ed. R. E. Fry, pp. 119–33. *SAA Papers No. 1*
14. Drennan, R. D. 1976. Fabrica San Jose and Middle Formative society in the Valley of Oaxaca. *Mem. Mus. Anthropol. Univ. Mich. No. 8*
15. Deleted in proof
16. Englebrecht, W. 1974. The Iroquois: archaeological patterning on the tribal level. *World Archaeol.* 6:52–65
17. Feinman, G. M. 1980. *The relationship between administrative organization and ceramic production in the Valley of Oaxaca, Mexico.* PhD thesis. City Univ. New York, NY. 537 pp.
18. Fish, P. R. 1978. Consistency in archaeological measurement and classification. *Am. Antiq.* 43:86–89
19. Flannery, K. V. 1976. Analysis of stylistic variation within and between communities. In *The Early Mesoamerican Village,* ed. K. V. Flannery, pp. 251–54. New York: Academic. 373 pp.
20. Friedrich, M. H. 1970. Design structure and social interaction: archaeological implications of an ethnographic analysis. *Am. Antiq.* 35:332–43
21. Gill, M. N. 1981. *The potter's mark: contemporary and archaeological pottery of the Kenyan southeastern highlands.* PhD thesis. Boston Univ., Boston, Mass. 244 pp.
22. Graves, M. W. 1981. *Ethnoarchaeology of Kalinga ceramic design.* PhD thesis. Univ. Ariz., Tucson. 360 pp.
23. Green, M. 1982. *Chipped stone raw materials and the study of interaction.* PhD thesis. Ariz. State Univ., Tempe. 360 pp.
24. Hantman, J. L. 1983. *A socioeconomic interpretation of ceramic style distribu-*

tions in the prehistoric Southwest. PhD thesis. Ariz. State Univ., Tempe

25. Hantman, J. L., Lightfoot, K. G. 1978. The analysis of ceramic design: a new method for chronological seriation. In *An Analytical Approach to Cultural Resource Management: The Little Colorado Planning Unit*, ed. F. Plog, pp. 38–63. *Ariz. State Univ. Anthropol. Res. Pap. No. 19*

26. Hantman, J. L., Plog, S. 1982. The relationship of stylistic similarity to patterns of material exchange. In *Contexts for Prehistoric Exchange*, ed. J. E. Ericson, T. K. Earle, pp. 237–63. New York: Academic. 321 pp.

27. Hill, J. N. 1970. Broken K Pueblo: prehistoric social organization in the American Southwest. *Anthropol. Pap. Univ. Ariz. No. 18*

28. Hill, J. N. 1977. Individual variability in ceramics and the study of prehistoric social organization. In *The Individual in Prehistory: Studies of Variability in Style in Prehistoric Technologies*, ed. J. N. Hill, J. Gunn, pp. 55–108. New York: Academic. 258 pp.

29. Hill, J. N. 1978. Individuals and their artifacts: an experimental study in archaeology. *Am. Antiq.* 43:245–57

30. Hodder, I. 1977. The distribution of material culture items in the Baringo district, western Kenya. *Man* 12:239–69

31. Hodder, I. 1979. Economic and social stress and material culture patterning. *Am. Antiq.* 44:446–54

32. Hodder, I. 1981. Society, economy, and culture: an ethnographic case study amongst the Lozi. In *Pattern of the Past*, ed. I. Hodder, G. Isaac, N. Hammond, pp. 67–95. New York: Cambridge Univ. Press. 443 pp.

33. Hodder, I 1982. *Symbols in Action*. New York: Cambridge Univ. Press. 244 pp.

34. Hole, F. 1978. Pastoral nomadism in western Iran. In *Explorations in Ethnoarchaeology*, ed. R. A. Gould, pp. 127–67. Albuquerque: Univ. New Mexico Press. 329 pp.

35. Irwin, G. J. 1978. Pots and entrepots: a study of settlement, trade, and the development of economic specialization in Papuan prehistory. *World Archaeol.* 9:299–319

36. Irwin, G. J. 1983. Chieftainship, kula, and trade in Massim prehistory. In *The Kula: New Perspectives on Massim Exchange*, ed. J. W. Leach, E. R. Leach. New York: Cambridge Univ. Press. In press

37. Jones, R. 1974. Tasmanian tribes. In *Aboriginal Tribes of Australia*, ed. N. B. Tindale, pp. 319–53. Berkeley: Univ. Calif. Press. 404 pp.

38. Krause, R. A., Thorne, R. M. 1971. Toward a theory of archaeological things. *Plains Anthropol.* 16:245–57

39. Layhe, R. W. 1977. *A multivariate approach for estimating prehistoric population change*. MA thesis. South. Ill. Univ., Carbondale, Ill. 95 pp.

40. LeBlanc, S. A. 1975. Micro-seriation: a method for fine chronological differentiation. *Am. Antiq.* 40:22–38

41. Leone, M. 1968. Neolithic autonomy and social distance. *Science* 162:1150–51

42. Longacre, W. A. 1964. Sociological implications of the ceramic analysis. In *Chapters in the Prehisotry of Eastern Arizona*, ed. P. S. Martin, J. B. Rinaldo, W. A. Longacre, L. G. Freeman, J. A. Brown, et al, 2:155–67. *Fieldiana: Anthropol. 53*

43. Longacre, W. A. 1970. Archaeology as anthropology: a case study. *Anthropol. Pap. Univ. Ariz. No. 17*

44. Longacre, W. A. 1981. Kalinga pottery: an ethnoarchaeological study. See Ref. 32, pp. 49–66

45. Martin, P. S., Plog, F. 1973. *The Archaeology of Arizona*. New York: Am. Mus. Nat. Hist. 422 pp.

46. Myers, T. P. 1975. Isolation and ceramic change: a case from the Ucayali River, Peru. *World Archaeol.* 7:333–51

47. Newton, D. 1974. The Timbira hammock as a cultural indicator of social boundaries. In *The Human Mirror*, ed. M. Richardson. Baton Rouge: Louisiana State Univ. 366 pp.

48. Plog, F. 1977. Archaeology and the individual. See Ref. 28, pp. 13–21

49. Plog, S. 1976. Measurement of prehistoric interaction between communities. See Ref. 19, pp. 255–72

50. Plog, S. 1978. Social interaction and stylistic similarity. *Adv. Archaeol. Method Theory* 1:143–82

51. Plog, S. 1980. *Stylistic Variation in Prehistoric Ceramics*. New York: Cambridge Univ. Press. 160 pp.

52. Plog, S. 1980. Village autonomy in the American Southwest: an evaluation of the evidence. See Ref. 13, pp. 135–46

53. Plog, S., Hantman, J. L. 1984. Multiple regression analysis as a dating method in the American Southwest. In *Spatial Organization and Exchange: Archaeological Survey on Northern Black Mesa*, ed. S. Plog. Carbondale: South. Ill. Univ. In press

54. Redman, C. L. 1977. The "analytical individual" and prehistoric style variability. See Ref. 28, pp. 41–53

55. Redman, C. L. 1978. Multivariate artifact analysis: a basis for multidimensional interpretations. See Ref. 8, pp. 159–92

56. Rice, P. M. 1980. Peten Postclassic pottery production and exchange: a view from Macanche. See Ref. 13, pp. 67–82

57. Rowe, J. H. 1959. Archaeological dating and culture process. *Southwest. J. Anthropol.* 15:317–24

58. Rubertone, P. E. 1978. *Social organization in an Islamic town: a behavioral explanation of ceramic variability.* PhD thesis. State Univ. New York, Binghamton. 188 pp.

59. Saitta, D. J. 1982. *The explanation of change in egalitarian society: a critique.* Presented at Ann. Meet. Soc. Am. Archaeol., 47th, Minneapolis

59a. Swarthout, J., Dulaney, A. P. 1978. *The great Cibola typological consensus test.* Presented at Cibola White Waré Conf., Flagstaff, Ariz.

60. Tuggle, H. D. 1970. *Prehistoric community relationships in east central Arizona.* PhD thesis. Univ. Ariz. Tucson. 169 pp.

61. Van der Leeuw, S. E. 1976. *Studies in the Technology of Ancient Pottery.* Amsterdam: Univ. Amsterdam. 424 pp.

62. Voss, J. A. 1980. *Tribal emergence during the neolithic of northwestern Europe.* PhD thesis. Univ. Mich. Ann Arbor. 371 pp.

63. Washburn, D. K. 1977. A symmetry analysis of upper Gila area ceramic design. *Pap. Peabody Mus. Archaeol. Ethnol.*, Vol. 68

64. Washburn, D. K. 1978. A symmetry classification of pueblo ceramic design. In *Discovering Past Behavior: Experiments in the Archaeology of the American Southwest,* ed. P. Grebinger, pp. 102–21. New York: Gordon & Breach. 279 pp.

65. Whallon, R. 1968. Investigations of late prehistoric social organization in New York State. In *New Perspectives in Archeology,* ed. S. R. Binford, L. R. Binford, pp. 223–44. Chicago: Aldine. 373 pp.

66. Wiessner, P. W. 1977. *Hxaro: a regional system of reciprocity for reducing risk among the Kung San.* PhD thesis. Univ. Mich. Ann Arbor. 404 pp.

67. Wiessner, P. W. 1982. Beyond willow smoke and dogs' tails: a comment on Binford's analysis of hunter-gatherer settlement systems. *Am. Antiq.* 47:171–78

68. Wilmsen, E. N. 1973. Interaction, spacing behavior, and the organization of hunting bands. *J. Anthropol. Res.* 29:1–31

69. Wobst, H. M. 1977. Stylistic behavior and information exchange. In *Papers for the Director: Research Essays in Honor of James B. Griffin,* ed. C. E. Cleland, pp. 317–42. *Anthropol. Pap. Mus. Anthropol. Univ. Mich.* No. 61

Ann. Rev. Anthropol. 1983. 12:143–64
Copyright © 1983 by Annual Reviews Inc. All rights reserved

PROFESSIONAL RESPONSIBILITY IN PUBLIC ARCHAEOLOGY

Thomas F. King

Advisory Council on Historic Preservation, Washington, D.C. 20005

INTRODUCTION

> *"Archaeology is the only branch of anthropology where we kill our informants . . ."* (16, p. 275).

The practice of archaeology creates a fundamental conflict of responsibilities. On the one hand, we want to keep our "informants," the sites we study, "alive"—intact so they can be studied further and continue to inform us. On the other hand, if we do not excavate and hence destroy them, such sites cannot inform us. This conflict has always been with us, but in recent years its urgency has intensified, and to it have been added new conflicts peculiar to the practice of "public archaeology." The result, as Plog (45, p. 10) pithily puts it, is that: "There is scarcely anyone involved in (public archaeology) who is not said to be in an inherently unethical position by those on the other side of one issue or another."

The literature on professional responsibility in public archeology remains thin, however, and mostly unpublished. A major book on the subject is in preparation (E. Green, in preparation), but will not be published until well after this article appears.

The term "public archaeology" was coined by C. R. McGimsey III in 1972 (40, p. 5). McGimsey's use of the term was inclusive:

> There is no such thing as "private archeology." Knowledge of (the) past . . . is essential to our survival, and the right to that knowledge is . . . a human birthright. . . . It follows that *no individual may act in a manner such that the public right to knowledge of the past is unduly endangered or destroyed.*

143

0066–4294/83/1015–0143$02.00

In the last decade, the term has come to be used more restrictively as a rough synonym for "conservation archaeology" (50) and for elements of "cultural resource management" and "historic preservation" (31). It is in this common sense that I will use it: to mean the practice of archaeology in connection with programs of land-use planning and development, supported by government agencies and regulated industries, usually via contracts. I will restrict my attention to the United States, where a pattern of ethical problems has developed to which I can speak with more authority than I can to those in other nations.

As late as 1961, American archaeology felt that it could get along with a fairly simple statement of professional responsibilities. The Society for American Archaeology in that year published a statement of professional standards that called on archaeologists to share access to collections and data, to publish results promptly, and to eschew trafficking in antiquities, digging other people's sites, and destroying, distorting, or concealing data (9). Within a decade, however, the last warm summers of archaeology's innocence had faded. With passage of the National Historic Preservation Act in 1966 and the National Environmental Policy Act in 1969, followed by the issuance of Executive Order 11593 in 1971, archaeology became intimately wrapped up in the planning of the federal government's activities. In 1974 the "Moss-Bennett" Act became law, resolving at last the question of whether federal agencies could use project funds to support archaeological work (31), and public archaeology was projected, pimply and doubt-ridden, into its vigorous but clumsy adolescence. By the end of the 1970s it was reliably estimated that over $200 million were being spent on archaeology throughout the nation each year. "Pure" academic/pedagogical archaeologists had become a minority, as archaeologists moved into jobs with federal, state, and local agencies, regulated industries, and consulting firms (13). These new worlds were strange ones, peopled by lawyers, contract officers, auditors, and bureaucrats, not to mention historians, architects, architectural historians, and others who shared or vied with archaeologists for the title "historic preservation professional," and special interest groups ranging from coal miners to radical American Indian groups and house museum buffs. The new environment was one of legal fine points, competing public and private interests, expectations of loyalty to agency or firm *uber alles,* overt and covert political action, and the heady but worrisome power, whether by law or bureaucratic fiat, to hold up multimillion dollar projects, determine the flow of contract money, and decide the fate of archaeological sites, historic buildings, and places of cultural importance to communities. Small wonder that questions of professional responsibility have arisen.

By 1975, concern about responsibility had developed enough to stimulate the first rather thorough effort to outline a general code of ethics (52), and to impel the several national archaeological groups to form a study committee. This committee gave rise to the Society of Professional Archaeologists (SOPA), which promulgated a detailed code of ethics and outlined standards of research performance (10, 32, 53). Every SOPA member or certificatee must meet basic educational and experiential requirements and agree to abide by the Code and Standards. A grievance procedure allows charges against members and certificatees to be investigated, leading where necessary to withdrawal of certification, while ensuring due process (10). As one of SOPA's founding parents, I think it performs an important function, and I will lean heavily on its Code and Standards in this discussion.

TO WHOM ARE PUBLIC ARCHAEOLOGISTS RESPONSIBLE?

In reviewing such literature as there is on professional responsibility, in talking to colleagues, and in simply pondering the matter, I have concluded that much of our difficulty in reaching consensus about it results from lack of agreement on the answer to a central question: to whom or what are we responsible? "Responsibility" does not exist in a vacuum; it requires an object to which one owes responsibility, if only in one's conscience. Few who talk about professional responsibility address very explicitly the object to which they are responsible; they *assume* a particular object or set of objects, and assume that any archaeologist claiming to be responsible must be responsible to the same object or set. In fact, the objects of our responsibility and the priority we assign to competing obejcts vary from person to person, and within a particular archaeologist from situation to situation.

At least six objects to which public archaeologists may be responsible can be identified. Some archaeologists cleave to only one, or to one at a time; most have several, even all, in their heads at once and assign them different priorities depending on circumstance. Juggling them can create real conflicts. Some handle these by becoming "true believers" in a particular object; others give up and become academicians or farmers; most muddle along and worry. The six objects that come to mind are:

1. *The Resource Base:* responsibility to archaeological sites.
2. *Companions-in-Arms:* responsibility to colleagues.
3. *Research:* responsibility to the advance of scholarship.
4. *Clients:* responsibility to those who pay the tab.
5. *The Law:* responsibility to legal and contractual obligations.
6. *The Living:* responsibility to nonarchaeologists with interests in archaeological sites or data.

I have left out a couple of obvious objects. One is "oneself." Self interest should not be discounted, but I think that for most archaeologists, responsibility to self and those dependent on one is a constant that needs no discussion. Those who elevate self-interest to paramountcy seldom do so overtly; instead they give their allegiance to a compatible external object, usually clients or the law. Strange as it may seem in a discussion of public archaeology, I have also not included "the public" as an object, because I find the term too amorphous to be useful. Every public archaeologist insists that he or she works in the public interest, but views the public through a different prism, thus focusing on some more limited object.

On the following pages I will discuss each object, what those who owe responsibility to each do and say about their obligations, and how responsibilities to different objects come into conflict. I will then try to draw conclusions and outline what may be needed to resolve such conflicts.

RESPONSIBILITY TO THE RESOURCE BASE

Responsibility to the continued "life" of our "informants"—to leaving archaeological data in the ground—is a major characteristic of public archaeologists. Recognition of this responsibility often has almost religious overtones. Consider, for instance, my own conversion experience:

> Over and over again, while watching the bulldozer slice through the wildflowers and churn up what could have been a thousand years' worth of banked research reserves . . . I felt appalled at having been bought off so cheap. . . . (W)e have stood by . . . and let the Corps of Engineers perpetrate another monstrous crime against . . . the entire settlement system of an extinct people. . . . No matter how successful the Buchanan Archaeological Project turns out to have been . . . , I have failed in my basic responsibility as an archaeologist (25, p. 10).

The central principle of responsibility to the resource base was articulated in 1974 by Lipe: "If our field is to last beyond a few more decades, we need to shift to resource conservation as a primary model" (37, p. 214).

"Conservation archaeology" features doing everything one can to avoid excavating sites, instead seeking to retain them in-place by redesigning projects that would damage them and by undertaking active conservation measures such as burying, fencing, and otherwise making sites inaccessible. Lipe's approach was very attractive to those of us who in the mid-1970s sought to integrate archaeology into the historic preservation movement, for which retention in place is a fundamental principle. It has also been attractive to development agencies, since it is often (though not always) cheaper to avoid a site than to pay for its excavation. Thus the primacy of preservation in place was broadly accepted (2), and the reponsibility to "actively support conservation of the archaeological resource base" became part of SOPA's Code of Ethics (53). The broad acceptance of responsibility to the resource base is illustrated by the

Society for American Archaeology's adoption, in 1980, of the following "basic principle": "(W)ise use (of archaeological resources) should be based on a principle of archaeological conservation of materials in their original deposit, complemented by well-designed research use as appropriate to provide information about our human history" (36, p. 165).

Responsibility to the resource base can, however, lead its advocates into some dubious policies. Consider, for example, the Powder River Basin of Wyoming and Montana. In this energy-rich area, many small surveys have been done in advance of oil, gas, and coal exploration, which involve drilling small wells or shafts at scattered loci. The Bureau of Land Management (BLM), which administers most federal lands in the Basin, follows a conservation philosophy featuring "protection through avoidance." If something archaeological is found in a drill-site survey, the drill-site is simply relocated to avoid the phenomenon. Drill rigs are mobile, so avoidance is easy. It follows that there is no reason to go through studies to determine what kind of phenomenon one is avoiding; if the consulting archaeologist says the thing is "archaeological," it is avoided. This being the case, it is a short step to the conclusion that one need not even describe the phenomenon; one need merely specify that it is archaeological. The predictable result, which has in fact occurred, according to knowledgeable sources (G. C. Frison, personal comunication, 1982), is that for large areas of the Basin which have been "surveyed," nothing is recorded except that certain locations are "archaeological sites". For any purpose other than short-term avoidance, such data are as useful as would be the diagnosis that a patient has "a disease" to a physician planning a program of therapy. For a BLM district archaeologist or an energy company's consultant, however, subscribing to a resource conservation ethic and dealing with an energy company that properly wants to pay bottom dollar for the work needed to clear its drill site, it is difficult to find justification for demanding more data. The phenomenon in question has been "conserved" by avoiding it; what else matters?

Not everyone has accepted the retention of data in place as their central responsibility. Early in "conservation archaeology's" life, L. E. Wildesen wrote:

(I)t must be confusing to legislators and agencies who are finally offering us the justification and the money to excavate when they are now told "we don't want to excavate—our techniques are still too crude." Most of what we now know about Indian culture history was obtained by even cruder techniques than we have now, and this . . . information provides the basis for our current hypothesis testing (56, p. 10). More recently, Wildesen has returned to the theme:
"(M)anagement by avoidance" . . . is becoming the standard recommendation of many archaeologists . . . faced with resolving resource conflicts. But this . . . is simply pseudomitigation. It is neither good resource management, nor good decision making. It may prevent harm to a specific archaeological resource today, but what of tomorrow? (58, p. 76).

Wildesen argues, in essence, that viewing "the resource base" as a unitary phenomenon to be preserved is simpleminded. She promotes instead what she calls "value conservation," involving the development of management strategies based in large measure on the research purposes to which a given site can be put (58).

RESPONSIBILITY TO COMPANIONS-IN-ARMS

The idea that a public archaeologist's major responsibility is to his or her colleagues takes many forms; at its most extreme it is akin to the now rather moribund Eleventh Commandment of the Republican Party: thou shalt not speak ill of thy fellows. On some levels, archaeologists tend not to take this very seriously; we are famous among practitioners of other disciplines for backstabbing and ill-speaking, and archaeologist vs archaeologist lawsuits have had a crippling effect on archaeological discourse in some areas (20a, 22). On the other hand, a problem that those who regulate archaeological projects face is that of getting one archaeologist to critique publicly the work of another; nattering behind the back is one thing, but as Plog has noted, "thou shalt not air dirty linen in public" (45).

The SOPA Code of Ethics lists a series of responsibilities that the archaeologist bears to colleagues. To paraphrase briefly, the archaeologist should:

(*a*) give appropriate credit to others;
(*b*) keep informed about developments in his or her field;
(*c*) prepare and disseminate reports promptly;
(*d*) cooperate with those having common interests;
(*e*) respect colleagues' interests in data in one's possession;
(*f*) comply with laws and the guidelines of professional organizations (53, p. 3).

Conversely, an archaeologist should not:

(*a*) falsely seek to injure a colleague's reputation;
(*b*) commit plagiarism;
(*c*) undertake research without provision for analysis and reporting;
(*d*) refuse a reasonable request for research data (53, p. 4).

Although most public archaeologists accept these prescriptions and proscriptions readily in the abstract, they are not always easy to adhere to in reality. For example, before the Air Force's plan to deploy the MX missile in Nevada and Utah aborted, a veritable army of archaeologists was hired by various Air Force subcontractors to survey different (and sometimes the same) parts of the planned system of "race tracks," bunkers, and service facilities. The subcontractors were usually subsidiaries of aerospace engineering firms, whose procurement and management practices strongly discourage the sharing of "proprietary" data. For many archaeologists employed by such firms, conforming to prescriptions *(c)*, *(d)*, and *(e)* and proscription *(d)* above virtually meant violating contract terms. To their credit, many did just that, but others could not. Prescription *(b)* is also a continuing troublemaker, particularly when construed in geographic terms. Since those who are best informed about developments in the archaeology of a given area are naturally those who work there regularly, does prescription *(b)* mean that only those who "know the territory" should seek and obtain contracts there? The territorial imperative has not often fared well in public archaeology, in the face of agency "fair" contracting practices and the simple volume of contract work, enough to swamp most state and regional populations of practitioners. The influx of "outsiders," often poorly prepared, into rich regional contract markets has certainly produced shoddy work in many cases, and has even more certainly resulted in the loss of useful information to regional research networks if not to the public generally. On the other hand, in theory at least, it has led to fruitful cross-pollination among regional groups. Wildesen argues (57) that the problem of territoriality could be solved through the use of more explicit contract specifications, better evaluations of proposals, increased negotiation of contract terms, and the development of more thoughtful bases for contract acquisition than pure turf marking. This may be so, but to make it happen would require great improvement in the quality both of contractors and of those who prepare contract specifications. In the meantime, despite its manifest logic, the idea embodied in SOPA's prescription *(b)* can and does serve as a basis for crude concepts of territoriality to which responsible archaeologists are expected by those within the territory to adhere, leaving those outside the territory almost no choice but to adopt equally crude patterns of "irresponsibility" if they wish to accept contracts.

Kent Flannery has raised a meatier responsibility to one's fellows with his question: "And what about other archaeologists with other hypotheses? . . . Don't you feel a little uncomfortable destroying data relevant to their problem while you're solving yours?" (16).

SOPA's Standards of Research Performance address this variant on the murder-of-informant theme by saying: "Insofar as possible, the interests of other researchers should be considered. For example, upper levels of a site should be scientifically excavated and recorded whenever feasible, even if the focus of the project is on underlying levels" (53, p. 5).

This fair and gentlemanly standard can be tricky to put into practice. Given a complex site subject to certain destruction by a development project, given a finite budget, how is an archaeologist really to balance his or her own research priorities against the need to honor the interests, often unstated and even unconceived, of other researchers? A surprizing number sacrifice research goals altogether, seeking to ensure that all sites, all stratigraphic levels, regardless of established or potential research value, are "scientifically excavated and recorded" to some arbitrarily defined extent. At the infamous New Melones project in California, for example, a large portion of a multimillion dollar budget went into very careful random sampling of sites without guidance from anything legitimately definable as a research design (14, 24). Practices like this have led to a belief, common among government and industrial contractees and fed by contractors with little interest in or capacity for research design, that the preservation laws require archaeological data recovery that is not problem-oriented. It follows that: "(p)resumably one who does research with contract monies is ripping off the client by charging more than is required for the client's purposes" (45, p. 10).

SOPA's Standards are not meant to sanction this kind of mindlessness. The Standards assume a research interest, and require that in pursuing it, we recall that other interests are possible, and do what is reasonable to allow them to be addressed in the future. What is reasonable can be debated long and hard. Flannery's Quandry will always be with us, because there is no way to disturb archaeological ground without threatening data pertinent to someone's research question. To escape the Quandry by abandoning focused research altogether in favor of undirected sampling is to commit archaeology to perpetual triviality.

RESPONSIBILITY TO RESEARCH

The archaeologist's responsibility to scholarly utility is perhaps the easiest responsibility to understand; naturally as archaeologists we are responsible for doing archaeology, in the best way we can, using the "archaeological resource base" skillfuly to advance legitmate scholarly research. This seems to have been the main responsibility perceived by McGimsey when he wrote:

> As more funds become available, freeing the archaeologist from the restriction of digging only where salvage archaeology is required, the archaeologists themselves must develop a broader view of their problems. . . . If we are to hope to recover a coherent story of the past and to preserve appropriate examples for the future, we must determine where we are going to dig with the funds available to us on the basis of a broadly drawn problem-oriented plan. . . . It is up to the practitioners of archaeology to develop. . . . state, regional, and national programs of research and development . . ." (40, p. 18).

The argument against a responsibility to do research is that the legal and business contexts in which public archaeology is done have nothing to do with research. Fitting, for example, says: "In a contractual situation, the research is being performed specifically for the buyer. That it may, at some time, contribute to the general fund of knowledge is incidental . . . (15, p. 356).

This kind of view provides the basis for Plog's sarcastic equation of research with exploitation (45). It seriously misconstrues the intent of the environmental and historic preservation statutes. On the whole, these address the esthetic, social, cutural, and economic values inherent in various kinds of historic properties no more explicitly than they do the research values in those we call archaeological; it does not follow that addressing any of these values is "incidental" to the processes created by the laws. On the contrary, addressing the values of 'historic properties, including their research values, must be central to these processes if they, and the statutes upon which they are based, are to have any meaning. If a property is valuable for the contribution its data can make to research, then the only logical construction of the protective statutes' intent is that we should consider preserving those data. Unlike some other characteristics of some historic properties—the contribution of an historic streetscape to a town's character, for example—archaeological data can in a way be preserved through consumption; by removing them from the ground and applying them to research problems, we realize their value and make this value available to the public in perpetuity. This is preservation just as much as is, say, the rehabilitation of an historic streetscape. The fact that realizing the research potential of an archaeological site may allow a particular scholar or portion of the discipline to advance toward solution of a research problem is no more "incidental" to the purpose of the statutes than is the pride that the people of the town feel for their refurbished Main Street or the economic stimulus the street's historic image gives to its retail establishments. As Plog has put it:

(I)f research is not a component of our effort, then what service are we providing the public? Does the legislation on which cultural resource management rests actually exist only so that we can provide the public with a list of sites or artifacts? (45, p. 11).

There are, however, circumstances under which one's responsibility to research can collide rather crushingly with other obligations. For example, if it is less expensive to preserve a site through avoidance than to excavate it, one need not be a strict devotee of the "resource base" school of responsibility to see that there are good economic arguments against committing the site to research. A more complicated and increasingly common form of conflict is exemplified by the semi-apocryphal "Elk Canyon sites." These sites, found during survey in advance of highway construction, were determined to be eligible for the National Register of Historic Places because of their value to research, and their excavation was proposed. The local "Lecompte Indians" objected, declaring themselves "not concerned with the study of ancient cultures and peoples" and adherents to the belief that "a Lecompte who unearths any previous Indian materials," or even sanctions such tampering, "violates one of the teachings of their religion and is cursed." The Lecomptes therefore requested that "the anthropological community as well as others respect their religious views and construct (the highway) without excavating and salvaging the artifacts and human remains found during construction" (3). Unable to find a way to avoid constructing over the sites, the highway department proposed to bury them without study, effectively closing them to research for the life of the highway. Maintaining a responsibility to realize the research value of the sites, the archaeological community protested vigorously, but lost (3); great disharmony was generated between the Lecomptes and the archaeological profession, but the sites were buried without study.

Responsibility to research can also create conflicts because one archaeologist's definition of research is not necessarily shared by others; if it were, we would be practitioners of a stultified science. Such a conflict occurred, for example, in a case that I fictionalized some years ago featuring Drs. Horseradish and Avocado, the former an "old school" culture historian, the latter a "new archaeologist." Dr. Horseradish, contracted to survey a proposed reservoir project area, found some 31 archaeological sites, only one of which—a deep, stratified site suitable for the study of local culture history—he judged to be significant enough to be excavated before inundation. When this decision was questioned by federal authorities, Dr. Avocado was brought in to test the smaller sites, which he viewed as having great value to the study of local settlement and subsistence systems. This simple description belies the controversy and loss of both data and money that in fact accompanied the project. The time of archaeologists and bureaucrats in several federal and state agencies was invested in argumentation, several separate contracts were let, thousands of dollars were spent, and the reservoir construction schedule was threatened, but in the end it remained unclear whether the research potential of the area had been effectively addressed (26).

In 1977, the Department of the Interior tried to resolve the problem of multiple research foci by saying, in its draft Moss-Bennett Act regulations:

> The program (of data recovery) should be conducted in accordance with a professionally adequate research design (which) should reflect. . . . a responsiveness to the need to recover from the property to be investigated, a usable sample of data on *all research problems* that reflect the property's research value, or a clear and defensible rationale for collecting data on a smaller range of problems" (21, emphasis added).

As one of the authors of the draft regulations, I can say that I now recognize our approach as a naive one that solved little or nothing, because research questions large and small, important and trivial, can be and promptly were spun out almost endlessly. In 1980 we tried to swing the pendulum back in the Advisory Council's archaeological handbook, defining and giving examples of significant research questions and flatly stating that:

It is not necessary, and is often counterproductive, to give the same level of effort to all study topics. The (data recovery) plan should consider all study topics but should establish and justify priorities for their investigation (2, p. 25).

This obviously reflects some shift in perspective, from one which demanded of archaeologists a justification for not addressing all conceivable research topics to one demanding justification for the topics selected. Increasingly, our tendency in the federal government is to assign to the archaeologist the burden of showing why it is in the public interest to address a given research topic. There remains some uncertainty about what to do if an archaeologist fails in this task; my own tendency is to support destruction of the site in question without study, because I feel that to do otherwise invites archaeologists to be cavalier about defining research goals, secure in the knowledge that they will still get money to dig a sample of the site or in some other mysterious way "mitigate the impact." From the standpoint of responsibility to the resource base, of course, such a tendency is anathema, and I feel about as comfortable about carrying it to its logical conclusion as Churchill doubtless did about ignoring German plans to bomb Coventry. Other solutions to the problem of focusing archaeology on significant research questions include the use of peer review panels (17), state or regional plans (29, 38, 43, 46, 55), and national or regional research topics (19, 28). It is safe to predict that this will be among public archaeology's hot topics of the early to mid-1980s, but it is not safe to predict an outcome.

RESPONSIBILITY TO CLIENTS

The public archaeologist's responsibility to his or her client has been more freely and explicitly debated than any other, largely thanks to James Fitting's willingness to articulate and defend a position that is widely held in practice but unpopular to espouse in public. Fitting's initial statement in support of "client oriented" archaeology (11) stimulated a vigorous response from Albert Goodyear (18) and then a full-scale attack by Raab and others (48a). Under the cover of these long-range salvos, I arranged for publication of an exchange of views between Fitting and Goodyear, on which I commented (15).

In brief, Fitting argues that when an archaeologist undertakes to perform a service for a client, the interests and needs of the client must become paramount:

If the client wishes to build a dam or a power plant, the goal of the archaeologist should be to provide an objective evaluation of the potential danger such a project might have on archaeological resources [sic]. The moral imperative is the objective evaluation, not the preservation, of the resources no matter how the archaeologist personally feels about the resources (11, p. 2).

This is a fair statement, and probably would not have generated any great excitement had Fitting not gone on to contrast "client orientation" with "problem orientation" and assert their mutual incompatibility. Fitting argues that problem orientation is the proper province of academic archaeologists operating "outside of the 'restrictive' confinements of the contract situation" (11, p. 13), but that academic institutions and their denizens, literally because of their commitment to pursuing research problems, are incapable of addressing the needs of clients effectively and honestly, thus leaving the field to the private consulting firms (12, pp. 86–90).

Raab and his colleagues isolated the fundamental flaw in Fitting's position with the observation that his approach: ". . . ignores the fact that archaeologists and clients have a relationship in the first place only because both are *subordinate to a public policy mandate to conserve archaeological resources*" (48a, p. 547).

One has not served one's client very well if one fails to help the client comply with that public policy, upon which to some extent the success of the client's venture depends. As I said in 1979, commenting on the Fitting-Goodyear debate:

> It seems to me that one has done one's duty by archaeological resources in the usual contract situation when one has gotten the best possible deal for them under the real temporal, fiscal, and political constraints that apply under the circumstances. One has done one's duty to one's client when one has shown how to give an acceptable deal to the archaeological resources without undue temporal, fiscal, or political impacts. There are certainly pragmatic problems that arise each time a deal is struck. . . . At risk of belaboring the obvious, I fail to see why the existence of these problems must be elevated to indicate inherent, insoluble incompatibility between academic science and service to clients (15, p. 360).

I do not mean to imply that Fitting has not identified a real issue. I think his perception that academic, problem-oriented archaeologists have difficulty competing with consulting firms for contracts is demonstrably a correct one. Certainly the bulk of archaeological projects that we at the Advisory Council review are carried out by private firms, not by academic institutions. These projects are not free from problem-orientation—far from it, though sometimes problems are addressed only because we who review the projects insist on it—but Fitting is probably right in his assumption that problem-oriented research can be most easily pursued in an academic environment. This is a matter for us in government to resolve. If we have created a market that selects against those most capable of realizing the research value of archaeological sites, we have erred badly and should seek changes. In the meantime, I think the SOPA Code of Ethics prescribes a reasonable stance with respect to clients:

An archaeologist shall:

(*a*) Respect the interests of his/her employer or client, so far as it is consistent with the public welfare and this Code and Standards;

(*b*) Refuse to comply with any request or demand of an employer or client which conflicts with the Code and Standards;

(*c*) Recommend to employers or clients the employment of other archaeologists . . . upon encountering archaeological problems beyond her/his own competence;

(*d*) Exercise reasonable care to prevent . . . revealing or using confidential (nonarchaeological) information . . . (53, p. 4).

In other words, an archaeologist should perform in accordance with a client's wishes provided these are not inconsistent with professional ethics and standards. Since the Code elsewhere requires that archaeologists represent archaeology and its results responsibly, be sensitive to the interests of living groups related to those studied through archaeology, support conservation of archaeological resources, respect the interests of colleagues, and respect pertinent laws, this stricture should lead archaeologists to advise clients of any potential conflicts with competing objects of professional responsibility, and seek to negotiate such conflicts away.

Only Pollyanna, however, would expect this to work easily and without rancor. The world of public archaeology is full of horror stories about archaeologists forced to avert their eyes while sites were destroyed or other outrages perpetrated, or lose their jobs or contracts. These stories are almost invariably impossible to verify, at least without exposing the endangered archaeologist to the wrath of his or her agency or firm, but there is every reason to believe many of them. The employee of a federal or state agency may actually be more vulnerable to this kind of pressure than is the contract archaeologist; the latter usually has some room to negotiate, and ironically is often a more highly qualified scholar, commanding more respect and possessed of more options than the agency archaeologist. The archaeologist assigned to a ranger district somewhere in the far west, often the holder of only a bachelor's degree and a little field experience, can ill afford to argue if told flatly that his or her job is on the line if he or she puts up too much of a fight for some threatened site. Like the problem of a wrongly selective contract market, this problem is one with which we who are involved in federal policy must grapple. The practicing archaeologist's responsibilities are well set forth in the SOPA Code and Standards; it may take a considerable amount of cunning to adhere to them, and in some cases one will fail. It is not the archaeologist's responsibility to adjust his or her ethics to those of the agency or client that he or she serves, however; it is our problem to so adjust the federal archaeology program to allow its practitioners to be honest.

There is one underlying truth in Fitting's position, however, that must be recognized by any public archaeologist, whether employee or contractor. With the partial exception of the National Park Service, no federal agency that funds public archaeology has archaeological research as its mission. To the agency or industry supporting an archaeological project, if not to the laws that require that support, the outcome and indeed the existence of the research is truly "incidental." The archaeologist who ignores an agency's or industry's central mission, or who denigrates it, is quite properly at peril. The archaeologist working for an agency or industry is responsible for cooperating in that agency's mission, seeking accommodation between that mission and the interests of archaeology. Many "horror stories" about agency/archaeologist conflicts, in my experience, involve unreasoning adherence by the archaeologist to some principle—that no project should ever go forward without prior field survey for archaeological sites, for example, or that no site regardless of significance should be sacrificed without salvage—that while perhaps defensible on professional grounds has little or no basis in law and fails to consider the interests and priorities that are central to the agency's mission. Government and business do important things other than archaeology, and the public archaeologist, like it or not, must be a part of their doing.

RESPONSIBILITY TO THE LAW

A certain unreadiness by archaeologists to comport with the requirements of laws and contracts has been politely deplored by a number of government agency writers, most eloquently by the Department of the Interior's Bennie C. Keel:

> Many managers are dismayed by the complaint from archaeologists that they are "scientists" and are not required to know the legal and regulatory framework under which this kind of work is conducted. That is nonsense (23, p. 166).
>
> A review of 125 contracts in force with the Interagency Archaeological Services - Atlanta during the final quarter of 1977 showed that. . . . 101 (81%) were technically in default. . . . (of which) 16 (16%) were overdue by four to 6.5 years. . . . Managers in other federal agencies indicate a similar condition, although they do not have contracts in such lengthy default (probably because only in the last few years have they begun writing archaeological contracts) (23, p. 167).

After several years of such embarassment and arm-twisting, and with the adoption by contracting agencies of an increasingly humorless approach to transgressions, public archaeologists on the whole have accepted the premise that executing a contract indicates acceptance of the responsibility to fulfill its terms. Most also acknowledge that their work must comport with the requirements of the laws and regulations that generate the work, though many cling to rather exotic notions of what such laws and regulations entail.

The trouble with seeing the letter of the law or the contract as the object of archaeological responsibility is that it invites mediocrity. Obviously the quality of research performed under contract is the product of both contract and contractor; if the latter sees his or her responsibility as being only to perform to the terms of the former, one source of high quality research results is eliminated, and the work will be only as good as the contract specifies. The contract, unfortunately, need not specify much excellence in order to comport with the literal requirements of the preservation laws. To "locate, inventory, and nominate to the Secretary all properties . . . that appear to qualify for inclusion on the National Register . . . ", a requirement of the National Historic Preservation Act (4), can require multiphase problem-oriented research (47), but it can also be simply a matter of walking stolidly over the ground recording potsherds. Determining a property's eligibility for the National Register can require real thinking and ingenuity, but it can also require only filling out forms neatly (6, 35, 48). Even the recovery of "significant scientific, prehistorical, historical, or archaeological data" in compliance with the Moss-Bennett Act (31) need not necessarily be an intellectually challenging activity; all too often, contracts for data recovery require only addressing such topics as:

> establishing a relative . . . chronology . . . , establishing site structure, function and type . . . , investigating probable site-to-site relationships . . . and integrating these into the regional context . . . , reconstructing the . . . depositional environment . . . (and) assessing the potential for presence of pollen . . . (27, pp. 49–50).

The above is contract boilerplate used by a major federal agency involved in archaeological contracting, applied to a whole range of data recovery projects without the bother of formulating research topics to which chronology, site structure, regional relationships, depositional environments, or pollen might be relevant.

The obvious solution to this problem is to improve the contracts, but this is not easily done. A plethora of agencies contracts for archaeological services, each with its own procurement policies and contracting procedures, which they do not lightly change. Contracts are written and administered by accountants, engineers, environmental and preservation specialists of many professional persuasions, and archaeologists who may claim the title on the basis of a bachelor's degree and a couple of field schools. The archaeological contracting system needs considerable reform, and perfection is unlikely in any case. To equate archaeological responsibility with adherence to contract terms is at best facile minimalism.

RESPONSIBILITY TO THE LIVING

One way that public archaeology is public is that it is practiced near and even within the living spaces of people. Surveys and salvage operations in advance of federally assisted urban development projects and sewer systems bring archaeologists into the hearts of cities. Federally supported economic development projects and federally licensed oil, gas, and coal extraction require studies that bring archaeologists onto Indian reservations. Public archaeology has brought archaeologists in from the distant mountains and deserts to the back-yards and streetcorners of America. Like it or not, we have had to recognize a responsibility to a number of archaeological public interests in archaeological sites and data.

My own experiences in relating archaeology to the interests of living groups have featured relations with several American Indian tribes, Native Hawaiians, Micronesians, and mainstream urban Americans with avocational interests in archaeology. I have found these experiences intensely rewarding for the friendships they have made possible, the enrichment they have provided to the archaeological data I collected, and the opportunities they have given me to make my work directly pertinent to the deeply felt needs of communities whose cultural integrity was threatened by modern development (33, 59). Other archaeologists have had similarly positive experiences with Indian and Eskimo groups (38a, 39, 44a), farm families (8), and urban neighborhoods (1). The increasing involvement of living social groups with the study and protection of the remains of their past has brought cultural anthropologists into increasing, fruitful interaction with archaeologists (7, 20, 51), resulting in research pro-jects of considerable breadth, interest, and relevance to modern society. Still other archaeologists have had the sensitivities of living communities forced upon them as a result of thoughtless or inadvertent transgressions, or have been used as whipping boys in local or national political stuggles over native power and self identity. Conflicts over treatment of human burials are the most famous examples of such encounters between the living and students of the dead (42, 54). Typically, archaeologists engaged in what they perceived to be standard research programs dealing with cemeteries or isolated burials have been sur-prised by the vigorous opposition of Indian groups, through the courts, through the legislatures, and sometimes through near-violent physical confrontations. Typically the archaeologists have beaten a hasty retreat from the initial encoun-ters, then fought back to something approaching parity.

The SOPA Code of Ethics phrases the archaeologist's responsibility to the living descendents of those we study in reasonable if somewhat passive and defensive terms: "An archaeologist shall . . . be sensitive to, and respect the legitimate concerns of, groups whose culture histories are the subjects of archaeological investigations" (53, p. 3).

I think most of us whose experiences with living communities have been relatively positive would subscribe to the rather more enthusiastic recom-mendations of the Society for American Archaeology's Airlie House sympo-sium on "Archaeology and Native Americans," which encouraged regular communication, training programs, joint development of cultural centers, and other mutual efforts to both advance knowledge of the past and make it serve the interests of modern communities (42).

Like other responsibilities, responsibility to the living can be carried to odd extremes. In California, for example, it seems to have become virtually impossible to turn a spade in pursuit of archaeology without having a paid "Native American Observer" looking on. There are occasions when such observers are completely appropriate (49), but for archaeologists to accede to being "observed" as a matter of course, in my view, reflects not responsibility but the opposite: a failure to take responsibility both for the legitimacy of one's own profession and for one's ability to practice it, unsupervised, in a manner sensitive to competing interests.

Responsibility to the living also brings archaeologists into contact with problems with which cultural anthropologists have long had to deal, but which archaeologists, thanks to their moribund subject matter, have in the past been able to ignore. Public archaeology is generally practiced with reference to projects that change land use and hence may have broad effects on social and cultural systems. If we with our anthropological training become aware that the project we are working on will have negative effects on the living descendents of the extinct society we are digging up, can we go on with our work without representing the interests of the living to the project's proponents? If we avert our eyes, can we claim adherence to the first Principle of Professional Responsibility set forth by the American Anthropological Association, which calls for us to put the interests of those studied first, and to do everything in our power to "protect their physical, social and psychological welfare and to honor their dignity and privacy" (5)? If we accept a responsibility to the living, we obviously accept the AAA's first principle, but if we recognize only a responsibility to do research, protect the resource base, satisfy our clients or fulfill our contracts, the principle is largely irrelevant.

Groups with cultural and genetic connections with the subjects of archaeological study are not the only living parties toward whom public archaeologists often accept some responsibility. There is a widely acknowledged though not too often acted upon responsibility to "involve the interested public" in research. Probably the most striking ongoing example of such involvement is the Alexandria (Virginia) Urban Archaeology Program, which involves some 300 volunteers on a regular basis in basic research, survey, and data recovery related to city planning needs (1). Many public archaeologists, however, especially those feeling primary responsibility to clients or contract terms, are reluctant to involve members of the public at all on the grounds that "it would be more trouble to supervise them than it would be worth," or because it would complicate a contractor's or contractee's management operations. Some whose main dedication is to the resource base fear that involving the public will lead to "pothunting." The last concern raises another question: does the "pothunter"— the private artifact collector—have any legimate claim on archaeological sites, and does the public archaeologist have any responsibility to the pothunter? Recent studies (34, 44) have suggested that private collectors share many interests and values with professional and amateur archaeologists, prompting some of us (30) to suggest that outreach to and cooperation with collectors might be both prudent and just.

CONCLUSIONS: PERSPECTIVE AND RESPONSIBILITY

Conflicts among public archaeologists about professional responsibility, in my experience, are more often the results of disagreement about the objects to which responsibility is properly owed than of straightforward irresponsibility or unprofessional behavior. A classic example is the case of the Papago Freeway in Phoenix, Arizona, which pitted Fred Plog and a number of supporters against the Arizona Department of Transportation (ADOT), the Federal Highway Administration, and ADOT's archaeological contractors. To greatly simplify the case's complexities, which Plog has discussed in some detail from his own perspective (45): Plog's central complaint against ADOT's contractors was that they were overwilling to acquiesce in a freeway project through two important Hohokam sites, implicitly because of political pressure and the potential for receiving large salvage contracts. Plog, on the other hand, was accused by his opposition of mischievously damaging archaeology's public image by allowing the discipline to be "used" in a lawsuit whose purpose was to stop the freeway. In the heat of battle, both sides were driven to actions that I think they would themselves find questionable in the cold light of reason, but I think the case began as, and was based upon, a simple disagreement about objects of responsibility. Plog and his cohort brought to the fray the belief that archaeologists owe their primary allegiance to conservation of the resource base, and they fought like tigers to keep any distrubance of the two sites from occurring. They also advanced a "responsibility to law" argument, that ADOT's contractors were assisting in activities that did not comport with the letter of the preservation statutes. The contrators advanced a client-oriented philosophy in which theirs was not to question the legality of the government's actions or the planning decisions the government had made, but to meet its needs. They also used a research responsibility argument, that by investing portions of the two sites in salvage excavations today, they would develop data to support more sophisticated research in the future. My own role was one of mediation, so it will be no surprise that I view neither side as being wholly "right" or "wrong." Both behaved with considerable responsibility, given the objects to which they acknowledged responsibility and the respective weights they assigned to each object. This is characteristic of the conflicts I see: resource-basers accuse researchers of selling out for contract dollars, researchers accuse resource basers of mindless adherence to ideology and agency policy at the expense of the discipline's intellectual life. Resource basers, unhappy to be thought anti-intellectual, shift the blame to government and clients with arguments based on contract terms and narrow interpretations of the preservation statutes. None of this is very productive.

I have suggested that all our objects of responsibility are real, and our conflicts arise when we allow them to become unbalanced. For my own part, I believe that our pervasive responsibility is to advance archaeological research toward defensible goals, tempered strongly by the responsibility to make archaeology, its resources, and its results relevant to the public both generally and on the community level. These preeminent responsibilities are tempered further by the need to preserve archaeological data in place, not because these data are sacred but because it makes sense to bank some resources for future study and because some data are embodied in sites that *are* sacred to groups to whom we should feel responsible. Somewhat less compelling but nonetheless real is our responsibility to colleagues, to the extent of recognizing ourselves as members of a community that maintains itself through mutual respect and toward whose goals we advance through cooperation, but *not* to the extent of allowing real or imagined peer pressure to stultify our thinking. I see responsibility to clients, contracts, and legal requirements as least definitive of behavior, because these objects of responsibility are mutable; they must not be ignored, but our efforts should be directed toward ensuring that they do not conflict with our more fundamental responsibilities. I would not, however, claim or desire to cling rigidly to this scaling of responsibilities, nor would I suggest that anyone else do so. Our need is to recognize the existence of competing but legitimate objects of responsibility, and establish mechanisms for deciding, in individual cases and as a rule under varying circumstances, how priorities should be established. Plog has called for an "ethics committee":

> . . . to which students, field workers, faculty, and others can go in comfort when ethical issues do arise—not in the belief that they will trigger a witch hunt, but in the belief that the committee will seek a short term resolution of the immediate problem and the long term development of mechanisms that will prevent such problems from arising again . . ." (45, p. 12)

SOPA could provide such a committee, but to make it work, I believe that three things would be needed. First, SOPA must become inclusive; everyone must submit to its review and certification. Second, to give its certifications clout, connections should be forged between SOPA and the agencies that give archaeologists jobs, review and design projects, and award contracts. These two steps would give SOPA a sanctioning power that would allow it to affect the ways archaeologists behave. At this point, however, my own recommendations make me worry. C. R. McGimsey III, the godfather of SOPA as he is of public archaeology, conceives of archaeology as composed of three concentric circles, the outermost consisting of pothunters and an undefined "lunatic fringe," the middle made up of those who "make every effort to practice 'proper' archaeology," and the innermost comprizing those who have attained real enlightenment, going on to say:

> It is the responsibility of this innermost circle to establish itself as a true profession, while encouraging the assistance and cooperation of the larger second circle and making an effort to educate the outer . . . (41, p. 379).

It is the innermost circle that to McGimsey should constitute the membership of SOPA; I am left uncomfortable with the recollection that in his time, Schliemann must have been part of the "lunatic fringe." SOPA must not take on the worst attributes of the American Medical Association; it must not become the "band of brethren" that McGimsey himself has rightly criticized. SOPA's third need, therefore, is to provide an institutionalized but "comfortable" alternative to the formal quasi-judicial process by which it now investigates and pronounces upon complaints against members and certificatees. SOPA should find a way to mediate, arbitrate, and help the profession learn from its conflicts. There is some movement in this direction today within SOPA's leadership, and I think it is vital that it go forward. Only the sort of "comfortable" forum that Plog proposes can air and resolve issues of professional responsibility without endangering the freedom of expression and innovation that is vital to archaeology's intellectual life and growth. The operation and use of such a forum must be based on the mature recognition that there are legitimate reasons for assigning contrasting priorities to different objects of responsibility in a given instance, and that disagreement with one's own assignment does not necessarily make one's opponent a rascal. SOPA's challenge, and the challenge of public archaeology in its definition of professional responsibility, is not to establish the proper boundaries between inner and outer circles of enlightenment but to decide in individual cases how best to balance our inherently conflicting responsibilities.

ACKNOWLEDGMENTS

I am grateful to Hester Davis, Robert L. Stephenson, and Leslie Wildesen for their provision of published and unpublished papers and for their suggestions; to Richard Leverty for assistance in gathering source material; and to Ronald Anzalone and Patricia Parker for review of drafts.

Literature Cited

1. Abramson, H. S. 1982. Digging up the secrets of our cities. *Hist. Preserv.* 34(3):32–37
2. Advisory Council on Historic Preservation. 1980. *Treatment of Archeological Properties: A Handbook.* Washington DC: Advis. Counc. Hist. Preserv. 39 pp.
3. Advisory Council on Historic Preservation. 1981. *Federal Projects and Historic Preservation Law: Participant's Course Book.* Washington DC: Advis. Counc. Hist. Preserv. 350 pp.
4. Advisory Council on Historic Preservation. 1981. *National Historic Preservation Act of 1966, as Amended.* Washington DC: Advis. Counc. Hist. Preserv. 21 pp.
5. American Anthropological Association. 1973. *Professional Ethics.* Washington DC: Am. Anthropol. Assoc.
6. Barnes, M. R., Briggs, A. K., Neilsen, J. J. 1980. A response to Raab and Klinger on archeological site significance. *Am. Antiq.* 45:551–53

6666

7. Blount, C. M., Johnson, A. H., Theodoratus, D. J. 1982. Ethnography and history in preservation research: views of CRM in California. *Contract Abst. CRM Archeol.* 3(1):29–34

8. Brown, M. 1974. The use of oral and documentary sources in historical archeology: ethnohistory at the Mott Farm. *Ethnohistory* 20(4):347–60

9. Champe, J. and others 1961. Four statements for archeology. *Am. Antiq.* 24:137–38

10. Davis, H. A. 1982. Professionalism in archeology. *Am. Antiq.* 47:158–63

11. Fitting, J. E. 1978. Client oriented archeology: a comment on Kinsey's dilemma. *Penn. Archaeol.* 48:12–25

12. Fitting, J. E. 1979. Further observations on archeology as business. In *Scholars as Contractors*, ed. W. J. Mayer-Oakes, A. W. Portnoy, pp. 86–90. Washington DC: Interagency Archeol. Serv. Dep. Interior

13. Fitting, J. E. 1982. The status of rescue archeology in North America. In *Rescue Archeology*, ed. R. L. Wilson, G. Loyola, pp. 173–90. Washington DC: Natl. Trust Hist. Preserv.

14. Fitting, J. E. 1982. The New Melones project: Murphy's Law in operation. *Contract Abstr. CRM Archeol.* 3(1):14–18

15. Fitting, J. E., Goodyear, A. C., King, T. F. 1979. Client-oriented archeology: an exchange of views. *J. Field Archeol.* 6:352–60

16. Flannery, K. V. 1982. The golden Marshalltown: a parable for the archeology of the 1980s. *Am. Anthropol.* 84:256–78

17. General Accounting Office. 1981. *Are Agencies Doing Enough or Too Much for Archeological Preservation? Guidance Needed.* Washington DC, US Gen. Account. Off. 102 pp.

18. Goodyear, A. C. 1978. A letter from Albert C. Goodyear. *Newsl. Soc. Prof. Archeol.* 2:1–2

19. Green, D. F., Plog, F. 1983. *Problem Orientation and Allocation Strategies for Prehistoric Cultural Resources on the New Mexico National Forests.* Cultural Resources Document No. 1. Albuquerque: US Forest Serv.

20. Hickman, P. P. 1977. *Country Nodes: An Anthropological Evaluation of William Keys' Desert Queen Ranch, Joshua Tree National Monument, California.* Washington DC: Natl. Park Serv. 109 pp.

20a. Horwatt, M. S., Kenny, T. S. 1980. *Petition for Writ of Certiori to the United States Court of Appeals for the Fourth Circuit, Loudoun Times-Mirror et al v. Arctic Company, Ltd. t/a Iroquois Reserach Institute.* Supreme Court of the

U.S., October term 1980 (cert. denied)

21. Interior Dept. 1977. Recovery of scientific, prehistoric, historic, and archeological data: methods, standards, and reporting requirements. *Fed. Regist.* 42:5374–83

22. Kaldenberg, R. 1980. Comment. In responses to "the trouble with archeology": part one. *J. Field Archeol.* 7:125–31

23. Keel, B. C. 1979. A view from inside. *Am. Antiq.* 44:164–70

24. Keel, B. C., Baker, B. L. 1980. *Status of New Melones mitigation program and recommendations for completion.* Washington DC: Natl. Park Serv. 55 pp. (manuscript)

25. King, T. F. 1972. Buchanan Reservoir: the last hurrah. *Soc. Calif. Archeol. Newsl.* 7(5):10

26. King, T. F. 1978. Allegories of eligibility: the determination of eligibility process and the capacity for thought among archeologists. In *Cultural Resources: Planning and Management*, ed. R. S. Dickens Jr., C. E. Hill, pp. 43–54. Boulder: Westview

27. King, T. F. 1981. Archeology for scholars or squirrels? *Proc. Am. Soc. Conserv. Archeol.*, pp. 48–55

28. King, T. F. 1981. The NART: a plan to direct archeology toward more relevant goals in modern life. *Early Man* Winter:35–37

29. King, T. F. 1982. Review of *Managing Archeology* (See Ref. 46). *Kiva* 47(3):181–84

30. King, T. F. 1982. The pothunter as an ally, not an enemy. *Early Man* Summer:38–40

31. King, T. F., Hickman, P. P., Berg, G. 1977. *Anthropology in Historic Preservation.* New York: Academic. 344 pp.

32. King, T. F., Lyneis, M. M. 1978. Preservation: a developing focus of american archeology. *Am. Anthropol.* 80:873–93

33. King, T. F., Parker, P. L. 1982. Tonnaachaw: a Truk village rediscovers its past. *Glimpses of Micronesia & the Western Pacific* 21(4):12–19

34. Klinger, T. C., Duncan, J. E. 1980. Stage 2 informant survey. In *Hampton*, assembler T. C. Klinger, pp. 39–52. Fayetteville: Arkansas Archeol. Surv. 101 pp.

35. Klinger, T. C., Raab, L. M. 1980. Archeological significance and the National Register: a response to Barnes, Briggs, and Neilsen. *Am. Antiq.* 45:554–57

36. Knudson, R. 1982. Basic principles of archeological resource management. *Am. Antiq.* 47:163–66

37. Lipe, W. D. 1974. A conservation model

for American archeology. *Kiva* 39:213–45

38. Lyneis, M. M. 1981. *Proc. Am. Soc. Conserv. Archeol.* 7, 1980–81. 47 pp.

38a. Maniery, J. G. 1982. An archeological site/ethnographic village: Central Sierra Miwok case study. *Contract Abst. CRM Archeol.* 3(1):19–26

39. McCartney, A. P. 1982. *Recycling prehistoric whale bone: a Canadian example*. Presented at Ann. Meet. Am. Anthropol. Assoc., 81st, Washington DC

40. McGimsey, C. R. III. 1972. *Public Archeology*. New York: Seminar. 265 pp.

41. McGimsey, C. R. III. 1981. Still a band of brethren? *Am. Antiq.* 46:378–80

42. McGimsey, C. R. III, Davis, H. A. 1977. *The Management of Archeological Resources*. Washington DC: Soc. Am. Archeol. 124 pp.

43. National Park Service ("Heritage Conservation & Recreation Service") 1980. *Resource Protection Planning Process*. Washington DC: Natl. Park Serv. 37 pp.

44. Nickens, P. R., Larralde, S. L., Tucker, G. C. Jr. 1981. *A Survey of Vandalism to Archeological Resources in Southwestern Colorado*. Denver: Bur. Land Manage.

44a. North Slope Borough Contract Staff 1979. *National Petroleum Reserve in Alaska: Native Livelihood and Dependence, a Study of Land Use Values Through Time*. National Petroleum Reserve in Alaska, Dep. Interior, Anchorage. 166 pp.

45. Plog, F. 1980. The ethics of archeology and the ethics of contracting. *Contract Abst. CRM Archeol.* 1(1):10–12

46. Plog, F. 1981. *Managing Archeology: a Background Document for Cultural Resource Management on the Apache-Sitgreaves National Forests, Arizona*. Albuquerque: US Forest Serv. 67 pp.

47. Plog, F., Tapman, K. C. 1982. *Cultural Resource Plan—McKinley Mine*. Denver: Pittsburg & Midway Coal Mining Co. 80 pp. (manuscript)

48. Raab, L. M., Klinger, T. C. 1977. A critical appraisal of 'significance' in contract archeology. *Am. Antiq.* 42:629–34

48a. Raab, L. M., Klinger, T. C., Schiffer, M. B., Goodyear, A. C. 1980. Clients, contracts, and profits: conflicts in public archeology. *Am. Anthropol.* 82:539–51

49. Reed, B., Mathiesen, K., Reed, S. 1982. Native American observer program, New Melones dam and reservoir, California. Washington DC: Natl. Park Serv. 12 pp. (manuscript)

50. Schiffer, M. B., Gumerman, G. J. 1977. *Conservation Archaeology*. New York: Academic. 495 pp.

51. Schneider, W. 1977. *Historic sites and the persistence of subsistence values*. Anchorage: Natl. Park Serv. 17 pp. (manuscript)

52. Smith, R. H. 1974. Ethics in field archaeology. *J. Field Archeol.* 1:375–83

53. Society of Professional Archeologists 1981. *Directory of Professional Archeologists*. Winston-Salem: Wake Forest Univ. 76 pp. 6th ed.

54. Talmadge, V. 1981. *State archeology programs and human burials: ethical and legal considerations*. Symp. presented at Ann. Meet. Soc. Am. Archeol., 46th, San Diego

55. Wendorf, F., ed. 1980. The Fort Burgwin report. *J. Field Archeol.* 7:248–53

56. Wildesen, L. E. 1975. Conservation vs. preservation of archeological sites. *Am. Soc. Conserv. Archeol. Newsl.* 2(2):9–11

57. Wildesen, L. E. 1979. *Getting us all together: cutural resources contracting in the Pacific northwest*. Presented at Ann. Meet. Soc. Am. Archeol., 44th, Vancouver

58. Wildesen, L. E. 1982. The study of impacts on archeological sites. *Adv. Archeol. Method Theory* 5:51–96

59. Wilke, P. J., King, T. F., Hammond, S. 1975. Aboriginal occupation at Tahquitz Canyon: ethnohistory and archeology. In *The Cahuilla Indians of the Colorado Desert: Ethnohistory and Prehistory*, ed. L. J. Bean. Ramona: Ballena. 73 pp.

Ann. Rev. Anthropol. 1983. 12:165–92
Copyright © 1983 by Annual Reviews Inc. All Rights reserved

CONCEPTS OF TIME IN QUATERNARY PREHISTORY

G. N. Bailey

Department of Archaeology, University of Cambridge, Downing Street, Cambridge, CB2 3DZ, United Kingdom

TIME AND ARCHAEOLOGY

Discussions of time in the archaeological literature have generally been dominated by problems of time measurement. Time concepts, however, have received little attention until recently (3, 11–13, 20, 38, 66, 72, 75, 80, 81, 93, 94, 97, 105, 114), even though they have been a longstanding source of interest to many other disciplines including philosophy, the natural and social sciences, history, and geography (1, 7, 15, 17, 18, 21, 33, 42, 43, 46, 48, 49, 52, 57, 87, 99, 110–112). To a large extent this is traceable to the difficulties of dating. It is only with the relatively recent development and widespread application of radiometric dating methods that archaeologists have begun to free themselves from technical preoccupations and to concentrate more fully on problems of process. Above all, new dating methods have demonstrated that human cultural history extends over a time span of at least two million years. This poses in a new way the issue of how we are to make use of knowledge about the past, what questions we should ask of it, and whether, by archaeological investigation of human activities over this time span, we can learn something new about human nature not available from other sources. I use the term quaternary prehistory here to emphasize an interest, in principle, in a time span of up to two million years.

The effect of time concepts on archaeological interpretation can be considered from two points of view. The first examines their influence on the thinking of archaeologists in their interpretation of past behavior. The second examines their influence on the thinking and behavior of prehistoric people and hence on the patterns which contribute to the archaeological record.

Contrasting notions of time are more or less implicit in archaeological thinking and have resulted in misguided rivalry between alternative approaches

165

to the interpretation of past behavior. Among the many different theoretical ideas that have entered the archaeological literature in the past 15 years, it is possible to discern a major polarity between "environmentalist" and "internalist" theories (62, 67, 92, 102, 103). Environmentalist theories, exemplified by ecological and palaeoeconomic schools of thought, derive their main inspiration from the natural sciences and emphasize ecological relationships and the determining or limiting effect of basic biological and environmental factors. Internalist theories, exemplified by neo-Marxist and structuralist schools of thought, derive their main inspiration from the social sciences and emphasize the inherent dynamic of social relations and structures of meaning.

In spite of attempts at integration, these two approaches are still frequently opposed to each other in language of moral fervor, as if they were irreconcilable gospels for archaeological salvation, mutually exclusive routes to intellectual maturity, alternative approaches to the *same* phenomena. A focus on the underlying time concepts indicates that this is misleading, and that these approaches have different objectives which refer to a large extent to *different* phenomena.

Cutting across this polarity are two sets of contrasts in the notion of time. The first is a difference of attitude about the relationship between the study of the present and the study of the past, and hence about the sorts of questions it is thought appropriate to ask about the archaeological record. On the one hand is the view that the past should be explained in terms of the present, reconstructed as if it were a series of "present moments" and thus "humanized" and made relevant to present-day social concerns. On the other hand is the view that the present should be explained in terms of the past, that the study of the past should be in terms of large-scale historical processes not obviously visible to the individual observer in a contemporary setting, processes which to some extent determine the present situation. I argue that these are not mutually exclusive notions which can be considered in isolation from each other, but that they are founded on two interrelated concepts of time—time as process and time as representation.

These environmentalist and internalist approaches are also founded on different notions about the sort of knowledge that can be acquired of the past: the environmentalist on the search for generalizations and a belief in the testability of hypotheses about past behavior; the internalist on the search for the unique qualities of particular events and situations and a rejection of some aspects of scientific methodology. I argue that this distinction is false and derives from ambiguities inherent in the principle of uniformitarianism. There are no epistemological grounds for separating knowledge of the past from knowledge of the present, and hence no epistemological grounds for preferring one type of knowledge or theory about past behavior over another.

The second contrast is between short time spans and long time spans and thus between short-term processes and long-term processes. In examining this contrast, I suggest that past behavior is not a single bounded entity which can be interpreted either in environmentalist or internalist terms, or in terms of some compromise between the two. Rather it represents an amalgamation and intersection of many different processes operating over different time spans and defined by different time boundaries. Environmentalist approaches tend to be associated with the study of long-term processes, internalist ones with short-term processes. I argue that this is a misleading juxtaposition, and that the interrelationships between different sorts of processes have been obscured by failure to clarify their temporal characteristics.

Time concepts have also been a major factor in the behavior of prehistoric people from the earliest period. An expanded temporal horizon is by common consensus a fundamental distinguishing characteristic of human behavior (30, 31, 42, 73). The development of distinctively human attributes, such as language, conceptual thought, and the coordination of social activities in time and space, are thought to be closely bound up with the three fundamental features of time experience: (a) succession—the sequence of events along a continuum; (b) duration—the span of events and of the intervals between them; and (c) simultaneity—the coordination of events according to a common time frame. Conscious recollection of past events and experiences, and the anticipation of future ones, is the very essence of what we mean by human intelligence, the means by which we model the environment around us and seek to adjust our relationship with it by internal or external modification. There are many hints that the human temporal horizon may have undergone a progressive expansion during the past two million years, initially through the evolution of more complex brain structures, and in more recent times through conceptual changes, notably in the gradual replacement of cyclical by linear conceptions of history (31, 90, 111, 118). The recent growth of interest in prehistory and futures research is the most recent manifestation of this process.

Time concepts, then, should be central to archaeological investigations of past behavior. They provide a unifying framework for discussing the different ways in which we as archaeologists think about past behavior, and a unifying framework for discussing the different sorts of past phenomena which are the objects of our archaeological investigations.

THE DUAL NATURE OF TIME

Time is a notoriously difficult concept and is frequently treated as if it were a dimension of space, whether at the cosmic level of space-time, or at the local level of everyday experience, as in the common practice of referring to the distance between locations in space as the time taken to travel between them, or in the description of temporal patterns in terms of spatial imagery (distance in time, location in time, time perspective). Despite this similarity, the dimensions of space and time are not interchangeable. Time is one-dimensional or linear, whereas space is three-dimensional. Time is also asymmetrical—it appears to flow irreversibly from past to future; whereas space is symmetrical and reversible.

Consider the contrast between a set of information presented as a three-dimensional model or a two-dimensional map and the same set presented as a series of written instructions. In the first case a variety of information is presented simultaneously and can be grasped as a totality or in many different combinations. In the second case the information is broken down into components which are then reformulated as a linear sequence. We could say with Whitrow (110) that space is presented to us all of a piece, whereas time comes to us bit by bit. Or in Fraisse's (42, p. 177) words: "Space is a collection of objects and it is these which largely determine the structure of perceived space. Time is the succession of changes, but each of these—apart from the present change—only exists for us as a memory or an anticipation; in other words they are *representations*. Space is primarily *presentation;* it is imposed on us" (italics in original).

The apparent linearity of time, then, appears to be a product of two factors: (*a*) succession or duration of events outside ourselves; (*b*) the way we think about these events by making mental representations of them. Thus time has a dual aspect—as sensation and as representation. In both respects time is a relational concept. It is partly a function of events and processes occurring, as it were, independently of our observations of them. It is also partly a function of the intellectual concepts by which we comprehend and express those events and processes. These two aspects of time are closely related: "it is not time itself but what goes on in time that produces effects. Time is not a simple sensation but depends on processes of mutual organisation uniting thought and action" (110, p. 39). There is no single time, but rather many different "times" and many different ways of representing them. What applies to time in general also applies to historical time in particular and to conceptions of the past.

Time as Process

The idea of different "times" is a reference to the different sorts of processes, be they cosmic, geological, physical, biological, social, psychological, or physiological, in terms of which time is defined: "processes do not 'occur over time', but *are* time" (87, p. 37). With reference to human activity, the notion of different sorts of time, such as linear, circular, reversible, directional, cumulative and so on, is really an imprecise way of referring to different sorts of processes (7). Insofar as time can be said to exist independently of process, it is a measuring device for comparing processes according to some common standard. "There is only one time, but there are many types of processes" (58).

Relativity theory has made familiar the idea that even the "one time" of the clock and the calendar is a relative concept. Nevertheless, it is convenient to accept the notion of a single time standard for events on this planet, the time of the solar calendar and radioactive clocks. We might call this "planetary time" to distinguish it from the universal time that may yet exist on the cosmic scale (111).

Time, unlike space, is irreversible. Or, if we are to be precise about terminology, the ultimate processes of the universe in terms of which we judge smaller-scale processes on this planet are thought to be irreversible. Thus time is said to flow like a river or to fly like an arrow. According to Gardner (46) and Whitrow (111), there are at least three irreversible processes or "arrows of time": (a) the recession of the galaxies (cosmological); (b) the tendency to entropy in closed systems (thermodynamic); and (c) information generating processes in open systems, such as biological evolution and the development of consciousness (psychological). This notion of the irreversibility of time is paradoxical. For if time is defined in terms of process, then it is technically incorrect to talk about reversible processes happening in irreversible time. It would be more accurate to say that some processes appear reversible when judged in terms of other processes. But by what standard are these other processes to be judged as irreversible? The possibility that the ultimate processes of life and the universe are reversible, or at least cyclical, is not apparently ruled out by present knowledge of particle physics. However that may be, past biological and cultural processes certainly seem to be irreversible to us from our present point of view. In part this is because our present consciousness is itself a product of these past processes—at the tip of the psychological arrow of time. We may seek to correct the distortions imposed by this limited time perspective in our imagination, but our knowledge of the past is necessarily influenced by the present point of view and has to be evaluated from a limited time perspective.

Time as Representation

Discussion of time as process implies a quasi-objective notion of events occurring independently of our observations and subject to distortion only because of our limited time perspective. But there is an additional subjective element. Kant's development of the idea that time is not given a priori but is an aspect of our intuition strongly influenced social anthropologists' ideas of time, and especially their discussion of attitudes to the past, through the work of Durkheim, who emphasized that concepts of time are social constructs (49). This is most clearly seen in nonliterate societies. Among the Nuer, for example, "time reckoning [beyond the annual cycle] is a conceptualization of the social structure, and the points of reference are a projection into the past of actual relations between groups of persons. It is less a means of coordinating events than of coordinating relationships, and is therefore mainly a looking backwards" (34, p. 108). "In primitive society . . . temporal concepts are inherently socio-spatial concepts" (58, p. 361), and "the past is inevitably swallowed up in the present" (49, p. 39), so that it represents a mythical projection of contemporary values and social relationships.

With the growth of technologies of literacy and ultimately of archaeological excavation and radiometric dating, the past acquires a certain independence from the present, but never fully escapes its influence. Literary documents and archaeological artifacts may refer to past events, but they are objects of the present. They may enable us to travel through time in our imaginations and to "visit" past events, but we do so though mental representations which are influenced by present concerns. "Archeology exists within our society's concepts of time and space, and all our findings take on meaning as a function of these vectors, not independently of them" (80, p. 25). This leads to various notions about the past as a symbolic resource, and about ways in which different versions of the past are used by different societies or different groups in society as a commentary on social issues and an additional weapon in political debate (2, 15). Different versions of the archaeological past may be preferred according to the climate of thought of the time, the perceived role of the archaeological discipline within the wider community, and the social and political standpoint of the individual archaeologist. This is not to imply that present values will necessarily impose particular interpretations regardless of the archaeological data, but rather that they will have an effect on the sort of archaeology that is pursued and the types of questions that are asked of it. One might refer to an interplay between past and present, or more precisely a dialogue between different versions of the past in the present. The past influences the present, but at the same time is interpreted in terms of present experience. Conversely, present experience may not be clearly understood until it has become past experience and can be viewed from a historical perspective. "Hence a sort of paradox: if the present has to be evaluated retrospectively, when it has become the past, the past has to be evaluated in the light of the present" (35, p. 61). There is, then, an interplay between processes and our conceptual representations of those processes, and that interplay is itself a process which forms part of the continuum of events.

The Elimination of Time

It is perhaps not surprising, in view of the difficulties of grasping the temporal dimension, that there has been a strong tendency at all levels of intellectual inquiry to reduce time to a dimension of space, or in some way to eliminate temporality (111). For example the "mythical time" of nonliterate societies is characterized by ritual imitation of actions and objects, presenting us with "the paradoxical situation that in his first conscious awareness of time man instinctively sought to transcend or abolish time" (110, p. 55). Post-Renaissance mathematicians and physicists, encouraged by idealist philosophers have been skeptical about the ultimate significance of time, preferring to treat it as a dimension of space.

There has been a similar tendency in biological and anthropological studies to eliminate historical time and to concentrate on patterns and processes which operate within the time span of contemporary observation, or which are believed to transcend the particular circumstances of time and place. For example, a major feature of social anthropological theory has been the search for synchronic structure in social behavior, whether in the structural-functionalism of Radcliffe-Brown or the structuralism of Lévi-Strauss (7, 47, 82, 91). The synchrony/diachrony polarity is treated rather differently in these two theories. For Radcliffe-Brown, synchrony refers to simultaneous relationships or patterns of relationships which persist through time, whereas diachrony refers to systematic change in the pattern of relationships and is excluded only through lack of historical data. For Lévi-Strauss, synchrony refers to principles of regularity and diachronic change to the largely incidental historical framework within which those regularities are expressed or transformed. These two structural approaches differ in their emphasis on material and mental phenomena respectively and in their respective attitudes to diachronic change. But they are nevertheless united in their belief in the possibility of achieving significant generalizations about human social life without reference to the past histories of the societies under study.

Ecological theories are likewise primarily focused on simultaneous relationships, or at best relatively short-term processes, as witnessed in the distinction sometimes made between "ecological" and "evolutionary" time (88). Evolutionary biology and its intellectual offspring, ethology and sociobiology, may be concerned with long-term change. However, these disciplines have traditionally been based on a neo-Darwinian theory of natural selection, in which long-term evolutionary patterns are thought to be wholly explainable in terms of small-scale selection processes.

This emphasis on comparison of contemporary cases is understandable in disciplines which lack data on past social and biological systems, and where "ahistorical" theories are to some extent made virtuous by necessity. However, a similarly tendency is also present in archaeological theorizing. In part this reflects the fact that archaeological data are inherently spatial in form. Many of the theoretical developments of the past decade, such as the explicit use of models (27), site catchment analysis (65, 96, 108), or spatial analysis (28, 68), were directly inspired by geographical ideas and texts (24, 25, 56). Multivariate statistics and programming procedures, in which time and space are treated as alternative axes in a coordinate system for plotting variability, also encourage the expression of temporal patterns in the form of spatial metaphor.

In part this tendency to eliminate time reflects the prevailing dependence of archaeological interpretation on concepts and theories derived from the literature of other disciplines, notably ecology and social anthropology, where the time dimension is greatly reduced in comparison with the archaeological record or largely ignored. It may be true that generalizations transcend time in the sense that they identify similarities between events or processes separate in time and space:

> events lose much, even all, of their meaning if they are not seen as having some degree of regularity . . . An historical fact thus shorn of its unique features escapes also temporality. It is no longer a passing incident, a sort of accident, but is, as it were, taken out of the flux of time and achieves conceptual stability as a sociological proposition (35, p. 49).

However, it does not follow that events and processes observed in the present are sufficient to indicate the nature of these timeless verities.

It is paradoxical that over a period when archaeological interpretation has drawn heavily on ahistorical theories from the natural and social sciences, these latter disciplines have begun to reexamine the historical dimension of their data as a legitimate stimulus to the development of theory. In the natural sciences, S. J. Gould (52–54) has challenged the view that macroevolutionary patterns in the paleontological record can be explained simply by extrapolation of microevolutionary principles. The theory of punctuated equilibria posits new causes at the level of macroevolution which are not opposed to the principles of microevolution, but which are not reducible to them either. Braudel (17, 18) is famous for a conception of human history as a series of layers, ranging from the deep and slowly changing processes of the natural environment to the more rapidly changing processes of social and individual activity, each layer in contact with the others but not reducible to them. Comparative sociology has also moved increasingly toward the analysis of historical data and the formulation of diachronic theories (1, 7, 48, 50, 83).

A number of archaeologists have expressed a belief in the operation of long-term processes not apparent in the short-term record (23, p. 1; 26, p. 9;' 36, p. 7; 38, p. 50, 53; 109). However, exploration of these processes has been hindered or overshadowed by a powerful resistance to the notion of historical generalization. Many other archaeologists have preferred to follow Radcliffe-Brown in their view of prehistoric archaeology as an idiographic discipline whose main goal is to establish "as acceptable certain particular or factual propositions or statements" (91, p. 1; see also 66, 106, 107).

This objection to generalizations stems in part from a belief that historical generalizations imply a degree of determinism incompatible with human creativity. The notion of time as process can, if taken to extremes, be held to imply that the present is determined by the past and therefore seems to deny any role to human choice or the creative intervention of individual action. The classic palaeoeconomic statement of a belief in the priority of long-term trends over "the noise of innumerable short term trivia" (64, p. 2) has been criticized on these grounds (70, 71, 104). A similar opposition influences debate in other disciplines. The theory of punctuated equilibria in paleobiology (54) is criticized by orthodox protagonists of the neo-Darwinian synthesis as an encouragement to Marxist doctrine (59), although the objection here is as much to the "revolutionary" implications of theory as to the invocation of macroevolutionary processes not visible in microevolutionary time. Popper's (89) attack on historical laws in the human sphere is inspired by, among other things, an antipathy, to Marxism (21a). Braudel's (17, 18) emphasis on the distinction between long-term "structures" and short-term "events" in human history is criticized for reducing individuals to the status of little more than accidents (8). The more extreme sociobiological theories of human behavior, which refer specific cultural practices to genetic factors, are vulnerable to similar criticisms in that they imply an underlying biological program which predetermines human activity (32).

An extreme historical determinism, which interpreted every action in the present as determined by processes in the past, would be logically untenable, since it would render superfluous the very process of intellectual inquiry by which it was sustained. However, objections to historical generalization on deterministic grounds—unless they are objections to generalizations of every sort—can only be upheld in relation to the particular class of historical generalizations described as unfolding models (48), in which the continuum of events is seen as a closed system, unfolding according to some preset design and totally insulated from subsequent intervention.

A far more pervasive restraint on archaeological generalization is the doctrine of uniformitarianism. This has come to be associated in the minds of many with two mutually reinforcing views: (a) that archaeological inference about prehistoric behavior is intrinsically unreliable, or less reliable than inference about contemporary behavior, since it works only with material data at least one step removed from the behavioral processes of ultimate interest; (b) that the sorts of processes and generalizations appropriate to the explanation of past behavior are the same as those derived from a study of contemporary behavior. In some senses this sort of uniformitarianism applies an important corrective to our distorted time perspective, which tends to exaggerate the importance and complexity of situations close to us in time at the expense of more remote epochs. However, this is easily translated into the view that the past *ought* to be reconstructed in the image of the present, thereby expressing in an extreme form the notion of time as representation. Such an extreme view, like extreme expressions of time as process, embodies a self-negating logic. Thus, by so emphasizing the similarities of past and present, it in effect denies the need to study the past at all, and denies to disciplines concerned with the study of the past any creative role as the source of novel generalizations about human behavior. So widespread and so confusing is the impact of uniformitarian philosophy in archaeology that it deserves detailed examination.

UNIFORMITARIANISM

Strictly speaking, uniformitarianism expresses a belief in universal principles which apply irrespective of time and place. However, it has come to be identified with a belief that we know the present better than the past and are therefore required to develop models which explain the past in terms of processes visible at the present day. A similar notion was used by nineteenth century geologists to remove the concept of divine intervention from the study of earth history, and ushered in an era of systematic inquiry unburdened by religious prejudice. Uniformitarianism had a similar liberating impact on the study of the human past, but in more recent times has had a stifling effect on archaeological theory. For, if the data relating to past behavior are unreliable and can only be interpreted in terms of present processes, then it seems to follow, as Trigger (106, 107) has argued, that we can never discover in the data of the past any generalizations that we do not already know. Consequently, archaeologists have only two choices: either we aspire to generalizations, in which case we are doomed to produce knowledge which is trivial; or we concentrate on the differences between events and situations, in which case we opt for the subservient role of an idiographic discipline, destined to consume the generalizations of others but never to produce any of its own. It is an odd paradox that such a self-negating logic should have gained any currency in the archaeological literature, and that a uniformitarian principle originally devised to encourage the study of the past and to emphasize the similarities between events, should come to be quoted as an authority for rejecting the study of the past and for concentrating on the differences between events.

This confusion has come about because uniformitarianism from its very inception was an ambiguous principle: "the uniformitarian assault was launched from two logically distinct platforms and the cardinal geologic principle arising from its victory is a dual conception" (51, p. 223). Methodological uniformitarianism asserts a belief in the spatial and temporal invariance of general laws, essentially as a procedural principle for bringing past events within the scope of empirical investigation. Substantive uniformitarianism asserts a belief in the uniformity of specific geological processes, notably that these occurred at the same rate in the past as at the present day. Both conceptions were important in the overthrow of catastrophist theory and the removal of the supernatural from geological explanation, and were thus closely linked in the minds of Lyell and his contemporaries. Gould (51) suggested that these terms should be abandoned, since the methodological variant is simply a statement of scientific method not confined to geologists, while the substantive variant has now been rejected as a theory of geological change. Nevertheless, it is useful to retain the distinction between methodological uniformities and substantive uniformities for purposes of archaeological discussion.

Methodological Issues

As an example of methodological uniformitarianism in action, let us examine the relatively simple case of quaternary climatic change. One way to proceed would be to analyze the varying proportions of different species of temperature-sensitive organisms in a stratigraphic column, for example marine foraminifera in a core of deep-sea sediment. The methodological unformity here is the assumption that the temperature preferences of the various species observed under present-day conditions have remained constant throughout the quaternary. It is important to emphasize that this assumption constitutes a theory, however much it might be corroborated by ecological and physiological analyses of modern organisms. In effect, a general principle established under present-day conditions for one set of phenomena—temperature preferences of marine organisms—is extrapolated to the past to investigate *another* set of phenomena—climatic change. It is in this sense that Gould refers to methodological uniformitarianism as a "warrant for inductive inference" (51, p. 226), as a means to an end rather than an end in itself.

Binford's (12) notion of "middle-range theory" is similar to this conception of methodological uniformitarianism. This is quite different from Trigger's (106, 107) reading of uniformitarianism, which implies that general principles established from present phenomena are extrapolated to the past record to explain particular instances of the *same* phenomena. If we were to use the modern temperature preferences of marine species to explain their past biogeographical distributions, it is indeed unlikely that we would learn much, apart from the unique qualities of particular distributions at different time periods and in different regions. At best we might hope to discover some anomalous distributions to cast doubt on the supposed universality of generalizations based on modern data.

Methodological uniformities may help to reconstruct various aspects of the past. However, they are unlikely, of themselves, to give rise to substantive theories of past phenomena. That would imply a dependence on induction, which is widely held to be an inadequate basis for creating a coherent body of theoretical knowledge, let alone a uniquely correct one (22). The application of methodological uniformities usually presupposes a more general framework of theory which determines what constitute relevant phenomena and relevant observations. Let us suppose that we already have a sustantive theory of climatic change which we wish to test against the paleoclimatic data supplied by marine foraminifera, for example the Milankovitch theory of climatic periodicity in relation to long-term variations in the geometry of the earth's orbit (60). In effect such a test would consist of contrasting one theory (the substantive) with another theory (the methodological). Testing in these circumstances is by no means straightforward, since a failed test might indicate only that the methodological theory was wrong, whereas a successful test might indicate only that it lacked the discriminatory power to distinguish between alternative substantive theories. Thus the methodological theory might itself be treated as a subsbtantive theory, to be tested against other theories, for example the theory of a uniform relationship between variations in oxygen isotope ratios and variations in continental ice volumes. This in its turn might raise further problems leading to a consideration of other theories, and so on. The reality of paleoclimatic interpretation is even more complex than this simplified illustration might indicate. It involves a large number of theories, including other theories of climatic change, theories about the interaction between regional and global climates, and about the interrelationship between different sorts of paleoclimatic indicators, as well as uniformitarian theories about sedimentation rates and radioactive decay processes employed in dating (60). Testing in this context might best be described as a search for consistency between logically distinct theories, the strength of the test being evaluated in relation to the number and scope of the interlocking theories. This interaction and intermeshing of many theories is characteristic of much empirical science and results in its cumulative strength as well as much of its provisional character.

The major conclusion I wish to draw from the above example at this point is that data from the prehistoric past, whether archaeological or otherwise, are in principle no more difficult to interpret than data in the present. It may be that the methodological theories used to facilitate interpretation of past phenomena are often, although by no means exclusively, derived from study of contemporary processes, hence the misleading notion that the past is that much further out of intellectual reach than the present. However, many other investigations require extrapolation from observable phenomena to unobservables, and thus the incorporation of intervening methodological theories or assumptions, whether the extrapolation is from artifacts to prehistoric behavior, from literary documents to the events they purport to describe, from human actions to human intentions, from verbal testimony to mental processes, or from the morphological characteristics of biological organisms to their genetic constitutions (22, 84, 116). Even observations with the naked eye require optical theories to establish the relationship between image and object.

From this point of view internalist theories of archaeological explanation are in principle no less viable than environmentalist theories. It is a common fallacy that reconstructions of subsistence and environment are relatively easy archaeological tasks, as if there were a simple correspondence between the archaeological data and the phenomena they refer to. This is simply not so. The inferences required to derive subsistence economy from archaeological food remains, or paleoenvironments from pollen or other paleoenvironmental in-dicators, involve no less complex theoretical considerations than those required to derive social organization from burial data or structures of meaning from pot decorations. It may be that there is a wider range of data sources and a larger network of interlocking theories that can be brought to bear to corroborate environmentalist theories. However, this is a separate point, and by no means well established. Certainly there are no good epistemological grounds for choosing between different sorts of questions and theories about past behavior. Attempts to discredit environmentalist theories on the grounds that they neces-sarily involve "elements of the straightforward positivist and Popperian posi-tions . . . and knowledge as a more or less accurate picture of the real world" (103, p. 174; 104) suggest either unfamiliarity with scientific theory or over-familiarity with bad examples of it. Attempts to discredit internalist theories on the grounds that they refer to intangible aspects of past behavior are equally suspect. One may choose between theories on other grounds, that they are more or less interesting or useful. Both of these are controversial criteria which cannot be justified in terms of reason or logic alone. But I shall nevertheless suggest a definition of usefulness in the next section.

Substantive Issues

A second major point which is clear from the paleoclimatic example discussed above is the importance of distinguishing between theory treated methodologi-cally as a means of investigating *another* theory and theory treated substantive-ly as the theory to be investigated. It is a commonplace that all observations are theory-dependent. But this is an ambiguous statement which can be understood in two ways, depending on whether one emphasizes the substantive or metho-dological context of investigation. Wylie's (116, p. 44) statement that "observations . . . acquire significance as relevant evidence only within a theoretical framework, generally the one which is under test" emphasizes the substantive aspect. Binford's comments on middle-range theory and his state-ment that "our methods for constructing the past must be *independent* of our theories for explaining the past" (12, p. 29, italics in original) emphasizes the methodological aspect.

Failure to clarify this distinction can lead to confusion. Wylie's statement can be misunderstood as endorsing circularity of argument unless it is strongly qualified. Binford (14) certainly implies some circularity in the structuralist program in his attack on Hodder's reliance on "empathetic understanding"—the uniformitarian assumption that human nature, mentality, and psychic responses in the past were the same as our own. Confusion occurs here because it is not clear whether the uniformitarian assumption is being expressed as a methodological theory or a substantive one. Structuralist archaeologists may wish to deny the validity of this distinction and to assert that the methodological theory by which they give meaning to the archaeological record and the substantive theory in terms of which they explain past behavior are one and the same. If they do so, however, they will rapidly remove the structuralist program beyond the pale of empirical investigation, or else cease to pursue their interests within the field of prehistoric archaeology. Conversely, Binford's statement may give rise to the misleading notion that methodological theory can provide a sufficient test if it is logically independent of the substantive theory being tested. This may be so, but it is obviously desirable that the methodological theory should also be correct, something which may not be clear at the time of the test. Emphasis on methodology is also vulnerable to the charge of induction and a belief that reconstructing the past without clearly specified a priori substantive aims will somehow lead to a uniquely correct view of past reality.

Ethnoarchaeological studies express something of this ambiguity in that they may be undertaken for two different purposes. One type of study examines processes or relationships which may be relatively uninteresting or even trivial in relation to an understanding of the modern society, for example the relationship between food waste and subsistence economy, but which provide a useful key for interpreting other processes in the archaeological past. Another type of study examines processes which are substantively interesting in their own right in that they say something new about the behavior of the modern society, for example about the use of material culture in social interaction. This substantive knowledge, in its turn, may be used in two different ways in archaeological interpretation. It may be generalized to the study of the past, that is, used in the form of analogy as a model for the substantive processes which operated in the past. Or it may be used in its own right as a case study in comparative analyses which include other independently derived case studies, archaeological as well as ethnographic.

The statement that processes in the present should be used to explain events in the past is then an ambiguous one. If we mean that such processes should be used methodologically to investigate other sorts of processes, that is one interpretation. If, however, we mean that processes in the present should be used substantively as a model of the processes which operated in the past, that is to subscribe to a particularist form of uniformitarianism which can be challenged on two grounds.

In the first place, the point of applying a uniformitarian principle to the past is that it should reveal the operation of processes that we cannot study in the present. Climatic change is an obvious example of a problem that cannot be meaningfully addressed except on a geological time span. The notion that there were processes operating in the past which we do not see operating in the present in no way conflicts necessarily with a strict definition of uniformitarianism as a belief in universal processes. One can imagine universal processes which operate so slowly that their effects are not visible on a short time span, or processes which have different effects under different conditions, or discontinuous or cumulative effects, none of which are apparent except over long time spans. Nor does the postulation of such processes obviate the study of the present, for they may lead to the discovery of new phenomena in the present, or give significance to phenomena whose meaning was previously obscure. They may also give rise to predictions about the future.

A more fundamental objection to the particularist version of uniformitarianism is that it assumes that the past in general and the archaeological record in particular are something given to experience, something "out there" that needs to be explained. However, the "facts" of prehistory, like other "facts," do not speak for themselves. There is no absolute commitment to recover the past in all its detail or to strive for complete explanations of it. Such concepts have no meaning except in relation to theoretical expectations. We do not reconstruct the past as an empirical exercise—as something given to observation—and then look for theories to explain the patterns so reconstructed. Or if we do so, we fall prey to a form of induction which is controverted by the theory-dependence of observations. Our initial theoretical interests will guide the choice of relevant data and hence the sorts of problems we choose to investigate in the archaeological past. Indeed, our initial theoretical interests will determine whether we study the archaeological past at all. For there is no absolute commitment to study the archaeological past unless it is relevant to the general theories we wish to investigate. Equally there can be no prospect of discovering long-term processes unless we look for them with appropriately devised theories. In the same way the boundary between the present and the past is not something independently given. We tend to speak as if this were so. But the "past" is a phrase used to refer to anything beyond the bounds of our current interests or techniques of observation. The past may be something that happened a fraction of a second ago, if our interest is in molecular processes, or billions of years ago, if our interest is in cosmic processes. The boundary between "present" and "past" is an arbitrary point, determined by the span of time over which given techniques of observation extend and by the nature of the processes under investigation. Therefore the notion of a fixed boundary between present time and past time must be abandoned as presupposing the very matters that require investigation.

To take processes in the present, i.e. happening over short time spans, as an explanation of the past, i.e. of processes happening over longer time spans, may result in knowledge which is in some sense true. But it is doubtful whether such knowledge can be regarded as useful in the sense of creating new theoretical knowledge. The use of the lengthy and uncertain procedures of archaeological analysis in this way to analyze short-term processes can be likened to the construction of a large and elaborate telescope on a satellite platform orbiting just beyond the earth's atmosphere. The telescope is then put to use, but instead of being directed outwards to explore the origins of the universe, it is directed earthward in order to demonstrate that, from the point of view of an individual observer standing on the ground, the earth's surface would appear to be flat.

None of this is to indicate a preference for environmentalist or internalist approaches to the explanation of prehistoric behavior. Both are vulnerable to the accumulation of useless knowledge in the above sense. Nor is it to deny or ignore the unique qualities which differentiate individual events and situations. For it is in the interplay between similarities and differences that many of the most fruitful generalizations may be found. It is rather to reaffirm the validity of the uniformitarian principle, not as an argument against the search for novel theories or generalizations in the archaeological past, but as a very powerful argument in its favor.

LONG-TERM PROCESSES

Discussion of the long term in archaeology has given rise to three notions. All have been encouraged by the palaeoeconomic literature, which has made the most explicit reference to long-term processes in justifying a theoretical position (3, 63, 64, 74). These three notions are: (a) that there are essentially only two scales of behavior—long-term and short-term; (b) that long-term processes are dominated by environmental and biological interactions, by relationships between genetics, demography, and economic exploitation of the natural environment, whereas short-term processes are dominated by social and psychological processes, by social rules and relationships and individual goals and motivations; (c) that behavior at these different scales requires different sorts of explanations expressing varying degrees of proximate or ultimate causation and varying emphasis on historical (in terms of the past), functional (in terms of the present), or teleological (in terms of the future) causes. There is some justification of this in that many environmental and biological interactions are prominent at large scales of organization, whereas many social and psychological processes are prominent at small scales. However, there are numerous essential qualifications of this position.

The Long Term and the Short Term

It is a characteristic argument in favor of environmentalist interpretations of behavior over long time spans that environmental and biological variation tends to occur relatively slowly or have effects which only become manifest after long intervals of time, so that the nature of the interaction between these variables and other features of human behavior only comes into focus over long time spans. Over the long time span of the glacial-interglacial cycle (about

100,000 years), for example, environments undergo immense changes and are a variable of major potential impact on human behavior. Over shorter time spans of years or decades, environmental change (apart from seasonal variation) may seem so slight that it can be treated as virtually a constant in the analysis of human behavior. Conversely, so it is argued, internalist approaches emphasize small-scale processes which vary rapidly over short time spans; but these are processes which are likely to fade out of focus over longer time spans because of the decreasing resolution of archaeological data and the increasing margin of error in dating methods as one moves farther back in time.

However, there are good reasons for supposing that environmental, biological, and social phenomena are each characterized by a series or hierarchy of different processes, representing different time scales of organization and operating over different time spans. Giddens, for example (48, p. 19), refers to "three intersecting planes of temporality involved in every moment of social reproduction": the flow of day-to-day life; the life cycle of the individual; and the development or persistence of social institutions which outlive the individual. Haldane (57) suggests five classes of biological processes defined by the different time depths over which they occur: molecular (up to a second); physiological (up to an hour); ontogenetic (up to a lifetime); historical (a number of lifetimes); and evolutionary (up to hundreds of millions of years). Butzer (20, p. 24 see also 77) refers to six typical "wavelengths" of environmental change, ranging from small-scale year-to-year fluctuations to large-scale geological cycles of millions of years duration. It may seem from these examples that social processes as a group are restricted to relatively short time spans in relation to environmental ones, while biological processes operate over the widest range. Nevertheless, there is also a zone of overlap, and this leads to a qualification of the long-term/short-term dichotomy in two ways.

In the first place, short-term environmental fluctuations, although far less dramatic in their effects than the long-term environmental cycles, can have a considerable impact on annual food yields and hence on short-term patterns of behavior. O'Shea (86) has identified institutionalized features of social behavior, among sedentary groups in particular, which seem to represent a response to these short-term environmental fluctuations through the operation of "social storage." Food surpluses are converted into durable nonfood tokens such as prestige goods through intercommunity exchange on a regional scale. These goods can later be reconverted into food through further exchanges, thereby serving as a form of "indirect" storage which helps to protect local groups against unpredictable short-term variations in food harvests. Among mobile groups, and especially hunter-gatherers, alliance networks seem to serve a similar function, providing an institutionalized network of social relationships over very wide areas which allows the rapid redistribution of personnel over the landscape in response to local resource fluctuations (44, 45,

76, 113). The time depth of the social process embodied in these institutions is unclear. But since they can involve relationships of delayed reciprocity between individuals scattered over very large areas, who may come into contact only infrequently, the time depth must presumably extend over at least several generations.

If environmental factors can have an impact over short time spans, the question naturally arises as to the impact of social and psychological factors over long time spans. Internalist interpretations of very long time spans, and especially social interpretations, tend to treat the long-term pattern as a succession of short-term processes. The effects of such a succession may be cyclical or cumulative, but these effects tend to be regarded as by-products of the social process rather than integral components of it. The question of long-term social processes is a very poorly explored area of study, and some possible further lines of inquiry are discussed in the next section.

Causation: Hierarchical and Interactive

If behavior is viewed as a hierarchy of processes, each level in the hierarchy being defined by different time depths, the question of causation can be considered from two points of view. One approach involves the notion of hierarchical causation, in which causes at one scale are treated as logically independent of causes at other scales (3, 16, 38, 53, 57, 69, 99). The emphasis here is on the differences between time scales and the analysis of each scale in its own terms in relation to the variables and relationships in focus at that scale. Variables operating over long time spans define broad channels for the more rapidly changing variables, but do not otherwise interact with them except in the negative sense of imposing general constraints on variation.

Hierarchical causation has obvious attractions where one is confronted with the juxtaposition of radically different scales of behavior. The relationship between environmental and social factors, for example, is frequently treated in these terms. Environmental factors are seen as supplying, at best, very broad negative constraints. These may eliminate social premises which create the conditions of their own demise because they specify the overexploitation of key environmental resources. But they are not otherwise thought likely to have any positive effect on the content or patterning of social process. Thus social behavior may vary widely in its own terms and in relation to causes which are quite independent of environmental factors (10, 39, 70). It has been argued that much of the hostility directed toward sociobiological theories has been provoked by their application at an inappropriate scale of organization, at the level of small-scale social or individual behavior, rather than the larger scales and longer time spans for which they seem best suited (16). Conversely, teleological explanations in terms of goal-seeking are more appropriate at smaller scales of activity.

Functional explanations of social behavior in terms of adaptation to environmental factors, if they are to be properly investigated, require an investigation of historical factors, and hence of time scales well beyond those normally available for social anthropological investigation. Hence the critique of adaptation concepts which originates in the social anthropological and sociological literature (48, 66, 70, 71, 103, 104) is not so much an argument for abandoning this type of explanation as for defining the scale of inquiry to which it is appropriate.

From a hierarchical point of view there is nothing contradictory in the idea of social behavior as an intersection of processes operating over different time spans, some of which can be explained in historical terms, some in functional terms, and some in teleological terms. The social institutions of social storage and alliance networks mentioned earlier certainly appear to include an adaptive component in that they clearly provide an advantage in environments subject to extreme, short-term resource fluctuations. Nevertheless, other factors are also involved as proximate causative agents. For example, the accumulation of nonfood tokens in systems of social storage may lead to differential accumulation of wealth, its transmission to subsequent generations, and hence to institutionalized social differentiation and centralization (86). Since nonfood tokens tend to lose their value through continued accumulation, there is a constant pressure for their upward conversion into more rare or more valuable items. These become the focus of manipulation by individuals for social and political ends, and thus dominate investigation at a proximate level of analysis.

Similarly, long-distance exchange relationships among hunter-gatherer groups frequently have a proximate motivation which is ritual or social in character. Over longer time spans, however, the ecological function of these social institutions is more obviously in focus. Alliance networks are prominent in the European record during the Last Glacial between about 30,000 and 10,000 years ago, and their distribution in time and space appears closely related to environmental variations during a period of generally severe climatic conditions (44, 45, 76). This does not mean that environmental stress is a sufficient explanation for the appearance of these prehistoric alliance networks, but it seems to have exerted a strong positive selection. Moreover, the occurrence of alliance networks had consequences which were biologically advantageous in that they allowed the maintenance of populations at low densities in marginal environments which would otherwise have been abandoned, as well as the large-scale colonization of extensive areas of northern Europe and Asia for the first time in the history of the human species.

Interactive causation refers to closely interrelated processes operating over similar or overlapping time-scales and the ways in which these interact and affect each other's behavior. Familiar under this heading are dialectical theories of social change which emphasize the mutual transformation of social structures and individual action, and the ways in which the intended and unintended consequences of individual actions modify the social context within which future actions occur (48, 66, 104). Fletcher's (39, 40) analysis of settlement space depends on an interactive process involving individuals and the material, spatial messages of their communities. The internal logical coherence of a group's material message system regulates the degree to which variation generated by individuals is tolerated. On the other hand, the constraints imposed by the structure of the message system will change over the longer term because of "accidental" errors in the transmission of knowledge from one generation to the next and the incorporation of other forms of idiosyncratic variation.

The above examples refer primarily to relatively short time spans of behavior and to social or psychological factors. But any combination of overlapping processes invites exploration in terms of interactive causation regardless of the total time span or the type of factors involved. One problem that might benefit from more detailed examination in these terms is the longer range consequences of individual decisions and social rules, consequences which extend beyond the time-horizon of individual and collective decision making. Decisions about mating and reproduction affect the size and genetic makeup of the next generation, and these in their turn provide the boundary conditions for the next generation of decisions. Exploitation of food resources, even of the simplest kind, has various effects on the exploited plants and animals, ranging from cyclical intergenerational changes in their demographic structure and consequent accessibility to future exploitation to more radical alterations of resource behavior and environment with cumulative effects over centuries or millenia. The alliance networks, discussed above, which became widespread in Eurasia during the Last Glacial, may have had further consequences in the context of large-scale environmental change during the early Postglacial, stimulating the intensification of food production and thereby acting as one factor in the development of agricultural economies (9). The example of prehistoric alliance networks suggests very strongly a pattern of reciprocal interaction between environmental and social changes over long time spans, and other long-term trends may be worth exploring in these terms.

Change and Continuity

The above discussion suggests that a major theme of interest in long time spans is in processes of *change*. However, as Renfrew (93, p. 266) puts it, long time spans offer two advantages, "allowing significant changes to occur" but also bringing out "certain regularities which would not have been visible with a narrower time focus." Interest in long-term patterning may be directed to two contrasting notions: large-scale change, major transformations of which our society is the cumulative outcome; and long-term stability, enduring qualities or regularities beneath the flux of change. The first emphasizes time as succession of events. It also emphasizes the past as seen from the present point of view—as a cumulative, directional process leading to the present. The second emphasizes time as duration and views the past as being in some sense independent of the present point of view, as transcending the particularities of time and place. Often the emphasis on change over longer time spans is in relation to behavior which appears stable in the short term, while the emphasis on continuity is in relation to stabilities which transcend a succession of states apparently separate and distinct in the shorter term. Typically this interplay between change and continuity is expressed in the form of a contrast between archaeological and ethnographic perspectives on similar phenomena.

One example of this contrast is the current archaeological view of hunters and gatherers in comparison with the now classic ethnograpic picture. In the latter the conception of a stable, unchanging way of life with strong in-built social, demographic, and energetic resistance to change except under the impact of external influence from more powerful economies has become almost a truism (78, 79, 98). The very notion of "hunter-gathererer" as a unitary and unifying category owes as much to social anthropological theory (100, 101) as to the ways in which archaeologists have chosen to classify the material record of prehistory. From the prehistoric point of view the picture is one of dynamic change with prehistoric hunter-gatherer groups expanding their habitat, changing their dietary preferences, and ultimately transforming themselves into farmers in many areas of the world. The pattern is one of cumulative development involving considerable variation in behavior—dynamic equilibrium at the very least, even though there is still much disagreement about the relative influence of genetic, environmental, demographic, technological, and social factors in this long-term process (5, 9, 11, 29). This dynamic view in its turn has reacted back on the interpretation of the ethnographic record and stimulated the search for the dynamic factors inherent in hunter-gatherer social organization (9, 71, 115).

Conversely, the classic palaeoeconomic view of the origins of agriculture (61, 63, 74) represents a move in the other direction, away from patterns of change, and toward the study of underlying continuities strongly reinforced by unchanging environmental constraints, a search for long-term constraints and phenomena stable in the long term which recalls the Braudelian emphasis on long-term structures. The basic "facts" of prehistory as a succession of distinct categories is directly challenged as the product of unwarranted theoretical preconceptions about behavior, whether in the form of the technological classification: Paleolithic, Mesolithic, Neolithic; or the economic classification: specialized hunting, broad-spectrum hunting and gathering, incipient agriculture, village farming (or other variations on this theme). Instead, the idea of a continuum of "man-resource relationships" is advocated, all subsumed under the general heading of symbiosis or husbandry. While the latter term was subsequently reexpanded into a series of distinct economic relationships (4, 74), the emphasis has generally been on the continuities in economic behavior and on the idea of change as variations on an underlying theme of continuity.

The dynamic view of hunter-gatherer behavior, for all its challenge to the unitary view of hunting and gathering as a single way of life, can still be criticized for implicitly accepting as given the distinction between hunter-gatherers and farmers, when this preconceived division is a matter which requires investigation in its own right. Conversely, palaeoeconomic interpretations are often weakened by confusion of methodological generalizations with substantive generalizations, and by assuming the very continuities they claim to have discovered in the archaeological record (6). Nevertheless, there is clearly some convergence between these two approaches, as well as a difference of emphasis. The potential interaction between them suggests the possibility of removing the somewhat artificial polarity between synchrony and diachrony, the general and the particular, the present and the past, in a pattern of interplay transformed and accelerated by virture of being transposed to the more varied time spans and time perspectives of the prehistoric record.

Long-term continuities have generally been emphasized in the context of environmentalist interpretations of past behavior. However, an example of an internalist approach may be found in Fletcher's (39–41) investigation of the relationship between the human sensory system and the use of settlement space. Analysis of modern and archaeological settlements in a wide variety of social, cultural, and technological contexts suggests fundamental uniformities in patterns of intrasettlement population density and in patterns of interaction between human message systems and the spatial environment within which they operate, uniformities which cannot be explained simply in terms of environmental resource levels or biological limitations. It may be that one of the more interesting consequences of rethinking structuralist and social theory in the context of long-term behavior patterns will be to demonstrate the enduring qualities of certain social and psychological processes as underlying process universals (19a), and hence their role in creating patterns of continuity rather than patterns of change.

PREHISTORIC TIME STRUCTURES

It is clear from the above discussion of long-term processes in the archaeological past that an understanding of them is closely related to an understanding of the time structures of prehistoric people—of their mental capacity to simulate events remote in time from immediate experience, and of the temporal horizons incorporated in their social relationships and economic activities. Systems of alliance and social storage, with their dependence on delayed reciprocity, are evidence of a future orientation which has both immediate practical consequences for day-to-day activity and longer-range consequence in terms of demographic patterns and environmental adaptation. Many other features of social and economic life are founded on the concept of investment in delayed returns among hunter-gatherer and agricultural groups alike (4, 115). Concepts of scheduling and logistic planning (11, 37), used in the organization of subsistence so as to facilitate optimal use of seasonally irregular food supplies, similarly attests to the practical effects of future orientation. Time-budgeting and the use of time as a resource to promote the efficiency of subsistence tasks develops a similar idea in the context of analyzing prehistoric technology (105), and this suggests another means of identifying some of the time structures implicit in prehistoric activities.

The notion of prehistoric time structures raises two sorts of problems. One is the precise time horizon implied by different sorts of activities. It is one thing to talk about future orientation in general, but quite another to specify in detail the time span implied by different sorts of future-oriented activities and the practical limitations and consequences attendant on their implementation. Future orientation can differ according to whether it refers to a time horizon minutes, months, or years into the future. It can also have different implications and different consequences according to whether it is related to subsistence activities, where deferred gratification may entail risks as well as advantages, or to ritual and symbolic acts such as burial of the dead or the construction of monuments.

A second and related issue is the question of long-term trends in time structures. The notion of a progressive expansion of the human temporal horizon throughout the quaternary period, implying some sort of cumulative trend, is intuitively attractive. But it is important in assessing any cumulative pattern to allow for the distortion of time perspective, which may give the illusion of a progressive trend leading from a "simpler" past to a more "complex" present.

It is a widely held consensus that a fully modern intellectual capacity for future-oriented activity was present from at least 30,000 years ago, in association with anatomically modern *Homo sapiens sapiens,* and that examples of such activity can be traced back at least to the Upper Paleolithic period (in European terms) with its evidence of economic intensification and rich artistic traditions. However, there are considerable uncertainties about the relationship between differences in brain size or morphology and mental abilities, and the anatomical and technological changes which define the Middle-Upper Paleolithic transition may be a misleading guide to a critical threshold in mental evolution (19, 45). It is also important to distinguish biological changes in brain capacity from conceptual changes. Evidence for a reduced time horizon in the activities of Lower and Middle Paleolithic groups might mean either that they were incapable of the required mental operations or that they had the ability but lacked the incentive to apply it.

Evidence of food-sharing from the earliest period (73), of burial ritual from Middle Paleolithic times onwards, and of complex reduction sequences in the manufacture of stone artifacts, all provide varying indications of future awareness, and suggest the sort of data that might be examined in more detail to shed further light on the nature of time structures. Oldowan pebble-tool assemblages made 2,000,000 years ago would have required quite rudimentary skills, but nevertheless they indicate more elaborate mental abilities and a broader time horizon than are implied by the concept of opportunistic flaking (55). Analysis of Acheulean hand-axe assemblages made 300,000 years ago suggests that their makers were fully capable of operational thought (117), which might imply that changes in general level of intelligence were not a factor in later developments. There is also evidence for an aesthetic and symbolic sense at about this time or earlier among *Homo erectus* populations (55, 85). However, the time structures implied by the flaking of a hand-axe are not necessarily the same as those implied by human burial or representational art. For example, a skilled flintknapper can complete a hand-axe in about 5 minutes. This is the minimal time horizon implied by its manufacture. Evidence for the collection of raw materials from an exotic source prior to manufacture, anticipation of use, and curation of the implement for re-use on subsequent occasions, would all modify this assessment.

Analysis of archaeological data in these terms has hardly begun, and the direction it might take can only be indicated here in the sketchiest fashion. But there is a wide range of data sources that might be treated in this way, including reduction sequences in the manufacture of stone artifacts and evidence of their use, movements of materials over tens or hundreds of kilometers across the landscape, and evidence of symbolic and artistic behavior. Through the development of such analyses it may eventually prove possible to unify the two separate strands of the present discussion: the subjective aspect of time, time as experienced by prehistoric people, and the objective aspect, time as it affects our interpretation of prehistoric behavior.

ACKNOWLEDGMENTS

I am grateful to Roland Fletcher, Paul Halstead, Hugh Mellor, Tim Murray, and Robin Torrence for persevering with an earlier draft and for many useful comments which helped to clarify the ideas presented here. Remaining obscurities are, as always, my own responsibility.

Literature Cited

1. Abrams, P. 1982. *Historical Sociology.* Shepton Mallet, England: Open Books
2. Appadurai, A. 1981. The past as a scarce resource. *Man* (NS) 16:201–19
3. Bailey, G. N. 1981. Concepts, time-scales and explanations in economic prehistory. See Ref. 102, pp. 97–117
4. Bailey, G. N. 1981. Concepts of resource exploitation: continuity and discontinuity in palaeoeconomy. *World Archaeol.* 13: 1–15
5. Bailey, G. N., ed. 1983. *Hunter-Gatherer Economy in Prehistory.* Cambridge: Cambridge Univ. Press
6. Bailey, G. N., Carter, P. L., Gamble, C. S., Higgs, H. P. 1983. Epirus revisited: seasonality and inter-site variation in the Upper Palaeolithic of north-west Greece. See Ref. 5, pp. 64–78
7. Barnes, J. A. 1971. Time flies like an arrow. *Man* (NS) 6:537–52
8. Beales, D. 1981. *History and Biography.* Cambridge: Cambridge Univ. Press
9. Bender, B. 1978. Gatherer-hunter to farmer: a social perspective. *World Archaeol.* 10:204–22
10. Bender, B. 1981. Gatherer-hunter intensification. See Ref. 102, pp. 149–57
11. Binford, L. R. 1980. Willow smoke and dogs' tails: hunter-gatherer settlement and archaeological site formation. *Am. Antiq.* 45:4–20
12. Binford, L. R. 1981. *Bones: Ancient Men and Modern Myths.* New York: Academic
13. Binford, L. R. 1981. Behavioral archaeology and the "Pompeii Premise". *J. Anthropol. Res.* 37:195–208
14. Binford, L. R. 1982. Meaning, inference and the material record. In *Ranking, Resource and Exchange,* ed. C. Renfrew, S. Shennan, pp. 160–63. Cambridge: Cambridge Univ. Press
15. Bloch, M. 1977. The past and the present in the present. *Man* (NS) 12:278–92
16. Bonner, J. T. 1980. *The Evolution of Culture in Animals.* Princeton Univ. Press
17. Braudel, F. 1972. *The Mediterranean and the Mediterranean World in the Age of Philip II.* Transl. S. Reynolds. London: Collins. (From French) 2nd ed.
18. Braudel, F. 1981. *On History.* Transl. S. Matthews. London: Weidenfeld & Nicolson. (From French)
19. Brown, R. W. 1981. Symbolic and syntactic capacities. See Ref. 118, pp. 197–204
19a. Bruner, J. 1981. Review and prospects. See Ref. 82a, pp. 256–62
20. Butzer, K. W. 1982. *Archaeology as Human Ecology.* Cambridge: Cambridge Univ. Press
21. Carlstein, T., Parkes, D.,. Thrift, N. eds. 1978. *Timing Space and Spacing Time,* Vols. 1, 2, 3. London: Arnold
21a. Carr, E. H. 1961. *What is History?* London: Macmillan
22. Chalmers, A. F. 1976. *What is this Thing called Science?* Univ. of Queensland Press
23. Childe, V. G. 1942. *What Happened in History.* Harmondsworth: Penguin
24. Chisholm, M. 1968. *Rural Settlement and Land Use.* London: Hutchinson. 2nd ed.
25. Chorley, R. J., Haggett, P., eds. 1967. *Models in Geography.* London: Methuen
26. Clark, J. G. D. 1954. *The Study of Prehistory.* Cambridge: Cambridge Univ. Press
27. Clarke, D. L., ed. 1972. *Models in Archaeology.* London: Methuen
28. Clarke, D. L., ed. 1977. *Spatial Archaeology.* London: Academic
29. Cohen, M. N. 1977. *The Food Crisis in Prehistory.* New Haven: Yale Univ. Press
30. Crook, J. H. 1980. *The Evolution of Human Consciousness.* Oxford Univ. Press
31. Davis, D. D. 1981. *The Unique Animal.* London: Prytaneum
32. Durham, W. H. 1979. Toward a coevolutionary theory of human biology and culture. In *Evolutionary Biology and Human Social Behavior,* ed. N. A. Chagnon, W. Irons, pp. 39–59. North Scituate, Mass: Duxbury
33. Elias, N. 1982. *The Civilizing Process, Vol. 2. State Formation and Civilization.* Transl. E. Jephcott. Oxford: Blackwell. (From German)
34. Evans-Pritchard, E. E. 1940. *The Nuer.* Oxford: Clarendon
35. Evans-Pritchard, E. E. 1961. *Anthropology and History.* Manchester Univ. Press. Reprinted in *Essays in Social Anthropology,* by E. E. Evans-Pritchard, 1962, pp. 46–65. London: Faber & Faber
36. Flannery, K. V. 1967. Culture history versus cultural process: a debate in American Archaeology. In *Readings from Scientific American: New World Archaeology: Theoretical and Cultural Transformations,* ed. E. B. W. Zubrow, M. C. Fritz, J. M. Fritz, pp. 5–8. San Francisco: Freeman
37. Flannery, K. V. 1968. Archaeological systems theory and early Mesoamerica. In *Anthropological Archaeology in the Americas,* ed. B. J. Meggers, pp. 67–87.

Washington DC: Anthropol. Soc. Washington

38. Fletcher, R. J. 1977. Alternatives and differences. In *Archaeology and Anthropology: Areas of Mutual Interest,* ed. M. Spriggs, pp. 49–68. Oxford: British Archaeol. Rep. Suppl. Ser. 19

39. Fletcher, R. J. 1977. Settlement studies (micro and semi-micro). See Ref. 28, pp. 47–162

40. Fletcher, R. J. 1981. Space and community behaviour: a discussion of the form and function of spatial order in settlements. See Ref. 82a, pp. 71–110

41. Fletcher, R. J. 1981. People and space: a case study on material culture. In *Pattern of the Past,* ed. I. Hodder, G. Isaac, N. Hammond, pp. 97–128. Cambridge: Cambridge Univ. Press

42. Fraisse, P. 1963. *The Psychology of Time.* Transl. J. Leith. New York: Harpers & Row. (From French)

43. Fraser, J. T., Parkes, D., Lawrence, N. 1981. *The Study of Time.* Vol. 4. New York: Springer

44. Gamble, C. S. 1982. Interaction and alliance in palaeolithic society. *Man* (NS) 17:92–107

45. Gamble, C. S. 1983. Culture and society in the Upper Palaeolithic of Europe. See Ref. 5, pp. 201–11

46. Gardner, M. 1982. *The Ambidextrous Universe.* Harmondsworth: Penguin. 2nd. ed.

47. Gellner, E. 1982. What is structuralisme? See Ref. 95, pp. 97–123

48. Giddens, A. 1981. *A Contemporary Critique of Historical Materialism.* London: Macmillan

49. Goody, J. R. 1968. Time II, social organization. *Int. Encycl. Soc. Sci.* 16:30–42

50. Goody, J. R. 1977. *The Domestication of the Savage Mind.* Cambridge: Cambridge Univ. Press

51. Gould, S. J. 1965. Is uniformitarianism necessary? *Am. J. Sci.* 263:223–28

52. Gould, S. J. 1977. Eternal metaphors of palaeontology. In *Patterns of Evolution as Illustrated by the Fossil Record,* ed. A. Hallam, pp. 1–26. Amsterdam: Elsevier

53. Gould, S. J. 1982. *Palaeontology and macroevolutionary theory.* Presented at Darwin Centen. Conf. "Evolution of Molecules and Men," Cambridge

54. Gould, S. J., Eldredge, N. 1977. Punctuated equilibria: the tempo and mode of evolution reconsidered. *Paleobiology* 3:115–51

55. Gowlett, J. A. J. 1982. *Mental abilities of early man: a look at some hard evidence.* Presented at Ann. Meet. Br. Assoc. Adv. Sci., Liverpool

56. Haggett, P. 1965. *Locational Analysis in Human Geography.* London: Arnold

57. Haldane, J. B. S. 1956. Time in biology. *Sci. Prog.* 44:358–402

58. Hallpike, C. R. 1979. *The Foundations of Primitive Thought.* Oxford: Clarendon

59. Halstead, L. B. 1982. Evolutionary trends and the phylogeny of the Agnatha. In *Problems of Phylogenetic Reconstruction,* ed. K. A. Joysey, A. E. Friday, pp. 159–96. London: Academic

60. Hays, J. D., Imbrie, J., Shackleton, N. J. 1976. Variations in the earth's orbit: pacemaker of the ice ages. *Science* 194:1121–32

61. Higgs, E. S., ed. 1972. *Papers in Economic Prehistory.* London: Cambridge Univ. Press

62. Higgs, E. S., ed. 1975. *Palaeoeconomy.* London: Cambridge Univ. Press

63. Higgs, E. S., Jarman, M. R. 1969. The origins of agriculture: a reconsideration. *Antiquity* 43:31–41

64. Higgs, E. S., Jarman, M. R. 1975. Palaeoeconomy. See Ref. 62 pp. 1–7

65. Higgs, E. S., Vita-Finzi, C. 1972. Prehistoric economies: a territorial approach. See Ref. 61, pp. 27–36

66. Hodder, I. R. 1982. Theoretical archaeology: a reactionary view. See Ref. 67, pp. 1–16

67. Hodder, I. R., ed. 1982. *Symbolic and Structural Archaeology.* Cambridge: Cambridge Univ. Press

68. Hodder, I. R., Orton, C. R. 1976. *Spatial Analysis in Archaeology.* Cambridge: Cambridge Univ. Press

69. Holly, B. P. 1978. The problem of scale in time-space research. In *Timing Space and Spacing Time,* Vol. 3: *Time and Regional Dynamics,* ed. T. Carlstein, D. Parkes, N. Thrift, pp. 5–18. London: Arnold

70. Ingold, T. 1980. *Hunters, Pastoralists and Ranchers: Reindeer Economies and their Transformations.* Cambridge: Cambridge Univ. Press

71. Ingold, T. 1981. The hunter and his spear: notes on the cultural mediation of social and ecological systems. See Ref. 102, pp. 119–30

72. Isaac, G. Ll. 1972. Chronology and the tempo of cultural change during the Pleistocene. In *Calibration of Hominoid Evolution,* ed. W. W. Bishop, J. A. Miller, pp. 281–430. Edinburgh: Scottish Academic Press

73. Isaac, G. Ll. 1981. Archaeological tests of alternative models of early hominid

behaviour: excavation and experiments. See Ref. 118, pp. 177–88

74. Jarman, M. R., Bailey, G. N., Jarman, H. N., eds. 1982. *Early European Agriculture*. Cambridge: Cambridge Univ. Press

75. Jochim, M. A. 1982. *Strategies for Survival*. New York: Academic

76. Jochim, M. A. 1983. Palaeolithic cave art in ecological perspective. See Ref. 5, pp. 212–19

77. John, B. 1980. Measuring time past. See Ref. 112, pp. 236–84

78. Lee, R. B. 1972. Work effort, group structure and land use in contemporary hunter-gatherers. In *Man, Settlement and Urbanism*, ed. P. J. Ucko, R. Tringham, G. W. Dimbleby, pp. 177–86. London: Duckworth

79. Lee, R. B., DeVore, I., eds. 1968. *Man the Hunter*. Chicago: Aldine

80. Leone, M. P. 1978. Time in American archeology. In *Social Archeology: Beyond Subsistence and Dating*, ed. C. L. Redman, M. J. Berman, E. V. Curtin, W. Y. Langhorne Jr., N. M. Versaggi, J. C. Wanser, pp. 25–36. New York: Academic

81. Leone, M. P. 1981. Archaeology's relationship to the present and the past. In *Modern Material Culture: the Archaeology of Us*, ed. R. A. Gould, M. B. Schiffer, pp. 5–14. New York: Academic

82. Lévi-Strauss, C. 1966. *The Savage Mind*. London: Weidenfeld & Nicolson

82a. Lloyd, B., Gay, J., eds. 1981. *Universals of Human Thought*. Cambridge: Cambridge Univ. Press

83. Macfarlane, A. 1978. *The Origins of English Individualism*. Oxford: Blackwell

84. Mellor, D. H. 1973. On some methodological misconceptions. See Ref. 92, pp. 493–98. London: Duckworth

85. Oakley, K. P. 1981. Emergence of higher thought 3.0–0.2 Ma b.p. See Ref 118, pp. 205–11

86. O'Shea, J. 1981. Coping with scarcity: exchange and social storage. See Ref. 102, pp. 167–83

87. Parkes, D., Thrift, N. 1980. *Times, Spaces and Places*. Chichester: Wiley

88. Pianka, E. R. 1978. *Evolutionary Ecology*. New York: Harper & Row. 2nd ed.

89. Popper, K. R. 1957. *The Poverty of Historicism*. London: Routledge & Kegan Paul

90. Porter, R. S. 1980. The history of time. See Ref. 112 pp. 5–44

91. Radcliffe-Brown, A. R. 1952. *Structure and Function in Primitive Society*. London: Cohen & West

92. Renfrew, C., ed. 1973. *The Explanation of Culture Change*. London: Duckworth

93. Renfrew, C. 1981. Space, time and man. *T. I. Br. Geogr. NS* 6:257–78

94. Renfrew, C. 1982. *Towards an Archaeology of Mind*. Cambridge: Cambridge Univ. Press

95. Renfrew, C., Rowlands, M. J., Segrave, B. A., eds. 1982. *Theory and Explanation in Archaeology*. New York: Academic

96. Roper, D. C. 1979. The method and theory of site catchment analysis: a review. In *Advances in Archaeological Method and Theory*, ed. M. B. Schiffer, 2:119–40. New York: Academic

97. Rowlands, M. J. 1982. Processual archaeology as historical social science. See Ref. 95, pp. 155–74

98. Sahlins, M. D. 1974. *Stone Age Economics*. London: Tavistock

99. Schumm, S. A., Lichty, R. W. 1965. Time, space and causality in geomorphology. *Am. J. Sci.* 263: 110–19

100. Service, E. R. 1962. *Primitive Social Organisation*. New York: Random House

101. Service, E. R. 1966. *The Hunters*. New York: Harper & Row

102. Sheridan, A., Bailey, G. N., eds. 1981. *Economic Archaeology*. Oxford: Br. Archaeol. Rep. Int. Ser. 96

103. Thomas, N. 1981. Social theory, ecology and epistemology: theoretical issues in Australian prehistory. *Mankind* 13(2): 165–77

104. Tilley, C. Y. 1981. Economy and society: what relationship? See Ref. 102, pp. 131–48

105. Torrence, R. 1983. Time budgeting and hunter-gatherer technology. See Ref. 5, pp. 11–22

106. Trigger, B. G. 1970. Aims in prehistoric archaeology. *Antiquity* 44:26–37

107. Trigger, B. G. 1978. The future of archaeology is the past. In *Time and Traditions*, pp. 37–52. Edinburgh: Univ. Press

108. Vita-Finzi, C., Higgs, E. S., with Harriss, D., Legge, A., Sturdy, D. 1970. Prehistoric economy in the Mount Carmel area of Palestine: site catchment analysis. *Proc. Prehist. Soc.* 36:1–37

109. Watson, P. J., LeBlanc, S. A., Redman, C. L. 1971. *Explanation in Archeology*. New York: Columbia Univ. Press

110. Whitrow, G. J. 1972. *What is Time?* London: Thames & Hudson

111. Whitrow, G. J. 1980. *The Natural Philosophy of Time*. Oxford: Clarendon. 2nd ed

112. Wilson, C., consult. ed. 1980. *The Book*

of Time. North Pomfret, Vt: David & Charles

113. Wobst, H. M. 1974. Boundary conditions for paleolithic social systems: a simulation approach. *Am. Antiq.* 39:147–78

114. Wobst, H. M. 1983. Palaeolithic archaeology: some problems with form, space and time. See Ref. 5, pp. 220–25

115. Woodburn, J. 1980. Hunters and gatherers today and reconstruction of the past. In *Soviet and Western Anthropology*, ed.

E. Gellner, pp. 95–107. London: Duckworth

116. Wylie, M. A. 1982. Epistemological issues in structuralist archaeology. See Ref. 67, pp. 39–46

117. Wynn, T. 1979. The intelligence of later Acheulean hominids. *Man* (NS) 14:371–91

118. Young, J. Z., Jope, E. M., Oakley, K. P., eds. 1981. *The Emergence of Man. Philos. Trans. R. Soc. London Ser. B* 292

Ann. Rev. Anthropol. 1983. 12:193–214

CONTEMPORARY HUNTER-GATHERERS: Current Theoretical Issues in Ecology and Social Organization

Alan Barnard

Department of Social Anthropology, University of Edinburgh, Edinburgh EH8 9LL, Scotland

The purpose of this review is to highlight those issues in recent studies which I believe are potentially the most significant for the advancement of our understanding of foraging societies generally. Like Orlove's review of ecological anthropology (91, p. 235), it is "critical" rather than "encyclopedic." To narrow the topic further, my primary concern is theoretical rather than ethnographic. Yet to some extent this is a false dichotomy, since theoretical issues inevitably rest on an ethnographic foundation and ethnographic findings almost inevitably stem from theoretical interest.

A further complication arises in deciding what issues in ecology and anthropology are especially relevant to the study of contemporary hunter-gatherers, as opposed to the study of any other contemporary peoples. In his summation of the proceedings of the Second International Conference on Hunting and Gathering Societies, Bernard Arcand stated boldly that "hunting and gathering societies" did not constitute a meaningful category. If I were totally in agreement, there would be little point in my going further with this review. Yet Arcand's deliberately provocative statement represents a view with which I have some sympathy. I will save discussion of this interesting problem until the end.

Other issues currently under debate include aspects of settlement patterns, subsistence ecology and "affluence," evolution and typology (which has seen some resurgence in the past 5 years), the application of sophisticated mathematical and ecological models to ethnographic data, problems in social organiza-

193

0066–4294/83/1015–0193$02.00

tion and cognition, and Marxist approaches. Several of these issues are of direct relevance to social anthropology generally, to archaeology and ethology, and to Marxist theory.

Readers interested particularly in the application of evolutionary ecological theory to hunter-gatherer populations should consult Winterhalder & Smith's recent book (140), which contains a number of theoretical essays of interest to both archaeologists and ethnologists, as well as useful case studies. My own views are perhaps more eclectic and more skeptical of ecological models than theirs, and therefore my review touches on different problems. Nevertheless, I recommend their short essay on perspectives in hunter-gatherer socioecology (114), and a similar recent paper by Hayden (47), as complements to this review.

The Conference Milieu and the Sociology of Hunter-Gatherer Studies

It would be misleading to consider new developments in any field as isolated intellectual achievements. The exchange of ideas in hunter-gatherer studies has taken place almost as much in conference meetings as in published work. Three major conferences have been held to date: "Man the Hunter" (Chicago, 1966), the "International Conference on Hunting and Gathering Societies" (Paris, 1978), and the "Second International Conference on Hunting and Gathering Societies" (Quebec, 1980). A third "International" is planned for Munich in 1983 and a fourth for an Australian venue in 1988.

In their preface to the *Man the Hunter* volume, Lee and DeVore speculated on the reasons why the participants at that meeting had taken up the study of hunter-gatherers: "We cannot avoid the suspicion that many of us were led to live and work among hunters because of a feeling that the human condition was likely to be more clearly drawn here than among other kinds of societies" (68, p. ix). This Rousseauian notion of natural purity and cultural pollution permeates the field of hunter-gatherer studies. Foragers are perceived as more "natural" and therefore, almost contradictorally, more "human" than other branches of humanity.

The Paris "International" reawakened the "Man the Hunter" spirit, although the extravagant plans to publish the complete proceedings of that conference were never followed through. Two of the three planned volumes were abandoned, but the third (58) has now been published. It deals with *politics,* in a suitably broad sense, and contains a useful introduction (59) and some 20 papers on decision making, exchange, relations between bands, relations between the sexes, ethnicity, applied anthropology and other issues. The Quebec symposium was both more intimate and more fragmented. Participants were divided into six workshops, ranging from "Social and Symbolic Structures" to "Survival and Transformation of Hunting and Gathering Societies in

Developed Nation States." A bound collection of the papers (30) was later distributed to participants but has not been made available commercially.

In addition to these large and well-known conferences, two smaller ones on related themes were convened in Ottawa in 1965 (26) and 1966 (27). The latter was not concerned exclusively with hunting and gathering societies, but several important papers on hunter-gatherers were included (see also 19, 132). Bicchieri's volume (17), although not based on conference proceedings, also provided extremely useful ethnographic summaries which were to give a stronger basis for comparative research. Finally, in 1978 a session of the American Anthropological Association meetings in Los Angeles dealt with hunter-gatherer socioecology. In general, the papers at this symposium were more theoretical and more geared to the interests of archaeologists than were the papers of the other major conferences. Winterhalder & Smith's book (140) is based on this symposium.

Each conference has consisted, to a very great extent, of younger scholars of each successive generation. The grand old women and men of preceding generations were present too, but younger scholars made major contributions both to discussion and to the growing literature of conference papers and publications. This has given hunter-gatherer studies a vitality lacking in many other subdisciplines of anthropology. Also contributing to the development of new ideas has been the deliberate international character of the events. The Paris and Quebec conferences brought Anglophone social, cultural, and ecological anthropologists face to face with some of the intricacies of Francophone structuralist and Marxist thought.

The Demise of the Steward-Service Typology

The Steward-Service typology of band societies has been remarkably resilient. It was first formulated by Steward in a 1936 article (115), which in considerably revised form is reprinted in *Theory of Culture Change* (117, pp. 122–50). It was later modified by Service (107), but its fatal flaw, the supposed widespread existence of the "patrilineal" or "patrilocal" band, still remained.

Briefly, Steward's original formulation (115) recognizes three types: patrilineal band societies, composite band societies, and matrilineal band societies. Steward tries to show that the patrilineal type is the most common. Patrilineal bands are defined as "politically autonomous, communally land owning, exogamous, patrilocal, patrilineal in land inheritance, and consisting theoretically or actually of a single lineage, which, however, comprises several households or elemental bilateral families" (115, p. 331). His examples include "N. W. Bushmen," Pygmy groups, Australian Aborigines, the Ona, and various California Indian groups.

Steward defines composite bands as "nonexogamous, bilateral in descent, lacking in rule of residence and consisting of several independent families"

(115, p. 331). In general, they are larger in population than patrilineal bands and occupy larger territories. His examples include "Southern Bushmen" generally, the Andaman Islanders, and a number of Canadian subarctic societies. Matrilineal band societies are not discussed and no examples are given, although uxorilocal residence is shown to affect group composition in societies otherwise classified as patrilineal or composite. Steward's theoretical interest in this paper is in trying to show the conditions under which each pattern can be expected to develop.

The most significant innovation in Steward's later version of this typology is his discussion of the uniqueness of Shoshonean band structure (117, pp. 101–21) in terms of his concept of "sociocultural integration" (116; 117, pp. 43–63). In hindsight, it was prophetic that Steward's own ethnographic region should yield an aberrant case. For in the 1960s and 1970s it would be shown by later fieldworkers that his orginal noncomposite, "patrilineal" type contains as many aberrant examples as typical ones.

In the meantime, Service (107, pp. 59–109) refined the model. His "patrilocal" band societies include essentially the same ones as Steward's "patrilineal." The new label is in some cases more accurate, but still misleading, and the weakness in the overall classification is demonstrated by Service's qualifications. The Philippine Negritos and the Semang are classified as "patrilocal," even though "the evidence is not very clear" (107, p. 62). For African Pygmies, "It could be argued that the patrilocal band organization was borrowed from the Negroes, or imposed by them" (pp. 62–63). Likewise, the "patrilocal" Bushmen "probably are not good examples of either patrilocal or composite bands" (p. 63). Service's later popular book on hunting peoples perpetuates the myth of the patrilocal band, even in its revised edition (108).

Service's "composite" type, although theoretically identical with Steward's, is shown to include peoples whom Service believes were originally patrilocal (or at least noncomposite): the Algonkians, Athapaskans, Yahgan, and Andaman Islanders (107, pp. 84–94). The Eskimo, together with the Shoshone, are classified as "anomalous" (107, pp. 94–107). In short, Steward and Service sowed the seeds for the destruction of their own model, but at the same time remained committed to its empirically groundless assumptions.

Yet in spite of this, their efforts were of great benefit. Their ideas helped to generate an unprecedented enthusiasm for ecological anthropology in general and hunter-gatherer studies in particular among young anthropologists of the 1960s and 1970s (28, p. 4). During this period, new generations of scholars gave the *coup de grace* to the patrilocal model. All over the world, societies of small community size were shown to be neither essentially virilocal nor patrilineal in any sense. "Flux," "flexibility," and "fluidity" became the new buzz words to describe their social organization (see e.g. 69, pp. 7–12).

Even so, this view is not shared by all scholars. On the basis of statistical cross-cultural comparisons, Ember (36, 37; cf Martin & Stewart 78) has tried to resurrect the patrilocal model: "Specifically, the data suggest that, contrary to current opinion, recent hunter-gatherers are typically patrilocal, typically have men contributing relatively more to subsistence than women, and typically have had fairly frequent warfare" (37, p. 447). What she fails to take into account is the inaccuracy of the early ethnographies on which her *Ethnographic Atlas* sample is based. The Nharo (Naron) and Hadza (Hatsa), for example, are cited in the *Atlas* as "virilocal" (88, p. 62), whereas recent ethnography (14, 141) suggests otherwise. Probably many more similar examples exist.

The Original Affluent Society

The ethnographic studies of the early 1960s led not only to the destruction of the old model (that of Steward and Service), but also to the generation of new ones. One such model emphasized the economic and social *advantages* of hunting and gathering and completely reversed the exaggerated assumption that foragers were perpetually on the verge of starvation, had little leisure time, and therefore failed to develop the forms of social organization associated with supposedly more advantageous means of production. On the contrary, foragers were more affluent than the armchair speculators had realized.

The data came from many societies, but probably none had more impact than the work of Marshall and Lee. Marshall's famous "Sharing, Talking, and Giving" paper (76) emphasized the exchange relations which redistribute wealth among the !Kung. Lee (60–64) in turn supplied the concrete evidence for !Kung leisure: the fact that each adult !Kung spends only two or three hours per day in activities directly related to subsistence. Initially this finding was derived from only a very limited period of detailed observation and based on a rather narrowly defined notion of "subsistence activity." But it was significant nevertheless, given the expectations of those who had assumed (without any evidence at all) that hunting and gathering were labor-intensive activities.

Although Lee, Marshall, and others provided the data, the most articulate formulation of the theory of hunter-gatherer affluence was that of Sahlins (101; 102; 103, pp. 1–39). He distinguishes two kinds of affluence: "the Galbraithian way" and "the Zen road to affluence." The former is the conventional conception which assumes that man's needs are great but his means limited. In this sense affluence is measured only in terms of goods produced or procured. Such a concept is applicable to the way in which people in market economies think, but not to most hunter-gatherer world views. Instead, foragers are prime exponents of "the Zen road to affluence." They do not value the accumulation of material goods. They are affluent because their needs are few and are easily satisfied by a relatively meager amount of labor time.

Sahlins attacks the ethnocentrism of earlier writers. *Bourgeois ethnocentrism,* he says, has led scholars to overemphasize material wealth in their formalist definitions of affluence. Likewise, *neolithic ethnocentrism* has given us a misleading picture of the development of agriculture. Far from reducing the amount of labor, the Neolithic Revolution demanded *more* labor than had previous, foraging lifestyles.

Settlement Patterns and Levels of Socioterritorial Organization

Ever since Mauss's pioneering essay on the Central Eskimo (80, 81), settlement patterns and socioterritorial organization have been dominant interests in the study of North American hunter-gatherers. Mauss attributed the causes of seasonal dispersal and aggregation to environmental factors and saw the effects in social differences, e.g. the simple, private religious observances of Eskimo summer family groups versus the ceremonial occasions of the winter band aggregations. Later writers on the Eskimo have stressed regional differences (e.g. 9, 25, 29).

In the 1960s and 1970s similar approaches were applied to subarctic ethnography (e.g. 49, 50, 57, 82, 98, 99, 112). Increasing emphasis was placed on task groups and on the definition of levels of organization in both kinship composition and territorial exploitation. The ethnography of other regions lagged far behind. Writing in 1963, Meggitt laments: "The blankest pages in our ledger are those dealing with [Australian] Aboriginal local organization" (83, p. 214). Although the problem was clearly evident in the 1960s, it is only relatively recently that Australianists have managed to redress this balance and concentrate more on empirical over ideological aspects of territorial organization (e.g. 92, 93, 148) or on the interrelations *between* these aspects of territorial organization (e.g. 121, 129).

Paralleling such ethnographic studies there is today a greater interest in models drawn not only from the study of human populations, but from work in animal ecology as well. Wilmsen (139), for example, utilizes Horn's (53) territorial model derived from the study of blackbirds. Wilmsen argues that stable food resources (e.g. evenly distributed vegetable foods) are best procured from dispersed locations and that unpredictably located food resouces (e.g. mobile herds of game) are best procured from centralized locations.

Similarly, Smith (113), drawing on a review of literature on animal feeding strategies (105), suggests a number of factors relating to group formation. He mentions three broad areas which entail these relations. In the first instance, aggregation may be of no benefit or even disadvantageous for foraging efficiency, while having compensatory benefits for the avoidance of predators, the defense of resources (cf 32) or reproductive strategies (cf 137, 138). In the second instance, groups may aggregate not because aggregation is beneficial in itself, but because a concentration of resources brings individuals or small groups together where such resources are located (cf 42, 147). This model, which is not unlike central place theory (23) in geography, would apply for example to Shoshone pinion harvests and fish runs or to !Kung aggregations at permanent waterholes in the dry season. The third and most complicated possibility is that aggregation in itself is directly advantageous for foraging activities. Smith cites as possible reasons increased encounter rate, increased capture rate, increased prey size taken, reduction in foraging area overlap, passive information sharing, active information sharing, and risk aversion.

Smith further discusses these models in terms of their application to ethnographic cases, with groupings or aggregations of varying sizes. He distinguishes four levels which he says should occur in all hunter-gatherer populations: "foraging groups" (task groups), "resource-sharing groups" (camps or local bands without territorial identity), "information-sharing groups" (not really groups at all, but networks), and "coresident groups" (any level of group which resides at a particular place at a particular time). Ironically, this applicative aspect of Smith's work tells us essentially that ethnographers have been on the right track all along in their empirical characterizations of group structure.

The next logical development in models of local organization would be the exploration of still more deductive procedures, based on the notion of logical possibilities. This may be of significant theoretical interest, especially to archaeologists who presently hover between trendy ethnographic analogies and antiquated "if I were a horse" methods of deduction. To take an example, with one relevant environmental factor (e.g. the seasonal distinction summer/winter) and one variable of social organization (aggregation/dispersal), four patterns of seasonal settlement could be generated (including permanent aggregation and permanent dispersal). All four can be found among Kalahari Bushman groups (12). If we add a second variable (e.g. upland/coastal lowland), 16 patterns are generated. While some of these may be unlikely, the probability is that more than just one, say, the summer-upland-dispersal/winter-coastal-aggregation model derived from Clark's (24) interpretation of Star Carr, will be viable.

Comparative Studies

THREE STYLES OF COMPARISON   It is impossible to establish ecological correlations without cross-cultural comparison, although some ethnographers have tried. Those who have grounded their theories about the relationship between environment and social organization in a comparative framework have employed three logically distinct methods: illustrative comparison, regional comparison, and global-sample comparison (104, pp, 53–74).

In ecological anthropology, illustrative comparison is a frequently used but dangerous technique. It is characterized by the use of casual or unsystematically chosen examples to illustrate, rather than test, hypotheses. The danger is that authors frequently assume that they *are* testing their hypotheses or finding correlations where none exist. Bicchieri (16), for example, compares three

African foraging societies: the net-hunting Mbuti, the Hadza, and some un-differentiated southern Bushman groups. His chosen variable is permissiveness of environment (that of the Mbuti is most permissive and that of the Bushmen is least permissive). Many of his specific comparisons do yield interesting ideas for future research. Nevertheless, these three cases constitute neither an ethnographic region nor a global sample. A regional-comparative study of Bushman societies would yield examples which are not consistent with his generalizations on ritual and belief, for example. Such a study of Bushman groups might effectively limit the number of ecological and cultural variables where Bicchieri's study does not; only then could a full explanation of causa-tive factors begin. Alternatively, a global sample of a statistically significant number of cases might yield a similar basis for correlative explanation.

In an earlier paper (12, pp. 131–32), I criticized Yellen (146, p. 48) on similar grounds. He suggests that a careful comparison of his own very thorough data on the !Kung with those of Gould (41) on Western Desert Aborigines would give correlations between the distribution of resources and settlement patterns. I argue that this is not the case. The !Kung, as Yellen notes, aggregate in the dry season and disperse in the wet season, but so do some Western Desert Aboriginal groups. Gould's Aborigines aggregate in the wet season and disperse in the dry season, but so do various Bushman groups not mentioned by Yellen (see e.g. 110, 119). Evidence for microenvironmental causes for radically different settlement patterns is strong for the Bushman, but the illustrative method will not provide it.

Even so, careful illustrative comparison with more limited objectives can raise interesting issues. Peterson's (94) discussion of territorial adaptations among the !Kung and Australian Aborigines is a case in point. He argues convincingly that there is greater similarity between the !Kung and desert Aborigines (Pintupi, Walpiri, and Aranda) than has often been supposed. Specifically, similarities in territorial organization have been obscured "be-cause the behaviour of the one people [!Kung] has been compared with the ideology of the other" (94, p. 124). While recognizing the obvious differences, Peterson suggests that there are marked similarities, both in rights in residence and resource allocation, and in the ways in which the two societies cope with demographic fluctuation. In a similar way, Turner's (127, 128, 130, 131) ingenious comparisons of Cree and Australian Aborigines have generated a new paradigm for the study of hunter-gatherer (and non–hunter-gatherer) social formations. This paradigm is based on the opposition between "kinship-confederational" (Australian) and "locality-incorporative" (Cree) principles. Although its use in limited comparative studies does not lead directly to any correlations, it has suggested new ways of approaching kinship, settlement patterns, and mythology.

Both global-sample comparison and regional comparison are superior to illustrative comparison for finding correlations. However, the global-sample method also has its drawbacks. Choosing a sample is the main problem. It must be suitably large, suitably global, and suitably diverse to offset the coincidence of common origin or diffusion between contiguous societies. Murdock, the founder of the method, has been well aware of this problem (88, pp. 1–6; 89).

REGIONAL COMPARATIVE STUDIES   The method of regional comparison implies careful control. It is conceivable that controlled comparison would not have to be regionally based, but certainly it is safer if it is. As I have argued above, two demographically similar hunter-gatherer populations do not constitute a controlled sample any more than do three disparate African foraging populations.

In the 1972 issue of the *Annual Review of Anthropology*, Heider (48, pp. 213–17) commends four "attempts to make environment the independent variable." Three of these deal with hunter-gatherers (29, 100, 126). Surprisingly, given the amount of data now available, few have followed this course. However, two attempts have been made with Kalahari Bushman data (12, 21), one with northern North American data (97), and one with Fuegian data (118), each of which has yielded interesting results and new theoretical insights. Stuart's paper (118) is particularly significant. Comparing the Ona and the Yahgan, he demonstrates the incompleteness of the patrilineal/composite distinction and substitutes a notion of flux between two ideal types: homeostatic and disequilibrium. The "patrilineal" bands of the Ona are seen as forming part of a relatively homeostatic system in which a small, transhumant human population hunted small herds of game. In contrast, the apparently "composite" features of Yahgan social organization, i.e. bilaterality, neolocality, a lack of local exogamy, and high population aggregates in outlying areas, imply a state of social disequilibrium possibly resulting from changes in environmental circumstances. Insights such as this are at least as likely to emerge from regional comparison as from more comprehensive but less detailed surveys of the entire world.

Marxist Approaches

The last two decades have seen a growing interest in Marxist theory in anthropology, and with it a growing confusion about its applicability to the study of hunter-gatherers. Marxist anthropology is often quite far removed from Marx's own interests; it has come to mean the science of applying rather nebulous underlying principles of dialectical materialism to ethnographic reporting and interpretation. This is all the more problematic when dealing with classless societies: either they are vestiges of a "primitive communist" mode of production (51, 56, 65, 66), or class-like structures based on age or sex must be found to complete the dialectic. Fortunately, Marxist hunter-gatherer specialists, unlike some of their West Africanist colleagues, have steered clear of the latter approach.

Instead, two general schools of thought have emerged, each of which claims to follow the spirit rather than the letter of Marx's *Capital*. I shall refer to these schools as "land and labor" and "structural and ecological" Marxism respectively.

LAND AND LABOR MARXISM   Meillassoux's (85–87) analysis of foraging society rests on Marx's (79, vol. I, pp. 174–80) distinction between land as an instrument of labor (in agricultural societies) and land as a subject of labor (in foraging societies). On the latter Meillassoux comments"

> It is sufficient for present purposes to say that the use of land as a *subject of labour* fosters a type of "instantaneous" production whose output is immediately available, allowing a process of *sharing* which takes place at the end of each enterprise. The hunters, once they share the common product, are free from any further reciprocal obligations or allegiance. The process gives no ground for the emergence of a social hierarchy or of a centralised power, or even the extended family organisation. The basic social unit is an equalitarian but unstable band with little concern for biological or social reproduction (86, p. 99; italics in original).

In contrast, the use of land as an instrument of labor "introduces a radical change into the entire social, political and ideological structures" (86, p. 99).

The distinction is important *for Meillassoux* as part of his argument that the development of agriculture implies control over people (the means of production) rather than simply control over land (the means of material reproduction). "Kinship," in the sense of family and lineage as productive units, emerges only with the development of agriculture and its consequent accumulation of surplus [for an alternative but complementary view, see (13, 15)]. Yet Meillassoux's paper is important *for hunter-gatherer studies* for a different reason, specifically for drawing attention to the fact that foraging economies are based on rights of access to land, rights to shared resources through various forms of exchange, and the relatively egalitarian forms of social structure (relations of production) which permit such economic activities. Meillassoux's assessment of the forager/nonforager or forager/postforager dichotomy foreshadows both Woodburn's typology of band societies (142, 144, 145) and recent ethnographic and theoretical discussions of forager, and particularly Bushman, reciprocity [(20, 31, 135, 136); for an overview of sharing customs in foraging societies, see (95)].

STRUCTURAL AND ECOLOGICAL MARXISM   Like Meillassoux, Godelier is an ethnographer of cultivators and a theorist on foragers. Both Meillassoux (85, 86) and Godelier (38, pp. 66–82; 39; 40, pp. 51–62) offer reanalyses of

Turnbull's (125) sketchy but nicely written Mbuti material and argue a case for the relative kinshiplessness of hunter-gatherers. Yet the theoretical work of Godelier and his followers is on the whole different from Meillassoux's, for it entails a more sophisticated understanding of ecological effects on social organization and an obvious debt to the best of both British functionalism and French structuralism. These debts and the apparent similarity between Godelier's approach and that of the substantivists have left Godelier seemingly vulnerable to Marvin Harris's recent attack (46, pp. 216–57). Godelier's structural Marxist approach is very different from Harris's infrastructural reductionism (see 90), and from Sahlins's substantivism as well (see 73), although there *are* peculiar similarities between Marxist and Stewardian theories of society.

Steward's "levels of sociocultural integration" (116; 117, pp. 43–63) resemble the Marxist notion (or notions) of "modes of production." Steward's "cultural core" (117 *passim*) and the implicit residual category of "cultural periphery" represent respectively notions not unlike "infrastructure" and "superstructure." Testart (120, 122, 123), a member of Godelier's *équipe*, has been particularly concerned with theoretical problems closely related to those in Steward's work, while other French writers, e.g. Bahuchet (5–8) in his descriptions of the Aka Pygmies, are pursuing practical research interests in the mainstream of cultural ecology.

The *differences* between Stewardian and Marxist views emerge when we look at concepts of evolution. Steward's "multilinear" evolutionism denies the utility of any concept of stages of evolution, which is so crucial to the Marxist interpretation of history (if not to Marxist interpretations of particular social formations). In Steward's view, the broad "universal" stages postulated by Leslie White and V. Gordon Childe "are so general that they are neither very arguable nor very useful" (117, p. 16), while nineteenth century "unilinear" evolutionism can be readily dismissed on empirical grounds. Modern Marxism wavers somewhere between universal and unilinear evolutionism, or even denies any commitment to determinist concepts of evolution (4, 71).

In my view, these different yet convergent interrests of cultural ecology and ecological Marxism highlight the incompleteness of both perspectives as presently formulated. There are two areas in which a more radical move away from incipient environmental and technological determinsim and evolutionism might be of benefit to Marxist analysis. The first is in the area of social transformation, where Marxism needs to be liberated from such ethnocentric notions as "precapitalist society." This notion is literally meaningless except in terms of an assumed norm of captialism, and its use implies a unilinear or universal evolutionary dichotomy (precapitalist/captialist) which is of very little significance for the study of the range of variation in human society.

The second area in which I would argue for a bolder approach is in the assessment of the relative importance of superstructure and infrastructure. Although cultural ecologists and Marxists agree on the primacy of infrastructure, the "cultural core," Marxists today are showing considerably greater interest in superstructure than cultural ecologists ever have. The problem is that there is still a tendency to regard these elements of culture as "peripheral"; this is a strange thing given that Marxism purports to be a theory of history. The fact is that Steward's phraseology is very misleading. It could be argued that the really central elements of a culture are those which are *not* affected by changes in environmental circumstances or technology, rather than those which are so affected. Social organization (perceived by Marxists as part superstructure and part infrastructure) is determined both by environmental constraints and by relatively fixed ideological premises, which will be found cross-culturally within a culture area and through time within a particular culture. This point comes out most clearly in Australian Aboriginal ethnography (74, 84).

The whole area of ecological and Marxist interpretations of social organization is presently one of major theoretical debate. Abruzzi (1, 2) propounds population pressure determinism and attacks Turnbull (126) for failing to provide evidence that the environment is as permissive as he (Turnbull) maintains, or that flux is a cultural rather than an ecological phenomenon. Godelier (39) finds the contradictions not in Turnbull's writings but in Mbuti society. He attacks cultural ecology for failing to see that classless foraging societies are sometimes plagued by contradictions between production and ideology. Legros (72) assesses precisely similar contradictions in Nunamiut society and argues that flexible and cognatic group structure hinders the cooperation required for collective hunting. Balikci (11) defends the traditional ecological perspective and charges Legros and Godelier with putting lofty theories ahead of the facts. Using a more empirical approach, he then comes to a conclusion not unlike that of Godelier and Legros. For Balikci the contradiction in foraging society, or at least in his Netsilik data, is between the rigid egalitarianism of the ideology and the "pecking order" hierarchy which can be observed in individual behavior (cf 10, pp. 173–93). The situation may be much more complicated in other foraging societies, however, as Biesele (18) and Silberbauer (111) show in their studies of Bushman political pressures (cf 64, 70, 77).

New Typologies

With the Steward-Service typology in tatters, a number of new typologies have appeared: Woodburn's (142, 144, 145), Testart's (123) and two by Watanabe (133, 134). Their significance lies not so much in classification in its own right, but rather in the issues which stem from the typology-making process.

WOODBURN'S TYPOLOGY   Woodburn has drafted a "preliminary formulation" (144, p. 115) of a bipolar typology: immediate return and delayed return.

His tentativeness refers not so much to the general distinction between these two concepts, but to the means of assessing the various ethnographies according to the distinction he draws.

Immediate-return economic systems are characterized by a behavior and attitude which rejects the notion of surplus. As Woodburn says in referernce to the Hadza, "Encumberances are unacceptable and people do not take on even short-term commitments which might provide a few additional days of desirable food" (144, p. 100).

Delayed-return systems, in contrast, allow for planning ahead. In this category are included part-time hunters, sedentary hunter-gatherers, fishermen who invest in boats or large-scale fish traps, trappers who invest in labor-intensive hunting traps, beekeepers, mounted hunters, and, perhaps anomalously (from my point of view), all Australian Aborigines. Part-time hunters are delayed return because the amounts of time and energy they put into horticulture or stock-keeping, even where these are relatively insignificant for subsistence purposes, necessitate a delayed-return social organization. Such a form of social organization, to turn the argument full circle, is one which encompasses task specialization sufficient to allow a surplus so that those engaged in long-term tasks are supported by those actively engaged in immediate pursuits. The same principle applies to the fishermen, trappers, beekeepers who use man-made hives, and hunters (such as the Plains Indians) who invest their time in keeping horses. Sedentary and semisedentary hunter-gatherers are delayed return because of the accumulation of property and of surplus which ensues from this way of life.

So why the Australian Aborigines? Woodburn's argument is that the Aboriginal men "maintain and transmit long-term rights over their female kin" and that Aboriginal social organization is "centrally and essentially connected with the maintenance, manipulation and transmission of these long-term rights" (144, p. 109). On the whole, food production in Australia resembles that of immediate-return producers in other parts of the world, but in light of Woodburn's wider view of production (which includes reproduction), Australian systems come to resemble instead those of delayed-return cultivators. In short, Australians "farm out" their women (144, pp. 108–9, cf pp. 107–11).

Significantly, Woodburn's model specifically rejects technology as a major factor and downplays the role of the environment. Societies with immediate-return systems have both the technology and the environments to engage in delayed-return activities, and delayed-return societies could similarly adapt to perform immediate-return activities. Ideology is the causative principle, although Woodburn himself emphasizes effects rather than causes. His primary interest is in the resultant forms of social organization. One of the major characteristics of immediate-return systems is their egalitarianism, which is lost in delayed-return systems (145; cf 143).

It is well worth pointing out that the immediate/delayed dichotomy is applicable not only to hunter-gatherers but to all societies. Some hunter-gatherers have immediate-return systems and others have delayed-return systems, but non–hunter-gatherers invariably and of necessity have systems of the latter type. Thus societies such as the Nuer, the Trobrianders, modern Japan, feudal Europe, subarctic Indians, and neolithic farmers are included in one type (delayed); and the !Kung, the Hadza, the Batek, the Malapantaram, and the Mbuti are included in the other (immediate).

In spite of Woodburn's tentative exposition, his theory is as bold and radical as any comparative economics has yet produced. Instead of a capitalist/precaptialist, civilized/savage, or producers/foragers dichotomy, we now have one which pushes the boundary between ourselves and our primitive contemporaries much more toward their end of the scale. This, above all else, is what makes Woodburn's typology so interesting.

TESTART'S TYPOLOGY   Testart (123), in a paper originally delivered at the Quebec conference, suggests a typology similar but with more distinctions than Woodburn's, and more clearly substantive (as oppsed to formal). Like Woodburn, he emphasizes the differences between hunting-and-gathering economies in terms of their relative reliance on non–hunting-and-gathering modes of subsistence, but he also takes particular account of the degree of contact hunter-gatherers have with herders and cultivators. Testart's paper gives a detailed account of the social organization of four types, the last including three subtypes:

Mounted hunter-gatherers of central Asia, Argentina, and the Great Plains of North America are characterized as extremely nomadic and relatively inegalitarian.

Storing hunter-gatherers include Northwest Coast Indians, western Siberians, and southeastern Siberians. These societies are characterized as sedentary, dense in population, inegalitarian, and developed in terms of exchange relations, warfare, and division of labor between the sexes.

Nonstoring, sedentary hunter-gatherers are few in number. The only definitive example cited is the Asmat of West Irian, but the semisedentary !Kung and various semiaccumulating societies are mentioned as having a tendency toward this form of socioeconomic organization. The importance of the type lies in its postulated occurrence in areas of relative abundance of resources, and therefore in its potential for the transformation to agriculture.

Nomadic hunter-gatherers are widespread but normally either "enclosed" (*enclavés*) or "circumscribed" (*circonscrits*). Enclosed nomads are egalitarian, but subordinate to the surrounding agricultural peoples on whom they depend for technology and trade. Typically, they use the language of and share other aspects of culture with their dominant neighbors. Examples include most Asian hunter-gatherers, African Pygmies, and the Bushmen of Angola. In contrast, circumscribed nomads are not economically or culturally dependent upon their neighbors. They occupy the marginal, less-fertile territories not utilzed by cultivators or pastoralists. Examples include North and South American hunter-gatherers and the Bushmen of southern Africa. Testart's residual subcategory of "others" belongs to the Australian Aborigines, characterized by cultural isolation and homogeneity.

Interestingly, both Woodburn's and Testart's typologies take the accumulation of surplus as the single most important typological distinction. Yet accumulation is seen as important not in its own right, but either as a result of a changing ethos which marks the difference between immediate-return systems and all others, or as a prerequisite for the transformations leading to social hierarchy. Though in my view less interesting for anthropology generally, Testart's classification is more directly relevant to the understanding of contemporary hunter-gatherer social organization. Ironically though, Testart himself sees the typology as a step toward refuting the existence of a "Neolithic Revolution" (123, pp. 213–15; cf 122, 124). He holds that surplus in foraging societies creates social hierarcy [for a contrasting view, see (65, 66)].

WATANABE'S TYPOLOGIES   Typologies which recognize a category of hunting and gathering societies either as a type itself or as a universe within which types are delimited are usually formulated either on the basis of mode of production (e.g. Woodburn's, Testart's) or on the basis of settlement pattern or social organization generally (e.g. Steward's, Service's, and the implicit typologies of those writers who speak of "band societies"). Watanabe's first typology (133, p. 70), proposed at the "Man the Hunter" conference, is of the latter kind. In this typology he recognizes six main types or a total of eight subtypes of hunter-gatherer social structure. Their defining characteristics stem from the relation between the seasonal cycle and what he terms the "residential shift patterns." The six or eight types are ordered on a scale of increasing residential stability from fully nomadic to permanently settled. Since that typology was in Watanabe's view tentative and has now been superseded, and since it is in my view of limited value, I will not discuss it further here.

In contrast, Watanabe's 1978 (134) typology is based on a new principle, not mode of production or settlement pattern, but "food habit." This typology identifies three major types of food habit on a spectrum from largely vegetarian to largely carnivorous.

His Type I is defined as "largely vegetarian." His examples are the Semang of mainland Malaysia and the Paliyans of south India. Both populations subsist primarily on root crops. Planned hunting is only a part-time activity.

Type II, "mixed diet" peoples, includes several subtypes, but their defining feature is that planned hunting is a "full-time" activity for men. Type II-A peoples have plant foods as staples. These include Type II-A-1 peoples, those for whom small game is more important than large game (he cites the Yiwara of Australia and the Shoshone, both with seed crops as staples); and Type II-A-2 peoples, for whom large game is more important (the nut-eating Bushmen, i.e. !Kung, and the root-eating Hadza). Type II-B peoples have animal foods as staples. This type again is subdivided. Type II-B-1 includes those groups with mammals as staples (e.g. the Kutchin and the Blackfoot, both land-mammal hunters). Type II-B-2 are those with fish as staples (e.g. the Koryak of Siberia and the Sanpoil of the Northwest Coast, both salmon-eaters).

Type III is defined as "largely carnivorous." For these peoples, plant-food collecting is a negligible activity. Watanabe's examples are the Nunamiut, who subsist on land mammals, and the Tareumiut, who subsist on sea mammals.

Watanabe explicitly relates his classification of hunting-and-gathering peoples to that of animals as herbivores, omnivores, and carnivores, although the subdivisions within his Type II indicate that the problem is more complicated than this. He concludes by noting that the spectrum of variation in hunter-gatherer food habits seems to be roughly correlated with the distribution of the world's climatic zones. Relatively carnivorous peoples tend to be found in the northern hemisphere, in cool climates, whereas relatively herbivorous peoples tend to be found in the southern hemisphere, in warm climates. This could have implications for the study of human prehistory.

It is interesting that Watanabe's typology is not formulated primarily on the basis of the kinds of plants gathered or animals hunted, but rather on the relative importance of gathering and hunting activities. This suggests that social organizational features are implicit in the typology, perhaps as a result of food-procuring activities. There is no space here to consider this problem, but future comparative research might do well to take the principles of Watanabe's classification into account.

Hunter-Gatherers: A Meaningful Category?

The existence of "hunter-gatherers" as a meaningful category for research entails two general fields of inquiry: first, the extent to which hunter-gatherers can be distinguished from non–hunter-gatherers, and secondly, the extent to which this distinction in subsistence pursuits is meaningful for the comparative study of other aspects of culture. For the purpose of this review, I shall confine my comments to the first field of inquiry [cf Arcand (3), who deals with both].

Ellen (35, pp. 170–76) has recently drawn attention to the difficulty in describing subsistence pursuits:

> Much confusion has been caused in the ethnographic and comparative literature by assuming ostensibly predominant subsistence techniques represent total subsistence strategies, and by a general use of excessively simple criteria for the description of life-support techniques. For example, we happily describe Eskimo, Hadza and Tasaday as "hunter-gatherers", the

Nuaulu, Gadio Enga, Iban and Hanunoo as "swidden cultivators", when the differences between them *in purely subsistence terms* are of as much social and ecological significance as those between populations to which we attach different labels (35, p. 170; italics in original).

As the subtitle of his book suggests, Ellen is interested in "the ecology of small-scale social formations," not in a narrowly defined concept of subsistence. He argues further (35, p. 174) that such activities as collecting firewood or appropriating resources for exchange also involve social and ecological consequences. Similar points are made by David Harris (43–45) in his descriptions of subsistence and trade in the Torres Strait Islands and Cape York Peninsula. He argues that the boundary between foraging and cultivation is not easily definable, and that trade networks further blur the distinction between social types.

Ingold (54, 55) considers an analogous case for a blurred distinction between hunting and herding. In his earlier paper (54) he outlines four forms of Lappish reindeer exploitation and the transformations between them. These include the exploitation of "domesticated" deer in a hunting economy, symbiotic pastoralism (individual ownership of deer and a "social contract" between these deer and their owners), predatory pastoralism (pursuer and pursued), and true stock-rearing. In his recent book, Ingold (55) gives a more theoretical model of the relationships between land, animals, economy, and ideology. In this, he defines three oppositions: the "hunting—pastoralism—ranching triangle." His point though is less concerned with fuzzy boundaries and more with explaining the logical distinctions between ideal types, distinctions through which we can explore the complex ecological relations between men and animals.

Finally, here it is important to consider the difference between viable foraging communities and dependent fringe-camp dwellers (former hunter-gatherers who attach themselves to a wider non–hunter-gatherer society). As Sahlins (103, pp. 8–9) points out, writers have sometimes been thinking of the latter when supposedly describing the former. A danger nowadays, however, is the tendency to *overemphasize* some of the differences between "pure" and part-time foragers. In the 1960s it was taken for granted that there were three levels of acculturation among Bushmen, for example: pure hunter-gatherers, clients of black pastoralists, and clients of white ranchers (60, pp. 11–37; 109). Bushmen associated with whites were erroneously assumed to be more acculturated than Bushmen associated with blacks, and the transition from foraging to stock-keeping was erroneously assumed to be irreversible. Recent ethnography among widely separated, "acculturated" Bushman groups has shown much greater dependence on hunting and gathering than had been supposed (22, 52), just as recent archival and archaeological work suggests a long history of herders becoming foragers and foragers becoming herders (33, 75, 106). Social change and acculturation are very complex problems, as hunter-gatherer specialists are only beginning to realize.

Conclusions

As I have implied throughout, the current status of hunter-gatherer studies is in disequilibrium. The interests of specialists are divergent, models and counter-models abound, and even the existence of hunter-gatherer studies as a definable subdiscipline is being questioned. My own views on the last issue aside, this is a beneficial state of affairs for progressive work, both specialized and rein-tegrative. *Man the Hunter* (67) was hailed by some reviewers (e.g. 34, 96) as if it were almost the final word on the subject; however, the last 15 years, and especially the last 5 years, have shown that this was not the case. New paradigms and exciting new debates are still arising, and there is every sign that this will continue for a long time to come.

ACKNOWLEDGMENTS

I would like to express my gratitude to Bernard Arcand, Asen Balikci, Megan Biesele, Elizabeth Cashdan, Roy Ellen, Dominique Legros, Richard Lee, David Riches, Jiro Tanaka, Alain Testart, Edwin Wilmsen, and James Wood-burn for providing me with offprints, references, and suggestions on the preparation of this article. In addition, my special thanks to Testart and Wilmsen, who gave valuable and careful criticisms of an earlier draft, and to David Damas, who some 12 years ago first inspired my interest in this topic.

Literature Cited

1. Abruzzi, W. S. 1979. Population pressure and subsistence strategies among the Mbuti Pygmies. *Hum. Ecol.* 7:183–89
2. Abruzzi, W. S. 1980. Flux among the Mbuti Pygmies of the Ituri Forest: An ecological interpretation. In *Beyond the Myths of Culture: Essays in Cultural Materialism*, ed. E. B. Ross, pp. 3–31. New York: Academic
3. Arcand, B. 1981. The Negritos and the Penan will never be Cuiva. *Folk* 23:37–43
4. Asch, M. I. 1979. The ecological-evolutionary model and the concept of mode of production. In *Challenging Anthropology*, ed. D. H. Turner, G. A. Smith, pp. 81–99. Toronto: McGraw-Hill Ryerson
5. Bahuchet, S. 1972. Étude écologique d'un campement de Pygmées Babinga. *J. Afric. trop. bot. appl.* 19(12):509–59
6. Bahuchet, S. 1975. Ethnozoologie des pygmées Babinga de la Lobaye, République Centraficaines. In *L'Homme et l'animal: Première colloque d'ethnozoologie*, pp. 53–61. Paris: Inst. Int. Ethnosci.
7. Bahuchet, S. 1978. Les constraintes écologiques en forêt tropicale humide: L'ex-

emple des Pygmées Aka de la Lobaye. *J. agric. tradit. bot. appl.* 25(4):1–29
8. Bahuchet, S. 1979. Utilisation de l'espace forestier par les Pygmées Aka, Chasseurs-cueilleurs d'Afrique Centrale. *Inf. sci. soc. / Soc. Sci. Inf.* 18(6):999–1019
9. Balikci, A. 1968. The Netsilik Eskimos: Adaptive processes. See Ref. 67, pp. 78–82
10. Balikci, A. 1970. *The Netsilik Eskimo.* Garden City, NY: Nat. Hist. Press
11. Balikci, A. 1980. Les contradictions au sein des bandes de chasseurs-cueilleurs. *Anthropol. soc.* 4(3):75–83
12. Barnard, A. 1979. Kalahari Bushman settlement patterns. See Ref. 19, pp. 131–44
13. Barnard, A. 1978. Universal systems of kin categorization. *Afr. Stud.* 37:69–81
14. Barnard, A. 1980. Sex roles among the Nharo Bushmen of Botswana. *Africa* 50:115–24
15. Barnard, A. 1981. Universal kin categorization in four Bushman societies. *L'Uomo* 5:219–37
16. Bicchieri, M. G. 1969. A cultural ecological comparative study of three African

foraging societies. See Ref. 26, pp. 172–79

17. Bicchieri, M. G., ed. 1972. *Hunters and Gatherers Today*. New York: Holt, Rinehart & Winston

18. Biesele, M. 1978. Sapience and scarce resources: Communication systems of the !Kung and other foragers. *Inf. sci. soc. / Soc. Sci. inf.* 17(6):921–47

19. Burnham, P. C., Ellen, R. F., eds. 1979. *Social and Ecological Systems*. London: Academic. A.S.A. Monogr. 18

20. Cashdan, E. A. 1980. Egalitarianism among hunters and gatherers. *Am. Anthropol.* 82:116–20

21. Cashdan, E. A. 1983. Territoriality among human foragers: Ecological models and an application to four Bushman groups. *Curr. Anthropol.* 24:47–66

22. Childers, G. W. 1976. *Report on the Survey/Investigation of the Ghanzi Farm Basarwa Situation*. Gaborone: Gov. Printer

23. Christaller, W. 1966 (1933). *Central Places in Southern Germany*. Transl. C. W. Baskin. Englewood Cliffs, NJ: Prentice-Hall

24. Clark, G. 1954. *Excavations at Star Carr*. Cambridge, England: Cambridge Univ. Press

25. Damas, D. 1968. The diversity of Eskimo societies. See Ref. 67, pp. 111–17

26. Damas, D., ed. 1969. *Contributions to Anthropology: Band Societies*. Ottawa: Natl. Mus. Can. Bull. 228

27. Damas, D., ed. 1969. *Contributions to Anthropology: Ecological Essays*. Ottawa: Natl. Mus. Can. Bull. 230

28. Damas, D. 1969. Introduction. See Ref. 27, pp. 1–12

29. Damas, D. 1969. Environment, history, and Central Eskimo society. See Ref. 27, pp. 40–64

30. *Deuxième congrès international sur les sociétés de chasseurs-collecteurs / Second International Conference on Hunting and Gathering Societies*. 1980. Quebec: Dep. anthropol. Univ. Laval

31. Draper, P. 1978. The learning environment for aggression and anti-social behavior among the !Kung. In *Learning Non-Aggression*, ed. A. Montagu, pp. 31–53. Oxford: Oxford Univ. Press

32. Dyson-Hudson, R., Smith, E. A. 1978. Human territoriality: An ecological reassessment. *Am. Anthropol.* 80:21–41

33. Ebert, J. I. 1978. Comparability between hunter-gatherer groups in the past and present: Modernization versus explanation. *Botswana Notes Rec.* 10:19–26

34. Elkin, A. P. 1969. Review of Ref. 67. *Oceania* 40:161–62

35. Ellen, R. 1982. *Environment, Subsistence and System*. Cambridge, England: Cambridge Univ. Press

36. Ember, C. R. 1975. Residential variation among hunter-gatherers. *Behav. Sci. Res.* 10:199–227

37. Ember, C. R. 1978. Myths about hunter-gatherers. *Ethnology* 17:439–48

38. Godelier, M. 1973. *Horizon, trajets marxistes en anthropologie*. Paris: François Maspero

39. Godelier, M. 1974. *Considérations théoriques et critiques sur le problème des rapports entre l'homme et son environment*. Presented at Conf. sur l'Homme et son Environment, Paris

40. Godelier, M. 1977. *Perspectives in Marxist Anthropology*. Transl. R. Brain. Cambridge, England: Cambridge Univ. Press (Transl. of Ref. 38)

41. Gould, R. A. 1969. Subsistence behaviour among the Western Desert Aborigines of Australia. *Oceania* 39:253–74

42. Harpending, H., Davis, H. 1977. Some implications for hunter-gatherer ecology derived from the spatial structure of resources. *World Archaeol.* 8:275–86

43. Harris, D. R. 1977. Subsistence strategies across Torres Strait. In *Sunda and Sahul: Prehistoric Studies in Southeast Asia, Melanesia and Australia*, ed. J. Allen, J. Golson, R. Jones, pp. 421–63. London: Academic

44. Harris, D. R. 1978. Adaptation to a topical rain-forest environment: Aboriginal subsistence in northeastern Queensland. In *Human Behaviour and Adaptation*, ed. N. G. Blurton Jones, V. Reynolds, pp. 113–34. London: Taylor & Francis

45. Harris, D. R. 1979. Foragers and farmers in the western Torres Strait Islands: An historical analysis of economic, demographic, and spatial differentiation. See Ref. 19, pp. 75–109

46. Harris, M. 1980 (1979). *Cutural Materialism: The Struggle for a Science of Culture*. New York: Vintage Books

47. Hayden, B. 1981. Subsistence and ecological adaptations of modern hunter/gatherers. In *Omnivorous Primates: Gathering and Hunting in Human Evolution*, ed. R. S. O. Harding, G. Teleki, pp. 344–421. New York: Columbia Univ. Press

48. Heider, K. G. 1972. Environment, subsistence, and society. *Ann. Rev. Anthropol.* 1:207–26

49. Helm, J. 1961. *The Lynx Point People: Dynamics of a Northern Athapaskan Band*. Ottawa: Natl. Mus. Can. Bull. 176

50. Helm, J. 1968. The nature of Dogrib socioterritorial groups. See Ref. 67, pp. 118–26

51. Hindess, B., Hirst, P. 1975. *Pre-Capitalist Modes of Production.* London: Routledge & Kegan Paul

52. Hitchcock, R. K. 1978. *Kalahari Cattle Posts.* Gaborone: Ministry of Local Government and Lands, Republic of Botswana. 2 vols.

53. Horn, H. S. 1968. The adaptive significance of colonial nesting in the Brewers blackbird *(Euphagus cyanocephalus). Ecology* 49:682–94

54. Ingold, T. 1974. On reindeer and men. *Man* (NS) 9:523–38

55. Ingold, T. 1980. *Hunters, Pastoralists and Ranchers: Reindeer Economies and Their Transformations.* Cambridge, England: Cambridge Univ. Press

56. Keenan, J. 1977. The concept of the mode of production in hunter-gatherer societies. *Afr. Stud.* 36:57–69

57. Leacock, E. 1969. The Montagnais-Naskapi band. See Ref. 26. pp. 1–17

58. Leacock, E., Lee, R., eds. 1982. *Politics and History in Band Societies.* Cambridge, England: Cambridge Univ. Press; Paris: Éditions de la Maison des Sciences de l'Homme

59. Leacock, E., Lee, R. 1982. Introduction. See Ref. 58, pp. 1–20

60. Lee, R. B. 1965. *Subsistence ecology of !Kung Bushmen.* PhD thesis. Univ. Calif., Berkeley

61. Lee, R. B. 1968. What hunters do for a living, or, how to make out on scarce resources. See Ref. 67, pp. 30–48

62. Lee, R. B. 1969. !Kung Bushman subsistance: An input-output analysis. See Ref. 27, pp. 73–94; Ref. 132, pp. 47–79

63. Lee, R. B. 1972. Work effort, group structure and land use in contemporary hunter-gatherers. In *Man, Settlement and Urbanism,* ed. P. J. Ucko, R. Tringham, D. W. Dimbleby, pp. 177–85. London: Duckworth

64. Lee, R. B. 1979. *The !Kung San: Men, Women and Work in a Foraging Society.* Cambridge, England: Cambridge Univ. Press

65. Lee, R. B. 1980. Existe-t-il un mode de production "fourrageur"? *Anthropol. soc.* 4(3):59–74

66. Lee, R. B. 1981. Is there a foraging mode of production? *Can. J. Anthropol. / Rev. Can. Anthropol.* 2(1):13–19 (Transl. of Ref. 65)

67. Lee, R. B., DeVore, I., eds. 1968. *Man the Hunter.* Chicago: Aldine

68. Lee, R. B., DeVore, I. 1968. Preface. See Ref. 67, pp. vii–ix

69. Lee, R. B., DeVore, I. 1968. Problems in the study of hunters and gatherers. See Ref. 67, pp. 3–12

70. Lee, R. B., DeVore, I., eds. 1976. *Kalahari Hunter-Gatherers: Studies of the !Kung San and Their Neighbors.* Cambridge, Mass/London: Harvard Univ. Press

71. Legros, D. 1977. Chance, necessity, and mode of production: A Marxist critique of cultural evolutionism. *Am. Anthropol.* 79:26–41

72. Legros, D. 1978. Instrumentalismes contradictoires de la logique des idéologies dans une formation sociale Inuit aborigène. *Anthropologica* (NS) 20(1/2):145–79

73. Legros, D. Copans, J. 1976. Est-il possible de synthétiser formalisme, substantivisme et marxisme en anthropologie économique? *Rev. can. sociol anthropol. / Can. Rev. Sociol. Anthropol.* 13(4):373–86

74. Maddock, K. 1973 (1972). *The Australian Aborigines: A Portrait of Their Society.* London: Allen Lane The Penguin Press

75. Marks, S. 1972. Khoisan resistance to the Dutch in the seventeenth and eighteenth centuries. *J. Afr. Hist.* 13:55–80

76. Marshall, L. 1961. Sharing, talking, and giving: Relief of social tensions among !Kung Bushmen. *Africa* 31:231–49. Reprinted in Ref. 70, pp. 349–71; Ref. 77, pp. 287–312

77. Marshall, L. 1976. *The !Kung of Nyae Nyae.* Cambridge, Mass / London: Harvard Univ. Press

78. Martin, J. F., Stewart, D. G. 1982. A demographic basis for patrilineal hordes. *Am. Anthropol.* 84:79–96

79. Marx, K. 1970 (1867, 1893, 1894). *Capital: A Critique of Political Economy.* Transl. S. Moore, E. Aveling. London: Lawrence & Wishart. 3 vols.

80. Mauss, M., with Beuchat, H. 1905. Essai sur les variations saisonnières des sociétés eskimos: Étude de morphologie sociale. *Année sociol.* 9(1904–5): 39–132

81. Mauss, M., with Beuchat, H. 1979. *Seasonal Variations of the Eskimo: A Study in Social Morphology.* Transl. J. J. Fox. London: Routledge & Kegan Paul (Transl. of Ref. 80)

82. McKennan, R. A. 1969. Athapaskan groupings and social organization in Central Alaska. See Ref. 26, pp. 93–114

83. Meggitt, M. J. 1963. Social organization: Morphology and typology. In *Australian Aboriginal Studies,* ed. W. E. H. Stanner, H. Sheils, pp. 211–17. Melbourne: Oxford Univ. Press

84. Meggitt, M. J. 1972. Understanding Australian Aboriginal society: Kinship systems or cultural categories? In *Kinship Studies in the Morgan Centennial Year*, ed. P. Reining, pp. 64–87. Washington: Anthropol. Soc. Washington

85. Meillassoux, C. 1967. Recherche d'un niveau de détermination dans la société cynégétique. *Homme et soc.* 6:95–105

86. Meillassoux, C. 1972. From reproduction to production. *Econ. Soc.* 1:93–105

87. Meillassoux, C. 1973. On the mode of production of the hunting band. In *French Perspectives in African Studies*, ed. P. Alexandre, pp. 187–203. London: Oxford Univ. Press for Int. Afr. Inst. (Transl. of Ref. 85)

88. Murdock, G. P. 1967. *Ethnographic Atlas*. Pittsburgh: Univ. Pittsburgh Press

89. Murdock, G. P. 1972. Anthropology's mythology. *Proc. R. Anthropol. Inst. 1971*, pp. 17–24

90. O'Laughlin, B. 1975. Marxist approaches in anthropology. *Ann. Rev. Anthropol.* 4:341–70

91. Orlove, B. S. 1980. Ecological anthropology. *Ann. Rev. Anthropol.* 9:235–73

92. Peterson, N. 1975. Hunter-gatherer territoriality: The perspective from Australia. *Am. Anthropol.* 77:53–68

93. Peterson, N. 1978. *Rights, residence and the relevance of flux in Australia*. Presented at Int. Conf. Hunting Gathering Soc., Paris

94. Peterson, N. 1979. Territorial adaptations among desert hunter-gatherers: The !Kung and Australians compared. See Ref. 19, pp. 111–29

95. Price, J. A. 1975. Sharing: The integration of intimate economies. *Anthropologica* (NS) 17(1):3–27

96. Reynolds, V. 1969. Review of Ref. 67. *Man* (NS) 4:658–60

97. Riches, D. 1982. *Northern Nomadic Hunter-Gatherers: A Humanistic Approach*. London: Academic

98. Rogers, E. S. 1963. *The Hunting Group—Hunting Territory Complex among the Mistassini Indians*. Ottawa: Natl. Mus. Can. Bull. 195

99. Rogers, E. S. 1969. Band organization among the Indians of Eastern Subarctic Canada. See Ref. 26, pp. 21–50

100. Rogers, E. S. 1969. Natural environment—social organization—witchcraft: Cree versus Ojibwa—a test case. See Ref. 27, pp. 24–39

101. Sahlins, M. D. 1968. Notes on the original affluent society. See Ref. 67, pp. 85–89

102. Sahlins, M. D. 1968. La première société d'abundance. *Les Temps modernes* 268 (Oct.):641–80

103. Sahlins, M. D. 1972. *Stone Age Economics*. Chicago/New York: Aldine-Atherton

104. Šarana, G. 1975. *The Methodology of Anthropological Comparisons*. Tucson: Univ. Ariz. Press (*Viking Fund Publ. Anthropol.* 53)

105. Schoener, T. W. 1971. Theory of feeding strategies. *Ann. Rev. Ecol. Syst.* 2:369–404

106. Schrire, C. 1980. An inquiry into the evolutionary status and apparent identity of San hunter-gatherers. *Hum. Ecol.* 8:9–32

107. Service, E. R. 1962. *Primitive Social Organization: An Evolutionary Perspective*. New York: Random House

108. Service, E. R. 1979. *The Hunters*. Englewood Cliffs, NJ: Prentice-Hall. 2nd ed.

109. Silberbauer, G. B. 1965, *Report to the Government of Bechuanaland on the Bushman Survey*. Gaberones: Gov. Printer

110. Silberbauer, G. B. 1981. *Hunter and Habitat in the Central Kalahari Desert*. Cambridge, England: Cambridge Univ. Press

111. Silberbauer, G. B. 1982. Political process in G/wi bands. See Ref. 58, pp. 23–36

112. Slobodin, R. 1962. *Band Organization of the Peel River Kutchin*. Ottawa: Natl. Mus. Can. Bull. 179

113. Smith, E. A. 1981. The application of optimal foraging theory to the analysis of hunter-gatherer group size. See Ref. 140, pp. 36–65

114. Smith, E. A., Winterhalder, B. 1981. New perspectives on hunter-gatherer socioecology. See Ref. 140, pp. 1–12

115. Steward, J. H. 1936. The economic and social basis of primitive bands. In *Essays in Anthropology in Honor of Alfred Louis Kroeber*, pp. 331–50. Berkeley: Univ. Calif. Press

116. Steward, J. H. 1951. Levels of sociocultural integration: An operational concept. *Southwest. J. Anthropol.* 7:374–90

117. Steward, J. H. 1955. *Theory of Culture Change: The Methodology of Multilinear Evolution*. Urbana: Univ. Ill. Press

118. Stuart, D. E. 1980. Kinship and social organization in Tierra del Fuego: Evolutionary consequences. In *The Versatility of Kinship*, ed. L. S. Cordell, S. Beckerman, pp. 269–84. New York: Academic

119. Tanaka, J. 1980 (1971). *The San, Hunter-Gatherers of the Kalahari: A Study in Ecological Anthropology*. Transl. D. W. Hughes. Tokyo: Univ. Tokyo Press

120. Testart, A. 1977. Les chasseurs-cueilleurs dans la perspective écologi-

que. *Inf. sci. soc / Soc. Sci. Inf.* 16(3/4):389–418

121. Testart, A. 1978. Bandes et clans en Australie: Pourquoi des clans patrilinéaires et localisés? *J. Soc. Océanistes* 34(61): 147–59

122. Testart, A. 1979. Pourquoi les sociétés de chasseurs-cueilleurs sont-elles des sociétés sans classes? *Anthropol. soc.* 3(1):181–89

123. Testart, A. 1981. Pour une typologie des chasseurs-cueilleurs. *Anthropol. soc.* 5(2):177–221

124. Testart, A. 1982. The significance of food storage among hunters and gatherers: Residence patterns, population densities, and social inequalities. *Curr. Anthropol.* 23:523–37

125. Turnbull, C. M. 1965. *Wayward Servants: The Two Worlds of the African Pygmies.* Garden City, NY: Nat. Hist. Press

126. Turnbull, C. M. 1968. The importance of flux in two hunting societies. See Ref. 67, pp. 132–37

127. Turner, D. H. 1978. Ideology and elementary structures. *Anthropologica* (NS) 20(1/2):223–47

128. Turner, D. H. 1978. *Dialectics in Tradition: Myth and Social Structure in Two Hunter-Gatherer Societies.* London: R. Anthropol. Inst. (Occas. Pap. 36)

129. Turner, D. H. 1980. *Australian Aboriginal Social Orgnization.* Canberra: Aust. Inst. Aboriginal Stud.; New York: Humanities Press

130. Turner, D. H., Wertman, P. 1977. *Shamattawa: The Structure of Social Relations in a Northern Algonkian Band.* Ottawa: Natl. Mus. Man, Mercury Ser.

131. Turner, D. H., Wertman, P. 1978. *A model of band societies.* Presented at Int. Conf. Hunting Gathering Soc., Paris

132. Vayda, A. P., ed. 1969. *Environment and Cultural Behavior.* New York: Nat. Hist. Press

133. Watanabe, H. 1968. Subsistence and ecology of northern food gatherers with special reference to the Ainu. See Ref. 67, pp. 69–77

134. Watanabe, H. 1978. Systematic classification of hunter-gatherers' food habits: An ecological-evolutionary perspective. *Minzokugaku Kenkyu* 43(2):111–37 (full text in Japanese, with English summary and tables)

135. Wiessner, P. W. 1977. *Hxaro: A regional system of reciprocity for reducing risk among the !Kung San.* PhD thesis. Univ. Mich., Ann Arbor. 2 vols

136. Wiessner, P. W. 1982. Risk, reciprocity, and social influence on !Kung San economics. See Ref. 58, pp. 61–84

137. Williams, B. J. 1968. The Birhor of India and some comments on band organization. See Ref. 67, pp. 126–31

138. Williams, B. J. 1974. *A Model of Band Society.* Washington: Soc. Am. Archaeol. Mem. 29. *Am. Antiq.* 39(4), Pt. 2, Mem. 29

139. Wilmsen, E. N. 1973. Interaction, spacing, behavior and the organization of hunting bands. *J. Anthropol. Res.* 29:1–31

140. Winterhalder, B., Smith, E. A., eds. 1981. *Hunter-Gatherer Foraging Strategies: Ethnographic and Archaeological Analysis.* Chicago/London: Univ. Chicago Press

141. Woodburn, J. 1968. Stability and flexibility in Hadza residential groupings. See Ref. 67, pp. 103–10

142. Woodburn, J. 1978. *Sex roles and the division of labour in hunting and gathering societies.* Presented at Int. Conf. Hunting Gathering Soc., Paris

143. Woodburn, J. 1979. Minimal politics: The political organization of the Hadza of North Tanzania. In *Politics in Leadership: A Comparative Perspective,* ed. W. A. Shack, P. S. Cohen, pp. 244–66. Oxford: Clarendon

144. Woodburn, J. 1980. Hunters and gatherers today and reconstruction of the past. *Soviet and Western Anthropology,* ed. E. Gellner, pp. 95–117. London: Duckworth

145. Woodburn, J. 1982. Egalitarian societies. *Man* (NS) 17:431–51

146. Yellen, J. E. 1976. Settlement patterns of the !Kung: An archaeological perspective. See Ref. 70, pp. 47–72

147. Yellen, J. E., Harpending, H. C. 1972. Hunter-gatherer populations and archaeological inference. *World Archaeol.* 4: 244–53

148. Yengoyan, A. A. 1976. Structure, event and ecology in Aboriginal Australia: A comparative viewpoint. In *Tribes and Boundaries in Australia,* ed. N. Peterson, pp. 121–32. Canberra: Aust. Inst. Aboriginal Stud.

Ann. Rev. Anthropol. 1983. 12:215-58

CURRENT DIRECTIONS IN WEST AFRICAN PREHISTORY

S. K. McIntosh and R. J. McIntosh

Department of Anthropology, Rice University, Houston, Texas 77251

INTRODUCTION

The tempo of prehistoric research in Africa has quickened remarkably during the past decade, necessitating important revisions in our understanding of the archaeological record. Africa's past in general is emerging as more complex, and more instructive from a comparative point of view, than earlier believed. With the more routine application of radiometric dating, old assumptions about chronology have fallen. Earlier it had seemed that Middle and Late Stone Age technologies appeared very late in sub-Saharan Africa compared with analogous Middle and Upper Paleolithic industries in Europe. This apparent lag led Graham C. Clark to declare in 1971 (51, p. 181) that much of Africa during the Late Pleistocene "remained a kind of cultural museum in which archaic traditions continued . . . without contributing to the main course of human progress." Recent dates demonstrate that technological innovations like flake tools produced on prepared cores, punch-struck blades, and burins appear in Africa at about the same time they did in Europe (20, 28, 269). Far from remaining a "cultural backwater," as Clark further suggested (51, p. 67), it now appears possible that microlithic technology, pottery, and cattle domestication were indigenous African developments.

Improved chronological resolution has also revealed that the pattern of technological change in Africa was frequently mosaic in character. Just as stone-tool using hunter-gatherers continued to inhabit regions subject to settlement by Iron Age farming groups up until this millennium in parts of Africa, so prepared core flake technology may have coexisted alongside backed microlithic technology in the prehistoric past (191). This complex situation is quite different from the more homogeneous pattern of technological change familiar from Europe.

0066–4294/83/1015–0215$02.00

For West Africa in particular, data is accumulating rapidly enough that syntheses written as recently as 1980 (e.g. 148) are already out of date. Other more detailed treatments published in the past 2 years have suffered the same fate, exacerbated by long time lags between writing and publication (7, 48, 126). This article is intended to update earlier synthetic works on West African prehistory (63, 160), including those concerned with specific periods, such as the Stone Age (32, 47, 220) or the Iron Age (162, 181), or with individual countries (11, 96, 103, 200, 219).

In addition to providing a broad outline of the most important discoveries of the past decade, we have tried to emphasize the emerging complexity of the archaeological record and the relevance of paleoclimatic change to interpreting it. Selectivity in presenting material was necessary, and we regret having to omit much substantial research. The general focus is on sites where controlled excavation or survey, dating programs, plus comprehensive descriptions of material culture and/or paleoeconomic and paleoenvironmental data have provided a crucial key to evaluating prehistoric remains within a wider region. The integration in the narrative of research in both francophone and anglophone countries has been a particular goal. In several cases, we have provided expanded discussions of recent French discoveries which may perhaps not become generally accessible to anglophone readers for a while.

We have defined West Africa as the land south of the Tropic of Cancer and west of a line drawn north from the Cameroun highlands (see Figure 1). In including the southern half of the Sahara in our discussion we follow precedents set by Andah (7) and Mauny (160). The northern boundary is clearly arbitrary, allowing others to limit their definition to sub-Saharan regions while recognizing that discussion of Saharan events, particularly in the Stone Age, is essential to understanding developments further south (220).

The portion of the archaeological record covered here extends from the Early Stone Age, whose earliest manifestations have not been dated in West Africa, through what may be termed the "prehistoric Iron Age." We have arbitrarily defined the end of this period as A.D. 1000, after which point historical documents, often quite detailed, supplement archaeological research as an important source of information on Saharan and sub-Saharan regions. Historical accounts of the forest regions do not, of course, become available for several more centuries. But even in these regions, oral histories are increasingly utilized to help interpret sites such as Ife, dating to the early centuries of this millennium.

West African prehistory, thus defined, is an immense topic. For substantial portions of it, both geographical and chronological, there is a critical lack of data from controlled excavations. As scientific investigation has increased in the past decade, however, several important themes have emerged.

One of these themes is the significance of paleoclimatic change for Stone

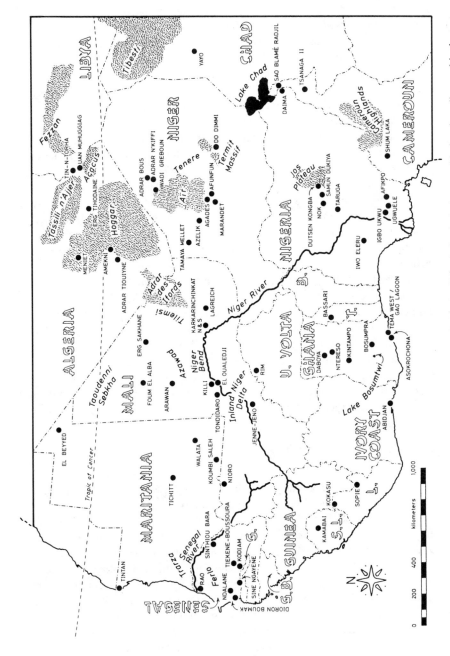

Figure 1 Map of West Africa showing the archaeological sties, palaeoclimatic data localities, and principal geographical regions discussed in the text.

Age adaptations. Much of the evidence comes from sites in the current Saharan and Sahelian zones where even small fluctuations in moisture can have dramatic consequences. On several occasions within the last 50,000 years, it appears that human populations in the Sahara adapted to periodically deteriorating climatic conditions by migrating, by modifying their subsistence base, or by becoming more mobile. It is possible, for example, that present-day nomadic pastoralists in the Sahara are the scattered remnant of an earlier, more populous, and more sedentary pastoral adaptation. While monocausal or deterministic explanations of prehistoric change in these areas are clearly to be avoided, the influence of major paleoclimatic shifts on human populations in large portions of West Africa is undeniable.

The complex and mosaic character of technological change in Africa has already been mentioned. This theme is clearly illustrated in West Africa by recent developments on the origins of metallurgy. Although earlier debate had centered on the question of indigenous innovation vs diffusion, it now appears that the combination of these two processes produced a uniquely African iron technology.

The most significant aspect of prehistoric Iron Age studies during the past decade has been the discovery that various large, complex sites, previously assumed to reflect the effect of Arab enterprise in developing trans-Saharan trade, in fact yield first millennium A.D. radiocarbon dates. It now appears that important developments in trade, social stratification, and even urban growth took place during this period. Increasing numbers of radiocarbon dates for towns and long-distance trade goods invalidate earlier views in which outside stimulus, in the form of Arab trans-Saharan commerce, was seen as the major factor in the emergence of high levels of sociopolitical organization in West Africa.

A Short Note on Terminology

The discussion of archaeological material in this review follows a logical chronological order beginning with the earliest traces of human occupation. The narrative for all pre-Iron Age material, for example, is arranged under the major headings of "Early," "Middle," and "Late Stone Age." These terms are employed, it should be stressed, informally. Their use in the formal nomenclature of African prehistory was officially abandoned at the Burg Wartenstein conference held in 1965 to revise and standardize the terminology of African prehistory (25). No alternative to these terms has yet been incorporated in the formal nomenclature, so many writers continue to use the old Stone Age divisions in the informal, broad sense of "general levels of cultural evolution, which may develop earlier in some regions or persist later in others" (49, p. 249). We follow this usage, while recognizing that these terms, however we may qualify them, still imply a chronological succession of industries that is sometimes inconsistent with archaeological reality (191, 192). There is a pressing need for a formal nomenclature that adequately reflects the complexity and variability of West Africa's archaeological record. This can only be achieved, as the Burg Wartenstein recommendations make clear (25), on the basis of comprehensive description and analyses of whole artifact assemblages from datable, primary context sites. Few investigations of this kind have been conducted in West Africa, although this situation is improving. For the time being, informal terminologies must suffice.

A complicating factor is the usage in the Sahara of French terminology broadly adapted from European prehistory (Lower, Middle, Upper and Terminal Paleolithic, Epipaleolithic, Neolithic). Differences in methodology and historical tradition are partly responsible for the divergence in French and Anglo-American approaches to nomenclature and archaeological description. Such differences are neither easily dismissed nor resolved, as the Burg Wartenstein discussions demonstrated (25). It is purely for simplicity's sake that we subsume the Lower and Middle Paleolithic under the headings Early and Middle Stone Age, respectively. All later Paleolithic material, plus the Neolithic in the Sahara, is included in the Late Stone Age section.

The use of the term Neolithic in Africa continues to be debated. Two definitions currently coexist somewhat uneasily. One is technological and applies in a general industrial sense to assemblages with pottery and ground stone (47, p. 565). The other is economic and includes only food-producing societies (116, p. 196; 233), and then perhaps only those with evidence of sedentary village life, stockherding, and agriculture (18). Additional confusion is created by those who mix the two by supposing that technological innovations like pottery are tangible evidence of economic change related to food production (34, p. 557). Since the earliest direct evidence for cultivated plants in West Africa postdates the appearance of pottery by 5000 years, such an assumption may not be warranted. We agree with Shaw (220) and Barich (18) that the appearance of pottery can be less ambiguously indicated by a term such as "ceramic Late Stone Age."

In discussions of chronology, this review follows the conventions observed in the Cambridge History of Africa (48). All Pleistocene results are presented as B.P. dates. Holocene C14 dates are normally given as uncalibrated B.C. or A.D. dates. Readers should refer to original sources for details on individual dates.

CLIMATE AND PALAEOCLIMATE

Tropical West Africa possesses a remarkable record of climatic and geomorphological change covering the past 30,000 years (see Figure 2). The record is slanted toward several localities well studied by interdisciplinary teams [espe-

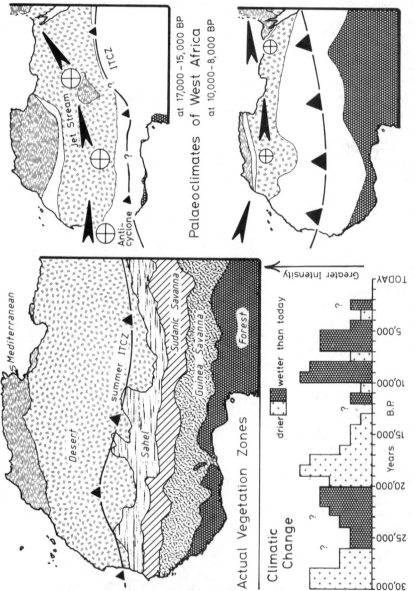

Figure 2 Parallel bands of climate and vegetation today and their very different disposition in the past, with an indication of some mechanisms responsible for those climatic shifts.

cially the Atlantic Saharan coast (27, 185, 268), Senegal and Niger Basins (163, 164, 255), Lake Chad Basin (80, 210, 211), and Lake Bosumtwi in Ghana (251)]. Recent climatic syntheses (108, 238, 239) and interpretations of meterological mechanisms (93, 131, 152, 154, 202, 204, 210) confirm this as a prime field of study for understanding the global circumstances of Quaternary climatic change. The interactions of atmospheric, oceanic, and continental systems which powered past climatic change are responsible also for today's climate and its unmistakable imprint on present human populations.

Climate

Rainfall and vegetation are distributed in West Africa in parallel east-west bands which reflect the position of atmospheric circulation cells. To the south, precipitation derives from moist Atlantic (so-called monsoonal) air traveling from the southwest and rising as it is warmed by the sun. This ascending air forms the equatorial side of the Hadley Cell. The warm air loses moisture (rain) as it rises; at a few thousand meters it moves polewise and then descends at the opposite side of the Hadley Cell as the desiccating NE Trades. The east-west front where moist air and the NE Trades meet and just south of which rain falls in the Inter-Tropical Convergence Zone (ITCZ). The front migrates north and south through the year, following the sun's apparent position over the Tropic of Cancer in summer and shifting south in winter. The summer maximum of the ITCZ's migration is on average 16°N latitude, and this maximum has shifted significantly in the past. Variations in the position, speed, and precipitation potential of the ITCZ (such as that experienced during the Sahel drought of 1967–1974) are caused by a complex interaction of the sun's seasonal position (107), speed and position of the Jet Stream of both hemispheres (152, 202, 204), the strength of desiccating anticyclonic systems on the equatorside of both Jet Streams (202, 204, 264), relative coolness of the southern hemisphere winter (152, 261), and ultimately by the relative size of the Antarctic and Arctic ice sheets (93, 131, 202, 204). As the effect of these variables on recent climate becomes better understood, enormous progress also has been made in attempts to reconstruct the regional effects of interacting climatic mechanisms during the late Pleistocene and Holocene. Such reconstruction will then allow more sophisticated modeling of the plant cover and faunal resources during the principal palaeoclimatic episodes than has so far been possible (135, 154, 261). The effect on modern vegetation of zonally organized precipitation is dramatic.

The equatorial coast is swept twice annually by the ITCZ, once on its moisture-charged northern migration and again as it moves south. Precipitation is plentiful (1400 mm or more) and evenly distributed through the year so that rainforest and root crops (yams, cassavas) grow in the south. But as one moves north into the Guinea (1400–1000 mm) and Sudanic (1000–400 mm) savannas, the long dry season under the influence of the NE Trades (Harmattan) encourages grasses rather than trees. The very short, single summer pass of the ITCZ over the Sahel (400–150 mm) ensures that evapotranspiration far exceeds total precipitation (250), and it is here that overgrazing and overcultivation contribute locally to the spread of the desert (54, 93, 118, 202). The Sahel supports a reduced harvest of savanna grains such as sorghum and millet; here pastoralism forms the livelihood of many. The progressive diminution of rainfall at approximately 200 mm per degree of latitude continues into the desert (dunes become active above ca 16°N latitude where rainfall is 150 mm or less). However, not all parts of the Sahara are hyperarid year-around, as some spring, winter, or autumn rain falls on the central massifs because of the "Saharan Depressions" (moisture-laden high-pressure anomalies at the interface of middle latitude cyclones and anticyclones) or because of occasional migration south of cyclonic winter rains from their usual position over the Mediterranean and Maghreb.

Pleistocene Palaeoclimate

The origin of the desert is difficult to date, but the Saharan core was hyperarid by at least the later Pliocene (154, 210, 237). East Atlantic sediment cores record many episodes of extreme deflation and dust transport during a generally dry Pleistocene (27, 73, 237). These alternated with conditions moist enough to support permanent lakes in the south Sahara (164, 210). Chronological resolution of these episodes improves appreciably only after 50,000 B.P.

Tropical West Africa was generally moist before ca 100,000 B.P. when, for example, the Senegal River fed massive lakes in the Ferlo and Trarza regions (163, 164). Evidence is strong for a severe arid period soon afterwards: the "Premier Erg" (dune sea) in the Chad Basin dates to ca 65,000 (81). This appears to be part of a remarkable system of dunes extending thousands of kilometers through the Sahara and Sahel, created sometime between 100,000 and >40,000 (250). Humid conditions followed, and Lake Chad rose to create its highest beach by ca 38,000 (80, 81, 211). At 30,000 another intense dry period is signaled by regression of the lake and aeolian reworking of basin sands, but by 22,000–20,000 Lake Chad had again grown to more than three times its present size. By 26,000 the lake began to receive moisture from both the southern monsoons and the northern "Saharan Depressions" (265). This lacustrine period is attested between 28,000–23,000 on the Mauritanian coast (268) and between 25,000–20,000 at other lakes on the Sahara's south and north margins (164, 202, 204, 237, 265); from 22,500 to 17,500 Lake Bosumtwi was a high lake with dilute waters (M. R. Talbot, personal communication).

The mechanisms responsible for these late Pleistocene shifts are now better understood than ever. It is clear that tropical West Africa never behaved as a unitary climatological system. The several environmental zones recognized today expanded, contracted, or disappeared entirely at different periods in response to one or more temporarily dominant meteorological forces which were succeeded by others with quite different effects. The end of the 100,000 to >40,000 B.P. hyperarid period coincides with an expansion of the Antarctic ice cap, strengthening the ITCZ and propelling monsoonal rains far to the north (202). The resulting pluvial ends at ca 30,000, coinciding with an Arctic icefield expansion which strengthened the northern Jet Stream and its attending (desiccating) anticyclonic system now located over the Sahara (204). The anticyclonic system weakened between 25,000 and 20,000, allowing precipitation to increase. But by the Late Glacial maximum (ca 18,000) low global temperatures (reducing evaporation over the Atlantic, hence preventing recharge of the monsoons) (93, 264), "continentality" caused by sea level drop (204), and increased coastal upwelling (185) considerably disorganized the ITCZ. The Arctic ice sheet's rapid expansion pushed the Jet Stream far south; the attending anticyclonic and cyclonic systems migrated south of their current position. Cyclonic rains bathed all North Africa, and the "Saharan Depressions" fed lakes and Mediterranean vegetation in the Saharan massifs during all but perhaps the worst of the hyperarid phase (81, 129, 203, 265). But a greatly expanded as well as more southerly anticyclonic system created a very dry and cold Sahel and southern Sahara, with precipitation only 15–20% of today (250, 264).

These southerly areas today bear the hallmark of the 20,000 to 12,000 dry period—massive and almost continuous fields of longitudinal dunes extending 4000 kilometers from the Atlantic littoral to the Sudan Republic (108, 202, 204, 251). At this time, the Sahara shifted 450–500 kilometers south (164, 265), dunes were active 6° latitude farther south than today (93), and the Chad, Senegal, and Niger Basins were subjected to dune erection over former lacustrine deposits (81, 163, 203, 210, 211, 237, 255). A low, saline Lake Bosumtwi (lowest level 17,500–15,000) lay in a landscape of grass savanna, where forest was reduced to valley remnants (251; M. R. Talbot, personal communication). As arid as this Late Glacial phase became, it was by no means as severe as that before 40,000.

Holocene Palaeoclimate

At the beginning of the Holocene (ca 12,000 B.P.) the rapid shrinking of the Arctic ice cap (93, 131) and global warming were complemented in West Africa by a weakening of the anticyclones (204, 264), expansion to the north of the moisture-charged ITCZ (93, 202, 238, 239, 261), and significant overlap of monsoons and "Saharan Depression" rains over northern Chad and the Saharan massifs (93, 129, 153, 202, 237, 264). Improvement was interrupted by short arid episodes at ca 11,500–11,200 and 10,500–10,000 (93, 129, 251). But by 10,000 stable pluvial conditions prevailed. Precipitation improved by 200–400% in the Sahel. Parts of the Sahara now receiving 5mm rainfall then received 250–400 mm (93, 238).

Temperatures rose very slowly and surface water loss declined as vegetation colonized former deserts, encouraging a favorable precipitation/evaporation balance. Nearly year-round precipitation maintained permanent streams in the Sahel and Mediterranean vegetation in the highlands (135, 155, 250). The Senegal and Niger rivers breached nearly stabilized barrier dunes, the sands of which were reddened as soils developed (108, 163, 164), and Lake "Megachad" formed at the +40 meter level (93, 210). To the south, forest recolonized the Bosumtwi region at ca 9000 and the lake was stable and high (251; M. R. Talbot, personal communication). The West African landscape was very different than today with many interdunal lakes in the Sahel, and Saharan meadowland supporting shallow lakes and permanent watercourses (especially in the highlands and adjoining areas). True desert was banished to the far north (135, 202, 204), to low-lying central regions such as the Taoudeni Sebkha (108, 237) and the East Atlantic coast (183, 185).

A short but significant dry phase at 8000–7000 B.P. is attested by severe drying of southern Saharan lakes and watercourses (131, 237), remobilization of dunes in the Sahel (164, 250, 265), and a rapid decline in the level of Lake Bosumtwi (251). Debate on causes for this dry episode continues (see 93, 131, 155), but it is highly significant that air temperature over West Africa, which was still quite cool during the early Holocene, at this time becomes as warm or warmer than today. Lake Chad now supported only tropical diatoms rather than the cold-tolerant and tropical mix of the lower Holocene (210, 211). Despite the return of pluvial conditions ca 7000 B.P. [signaled by lake level rises at Adrar Bous and Lake Bosumtwi (50, 251)], the onset of higher temperatures signals the beginning of a slow, nonlinear decline to present arid conditions. Temperature increases soon created an unfavorable evaporation profile (93, 153) and rainfall in the Sahel and Southern Sahara became more episodic. As a result, streams that once flowed year-round became increasingly seasonal and temporary (155, 250). Various localities experienced appreciable lake level declines at 4500–3500 (129, 172, 250, 251), coinciding with general East African lake regression (178, 238, 239). Humid episodes at ca 3500–3000 (155, 178, 250, 265) and 2500–2000 (129, 265) are of short duration and perhaps local effect only.

By 2000 the Sahara and Sahel were as dry or drier than today and the effects of deforestation, overcultivation, and overgrazing were felt even in the forest and savanna regions (93). Research on the most recent periods (54, 93, 118, 155, 178) concerns the apparent correlation between climatic improvement in West Africa and cooling in the upper latitudes (such as during the "Little Ice Age" of the sixteenth through eighteenth centuries A.D.), predicting future effects of CO_2 concentration in the atmosphere and of local human abuse of the land.

This brief summary of Late Quaternary climate change can only hint at the sense of accomplishment researchers have felt as simplistic theories such as the Glacial-Pluvial synchrony or monolithic latitudinal shifts of climatic bands during the Pleistocene are discarded and the great complexity of meterological interactions is appreciated. Certain methodological problems with the use of Saharan pollens (261, 265), diatoms (211), and radiocarbon dates on shell and precipitated carbonate (177, 202, 210) plague researchers still—but the overall picture after ca 30,000 has begun to come nicely into focus. Greatly needed now is that fine detail of local palaeo-environment which the archaeologist can provide. Collaboration between archaeologist and geomorphologist has been rare in West Africa. In those few cases where it has occured [e.g. Clark in the Tenere of Niger (50) or Petit-Maire on the East Atlantic coast (183–185) and central Sahara (189, 190)]—results have been exemplary.

THE EARLY STONE AGE

Compared with the eastern and southern parts of the continent, studies of Pre-Acheulean and Acheulean industries in West Africa have had little impact on our understanding of the Early Stone Age (ESA). The East African Rift Valley situation, where rapid late Tertiary/Early Quaternary sedimentation was followed by faulting and exposure of those sediments, (127), is matched nowhere in West Africa. Pliocene and Pleistocene sediments are especially rare in West Africa south of the Sahara. Farther north, they are present up to 600 m deep in the vast Chad basin. Eroding deposits of this formation at Yayo yielded the heavily fossilized "Tchadanthropus" skull fragment, initially identified as an Australopithecine (58). The fossil is now recognized as more similar to *Homo erectus* in significant aspects (122, p. 122), which accords with the suggestion that the Yayo fauna is approximately coeval with Upper Bed II at Olduvai (ca 1 m.y.) (29, p. 35). Unfortunately, Chad formation exposures are limited, so much material presumably lies deeply buried.

Most of the evidence for makers of Oldowan-type and Acheulean tools in West Africa comes from surface finds (128). More rarely, collections have been made from test pits in river gravels or terraces where lithics have been redeposited. Materials recovered from erosion surfaces or secondary deposition contexts pose problems because they cannot be assumed to represent fully the original assemblage. Indeed, the various pieces found together may not even be contemporaneous. The initial problems presented by these contexts have frequently been exacerbated by preferential collection of "diagnostic" tool types for relative dating purposes. As a result, very few ESA assemblages in West Africa have been subject to systematic collection and comprehensive description and analysis. Not only is assemblage composition and variability poorly understood, but the chronological framework for the West African ESA remains extremely rudimentary.

Pre-Acheulean lithics have been identified at a scatter of sites from the present forest region to the Sahara (63, pp. 92–98; 157; 219, p. 25). The man-made nature of some of the pebble-choppers collected by Davies in Ghana has been disputed, however (245). Some other Pre-Acheulean attributions, based on the identification of a few isolated core-choppers, are also suspect since these tools may be present in West African assemblages of any period (47, p. 534). It is certainly reasonable to suppose that the distribution of early stone tool makers ca 2.5–1.5 m.y. ago extended throughout suitable portions of the African dry savanna biotope. However, no direct evidence of their activities has yet been recovered in West Africa from an undisturbed context of demonstrably Pliocene/early Pleistocene age.

Acheulian industries are found throughout the central and southern Sahara, associated with fine-grained lake or swamp sediments or in older alluvial terraces of main drainage systems. A grassland/scattered woodland habitat is suggested by the large ungulate fauna accompanying Acheulian handaxes, cleavers, and discoids at the site of Erg Tihodaine (32, pp. 42–45). Bifaces numbering in the thousands at El Beyyed indicate that favorable Saharan locales may have supported relatively stable populations over a long period of time (47, p. 538). These and other major biface sites in the Sahara [see (47) for an excellent summary] have only been surface collected, often in a highly selective way.

South of the Sahara, the Acheulian is thus far very poorly represented in Senegal (67) and absent in Liberia, Sierra Leone, and lowland Ivory Coast (247, p. 38). Putative Acheulian occurrences cluster in southeastern Ghana and central Togo along the Atakora highlands (63, p. 104). However, the best examples of fully characterized assemblages come from the Jos Plateau in Nigeria, where hundreds of bifaces were discovered as a result of tin mining in alluvial deposits (219). Against this backdrop of isolated surface finds and secondary deposits, the recent discovery in eastern Nigeria of what appears to be a major Acheulian handax quarry site and factory is of great importance. Excavations at Ugwuele have produced prodigious quantities of processed stone, especially broken and unfinished handaxes (8). The brittle character of the Ugwuele dolerite outcrop probably accounts for the many discards (9).

Dates for West African Acheulian assemblages are scarce. Until recently, the single available date was a C14 determination run on wood from the alluvial deposits at Nok (219, p. 29). At 39,000 B.P., it clearly represented a minimum age only. Now two burned flint bifaces from Lagreich in the Malian Sahara have been thermoluminescence dated to 282,000± 56,000 B.P. (74). In the Libyan Fezzan, a team led by Petit-Maire observed Late Acheulian and Mousterian artifacts in lacustrine shell deposits uranium dated to 140,000–

90,000 B.P. (100, 187). If these dates do prove to bracket the Early/Middle Stone Age interface in the Fezzan, this Saharan chronology will accord with sequences elsewhere in Africa, where this boundary dates between 200,000–100,000 B.P. (20, 269).

POST-ACHEULIAN INDUSTRIES: MIDDLE STONE AGE AND SANGOAN

Sterile, windblown sands overlie late Acheulian deposits at various Saharan sites, testifying to the onset of extremely arid conditions. The eariest known post-Acheulian flake industries have been found stratified above these aeolian sediments, probably representing a repopulation of the region as more humid conditions returned. Two kinds of Middle Stone Age (MSA) industries have been identified in the present Sahara: *Mousterian,* with high frequencies of scrapers and points produced on flakes struck from prepared cores; and *Aterian,* a closely related industry with a substantial percentage of bifacially tanged forms and a variable blade element (32, pp. 26–31; 49, p. 262; 254). In North Africa and Egypt, Aterian tanged tools have been found stratified above Mousterian assemblages (32, pp. 23–36; 270). Within the West African Sahara, however, only Adrar Bous has provided stratigraphic evidence for a possible Mousteroid facies underlying the Aterian (50). Too few Mousterian occurrences are known from the Sahara to determine whether the Aterian there represents a derivative industry or, alternatively, a largely contemporary special activity facies, involving the hafting of a variety of tools in sockets or split shafts (49, p. 259).

Aterian lithics are widely distributed north of 15°N at open sites adjacent to lacustrine and swamp sediments and in the valleys of major water courses. Because most of the Saharan assemblages are surface collections, dating is difficult. In the Aïr, redeposited Aterian artifacts occur in cross-bedded sediments dated to 18,500 B.P. (167). Several North African dates between 40,000–25,000 B.P. provide a useful basis for extrapolaton (32, p. 33). However, Wendorf & Schild (270, p. 234) advocate rejecting all existing absolute dates for the Aterian, citing their evidence from the Western Desert of Egypt that Aterian chronology exceeds the limits of the radiocarbon method. This being the case, they argue, datable materials can be seriously contaminated by the slightest trace of carbonates or brief surface exposure. Clark (47, p. 550) concurs that the Saharan MSA probably ended by 40,000 B.P. Almost all authors agree that it had certainly ended by the start of the hyperarid phase that began ca 30,000 B.P. Hugot's conviction (124, 126) that the Aterian is a Terminal Palaeolithic industry lasting as late as 9000–7000 B.P. in the southern Sahara has been largely discredited.

In a number of locales, Aterian horizons are heavily deflated by wind erosion or, as at Adrar Bous (50), topped by dune deposits, indicating renewed aridity. This same arid phase may be represented south of the Sahara by thick deposits of wind-blown sand on the Accra plains of Ghana. Stratified underneath, at the sites of Asokrochona and Tema West, are undisturbed post-Acheulian occupation levels. The 12,600 lithics recovered by Nygaard from Asokrochona constitute the first complete post-Acheulian assemblage excavated from an undisturbed occupation context in West Africa (179). At Tema West a very similar industry occurs, and it is overlain by a MSA assemblage of quite different character (S. Nygaard, in preparation). Both sites provide a consistent paleoclimatic picture in which occupation took place during dry savanna conditions similar to those prevailing today on the Accra plains. Geological features created during significantly drier conditions occur immediately below and above occupation levels at both sites (179; S. Nygaard, in preparation).

The Asokrochona assemblage and the earliest Tema West material comprise a large percentage of unmodified quartz flakes, chunks, and chips, plus a tool kit of scrapers, choppers, picks, and spheroids, all manufactured on quartz cores. Levallois technique appears to be absent. Comparable tools are reported from savanna regions elsewhere in West Africa (63, 235, 246). These relatively heavy-duty, crude, core-tool assemblages in West Africa have frequently been termed Sangoan, referring to apparently similar industries first identified in East Africa (49, p. 288). Because so many Sangoan assemblages result from selective surface collections, it has been unclear whether the heavy-duty picks and core scrapers represent a temporally discrete cultural episode or a facies of material culture that recurred intermittently throughout late Acheulean and post-Acheulian times. Clark (49, p. 288) favors the latter, interpreting the Sangoan as a special activity facies, possibly wood-working, of the MSA. Several authors prefer to avoid applying the term to West African assemblages until much more quantitative description and paleoclimatic analysis have been undertaken at systematically excavated sites (267; S. Nygaard, in preparation).

Post-Acheulian assemblages lacking a heavy-duty core tool component and possessing flake tools produced from Levallois prepared cores are also documented in sub-Saharan West Africa. Very little is known of these, referred to simply as MSA industries. The best-described MSA material to date comes from secondary deposition contexts in Nigeria (3, 4) and northern Cameroon (156, pp. 67–95), where radiocarbon dates unfortunately have proved unsatisfactory. Relevant new discoveries elsewhere include a flake assemblage with Levallois technique stratified above a core tool assemblage at Tema West (S. Nygaard, in preparation) and the report of an assemblage containing both "Sangoan" and Levallois flake elements in southern Ivory Coast (43). These finds, preliminary as they are, encourage the tempering of traditional emphasis on culture-stratigraphic succession with an appreciation of post-Acheulian assemblage variability.

LATE STONE AGE

Aceramic Industries in the Sahara

During the hyperarid episode lasting from 20,000–12,000 B.P., the Sahara down to 15°N apparently was uninhabited. Most of the population in West Africa at that time probably lived south of 11°N. When wadi channels began to flow with water again between 10,000 and 8,000 B.C., grasslands and large grazing mammals repopulated the Sahara, as, presumably, did hunter/collectors. Archaeological traces of these groups are rare, however. They are probably represented by small scatters of punched blade industries known from a handful of Saharan sites. This industry is well described at Wadi Greboun in the Aïr (45), where a small group of hunter/collectors camped briefly on the banks of an early Holocene lake. Similar aggregates with distinctive, assymetrically shouldered Ounanian points have been found at Adrar Bous, near Arawan, and further north in the Fezzan and Maghreb (16, 45). It appears that these industries are earlier than 6500 B.C. Confirmation of this chronology has recently come from Roset's work (207a) in the Temet Basin in the northeast Aïr, where a blade industry associated with stone bowls and pestles has been dated to about 7600 B.C. In Egypt's Western Desert, Terminal Paleolithic industries with backed bladelets and Ounanian points date to 7000–6800 B.C. and apparently represent the first occupation of the area since the Aterian (270, pp. 108–10, p. 277). The affinity of these blade and bladelet industries with earlier Epipaleolithic material in North Africa indicates that large parts of the Sahara were recolonized from the North in the early Holocene (47, p. 564). Mori (169) has suggested that the well-known Saharan rock engravings of elephants and wild buffalo *(Homioceras (Bubalus) antiquus)* were created at this time. Muzzolini, however, argues that the so-called *Bubalus* style is contemporaneous with other Saharan rock art dating to the second half of the Holocene (174, 175).

Saharan Ceramic Industries

The industries which apparently succeeded these punched blade industries in the Sahara have received much attention, focusing on one of their most distinctive characteristics: round-bottomed pottery, made in simple basket-like shapes and decorated by impressing or dragging a comb, fishbone, or awl into the wet clay surface. The most extraordinary aspect of this pottery is its enormous distribution in both time (eighth to second millennia B.C.) and space (the entire Sahara south of the Tropic, extending along the upper Nile Valley and into the East African Rift Valley lakes region). The pottery figures prominently in two conceptions of the Saharan Late Stone Age (LSA) that have become firmly entrenched in the literature: Camps' (32, 34) formulation of the *Saharo-Sudanese Neolithic* and Sutton's *Middle African Aqualithic* (240–242). In addition to the distinctive pottery, both formulations identify several other defining features including bone harpoons and an abundance of fish remains, with preferential site location along ancient lakes, depressions, and wadis. Camps and Sutton suggest that these elements reflect establishment of culturally related Negroid groups throughout the tropical Sahara which endured until aridity became pronounced in the second millennium B.C. Both accommodate the appearance of domestic cattle and sheep/goat sometime after 5000 B.C. within a framework of increasing regional variation through time.

Camps and Sutton interpret the nature of the economic adaptation reflected at these widely distributed sites quite differently, however. Camps insists that pottery is directly associated with changes in food habits due to agriculture (34, p. 555). Hence, the Saharo-Sudanese tradition is identified as Neolithic, despite the admitted absence of any direct evidence prior to 2000 B.C. for cultivated plants at sites west of Lake Chad (34, p. 556). Pre-Neolithic pottery is of course well known in the Old World from the Jomon (Japan) and Ertebolle (Denmark) cultures. Sutton views pottery as part of a "soup, porridge, and fish stew revolution" (240, p. 530), representing a new technology for processing wild resources. His Aqualithic formulation is deliberately "anti-Neolithic" (242, p. 322), emphasizing the success of the aquatic way of life while refuting food production as "an inevitable or an ideal direction of development" (241, p. 32).

Both Sutton's and Camps' formulations have been criticized for being overly generalizing, given the considerable archaeological variability involved (62, p. 616; 149; 220, p. 71). Maitre (151, p. 718) denounces as "an absurdity" the idea of a single cultural ensemble persisting several millennia over a large part of the Sahara. He suggests (149, 150) that the use of bone harpoons and wavy line (sinuous dragged comb) and dotted wavy line (impressed curved comb) pottery as "fossiles directeurs" is largely responsible for generating a misleading picture of general uniformity. Far more attention needs to be paid to the other punctate, rocker, and straight comb impressions that predominate at nearly all Saharan sites. When all ceramic elements are considered, significant local differences can appear (150). Lithic assemblages also reveal enormous intersite diversity, ranging from the blade-based industries of the Acacus (17) to the ruder flake industries of the Hoggar (150) or the microliths in the Aïr (226) and at Early Khartoum (13). Within the Saharo-Sudanese Neolithic and the Aqualithic formulations, however, lithic assemblages are downplayed as sources of valuable information on cultural traditions and activities (32, p. 234; 241, p. 28). Neither concept, as currently laid out, adequately reflects the complex and variable LSA situation revealed by recent Saharan research.

8000–5500 B.C.   Recent excavations confirm that the earliest use of pottery at Saharan sites coincides with a humid period in the eighth and seventh millennia B.C., when Saharan lakes reached their highest Holocene levels. The

early dates present the possibility that the round-based pottery was an indigenous African development (34, p. 263; 116; 117; 241, p. 29). The earliest
Saharan pottery sites known so far occur along wadis in the central massifs (17,
31, 151, 207a, 207b). The accompanying lithics are regionally distinct and late
Paleolithic or EpiPaleolithic in character (17, p. 151; 150); bifacial retouch and
polished stone are absent. All sites have significant numbers of grinding stones,
apparently for processing wild grains. Hunting was also a major element of the
economy. At Ti-n-Torha, Barbary sheep constituted up to 70% of the mammalian fauna in the seventh millennium (17), raising the possibility of specialized
hunting or even herding (53, p. 155). There is no evidence that domesticated
cattle, identified at late seventh millennium impressed pottery sites in Western
Egypt (270, p. 277), had penetrated the Saharan highlands by this time.

The available evidence for the earliest pottery-using Saharan groups does not
yet confirm the existence of a widespread aquatic or lacustrine adaptation in the
seventh millennium, as proposed by Smith (230, 233) and Sutton (240–242)
and uncritically accepted by others (148). Impressed pottery, bone harpoons,
and intensive exploitation of aquatic resources are the hallmarks of this proposed early adaptation. To date, none of the Saharan highland sites has produced
bone harpoons or evidence of an economy based predominantly on aquatic
resources, although some fishing was done at Ti-n-Torha and Amekni (17, 31).
No evidence of this kind has yet been unambiguously dated earlier than 5500
B.C. anywhere in the Sahara. The isolated, eighth millennium date for Tamaya
Mellet, referred to by Smith (231, p. 140) must be rejected for several reasons,
including the absence of information on the relation of the dated sample to
artifacts at the site. The harpoon and pottery sites in the Azaouad (Mali), which
Smith cites (231, p. 140) as characteristic of this early lacustrine tradition, have
recently been dated to ca 5000 B.C. (186). Smith's uncertainly dated Adrar
n'Kiffi site was occupied sometime between 5500–4000 B.C. (226, p. 190).

Older fishing sites may yet turn up along early Holocene lake margins. Their
apparent sparseness might be accounted for in some areas by the destruction
and reworking of Holocene high lake deposits during subsequent wet phases.
Some evidence for this exists at Tichitt (123). Alternatively, it is possible that
intensive exploitation of aquatic resources by pottery-using groups in the
Sahara occurred only after 5500 B.C., perhaps correlated in some still obscure
way with the end of an arid phase dated between 6000–5000 B.C.

5500–2500 B.C.   After this, sites with aquatic fauna including fish *(Clarias*
and *Lates* especially), molluscs, hippo, and crocodile are common in the
Sahara until aridity becomes locally pronounced after ca 2500 B.C. Although
discussion of these sites has tended to focus on a small number of superficially
similar features, as mentioned above, the differences among them remain
intriguing. At midden sites like those studied by Gallay (97) and Petit-Maire's

team (186) near Arawan (Mali), aquatic resources clearly constitute a substantial portion of the subsistence base. Grindstones are rare, and other lithic elements are poorly elaborated in comparison with the bone industry, which includes harpoons.

Further to the northeast in Mali, the lacustrine sites at Erg Sakhane suggest a more diversified economy, with large numbers of grindstones for grain processing, as well as fishing and occasional hunting of ungulates (190). The sites closest to the Holocene lake at Sakhane are extensive occupation sites with stone structures and fireplaces (190).

By contrast, sites at Adrar n'Kiffi consist of small microlithic and pottery scatters associated with diatomite deposits containing harpoons and the bones of fish, crocodile, hippo, and turtle (226). At other fishing sites, like Adrar Tiouiyne, bone harpoons seem to have been replaced by tiny, barbed stone points (32, p. 237). Nor are there any bone harpoons at Amekni rock shelter in the Hoggar, where broad spectrum fisher-hunter-collectors repeatedly camped during the seventh to fourth millennia B.C. (31).

One of the most elusive questions for this period concerns the extent to which these diverse "aquatic" and fisher-hunter-collector economies were contemporaneous with cattle and ovicaprid herding economies established in the central Sahara by 4000 B.C. Did these constitute chronologically distinct adaptations as Clark (47, pp. 565–67) implies by dividing the Saharan LSA into a Prepastoral and a Pastoral phase? Or were they different ways of life, possibly overlapping in time, pursued by "quite separate peoples maintaining distinct cultural traditions" (241, p. 30)? Alternatively, pastoral and "aquatic" sites may in some cases represent seasonal aspects of a mixed economy.

Investigation of these questions hinges on the ability to ascertain when domestic cattle are present in the faunal remains at a given site. This is rarely easy, given the normally fragmented and decalcified condition of what often are small archaeological samples, and the osteological similarity of the small African buffalo *(Syncerus Caffer nanus)* to domestic cattle (37, p. 280). The earliest accepted identifications of domestic *Bos* come from the sites of Adrar Bous, where an entire skeleton was recovered (36), and Uan Muhuggiag, which produced a nearly complete frontal (168). Both samples date to the early fourth millennium B.C.

The best evidence for Saharan pastoralism continues to be the prolific rock paintings in the northern massifs of Tassili n-Ajjer and Tadrart Acacus (140, 168). Herds of cattle numbering up to 100 are shown with domestic traits such as spotted hides and a variety of horn shapes. Some have rope leads around their neck. Unfortunately, rock art is hard to date, since associated occupation deposits cannot be assumed to be contemporary (175, p. 30) unless painted material is actually found in the deposits. This was the case at Uan Muhuggiag, where a rock slab with painted cattle broke off from a rock overhang and became incorporated in deposits dated to the early third millennium B.C. (168).

The archaeological sequence at Adrar Bous (50) sheds some light on the appearance of pastoralism in the central Saharan massifs. After occupation by nonpastoral groups, perhaps in the late sixth millennium, Adrar Bous appears to have been abandoned during a dry phase, evidenced by a fall in lake level of at least 5 m and minor dune formation. As the climate became more humid in the early fourth millennium, the site was reoccupied by pastoralists whose material culture and economy resembled, in certain aspects, that of the earlier "aquatic" sites. On this basis, Smith (226, p. 191) suggests that the early Adrar Bous pastoral assemblage (identified as part of the Tenerean facies of the Saharo-Sudanese Neolithic) does not represent a migration of new groups from elsewhere. Rather, earlier traditions have been modified to include domestic livestock. It will be interesting to see if this continuity is confirmed at other Tenerean sites, identified throughout a vast area east of the Aïr (60, 199, 206, 207). Unfortunately, no other Tenerean sites to date have been investigated and reported to the same standard as Adrar Bous.

Both Clark (46) and Smith (231) theorize that the shift to pastoralism was related to increasing desiccation in the Sahara after 4000 B.C. Domestication may have been a response to resource depletion near lake basin and river valley habitats which potentially supported fairly high population densities by 6000 B.C. "Acquisition of stock would have made it possible to maintain and even increase population densities by providing a "stored" source of animal protein that would have significantly reduced the problem of the famine season, not only through the regular supply of meat, but also through use of milk and blood" (47, p. 567).

However, the appearance of domestic cattle in the Aïr during or immediately after a dry phase can be contrasted with the situation at the Nabta Playa sites in western Egypt where the earliest domstic stock is associated with climatic amelioration and moister conditions (270, pp. 160–63). Wendorf & Schild (270, p. 337) suggest that Saharan pastoralists were the source of the Nabta Playa domestic cattle, which occur in a Terminal Paleolithic context dated to the early seventh millennium B.C. Clearly, we cannot yet be sure of the date at which cattle first appear in the Sahara outside the central massifs. We are thus a long way from understanding the process by which livestock was incorporated into the subsistence economy in Africa.

The origin of early Saharan cattle is problematic as well. Epstein (82, pp. 213, 314, 555) believed that humpless longhorn cattle were introduced from southwest Asia in the late fifth millennium B.C., followed two or more thousand years later by the introduction of humpless shorthorn (brachyceros) forms. This is hard to reconcile with the early dates for cattle at Nabta Playa and the fourth millennium specimens from Uan Muhuggiag and Adrar Bous, both of which are claimed to be short-horned (36, 168). Consequently, many consider local domestication from wild North African *Bos* to be more likely (36, 229). The North African *Bos* stock was large, with long, forward-curving horns *(Bos primigenius)*. Another wild species, *Bos ibericus*, was very similar but smaller, and may merely be the female of *Bos primigenius* (229, p. 492). All the domestic specimens recovered so far from Saharan excavations have been smaller, shorter-horned varieties, suggesting that the domestication process, if indigenously achieved, involved body size reduction and selection for new horn shapes and sizes. The variety of horns depicted in the rock paintings range from long and lyre-shaped (sometimes identified as a separate domestic taxon, *Bos africanus*) to short and forward curving [referred to by some as *Bos brachyceros,* although this assignation is strenuously rejected by Muzzolini (174, 176)]. Far more faunal material from both wild and domestic African *Bos* needs to be found and methodically examined and described [as Grigson did for European specimens (105, 106)] before we can progress in the debate over the identification of domestic taxa and their origins.

The issue of ovicaprid origins is more straightforward. No wild progenitors are thought to have existed on the continent, so sheep/goat must have been introduced from elsewhere. Possible routes include a westward spread from the Near East via Egypt (82, p. 79) or the maritime expansion of ovicaprid herders along the North African Coast. There is some evidence from North Africa that the appearance of ovicaprids there preceded domestic *Bos* (229, p. 495). For the Sahara, however, the chronological relation of domestic sheep/goat and cattle is unknown.

Seasonal movements were probably necessary for the Saharan LSA pastoralists, given the large daily water requirements of cattle. Several authors have speculated on the nature and extent of these movements, extrapolating from case studies of modern Saharan and Sahelian pastoralists (47, 143, 232, 234). Some differences may be expected between the LSA and the modern pastoral adaptation, of course, since the LSA Saharan environment was more favorable and supported a much higher biomass than the marginal areas with which modern pastoralism is often associated. Nevertheless, ethnographic models can be used to generate predictions concerning LSA site distributions and resource scheduling which are applicable to the archaeological record. Haaland (110, 111) has used this methodology along the Sudanese Nile, demonstrating that two contemporaneous sites differing in size, location, subsistence, and tool kit probably represented seasonal occupations by a single herding-fishing-collecting group. Some of the Saharan fishing and herding sites may have similarly functioned as separate seasonal components of an integrated economy. The massive *Arca* shell middens created between 4500–1500 B.C. on the Mauritanian coast at sites like Tintan (183, 184) and the grain processing sites around Foum el Alba [abundant grindstones and pottery, but very few fish and no large mammal bones (186)] also need to be considered from a possible seasonal perspective. Of course, not all intersite differences reflect seasonality. Within the West African Sahara from 5500–2500 B.C., different cultural traditions and adaptations almost certainly existed. Pastoralism, although widespread, may not have penetrated some areas of the desert for millennia after its first appearance in the central highlands. Smith (233) reminds us that hunter-collectors persisted in western Mauritania until this century.

2500–0 B.C.   The humid conditions prevailing throughout much of the Sahara in the fourth and third millennia permitted substantial population growth, to judge from the density of sites occupied during this period (188). The impact on these groups of increasing aridity, evidenced locally after 2500 B.C., and possibly exacerbated by the effects of overgrazing, was profound. Sites like Adrar Bous were abandoned (2400 B.C.) as lakes dried up and cattle herds became difficult to maintain (47, p. 568). Better-watered parts of the central massifs may have provided some refuge, and scattered, increasingly nomadic groups may have remained in the lowlands. But many pastoralists presumably followed retreating water supplies toward the south. Smith (228) argues that migration of the tsetse belt southward from 17°N at this time may have opened up parts of the Sahel and Sudanic zones to colonization by pastoral groups. In the Tilemsi Valley, for example, the sites of Karkarichinkat South and North were first occupied in the second millennium by herder-fisher-collectors bearing a material culture with Saharan affinities (224). Farther east, other herder-fisher-collector groups continued to move southward, it appears, colonizing the clay plains exposed by receding Lake Chad before the early first millennium B.C. Here the early settlers at Daima (56) and Sao Blamé Radjil (137) used grindstones and bone harpoons and made clay figurines of cattle and sheep similar to those from several other roughly contemporaneous sites in the southern Sahara and Sahel (102; 125, p. 509; 227). It is possible that pastoralists penetrated even beyond the Sahel belt, using tsetse-free corridors during the dry season. The bones of small domestic cattle and dwarf goat dating to the mid-second millennium B.C. have been recovered from Kintampo in northern Ghana (37). From the culturally related, approximately contemporary site of Ntereso, Davies found almost 100 hollow-based points of a type thus far known only from the Sahara, as well as bone harpoons and dwarf goat bones (64).

Increasing aridity after 2500 B.C. in the Sahara was interrupted by a short humid episode ca 1500 B.C. (155, 164, 172). The western Sahara was particularly attractive to human occupation at this time (184). In western Mauretania, sites with economies based on grain processing (abundant grindstones), hunting (warthog and wild ungulates), and domestic stock-herding date to this period (184, pp. 233–34; 266). So do the pastoralist settlements distributed along the escarpment between Tichitt and Walata. Munson's work showed that the Tichitt inhabitants pursued a mixed subsistence strategy of herding cattle and goat, fishing, hunting, and collecting for 400 years along successively lower beach ridges of the slowly desiccating lake (170, 172). The disappearance of aquatic resources from the archaeological record at Tichitt is immediately followed by the appearance of domestic cereals, a phenomenon to which we shall return presently. The rapid incorporation of cereals into the economy apparently stabilized the subsistence base and actually permitted population growth, to judge from the increased size of the archaeological sites (5, 171). Claims for the urban nature of the larger Tichitt sites (125) cannot be evaluated here in the absence of excavation reports demonstrating accepted features of early urbanism, such as permanent settlement and occupational specialization. By 900 B.C., the lake dried up completely, and sites became smaller and more ephemeral. LSA settlement at Tichitt ended by 400 B.C., possibly influenced by the arrival of horse-riding nomads from the north (171). Past this point, throughout the Sahara, occupation sites of any kind become extremely rare. The persistence of highly mobile human groups in the desert throughout the terminal LSA and Iron Age is attested mainly by thousands of stone-covered tombs from this period, as well as by rock art (165, 166, 201).

Late Stone Age in Sub-Saharan Regions

Late Pleistocene and Holocene climatic fluctuations also affected LSA populations in sub-Saharan regions, although perhaps not as dramatically as in the Sahara. The consequences of fluctuating rainfall and shifting vegetational boundaries on the economies and population density of these groups have been hard to document owing to poor preservation of organic materials and the problem of identifying sites in heavily vegetated terrain.

Unlike the Sahara, which was hyperarid and apparently unoccupied for many millennia between the last MSA and the earliest LSA habitation, the southernmost regions of West Africa probably saw an unbroken development of these industries. The LSA over much of this area is represented by microlithic industries. The date at which this technology appeared in West Africa is unknown, but it was present in central Africa by 40,000 B.P. (263). At Iwo Eleru rock shelter, located just inside the Nigerian forest, basal deposits containing a microlithic industry date to 9200 B.C. (214). The numerous geometric microliths at Iwo Eleru may have been slotted into arrowshafts to make points and barbs (220, p. 58). Clarke (52, p. 452) reminds us, however, that microliths can just as frequently be "employed in composite tools for plant gathering, harvesting, slicing, grating, plant-fibre processing for lines, snares, nets and traps, shell openers, bow-drill points and awls." The presence of a high gloss along the edge of trapezoids from Iwo Eleru is interesting in this regard (219, p. 49). A number of other sites with aceramic microlithic assemblages are known from West Africa, although the frequency of geometrics and other tool classes varies greatly from site to site (6; 84; 87; 94; 95; 205; 220, pp. 66–67; 248; 272). Few of these besides Iwo Eleru have been dated, although an important sequence at Shum Laka, Cameroun begins with a microlithic industry dated to the seventh millennium B.C. (66, p. 2). Microliths continue throughout the deposits, joined ca 5000 B.C. by large basalt blades and hoe-like tools. This is roughly contemporary with the appearance of large flaked axes at Iwo Eleru (214). The fauna from Shum Laka (monkeys, gorilla) indicates a forested environment, thereby weakening the suggestion that microlithic industries were generally confined to the savanna. (220).

Microlithic assemblages accompanied by ceramics and ground stone occur stratified above aceramic microlithic industries at several widely distributed sites (84, 214, 225, 248, 274). These innovations appear by the late fifth millennium B.C. at Shum Laka (66) and by the fourth millennium at Iwo Eleru (214), Bosumpra (225), and Dutsen Kongba (274), although the dating for this last site is somewhat confused. Whether the appearance of pottery and ground stone signals a shift in economy or a movement of ideas or peoples from the north is unknown. Ceramic microlithic sites are broadly distributed in West Africa (220, p. 67) from Senegal (70) and the Malian Sahel at Nioro (90) to the forest regions of Liberia, Nigeria, and Cameroun. This technological base endured into the first millennium A.D. at rock shelter sites in the Liberian forest (94) and Sierra Leone (14).

Rather crude-looking small, quartz flake industries associated with shell middens in coastal Ghana and Ivory Coast may be related to these widespread microlithic industries. In discussing the industry from the Gao Lagoon (Ghana) midden, dated between 4000–2000 B.C. (30, p. 7), Nygaard points out that standard microlithic forms are rare, although the tools are made on quite small flakes (180). Chenorkian (40, 41) uses the term "generally microlithic" to describe very similar industries from Ivory Coast middens dated from 1500 B.C. to A.D. 1300 (161) and from other coastal and inland sites. He suggests (40) that the poor quality of the quartz is responsible for the crude appearance of these industries. Near Abidjan, an aceramic industry of this type was recently dated to 13,000 B.P. (42).

Elsewhere in Ghana and Ivory Coast, another kind of LSA assemblage becomes prominent ca 1500 B.C. Characterized by enigmatic, scored soft-sandstone "rasps," polished stone axes and bracelets, and undistinguished microlithic component, grindstones, and comb-impressed pottery (91), the "Kintampo Industry" is best known from the forest and savanna of central Ghana, but its distribution also extends to Ivory Coast and southern Ghana (11, p. 64; 243). The origins of the Kintampo Industry are obscure, although the Sahara (64) and Ivory Coast (92, p. 220) have been suggested as source areas.

A handful of LSA sites have revealed nonmicrolithic industries in which large flaked or ground stone axes, picks, and celts form a prominent element (6,

44, 57, 115). Some of these large tools may have been used to dig tubers such as yams. Atherton (15) suggests that the double-edge ground or flake celt was used as a wood adze. It is interesting that ceramic assemblages of this kind apparently succeed aceramic microlithic industries at the widely separated sites of Rim (6) and Afikpo (220, pp. 64–65). The meaning of this shift, and the relation of these assemblages to the better-represented microlithic industries remains unclear.

The Origins of Agriculture

There is at present no unequivocal direct evidence for domesticated plants at any West African site before 2000 B.C. Contrary to some authors' convictions (34, pp. 555, 567), the presence of pottery and grinding stones at many LSA Saharan sites does not demonstrate that agriculture, rather than wild grain collection, was practiced. Claims for agriculture in the Hoggar, based on two pollen grains of "cultivated *Pennisetum*" millet from Amekni (32, p. 226) and one grain of a "cultivated grass" from Meniet have been discounted (216, pp. 112–13). The difficulties with distinguishing pollens of domesticated grasses from their wild relatives in African samples are widely acknowledged in the literature (142; 236; p. 520; 261). Pottery impressions from Adrar Bous of a single grain of *Brachiaria* (Guinea millet) and sorghum were initially believed to be cultivated forms, suggesting that agriculture was practiced in the Aïr as early as 4000 B.C. Both impressions are now thought to represent wild forms (217, p. 102).

The lack of direct evidence for early agriculture may of course reflect the failure of archaeologists to collect paleobotanical evidence systematically, using flotation or screening. Yet the recovery, nevertheless, from numerous Saharan sites of wild grains and seeds, particularly *Celtis* (hackberry) and *Zizyphus* (jujube) (32, pp. 234–37), presents the possibility that cultigens are not present at these sites, and agriculture is a genuinely late development in West Africa. It may be the case that, at least in the cereal grass belt of West Africa, pastoralism predated agriculture by several millennia. Such a situation would profoundly alter our understanding of the evolution of pastoralism, now generally believed to be an offshoot of agricultural systems.

So far, only three sites, all postdating 2000 B.C., have provided definite proof of domestic cereals. Investigations currently in progress on surface sherds from Karkarichinkat South (occupied between 2000–1500 B.C.) (224) have revealed impressions of both wild and domesticated pearl millet *(Pennisetum americanum)* and Guinea millet *(Brachiaria deflexa)* (233). Among the botanical remains recovered by flotation from third century B.C. levels at Jenne-jeno, domesticated *Pennisetum,* sorghum, and African rice *(Oryza glaberrima)* have recently been identified (J. Harlan and J. Scheuring, personal communication). This is the earliest sorghum yet identified in Africa, supporting Harlan & Stemler's (114) hypothesis that domestic sorghum had reached West Africa by the first millennium B.C. The rice at Jenne-jeno is too late to be of use in evaluating Portères' (193) claim that the initial domestication took place ca 1500 B.C. in the Inland Niger Delta. Thus far, however, archaeological reconnaissance undertaken in the central Delta by various researchers (19, 21, 147) has failed to reveal any trace of LSA habitation.

Grain impressions on pottery from several sites associated with the lakebed at Tichitt provide more detailed, diachronic information on the shift to cultivation. Munson (170) has shown that Tichitt's herder-fisher-hunter-collectors increased their exploitation of wild grain resources ca 1100–1000 B.C., as the lake dried up and fish disappear from the archaeological record. Immediately thereafter, in the period 1000–900 B.C., domestic *Pennisetum* appears, constituting over 60% of the total identifiable grain impressions on the pottery (170). The shift at Tichitt from intensive collecting of wild grains to reliance on cultigens is intriguing because of its lateness, its rapidity, and its relation to severe climatic deterioration. Opinions are mixed as to whether the transition at Tichitt involves the adoption of plants already domesticated elsewhere (113, p. 626; 170) or in situ domestication under particularly strong selective pressures (236, p. 514). Either way, agriculture at Tichitt clearly represents a response to environmental stress, a fact not overlooked by authors interested in the processual aspects of economic change in West African prehistory (46; 170; 220, pp. 74–75; 236).

A notable aspect of West African domestication is its noncentric pattern (112), referring to the dozens of locally important West African domesticated crops which must have arisen in many different areas from intensive manipulation of local plants. The West African mosaic of locally important staple crops includes several different genera of millets, plus sorghum, African rice, fonio, and groundnuts, not to mention the southern savanna and forest regions staples such as yams, cowpeas, and treecrops (198). The concept that early agricultural experimentation took place within a broad expanse of Sahel and savanna in West Africa has largely replaced earlier ideas of an agricultural "center of origin" located in the Saharan highlands (121, 170) or on the Upper Niger (173).

Little is known of the development of cultivation in the more humid zones of West Africa. Archaeological evidence for the major indigenous staple crop of the southern savanna and forest, yams, remains elusive. Although a high antiquity for yam domestication has been claimed (59), direct archaeological evidence for use of the tuber is nonexistent. Oil-palm *(Elaeis guineensis)* kernels have been found at several southern savanna sites dated to the third and second millennia B.C. (92, 94, 225), but it is impossible to say whether they came from trees that were being deliberately planted, cultivated, or protected. It is similarly impossible to say whether the cowpeas *(Vigna unguiculata)* at

Kintampo (92) were cultivated or not. Extrapolating from the presence of possible cultigens at Kintampo, Flight proposes that yam-cereal agriculture was established at the site. He further suggests that yam-cereal cultivation, developed within the savanna-forest mosaic, may be the primary form of agriculture in sub-Saharan Africa. Others consider it more likely that cereals were initially domesticated in less humid areas than the forest-savanna margin where yams were probably first cultivated. Alexander & Coursey (2, p. 421) suggest that yam cultivation may have occurred only after the idea of cultivation was introduced by northern cereal growers. It is also possible that cereal and yam domestication originated quite independently, millennia apart, in response to different factors operating on different ecosystems (196; 217, pp. 75–76).

In any case, agriculture at Kintampo sites is not improbable, given the evidence for domestic livestock (37) and a settlement pattern comprising, where information is available at open-air sites, small semisedentary villages of 4–7 rectilinear wattle and daub houses (10, 64, 78, 79).

THE DEVELOPMENT OF METAL-USING SOCIETIES

Over large parts of West Africa, the LSA seems to be directly succeeded by Iron Age assemblages, with no intervening period of copper or bronze use (exceptions will be discussed below). The earliest reliable dates for the use and working of iron in West Africa come from central Nigeria, just south of the Jos Plateau. The sophisticated Nok-style terracottas associated with these early Iron Age assemblages are well known (88, 222). After some initial confusion over very early radiocarbon dates for iron objects recovered from alluvial deposits at the type site of Nok (212), excavations at nonalluvial Nok sites, such as the iron-smelting site of Taruga (86) and Samun Dukiya (85), have produced a convincing cluster of seven radiocarbon dates in the sixth to second centuries B.C. (30). Thermoluminescence dates from a number of other Nok sites also fall within this range. (30).

Very few areas outside the Nok region have produced first millennium B.C. dates for Iron Age assemblages. South of Agades, a French salvage archaeology program has located over 40 sites with iron and slag and broadly similar material culture (characteristic items include stone scrapers, axes, and points, as well as a popular everted-rim pot decorated overall with twine roulette). Dates on charcoal from three of these sites ranged from the fifth to first centuries B.C. (104). Farther east, in the Termit Massif, smelting sites at Do Dimmi date as early as the seventh century B. C. (30, p. 10; 197, p. 184; 199). Evidence that iron technology had spread into Mali comes from Jenne-jeno, where the earliest traces of permanent settlement found so far date to the third century B.C. and are associated with iron and furnace slag (147). Unlike the

Niger sites, however, stone tools other than grindstones are absent. By the end of the first millennium B.C., iron is also attested in northern Ghana at Daboya in an assemblage similarly devoid of lithics, save grinders. As one of the few known sites comprising both LSA and IA deposits, Daboya may prove crucial to our understanding of this transition in West Africa (244; P. L. Shinnie and F. Kense, in preparation).

Origins of Metal Technology

The origins of this early iron technology are not well known. Some authors have seized upon the third and second millennium B.C. dates from the Nok Valley gravels to argue that iron-smelting was independently invented in central Nigeria ca 3500 B.C. (75, 77). This hypothesis assumes that the early radiocarbon results accurately date the iron artifacts at Nok. Most authorities agree, however, that the wide range of dates is attributable to alluvial mixing.

One of the major obstacles to a theory of independent discovery of iron in West Africa has been the apparent lack of any metallurgical tradition preceding the use of iron on the subcontinent. The role of copper smelting in the development of sohisticated pyrotechnology necessary for the reduction of iron ore has been recently emphasized (271). This view holds that the discovery of iron metallurgy was the ultimate consequence of the use of iron ores as a flux to facilitate the separation of molten reduced copper from copper ores (39). The discovery process must have been a long one. Since iron, unlike copper, was usually smelted below its melting point in antiquity, it bore little compelling resemblence after smelting to its final, usable form. Much heating and forging were required to achieve a utilitarian metal. Given the complex nature of iron, it is hard to credit the suggestion that knowledge of smelting could have been gained in West Africa through the experience of pot-firing in pits (77).

The recent discovery of early copper-using sites in the region of Agades has rekindled the question of a West African metallurgical tradition culminating in the discovery of iron. Sites with surface evidence of a copper industry have been located in two regions of Niger: northwest of Agades around Azelick (23), and southeast of Agades with a very important series of sites at Afunfun (22). Thirty-four C14 dates, many on charcoal from furnaces, reveal that copper working in these two regions was practiced throughout the last two millennia B.C. (104).

There are several interesting features of this enduring metallurgical tradition. First, none of the hearth pits filled with charcoal and copper drops is associated with any archaeological deposits suggesting permanent settlement. Associated pottery is strongly reminiscent of the Saharan LSA pottery in the same region. Stone tools continue to be used alongside the small copper pins, spatulas, and points (104). Second, throughout its 2000 year duration, the industry appears to have exploited the abundant native copper in the two regions investigated.

Metallurgical analyses of copper and slag from numerous hearth pits have revealed no evidence of copper ore smelting. Rather, metallic copper was apparently extracted from local rocks by crushing and then melted (260). Objects were fashioned by the use of simple one-piece molds or by heating and working. A similar copper industry has also been documented in western Mauretania dating from the ninth to fifth centuries B.C. (133). In Niger, the presence of arsenic as a natural impurity in the copper made the worked metal significantly harder and more useful than pure copper. The discovery of several bronze pieces may indicate that the alloying of copper with tin (from the neighboring Aïr region) may have soon been locally achieved, possibly by adding tin to the crucible under reducing conditions (259). Alternatively, the bronze pieces may be imports. The early copper industry in Niger thus lacks advanced pyrotechnology, such as copper smelting and the use of available iron ores as a flux. In the opinion of Tylecote (259) and van der Merwe & Avery (262), this argues against the local development of iron technology out of copper extraction.

It remains far more likely that iron was introduced to West Africa from the outside. It was earlier believed that a probable source area for the diffusion of iron technology was Meroe in the Republic of Sudan. Immense slag heaps, some 150 m long, still dominate the site, attesting to Meroe's importance as an early industrial center. Inspired by these mounds, the myth of diffusion from Meroe persisted for years in the virtual absence of direct supporting evidence (256). The slag mounds now appear to date to the first two centuries A.D., and the furnace type involved was a Roman-type, slag-tapping shaft furnace (258). Earlier iron smelting at Meroe, documented from the third century B.C. and perhaps earlier (223), was achieved in small bowl furnaces. The contemporaneous low-shaft Taruga furnaces are more technologically advanced than the earliest Meroitic furnaces (257).

It is more probable that West African Iron technology was introduced from North Africa where iron-using Phoenicians founded trading colonies like Carthage and Leptis Magna from the ninth to seventh centuries B.C. Carthaginian-style bronze jewelry found in a sixth century B.C. context in western Mauretania suggests the existence of contacts between Punic North Africa and the Southern Sahara (132, p. 168; 134, p. 214). Berber tribes, such as the chariot-driving Garamantes mentioned by Herodotus, may have been the Saharan intermediaries through whom the knowledge of iron passed (162, pp. 277–86). Some authors suggest that the distribution of rock art depicting horse-drawn chariots in the Fezzan, Tassili, Hoggar, Adrar des Iforas, and Western Mauretania outlines the route of north-south contact [for full bibliography see (35)]. Views on the nature of these contacts vary: some believe they were regular (194) and involved extensive Phoenician trade (181). Others deny that regular trans-Saharan traffic or significant trade was possible before the introduction of the camel in the early centuries A.D. (99, 136, 162). Camps (33) rejects the idea of chariot "routes" altogether by noting that the concentration of rock art along a north-south axis reflects the distribution of rocky massifs and outcrops in the Sahara rather than any system of prehistoric highways. That goods from the Mediterranean world actually did penetrate south of the Sahara in the first millennium B.C. is demonstrated by two Hellenistic glass beads from first and second century B.C. deposits at Jenne-jeno in Mali (S. Goldstein, personal communication). This discovery unfortunately sheds no light on how they reached the Niger.

In any case, a Punic source for West African metallurgy cannot be regarded as firmly established. In the absence of comparative data on iron furnaces and technology in Punic North Africa, it can only be regarded as "the least improbable view to date" (62).

Other important questions about early iron in West Africa are now being raised. Once established by 500 B.C. in Niger and Nigeria, for example, how did iron metallurgy spread? A number of factors, including usefulness of iron in the local economy, access to good quality ores, and the cultural costs of working iron or trading for finished objects may have influenced the speed of iron adoption in different areas (1). Sites with both LSA and Iron Age (IA) components are clearly the most useful for dating the transition to iron use in a given area, but few of these have been excavated. At several rock shelters in Sierra Leone and Liberia, iron was not present in levels earlier than the late first millennium A.D. (14, 94). Iron may be similarly late at Daima in northeastern Nigeria, where the LSA-IA transition appears to coincide with a significant decline in bone tools and ground stone axes in levels dated to the fifth century A.D. (55). Dating of levels directly associated with iron has been problematic, however, permitting no unambiguous conclusions about its chronology (56). Currently, the most reliable radiocarbon dates for iron in the region of northeastern Nigeria, southern Chad, and northern Cameroun are all later than 400 A.D. (61). The third century A.D. date cited by Calvocoressi & David (30) for iron objects associated with stone ax factory debris at Tsanaga II is now regarded sceptically by Marliac (158).

Categorical statements about the spread of iron in West Africa cannot be made on the basis of the small number of systematically excavated and dated sites with IA components. Nevertheless, available data are consistent with a mosaic pattern of acceptance, involving different local processes and chronologies (162, p. 332). Late Stone Age "survivals" were of course known up until this century in parts of Africa.

Local innovation in early African iron technology has recently emerged as an exciting and important issue. Even if West Africa may have adopted the earliest iron technology from a Mediterranean source, it scarcely did so passively. Recent research suggests that local metallurgists quickly elaborated on the technology, possibly incorporating ideas from existing copper extraction. The early Taruga smelting furnaces, for example, bear a strong resemblance to the late Copper Age furnaces at Afunfun (259). By the end of the first millennium B.C., an extraordinary variety of furnace designs and smelting approaches had been developed in West Africa, including bowl furnaces, bellows-blown shaft furnaces, and induced draft furnaces. There is now evidence from West Africa that some of these early furnaces were producing steel.

The process by which some African smelters created a bloom of high carbon steel directly in the smelting furnace has been recorded ethnographically among the Haya of Tanzania and recreated ethnoarchaeologically by Schmidt (209). A critical innovation of the process was the insertion of tuyeres deep into the blast so that the air inside was preheated, permitting smelting temperatures as high as 1500°C. to be achieved. Products of this process were first identified archaeologically in Tanzania, possibly dating to the first millennium B.C. (209). Now artifacts of medium carbon steel with a homogeneously carburized structure have been identified in second century B.C. contexts at Jenne-jeno, Mali (R. L. Tylecote, personal communication). Similar material has also been identified at Taruga, although most of the pieces analyzed were forged products of soft wrought iron (262).

Tylecote (259) and Willet (273) suggest that metallurgical innovation, particularly in copper technology, may have continued through the first millennium A.D. It is possible that local experimentation with copper smithing techniques (annealing, casting, chasing) and alloys culminated in the sophisticated *cire perdu* masterpieces dated as early as the ninth century at Igbo Ukwu (213).

Although many questions remain concerning the spread and elaboration of iron working, we can state with certainty that acceptance of the technology had far-reaching consequences for West African societies. In those areas lacking suitable stone for adzes and hoes, iron agricultural tools may have opened up large amounts of new land to tillage. The creation of demand for high-quality iron or ores probably fostered intensified trade contacts, with the concomitant appearance of specialized iron production centers or the elaboration of specialized castes of smiths. In many West African cultures today the blacksmith caste is an institution of fundamental significance to the texture of society. Blacksmiths figure prominently in the creation myths and oral traditions of many groups and are often regarded as imbued with mystical powers (12). The origins of social stratification in parts of West Africa may thus be intimately linked to the introduction of iron. Of interest is de Barros' current archaeological study of the effects of iron production in the Bassar region (Togo) on settlement patterns, trade, and specialization (65; P. de Barros, personal communication).

The potentially dramatic impact on fragile West African environments of fuel-hungry smelting industries has been discussed by Goucher (101) and Haaland (109). Schmidt & Avery (209) suggest that the necessity for fuel conservation may have sparked technological innovation in some areas.

EMERGENCE OF COMPLEX SOCIETIES BEFORE 1000 A.D.

From the beginnings of iron use until the historical period is inaugurated by Arab penetration of the West African Sahel at the end of the first millennium A.D., we know little in detail about the evolution of West African societies. Yet it is clear that changes of great importance were occurring in certain regions during this period, transforming the noncentralized societies of the Late Stone Age into highly stratified systems with power and wealth concentrated in the hands of god-like kings. By 1000 A.D., large areas of West Africa were organized into empires, such as the Empire of Ghana, replete with armies, cities, craft industries and long-distance trade. When and why did this happen? For many years it has been widely assumed that much of the impetus for the development of West African complex societies came from outside stimulation of the indigenous economy as North African Arabs initiated,in the late eighth century A.D., trans-Saharan trade for gold and slaves from sub-Saharan regions. During the past decade, however, controlled excavations incorporating radiocarbon dating programs have revealed evidence of complex social stratification, long-distance trade, and even urbanism in West Africa by the mid-first millennium A.D. (72).

Work by several different research teams at funerary monuments, occupation sites, and specialized iron production centers along the middle Niger has provided insights concerning the emergence of complex societies during this period. Excavations at the massive tumuli (up to 150 m diameter and 15 m high) in the lake region of the lower Inland Delta have produced four radiocarbon dates between A.D. 600–1000 (160, p. 110; 208). These erosion-resistant monuments, with their deliberately fired surfaces, were first investigated early this century. Desplagnes' excavations resulted in the only published excavations to date of burial chambers within the tumuli (160, pp. 96–77). The rich burials at El-Oualedji were accompanied by iron tools and jewelry, copper bracelets and earrings, pottery and food offerings. The Killi mound contained 25–30 adults and children who apparently had been pushed or thrown into the tomb. These findings of a wooden burial chamber with rich grave goods and probable human sacrifices closely resemble the burial ritual for the pagan king of the Ghana Empire which the Arab geographer al-Bakri described in 1067 A.D.

At Tondidaro, tumuli dated to the seventh century are associated with extensive alignments of megaliths with carved phallic and geometric motifs (160, pp. 129–34). The date of the megaliths is unknown. Other associations of tumuli and megaliths occur throughout the lakes region, but Tondidaro is the most important. Unfortunately, it was vandalized by French officials earlier this century and little remains in situ for archaeological study.

Pottery very similar to the red-slipped tumulus pottery with its white painted or comb-impressed geometric designs has also been found in the upper Inland Niger Delta at the occupation site of Jenne-jeno. Not far from this site, probable funerary tumuli have been discovered but not yet excavated (147, p. 361). In addition to providing evidence of cultural contacts along the Niger in the first millennium, the 5.5 m stratified sequence at Jenne-jeno has yielded insights into the processes by which certain West African cultures expanded and became markedly more complex during this period. According to 28 radiocarbon dates (144), the site represents over 1500 years of continuous Iron Age occupation. Recent excavations confirm earlier claims that the site expanded rapidly in size in the first millennium A.D., reaching a maximum area of 33 hectares by A.D. 800, and then experiencing gradual abandonment after 1150 (145). This pattern of growth and decline is mirrored by hinterland settlements around Jenne-jeno, where site density in the period 700–1100 was almost ten times greater than the density of occupied villages today (147). Most of these sites were apparently abandoned by 1400, for unknown reasons.

Jenne-jeno's location at the interface of two major ecotopes (dry savanna and sahel) on a floodplain lacking important resources encouraged interregional exchange. Iron and stone from sources at least 50 km distant occur in the lowest deposits. The appearance of copper by 400 A.D., presumably from the nearest Saharn sources, and of savanna gold by 800 A.D. brackets a period of rapid site expansion, culminating in construction of a city wall 2 km long. It has often been assumed that long-distance trade in gold and copper between Saharan and sub-Saharan regions did not really develop until the Arabs organized the "Golden Trade of the Moors" (26). The Jenne-jeno evidence suggests the existence of an earlier indigenous trade. This is supported at Marandet in the Aïr, where sixth and seventh century dates were obtained on charcoal from refuse heaps containing over 40,000 crucibles used in working a remarkable variety of copper alloys (38, 141, 197, 273). Unfortunately, Lhote's work at this important site has been severely criticized (96).

Early development of the middle Niger region as a major transport axis would account for the growth of Jenne-jeno, at the southwest extreme of the Inland Delta, as an exchange point for Saharan copper and salt, and savanna gold, iron, and agricultural produce. The appearance of rich tumuli in the lakes region would also reflect the effects of trade, possibly among groups in a position to control the flow of goods. The homogeneity of material culture throughout a large area of the Inland Delta from 700–1400 A.D. may indicate a degree of admnistrative control, ensuring a stable political environment for exchange (147, p. 443). Research by Bedaux et al (21) and Barth (19) at sites up to 100 km downriver from Jenne-jeno has revealed a material culture, radiocarbon dated between 900–1400 A.D., that is virtually indistinguishable from contemporaneous items at Jenne-jeno. Similar, though not identical, material comes from the Mema region bordering the Inland Delta (109, 182, 249). Haaland (109) suggests that the region's iron industry, dated to 800–1150 at sites associated with huge slag mounds, was controlled by the Empire of Ghana. Excavations conducted by Robert and Berthier at Koumbi Saleh, the putative capital of the Empire, may verify the existence of relations between that town and the Mema/Middle Niger. Findings presented so far indicate that an urban center had emerged at Koumbi Saleh by the early ninth century. Pre-urban occupation deposits, dating back to the seventh century, extended a meter under the early urban levels (24, 83). It seems likely that the emergence of specialized industrial centers in the Mema, the consolidation of the Soninke Empire of Ghana, and the rise of Soninke trade towns like Jenne-jeno along the Niger were all intimately related to the develoment of indigenous long-distance trade in the first millennium A.D. (146).

A strikingly similar picture of first millennium developments is beginning to emerge along the Senegal River, although far fewer details are available. At mound sites like Sinthiou Bara along the middle Senegal, excavations by Ravisé and Thilmans have revealed that copper, brass, and silver were reaching the area as early as the sixth century A.D. (76, p. 462). Copper-based bracelets and small bells from undated sites in southern Mauretania and from sites farther down the Senegal River closely resemble the Sinthiou Bara material (252), possibly reflecting long-distance trade networks (72, p. 162). Somewhere along this stretch of the middle Senegal, the trading empire of Takrur arose by the tenth century.

In the Ferlo region south of the river, numerous iron-smelting sites have been inventoried but not yet investigated (159). Throughout the northwest quadrant of Senegal, earthen funerary tumuli called *mbanar* abound. Over 6800 monuments, varying in size from 3 to 80 m diameter and up to 10 m in height, have been located at a total of 1446 sites (159). These figures do not include the many shell tumuli constructed atop shell middens in the Sine-Saloum estuarine region (71). Excavations of earthen tumuli at Ndalane and Rao and several shell tumuli at Dioron Boumak revealed collective inhumations often accompanied by grave furnishings of iron, copper, brass, and gold (68, 71, 130). The few available radiocarbon dates suggest a tumulus chronology encompassing the eighth to twelfth centuries (68, 76).

Megalithic funerary monuments overlap with tumuli in both time and space. Available dates range from the sixth to eleventh centuries A.D. and later (69), refuting earlier ideas that the Senegambian monuments derived from Iberian megalithic influences in the second millennium B.C. (119). Throughout the megalithic zone, the basic pattern of a circular funerary monument associated with one or more megalithic standing stones placed several meters to the east recurs. The nature of the circular monument varies, however. While earthern tumuli are most common in the northwest part of the megalithic zone, circles up to 10 m diameter of shaped laterite megaliths are well known in the central part. Farther east, stone tumuli and stone circles appear, constructed out of fist-sized blocks of unworked laterite. Since standing stones may or may not be associated with any given monument, many of the 16,000+ "megalithic" monuments known have no megalithic components. The frequent co-occurrence of two or more types of monument at the same site nevertheless suggests a close linkage among earthen tumuli, megalithic circles, stone circles, and stone tumuli. This is supported by the close ressemblance of "megalithic" and "tumulus" pottery in the area where these distributions overlap (98). Hill (120) proposes grouping all these monuments within a single Senegambian Monument Complex. Structural variations among monuments may reflect symbolic, functional, or temporal differences, but with systematic excavations accomplished at only five out of 1900 known sites, it is too soon to draw meaningful conclusions.

Thilmans et al (253) and Gallay (98) have excavated several different types of megalithic monuments, revealing substantial variability in burial treatment. At Tiékéné-Boussoura and Kodiam, individual monuments contained one to six burials unaccompanied by grave goods (253). Farther west, three excavated megalithic circles at Sine Ngayen contained collective inhumations of up to 59 individuals, including men, women and children. Some wore iron or copper jewelry or were accompanied by iron spears. Many appeared to have been simultaneously interred, suggesting human sacrifice on a considerable scale (253).

The first millennium dates for commerce, towns, and labor intensive funerary monuments in Mali and Senegal have necessitated reevaluation of discoveries earlier regarded as anomalous. At the site of Igbo Ukwu, situated on the forest fringe of eastern Nigeria, Shaw's excavations uncovered a stunning array of cast bronze vessels and finely crafted copper objects (213, 218). One of the excavation units revealed the burial chamber of a high-ranking individual, whose regalia included a bronze staff and wisk, chased copper pectoral and crown, and over 100,000 glass beads. Wood from the burial chamber has been dated to the ninth century A.D.

The large quantities of imported glass beads imply trading connections reaching into the Mediterranean world. The four ninth-century radiocarbon dates for Igbo Ukwu were initially dismissed by many scholars as centuries too early for such trade contacts to have reached the Nigerian forest [see (215) for discussion]. These dates no longer seem inplausible in light of the growing evidence for an extensive pre-Arab trade (72, 144, 146, 147, 195). The rapid and early dispersal of North African trade goods far into the interior suggests that Arab commerce was effectively grafted onto a preexisting infrastructure of

Saharan and sub-Saharan networks. A similar model might be profitably applied to other Nigerian forest sites, such as Ife, where a prospering first millennium trade in kola may have contributed to the emergence of Ife by 1100 as a religious center supporting a royal court (221). Additionally, well-known sites such as Niani (89) and some of the larger "Sao" sites (137–139) may reveal comparable developments in the late first millennium once their early Iron Age chronologies are better understood. It is increasingly clear that much of West Africa's rapid development in the centuries after Arab penetration can be properly accounted for only in the context of earlier, indigenous processes of trade expansion, increasing social stratification, and urbanism.

CONCLUSIONS

A recurring theme in this review is the inadequacy of simplistic stadial models for West African prehistoric cultural change. As more archaeological and palaeoecological detail is known, the true complexity of events emerges. Palaeoclimate researchers have jettisoned the notions of Glacial-Pluvial correspondence and simple latitudinal isohyet shifts during major episodes of cimatic change. The picture emerges of significant regional and even intraregional variability during all major periods. It is no longer advisable to predict the ecological profile of one area by reference to that of another hundreds much less thousands of kilometers away, regardless of currently similar conditions.

With the decline of these broad palaeoclimatic schemes, existing overly generalized stadial concepts of West African prehistory seem increasingly inappropriate. Formulations such as the Saharo-Sudanese Neolithic and the Aqualithic currently obscure significant variation in the evidence of local adaptations. Similarly, it is only by appreciating the local scene that we can understand the noncentric, mosaic pattern of indigenous food crop domestication. Assumptions about the spread of iron technology may also require revision. Rather than diffusing along a broad, ever-expanding front, iron may have been adopted early in some places, late in others, and in significant ways subjected to intense innovative impulses at the local level. The role played by an early, possibly indigenous copper technology in fostering this complex process of metallurgical adaptation needs investigation. And likewise, the picture of early complex societies and institutions recently has radically changed. Gone are the obligatory outside stimuli to states, urbanism, and long-distance trade. These developments now appear very early in an entirely comprehensible local context.

Future directions of West African prehistoric research will require new methodologies and new terminologies. With the decline of the monolithic models of implied pan-continental cultural stages we now need intensive, multidisciplinary research on local processes of change and adaptation. All convincing and enduring conclusions about processes of change are built upon detailed cultural historical sequences. West Africa, however, has been so underpopulated by prehistorians in comparison to Europe, the Americas, and much of Asia that we still lack the fine-grained chronological control on local processes that are taken for granted in those other continents. But sterile stadial culture histories will not work here; terms such as the MSA or LSA (and stratification of those stages into "early," "middle," etc) may reflect the archaeological reality of some parts of the world, but they inadequately describe West Africa's complex evolution. Research into West Africa's past is embarking in exciting directions as a newly emergent corps of West African archaeologists, with a demonstrated interest in documenting the regional context, collaborate with international interdisciplinary research teams. This collaboration will affirm West Africa's position as one of the world's most dynamic and individual theaters of prehistoric process and change.

ACKNOWLEDGMENTS

We are grateful to the many scholars who generously provided information and research material for this review. Special thanks also go to Brian M. Fagan for comments on content and style on a preliminary draft of this paper. Barbara Podratz's achievements in typing the manuscript were little less than heroic.

Literature Cited

1. Alexander, J. 1980. The spread and development of iron-using in Europe and Africa. *Proc. Panafr. Congr. Prehist. Quat. Stud., 8th, Nairobi*, ed. R. E. F. Leakey, B. A. Ogot, pp. 327–30
2. Alexander, J., Coursey, D. G. 1969. The origins of yam cultivation. In *The Domestication and Exploitation of Plants and Animals*, ed. P. J. Ucko, G. W. Dimbleby, pp. 402–25. London: Duckworth
3. Allsworth-Jones, P. 1980. The Middle Stone Age industry from Zenabi, northern Nigeria. See Ref. 1, pp. 244–47
4. Allsworth-Jones, P. 1980. The Middle Stone Age north of the Jos Plateau: a preliminary report on the finds and their context. *West Afr. J. Archaeol.* 10: In press
5. Amblard, S. 1981. *Le Dhar Tichitt-Walata (République Islamique de Mauritanie): architecture et industrie lithique*. Presented at Colloq. Assoc. Ouest-Afr. Archaeol., 3rd, Dakar
6. Andah, B. W. 1978. Excavations at Rim, Upper Volta. *West Afr. J. Archaeol.* 8:75–138
7. Andah, B. W. 1981. West Africa before the seventh century. In *Ancient Civil-*izations of Africa, ed. G. Mokhtar, UNESCO Gen. Hist. Afr. 2:593–619. Berkeley: Heinemann-UNESCO 2 vols.
8. Anozie, F. N. 1982. *Recent archaeological discoveries in south-eastern Nigeria*. Presented at Ann. Congr. Hist. Soc. Nigeria, 27th, Port Harcourt
9. Anozie, F. N., Chikwendu, V. E., Umeji, A. C. 1978. Discovery of a major prehistoric site at Ugwuele-Uturu, Okigwe. *West Afr. J. Archaeol.* 8:171–76
10. Anquandah, J. 1976. Boyasi Hill—a Kintampo Neolithic site in the forest of Ghana. *Sankofa* 2:92
11. Anquandah, J. 1982. *Rediscovering Ghana's Past*. Accra: Longmans
12. Ardouin, C. D. 1978. La caste des forgerons et son importance dans le Soudan Occidental. *Etud. Maliennes* 24:1–32
13. Arkell, A. J. 1949. *Early Khartoum*. London: Oxford Univ. Press
14. Atherton, J. H. 1972. Excavations at Kamabai and Yagala rock shelters, Sierra Leone. *West Afr. J. Archaeol.* 2:39–74
15. Atherton, J. H. 1980. Speculation on functions of some prehistoric archaeo-

logical materials from Sierra Leone. In *West African Culture Dynamics: Archaeological and Historical Perspectives*, ed. B. K. Swartz, R. E. Dumett, pp. 259–75. The Hague: Mouton

16. Aumassip, G. 1973. Civilisations pré-néolithique des régions Sahariennes. *Proc. Panafr. Congr. Prehist. Quat. Stud., 6th, Dakar*, ed. H -J. Hugot

17. Barich, B. 1974. La serie stratigraphica dell'uadi Ti-n-Torha. *Origini* 8:7–182

18. Barich, B. 1980. Pour une definition du Néolithique en Afrique du Nord et au Sahara. See Ref. 1, pp. 271–72

19. Barth, H. K. 1977. L'age de la civilisation des tumulus et des anciens habitats du Delta Intérieur du Niger (Mali). *Notes Afr.* 155:57–61

20. Beaumont, P. B., de Villiers, H., Vogel, J. C. 1978. Modern man in sub-Saharan Africa prior to 49,000 years B.P.: a review and evaluation with particular reference to Border Cave. *South Afr. J. Sci.* 74:409–19

21. Bedaux, R. M. A., Constandse-Westermann, T. S., Hacquebord, L., Lange, A. G., van der Waals, J. D. 1978. Recherches archéologiques dans le Delta Intérieur du Niger. *Palaeohistoria* 20:92–220

22. Bernus, S., ed. 1979. *Programme archéologique d'urgence, In Gall-Tegidda n'Tesemt. Document de la Mission R. C. P. 322.* Niamey: ORSTOM

23. Bernus, S., Gouletquer, P. 1976. Du cuivre au sel, recherches ethnoarchéologiques sur le région d'Azelik. *J. Afr.* 46:7–68

24. Berthier, S. 1981. *Fouille d'un ensemble d'habitations quartier de la mosquée. Site de Koumbi Saleh.* Presented at Colloq. Assoc. Ouest-Afr. Archaeol., 3rd, Dakar

25. Bishop, W. W., Clark, J. D., eds. 1967. *Background to Evolution in Africa.* Chicago: Univ. Chicago Press

26. Bovill, E. W. 1968. *The Golden Trade of the Moors.* Oxford: Oxford Univ. Press. 2nd ed.

27. Bowles, F. A. 1975. Paleoclimatic significance of quartz/illite variations in cores from the eastern equatorial North Atlantic. *Quat. Res.* 5:225–35

28. Butzer, K. W. 1978. Sediment stratigraphy of the Middle Stone Age sequence at Klasies River Mouth, Tsitsikama Coast, South Africa. *South Afr. Archaeol. Bull.* 33:141–51

29. Butzer, K. W. 1982. The palaeoecology of the African continent. See Ref. 48, pp. 1–69

30. Calvocoressi, D., David, N. 1979. A new survey of radiocarbon and thermoluminescence dates for West Africa. *J. Afr. Hist.* 20:1–29

31. Camps, G. 1968. *Amekni, Néolithique Ancien du Hoggar.* Mem. Cent. Rech. Anthropol. Prehist. Ethnol. 10. Algiers: CRAPE

32. Camps, G. 1974. *Les Civilisations Préhistoriques de l'Afrique du Nord et du Sahara.* Paris: Doin

33. Camps, G. 1981. *Le cheval et le char dans la préhistoire Nord-Africaine et Saharienne.* Trav. Lab. Anthropol. Prehist. Ethnol. Pays Mediterr. Occident. 1981:1–12

34. Camps, G. 1982. Beginnings of pastoralism and cultivation in northwest Africa and the Sahara: Origin of the Berbers. See Ref. 48, pp. 548–612

35. Camps, G., Gast, M., eds. 1983 *Les Chars Préhistoriques du Sahara: Archéologie et Technique d'Attelage.* Aix-en-Provence: Ed. Univ. Provence. In press

36. Carter, P. L., Clark, J. D. 1976. Adrar Bous and African cattle. *Proc. Panafr. Congr. Prehist. Quat. Stud., 7th, Addis Ababa,* ed. B. Abebe, J. Chavaillon, J. E. G. Sutton, pp. 487–93

37. Carter, P. L., Flight, C. 1972. A report on the fauna from the sites of Ntereso and Kintampo Rock Shelter Six in Ghana: with evidence for the practice of animal husbandry during the second millennium B.C. *Man (NS)* 7:278–82

38. Castro, R. 1974. Examen de creusets de Marandet (Niger). *Bull. Inst. Fondam. Afr. Noire Ser. B* 36:667–73

39. Charles, J. A. 1980. The coming of copper and copper-based alloys and iron: a metallurgical sequence. See Ref. 271, pp. 151–81

40. Chenorkian, R. 1979. *Prospections préhistoriques en Côte d'Ivoire. Les sites de Ehania-Krinjabo and Kong.* Trav. Lab. Anthropol. Prehist. Ethnol. Pays Mediterr. Occident.

41. Chenorkian, R. 1981. *Note sur l'industrie lithique de l'amas coquiller de N'Gaty (Basse Côte d'Ivoire).* Trav. Lab Anthropol. Prehist. Ethnol. Pays Mediterr. Occident, pp. 1–5

42. Chenorkian, R., Delibrias, G., Paradis, P. 1982. *Une industrie microlithique datée de 13050 BP environ découverte en Côte d'Ivoire dans la "terre de barre".* Trav. Lab. Anthropol. Prehist. Ethnol. Pays Mediterr. Occident. In press

43. Chenorkian, R., Paradis, G. 1981. *Une industrie paléolithique découverte dans la "terre de barre" d'une terrasse proche d'Anyama (Région d'Abidjan).* Presented at Colloq. Assoc. Ouest Afr. Archecol., 3rd, Dakar

44. Chikwendu, V. E. 1979. The occurrence of waisted stone adzes/axes in E. Nigeria. *Nyame Akuma* 14:44–48

45. Clark, J. D. 1976. Epi-Palaeolithic aggregates from Greboun Wadi, Aïr, and Adrar Bous, northwestern Ténéré, Republic of Niger. See Ref. 36, pp. 67–78

46. Clark, J. D. 1976. Prehistoric populations and pressures favoring plant domestication in Africa. In *Origins of African Plant Domestication*, ed. J. R. Harlan, J. M. de Wet, A. B. Stemler, pp. 67–105. The Hague: Mouton

47. Clark, J. D. 1980. Human population and cultural adaptations in the Sahara and Nile during prehistoric times. In *The Sahara and the Nile*, ed. M. A. Williams, H. Faure, pp. 527–82. Rotterdam: Balkema

48. Clark, J. D., ed. 1982. *The Cambridge History of Africa. Vol. 1: From Earliest Times to c. 500 BC*. Cambridge: Cambridge Univ. Press

49. Clark, J. D. 1982. The cultures of the Middle Palaeolithic/Middle Stone Age. See Ref. 48, pp. 248–340

50. Clark, J. D., Williams, M. A., Smith, A. B. 1973. The geomorphology and archaeology of Adrar Bous, Central Sahara: a preliminary report. *Quaternaria* 17:245–98

51. Clark, J. G. D. 1971. *World Prehistory: A New Outline*. Cambridge: Cambridge Univ. Press. 2nd ed.

52. Clarke, D. 1977. Mesolithic Europe: the economic basis. In *Problems in Social and Economic Archaeology*, ed. G. G. Sieveking, I. H. Longworth, K. E. Wilson, pp. 449–81. London: Duckworth

53. Close, A. E. 1980. Current research and recent radiocarbon dates from northern Africa. *J. Afr. Hist.* 21:145–67

54. Cloudsley-Thompson, J. L. 1978. Human activities and desert expansion. *Geogr. J.* 144:416–23

55. Connah, G. 1976. The Daima sequence and the prehistoric chronology of the Lake Chad region of Nigeria. *J. Afr. Hist.* 17:321–52

56. Connah, G. 1981. *Three Thousand Years in Africa*. Cambridge: Cambridge Univ. Press

57. Coon, C. S. 1968. *Yengema Cave Report*. Mus. Monogr. Univ. Mus., Univ. Pennsylvania

58. Coppens, M. Y. 1961. Le Tchadanthropus. *L'Anthropologie* 70:5–16

59. Coursey, D. G. 1976. The origins and domestication of yams in Africa. See Ref. 46, pp. 383–408

60. Courtin, J. 1968. Le Tenéréen du Borkou, Nord-Tchad. In *La Préhistoire:*

Problems et Tendences, ed. F. Bordes, D. de Sonneville-Bordes, pp. 133–38. Paris: CNRS

61. David, N. 1976. History of crops and peoples in north Cameroon to A.D. 1900. See Ref. 46, pp. 223–67

62. David, N. 1980. Early Bantu expansion in the context of Central African prehistory: 4000–1 BC. In *L'Expansion Bantoue*, ed. L. Bouquiaux, pp. 609–47. Soc. Et. Linguist. Anthropol. Fr., Numero Spec. 9

63. Davies, O. 1967. *West Africa Before the Europeans*. London: Methuen

64. Davies, O. 1980. The Ntereso culture in Ghana. See Ref. 15, pp. 205–25

65. de Barros, P. 1981. The iron industry of Bassar. *Nyame Akuma* 18:57–58

66. de Maret, P. 1982. New survey of archaeological research and dates for West-Central and North-Central Africa. *J. Afr. Hist.* 23:1–15

67. Descamps, C. 1978. *Etat des connaissances sur le Paléolithique au Sénégal*. Presented at Colloq. Assoc. Ouest-Afr. Archaeol., 2nd, Bamako

68. Descamps, C. 1979. Sites protohistoriques de la Sénégambie. *Ann. Fac. Lett. Sci. Hum. Univ. Dakar* 9:305–13

69. Descamps, C. 1981. Note sur le mégalithisme Sénégambien. In *Le Sol, La Parole, et l'Ecrit*, ed. J. P. Cretien, J. Devisse, C. H. Perrot, Y. Person, 1:29–36. Soc. Fr. Hist. Outre-Mer. 2 vols.

70. Descamps, C. 1982. Quelque reflexions sur le néolithique du Sénégal. *West Afr. J. Archaeol.* In press

71. Descamps, C., Thilmans, G., Thommeret, Y. 1974. Données sur l'edification de l'amas coquiller de Dioron Boumak (Sénégal). *Bull. Assoc. Sénégalaise Etude Quat. Afr.* 41:67–83

72. Devisse, J. 1982. L'Apport de l'archéologie à l'histoire de l'Afrique Occidentale entre le Vᵉ et le XIIᵉ siècle. *C. R. Acad. Inscriptions B.-Lett.* 1982:156–77

73. Diester-Haass, L. 1976. Late Quaternary climatic variations in northwest Africa deduced from East Atlantic sediment cores. *Quat. Res.* 6:299–314

74. Diop, A. 1980. Une nouvelle datation de l'Acheuléen en l'Afrique de l'Ouest. *Ann. Fac. Lett. Sci. Hum. Univ. Dakar* 10:283–91

75. Diop, C. A. 1976. L'Usage du fer en Afrique. *Notes Afr.* 152:93–95

76. Diop, C. A. 1977. Datations par la méthode du radiocarbone, Série IV. *Bull. Inst. Fondam. Afr. Noire Ser. B* 39:461–70

77. Diop, L. M. 1968. Métallurgie traditionelle et l'âge du fer en Afrique. *Bull.*

Inst. Fondam. Afr. Noire Ser. B 30:10–37

78. Dombrowski, J. 1976. Mumute and Bonoase-two sites of the Kintampo industry. *Sankofa* 2:64–71
79. Dombrowski, J. 1980. Earliest settlements in Ghana: the Kintampo industry. See Ref. 1, pp. 261–62
80. Durand, A. 1982. Oscillations of Lake Chad over the past 50,000 years. New data and new hypothesis. *Palaeogeogr., Palaeoclimatol., Palaeoecol.* 39:37–53
81. Durand, A., Mathieu, P. 1980. Evolution paléogéographique et paléoclimatique du bassin tchadien au Pleistocene supérieur. *Rev. Géol. Dyn. Geogr. Phys.* 22:329–41
82. Epstein, H. 1971. *The Origins of the Domestic Animals of Africa.* New York: Africana. 2 vols.
83. Evin, J., Marien, G., Pachiaudi, C. 1979. Lyon Natural Radiocarbon Measurements VIII. *Radiocarbon* 21:429–31
84. Eyo, E. 1972. Rop rock shelter excavations 1964. *West Afr. J. Archaeol.* 2:13–16
85. Fagg, A. 1972. Excavation of an occupation site in the Nok Valley, Nigeria. *West Afr. J. Archaeol.* 2:75–80
86. Fagg, B. E. 1969. Recent work in West Africa: new light on the Nok culture. *World Archaeol.* 1:41–50
87. Fagg, B. E. 1972. Rop rock shelter excavations, 1944. *West Afr. J. Archaeol.* 2:1–12
88. Fagg, B. E. 1978. *Nok Terracottas.* London: Ethnographica
89. Filipowiak, W. 1979. *Etudes Archéologiques sur la Capitale Médiévale du Mali.* Szczecin: Muzeum Narodowe
90. Fitte, P. 1959. Contribution à l'étude du préhistoire du Soudan occidental. *Bull. Soc. Prehist. Fr.* 58:453–55
91. Flight, C. 1973. Prehistoric sequence in the Kintampo area of Ghana. See Ref. 16, pp. 68–69
92. Flight, C. 1976. The Kintampo culture and its place in the economic prehistory of West Africa. See Ref. 46, pp. 211–21
93. Flohn, H., Nicholson, S. 1980. Climatic fluctuations in the arid belt of the 'Old World' since the Last Glacial maximum; possible causes and future implication. *Palaeoecol. Afr.* 12:3–21
94. Gabel, C. 1976. Microlithic occurrences in the Republic of Liberia. *West Afr. J. Archaeol.* 6:21–35
95. Gabel, C., Borden, R., White, S. 1975. Preiminary report on an archaeological survey of Liberia. *Liberian Stud. J.* 2:87–105

96. Gado, B. 1981. La recherche archéologique et historique au Niger: Bilan, perspectives en archéologie et en histoire précoloniale. *Rech. Pedagog. Cult.* 9(55):33–41
97. Gallay, A. 1966. Quelques gisements néolithiques du Sahara Malien. *J. Soc. Afr.* 36:167–208
98. Gallay, A., Pignat, G., Curdy, P. 1981. *Contribution à la connaissance du mégalithisme Sénégambien: Mission du Département d'Anthropologie au Sénégal, Hiver 1980–81.* Geneve: Univ., Dep. Anthropol.
99. Garrard, T. F. 1982. myth and metrology: the early trans-Saharan gold trade. *J. Afr. Hist.* 23:443–61
100. Gaven, C., Hillaire-Marcel, C., Petit-Maire, N. 1981. A Pleistocene lacustrine episode in southeastern Libya. *Nature* 290:131–33
101. Goucher, C. L. 1981. Iron is iron 'til it is rust: trade and ecology in the decline of West African iron-smelting. *J. Afr. Hist.* 22:179–89
102. Gouletquer, P., Grébenart, D. 1979. Figurines en terre cuite de néolithique de la région d'Agadez (République du Niger). *Bull. Soc. Prehist. Fr.* 76:91–96
103. Grébenart, D. 1979. La préhistoire de la République du Niger: Etat actuel de la question. In *Recherches Sahariennes,* ed. G. Camps, pp. 37–70. Paris: CNRS
104. Grébenart, D. 1981. *Vues générales sur les débuts de la métallurgie du cuivre et du fer.* Presented at Congr. Int. Cienc. Prehist. Protohist., 10th, Mexico City
105. Grigson, C. 1974. The craniology and relationships of four species of *Bos*: 1. Basic craniology: *Bos tauris L.* and its absolute size. *J. Archaeol. Sci.* 1:353–79
106. Grigson, C. 1978. The relationship between *Bos primiginius* and *Bos taurus*. *J. Archaeol. Sci.* 5;123–52
107. Grove, A. T. 1978. *Africa.* Oxford: Oxford Univ. Press. 3rd ed.
108. Grove, A. T., Warren, A. 1968. Quaternary landforms and climate on the south side of the Sahara. *Geogr. J.* 134:194–208
109. Haaland, R. 1980. Man's role in the changing habitat of Mema during the Old Kingdom of Ghana. *Norw. Archaeol. Rev.* 13:31–46
110. Haaland, R. 1981. *Migratory Herdsmen and Cultivating Women. The Structure of Neolithic Seasonal Adaptation in the Khartoum Nile Environment.* Bergen: (Private)
111. Haaland, R. 1981. Seasonality and division of labour: a case study from Neolithic sites in the Khartoum Nile environment. *Norw. Archaeol. Rev.* 14:44–59

112. Harlan, J. R. 1971. Agricultural origins: centers and non-centers. *Science* 174:468–74

113. Harlan, J. R. 1982. The origins of indigenous African agriculture. See Ref. 48, pp. 624–54

114. Harlan, J. R., Stemler, A. B. 1976. The races of sorghum in Africa. See Ref. 46, pp. 465–78

115. Hartle, D. D. 1980. Archaeology east of the Niger: a review of cultural-historical developments. See Ref. 15, pp. 195–203

116. Hays, T. R. 1975. Neolithic settlement of the Sahara as it relates to the Nile Valley. In *Problems in Prehistory: North Africa and the Levant,* ed. F. Wendorf, A. Marks, pp. 193–204. Dallas: SMU Press

117. Hays, T. R. 1980. The Sahara as a center of ceramic dispersion in northern Africa.. See Ref. 15, pp. 183–94

118. Hecht, A. D., ed. 1979. Paleoclimatic research: status and opportunities. *Quat. Res.* 12:6–17

119. Hill, M. H. 1978. Dating of Senegambian megaliths: a correction. *Curr. Anthropol.* 19:604–8

120. Hill, M. H. 1981. The Senegambian Monument Complex: current status and prospects for research. In *Megaliths to Medicine Wheels: Boulder Structures in Archaeology.* ed. M. Wilson, K. L. Road, K. J. Hardy, pp. 419–30. Proc. Ann. Chacmool Conf., 11th, Calgary

121. Hobler, P., Hester, J. J. 1969. Prehistory and environment in the Libyan desert. *South Afr. Archaeol. Bull.* 23:120–30

122. Howell, F. C. 1982. Origin and evolution of the African hominidae. See Ref. 48, pp. 70–156

123. Hugot, G. 1981. Les lacs Quaternaires du Sahara meridional: l'example de Tichitt (Mauritanie). In *Préhistoire Africaine. Mélanges Offerts au Doyen Lionel Balout,* ed. C. Roubet, H-J. Hugot, G. Souville, pp. 263–73. Paris: Ed. Assoc. Diffusion Pensée Fr.

124. Hugot, H-J. 1967. Le paléolithique terminal dans l'Afrique de l'Ouest. See Ref. 25, pp. 529–55

125. Hugot, H-J. 1972. Les communautés néolithiques urbaines de Tichitt (Mauritanie). *Rev. Fr. Hist. Outre-Mer* 59:506–12

126. Hugot, H-J. 1981. The prehistory of the Sahara. In *Methodology and African Prehistory,* ed. J. Ki-Zerbo, UNESCO Gen. Hist. Afr., 1:585–610. Berkeley: Heineman-UNESCO 2 vols.

127. Isaac, G. L. 1976. East Africa as a source of fossil evidence for human evolution. In *Human Origins: Louis Leakey and the East African Evidence,* ed. G. L. Isaac, E. R. McCown, pp. 121–38. Menlo Park, Calif: Benjamin

128. Isaac, G. L. 1982. The earliest archaeological traces. See Ref. 48, pp. 157–224

129. Jäkel, D. 1979. Run-off and fluvial formation processes in the Tibesti Mountains as indicators of climatic history in the Central Sahara during the late Pleistocene and Holocene. *Palaeoecol. Afr.* 11:13–44

130. Joire, J. 1955. Découvertes archéologiques dans la région de Rao. *Bull. Inst. Fondam. Afr. Noire Ser. B* 17:249–333

131. Klaus, D. 1980. Climatological aspects of the spatial and temporal variations of the southern Sahara margin. *Palaeoecol. Afr.* 12:315–31

132. Lambert, N. 1967. Objets en cuivre et néolithique de Mauritanie Occidentale. See Ref. 16, pp. 159–74

133. Lambert, N. 1971. Les industries sur cuivre dans l'Ouest Saharien. *West Afr. J. Archaeol.* 1:9–21

134. Lambert, N. 1981. L'Apparition du cuivre. Les civilisations préhistoriques. See Ref. 69, pp. 213–26

135. Lauer, W., Frankenberg, P. 1980. Modelling of climate and plant cover in the Sahara for 5,500 BP and 18,000 BP. *Palaeoecol. Afr.* 12:307–14

136. Law, R. C. 1967. The Garamantes and trans-Saharan enterprise in Classical times. *J. Afr. Hist.* 8:181–200

137. Lebeuf, A. M. 1981. Recherches archéologiques dans les basses vallées du Chari et Logone (Cameroun septentrional). *Rech. Pedagog. Cult.* 9(55):42–46

138. Lebeuf, J-P. 1980. Travaux archéologiques dans les basses vallées du Chari et du Logone (1936–1980). *C. R. Acad. Inscriptions B.-Lett.* 1980:636–56

139. Lebeuf, J-P., Lebeuf, A. M., Treinen-Claustre, F., Courtin, J. 1980. *Le Gisement Sao de Mdaga (Tchad). Fouilles 1960–1968.* Paris: Soc. Ethnol.

140. Lhote, H. 1961. The rock art of the Maghreb and Sahara. In *The Art of the Stone Age,* ed. H-G. Bandi, pp. 99–152. New York: Crown

141. Lhote, H. 1972. Recherches sur Takedda, ville décrit par le voyageur arab Ibn Battouta et située en Aïr. *Bull. Inst. Fondam Afr. Noire Ser. B* 34:429–70

142. Livingstone, D. 1978. *Interactions of food production and changing vegetation in Africa.* Presented at Ann. Meet. Am. Anthropol. Assoc., 77th, Los Angeles

143. McHugh, W. P. 1974. Cattle pastoralism in Africa—a model for interpreting archaeological evidence from the eastern Sahara desert. *Arct. Anthropol.* 11:236–44 (Suppl.)

144. McIntosh, R. J., McIntosh, S. K. 1982. The 1981 season at Jenne-jeno: preliminary results. *Nyame Akuma* 20:28–32
145. McIntosh, R. J., McIntosh, S. K. 1983. Forgotten tells of Mali: new evidence of urban beginnings in West Africa. *Expedition* 25(2):35–46
146. McIntosh, S. K. 1981. A reconsideration of Wangara/Palolus, Island of Gold. *J. Afr. Hist.* 22:145–58
147. McIntosh, S. K., McIntosh, R. J. 1980. *Prehistoric Investigations in the Region of Jenne, Mali*. Oxford: BAR 2 vols.
148. McIntosh, S. K., McIntosh, R. J. 1981. West African prehistory. *Am. Sci.* 69:602–13 .
149. Maitre, J. P. 1972. Notes sur deux conceptions traditionalles du néolithique Saharien. *Libyca* 20:125–36
150. Maitare, J. P. 1974. Nouvelles perspectives sur la préhistoire récente de l'Ahaggar. *Libyca* 22:93–143
151. Maitre, J. P. 1976. Contribution à la préhistoire récente de l'Ahaggar dans son context Saharien. *Bull. Inst. Fondam. Afr. Noire Ser. B* 38:46, 716–89
152. Maley, J. 1973. Mechanisme des changements climatiques aux basses latitudes. *Palaeogeogr., Palaeoclimatol., Palaeoecol.* 14:193–227
153. Maley, J. 1977. Palaeoclimates of Central Sahara during the early Holocene. *Nature* 269:573–77
154. Maley, J. 1980. Les changements climatiques de la fin du Teriaire en Afrique: leur conséquence sur l'apparition du Sahara et de sa vegetation. See Ref. 47, pp. 63–86
155. Maley, J. 1982. Dust, clouds, raintypes and climatic variations in tropical North Africa. *Quat. Res.* 18:1–16
156. Marliac, A. 1973. Prospection archéologique au Cameroun. *Cah. ORSTOM* (Ser. Sci. Hum.) 10:47–114
157. Marliac, A. 1978. L'Industrie de la haute terrasse du Mayo Louti: note préliminaire sur le site de Mokorvong au Cameroun septentrional. *Cah. ORSTOM* (Ser. Sci. Hum.) 15:367–77
158. Marliac, A. 1983. L'Age du fer au Cameroun septentrional: données chronologiques nouvelles sur le Diamaré. *J. Afr.* 51: In press
159. Martin V., Becker, C. 1974. Vestiges protohistoriques et occupation humaine au Sénégal. *Ann. Demogr. Hist.*, pp. 403–29
160. Mauny, R. 1961. *Tableau Géographique de l'Ouest African au Moyen Age: d'Après les Sources Ecrites, la Tradition et l'Archéologie*. Mem. Inst. Fondam. Afr. Noire 61. Dakar: IFAN
161. Mauny, R. 1973. Datation au carbone 14 d'amas artificiels de coquillages des lagunes de basse Côte d'Ivoire. *West Afr. J. Archaeol.* 3:207–14
162. Mauny, R. 1978. Trans-Saharan contacts and the Iron Age in West Africa. *The Cambridge History of Africa*, ed. J. D. Fage, 2:272–341. Cambridge: Cambridge Univ. Press. 8 vols.
163. Michel, P. 1973. *Les Bassins des Fleuves Sénégal et Gambie, Etude Géomorphologique* Paris: Mem. ORSTOM 63
164. Michel, P. 1980. The southwestern Sahara margin: sediments and climatic changes during the recent Quaternary. *Palaeoecol. Afr.* 12:297–306
165. Milburn, M. 1978–1979. On the study of Libyan and Saharan stone structures as a possible means of researching early desert trade and contacts. *Almogaren 9–* 10:107–34
166. Milburn, M. 1981. Western Aïr and Timersoï: a contribution to stone monument typology. See Ref. 69, pp. 47–64
167. Morel, A. 1981. Formes, formation superficielles et variations climatiques récents dans les massifs centraux de l'Aïr. *Palaeoecol. Afr.* 13:189–98
168. Mori, F. 1965. *Tadrart Acacus. Arte Rupestre e Culture del Sahara Preistorico*. Torino: Guilio Einaudi
169. Mori, F. 1974. The earliest Saharan rock engravings. *Antiquity* 48:87–92
170. Munson, P. J. 1976. Archaeological data on the origins of cultivation in the southwestern Sahara and their implications for West Africa. See Ref. 46, pp. 187–209
171. Munson, P. J. 1980. Archaeology and the prehistoric origins of the Ghana Empire. *J. Afr. Hist.* 21:457–66
172. Munson, P. J. 1981. A late Holocene (c. 4500–2300) climatic chronology for the southwest Sahara. *Palaeoecol. Afr.* 13:53–60
173. Murdock, G. P. 1959. *Africa, Its Peoples and Their Culture History*. New York: McGraw-Hill
174. Muzzolini, A. 1980. Boeuf (Préhistoire). *Encyclopédie Berbère* 27:1–16. Aix-en-Provence: Lab. Anthropol. Préhist. Ethnol. Pays. Mediterr. Occident.
175. Muzzolini, A. 1981. La datation des premiers boeufs domestiques sur les figurations rupestres au Sahara central. La Période "Bubaline". *Bull. Assoc. Int. Etud. Préhist. Egypt.* 3:15–37
176. Muzzolini, A. 1981. Les premiers boeufs domestiques au Sahara central: les documents des fouilles. *Bull. Soc. Meridionale Spéléol. Préhist.* 21:19–34
177. Muzzolini, A. 1982. Les datations au 14-C sur roches carbonatées en zone aride: corrections à appliqué et incertitudes. *Archaeometry* 24:85–96

178. Nicholson, S. E. 1980. Saharan climates in historic times. See Ref. 47, pp. 173–200

179. Nygaard, S., Talbot, M. R. 1976. Interim report on excavation at Asokrochona, Ghana. *West Afr. J. Archaeol.* 6:13–19

180. Nygaard, S., Talbot, M. R. 1977. First dates for coastal sites near Kpone, Ghana. *Nyame Akuma* 11:29–30

181. Oliver, R. A., Fagan, B. M. 1975. *Africa in the Iron Age.* Cambridge: Cambridge Univ. Press

182. Person, A., Valladas, H., Fontes, P., Barry, I., Saliège, J. F. 1981. *Prospection archéometrique de sites du Delta Intérieur du Niger.* Presented at Colloq. Assoc. Ouest Afr. Archaeol., 3rd, Dakar

183. Petit-Maire, N. 1979. Cadre écologique et peuplement humain: le littoral ouest-Saharien depuis 10,000 ans. *Anthropologie* 83:69–82

184. Petit-Maire, N. 1979. *Le Sahara Atlantique à l'Holocène. Peuplement et Ecologie.* Mem. Cent. Rech. Anthropol. Préhist. Ethnol. 28. Algiers:CRAPE

185. Petit-Maire, N. 1981. Aspects of human activity in the coastal occidental Sahara in the last 10,000 years. In *Sahara: Ecological Change and Early Economic History,* ed. J. A. Allan, pp. 81–91. London: Menas

186. Petit-Maire, N. 1982. Paléoenvironnements holocènes du Sahara Malien. In *Complément 1980–1981 aux Notices, Titres et Travaux Précédemment Fournies.* ed. N. Petit-Maire, pp. 13–31. Marseille: Lab. Geol. Quat.

187. Petit-Maire, N., ed. 1982. *Le Shati. Lac Pleistocene du Fezzan (Libye)* Paris: CNRS

188. Petit-Maire, N., Casanova, J. 1980. Essai d'interprétation critique de la repartition de dates isotropiques, example: peuplement et climates de l'Afrique du Nord du Sahara à l'Holocène. *Bull. Mus. Anthropol. Monaco* 24:57–70

189. Petit-Maire, N., Delibrias, G., Gaven, C. 1980. Pleistocene lakes in the Shati area, Fezzan. *Palaeoecol. Afr.* 12:289–95

190. Petit-Maire, N., Riser, J. 1981. Holocene lake deposits and palaeoenvironments in Central Sahara, NE Mali. *Palaeogeogr., Palaeoclimatol., Palaeoecol.* 35:45–61

191. Phillipson, D. W. 1980. Technological disparity, or the contemporaneity of diverse industries. See Ref. 1, pp. 15–16

192. Phillipson, D. W. 1982. The Later Stone Age in sub-Saharan Africa. See Ref. 48, pp. 410–77

193. Portères, R. 1976. African cereals: eleusine, fonio, black fonio, teff, *Brachiaria paspalum, Pennisetum,* and African rice. See Ref. 46, pp. 409–52

194. Posnansky, M. 1971. Ghana and the origins of West African trade. *Afr. Q.* 11:110–25

195. Posnansky, M. 1980. Trade and the development of the state and town in Iron Age West Africa. See Ref. 1, pp. 373–75

196. Posnansky, M. 1983. Early agricultural societies in Ghana. In *From Hunters to Farmers,* ed. J. D. Clark, S. A. Brandt. Berkeley: Univ. Calif. Press. In press

197. Posnansky, M., McIntosh, R. J. 1976. New radiocarbon dates for northern and western Africa. *J. Afr. Hist.* 17:161–95

198. Purseglove, J. W. 1976. The origins and migrations of crops in tropical Africa. See Ref. 46, pp. 291–309

199. Quéchon, G., Roset, J. 1974. Prospection archéologique du Massif de Termit (Niger). *Cah. ORSTOM (Ser. Sci. Hum.)* 11:85–104

200. Raimbault, M. 1981. Les recherches archéologiques au Mali. *Rech., Pedagog., Cult.* 9 (55):16–25

201. Reygasse, M. 1950. *Monuments Funéraires Préislamiques de l'Afrique du Nord.* Paris: Arts et Métiers Graphiques

202. Rognon, P. 1976. Essai d'interprétation des variations climatiques au Sahara depuis 40,000 ans. *Rev. Geogr. Phys. Geol. Dyn.* 18:251–82

203. Rognon, P. 1980. Une extension des déserts (Sahara et Moyen-Orient) au cours du Tardiglacaire (18,000–10,000 ans B.P.). *Rev. Geogr. Phys. Geol. Dyn.* 22:313–28

204. Rognon, P., Williams, M. A. 1977. Late Quaternary climatic changes in Australia and North Africa: a preliminary interpretation. *Palaeogeogr., Palaeoclimatol., Palaeoecol.* 21:285–327

205. Rosenfield, A. 1972. Microlithic industries of Rop rock Shelter. *West Afr. J. Archaeol.* 2:17–28

206. Roset, J. P. 1974. Un gisement néolithique ancien près de Fachi (Erg du Ténéré). *Cah. ORSTOM (Ser. Sci. Hum.)* 11:105–10

207. Roset, J. P. 1978. Poteries néolithiques du Ténéré, 1. la région de l'Adrar Chiriet. *Cah. ORSTOM (Ser. Sci. Hum.)* 15:379–406

207a. Roset, J. P. 1982. *New data on the south Saharian neolithisation problem: Aïr and Ténéré in Niger.* Presented at INQUA Cong. 11th, Moscow

207b. Roset, J. P. 1982. Tagalagal: un site à céramique au Xe millénaire avant nos jours dans l'Aïr (Niger). *C. R. Acad. Inscriptions B-Lett.* pp. 565–70

208. Saliège, J-F., Person, A., Barry, I., Fontes, P. 1980. Premières datations de tumulus préislamiques au Mali: site mégalithique de Tondidarou. *C. R. Acad. Sci. Paris Ser. D* 291:981–84

209. Schmidt, P., Avery, D. 1978. Complex iron smelting and prehistoric culture in Tanzania. *Science* 201:1085–89

210. Servant, M., Servant-Vildary, S. 1980. L'Environnement quaternaire du Bassin du Tchad. See Ref. 47, pp. 133–62

211. Servant-Vildary, S. 1979. Paléolimnologie des lacs du Bassin Tchadien au Quaternaire récent. *Palaeoecol. Afr.* 11:65–78

212. Shaw, C. T. 1969. On radiocarbon chronology of the Iron Age in sub-saharan Africa. *Curr. Anthropol.* 10:226–31

213. Shaw, C. T. 1970. *Igbo Ukwu: An Account of Archaeological Discoveries in Eastern Nigeria.* London: Faber & Faber. 2 vols.

214. Shaw, C. T. 1973. Finds at the Iwo Eleru rock shelter, western Nigeria. See Ref. 16, pp. 190–92

215. Shaw, C. T. 1975. Those Igbo-Ukwu radiocarbon dates: facts, fictions and probabilities. *J. Afr. Hist.* 16:503–17

216. Shaw, C. T. 1976. Early crops in Africa: a review of the evidence. See Ref. 46, pp. 107–53

217. Shaw, C. T. 1977. Hunters, gatherers and first farmers in West Africa. In *Hunters, Gatherers and First Farmers Beyond Europe,* ed. J. V. Megaw, pp. 69–125. Leicester: Leicester Univ. Press

218. Shaw, C. T. 1977. *Unearthing Igbo-Ukwu.* Ibadan: Oxford Univ. Press

219. Shaw, C. T. 1978. *Nigeria. Its Archaeology and Early History.* London: Thames & Hudson

220. Shaw, C. T. 1978–1979. Holocene adaptations in West Africa: the Late Stone Age. *Early Man News* 3–4:51–81

221. Shaw, C. T. 1981. Ife and Raymond Mauny. See Ref. 69, pp. 109–35

222. Shaw, C. T. 1981. The Nok sculptures of Nigeria. *Sci. Am.* 244:154–66

223. Shinnie, P. L. 1977. *Excavations at Meroe and trade connections.* Presented at Panafr. Congr. Prehist. Quat. Stud., 8th, Nairobi

224. Smith, A. B. 1974. Preliminary report of excavations at Karkarichinkat Nord and Karkarichinkat Sud, Tilemsi Valley, Republic of Mali, Spring 1972. *West Afr. J. Archaeol.* 4:33–55

225. Smith, A. B. 1975. Radiocarbon dates from Bosumpra Cave, Abetifi, Ghana. *Proc. Prehist. Soc.* 41:179–82

226. Smith, A. B. 1976. A microlithic industry from Adrar Bous, Tenere Desert, Niger. See Ref. 36, pp. 181–96

227. Smith, A. B. 1978. Terracottas from the Tilemsi Valley, Mali. *Bull. Inst. Fondam. Afr. Noire Ser. B* 40:223–34

228. Smith, A. B. 1979. Biogeographical considerations of colonization of the lower Tilemsi Valley in the second millennium B.C. *J. Arid Environ.* 2:355–61

229. Smith, A. B. 1980. Domesticated cattle in the Sahara and their introduction into West Africa. See Ref. 47, pp. 489–501

230. Smith, A. B. 1980. The Neolithic tradition in the Sahara. See Ref. 47, pp. 451–65

231. Smith, A. B. 1980. Saharan and Sahel zone environmental conditions in the late Pleistocene and early Holocene. See Ref. 1, pp. 139–42

232. Smith, A. B. 1981. *The ethnoarchaeology of pastoralism in the Saharan and Sahel zones of West Africa.* Presented at Colloq. Assoc. Ouest Afr. Archaeol., 3rd, Dakar

233. Smith, A. B. 1983. Origins of the Neolithic in the Sahara. See Ref. 196

234. Smith, S. E. 1980. The environmental adaptation of nomads in the West African Sahel: a key to understanding prehistoric pastoralists. See Ref. 47, pp. 467–87

235. Soper, R. C. 1965. The stone age in northern Nigeria. *J. Hist. Soc. Nigeria* 3:175–94

236. Stemler, A. B. 1980. Origins of plant domestication in the Sahara and the Nile Valley. See Ref. 47, pp. 503–26

237. Street, F. A., Gasse, F. 1981. Recent developments in research into the Quaternary climatic history of the Sahara. See Ref. 185, pp. 7–28

238. Street, F. A., Grove, A. T. 1976. Environmental and climatic implications of late Quaternary lake-level fluctuations in Africa. *Nature* 261:385–90

239. Street, F. A., Grove, A. T. 1979. Global maps of lake-level fluctuations since 30,000 yr. B.P. *Quat. Res.* 12:83–118

240. Sutton, J. E. 1974. The aquatic civilization of Middle Africa. *J. Afr. Hist.* 15:527–46

241. Sutton, J. E. 1977. The African aqualithic. *Antiquity* 51:25–34

242. Sutton, J. E. 1980. Aquatic reflections. See Ref. 1, pp. 321–22

243. Sutton, J. E. 1980–1981. Kintampo 'cigars' in Ivory Coast. *Archaeol. Ghana* 2:11–13

244. Sutton, J. E. 1982. Archaeology in West Africa: a review of recent work and a further list of radiocarbon dates. *J. Afr. Hist.* 23:291–313

245. Swartz, B. K. 1972. An analysis and evaluation of the Yapei Pebble Tool industry, Ghana. *Int. J. Afr. Hist. Stud. Notes Doc.* 2:265–70

246. Swartz, B. K. 1974. A stratified succession of stone age assemblages at Hohoe, Volta Region, Ghana. *West Afr. J. Archaeol.* 4:57–81
247. Swartz, B. K. 1980. The status of Guinea Coast paleoarchaeological knowledge as seen from Legon. See Ref. 15, pp. 37–40
248. Szumowski, G. 1956. Fouilles de l'abri sous roche de Kourounkorokalé (Soudan Francais). *Bull. Inst. Fondam. Afr. Noire Ser. B* 18:462–508
249. Szumowski, G. 1957. Fouilles au Nord du Macina et dans la région de Ségou. *Bull. Inst. Fondam. Afr. Noire Ser. B* 19:224–58
250. Talbot, M. R. 1980. Environmental responses to climatic change in the West African Sahel over the past 20,000 Years. See Ref. 47, pp. 37–62
251. Talbot, M. R., Delibrias, G. 1980. A new late Pleistocene-Holocene water-level curve for Lake Bosumtwi, Ghana. *Earth Planet. Sci. Lett.* 47:336–44
252. Thilmans, G. 1977. Sur les objets de parure trouvés à Podor (Sénégal) en 1958. *Bull. Inst. Fondam. Afr. Noire Ser. B* 39:669–94
253. Thilmans, G., Descamps, C., Khayat, B. 1980. *Protohistoire du Sénégal, Les Sites Mégalithiques.* Mem. Inst. Fondam. Afr. Noire 91. Dakar:IFAN
254. Tixier, J. 1967. Procédés d'analyse et questions de terminologie concernant l'étude des ensembles industriels du paléolithique récent et de l'epipaléolithique dans l'Afrique du Nord-Ouest. See Ref. 25, pp. 771–820
255. Tricart, J. 1965. *Rapport de la Mission de Reconnaissance Géomorphologique de la Vallée Moyenne du Niger.* Mem. Inst. Fondam. Afr. Noire 72. Dakar: IFAN
256. Trigger, B. G. 1969. The myth of Meroe and the African Iron Age. *Afr. Hist. Stud.* 2:23–50
257. Tylecote, R. F. 1975. Iron smelting at Taruga, Nigeria. *J. Hist. Metall. Soc.* 9:49–56
258. Tylecote, R. F. 1975. The origin of iron smelting in Africa. *West Afr. J. Archaeol.* 5:1–10
259. Tylecote, R. F. 1982. *Early metallurgy in West Africa.* Presented at CNRS Conf. Operation Metall. Ancienne Actuelle, Paris
260. Tylecote, R. F. 1982. Early copper slags and copper-based metal from the Agadez region of Niger. *J. Hist. Metall. Soc.* 16: In press
261. van Campo, M. 1975. Pollen analysis in the Sahara. See Ref. 116, pp. 45–64
262. van der Merwe, N. J., Avery, D. H. 1982. Pathways to steel. *Am. Sci.* 70: 146–55
263. van Noten, F. 1977. Excavations at Matupi Cave. *Antiquity* 51:35–40
264. van Zinderen Bakker, E. M. Sr. 1980. Comparison of late-Quaternary climatic evolution in the Sahara and the Namib-Kalahari region. *Palaeoecol. Afr.* 12: 381–94
265. van Zinderen Bakker, E. M. Sr., Maley, J. 1979. Late Quaternary paleoenvironments of the Sahara region. *Palaeoecol. Afr.* 11:83–104
266. Vernet, R. 1981. *Un site néolithique de Mauritanie occidentale: Khatt Lemaiteg.* Presented at Colloq. Assoc. Ouest.-Afr. Archaeol., 3rd, Dakar
267. Wai-Ogosu, B. 1973. Was there a Sangoan industry in West Africa? *West Afr. J. Archaeol.* 3:191–96
268. Weisrock, A. 1980. The littoral deposits of the Saharan Atlantic coast since 150,000 years B.P. *Palaeoecol. Afr.* 12:227–87
269. Wendorf, F., Laury, R. L., Albritton, C. C., Schild, R., Haynes, C. V., et al. 1975. Dates for the Middle Stone Age of East Africa. *Science* 187:740–42
270. Wendorf, F., Schild, R. 1980. *Prehistory of the Eastern Sahara.* New York: Academic
271. Wertime, T., Muhly, J. D., eds. 1980. *The Coming of the Age of Iron.* New Haven: Yale Univ. Press
272. Willett, F. 1962. The microlithic industry from Old Oyo, western Nigeria. *Proc. Panafr. Congr. Prehist. Quat. Stud., 4th, Kinshasa,* pp. 261–72
273. Willett, F. 1981. The analysis of Nigerian copper alloys: retrospect and prospect. *Crit. Arte Afr.* 46:35–49
274. York, R. N. 1978. Excavations at Dutsen Kongba, Plateau State, Nigeria. *West Afr. J. Archaeol.* 8:139–163

Ann. Rev. Anthropol. 1983. 12:259–84

HUMAN HEAT TOLERANCE:An Anthropological Perspective

Joel M. Hanna

Departments of Physiology and Anthropology, University of Hawaii at Manoa, Honolulu, Hawaii 96822

Daniel E. Brown

Department of Anthropology, University of Hawaii, Hilo, Hawaii 96720

INTRODUCTION

Within the complex of characteristics which we recognize as distinctly human are usually listed bipedalism, hairlessness, a large brain, and a symbolic linguistic ability. Each of these characteristics is genetically coded and probably represents a response to selective pressures at some time in the past. In each case we see a continuation and elaboration of adaptive patterns which characterize the order Primates.

Among our human adaptations we must also include the ability to tolerate heat. Human heat tolerance is the result of a series of adaptations which have been genetically encoded. All normal members of the species are born with a highly specialized complex of thermoregulatory sweat glands and a sensitive control system. It is a plastic system whose response and efficiency becomes more pronounced with prolonged and intense stimulation. The ability to respond to heat is seen in all extant human populations, regardless of the environment in which they now live or how many generations they have been removed from the heat (22). For those groups living in hot environments, the employment of cultural mechanisms has served as a buffer mediating between the hot macroenvironment and the organism. Still it is clear that physiological adaptations remain of paramount importance in daily survival (80). As is the case with other human characteristics, we seem to have taken advantage of our primate heritage, and with the aid of selection, extended our capacity beyond that of the other members of the order.

259

0066–4294/83/1015–0259$02.00

In this paper we will consider several aspects of heat tolerance and adaptation. First we take an evolutionary perspective, relating human heat tolerance to that of other animals and considering how it could have occurred. Then there is a discussion of hot environments and heat exchange with them. Finally, we examine the response to heat of contemporary humans and discuss various factors which influence individual response.

EVOLUTIONARY CONSIDERATIONS

Mammals have evolved a number of adaptations to enhance survival in hot environments. These include thick coats of hair, spreading of saliva over the surface of the body, perspiration, temporary storage of heat through increasing body temperature, panting, and heat avoidance by seeking refuge in the shade or underground (90, 105). Many species combine several of these adaptations to enhance heat tolerance. Camels, for example, have thick hair, store significant amounts of heat (to be released at nighttime), perspire, and drink large quantities of water. These techniques can be employed individually or in combination as the situation requires (90). The order Primates has generally been conservative and has employed fewer mechanisms. Prosimians and New World monkeys rely upon the primitive mammalian pattern of saliva spreading accompanied by panting. This combination is not particularly effective for primates because they cannot survive above ambient temperatures of 38°C (59, 94). Some prosimians and New World forms have also adopted a nocturnal schedule to avoid heat.

Old World monkeys, apes, and humans have evolved in a different direction through elaboration of thermoregulatory sweat glands dispersed over the surface of the body. These specialized glands, called eccrine glands, are also found in the lower primates, but at a much lower density, and they produce measurable perspiration only on the palms, soles, and the volar surfaces of the tail (94). Their function seems to be tactile rather than thermoregulatory and their contribution to the maintenance of body temperature is negligible (56). At some point after the separation of the New World from the Old World monkeys, selection favored the development of a greater heat tolerance. This was accomplished by wetting of the general body surface with eccrine glands becoming more dispersed, more numerous, and more active. This was an effective development allowing macaques and baboons to survive at environmental temperatures exceeding 40°C (48, 69). Humans show a continuation of this trend, with the highest capacity for heat loss through evaporation of perspiration exceeding that of monkeys by a significant amount (23). Unfortunately, physiological studies have not been extended to other types of monkeys (tropic forest dwellers, for example) or to the great apes, but on the basis of the anatomical distribution of eccrine glands, these primates also seem inferior to humans in sweat capacity (73, 95).

The evolutionary events leading to our high level of heat tolerance remain obscure; however, it seems safe to assume that the adaptation occurred in a hot environment with daily accessibility to drinking water and probably involved periodic bouts of intense physical activity. That a hot environment was involved seems obvious. Eccrine glands are thermoregulatory so that an increase in capacity, number, and distribution would suggest selection for heat. It is difficult to determine, based on current human physiological adaptations alone, whether human heat tolerance developed under hot-dry or hot-wet conditions. Evaporation of perspiration, and thus cooling power, is most effective in dry conditions, making an adaptive strategy emphasizing enhanced eccrine gland activity appropriate for hot-dry conditions (27). On the other hand, the need for a constant and plentiful water supply to provide a substrate for perspiration can be a great limitation for humans in dry heat. Evaporation is not so effective in a hot-humid environment, but since water is usually easily available, prodigious sweating over the entire body surface will maximize evaporative cooling without leading to fatal dehydration.

One must turn to the fossil record for information concerning the conditions under which humans may have developed their heat adaptations. The oldest unambiguous evidence for hominid remains stem from areas of eastern and southern Africa which at present are savanna or open woodland environments (14). It seems likely that similar environmental conditions were present in these areas during Plio-Pleistocene times. In the lower Omo basin, for instance, palynological studies suggest that xerophytic plants predominated about 2.0 million years ago (7), with grassland environments mixed with shrubs and some trees (12). Also, existing presently, as well as in the Plio-Pleistocene, are a variety of microenvironments, including those associated with rivers, streams, and lakes, where water favored limited woodlands. Plio-Pleistocene hominid sites from East Africa are generally found near water sources (e.g. Olduvai Gorge, Hadar, Lake Turkana), whereas later habitations were often located in drier areas (50).

Looking beyond the Plio-Pleistocene into the Early Miocene, much of East Africa was probably heavily forested, with later Miocene uplifting of the Rift Valley highlands creating a rain shadow which led to the drier climates of later times. The drying trend, which is marked by an increase in faunal turnover, began about 16 million years ago (98). It may have been during this period that hominid ancestors were first confronted with hot-dry environmental conditions. Thus, it may well be that early hominid evolution took place under hot-dry conditions. This, however, is far from certain.

More clearly implicated by the development of rapid response and high capacity of eccrine glands in acclimatized human subjects is selection for high levels of physical activity. The rapid response and high capacity in acclimatized man implicates selection for the high heat loss required during intensive physical activity. Well acclimatized humans can sustain a perspiration rate of 2*l* per hour (51). This is adequate to lose 1200 kcal of heat per hour or the equivalent of the heat generated by running 12 miles per hour or running 5-minute miles. This exceeds most levels of activity. For short time periods, a sweating rate of 4l per hour has been reported (23). This represents a heat loss potential above our ability to produce heat through working. This excess capacity for heat loss is probably related to high levels of heat production associated with intense work of short duration.

There is a curious problem in that heat loss is related to water availability. In order to dissipate the large quantities of heat associated with intense work, equal quantities of water must be consumed. Yet men cannot store water nor can they dehydrate to a significant degree. Humans have a limited capacity to dehydrate. Less than 3 percent of body water can be lost with no decrease in function (63), and for longer duration of heat loss, water must be replenished continuously, a significant limiting factor. Additionally, there is a problem of replacement. Most other animals can drink prodigious quantities of water after exposure to heat and so replace that lost through evaporation (1). Humans do not have this capacity. We are limited to about 1l at a time, which is scarcely the amount of water lost during an hour's moderate work (90). It is not clear why we do not have a larger capacity for rehydration considering the high capacity of the sweat glands. Furthermore, even if water is readily available, men working in the heat will drink less than that lost through perspiration. Adolph (1) has called this voluntary dehydration. Voluntary dehydration has been seen during work in the heat under a variety of conditions ranging from heavy industrial tasks (41) to primitive village agriculture in New Guinea (9). There is a gradual dehydration so by the end of the working period those involved have sustained significant water loss. This deficit is gradually replaced during meals and at other times so that rehydration is complete by the next day (40). Thus, there is a partial uncoupling of thirst from actual water requirements. This means that activity level will not be directly tied to and limited by water availability. These then are major elements of human heat tolerance: high capacity for heat loss, availability of water, and a loss of sensitivity for immediate water need.

In an evolutionary perspective there are several situations in which this complex of adaptations could have occurred. First, an adequate technology may have existed such that water could be carried, perhaps in large bird eggs or in gourds. The !Kung San employ such technology today (68); however, it is difficult to envision primitive men carrying several kilograms of water, while periodically engaging in vigorous activity. A second possible situation involves a thorough knowledge of the environment, its flora and fauna. Precise knowledge of surface water and plant resources would allow movement from place to place. Contemporary San and Australian aborigines have been able to acquire adequate amounts of water in this manner (68).

A third solution is to remain within a day's range of a water supply. Hunters or foragers could thus leave in the morning and return in the evening or, if necessary, the next evening. This would set conditions for voluntary dehydration and favor the uncoupling of thirst from water deficit. In the perspective of human evolution, some anthropologists (18, 61) have suggested that the establishment of a home base with daily foraging and return was a major step in human social evolution. A certain supply of water would contribute to the establishment of a home base. If a home base near water were established, several other benefits would accrue. The proximity of water and associated vegetation would provide a cool microclimate. This would be especially helpful to the very young, who have a limited heat tolerance because of an inadequate sweating capacity, and to pregnant women, who have the additional heat load of several kilograms of tissue which is metabolically very active. Remaining at a home base would have benefited these important segments of the population by reducing their thermal burden.

Several anthropologists, including Coon (17), LeBarre (54), and Montagu (67), have attempted to tie heat tolerance to hair loss. The basic argument is that body hair impedes heat loss, and its removal permits free circulation of the air to the skin allowing greater evaporation. Newman (70) objects, arguing that (a) there is no evidence to support a hair coat as a barrier to heat loss, and (b) removal of hair exposes the body surface to solar heat gain and may actually increase heat load. The first point has not been supported by experimental evidence. Weiner (101) has cited experimental evidence showing a direct relationship between thickness of hair coat and heat loss. The hair coat is especially undesirable at low levels of air movement where it restricts evaporation. Similarly, a recent study of macaques by Johnson & Elizondo (48) shows that the hair coat of the rhesus monkey may be a significant barrier to heat dissipation when compared to hairless man. With respect to Newman's second point, there is little doubt that exposure of the skin to solar radiation increases body heat load. In hot, dry conditions, clothed men are more tolerant than unclothed men. If heat tolerance and hair loss are related, we suggest the selection must have occurred during bouts of strenuous activity when solar heat gain is less critical than immediate heat dissipation. This may represent a trade between acceptance of an increased heat load due to radiation and an ability for rapid heat loss. Such conditions could have been bursts of running in pursuit of game or strenuous digging of roots and tubers, activities not typically observed in nonhuman primates.

An alternative relationship between hair loss and heat tolerance has been suggested by Robertshaw (79). He suggests "It has been speculated that eccrine sweating in man became necessary because of the loss of hair and that glands previously confined to the glabrous surfaces of the palms and soles spread to the other parts of the skin surface (p. 119)." While this hypothesis cannot simply be rejected, the high density of eccrine glands over the skin surface (relative to other mammals) is a characteristic of Old World monkeys and the great apes (73, 95). It would thus seem that loss of hair has simply enhanced their effectiveness rather than causing them to spread. Regardless of how the development of heat tolerance and hair loss are related, they are complementary.

HOT MACROENVIRONMENTS

An understanding of biological and cultural heat adaptations requires a knowledge of heat exchange and some salient characteristics of the environment in which it occurs. Adaptive responses involve the creation and maintenance of a favorable microclimate within a larger and more stressful macroclimate. The microclimate acts as a buffer, restricting heat gain while promoting heat loss. The center of the system is the human body, the core of which includes the brain, lungs, viscera, and other organs which function only within a narrow temperature range. Elevation of core temperature by only a few degrees is fatal. The core is surrounded by a shell of other tissues—the muscles and skin—whose temperature is variable (11, 51, 58). The shell interacts directly with the microclimate to facilitate heat loss.

Humans generate heat by normal metabolic processes and must ultimately lose this heat to the macroenvironment in order to maintain a constant internal body temperature. The effectiveness of the heat removal process depends, in large part, on the gradient of heat between the body core and the external environment. In simple terms, human ability to adjust to heat depends on only three factors: the magnitude of the heat gradient between the macroenvironment and the body core, the rate of heat exchange between the interior and skin surface, and the rate at which metabolic heat is produced. Various aspects of the macroenvironment clearly have a direct effect on the first two factors, and they may also have an indirect effect on the rate of metabolic heat production by limiting the types or amount of physical work that humans can perform.

An initial understanding of how environmental features can affect human heat tolerance may be gained through examination of the processes of heat transference between the body and the macroenvironment. These processes are radiation, conduction, convection, and evaporation.

Heat Exchange with the Environment

RADIATION   Radiative heat exchange occurs between objects in line of sight of each other. Heat is exchanged through the gain or loss of electromagnetic energy at a wide span of wavelengths. Energy is emitted from one object to another, and thus heat is lost from the first object. Net radiative heat change, or the difference between energy lost through emission and gained through absorption, depends upon an object's temperature and reflectance, the temperatures and reflectances of all objects visible to it, the surface area of the object, and the surface area of features visible to the object (46, 51).

For human heat adaptation, the most significant type of radiative heat transfer is between the sun and the body surface. The amount of solar radiation at the earth's surface, or insolation, varies depending upon season, latitude, time of day, amount of moisture and dust in the atmosphere, and altitude (71, 85). Interestingly, direct solar radiative heat gain in standing individuals, particularly in the tropics or during summer, is less around noon than at about 9 AM or 3PM, since less area is exposed to the sun at noon (97). Another consideration in solar radiative heat gain is the reflectance of the skin, which significantly differs among individuals and between populations. "White" skin reflects about 30–40 percent of total solar radiation, while "black" skin reflects 18 percent or less (37).

CONDUCTION   Conduction is a process similar to diffusion, involving molecule-to-molecule transferal of heat between surfaces that are in physical contact with each other. The amount of thermal conductance depends upon temperature differences between touching surfaces, the area of contact between them, and the thermal conductivity of the materials (20, 32).

In consideration of human heat gain or loss through conduction, the chief route is through body surface contact with the ground (or floor). Conductive heat exchange is maximized in the supine position and minimized when standing. Conductive heat gain from surfaces with temperatures above that of the body core may be minimized by wearing sandals or shoes made of material with low thermal conductivity (high insulation) and maintaining a standing posture. Of the four processes of heat exchange between the skin surface and the macroenvironment, conduction usually has the least significance for human adaptation (36).

Within the organism the process of conduction is the major means for heat transfer from the body core to the surface. Heat is conducted through layers of tissue or via the blood. The thickness and composition of the shell therefore can greatly influence the rate of heat exchange between the core and the environment.

CONVECTION   Convective heat transfer refers to the exchange of heat between an object and a moving fluid (liquid or gas). This is frequently divided into two types of heat exchange: natural (or free) convection and forced convection. Natural convection occurs when an object is in contact with a calm, non-moving gas or liquid. The temperature difference between the object and the fluid causes vertical movements of the fluid due to density-buoyancy effects (62). Forced convection occurs when some outside force causes the fluid to move (e.g. in air, barometric pressure differences or electric fans may cause this movement). With forced convection, natural convection becomes of negligible importance (37). If air temperature is lower than body core temperature, convective heat loss can be elevated by artificially increasing air velocity or by exposing the maximum amount of body surface area to natural air movements. On the other hand, with air temperature above 38°C, any breeze will increase heat load and at above 45°C air convection will add more heat than can be lost by evaporation (8).

EVAPORATION   When a substance is converted from a liquid to a gas under isothermal conditions, energy in the form of heat is required to drive the process. This energy requirement, the latent heat of vaporization, has a characteristic value for a unit mass of a given substance at a given temperature. The latent heat of vaporization of water is approximately 0.58 kcal/g at 30°C (32), hence a liter of water will remove 580 kcal of heat.

Evaporation of water from the skin surface is dependent on skin temperature, water vapor pressure of ambient air, the surface area of exposed skin, and the amount of water available for evaporation on the skin surface. The principle means by which humans provide moisture for evaporative cooling is by active perspiration from eccrine glands. Additionally, water used to humidify air in the respiratory tract, insensible perspiration (diffusion of water to the skin surface), and the behavioral application of water to the skin surface all add to evaporative heat loss.

Heat Balance

Body heat content as related to heat exchange with the environment may be represented by the following equation (11, 51):

$$M_b + M_a \pm S = E \pm R \pm K \pm C$$

The left side of the equation is a summary of body heat production and content. M_b is basal heat production and is thus the amount of heat generated by living tissue at rest. M_a is additional heat produced through physical activity. S is the amount of heat contained by the body. In the heat S may be increased to reduce strain on the heat loss effectors. On the right side of the equation are the avenues of heat exchange discussed above: E, R, K, and C are evaporation, radiation, conduction, and convection respectively. Excluding S, over any short period of time the equation may be unbalanced, but to maintain equilibrium the two sides must balance in the long term.

Several variables in the macroenvironment have important, direct effects on heat exchange. These include: ambient temperature, insolation (and thus cloudiness and particulate matter in the atmosphere), temperatures and reflectances of objects in line-of-sight, the surface areas of these objects, temperature and thermal conductivity of the ground, wind velocity, and water vapor pressure (or humidity) of the air. A number of biometeorological indices have been developed, such as comfort indices, to sum the factors in the macroenvironment contributing to heat stress; these indices are useful only for specific purposes and under specific conditions (28, 34, 51). For adaptive considerations, air temperature and humidity are perhaps the most important factors and are the variables used for dividing the macroenvironment into two major types of significance for human heat tolerance: hot-dry and hot-humid environments.

Hot-Dry Macroenvironments

Hot-dry climates are represented in the extreme by hot deserts, although many nondesert areas such as savannas, or the Intermediate Tropical Zone, are seasonably hot-dry. It is in hot-dry climates that environmental temperatures above that of the body core are most frequently encountered. Under these conditions it is possible to gain body heat by convection and conduction.

A primary feature of hot deserts is their dryness. Deserts can be defined as land areas where the annual rainfall in centimeters is a smaller number than the mean annual temperature in degrees Celsius plus 16.5 (39). The aridity permits high insolation values because of the usually dry, cloudless skies, and thus desert environments have a high solar radiative heat load (26). Deserts are also exceedingly hot in mid-day. Records from North Africa indicate temperatures of 80°C are not uncommon (15). The high daytime temperature in deserts tends to increase air movement, leading to increased convective heat gain. Conversely, cloudless night skies favor the rapid reradation of heat into space, resulting in cool nights (2, 15). Hot deserts are also characterized by sparse vegetation and therefore shade and humid microenvironments are rare. Human adaptation to hot deserts then must also extend beyond heat adaptation: low availability of food (both caloric and protein) and water (8, 90) resources also become significant limiting factors. Even when water is available, it may be unusable because of high salinity (8, 100), and the cool nights may necessitate adaptations to cold stress as well as to heat.

Some regions not usually considered as deserts are seasonally hot-dry. These include: many tropical grassland regions with alternating wet and dry seasons; hot steppes, which are characterized by extreme variability in precipitation, often with low predictability; temperate or cool deserts, with summer temperatures as high as those found in hot deserts; and temperate steppes with short, hot summers (64, 100). These seasonally hot-dry areas tend to have more vegetation than hot deserts because rainfall, when it occurs, is more frequent during cool seasons when there is less evaporation (100). This lowered evaporation rate during part of the year makes water more available to human inhabitants.

During hot-dry seasons these regions, like hot deserts, are characterized by hot days and cold nights, although the ranges are not so extreme.

Hot-Humid Macroenvironments

Hot-humid areas differ in several ways from the hot-dry environments discussed above. Because of cloudiness and moisture in the atmosphere, insolation values are lower, and thus ambient temperatures are lower. Concomitantly, the more opaque atmosphere limits reradiation of heat from the ground, favoring warmer nighttime temperatures. Temperature variations tend to be less extreme and seldom rise above human body core temperature. While tropical rainforest is the extreme representation of hot-humid zones, hot-wet environments also include a wide distribution of local climates, some of which may be seasonally cold and dry as well (38).

For human heat adaptation, the primary problem in humid environments is the reduced effectiveness of evaporation as a cooling mechanism. However, because objects in line-of-sight are usually cooler than body core temperature, especially when there is extensive vegetation cover (55), radiative heat loss occurs. Convective cooling is also very important, as air temperature is also lower than core temperature. Because of this, microclimate ventilation is an important consideration in hot-wet environments.

Because of the high humidity, vegetation is extensive and diverse (16, 54). Shade and water are usually plentiful for humans, permitting reduction of solar heat gain and the replenishing of body water lost in perspiration (70). Another potential problem is the relatively constant diurnal temperature. Intensive activity cannot be scheduled to cool parts of the day as is common in hot-dry areas. Human parasites and disease factors find hot-humid conditions congenial, and thus such water-associated infections as malaria, trypanosomiasis, schistosomiasis, enteric diseases, as well as many fungal and nematode infections, are prevalent (10). These infections can add to the heat burden by virtue of their febrile effects.

MICROENVIRONMENTS

Moran (68) has defined microclimate as "The climatic condition, especially the temperature, nearest the individual. Refers to the creation of environmental conditions different from those in the general area." For humans in heat, the ideal microclimate is below skin temperature, has a vapor pressure favoring evaporative heat loss, and is protected from conductive, convective, and radiation heat gain. It is within this extrasomatic zone that behavioral and social adaptations play a major role by maintaining a favorable microclimate within the microenvironment.

The goal of these adaptations is to maintain a cool and relatively dry shell of air about major portions of the body surface to facilitate heat loss. The physiological adaptations to be discussed later facilitate heat transfer from the core and working muscles into this microenvironment so that thermal equilibrium of the core can be maintained.

Microenvironment Adaptations to Dry Heat

Human adaptive techniques include material cultural adjustments and behavioral adaptations. Material culture provides habitations and clothing which establish a favorable microclimate and counter the high potential of radiation, convection, and conductive heat gain. Behavioral techniques center largely upon avoidance.

Material cultural adaptation to hot-dry environments are similar to those observed in cold environments. Lee (56), Rapoport (77), Wulsin (106), and Moran (68) have discussed housing and may be consulted for details. There are a number of techniques which seem common to hot-dry areas. 1. Houses are constructed to delay the entry of heat. High heat capacity materials such as adobe and stone are desirable because they can absorb large amounts of heat before passing it into the interior. The stored heat is lost at night by radiation and convection. The net effect is to dampen temperature fluctuations so that interior temperatures remain moderate. An added bonus is warm indoor temperatures during the cool evening. Houses of the Pueblo Indians of the Southwest provide a good example of the application of this principle. 2. A simple alternative to massive construction is excavation into the earth. The mean temperature of the subsoil is more comfortable than the surface with its extreme variations and is much cooler during the day. Rapoport (77) has described Middle Eastern communities with the entire village constructed several meters beneath the surface. Pit houses in the American Southwest and elsewhere are examples. 3. If habitation is to be above ground, a compact geometry minimizing surface area to internal volume is desirable. This proportionally reduces solar heat gain as well as convective heat gain from desert winds. 4. Houses can also be built close together, thereby increasing the internal volume with a disproportional increase in surface area. Such compact building also provides for mutual shading of some exterior walls and provides wind protection. This can be extended to villages and towns with multiple-story houses and canyon-like streets. 5. Limiting the size and number of windows, as well as provisioning them with shutters, reduces convective and radiative heat entry. 6. Painting in a light color or whitewashing reflects much radiation and reduces radiative heat gain. 7. If adequate water is available, plants can be used as primitive air conditioners by taking advantage of their transpiration, planting them close to walls for shade and cooling. Rapoport describes an ingenious tropical Spanish design employing plants. The house design includes two courtyards with a gallery extending between them. One courtyard is of flagstone and the other well planted. As the sun warms the stoneyard, air rises pulling the cooler air through the structure by convection. 8. Kitchens and cooking areas can be built away from residential structures to prevent heat entry.

Clothing is a second aspect of material culture which provides protection against the extremes of the macroclimate. Although clothing reduces abrasions and prevents sunburn, an equally important effect is to reduce solar heat gain (2). This, in turn, reduces the level of perspiration required to maintain equilibrium. Henschel & Hanson (42) have shown that well-acclimatized men wearing an army desert uniform perspire 30 percent less than unclothed men at rest. This represents a reduction in heat load of about 165 kcal/hr. There are also benefits in terms of reduced core temperature and heart rate. Adolph (2) calculates wearing clothing in the desert gives about half the protection of an awning or a building.

Desert clothing has adaptive value in that it stops radiation at some distance from the skin surface and converts it to heat which can then be lost into the air. Additionally, the insulative effects of trapped air reduce heat transmission to the skin surface (2). The addition of a light reflective surface may reduce heat gain even more.

Clothing is less advantageous at work than at rest because of the need to lose internally generated heat. Henschel & Hanson (42) calculate the sweat reduction as about 15 percent at work. Design principles for hot desert garments are also similar to those for cold climates (51). The material should be permeable to water permitting evaporation, but should act as a barrier to radiation and convective heat gain. Loose fitting, baggy clothing is desirable in that it favors ventilation and evaporation from the skin surface. A light-colored external garment may reflect radiation, reducing heat gain. Wulsin (106) has discussed the application of some of these principles by residents of hot desert areas.

Microenvironment Adaptations to Humid Heat

In the humid tropics, the problems associated with heat are quite different. Solar radiation is less of a problem as temperatures are lower than in the desert. The major thermoregulatory problem is the high humidity which reduces the effectiveness of evaporative heat loss (70).

Houses are constructed for shade and protection from rain, yet they must provide adequate ventilation. The dominant feature is the roof. Ideally, it is a huge parasol with steeply sloping sides to shed rainfall and large overhangs to provide the maximum protection. Materials of a low heat capacity are favored because diurnal temperature variation is not great and heat storage provides no benefit (77). Grass or thatch are ideal because solar radiation striking a damp roof evaporates water and aids in cooling. Humid tropic houses normally have a long, narrow geometry to achieve maximum ventilation. In some cases, elevated platforms may be employed to escape rain puddling and to allow more adequate convective cooling. A variation is seen in Polynesia where elevated stone platforms move the living floor several meters above ground level. Conductive heat transfer into the subsoil may aid in maintaining a cool microenvironment.

The obvious problem in constructing houses in the humid tropics is how to provide for privacy while retaining unrestricted ventilation. The privacy can be solved with curtains, blinds, or other movable temporary partitions. In some cases, permanent walls made of loosely joined bamboo or similar material are a compromise, allowing some degree of privacy but also permitting an appreciable degree of air flow.

There is a single simple rule for humid tropical clothing—the least amount possible. Given the high humidity and modest solar heat input, it is desirable to leave most of the skin uncovered (80).

There are a variety of other behavioral adaptations to the heat, including culturally sanctioned behavior, special foods and drinks, behavior scheduling, etc. These will not be considered here because of space limitations, but they have been reviewed elsewhere (36, 68, 76, 77, 106).

BIOLOGICAL ADAPTATIONS TO HEAT

If the temperature of the microenvironment cannot be maintained at comfortable levels, a series of physiological responses is initiated. These increase heat loss via evaporation and enhance heat transfer from the core to the shell. At ambient temperatures between 24–29°C, most resting unclothed humans are in thermal equilibrium such that metabolic heat is dissipated by a combination of factors discussed above (51). As ambient temperature increases, there is a gradual increase in body heat content, and the thermoregulatory centers in the brain begin a series of responses to increase conductive heat transfer from the core to the shell and to evaporate water from the surface.

Dermal Blood Flow

The initial response to increased body heat content is an elevated dermal blood flow. Venous blood flow is shifted from internal veins to superficial veins where it can be cooled before entering the core. There is a compensatory vasoconstriction in other areas to maintain blood pressure (107). This presents an efficient and metabolically economical mechanism for rapid transfer of heat to the shell. Peripheral skin blood vessels dilate under the influence of the sympathetic nervous system and an as yet unidentified transmitter (21, 84). The active vasodilation caused by transmitter accounts for most of the increased surface blood flow, and according to Rowell (88), is regulated by central core temperature. As blood flow increases through direct arteriovenous shunts, large quantities of blood are shifted into the extremities, especially the hands and feet. These are superb heat exchangers by virtue of their large surface areas and low metabolic heat production (5). The general increase in skin temperature also is beneficial in promoting loss of heat from the surface by radiation and convection.

Cardiovascular Response

The increased surface blood flow may induce an increase in cardiovascular activity, specifically increases in heart rate and blood pressure. The tachycardia seems to be a response to pooling of blood in cutaneous circulation (81, 107). If physical activity is required, the strain on the heart is increased. It must maintain flow to working muscles as well as to the skin. In acute exposure to heat, it is this increased cardiovascular strain which leads to fatality and accounts for the excess deaths of the elderly and young during heat waves (24).

Perspiration

As skin temperature increases, the sweat glands begin to function. This occurs at about 35°C skin temperature, but the starting point is subject to considerable individual variation (35). The appearance of perspiration is not uniform but the pattern is regional, starting on the trunk and progressing distally to include the extremities (44). The sweating mechanism will be carefully matched to thermal needs. When sweating has been adequate to reduce the temperature of blood perfusing the thermoregulatory center, the rate of production will be reduced until an equilibrium is established. If core temperature continues to climb, however, sweat producton may not continue to increase. Before the surface is completely saturated, hidromeiosis (sweat gland fatigue) can occur and reduce output. Hidromeiosis probably results from blockage of duct openings because of hydration of the surrounding skin (51) since it appears in humid exposures more frequently than dry exposures.

Thus, the physiological response of humans to a hot ambient temperature is rather simple: blood is shifted to the surface, cardiovascular activity maintains blood flow and rapid heat transfer within the organism, while sweating physically removes heat from the skin surface.

Eccrine Glands

The effectiveness of human evaporative heat loss is the work of the eccrine sweat glands. These are so specialized and developed in humans that Montagna (66) considers them one of our characteristic organs. They can be contrasted with apocrine sweat glands which are found in the skin of most mammals. Apocrine glands are associated with hair follicles, secrete a lipid rich, viscous fluid, and are poorly innervated (53, 79, 89). In mammals such as the horse and the sheep, they produce thermal sweat (90, 105). In primates a phylogenetic trend is seen as the ratio of eccrine to apocrine glands increase from prosimians to man (73, 95). In humans, eccrine glands are spread over the surface and apocrine glands are confined to the axilla and groin (13, 53).

Eccrine glands consist of a coiled region within the dermis and a duct through the epidermis to the surface of the skin. The innermost coiled portion secretes a fluid similar to plasma, and the coiled and tubular portions contain a series of active transport systems to reabsorb some solutes (13). The glands are sensitive to acetylcholine and to circulating hormones such as aldosterone, so that the composition of the final fluid reflects general body water and electrolyte balance as well as immediate thermal needs.

Eccrine glands are found on the hairless portions of the body surface at densities ranging from 52 glands/cm^2 on the thigh to 240/cm^2 on the dorsum of the hand. These densities exceed those reported for other animals (102). In terms of heat loss, their effectiveness can be appreciated from the following: a horse can perspire at a rate of 100 gm/m^2/hr, a camel at 250 gm/m^2/hr, and a human in excess of 500 gm/m^2/hr (27).

The activity of eccrine glands is regulated by the sympathetic nervous system with acetylcholine serving as the postsynaptic transmitter. The function of the glands is under complex control with local skin temperature and central core temperature playing roles (51). The central receptors in the hypothalamus monitor body heat content carefully, such that a small increase in the temperature of the blood perfusing the hypothalamus leads to a rapid onset of thermal perspiration over large areas of the body. The central hypothalamic center is presumably involved in control of patterned, nonthermal eccrine function such as emotional and gustatory sweating (13). Local heating of the skin also causes local thermal sweating (29), and under many circumstances it can be more important than central input (57). Drugs and hormones can also mediate sweating.

Factors Influencing Individual Response

ACCLIMATIZATION   Of the myriad of factors known to influence individual response to heat, the state of acclimatization is without doubt the most important. Acclimatization seems to be a universal human capacity, and degree of acclimatization is a major contributor to individual variation in response. The process of acclimatization is illustrated in a study reported by Strydom & Wyndham (96). Twelve white South African men from temperate regions with no recent heat exposure served as subjects. They were required to perform moderate work (1560 ft.lb/min, 212 m.kg/min) in a hot, humid environment (33/34°C; 90/93°F wet/dry) for a period of 4 hours. The work consisted of stepping onto a box at a rate of 12 times per minute. Their responses are shown in Figure 1 and are characteristic of acute heat response in unacclimatized humans. Sweating rate is low, heart rate is high—approaching maximum levels—and core temperature reaches pathological levels. Several of the men could not complete the test.

The acclimatization procedure involved repeating the test each day for 10 consecutive days. The changes are also recorded in Figure 1. Sweat rate has

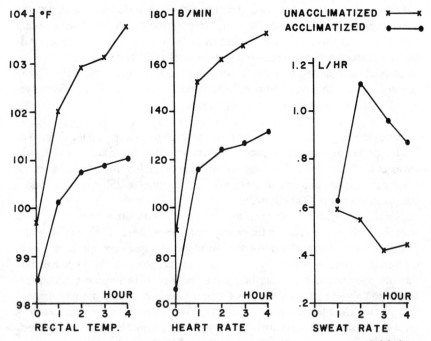

Figure 1   Physiological changes during acclimatization to heat. Responses are recorded during a 4-hour work period in a hot, humid environment. Acclimatization leads to increased sweat loss, which reduces core temperature and cardiovascular stress. After Strydom & Wyndham (96).

doubled and the resulting increase in heat loss has reduced cardiovascular activity and reduced core temperature. These observations have been repeated in a number of studies (23, 29, 60, 107). The actual exposure time required is less than 100 minutes per day (60) irrespective of the thermal environment for the rest of the day.

The remarkable aspect of the acclimatization response is the ease by which it is accomplished. It is rapid, effective, and will occur even though the trials are performed in a temperate climate in winter. Furthermore, all normal people who have been tested can acclimate. As Edholm & Weiner (22, p. 151) note, "even with long continued life in temperate or cold climates over many generations without exposure to hot or tropical conditions, the ability to acclimatize is retained." Studies on macaques (47) have confirmed that a similar, but less dramatic acclimatization may occur in other primates.

The major factor promoting acclimatization is an increase in sweat gland output and an increase in sensitivity to the thermal environment. Sweating begins at a lower skin temperature (5, 51), the capacity for production is increased by severalfold, and "inactive" glands may be activated (52). This permits core temperature to remain at a lower value and concomitantly reduces circulatory strain (87). In addition to a higher output of perspiration, there is a reduction in sodium and chloride loss (83). This may reflect general body water balance rather than sweat gland adjustment (103). However, the end result is the same. Acclimatization yields a greater electrolyte economy through a reduction in sodium and chloride loss in sweat. The kidneys also reduce sodium loss and respond rapidly with a reduction in water loss if dehydration occurs (90).

The stimulus for acclimatization is closely related to physical activity, because natural acclimatization is always accompanied by work. However, in a series of laboratory studies, Fox (29) demonstrated that acclimatization will develop in proportion to the degree of rise in body temperature. Fox and associates developed a plastic suit which enabled the temperature of a resting individual to be raised to any level and maintained in a steady state. Acclimatization changes paralleled those seen in other studies, confirming that elevated temperature and not work was the acclimatizing stimulus (29).

Acclimatization also seems to involve a change in pattern of sweat gland recruitment. Hofler (44) found that unacclimatized men sweated most profusely about the trunk and gradually recruited sweat glands from the limbs and other parts of the body surface. After acclimatization, the pattern was reversed such that sweating was most perfuse about the limbs with the trunk being recruited later. The higher surface area to mass ratio of the limbs and their lower level of metabolic activity makes them potentially better sources for loss of metabolic heat. Such a reversal in pattern of recruitment would provide a much more efficient vector for heat loss at no increase in energy expenditure and could actually reduce the perspiration required to maintain thermal equilibrium (36).

In summary, humans acclimate to heat in a rapid and effective manner. Acclimatization involves increased sweating which reduces body temperature and circulatory strain. The stimulus is elevated body temperature for short periods over several consecutive days. In addition to a higher rate of perspiration, acclimatization also involves a greater sensitivity to environmental heat, as evidenced by the lower temperature at which sweating begins, as well as a redistribution of recruitment patterns and a greater sodium and chloride economy.

Anecdotal observations may cause us to question the idea that acclimatization leads to increased sweating because newcomers to the topics seem to perspire more than indigenes. Newcomers are most likely storing more heat and beginning to perspire at higher skin and core temperatures than natives, hence they have greater heat stores to lose. This requires more perspiration once sweating begins.

AGE   There is a close relationship between an individual's age and heat tolerance. Development of sweat gland function in youth and reduction in cardiovascular functions in the aged are the major factors involved. Neonates are extremely vulnerable to extreme heat because their sweating capacity is limited. All sweat glands are formed at birth, but many are inactive. Hey & Katz (43) estimate that a newborn's sweat glands produce only one third the adult levels of perspiration, even though they are more densely packed. This reduced capacity puts them at risk for heat-related problems. Ellis (24) has shown that during a 15-year period in the U.S., the heat-aggrevated death rates in infants under a year of age was the highest of any age group save those over 50.

As the child grows, the integument stretches, density of sweat glands fall, and capacity increases. Essential to the process is activation of formed glands. Kuno (53) has summarized evidence suggesting a critical period in the first 2 ½ years during which time activation occurs. It is during this period that the sweating capacity of children increases. Because there seems to be no additional activation, this developmental phenomenon has been used to account for the observation that natives in hot climates have more active glands than those from temperate climates (53). Exposure to heat during infancy is presumably the activating stimulus. Knip (52) has recently summarized evidence that deactivation and reactivation may occur in adulthood.

Older adults are at highest risk for heat-induced death (24). The major problem seems to be lack of acclimatization and reduced physical activity in the elderly. The elderly who maintain physical condition fare as well as middle-aged men in moderate heat (19, 82). It is only at high levels of physical activity in the heat that the fit and healthy older individual may be less tolerant (82).

SEX DIFFERENCES   A large number of studies have compared men and women in humid and dry heat with the general conclusion that both sexes respond to heat and acclimatize in the same manner, but women tend to begin sweating at a higher skin temperature, sweat less, and store more heat (30, 91, 108). Weinman et al (104) reported that at equal exercise intensity active women had better performance in humid heat than inactive men. When the sexes are matched in terms of physical fitness and level of work, there are only trivial differences in the heat (45, 49, 72). Horstman & Christensen (45) have presented evidence that active women may acclimatize at a faster rate, but again the difference seems trivial. Thus, with respect to heat tolerance, there seems to be no important difference between the sexes if physical condition is equal.

PHYSICAL ACTIVITY   Physical activity leads to physical fitness which is closely related to heat tolerance. Well-trained men more easily tolerate heat, and training actually enhances the level of heat tolerance (33, 74). Training is beneficial even if it takes place in a temperate environment with no ambient heat load (75). The opposite is also true—acclimatization to heat has a positive effect on work performance and improves maximum work capacity (92). As we have noted previously, "Physical fitness and heat tolerance both involve greater sweating and improvement in cardiovascular function so they probably cannot be separated" (36).

BODY SHAPE AND PROPORTION   Among the earliest established correlates of human variation were the "ecological rules" of Allen and Bergmann. These rules hold that peoples living in warm climates have longer extremities and a lesser body mass than those living in cold climates. Roberts (78) has summarized the data and arguments. The underlying assumption is that a higher surface area to mass ratio in homeotherms is beneficial in terms of heat loss. There are a number of qualifications which limit the usefulness of this attractive hypothesis. Malnutrition and infectious disease are epidemic in the tropics, and these could reduce body size and proportions. These notwithstanding, stature, weight, and limb length are phenotypically plastic and have a significant environmental input. In this context, studies of growth are helpful. Eveleth (25) studied American middle-class children reared in Brazil and found them to be more linear than expected. Stinson & Frisancho (93) compared the children of Andean migrants to the Amazon jungle with children living in the Andes. Those reared in the jungle were more linear, the length of the extremities clearly greater. Dietary factors, parasitic infection, or selective migrations could play some critical role; however, the lengthening of extremity in tropical areas is part of a developmental process. This corresponds to evidence from animal studies. Whittow (105) describes pigs reared outdoors in a cold environment as having shorter legs than littermates reared within a heated enclosure. The mechanism is probably blood flow to the developing extremities. In the cold, body thermal balance takes precedence, so blood flow is reduced and full genetic potential is not reached. In a warm environment the full potential is realized.

A linear body build is of advantage in hot climates if it promotes heat loss; however, this advantage is limited to some conditions. Experimental studies in climatic chambers show body temperature responds most obviously to level of physical activity (51) and that level of physical fitness is more important than surface area to mass proportions (4). During mild heat exposure surface area does provide an advantage for heat loss (92), but as ambient temperature increases, linear individuals may actually be at a disadvantage. At high environmental temperatures, the heat gain via convection and radiation can be greater than the heat loss advantage conferred by the greater surface area, thus a more compact body build may be favored (4).

Despite the simplicity and attractiveness of Bergmann's and Allen's rules for exploration of variation in human body form, a thermal explanation cannot be accepted uncritically. Other factors such as physical activity are more important than body shape during work. Also, body shape can be modified by disease, malnutrition, and other factors; and there also remains the possibility that extremity exposure to cold during the development process is more important than thermal demands during work in shaping final body configuration.

BODY FAT   Excess body fat is probably detrimental in hot climates. Heavier individuals are more subject to heat-related death (58) and have greater stress during heat acclimatization (58, 65, 86). Reduced physical activity may be involved, but obesity per se may also play a role. Bar-Or et al (4) studied obese and lean women working in six environmental conditions ranging from cool to hot. In all conditions, the obese women sweated more profusely, stored more heat, and maintained higher heart rate: Fat did not appear to hinder heat transfer from core to shell because skin temperatures were also higher in the obese. The investigators suggested several factors linking obesity to heat tolerance. First and least important was surface area to mass ratio. As noted previously, at higher temperatures the obese obtain some advatage through lower environmental heat gain. Second, adipose tissue has less water than other tissues and hence can absorb less heat. This promotes a greater heat load on nonfat tissue and reduces heat tolerance. Third, obese individuals have lesser cardiovascular fitness than nonobese. Even if there are no pathological problems, obesity leads to an increased blood volume which is distributed to adipose tissue (99). This places greater strain on the cardiovascular system.

SKIN COLOR   While skin color seems to vary in response to the ultraviolet level in solar radiation (31), thermobiologists have also considered its potential influence on heat regulation (55). White and dark skin are similar in terms of thermal exchange except, all else being equal, dark skin absorbs 30 to 40% more sunlight than white skin (6, 37). This must be dissipated as heat. Baker (3) reported that when blacks and whites are tested unclothed in the desert, blacks seem to show higher level heat storage than whites, presumably because of greater heat gain via radiation. There has been no confirmation of this observation. The thermal advantage of white skin was slight, and we agree with Blum (6, p. 54), "it seems necessary to assume that the possession of dark skin should be a disadvantage to the Negro, as regards to heat load and life in hot desert areas, but that the disadvantage is not a great one and probably of little importance under his usual condition of life."

ETHNICITY   The influence of ethnicity on the ability to tolerate heat has been the subject of much speculation in the anthropological as well as in the popular literature. Implicit has been the assumption that people indigenous to hot environments are better able to tolerate heat than non-natives. The phenomenon of acclimatization has been largely unappreciated and the existing differences magnified. In some cases adaptation to a hot climate has been viewed as an adaptation to solar radiation rather than to heat. European literature, for example, focused upon the "actinic" or "chemical" rays of the sun (76). Protecting fair-skinned residents from these rays required heavy clothing and special spinal pads which simply impaired heat loss. Darker-skinned, less clothed natives tolerated the heat with greater ease.

Only recently have controlled experimental investigations begun to unravel ethnic differences in heat tolerance. People living in all major hot zones have been studied, and we have outlined details of this work in an earlier paper (36). In general, all people studied are capable of acclimatizing and achieving a high level of heat tolerance. This does not mean that all people respond in a similar manner. Some sweat more profusely, some tend toward greater heat storage, but the observed differences are generally small and not important for survival. The conclusions of Strydom & Wyndham (96) are probably still valid: differences in the state of acclimatization are probably more important than any other factor in producing differences in heat tolerance.

With this point in mind, we should consider the one ethnic factor which has emerged in several studies. Well-acclimatized Europeans show a tendency toward higher levels of sweat production than do natives of hot climates in similar states of acclimatization. The reported differences are usually small, but Strydom & Wyndham (96) observed rates of well-acclimatized Europeans to exceed those of similarly acclimatized Bantu by up to 250 cc per hour (Figure 2). The accumulated difference was over 600 cc in 4 hours. If Europeans do indeed perspire more heavily, there are a number of possible causes. One is that the Europeans are drinking more, hence maintaining a higher level of hydration. Alternatively, there may be a more "economical" sweating pattern in indigenes as has been previously suggested. It does not seem to be related to sweat gland density for density of functioning sweat glands does not seem to have an ethnic component (52). Regardless of the locus or even the reality of the phenomenon, Euporeans tolerate heat as well as any other people studied, and the work on ethnic variation has reinforced the view that intense selection for heat tolerance antedates contemporary human ethnic variation.

CONCLUSIONS

Humans are remarkably well adapted to tolerate heat whether derived from environmental or from metabolic sources. This adaptation apparently developed early in hominid evolution and permitted successful colonization of

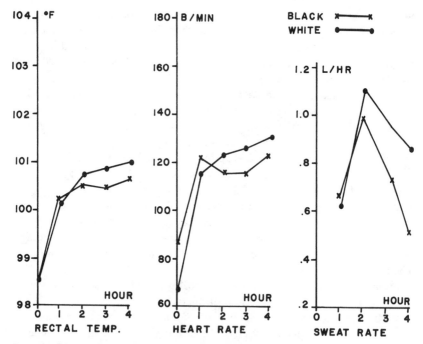

Figure 2   Ethnic differences in response to heat are seen when well-acclimatized black and white men are compared in a hot environment. The white men sweat more profusely, but maintain similar core temperatures and heart rates. These data are presented by Strydom & Wyndham (96). Other studies have yielded similar—but less extreme—differences.

savanna and other hot environments. Apparently, the selective pressures were very stong and included a behavioral component with high levels of physical activity. The major adaptation was a high-capacity sweating response, an improvement upon specialized sweat glands existing in the order Primates. The adaptation came with a price, however: the necessity for a reliable daily water supply. We have speculated that the necessity for water may have contributed to the establishment of a home base for hominid social groups. This base, in turn, may have been a critical factor in human sociocultural evolution.

In contemporary humans, cultural activities are an important means for adjustment to many environmental problems, yet biological adaptations seem of primary importance in adaptation to heat. These include cardiovascular adjustments and diversion of blood flow to surface areas which facilitate heat loss accompanied by active sweating and evaporative heat loss. Repeated exposure results in improvement in the system with a quicker onset, higher rate and increased sweating capacity. It is this ability to acclimatize found in all humans which accounts for most of the individual variation in response to heat.

Literature Cited

1. Adolph, E. F. 1947. The human body and the desert. In *Physiology of Man in the Desert*, ed. E. F. Adolph et al, pp. 16–32. New York: Wiley
2. Adolph, E. F. 1949. Desert. In *The Physiology of Heat Regulation and the Science of Clothing*, ed. L. W. Newburg, pp. 330–38. Philadelphia: Saunders
3. Baker, P. T. 1958. Racial differences in heat tolerance. *Am. J. Phys. Anthropol.* 16:282–305
4. Bar-Or, O., Lundergren, H. M., Buskirk, E. R. 1969. Heat tolerance in exercising and obese women. *J. Appl. Physiol.* 26:403–9
5. Belding, H. S., Hatch, T. F. 1963. Relation of skin temperature to acclimatization and tolerance to heat. *Fed. Proc.* 22:881–83
6. Blum, H. F. 1961. Does the melanin pigment of human skin have adaptive value? *Q. Rev. Biol.* 36:50–63
7. Bonnefille, R. 1976. Palynological evidence for an important change in the vegetation of the Omo basin between 2.5 and 2 million years ago. In *Earliest Man and Environments in the Lake Rudolf Basin*, ed. Y. Coppens et al, pp. 421–31. Chicago: Univ. Chicago Press
8. Briggs, L. C. 1975. Environment and human adaptation in the Sahara. In *Physiological Anthropology*, ed. A. Damon, pp. 93–129. New York: Oxford Univ. Press
9. Budd, G. M., Fox, R. H., Hendrie, A. L., Hicks, K. E. 1972. A field survey of thermal stress in New Guinea villages. *Philos. Trans. R. Soc. London Ser. B* 268:393–400
10. Burnet, M., White, D. O. 1972. *Natural History of Infectious Disease*. Cambridge: Cambridge Univ. Press. 4th ed.
11. Burton, A. C., Edholm, O. G. 1955. *Man in a Cold Environment*. London: Arnold
12. Carr, C. J. 1976. Plant ecological variation and pattern in the lower Omo basin. See Ref. 7, pp. 432–67
13. Champion, R. H. 1970. Sweat glands. In *An Introduction to the Biology of the Skin*, ed. R. H. Champion, T. Gillman, A. J. Rook, R. T. Simms, pp. 175–83. Philadelphia: Davis
14. Clark, J. D. 1980. Early human occupation of African savanna environments. See Ref. 38, pp. 41–71
15. Cloudsley-Thompson, J. L. 1964. Terrestrial animals in dry heat: Introduction. In *The Handbook of Physiology, Vol. 4: Adaptation to the Environment*, ed. D. B.

Dill, pp. 447–50. Baltimore: Williams & Wilkins
16. Connell, J. H. 1978. Diversity in tropical rain forests and coral reefs. *Science* 199:1302–10
17. Coon, C. S. 1955. Some problems of human variability and natural selection in climate and culture. *Am. Nat.* 89:257–80
18. DeVore, I. 1964. The evolution of social life. In *Horizons in Anthropology*, ed. S. Tax, pp. 25–36. Chicago: Aldine
19. Dill, D. B., Consolazio, F. C. 1962. Responses to exercise as related to age and environmental temperature. *J. Appl. Physiol.* 17:645–48
20. Eckert, E. R. G., Drake, R. M. Jr. 1972. *Analysis of Heat and Mass Transfer*. New York: McGraw-Hill
21. Edholm, O. G., Fox, R. H., McPherson, R. 1957. Vasomotor control of cutaneous blood vessels in the forearm. *J. Physiol.* 139:455–65
22. Edholm, O. G., Weiner, J. S. 1981. Thermal physiology. In *The Principles and Practice of Human Physiology*, ed. O. G. Edholm, J. S. Weiner. London: Academic
23. Eichna, L. W., Park, C. R., Nelson, N., Horvath, S. M., Palmes, E. D. 1950. Thermal regulation during acclimatization to a hot dry environment. *Am. J. Physiol.* 163:585–87
24. Ellis, F. P. 1972. Mortality from heat illness and heat-aggrevated illness in the United States. *Environ. Res.* 5:1–58
25. Eveleth, P. B. 1966. The effects of climate on growth. *Ann. NY Acad. Sci.* 134:750–59
26. Fitzpatrick, E. A. 1979. Radiation. In *Arid-Land Ecosystems: Structure, Functioning and Management*, ed. D. W. Goodall, R. A. Perry, 1:347–72. Cambridge: Cambridge Univ. Press
27. Folk, G. E. 1976. *Textbook of Environmental Physiology*. Phildelphia: Lea & Febiger
28. Fox, R. H. 1965. Heat. In *The Physiology of Human Survival*, ed. O. G. Edholm, A. L. Bacharach, pp. 53–80. London: Academic
29. Fox, R. H., Goldsmith, R., Hampton, I., Hunt, T. 1967. Heat acclimatization by controlled hyperthemia in hot dry and hot wet climates. *J. Appl. Physiol.* 22:39–46
30. Fox, R. H., Loftedst, B., Woodward, P., Eriksson, E., Werkstrem, B. 1969. Comparison of thermoregulatory function in men and women. *J. Appl. Physiol.* 26:444–53

31. Frisancho, A. R. 1979. *Human Adaptation*. St. Louis: Mosby
32. Gates, D. M. 1980. *Biophysical Ecology*. New York: Springer
33. Gisolfi, C., Robinson, S. 1969. Relation between physical training, acclimatization and heat tolerance. *J. Appl. Physiol.* 26:530–34
34. Givoni, G. 1974. Biometeorological indices. In *Progress in Biometeorology. Vol. 1, Part 1A. Micro- and Macro-Environments in the Atmosphere: Their Effects on Basic Physiological Mechanisms of Man*, ed. S. W. Tromp, pp. 138–45. Amsterdam: Swets & Zeitlinger BV
35. Goldman, R. 1978. Prediction of human heat tolerance. In *Environmental Stress: Individual Human Adaptations*, ed. L. J. Folinsbee, J. A. Wagner, J. F. Borgia, B. L. Drinkwater, J. A. Gliner, J. F. Bedi, pp. 53–70. New York: Academic
36. Hanna, J. M., Brown, D. E. 1979. Human heat tolerance: Biological and cultural adaptations. *Yearb. Phys. Anthropol.* 22:163–86
37. Hardy, J. D. 1949. Heat transfer. See Ref. 2, pp. 78–108
38. Harris, D. R. 1980. Tropical savanna environments: definition, distribution, diversity, and development. In *Human Ecology in Savanna Environments*, ed. D. R. Harris, pp. 3–27. London: Academic
39. Healy, J. R. 1968. *Inventory of Research on Desert Regional Types*. Tucson: Office Arid Lands Stud., Univ. Ariz.
40. Henschel, A. 1964. Minimal water requirements under conditions of heat and work. In *Thirst*, ed. M. J. Wayner, pp. 19–28. New York: Macmillan
41. Henschel, A., Coppola, S. A. 1972. *Occupational Exposure to Hot Environments*. Washington DC: US Dep. HEW
42. Henschel, A., Hanson, H. E. 1959. Heat stress in a desert environment. *Proc. Am. Soc. Mech. Eng.* 210:1–4
43. Hey, E., Katz, G. 1969. Evaporative water loss in the newborn baby. *J. Physiol.* 210:1–4
44. Hofler, W. 1968. Changes in regional distribution of sweating during acclimatization to heat. *J. Appl. Physiol.* 25:503–6
45. Horstman, D. H., Christensen, E. 1982. Acclimatization to dry heat: Active men vs active women. *J. Appl. Physiol.* 52:825–31
46. Incropera, F. P., DeWitt, D. P. 1981. *Fundamentals of Heat Transfer*. New York: Wiley
47. Johnson, G. S., Elizondo, R. S. 1975. A thermal balance study in *Macaca mulatta* before and after heat acclimatization. *Fed. Proc.* 34:455 (Abstr.)
48. Johnson, G. S., Elizondo, R. S. 1979. Thermoregulation in *Macaca mulatta*: a thermal balance study. *J. Appl. Physiol.* 46:268–77
49. Kamon, E., Avellini, B. 1979. Responses to heat of men and women equal in surface area and aerobic capacity. *Fed. Proc.* 38:1296. (Abstr.)
50. Kennedy, G. E. 1980. *Paleo-Anthropology*. New York: McGraw-Hill
51. Kerslake, D. M. 1972. *The Stress of Hot Environments*. Cambridge: Cambridge Univ. Press
52. Knip, A. S. 1977. Ethnic studies on sweat gland counts. In *Physiological Variation and its Genetic Basis*, ed. J. S. Weiner, pp. 113–23. New York: Halsted
53. Kuno, Y. 1956. *Human Perspiration*. Springfield: Thomas
54. LaBarre, W. 1964. Comments on the human revolution. *Curr. Anthropol.* 5:147–50
55. Ladell, W. S. S. 1964. Terrestrial animals in humid heat: Man. See Ref. 15, pp. 625–59
56. Lee, D. H. K. 1964. Terrestrial animals in dry heat: Man. See Ref. 15, pp. 551–82
57. Leibert, J., Candas, V., Vogt, J. 1979. Effect of rate of change in skin temperature on local sweating rate. *J. Appl. Physiol.* 46:306–11
58. Leithead, C. S., Lind, A. R. 1964. *Heat Stress and Heat Disorders*. Phildelphia: Davis
59. LeMaho, V., Goffart, M., Rochas, A., Felbabel, H. 1981. Thermal regulation in the only nocturnal Simian: the night monkey *Aotus trivirgatus*. *Am. J. Physiol.* 240:R156–65
60. Lind, A. R., Bass, D. E. 1963. Optimal exposure for development of heat acclimatization. *Fed. Proc.* 22:705–8
61. Lovejoy, C. O. 1981. The origin of man. *Science* 211:341–50
62. Lowry, W. P. 1969. *Weather and Life*. New York: Academic
63. Marriott, H. L. 1950. *Water and Salt Depletion*. Springfield: Thomas
64. McGinnies, W. G. 1979. Arid-land ecosystems—common features throughout the world. See Ref. 26, pp. 299–316
65. Minard, D., Copman, L. 1963. Elevation in Body Temperature. In *Health in Temperature: Its Measurement and Control in Science and Industry*, ed. J. D. Hardy, pp. 527–43. New York: Reinhold
66. Montagna, W. 1962. *The Structure and Function of Skin*. New York: Academic

67. Montagu, M. F. A. 1964. Natural selection and man's relative hairlessness. *J. Am. Med. Assoc.* 187:356–57
68. Moran, E. F. 1982. *Human Adaptability.* Boulder, Colo: Westview Press
69. Newman, L. M., Commings, E. G., Miller, J. H., Wright, M. 1970. Thermoregulatory responses of baboons exposed to heat stress and scopolamine. *Physiologist* 13:217–18
70. Newman, R. W. 1970. Why is man such a sweaty, thirsty, naked animal: a speculative review. *Hum. Biol.* 42:12–27
71. Nieuwolt, S. 1977. *Tropical Climatology.* London: Wiley
72. Paolone, A. M., Wells, C. L., Kelly, G. T. 1978. Sexual variations in thermoregulation during heat stress. *Aviat. Space Environ. Med.* 49:715–19
73. Perkins, E. M. 1975. Phylogenetic significance of the skin of New World monkeys. *Am. J. Phys. Anthropol.* 42: 395–424
74. Piwonka, R., Robinson, S. 1967. Acclimatization of highly trained men to work in severe heat. *J. Appl. Physiol.* 22:2–12
75. Piwonka, R., Robinson, S., Gay, V., Manalis, L. 1965. Preacclimatization of men to heat by training. *J. Appl. Physiol.* 20:379–84
76. Planalp, J. M. 1971. *Heat Stress and Culture in North India.* Spec. Tech. Rep. US Army Inst. Environ. Med., Natick, Mass.
77. Rapoport, A. 1969. *House Form and Culture.* Englewood Cliffs, NJ: Prentice Hall
78. Roberts, D. F. 1972. *Climate and Human Variability.* Reading, Mass: Addison-Wesley
79. Robertshaw, D. R. 1979. Apocrine glands. In *Dermatology in General Medicine,* ed. T. B. Fitzpatrick, A. Z. Eisen, K. Wolff, I. M. Friedberg, K. F. Austey, pp. 118–21. New York: McGraw Hill
80. Robinson, S. 1949. Tropics. See Ref. 2, pp. 338–50
81. Robinson, S. 1972. Cardiovascular and respiratory reactions to heat. In *Physiological Adaptations,* ed. M. K. Yousef, S. M. Horvath, R. W. Bullard, pp. 77–98. New York: Academic
82. Robinson, S., Belding, H. S., Consolazio, F. C., Horvath, S. M., Turrell, E. S. 1965. Acclimatization of older men to work in heat. *J. Appl. Physiol.* 20:583–86
83. Robinson, S., Robinson, A. H. 1954. Chemical composition of sweat. *J. Physiol.* 34:202–20
84. Roddie, I., Shepard, J., Whelan, R. 1957. The contribution of constrictor and dilator nerves to skin vasodilation during body heating. *J. Physiol.* 136:489–97
85. Rosenberg, N. J. 1974. *Microclimate: The Biological Environment.* New York: Wiley
86. Ross, F. 1966. Medical problems related to the hostile environment, III: problems related to heat. *Southwest. Med.* 47:137–48
87. Rowell, L. B. 1974. Human cardiovascular adjustments to exercise and thermal stress. *Physiol. Rev.* 54:75–159
88. Rowell, L. B. 1978. Human adjustments and adaptations to heat stress—where and how? See Ref. 35, pp. 1–27
89. Sato, K. 1977. The physiology, pharmacology and biochemistry of the eccrine sweat gland. *Rev. Biochem. Physiol. Pharmacol.* 79:51–132
90. Schmidt-Nielsen, K. 1964. *Desert Animals.* Oxford: Oxford Univ. Press
91. Shapiro, Y., Pandolf, K. B., Avellini, B. A., Pimentel, N. A., Goldman, R. F. 1980. Physiological responses of men and women to humid and dry heat. *J. Appl. Physiol.* 49:1–8
92. Shvartz, E., Shapiro, Y., Magazanik, A., Meroz, A., Birnfeld, H., et al. 1977. Heat acclimatization, physical fitness and responses to exercise in temperate and hot environments. *J. Appl. Physiol.* 43:678–83
93. Stinson, S., Frinsancho, A. R. 1978. Body proportions of highland and lowland Peruvian Quechua children. *Hum. Biol.* 50:57–68
94. Stitt, J. T., Hardy, J. D. 1971. Thermoregulation in the squirrel monkey. *J. Appl. Physiol.* 31:48–54
95. Straus, W. L. 1950. Microscopic anatomy of the skin of the gorilla. In *Anatomy of the Gorilla,* ed. W. K. Gregory, pp. 214–21. New York: Columbia Univ. Press
96. Strydom, N. B., Wyndham, C. H. 1963. Natural state of heat acclimatization of different ethnic groups. *Fed. Proc.* 22: 801–9
97. Terjung, W. H., Louie, S. S.-F. 1971. Potential solar radiation climates of man. *Ann. Assoc. Am. Geogr.* 61:481–500
98. Van Couvering, J. A. H., Van Couvering, J. A. 1976. Early Miocene fossils from East Africa: Aspects of geology, faunistics and paleoecology. In *Human Origins: Louis Leakey and the East African Evidence,* ed. G. L. Isaac, E. R. McCown, pp. 155–207. Menlo Park, Calif: Benjamin
99. Vaughan, R. W., Conahan, T. J. 1980. Cardiopulmonary consequences of morbid obesity. *Life Sci.* 26:1–9

100. Walton, K. 1969. *The Arid Zones*. Chicago: Aldine
101. Weiner, J. S. 1971. *The Natural History of Man*. Garden City, NY: Doubleday Anchor
102. Weiner, J. S. 1977. Human ecology. In *Human Biology*, ed. G. A. Harrison, J. S. Weiner, J. M. Tanner, N. S. Barnicot, pp. 389–484. New York: Oxford
103. Weiner, J. S. 1977. Variation in sweating. See Ref. 52, pp. 125–37
104. Weinman, K., Slabochora, Z., Bernaur, E., Morimoto, T., Sargent, F. 1967. Reactions of men and women to repeated exposures to humid heat. *J. Appl. Physiol.* 22:533–38
105. Whittow, G. C. 1973. Evolution of thermoregulation. In *Comparative Physiology of Thermoregulation*, ed. G. C. Whittow, 3:202–58. New York: Academic
106. Wulsin, F. R. 1949. Adaptations to climate among non-European peoples. See Ref. 2, pp. 3–69
107. Wyndham, C. H., Benade, A. J. S., Williams, C. G., Strydom, N. B., Goldin, A., Heynes, A. J. 1968. Changes in central circulation and body fluid spaces during acclimatization to heat. *J. Appl. Physiol.* 25:586–93
108. Wyndham, C. H., Morrison, J. F., Williams, C. G. 1965. Heat reaction of male and female Caucasians. *J. Appl. Physiol.* 20:357–64

Ann. Rev. Anthropol. 1983. 12:285–304

ADAPTATION TO HIGH ALTITUDE

Lorna Grindlay Moore

Department of Anthropology, University of Colorado, Denver Campus, Denver, Colorado 80202; Cardiovascular Pulmonary Research Laboratory, University of Colorado Health Sciences Center, Denver, Colorado 80262

Judith G. Regensteiner

Department of Anthropology, University of Colorado, Boulder Campus, Boulder, Colorado 80309

INTRODUCTION

The high altitude environment poses a severe challenge for human adaptation. The availability of our most vital nutrient, oxygen, is reduced at high altitudes. Human beings cannot live without oxygen for more than a few minutes, yet its supply is reduced by one-half at the highest altitudes at which human populations live. Most human beings live today and have lived in the past at sea level. However, approximately 20 to 30 million people live and successfully reproduce at elevations over 2500 m (2). How has adaptation to high altitude been achieved? Are problems encountered for adaptation to high altitudes in contemporary populations? By what mechanism(s) does high altitude adaptation take place?

This article reviews recent studies of the effects of high altitude which pose problems for human adaptation. "Recent" is considered to mean published within the past 6 years, although exception is made for a few pre-1978 reports where no more recent publication has appeared. "High altitude" is arbitrarily defined as elevations above 2500 m. The problems of adaptation are discussed in the integrating framework of the human life cycle. Emphasis is placed throughout the article on the role played by the physiological system of oxygen transport for mediating effects of high altitude and identifying mechanisms by which adaptation may occur.

285

0066–4294/83/1015–0285$02.00

Challenges of High Altitude

Populations residing at elevations above 2500 m live in four regions of the world: the Rocky Mountains in North America, the Andes of South America, the Ethiopian Highlands of Eastern Africa, and the Himalayas of South-Central Asia (Figure 1). The primary challenge in each of these high altitude environments is the decrease in oxygen availability or hypoxia. Oxygen availability is determined by the pressure by which oxygen exists in the atmosphere. Atmospheric pressure, in turn, is determined by the weight of the air pressing on the earth's surface. Human beings at sea level live also at the bottom of a sea of air; at higher altitudes, the weight and hence the pressure of oxygen in the air is lessened (Figure 2).

The hypoxia of high altitudes cannot be modified readily by culture. This distinguishes hypoxia from other attributes of the high altitude environment which can be and routinely are modified by culture: cold, dryness, increased ultraviolet radiation, rugged terrain, and shortened growing season. Temperature drops approximately 0.5°C for each 100 m gain in elevation as a result of the decrease in atmospheric pressure. Cool temperatures, generally low rainfall, and large diurnal temperature variation cause dryness and a shortened growing season. The thinner atmosphere is less effective in screening out solar rays and thus increases ultraviolet radiation. Rugged terrain typifies mountainous environments.

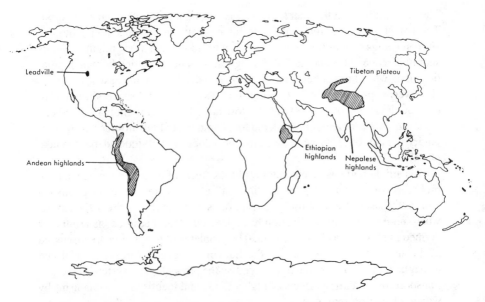

Figure 1   The high altitude (>2500 m) regions of the world (from 55)

The challenge of hypoxia is not confined to high altitude but is shared by a broad spectrum of heart, lung, and blood diseases which interrupt the complex chain of events required to transport oxygen to the tissues. The effects of hypoxia may be more easily understood at high altitude than in disease states where complications are introduced by the presence of the disease itself. For instance, understanding hypoxic pulmonary hypertension in diseases such as cystic fibrosis and chronic bronchitis has been aided by studies of pulmonary hypertension at high altitudes. Therefore, studying the effects of hypoxia at high altitudes may also be relevant for understanding the causes and potentially identifying treatments for heart, lung, and blood disorders.

Human Adaptation

Theodosius Dobzhansky defined an adaptation as "a feature of structure, function, or behavior of the organism which is instrumental in [enabling it] to live and to reproduce in a given environment" (12, p. 111). In this article, high altitude adaptation is viewed as a biologically based process by which individuals respond to the hypoxia of high altitude in order to be able to live and reproduce. No assumptions are made as to whether the mechanisms underlying

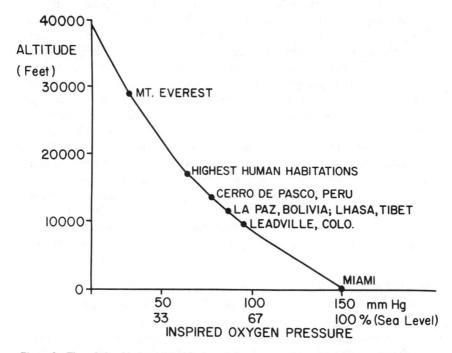

Figure 2   The relationship between altitude and the pressure of oxygen in the atmosphere or inspired air (from 31).

the adaptations being discussed are genetic, acquired, or some combination of both, as these mechanisms, in the case of high altitude, are seldom known. Also, it is not possible to draw distinctions between current utility and historical genesis in governing the derivation of adaptations, important as such distinctions are (20). Biological responses to hypoxia are considered because they are the principal avenue for responding to hypoxia which, in turn, is the primary challenge of the high altitude environment. The individual human being is the unit of study because it is the individual who lives and reproduces and the individual on whom the effects of hypoxia can be most easily observed. Adaptation can also be viewed on other levels. On the level of a gene, adaptation occurs as deleterious genes are eliminated or reduced in frequency by natural selection. Adaptation on the level of the population is reached as favored genes reach their appropriate frequencies. Ultimately, a view of adaptation on the individual (or any single) level needs to be supplemented with views which incorporate other levels and behaviorally based as well as biological strategies.

The study of human adaptation is complicated by the fact that a single scientist or scientific team only studies events over a limited period of time, yet adaptation is a process occurring over many generations. Studies of high altitude may be useful for clarifying the process of adaptation in two ways. First, piecing together the effects of high altitude in the context of the human life cycle provides a picture of the process as it occurs within one generation. Viewing the relationship between the effects of high altitude on the parental and offspring life cycles permits generalizing about the process of adaptation from one generation to the next. Second, populations have been present at high altitudes for different lengths of time and hence constitute "natural laboratories" for the study of adaptation. Residents of high altitudes in North America are essentially migrants from low altitudes, having come from low altitudes in either the current or the past one or two generations. Amerindian populations in South America have lived in highland regions for approximately 20,000 years (18). The Himalayan regions have been occupied by human (or hominid) populations for the longest period, possibly for as many as 500,000 years (47). Thus, a comparative study of high altitude populations along this time gradient may be able to elucidate the long-term process by which adaptation has occurred.

Human Life Cycle

The human life cycle refers to the predictable series of events which characterize a person's life: conception, birth, maturation, and death. Interspersed between these events are the familiar periods of embryonic, fetal, infant, childhood, adolescent, adult, and old age development.

The model of the human life cycle can be used in a variety of ways for interpreting the determination of health and disease (1, 46). The model is used here as a context in which to view problems of high altitude adaptation (Figure 3). An effort is made to avoid the limitations of a linear model in which human development is viewed narrowly as a series of events only affecting the course of one person's life. The model used here incorporates a period of overlap between the parent's, particularly the mother's, and the offspring's life cycles (Figure 3). In keeping with the definition of adaptation, effects of high altitudes which pose problems for high altitude adaptation need to influence fertility and/or mortality. Factors influencing the chance of conception (fecundity) and the production of live offspring determine fertility. Strictly speaking, mortality encompasses survival from birth to the end of the reproductive period. In a broader sense, mortality in later years can also be considered relevant for adaptation since persons in older generations can influence opportunities for the reproduction of the young.

Oxygen Transport System

The purpose of the oxygen transport system is to deliver oxygen to the tissues. Responses of the oxygen transport system can increase the amount of oxygen available to the tissues and thus compensate, at least in part, for the effects of high altitude. The oxygen transport system consists of three components: 1. the lungs, 2. heart and blood vessels, and 3. blood (Figure 4). The volume of air breathed by the lungs determines the oxygen pressure or tension in the lung alveoli. Vital capacity sets the upper limit on the amount of air which can be

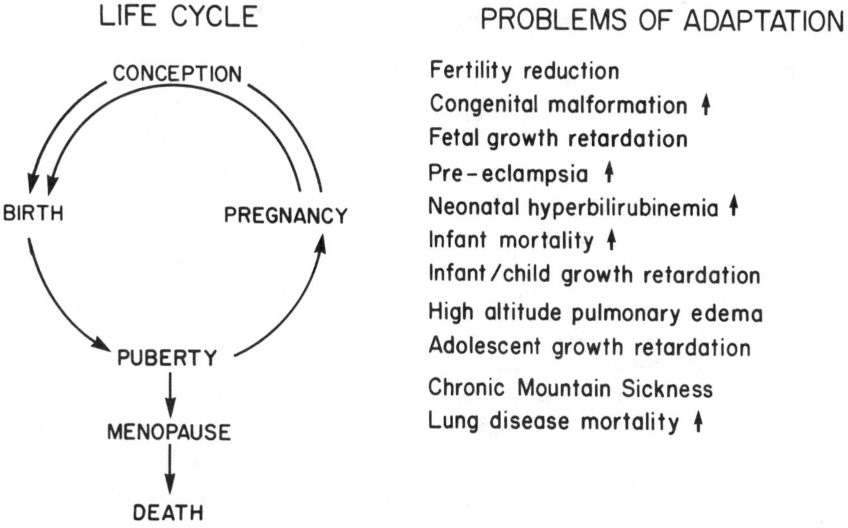

LIFE CYCLE

CONCEPTION

BIRTH

PREGNANCY

PUBERTY

MENOPAUSE

DEATH

PROBLEMS OF ADAPTATION

Fertility reduction
Congenital malformation ↑
Fetal growth retardation
Pre-eclampsia ↑
Neonatal hyperbilirubinemia ↑
Infant mortality ↑
Infant/child growth retardation
High altitude pulmonary edema
Adolescent growth retardation

Chronic Mountain Sickness
Lung disease mortality ↑

Figure 3 Effects of high altitude which pose problems for human adaptation occur at different phases of the human life cycle. Each problem of adaptation is discussed in the text. Arrows indicate interrelationships between the life cycle events.

moved in or out of the lungs. The level of ventilation, or volume of air normally breathed per minute, is regulated by ventilatory control centers in the brainstem and peripheral chemoreceptors. Diffusing capacity determines the ease with which oxygen can diffuse across the alveolar membranes into the blood. The heart pumps the blood which picks up the oxygen from the lungs and distributes it throughout the body via blood vessels. The cardiac output is the volume of blood pumped per minute. The distribution of blood flow is regulated by the resistance and blood pressure in the various blood vessels. Oxygen is transported in the blood while reversibly bound to hemoglobin. Hemoglobin-oxygen affinity determines the ease with which oxygen can be bound and unbound from hemoglobin. The total capacity for carrying oxygen is set by the volume and hemoglobin concentration of the blood. Succinctly, oxygen transport is the product of arterial oxygen saturation, blood oxygen carrying capacity, and cardiac output.

HUMAN LIFE CYCLE AND PROBLEMS OF HIGH ALTITUDE ADAPTATION

Prenatal Events and Infancy: Conception to 1 year of age

Birth is a pivotal event in the human life cycle. It requires the occurrence of conception and a lengthy period of gestation before the offspring is sufficiently mature to sustain life in the "outside" world. Events prior to birth fall within both the offspring's and the parent's life cycles. Conception is a parental act; gestation for the offspring is pregnancy for the mother. Factors influencing the chance of conception (fecundity), as well as the production of live offspring (fertility), are involved and, in practice, difficult to separate. Considerations affecting survival after birth (mortality) may also influence reported fertility since births may not be recorded when the infant dies shortly after being born.

FECUNDITY   High altitude influences prenatal development, but it is not always clear as to whether the effect of high altitude is on fecundity, fertility, and/or infant mortality. Acute high altitude exposure has been associated with changes in the reproductive system that may result in impaired fecundity. Decreased gonadal function has been inferred from reductions in sperm count, pituitary gonadotropins, and testosterone excretion in males, but hormonal changes have not been confirmed in more recent studies (62). Pituitary gonadal hormones are not decreased in natives from high compared to low altitudes (3). Thus, only limited data are available (especially on women), and they do not argue in favor of a reduction in fecundity in at least native high altitude populations.

FERTILITY, CONGENITAL MALFORMATIONS   Direct studies on fertility are difficult to conduct. Careful monitoring of the number of spontaneous abor-

<u>OXYGEN TRANSPORT SYSTEM</u>   <u>COMPONENTS</u>

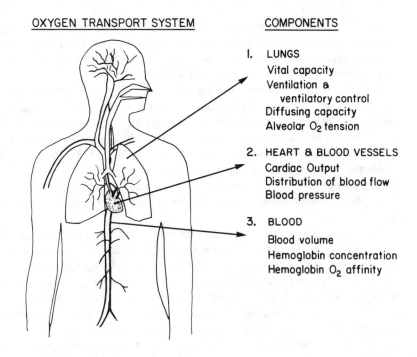

I. LUNGS
    Vital capacity
    Ventilation &
        ventilatory control
    Diffusing capacity
    Alveolar O_2 tension

2. HEART & BLOOD VESSELS
    Cardiac Output
    Distribution of blood flow
    Blood pressure

3. BLOOD
    Blood volume
    Hemoglobin concentration
    Hemoglobin O_2 affinity

Figure 4 The oxygen transport system consists of three components: the lungs, heart and blood vessels, and blood. Each component can influence the amount of oxygen which is ultimately delivered to the tissues in the ways listed.

tions is required and, while theoretically feasible (41), is not easily performed. The incidence of congenital malformations is slightly (1.4 times) but significantly increased at high (>3740 m) compared to low altitudes in Peru, suggesting that hypoxia may be a teratogenic agent for human beings as well as for other species (28). Indirect studies also suggest an impairment of fertility at high altitude. Sixteenth century Spanish historians reported that the Spanish colonizing the Andean region had great difficulty having children. Migration from high to low altitudes increases completed fertility (the total number of children born), suggesting that residence at high altitude reduces fertility (29). Studies of birth records show that women at high altitudes in Andean countries report fewer live births than do their low altitude counterparts. However, the records are likely to underestimate fertility, especially in highland areas where infant mortality is high. This possibility is supported by a detailed analysis of fertility and mortality at high, medium, and low altitudes in Boliva (13). There were no altitude-related differences in fertility, but a reduction in the number of surviving children occurred at high altitude because of greater early childhood mortality. The likelihood that fertility is not reduced by high altitude hypoxia is further supported by a recent comparative Himalayan study (18a).

FETAL GROWTH RETARDATION   The clearest prenatal influence of high altitude is a reduction in infant birth weight. Data collected in North and South America over the past 25 years shows an approximately 100 gram decrease in birth weight for each 1000 m elevation gain (Figure 5).

Comparable lengths of gestation and lower birth weights at each gestational age at high and low altitudes in Colorado points to fetal growth retardation rather than shortened gestation as the cause of the decrease in birth weight (39). Babies born at high altitude are shorter as well as lighter, and the effects of high altitude are more pronounced in male than female births (23). High altitude newborns also present signs of neurological and behavioral immaturity in comparison to newborns at low altitude (59). Reduction in prenatal growth occurs in other mammalian as well as avian species under hypoxic conditions (40).

The precise mechanism responsible for the growth retardation at high altitudes is not clear. The fetus even at sea level lives in an hypoxic environment (by adult standards). Growth rate is extremely rapid during intrauterine life. Possibly, exaggerated fetal hypoxia at high altitudes reduces fetal oxygen supply and the metabolism of nutrients needed to sustain extremely rapid growth. Because the fetus is wholly dependent on its mother for supplying oxygen and other nutrients, one hypothesis to account for fetal growth retardation at high altitude is that it is caused by a failure of maternal adaptation during pregnancy. Several lines of investigation have been conducted recently which support this hypothesis. Haas and co-workers (25) found that Amerindian

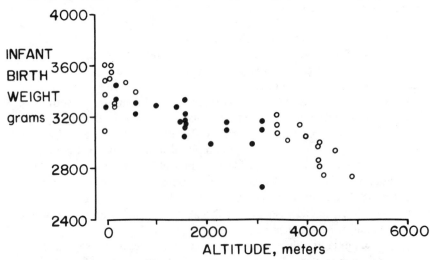

Figure 5   Birth weights in North America (closed circles) and South America (open circles) decrease over a continuum of nearly 5000 m. Data are presented from all published studies including measurements of birth weights at both high and low altitudes. [Redrawn from (39) with the addition of data from (4, 9, 26, 42, 59).]

(Quechua and Aymara) women deliver larger babies at high altitude than non-Indian women. Variation in infant birth weight was not attributable to differences in maternal body size or nutrition but was associated with lower hemoglobin concentrations (24). Data from Moore and her colleagues (43, 45) showed that differences in maternal oxygen transport during high altitude pregnancy relate to fetal growth. Mothers of full-term, smaller babies (<2900 g) compared to mothers of full-term, larger babies (>3500 g) at high altitude in Colorado breathed less, had falling hemoglobin concentrations from early to late gestation, and were more often smokers. Thus, maternal characteristics affecting oxygen transport during pregnancy may be important adaptations for maintaining fetal growth and, by extension, well-being at high altitude.

PRE-ECLAMPSIA   Recent studies also support the possibility that fetal well-being may be compromised by effects of high altitude acting to increase maternal complications of pregnancy. A more than fourfold increase in the incidence of pre-eclampsia occurs at high altitudes in Colorado (42). Pre-eclampsia is among the leading contributors to fetal and maternal mortality today. Possibly a failure of maternal oxygen transport is involved in the etiology of pre-eclampsia, as study results showed an altitude-associated rise in blood pressure even during normal pregnancies and an inverse relationship between maternal arterial oxygen saturation and the degree of hypertension present at high altitude.

INFANT MORTALITY   Infants born at high altitudes are less likely to survive than infants born at low altitudes. Under conditions of comparable medical care in Colorado, infant mortality was nearly two times greater at high than low altitudes (39). An increased number of deaths due to respiratory disease among preterm infants was the most important factor in causing the increased mortality. Low infant birth weight per se was not associated with increased mortality under conditions of nearly optimal medical care in Colorado. However, the possibility exists that reductions in infant birth weight might adversely affect survival where medical care was more limited.

The influence of birth weight on survival may differ at high compared to low altitudes. Despite lower birth weights at 3860 m than at 600 m in Peru, Beall (4) found that infant mortality was not greater at high altitudes, as has been previously reported, but lower overall and lower at virtually every birth weight. Optimum birth weights for survival were calculated using a complex mathematical model and found to be lower at high than at low altitudes but still higher than the average high altitude birth weight. Possibly, therefore, fetal growth retardation is less disadvantageous at high than at low altitudes.

HYPERBILIRUBINEMIA   Neonatal problems, specifically hyperbilirubinemia (the presence of excessively elevated bilirubin levels in the first week after birth), occur more frequently at high altitudes. Neonatal hyperbilirubinemia may lead to brain damage (kernicterus) and even death. Its incidence at 3100 m in Colorado was found to be twice that at 1600 m and nearly four times greater than sea level values (10). The increased occurrence of hyperbilirubinemia was not a result of fetal growth retardation, as its incidence was the same in low and full birth weight babies, but rather implied that other, adverse effects of high altitude existed during the neonatal period.

INFANT GROWTH RETARDATION   The first year after birth is a period of rapid growth and development. Body size continues to be smaller at high altitudes during infancy, but motor development is comparable in highland and lowland Andean populations (23). Longitudinal study has shown that the cause of the lower body weight was traceable to the persistence of lower birth weights rather than to postnatal growth retardation since high altitude infants gained weight at the same rate as low altitude infants (26). Infants also remained shorter during the first nine months but experienced a late acceleration such that they were taller at the end of the first year. Despite lower body weights, high altitude infants were fatter than low altitude infants, suggesting that high altitude affects body composition as well as body size during infancy.

SUMMARY   The infant born at high altitude has a decreased chance of survival. The period of transition from intrauterine to extrauterine life is associated with high mortality at any altitude; high altitude appears to further compromise survival during this sensitive period. The factor(s) at high altitude responsible for impairing infant survival is not clear. Recent studies are consistent with the possibility that diminished oxygen supply *in utero* increases the occurrence of fetal and pregnancy-related complications which, in turn, increase mortality shortly after birth. A failure of maternal oxygen transport may underlie the prenatal and early postnatal complications observed. However, it is not clear whether all the effects of high altitude seen during prenatal and early postnatal life constitute problems or whether some are solutions for adaptation to high altitudes. In addition, the effects of high altitude may vary at different periods of the life cycle and in different populations. For instance, growth retardation may threaten prenatal survival but facilitate postnatal development, and it may not have the same consequences for adaptation in different populations. Future studies should be directed at determining the precise mechanisms underlying the effects of high altitude observed and their actual consequences for adaptation to high altitude.

Childhood and Adolescence: 1 to 20 years of age

GROWTH RETARDATION   Childhood and adolescence are periods of continued body growth and development although the rate of growth is not as rapid as during prenatal life and infancy. Several investigators have stressed the importance of events occurring during these periods because the opportunity exists during periods of growth and development for the environment to modify the expression of inherited potentials (14). Also, alterations in growth during early stages of the human life cycle lay the foundation for future development (26).

Numerous studies have reported smaller body sizes, reduced growth rates, and alterations in body shape during childhood and adolescence in Andean populations (5, 16, 50, 52, 53). Male and female height is shorter and weight is lower in highland than lowland Andean populations due to the appearance of a late, poorly defined adolescent growth spurt (16). The period of growth is prolonged into the third decade but is not sufficient to attain low altitude values. No secular increment in adult body size has occurred in highland Peru over the past 35 years (19). Growth during childhood is also diminished at high compared to low altitudes in children of Amerindian and of European ancestry (5, 50, 60, 61). The degree of retardation in body height and weight among Amerindian children is less than that present during adolescence (5). The appearance of secondary sexual characteristics is also delayed in highland Peruvian populations although the age of sexual maturation appears to have become younger over the past 35 years (15, 19). Chest size relative to body size increases with altitude although little change occurs in absolute dimensions. Increased total lung capacity parallels the changes in relative chest size. The greatest increase occurs in the functional residual capacity component (63). Forced vital capacity is greater as well, particularly when the smaller body sizes are taken into account (36, 51), Alterations in body growth and shape appear to be a response to high altitude hypoxia rather than to other attributes of the high altitude Andean environment such as poor nutrition and/or medical care (5, 16, 56). The reduction in body size is likely to be developmental rather than genetic in origin since high altitude attributes are acquired by persons of low altitude ancestry (60, 61), and low altitude attributes are acquired by migrants from high altitudes (5). The relative increase in chest and lung dimensions at high altitudes may be under a different set of controls than height and weight, although the precise nature of the controls is unclear (51, 53). Both developmental (16) and genetic (5, 53) explanations have been advanced. A problem for distinguishing between them is that it is difficult to differentiate the effects of duration of high altitude exposure from the effects of the age at which exposure began. It is also unclear as to whether the larger chest and lung dimensions reflect selective preservation or enhancement of their growth or whether the effects of high altitude are acting directly on the chest or through morphological changes in the heart and lungs.

Studies of the effects of high altitude on growth in Ethiopian, Himalayan, and North American populations present a more equivocal picture. Advanced rather than retarded growth characterizes high altitude (3000 m) children in Ehtiopia, but the effects of hypoxia may be obscured by better health and nutrition-related conditions at high altitudes (7). Studies from Nepal (54) show that high altitude Sherpas have the same body and chest dimensions as Tibetans born and raised at low altitude. However, the comparison is complicated by the fact that the Tibetans were derived from populations living at elevations comparable to those inhabited by the Sherpas (approximately 3500 m). Skeletal development in both Himalayan groups is slow relative to U.S. standards. Chest circumference (both in absolute terms and relative to body size) is the same in the Sherpas and Tibetans (54) but decreased compared to highland Peruvians (16). Forced vital capacity among Sherpas is less than among Europeans in absolute terms but the same in relation to body size (27). Further, growth of pulmonary function as measured by forced vital capacity does not appear accelerated relative to body growth among Tibetans (4a). Childhood and adolescent growth has not been studied in North American high altitude populations. Forced vital capacity of Colorado residents at 3100 m is the same as values predicted at sea level. Higher forced expiratory volumes and flow noted in the high altitude residents were due to the decrease in air density (32), as has also been observed in Peruvian studies (63). Thus, the patterns of growth and development observed in Himalayan, Ethiopian, and North American highlanders are not entirely consistent with observations from the Andean area. The explanation for this apparent discrepancy may reside in health and nutrition-related differences between high and low altitude regions, the length of time during which the populations have resided at high altitudes, and/or the elevations being considered. Many Andean residents live at substantially higher elevations than the Ethiopians, North Americans, or even the Sherpas, whose mean population centers are at 2600 m in Solu and approximately 3600 m in the Khumbu (P. Hackett, personal communication).

It is far from clear whether or not the childhood and adolescent growth retardation seen in Andean and possibly also Himalayan populations should be considered a problem or a solution for adaptation to high altitude. The effects of growth retardation during infancy and fetal life are also equivocal, although at least fetal growth retardation is usually thought to be disadvantageous. One indication in favor of an adaptive value for smaller body size is that a larger proportion of infants born to smaller-sized parents survived in comparison to the proportion of surviving infants born to larger-sized parents living under poor socioeconomic conditions in highland Peru (17). However, the smaller body sizes observed were not necessarily the result of high altitude-induced growth retardation, and a comparable advantage for smaller body sizes might not exist under the broader range of cultural conditions present at high altitude. Enlarged chest dimensions relative to body size appear present only among Andean populations where they may be adaptive insofar as they contribute to increased pulmonary diffusing capacity. No studies have been performed, however, in which an adaptive advantage of increased diffusing capacity has been directly demonstrated (63).

HIGH ALTITUDE PULMONARY EDEMA   High altitude pulmonary edema is a rare, but possibly fatal, disease which occurs typically among young high altitude residents after brief sojourn at sea level and rapid reascent to altitudes over 2700 m. Its estimated incidence ranges from 1–6% among high altitude residents under 21 years of age in North and South America and from 2–15% among sea level military personnel during initial high altitude exposure in India (22). Many consider that it is an extreme form of acute mountain sickness (37). Symptoms of high altitude pulmonary edema include shortness of breath, undue fatigue, cough, and upon examination, cyanosis, tachycardia, and rales. Without treatment with supplemental oxygen or by descent, the pulmonary edema may become extensive, impair blood oxygenation and cause mental confusion, loss of consciousness, coma, and death. The requirement that the ascent be rapid probably made high altitude pulmonary edema (and acute mountain sickness) rare before the advent of automobiles or aircraft, but not necessarily nonexistent, because rapid altitudinal changes are known to have been made on foot by the Incas.

The pathogenesis of high altitude pulmonary edema remains a fascinating problem for physiologists (22, 37). Severe pulmonary hypertension is known to be present, but its precise cause and relationship to the accumulation of fluid in the lungs (edema) are not fully understood. Repeated occurrences of high altitude pulmonary edema within the same person and within families suggest a familial, possibly genetic determination of individual susceptibility to the disease. Greater susceptibility in some individuals in turn may stem from factors acting to increase the stimulus (i.e. lowered arterial oxygen tension) or the response (i.e. increased pulmonary vascular reactivity). Exaggerated hypoxemia at high altitude in persons known to be susceptible supports the first possibility (30). Possibly the control of a person's ventilatory response to hypoxia, already known to be under genetic control (8), is the important factor in deciding individual susceptibility (21). Evidence also exists in favor of increased pulmonary vascular reactivity as underlying differences in individual susceptibility. Genetic control of pulmonary vascular reactivity has been elegantly demonstrated in cattle (11). Pulmonary arterial pressures increase with altitude, but when compared at a given altitude and arterial oxygen tension, pulmonary arterial pressures are greater among high altitude residents of the

United States and Europe than of Andean countries (57). Possibly genes which increase pulmonary vascular reactivity prompt the occurrence of high altitude pulmonary edema and, as a result, have been eliminated from Andean populations by natural selection. There is also evidence against pulmonary vascular control as being the key determinant. Increased pulmonary vascular reactivity has not been a consistent finding in studies of persons susceptible to high altitude pulmonary edema. However, reentry to high altitude, as often occurs prior to the development of high altitude pulmonary edema, may alter pulmonary vascular control and influence whether or not a person exhibits increased pulmonary vascular responsiveness (22).

SUMMARY Influences of high altitude during childhood and adolescence clearly exist and are among the most studied effects of high altitude. Yet important questions remain. Are the smaller body sizes and/or larger chest dimensions of Andean populations adaptive? Are the patterns of growth retardation and alteration observed universal or do they vary among the different high altitude populations of the world? High altitude pulmonary edema is a clear instance of a problem of adaptation to high altitude. Its causes remain obscure and worthy of further study.

Adulthood and Old Age: 21 years of age to death

CHRONIC MOUNTAIN SICKNESS Beginning at approximately age 30, some long-term residents of high altitude may develop chronic mountain sickness (also termed excessive polycythemia, Monge's disease, or chronic *soroche*). The disease occurs almost exclusively in males and has been reported in North American, Andean, and recently Tibetan populations (S.Y. Huang, personal communication). Persons with chronic mountain sickness complain of severe headaches and inability to think clearly and are more hypoxemic (lower arterial oxygen tensions) than normal persons at the same altitude. They develop excessive polycythemia as a result of the stimulating effects of hypoxemia on red blood cell production. Greater red cell production increases hematocrit and raises blood viscosity which, in turn, imposes a greater workload on the heart. In time, the disease may result in a fatal stroke or heart failure unless the hematocrit is lowered by repeated phlebotomy ("bleeding") or descent.

The cause of the hypoxemia among persons with chronic mountain sickness is unclear. Two possibilities were investigated in recent studies in Leadville, Colorado (3100 m): lung disease and reduced level of ventilation (35). In one-half of the cases present, hypoxemia was attributable to the effects of lung disease. Mismatching of ventilation and perfusion as occurs with lung disease resulted in a widened alveolar-arterial difference for oxygen tension and lower arterial oxygen tensions. The other one-half of the patients had normal lungs; their hypoxemia was due to reduced levels of ventilation. These persons have lost the acclimatization to high altitude which normally maintans high levels of resting ventilation in the face of diminished arterial carbon dioxide tensions. An abnormal, shallow breathing pattern occurred in these persons as well. Blunted hypoxic ventilatory responses characterized the persons with chronic mountain sickness but were present in normal, long-term residents of high altitude as well. Thus, it appeared that blunted hypoxic ventilatory response did not cause the hypoxemia but permitted hypoxemia from other causes to persist.

Treatment with the female hormone progesterone has proved an effective therapy for chronic mountain sickness (34). Progesterone, a respiratory stimulant, raised daytime ventilation and levels of arterial oxygenation while lowering hematocrit. Progesterone was also an effective means for raising arterial oxygen saturation during sleep (33).

LUNG AND HEART DISEASE   Mortality from emphysema is higher in Colorado, Wyoming, and New Mexico than in the rest of the United States. These are the only states whose populations live above an average elevation of 1515 m, raising the question as to whether high altitude adversely affects survival from lung disease. Examination of death records of Colorado and in the nation as a whole has shown that age-standardized mortality from emphysema and chronic bronchitis nearly doubles over a 3000 m elevation range (44). Emphysema deaths at higher altitudes in Colorado occurred at a younger age, after a shorter duration of illness, and more commonly from cor pulmonale (right heart failure) than at lower altitudes where pneumonia was more common as the immediate cause of death. Thus, the course of emphysema appears to be altered at high altitudes such that a failing right heart caused death to occur at an earlier stage of the disease than at low altitude. The mechanism by which high altitude residence interacts unfavorably with survival is unknown but may stem from augmented pulmonary hypertension caused by the hypoxia of lung disease added to the hypoxia of high altitude.

Contradictory findings have been reported regarding the effects of high altitude on mortality from heart disease. Mortality from coronary heart disease has generally been lower in the U.S. mountain states than in the nation as a whole. A serial decline in age-standardized rates occurred from the lowest to the highest altitude counties in New Mexico, amounting to an approximately 30% reduction over a 900–2130 m elevation range (48). However, no decline in mortality from heart disease occurred from the lowest to the highest elevations in Colorado (49). Anecdotal reports from Andean, Caucausus, and Karakoram regions claim exceptional longevity and reduced mortality from cardiovascular disease but are difficult to evaluate in the absence of adequate data.

There is a smaller proportion of older-aged persons in high altitude compared to low altitude regions in Andean, Himalayan, and Rocky Mountain regions. In Colorado the proportion of persons over the age of 65 declines from 15% at elevations below 1400 m to 5% at elevations above 2500 m (58). The reduction in the numbers of elderly could be traced to the departure of the elderly by death or migration or to a relative increase in the numbers of younger-aged persons. In Colorado the most important factor is increasing migration from high to low altitude areas after the age of 50 (58). Migration of older-aged persons from high to low altitude areas may also be responsible for reducing the proportion of elderly persons in Andean regions where marginal subsistence economies may make nonproductive adults burdensome (38). The observation that many older persons leave their high altitude places of residence is surprising in light of the fact that nationwide, older-aged persons tend not to leave the area in which they spend their middle years (6).

Health-related reasons prompt older people's departure from high altitudes in Colorado (58). Interviews conducted with middle- and older-aged persons show that health problems become increasingly important reasons for departure with advancing age at high but not at low altitudes. (Older-aged persons living at low altitudes move in order to live nearer family members.) Cardiovascular and/or lung diseases were the most common health problems cited by high altitude migrants, occurring in approximately one-half of the cases. Older persons noted improvement in their health after leaving high altitudes, but no effects on their health were noted by persons leaving low altitudes.

SUMMARY   Problems of adaptation to high altitude continue to occur during adulthood and old age. Chronic mountain sickness and increased mortality from lung disease are clear indications of adaptive failure. Lung disease, a problem for high altitude adaptation in its own right, also appears to be responsible for the underlying hypoxemia in some cases of chronic mountain sickness. It is not known what causes the loss of acclimatization, and hence the hypoventilation in persons who develop chronic mountain sickness with normal lungs. Gender-related factors may be involved since females appear to be protected from chronic mountain sickness as well as, possibly, from chronic lung disease (46). Adverse effects of high altitude during old age (>50 yrs of age) occur after the completion of the reproductive period and hence may not be as significant for the process of adaptation as events occurring in younger age groups. However, their effect should not be discounted, because the male reproductive period may continue into old age and also older-aged persons may indirectly influence reproduction by younger-aged persons through, for example, control of resource distribution. Self-selection appears to operate in older-aged persons at least in Colorado such that the unhealthy migrate and healthy persons remain at high altitudes. Future studies should be directed at determining whether self-selection operates in other high altitude populations.

SUMMARY AND CONCLUSIONS

Recent studies point to a series of problems that exist from conception through old age for adaptation to high altitudes. These are:

1. possible, modest reductions in fertility;
2. a small increase in the incidence of congenital malformations;
3. substantial problems of pregnancy, gestation, and neonatal life;
4. growth retardation from infancy through adolescence;
5. high altitude pulmonary edema;
6. chronic mountain sickness;
7. increased emphysema mortality.

Several issues appear in these studies which require further study:

1. There is need to determine whether the effects of high altitude are problems or solutions for adaptation to high altitude, and whether their consequences are the same in all high altitude populations.
2. The physiological system of oxygen transport is well suited to respond adaptively at high altitudes by compensating for the reduced oxygen availability. Yet only rarely has the adaptive value of oxygen transport responses been directly demonstrated. Useful beginnings for these kinds of studies have been made in attempts to determine whether failures of oxygen transport are responsible for the complications of pregnancy and fetal life, high altitude pulmonary edema, and chronic mountain sickness observed at high altitudes.
3. Lung disease constitutes a continuing problem for high altitude adaptation, causing mortality at several different phases of the life cycle and prompting older persons' departure. Mechanisms responsible for the adverse effects of high altitude on survival from lung disease and the range of effects stemming from lung disease require further study.

In conclusion, recent studies have generated important findings about effects of high altitude which pose problems for high altitude adaptation. Important questions remain to be explored in future studies, particularly in regard to mechanisms responsible for the observed effects of high altitude and to their adaptive significance. Persons interested in high altitudes and in the process by which adaptation occurs are likely to benefit from such future research efforts.

ACKNOWLEDGMENTS

Grant support was provided by the Colorado and American Heart Associations (80–837) and the National Institutes of Health (HL 14985) for studies conducted by L. G. Moore and J. Regensteiner. Sabbatical leave provided by the University of Colorado, Denver Campus, made possible the writing of this review. Michele L. Jones and Eva Toyos produced the manuscript and figures in finished form.

Literature Cited

1. Aldrich, R. A. 1976. A life science for epoch B. In *The Nature of a Humane Society*, ed. H. Oberttress. Philadelphia: Fortress
2. Baker, P. T. 1978. The adaptive fitness of high altitude populations. In *The Biology of High Altitude Peoples*, ed. P. T. Baker, pp. 317–46. Cambridge: Cambridge Univ. Press. 357 pp.
3. Bangham, C. R. M., Hackett, P. H. 1978. Effects of high altitude on endocrine function in the Sherpas of Nepal. *J. Endocrinol.* 79:147–48
4. Beall, C. M. 1981. Optimal birth weights in Peruvian populations at high and low altitudes. *Am. J. Phys. Anthropol.* 56: 209–16
4a. Beall, C. M. 1983. Functional and morphological growth and development of high altitude natives: Comparison of findings among Himalayan and Andean populations. *Am. J. Phys. Anthropol.* 60:172
5. Beall, C. M., Baker, P. T., Baker, T. S., Haas, J. D. 1977. The effects of high altitude on adolescent growth in southern Peruvian Amerindians. *Hum. Biol.* 49: 109–24
6. Brody, S. J. 1980. The graying of America. *Hospitals* 54:63–66
7. Clegg, E. J., Pawson, I. G., Ashton, E. H., Flinn, R. M. 1972. The growth of children at different altitudes in Ethiopia. *Philos. Trans. R. Soc. London Ser. B* 264:403–37
8. Collins, D. D., Scoggin, C. H., Zwillich, C. W., Weil, J. V. 1978. Hereditary aspects of decreased hypoxic response. *J. Clin. Invest.* 62:105–10
9. Cotton, E. K., Hiestand, M., Philbin, G. E., Simmons, M. 1980. Re-evaluation of birth weights at high altitude. *Am. J. Obstet. Gynecol.* 138:220–23
10. Crnic, L. S., Newberry, M. A., Moore, L. G. 1983. High altitude hyperbilirubinemia. *Clin. Res.* 31:134A
11. Cruz, J. C., Reeves, J. T., Russell, B. E., Alexander, A. F., Will, D. H. 1980.

Embryo transplanted calves: the pulmonary hypertensive trait is genetically transmitted. *Proc. Soc. Exp. Biol. Med.* 164: 142–45
12. Dobzhansky, T. 1968. Adaptedness and fitness. In *Population Biology and Evolution*, ed. R. C. Lewontin, p. 111. Syracuse: Syracuse Univ. Press. 205 pp.
13. Dutt, J. S. 1980. Altitude and fertility: the confounding effect of childhood mortality—a Bolivian example. *Soc. Biol.* 27:101–13
14. Frisancho, A. R. 1975. Functional adaptation to high altitude hypoxia. *Science* 187:313–19
15. Frisancho, A. R. 1976. Growth and morphology at high altitude. In *Man in the Andes*, ed. P. T. Baker, M. A. Little, pp. 180–207. Stroudsburg: Dowden, Hutchinson & Ross. 482 pp.
16. Frisancho, A. R. 1978. Human growth and development among high altitude populations. See Ref. 2, pp. 117–72
17. Frisancho, A. R., Sanchez, J., Pallardel, D., Yanez, L. 1973. Adaptive significance of small body size under poor socio-economic conditions in southern Peru. *Am. J. Phys. Anthropol.* 39:255–62
18. Garruto, R. M., Hoff, C. J. 1976. Genetic history and affinities. See Ref. 15, pp. 98–114
18a. Goldstein, M. C., Tsarong, P., Beall, C. M. 1983. High altitude hypoxia, culture, and human fecundity/fertility: A comparative study. *Am. Anthropol.* 85: 28–49
19. Gonzales, G., Crespo-Retes, I., Guerra-Garcia, R. 1982. Secular change in growth of native children and adolescents at high altitude. *Am. J. Phys. Anthropol.* 58:191–95
20. Gould, S. J., Vrba, E. 1982. Exaptation—a missing term in the science of form. *Paleobiology* 8:4–15
21. Grover, R. F. 1980. Speculations on the pathogenesis of high altitude pulmonary edema. *Adv. Cardiol.* 27:1–5

22. Grover, R. G., Hyers, T. M., McMurtry, I. F., Reeves, J. T. 1979. High altitude pulmonary edema. In *Pulmonary Edema*, ed. A. P. Fishman, E. M. Renkin, pp. 229–40. Am. Physiol. Soc.

23. Haas, J. 1976. Prenatal and infant growth and development. See Ref. 15, pp. 161–79

24. Haas, J. D. 1980. Maternal adaptation and fetal growth at high altitude. In *Social and Biological Predictors of Nutritional Status, Physical Growth, and Neurological Development*, ed. L. S. Greene, F. S. Johnston, pp. 255–88. New York: Academic

25. Haas, J. D., Frongillo, E. A., Stepick, C. D., Beard, J. L., Hurtado, L. 1980. Altitude, ethnic, and sex difference in birth weight and length in Bolivia. *Hum. Biol.* 52:459–77

26. Haas, J. D., Moreno-Black, G., Frongillo, E. A., Pabon, J., Pareja, G., et al. 1982. Altitude and infant growth in Bolivia: a longitudinal study. *Am. J. Phys. Anthropol.* 59:251–62

27. Hackett, P. H., Reeves, J. T., Reeves, C. D., Grover, R. F., Rennie, D. 1980. Control of breathing in Sherpas at low and high altitude. *J. Appl. Physiol: Respir. Environ. Exercise Physiol.* 49:374–79

28. Herrera, R., Li Lora, J. A., Ingalls, T. H., Marticorena, E. 1977. Malformaciones congenitas del recien nacido el la altura. *Arch. Biol. Andina* 7:95–101

29. Hoff, C. J., Abelson, A. E. 1976. Fertility. See Ref. 15, pp. 128–46

30. Hyers, T. M., Scoggin, C. H., Will, D. H., Grover, R. F., Reeves, J. T. 1979. Accentuated hypoxemia at high altitude in subjects susceptible to high altitude pulmonary edema. *J. Appl. Physiol: Respir. Environ. Exercise Physiol.* 46:41–6

31. Kryger, M. 1980. Breathing at high altitude: lessons learned and application to hypoxemia at sea level. *Adv. Cardiol.* 27:11–26

32. Kryger, M., Aldrich, F., Reeves, J. T., Grover, R. F. 1978. Diagnosis of airflow obstruction at high altitude. *Am. Rev. Respir. Dis.* 117–:1055–58

33. Kryger, M., Glas, R., Jackson, D., McCullough, R. E., Scoggin, C., et al. 1978. Impaired oxygenation during sleep in excessive polycythemia of high altitude: Improvement with respiratory stimulation. *Sleep* 1:3–17

34. Kryger, M., McCullough, R. E., Collins, D., Scoggins, C. H., Weil, J. V., et al. 1978. Treatment of excessive polycythemia of high altitude with respiratory stimulant drugs. *Am. Rev. Respir. Dis.* 117:455–64

35. Kryger, M., McCullough, R., Doelkel, R., Collins, D., Weil, J. V., et al. 1978. Excessive polycythemia of high altitude: Role of ventilatory drive and lung disease. *Am. Rev. Respir. Dis.* 118:659–66

36. Lahiri, S., Delaney, R. G., Brody, J. S., Simpser, M., Velasquez, T., et al. 1976. Relative role of environmental and genetic factors in respiratory adaptation to high altitude. *Nature* 26:133–35

37. Lockhart, A., Saiag, B. 1981. Altitude and the human pulmonary circulation. *Clin. Sci.* 60:599–605

38. Mazess, R. B. 1975. Human adaptation to high altitude. In *Physiological Anthropology*, ed. A. Damon, pp. 167–209. London: Oxford Univ. Press. 367 pp.

39. McCullough, R. E., Reeves, J. T., Liljegren, R. L. 1977. Fetal growth retardation and increased infant mortality at high altitude. *Arch. Environ. Health* 32:36–39

40. Metcalfe, J., McCutcheon, I. E., Ettinger, T. B., Welch, J. E. 1982. Organ growth and oxygen supply in the avian embryo. *Fed. Proc.* 1255:505

41. Miller, J. F., Williamson, E., Glve, J., Gordon, Y. B., Grudzinskas, J. G., et al. 1980. Fetal loss after implantation. A prospective study. *Core J. Obstet./Gynecol.* 1:2

42. Moore, L. G., Hershey, D. W., Jahnigen, D., Bowes, W. 1982. The incidence of pregnancy-induced hypertension is increased among Colorado residents at high altitude. *Am. J. Obstet. Gynecol.* 144:423–29

43. Moore, L. G., Jahnigen, D., Rounds, S. S., Reeves, J. T., Grover, R. F. 1982. Maternal hyperventilation helps preserve arterial oxygenation during high altitude pregnancy. *J. Appl. Physiol: Respir. Environ. Exer. Physiol.* 52:690–94

44. Moore, L. G., Rohr, A. Z., Maisenbach, J. K., Reeves, J. T. 1982. Emphysema mortality increases in Colorado residents at high altitude. *Am. Rev. Respir. Dis.* 126:225–28

45. Moore, L. G., Rounds, S. S., Jahnigen, D., Grover, R. F., Reeves, J. T. 1982. Infant birth weight is related to maternal arterial oxygenation at high altitude. *J. Appl. Physiol: Respir. Environ. Exercise Physiol.* 52:695–99

46. Moore, L. G., Van Arsdale, P. W., Glittenberg, J. E., Aldrich, R. A. 1980. *The Biocultural Basis of Health*. St. Louis: Mosby. 278 pp.

47. Morpurgo, G., Arese, P., Bosia, A., Pescarmona, G. P., Luzzana, M., et al. 1976. Sherpas living permanently at high altitude: a new pattern of adaptation. *Proc. Natl. Acad. Sci. USA* 73:747–51

48. Mortimer, E. A., Monson, R. R., Mac-Mahon, B. 1977. Reduction in mortality from coronary heart disease in men residing at high altitude. *N. Engl. J. Med.* 296:581–85

49. Morton, W. E. 1977. Coronary heart disease at high altitudes. *N. Engl. J. Med.* 297:60–62

50. Mueller, W. H., Murillo, F., Palomino, H., Badzioch, M., Chakraborty, R., et al. 1980. The Aymara of Western Bolivia: V. growth and development in an hypoxic environment. *Hum. Biol.* 52: 529–46

51. Mueller, W. H., Schull, V. N., Schull, W. J., Soto, P., Rothhammer, F. 1978. A multinational Andean genetic and health program: growth and development in an hypoxic environment. *Ann. Hum. Biol.* 5:329–52

52. Mueller, W. H., Yen, F., Rothhammer, F., Schull, W. J. 1978. A multinational Andean genetic and health program: VI. physiological measurements of lung function in an hypoxic environment. *Hum. Biol.* 50:489–513

53. Palomino, H., Mueller, W. H., Schull, W. J. 1979. Altitude, heredity and body proportions in northern Chile. *Am. J. Phys. Anthropol.* 50:39–50

54. Pawson, I. G. 1977. Growth characteristics of populations of Tibetan origin in Nepal. *Am. J. Phys. Anthropol.* 47:473–82

55. Pawson, I. G., Jest, C. 1978. The high altitude areas of the world and their cultures. See Ref. 2, pp. 17–46

56. Picon-Reategui, E. 1976. Nutrition. See Ref. 15, pp. 208–36

57. Reeves, J. T., Grover, R. F. 1975. High altitude pulmonary hypertension and pulmonary edema. In *Progress in Cardiology;* ed. P. Yu, J. Goodwin, pp. 99–145

58. Regensteiner, J., Moore, L. G. 1983. Cardiovascular-pulmonary disease is a cause of migration from high to low altitude in Colorado. *Am. J. Phys. Anthropol.* 60:243

59. Sacro-Pollitt, C. 1981. Birth in the Peruvian Andes: physical and behavioral consequences in the neonate. *Child. Dev.* 52:839–46

60. Schutte, J. E., Lilljeqvist, R. E., Johnson, R. L. 1983. Growth of lowland native children of European ancestry during sojourn at high altitude (3200 m). *Am. J. Phys. Anthropol.* 61: In press

61. Stinson, S. 1982. The effect of high altitude on the growth of children of high socioeconomic status in Bolivia. *Am. J. Phys. Anthropol.* 59:61–71

62. Vander, A. J., Moore, L. G., Brewer, G., Menon, K. M. J., England, B. G. 1978. Effects of high altitude on plasma concentrations of testosterone and pituitary gonadotropins in man. *Aviat. Space Environ. Med.* 49:356–57

63. Velasquez, T. 1976. Pulmonary function and oxygen transport. See Ref. 15, pp. 237–60

Ann. Rev. Anthropol. 1983. 12:305–33

BIOMEDICAL PRACTICE AND ANTHROPOLOGICAL THEORY: Frameworks and Directions

Robert A. Hahn

Department of Psychiatry and Behavioral Sciences, University of Washington, Seattle, Washington 98195

Arthur Kleinman

Department of Anthropology, Harvard University, Cambridge, Massachusetts 02138

INTRODUCTION

The exploration of "Western" medicine—"Biomedicine"—extends a new frontier in medical anthropology. Anthropologists have returned from abroad to follow trails blazed by sociological pioneers (55, 135). The anthropological venture of self-examination has encountered resistance from our medicine itself (136a) as well as from the anthropological community (142), even its medical division (78). Such resistance attests to the powers of Biomedicine as a sociocultural system and to the epistemological difficulties of reflexive anthropology, in which one's own society provides at once the perspective and the subject of one's examination.

By the name *Biomedicine* we refer to the predominant medical theory and practice of Euro-American societies, a medicine widely disseminated throughout the world (191). Each of its many denominations, "Western," "Cosmopolitan," "Modern," "Scientific," "Allopathic," and "Biomedicine" as well, captures ones of its characteristics, while misleading us in other ways. While Biomedicine may have its principal origins in Western civilization, and has even been a leading edge of modernism (117), it has incorporated and now penetrates other traditions as well (146, 191). Even though it is widespread, the exclusive erudition and catholicism connoted by "Cosmopolitan" (42a, 105a) is inaccurate. Biomedicine may have appeared more recently and changed more

305

rapidly than many other traditions, but nonetheless these other traditions also manifest contemporary, "modern" versions (37, 105). Moreover, non-Western ethnomedicines evidence "scientific" approaches, while Biomedicine discloses certain magical nonrational elements (17, 19, 140). We use "Biomedicine" as a name for this medicine, referring to its primary focus on human biology, or more accurately, on physiology, even pathophysiology. Other medicines, e.g. contemporary Chinese (57a, 95), demonstrate a similar focus, though cast in a different orientation. Thus, Biomedicine is the version of bio-medicine founded and dominant in Euro-American societies and spread widely elsewhere.

In claiming that Biomedicine is a sociocultural *system,* we assert that this medicine consists of distinctive elements that interact in a manner which separates them from other systems within society. In that Biomedical practitioners believe that their domain is distinct from morality and aesthetics, and from religion, politics, and social organization, this form of medicine may be a more discrete system than others. Social scientists discern interconnections between these domains, however, which practitioners usually deny or ignore.

In claiming that the system is a *sociocultural* one (78), we assert that it is not simply a natural phenomenon but an artifact of human society, founded in a cultural framework of values, premises, and problematics, explicitly and implicitly taught by the communications of social interaction and then enacted in a social division of labor in institutional settings. Biomedicine, then, is an *ethnomedicine,* albeit a unique one. In making this claim we do not deny a natural connection. Biomedicine and other sociocultural systems continually remake nature, including human nature; but nature reciprocally constrains what can be made of it. Biomedicine is thus the product of a dialectic between culture and nature. By making this dialectic a central focus, medical anthropology, we aver, will confront general anthropological theory with a vital problematic and offer a subject matter for its exploration.

To elucidate the relevance of the anthropological study of Biomedicine for general anthropological theory, we begin by formulating a classification of theoretical positions in anthropology. We then return to survey research on Biomedicine as a sociocultural system, exemplifying several of these theoretical positions, explicit and implicit, which underlie the range of this research. We explore the fit between theory and findings, and recommend a framework and directions for future anthropological research. We suggest that the practice (and theory) of medicine inherently incorporates anthropological principles which should be explicitly formulated, and which could present a program for an anthropological reform of Biomedicine.

A PARADIGM OF ANTHROPOLOGICAL THEORIES

A continuum of theories can be discerned among anthropological accounts of human phenomena. The continuum ranges from one extreme stance which posits a material essence and explanation for all phenomena, to another extreme which posits an ideal, mental, or experiential essence and explanation. Inherent in any theory is an *ontology* (an understanding of the the basic elements theorized about), an *epistemology* (an understanding of the sources and processes of knowledge) and a *moral* and *aesthetic* order. These elements may be more or less consistent with one another. While alternate schematizations of anthropological theories are certainly possible, the one we propose is especially appropriate in the realm of medicine in which the tension between materiality and ideation is prominent. This continuum, moreover, effectively distinguishes the central features of many theoretical positions, including radically divergent ontologies, epistemologies, moralities, and aesthetics.

Excluding the opposed materialist and idealist poles, both reductionist, we distinguish three (emergentist) positions acong the continuum. All the positions we depict are ideal types—self consistent systems of belief, each of which follows an internal logic. The theories actually formulated by anthropologists conform to these ideal types to varying degrees; some theories fall between the positions we distinguish. We are here conducting exploratory ethnography among our colleagues and ourselves, attempting to portray a range of "world views" at home. Our interest is more to promote the theoretical development of the anthropological study of medicine, including Biomedicine, than to make definitive claims about the positions of anthropological colleagues.

Materialism

Materialist theory posits that all phenomena or reality, including "knowledge" itself, are essentially material, that what may appear to be nonmaterial "things" are not really so, and that all that there is to be explained must also be explained in terms of the material (and the only) world. In this concrete theory, while one may talk of nonmaterial events, e.g. "consciousness" and "culture," such talk is loose and can and should more rigorously be translated to its veridical, material form, thus perhaps, into "neuronal firings" and "observable behaviors."

The gathering momentum in the growth of science at the turn of the twentieth century fostered both the victory of Biomedicine over competitors and the emergence of a new form of positivism (176). Analysis replaced synthesis, a focus on single concrete causes vanquished vision of the whole, physicalism severely weakened vitalism (122). Biomedicine became a paradigmatic exemplar of these materialistic tendencies. Thus R. W. Wilcox (188), the first president of the American Congress on Internal Medicine, proclaimed the dependence of medicine on the natural sciences and their "legitimate appplications to that complex category of physiochemical relationships which we call life. . . ." Neopositivists similarly sought to properly and radically reduce all that was justifiably known to its true, physical, observable basis—to the rock-bottom foundation; "metaphysics" and judgment would thus be dispelled, relegated to the realm of vacuous nonsense.

The effects of this form of positivism spilled over from philosophy into physics, various forms of psychology, and even into social science: an insistence on "operationalism," "objective" behavior, and an eschewal of abstract theorizing in preference for purportedly more rigorous empirical, observational descriptions.

Yet positivism did not penetrate anthropology as deeply as it did the "natural" sciences and psychology, e.g. psychophysics and behaviorism. We are not aware of anthropologists avowing materialistic ontologies or epistemologies in the strict sense. Perhaps the power and varieties of cultural phenomena themselves defy any such reduction. Only sociobiology appears to approximate the materialist position, as when its leading spokesman (189) writes: "The central idea of the philosophy of behaviorism, that behavior and the mind have an entirely materialist basis subject to experimental analysis, is fundamentally sound."

Even those anthropological divisions called "Biological," "Physical," "Physiological," "Nutritional," "Behavioral," and so on, do not claim exclusive power for their particular disciplines, e.g. that anthropology *is* biology. Rather, the names of these fields of investigation refer to aspects of human affairs. They (27, 39) commonly ascribe to culture an ontological standing of its own, and, though they may not develop this notion, they are at least aware of its interactive powers. Materiality is thus assumed to be only one aspect of a larger system.

Epiphenomenal Materialism

Nonmaterial "things," e.g. relationships, ideas, values, and feelings, are posited to exist, but they are explained in terms of material phenomena, which may then be said to "underlie" them. Conversely, the nonmaterial things are held not to explain material phenomena either to any degree at all, or to any significant degree. The causality is one-way.

In anthropology, this position is maintained under several rubrics: cultural materialism (80), technoenvironmental or technoeconomic determinism (186), cultural ecology (2a, 169). Marx is sometimes said to support such a theory, a version of Marxism also described as "vulgar materialism" (62). Sociobiology (189) also makes epiphenomenal materialist claims.

Harris's (80a) formulation of an ephiphenomenal position, while not necessarily correct, is perhaps the most thoroughly explicit and self-consistent version of such a theory. Harris proposes an ontology of cultural as well as noncultural "things." He develops a (nonrelativistic) epistemology for research—problematic for a position which claims principal material determination of cultural phenomena, including knowlege itself. His research strategy follows the guiding hypothesis that the environment and technological capabilities of a society are the principal determinants of its cultural forms, and that the reverse effects are minimal in comparision. He calls for an investigation of this primary causal relation.

Material-Ideal Interactionism or "Aspectualism"

These theories posit the material and the ideal to be either (dualistically) separate sorts of "things," or (monistically) distinct aspects of common "things," "events," or some such elementary entity. They claim, moreover, that the causality or interaction of these things or aspects is essentially mutual rather than one-way. Thus we might speak of a material-ideal dialectic or of subjective materialism.

Godelier (68) presents a seminal dual aspect theory of society—his version of Marx, called by Harris (80) "structural Marxism." In his formulation, the material and the ideal do not appear separately in human affairs. He claims (68, p.764) that " . . . right at the heart of man's most material relationships with the material nature surrounding him lies a complex body of representations, ideas, patterns, etc, which I call *idéel* realities . . .," that "social relations . . . are simultaneously a material and an ideal reality," and that thought is no "less material than the rest of social life."

Double aspects are manifest also in what Godelier terms the "functions" of infrastructure and superstructure. In contrast to other Marxists, Godelier contends that infrastructure and superstructure are not essentially societal levels, different things, or institutions; rather they are functions within institutions. Thus Godelier asserts that while the economy "determines" the superstructure, the superstructure itself "dominates" the infrastructure.

For Godelier, as for Marxists more generally (for review see 80), conflicts among social classes are the principal force of social change. In one version of Marxism, "dialectical materialism," social processes conflict with one another in a manner described in the terms of logical discourse as "contradictions." Contradictions cannot endure, and in their resolution they engender new contradictions which then fuel further societal change.

The formulation of Giddens (66) approximates that of Godelier. It embraces three elements—meaning, morality, and power—and focuses on a double aspect of structure: structure is created in the process of human interaction, and it provides the elements to which such interaction responds. Humans do not create reality from nothing, but rather transform the material of nature. Social science is reflexively regarded as itself a social enterprise susceptible to the same analytic scrutiny.

Marxist versions which embrace both ideal and material realms (e.g. 66, 68) have considered both international relations and nation-statewide relations in the analysis of specific institutions such as medicine. Marxists (22, 59, 103,

132, 178) have been sharp critics of functionalist, symbolic interactionist, and culturalist medical social sciences, as well as of Biomedicine itself (but less of their own position). This approach is also amenable to the systems formulation (20, 21, 44), though its practitioners might resist the positivistic connotations of this perspective.

Functionalist theories display several material-ideal interactionist versions. That of Malinowski (118) begins with material needs which may be functionally satisfied by different parts of culture. The "structural-functionalism" of Radcliffe-Brown brackets materiality and examines interrelationships among elements of social organization. Functionalism, whatever elements it may embrace, is also susceptible to systems formulations (25).

Epiphenomenal Idealism

This position posits both material and ideal things, but, at least in accounting for social phenomena, gives causal or explanatory weight to the realm of the ideal. Human diseases are conceived and born in human thought (156), whereas bacteria themselves may have other sources. In this theory, causality itself may be denied as important or even relevant. Parsons' (135) version of functionalism has been characterized as idealistic (66) inasmuch as he holds that human affairs in essence are generated by actors who have incorporated the principles and values of their consociates.

Explicitly opposed to this position is the symbolic interactionist school, which has fostered another major movement in medical sociology (6, 60, 61, 173). The interactionist approach, and its opposition to functionalism, has been prominent in the all-too-rare theoretical discussions about medicine. Interactionists acknowledge, but essentially ignore, material conditions. They are principally concerned with the way in which the society of interacting persons engages in the production of both the "selves" of persons and their social environments. The productive process is not one deriving from stable internal norms, but is rather one of continuing negotiation between persons and their environments, both of which are thus continuously reconstructed through this process. Indeed, in some formulations (e.g. 69), the self is not a stable, or even an internal entity, but rather a series of socially conditioned presentations.

Another group of theories which regard human social life as epiphenomenal to human ideation is "culturalism." The members of societies carry "in their heads" systems of ideas, values, and rules of action—cultures, which somehow generate their actions, symbolic (but nevertheless real) actions. Consideration of material conditions is again suspended. "Ethnoscience," "cognitive anthropology," and the "new ethnography" were formulations of such a perspective: cultural anthropological analysis consisted, according to this view, of the detailed description of what one had to know (or feel) to behave as natives do [e.g. (72b); see also Winch (190), who purported to follow Wittgenstein, and Kuhn (101)].

A kindred position is that of Geertz (65), who maintains that anthropolgists should be concerned with meaning, and thus with interpretation, but not with causation. Under such an approach, epistemological canons are quite different from those under material-ideal interactionist or more materialist approaches. The "structuralist" positions of Sahlins (153a) and Lévi-Strauss (107) approximate that of Geertz as well as that of straightforward idealism. [The later Lévi-Strauss appears to argue for a materialist (i.e. biology of the brain) underpinning of the dualist categories of thinking.]

Idealism

Idealist social observers maintain that material phenomena are "real" because they are socially constructed (9). While it is not clear that in practice social observers actually adopt a thorough-going idealistic ontology, some theorists at least write in a manner which strongly suggests this view. Phenomenological sociologists and anthropologists often present themselves in this way, claiming to "bracket" (154) their own world views and realities in the analysis of others. Berger & Luckmann (9) claim that epistemological and methodological considerations are distinct from and not necessary for the development of a sociology of knowledge (which considers the social construction of reality). Thus, while the subjects one studies, according to this perspective, are mired in their constructed reality, the phenomenological observer has the power to willfully suspend belief for pure investigative purposes. Phenomenological sociologists have argued well for the social bases of commonsense reality, for the multiplicity of such realities (154), and for the communal sharing of cultural epistemologies (86a).

ANTHROPOLOGICAL STUDIES OF BIOMEDICAL PRACTICE

We now turn to review research on the practice of Biomedicine. We are especially concerned with the relevance of Biomedicine for anthropological theory. Thus we focus on the theoretical background of contributing social science studies, in search of a framework to encompass what is known, and to suggest further research.

As evidence for the sociocultural status of Biomedicine, we examine five of its features: a distinctive domain and system of ideas, that is "medicine"; a division of labor (i.e. medical specialties); corresponding roles, rules of practice and interaction, and institutionalized settings; a means of "socialization" by which this domain and its procedures are taught and reproduced; and an enterprise of knowledge construction (i.e. Biomedical research). Functionalist, interactionist, and Marxist perspectives predominate in the research in these areas; cultural analyses have appeared more recently. Recall that in calling Biomedicine "a sociocultural system," we do not deny its physical, material reality. Rather, we are exploring its sociocultural *aspect*. We propose that this distinction will then allow an investigation of the mutual powers of material and social-ideological aspects of this phenomenon.

The Domain of Medicine

While we have used the name Biomedicine to signal the focus of this ethnomedicine on human physiology, its practitioners (and its patients) refer to it simply as "medicine." (It is *the* medicine, real medicine; only other ethnomedicines are specially denominated, "osteopathic medicine," "Chinese medicine," "homeopathic medicine.") To a degree perhaps unique to segmented Western society, the participants of this ethnomedicine emphatically distinguish their medicine from other aspects and institutions of their society. Other than its science and its technology, Biomedicine is held to be clearly separate from religion, politics, economics, the arts (with token exception), aesthetics and morality. And, while connections between these realms and Biomedicine are becoming increasingly apparent (33, 55, 64, 96, 194), still practitioners claim that "medicine" can be delimited as an autonomous domain (157).

Stedman's Medical Dictionary (164), compiled by and as a guide to the medical community, defines "medicine" as:

> "1. A drug. 2. The art of preventing or curing diseases; the science that treats of disease in all its relations. 3. The study and treatment of general diseases or those affecting the internal parts of the body, distinguished from surgery."

Striking in this definition is the predominance of the concrete: The primal sense of "medicine" is "a drug." Other senses are concerned with diseases and the body. The central concern of Biomedicine is not general well-being, nor individual persons, nor simply their bodies, but their bodies in disease. Kleinman et al (97) have noted that while patients suffer "illness" (the patient's construal of affliction), physicians treat "disease" (their reduction of problems in the patient's life world to disordered physiology). The core, rational discipline of Biomedicine is "internal" medicine (75), most often called simply "medicine" (Stedman's definition 3.).

Stedman's (164) defines "disease" as

> "1. Morbus; illness, sickness; an interruption, cessation, or disorder of body functions, systems, or organs. 2. A disease entity, characterized usually by at least two of these criteria: a recognized etiologic agent (or agents); an identifiable group of signs and symptoms; consistent anatomical alternations."

Again concreteness and operationalism, the connection of concept and "entity," is a definitional theme. Rather than human value, statistical deviation from physical norms seems to be the defining criterion of pathology (etymologically, "the science of suffering"). Medicine, as the restoration of altered anatomy or physiology, is thought to be a logical, value-free activity (48, 71, 89, 128a, 137, 195).

Illness is generally though of as a "natural" occurrence (and not, as anthropologists might insist, as a social product). Similarly, when patients improve without medical intervention, they are said to manifest "natural remission." Thus, at least metaphorically, there is no space allotted to society and its relations between the forces of nature and the powers of medicine (139, 180a). Attempts to recognize the experience and contexts of patients' suffering (50) have generally regarded this subjective realm as peripheral to the real work of medicine, i.e. restoration of physiological homeostasis.

Robbins' very influential text, *Pathological Basis of Disease* (150), begins with the credo that, with the possible exception of illness "having emotional or functional causes," " . . . behind every organic illness there are malfunctioning cells. Indeed it is more correct to say that when a sufficient number of cells become sick, so does the patient." Similarly, medical theorist Feinstein (50, 51), explicitly building "clinical science," directs his search for a foundation toward "paraclinical entities," the bedrock of disease, the atom of suffering (see also 157).

Physical reductionism is a central tenet of Biomedicine (46, 75, 119). This medicine also radically separates body from nonbody; the body is thought to be knowable and treatable in isolation. Such work is held to be valuable as an end in itself. Despite evidence to the contrary (35), most observers (e.g. 175) discern a passionate devotion to the preservation of (physiologically defined) "life" at all costs. The object of internal medicine is neatly defined by some practitioners (75) as "physiological integrity."

Biomedical practitioners proclaim the foundations of their theory and practice to lie in art as well as in science. The art of medicine emerges in the intuitive application of scientific principle to individual patients whose conditions fit the scientific generalities only to degrees of varying uncertainty; or the art is that peripheral, "nonmedical" aspect of medicine which deals with "patient care" and "bedside manner," purportedly matters of heart, spirit, and intuition. In most medical texts, the art of medicine is given the briefest mention relative to the great detail of medical science; this proportion attests to both the interest in and the development of the art.

Even the clinical practice of medicine is thought to share the basic qualities of experimentation (50), while observers of medical practice have shown the limits of logic in a "bounded rationality" (43, 139). The Biomedical response to error (18) may take the form of silence (134) or an ascription to the patient's anatomy (18, 55). The predominant paradigm of this ethnomedical clinical science is Platonic realism, an orientation to disease "entities" or "lesions";

even states of relative ignorance are reified in nosological categories such as "idiopathic" such-and-such disease, "essential" or "primary hypertension," (i.e. cause unknown), and "typical atypical pneumonia." The power of this paradigm in constructing clinical reality is well demonstrated in recent anthropological research in medical settings (139).

Biomedical Division of Labor

Corresponding to the distinctive domain of Biomedicine and its epistemology is an elaborate division of labor. Preeminent practitioners (61) are called "physicians" or "(medical) doctors." Also participating in Biomedical institutions (in far greater numbers—more than 95%) are the incumbents of several other roles whose relations with physicians are matters of controversy and change: "nurses" of various stripes, "pharmacists," "physicians assistants," "technicians," clerical and maintenance "staff," "public health" workers, "psychologists," "social workers," and "administrators."

Biomedicine established its legal status as a virtual medical monopoly following the turn of this century and the signal "Flexner Report" of 1910 (53). Brown (22), Berliner (11), and others have argued that Biomedicine's power was established by collaboration of the American Medical Association ("scientific," "regular," or "allopathic" physicians) and the power elite, because this medicine and its "public health" served their interests in enhancing productivity and palliating the complaints of workers. Marxist theorists have claimed that the individualism and the corporeal, physiological paradigm of Biomedicine, paralleling the interest in mechanical efficiency (133a) in the capitalist ideology itself, diverted attention away from social sources of pathology, including the workplace and the larger politicoeconomic order. These theorists (92, 132, 179; see also 4) assert that the contending, "contradictory" forces of capitalism dialectically generate responses which in turn engender further contradiction, *ad revolutionam.*

Recent political science and economic analyses lend support to certain, but by no means all, of the Marxist contentions. For example, Stone (171) analyzes the role of physicians as gatekeepers for redistributive politics in the United States, where physician legitimization of illness has become the chief means of certifying welfare eligibility and thereby distributing economic support to the poor. Stone (170) discloses the latent political function served by illness-testing (as opposed to means-testing) and medical certification, " . . . such as allowing welfare programs to be responsive to political unrest, siphoning off opposition to controversial policies by the granting of medical exemptions to opponents, and reducing political conflict by using physicians as arbiters." But she also demonstrates that Biomedicine itself has repeatedly attempted to avoid being pressed into these political activities by larger societal forces. Yelin et al (192) show that the chief determinants of whether workers with disability return to

work are neither demographic factors nor doctor-determined medical conditions, but local conditions in the workplace (see also 10).

Within Biomedicine, among its elite core of licensed physicians, there are
further divisions of labor (and ideology and practice). *Biomedicine is not one,
but many medicines*. The American Board of Medical Specialists (3) notes 22
"speciality boards," 67 areas of medical practice, and others in contention (see
113). A reader of earlier medical anthropology might not recognize this
diversity, since Biomedicine has frequently been taken as monolithic and
unchanging (e.g. 141).

Within the hierarchy of medical specialties, status and power accord with the
therapeutic techniques employed and the parts of patients treated. Internal
medicine is the rational, surgery the technical pinnacle of medical practice. The
two are often felt to be exclusive and competitive; yet even within each there are
more interventionalist and more rationalist strains (99). In medicine generally
(Stedman's definition 2), the seemingly concrete "procedures" of surgery are
commonly valued far more than the "only talk" therapies of some forms of
psychiatry, which may even approach what some physicians refer to as "doing
nothing." Within each branch also, higher status is granted to the heart (cardiology and cardiac surgery) than to the kidneys (nephrology and urology) or the
digestive tract (gastroenterology and proctology), corresponding in part to the
cultural symbolism of these body parts. Financial (both salaries and insurance
payments) and other symbolic rewards generally accord with these divisions as
well as with the use of high technology.

The division of labor within Biomedicine is the product of an ongoing
politics of legitimization. Stevens (168) has charted the struggle within medicine which divided up and certifed some "specialities," suppressing others.
Chase (28) has suggested a rough chronology for the development of specialties, involving the invention of new devices or techniques, organizations for
their dissemination and instruction in their use, and licensure. Through these
productive struggles, the society of medicine reconstructs the subject of medicine itself, the human body and its pathologies—thus a politicized body,
bearing the divisions, wounds, and scars of social life. Wennberg & Gittelson
(185), following others (147), have recently demonstrated how the "needs" of
the medical community create those of patients; rates of surgery, and thus of
pathology, correspond not just with rates of patient morbidity, but with the
numbers of physicians in the community, their styles of practice, and the
number of hospital beds available. For every carefully conducted study by
social scientists in medicine like the above, however, there are numerous others
in which a simplistic, reverse ethnocentric, and sometimes paranoid ideology
of social scientist *against* medicine has obscured more than it has revealed.
Fortunately, many recent ethnographies of Biomedicine successfully avoid this
polemic and offer a more discriminating understanding of how the many

medicines construct distinctive practices (as well as "diseases"), sometimes as direct expressions of encompassing cultural meanings, other times as autonomous institutional constructions, but almost always as interactions between types of medicine, types of trouble, and types of society (1, 1a, 17a, 26, 63, 71, 83, 84, 95, 111, 128a, 148, 175, 183a, 197).

The Social Relations of Biomedicine

Although Biomedicine establishes its own particular roles and rules, these clearly take origin from ancient models and broader social currents. The privileged, private, and paternalistic doctor/patient dyad of contemporary Biomedicine (82) is a prime example, reflecting Hippocratic roots. More recently it has been argued (145) that contemporary medicine is part of the more pervasive "therapeutic" which has triumphed as part of a cultural revolution in which a fascination with the manipulation of technical means has obscured the consideration of ends. In the development of Western society and culture, medicine has both responded to broader cultural paradigms and social pressures and been a leading edge in cultural and social change (117).

The preeminent practitioners, the physicians and specialists among them, encounter themselves, their colleagues, their patients, and other consociates in characteristic ways—some noted in explicit rules, others implicit, observable regularities. Some of these rules and regularities may be ascribed to roles, others to settings of action, some to both. It is by means of these multiplex relations, relations of production, that the work of medicine is effected (163).

Physician's treatment of themselves, though of course highly variable, is notoriously hard—in work, in mental and physical health, and in relations with others (138). Familial or other intimate relations often suffer in consequence. This characteristic is of special significance if one considers the healing relation as an interaction in which the personal qualities of participants in part determine the outcome (5, 165).

In relations with patients, the normal conventions are in part suspended to allow a one-way exploration of the patient's intimate features which may be relevant to his/her current problem. Fox (55) aptly describes this attitude of interested distance as "detached concern." Similarly, what physicians call "listening to the patient" and "taking the history" are medicalized tasks directed not at the patient's life world, but at diagnostic evidence (75). Medical training and general attitudes toward medicine and its physicians engender a stance often described as "paternalistic," in which a logical necessity of medical disturbance is regarded as far more significant than the subjective judgment of the patient. Moreover, contact in which no "procedure" is enacted may be referred to as "bedside manner," "just social," or "doing nothing." Placebo therapies, regarded as medically inefficacious, may be applied punitively (73).

The relations of Biomedicine may be regarded as a social system (engaged in a larger social system) in which there is an exchange (14, 121) of valued and disvalued "things" (and intangibles), including "goods," services, but also power, respect, knowledge, and status. A heightened form of exchange, organ transplantation, involves "the gift of life" itself (57). The flow of things may maintain, but may also alter the system. Within Biomedicine, work itself is exchanged in the forms of "consultation" and "referral"; patients and knowledge are thus moved through the system. Such transactions signal and create the careers of those who make them (79, 79a). New knowledge also diffuses along the lines of the social structure of this system (32). And, central to the enterprise of medicine itself, in the healing encounter there are exchanges also. Some of these are explicitly recognized by practitioners who thus refer to themselves (in concrete fashion) as "providers" who "deliver" "health care." The reciprocal transfer of goods, in money, knowledge, relations, and other symbolic forms, is important and less often recognized (172).

In a wide variety of Biomedical contexts, social analysts have described ritual, the repetitive aspect of people's behavior which is extraneous to its technical or instrumental objectives, yet which is often held to be efficacious. In an experimental setting of research medical practice, Fox (56), following Malinowski (118a) observed "scientific magic" which seemed to alleviate the anxieties of uncertainty at the frontiers of medical knowledge. Similary, Bosk (19) notes a series of rituals, such as "gallows humor" and "hyperrealism," which provide a medium for expressing, communicating, and managing the difficulties of medical work. Katz (91) describes the rituals of purification undergone in surgery, and Henslin & Biggs (85) describe the stages by which a physician transforms a woman patient into "a pelvic" during a check-up examination. Rituals are analyzed as sociocultural conventions which serve (that is, *function* in the capacity) to minimize the difficulties inherent in medical work.

Social observers of Biomedicine have taken a wide range of theoretical positions in explaining the social relations of this (and other) ethnomedicines. Parsonian functionalists explore the roles of Biomedicine and their inherent expectations, inculcated by the social relations of "socialization," and then called forth in appropriate settings. The spring is wound and then released; persons embody norms which then generate their "actions." Parsons formulated the justly classical statement of the "sick role" and the role of physician, also justly criticized and revised (29, 61, 123, 124, 160, 174) and revisited by Parsons (135a). Chronic illness, conflict, negotiation, and system change are difficult in the Parsonian scheme.

The symbolic interactionist position, in its extreme form, contradicts the Parsonian vision in that actions are generated not from the insides of persons who respond to settings, but simply by the settings themselves. Goffman (e.g.

69) sometimes writes with this implication. The "labelling theory" of "secondary deviance" (182, 183; see also 74) claims that at least mental illnesses are the products of social expectations rather than simple internal, individual disorder (or some interaction between the two). Less radical versions of interactionism note the importance of ongoing negotiation in social settings for the determination of both the interacting "selves" and their actions. Physicians and patients act as they do because of expectations about their roles in the settings they are in; their actions recreate those settings and "rules" through negotiation. Thus Strauss et al (173) analyze "The Hospital and its Negotiated Order" to show how explicit, formal rules in a psychiatric hospital are constantly negotiated, thus perpetually reconstructing the social order, in the pursuit of vague institutional as well as individual goals (see also 60, 61).

Mishler (128) examines doctor-patient relationships in terms of discourse analysis between "voice of medicine" and "voice of the life world" (see also 134, 139). Sociolinguistic analysts of Biomedical discourse tend to document the dominance of the medical voice. Similarly, there is a tradition of cultural constructionist analysis of the conflicting interpretations of disease (by practitioners) and illness (by patients) that demonstrates the role of institutional ideology in the clinical construction of social reality and process of negotiation of that reality (16, 17a, 63, 84, 95).

Marxists, both epiphenomenal materialists and material-ideal interactionists, insist on the importance of society-wide (indeed world-wide) relations and forces of production in accounting for social relations (and even self-understanding) in the different parts of society, e.g. its medicine. Of course, they are not the only ones to demonstrate this relationship of macro social forces to micro social affairs. Not only the processes of "socialization," but also the range of social settings are to be explained by society-wide processes of production, of which medicine is only an element. The studies of Waitzkin and colleagues (181) and Navarro (132) provide evidence that the broader social order is reproduced in the Biomedical division of labor and its doctor-patient relations; the legitimization of this social order is also reproduced in the Biomedical setting (see also 194).

"Socialization": The Reproduction of Biomedicine

Not only is the work of medicine transacted through a complex of regular, rule-following, and ritual social interaction, but this "social system" is reproduced, taught to newcomers by means of partly overlapping social relations known within this system itself as "medical education." While social observers have most often analyzed the reproduction of Biomedical relations by focusing on this formally delimited "medical education" (thus adopting the Freudian and Parsonian wind-up models of Biomedicine itself), we suggest that significant "socialization" both preceeds and follows this formal education; social life is perpetual socialization. There are no explicit rules of the beginning, mature, and later stages of the medical professional life cycle. Moreover, socialization does not simply reproduce the system as it exists (reduplication, whatever it may mean, is implausible); rather, transformation is likely to be the standard.

Medical education, internship, and residency must number among the most arduous of rituals ever devised by humankind. In the ethnomedical theories of many other societies, the knowledge and powers of healing derive from spiritual forces of the universe, often achieved by means of participation in the affliction which the healer then learns to heal; in the disenchanted theory of our society and its ethnomedicine, the "art and science" of medicine are learned by individuals themselves through intense practice and hard work—the absorption of vast learning.

It is through medical education that neophytes are transformed into experts and channeled into the various divisions of medical practice. The same theoretical positions which are professed to account for the social organization of Biomedical practice as a whole have been applied as well to its reproductive system—its socialization. Thus, in the mode of Parsonian functionalism, Merton et al's (126) study of *The Student Physician* focuses on the student's internalization of the principles of medical practice, examining also some earlier sources of orientation to a medical career. Fox (55) portrays the way in which students undergo "training for uncertainty," the adoption of the noted stance, "detached concern," and various aspects of medical morality, attitudes toward self, others, and time. These habits are then carried into and through medical practice (and research).

In the interactionist tradition, Becker et al's study of *Boys in White* (6) claims (see 106a) that a long-term learning of a medical orientation and practice is incidental to "medical education," of which the primary result is a "student culture" oriented to surviving and passing of the training itself. Students learn to effectively cooperate and compete with each other, to study and treat patients in a manner that appears competent. Yet, despite their claim for the overwhelming determining powers of current environments in social life, Becker et al still note both residual precedents and persisting consequences of this training.

These seminal functionalist and interactionist works have spawned a host of further studies (see 15) including some of postmedical education, internship, and residency (24, 34, 110, 127, 130, 159). Much recent research is empiricist, and there have been few innovations to match the changes in medical education itself (55).

Marxists have also examined medical education—as the reproduction not simply of Biomedicine, but of the politicoeconomic, social, and ideological order of capitalism itself. While not (often) themselves engaging in empirical field studies, they have claimed that the similarities between the hierarchy of professionals within medical training and the socioeconomic distinctions within the broader society (132), the beliefs and attitudes taught and learned through medical education, even such "deviant" ideologies as "holistic medicine" and "self-care" (12), also serve and perpetuate capitalist interests (180).

Strangely, many social observers have left the disciplined analysis of the development of Biomedicine to historians, as if the dynamics of social change were distinct from those of quotidian social life and not the proper study of anthropology or sociology. With the exception of Foucault (54) and Starr (163), it has been principally Marxists who have explored the larger picture. They have noted the way in which Biomedicine has developed in tandem with the (international) development of capitalism over the last century (11, 22). Programs of "international aid" promote capitalist interests while contributing to the "underdeveloment" of third world peoples (11, 132), even following the severance of colonial ties (103). In the Marxist historical dynamic, the contradictions of Capitalism foster preferred solutions which bear further contradictions (180a).

Much of the extensive work on the sociopolitical, socioeconomic, and historical aspects of Biomedicine we only mention (e.g. 42, 143, 152) since it is difficult to determine what in fact are the guiding theoretical frameworks in these contributions. Much of this work is neither theoretically informed nor reciprocally contributes to theoretical development.

The Production of Biomedical Knowledge: Research

There has been a movement within the history of science to critically assess the social production of scientific knowledge (125, 196). Kuhn's (101) well-known *The Structure of Scientific Revolutions* could be cited as an attempt to create an historical anthropology of the cultural paradigms of scientific practice. Foucault's studies of medicine and psychiatry (41) have contributed to this line of analysis, though their concern is broader than science per se. Schutz's (154) comparison of scientific and commonsense rationality, which has stimulated so much work on lay versus professional constructions of clinical reality (17a, 61, 88, 90, 96) has not thus far given rise to a substantial tradition of studies of the work of science.

More than a decade ago, one began to hear the evocative phrase, "anthropology of science," but little work has been forthcoming in this direction. Previously, Fox (56), working in the Parsonian tradition, engaged in ethnographic studies to portray the culture of a clinical research and practice setting, and the personal functions of its relationships. More recently, Latour & Woolgar (104) have given a most provocative ethnographic account of a Biomedical research group's production of biological "fact." Here culturalist and Marxist interpretations are joined to uncover the social processes underlying the creation of scientific knowledge. Inasmuch as "laboratory life," including even its equipment, are portrayed as existing only in socially evolved ideation, the underlying tenor of this study is idealist. Beside the Latour and Woolgar study, Young's (194) prolegomenon to an analysis of the discourse on stress—which has become a key concept at the margin of Biomedicine—indicates how an interpretive anthropology might proceed to create such a field (see also 106, 115). The syncretist expansion of Biomedical research concerns to include sociocultural considerations makes this a subject of great theoretical as well as practical importance (see 94).

NEW DIRECTIONS IN THE ANTHROPOLOGY OF BIOMEDICINE

While participants in Biomedicine have often been blind to the ideal and cultural facets of their work, and while social science observers in the settings of Biomedicine have commonly ignored its materiality, we believe that comprehensive participant-observation in the variety of Biomedical settings couples recognition of the powers of nature and culture and their interactions. *We consider the dialectic of nature and culture to be one of the primary theoretical problematics of medical anthropology.* Medical anthropology acts at a vital intersection of body, mind, and community. It thus embraces a range of anthropological concerns, biological and ecological, cultural and symbolic, personal and social. It does so, moreover, at a point of widespread human concerns, commonly of daily import, often of cosmological significance: health and well-being, pathology and suffering. The concentration of significant dimensions in the settings of medicine makes this a rich arena for exploration of societal and human "nature" and their limits. We thus broach the vital anthropological tension between universalism and relativism.

The nature-culture dialectic operates both at levels of society as a whole and of its individual members. The members and groups within societies collaboratively construct their ethnomedical (and other cultural) realities, including their understandings of the shapes and forms of disease and illness, their theories of etiology and therapy, and their rules for proper response to these conditions—e.g. "the sick role" and the lay, professional, and folk healing roles (96). This socially constructed ethnomedical culture guides societal members (e.g. patients and healers) in their construals and responses to environmental conditions; the consequent responses in turn fundamentally shape this environment by distributing societal members in time, space, and activity. Society thus both *constructs* understandings and *produces* the events of disease/ illness and of healing. Yet both the construction of ethnomedical ideologies and the concomitant production of social and enviromental conditions are constrained by material conditions which are malleable only to some degree. Knowledge is constructed by material means—the human body and its epistemic instruments (measuring devices, calculators, and other indices). Moreover, the knowledge produced must correspond in some rough degree to its subject, or it will guide producers pathologically astray, even to self-destruction; objective material and social conditions thus provide a form of social reality testing. Anthropologists must explore the material constraints on the social construction and production of "reality," and the reciprocal shaping of nature by its social production and construction. The settings of Biomedicine provide a fertile field for such a basic research.

The nature-culture dialectic appears in another dramatic fashion in medical settings—in the mind-body interactions within individual persons. Beliefs (thus culture) can heal the believer, as in the "placebo" phenomenon (20, 58, 77, 129); they can also be pathogenic (84); and they are reported to kill as well [(45, 109); for a critique, see (108)]. Anthropologists, as preeminent students of symbols, should explore the ways in which symbols are literally embodied in persons. They should discover the limits to theories advocating the powers of expectation, as in "labeling theory" (183; see 74, 131), "culture-bound syndromes" (148, 194), and the "constructionist" theory of emotion (93, 116, 151). Anthropologists have begun to explore the powers of Biomedial ideologies and relations in both healing and pathology (75, 84, 98, 111; see also 162). The very diversity of Biomedicine—its various practitioners and multiple settings—provides an appropriate laboratory for research on mind-body and society interrelations.

Clearly we contend that the material-ideal interactionist framework will emerge as the one most valid in the anthropological account of human and social affairs. We support the *aspect* version of this framework, in which society, mind, and body are not, in Cartesian fashion, separate sorts of entities which interact, but rather aspects common to human events. Thus, with respect to medicine, pathological conditions are not exclusively psychosomatic *or* somatopsychic; rather, all human conditions share psychological, social, and physiological aspects. We are recommending Biomedicine and comparative medical anthropology as testing grounds for this theory.

We maintain that an anthropological theory of medicine and ethnomedicine should cover a broad range of questions, including the dialectics of culture and nature. Such a theory must account for the sources or causes, the distribution, and the consequences of medical ideologies, practices, and institutions, as well as of diseases/illnesses, their courses, and their remedies.

Biomedicine provides a crucial experiment, a "test case," for any cross-cultural, comparative theory of ethnomedicine, for it is highly distinctive, contrasting with most traditional, "non-Western" ethnomedicines in fundamental ways. The anthropological study of Biomedicine affords a unique opportunity to understand the implications and limits of technological development, high specialization, an institutionalized mind/body/society division, an elaborate corporeal and reductionist focus, and powerful social instrumentalities for the enculturation and control of participants. Any general theory of relations between the broader society, its medical "part," and the conditions of its members must take this greatly elaborated ethnomedicine into account. In this regard, the differences among forms of Biomedicine, e.g. Euro-American Biomedicine and contemporary Chinese "scientific" medicine, and between Biomedicine in Western and non-Western settings (e.g. 112, 184) are also of great interest.

Biomedicine is not only of basic substantive importance, but of methodological interest as well. The Biomedical nosology and its guiding theory have served as methodological grids not only in epidemological and clincal research within Biomedicine itself, but also in anthropological research. Anthropologists are indebted for this borrowed framework which has provided a vast classification of pathologies, etiological principles and methods of study. Yet the Biomedical framework has also significantly obstructed the wide anthropological and comparative study of disease/illness, healing, and ethnomedicine, because it has ethnocentrically devalued, if not excluded, the knowledge of other ethnomedicines, including lay beliefs and practice. Some basic assumptions underlying the Biomedical framework contradict those of anthropology. Thus we consider as a mandate of medical anthropology the revision of the Biomedical framework to construct a universal comparative theory of suffering and healing.

In pursuit of these questions we make several recommendations:

1. In parallel with a focus on the nature-culture dialectic as a primary theoretical problematic for medical anthropology, *we recommend the strategic integration of medical and anthropological epistemologies as a primary methodological problematic of this field.* The logical strengths of epidemiology should be integrated with the powers of systematic ethnographic insight into local social order, and the narrow rigor of clinical research should be expanded to encompass the personal and social realms of belief, value, and norm. Sociocultural phenomena such as the social production of disease and the placebo effect may then be included within medical theory and practice rather than excluded either as "nonmedical" or as "controls" for purportedly more real effects. Methodologies combining ethnography and cultural analysis with epidemology and clinical research techniques are being applied in non-Western settings (49, 72, 86, 95, 120, 153), and there is every reason to see such approaches applied in interdisciplinary research in Western Biomedicine settings as well (e.g. 23).

2. We recommend five heuristics for anthropological research on Biomedicine (and other ethnomedicines):

(a) *Systems theory* (25) is useful for the comprehensive analysis of phenomena comprised of complex, many-level interactive elements, more or less loosely bounded from their environment. Systems theory has been proposed to consider the levels of phenomena of health and pathology, from the physicochemical, through the psychological, to the social and broader ecological (21). More specifically, it has been applied to the study of medical institutions (158). We recommend the application of systems theory within levels of medical phenomena, for example, the international relations of medicine and development (e.g. 38, 52). Biocultural interactions between levels, e.g. the symbolic or social and the physiological (e.g. 36, 40, 77, 133, 167), are an especially important field for the application of systems theory.

(b) *Exchange theory* (e.g. 14, 187) analyzes social life as a system in which a range of "things" are transferred among persons: the study of exchange in social life, even of social life as exchange, has a venerable history in the work of Mauss, Malinowski, and, more recently, of Lévi-Strauss. In the settings of Biomedicine, exchanges of material goods (177), knowledge, attitudes (e.g. respect, disregard), and other symbols (e.g. money), are common among participants, both within interpersonal encounters, e.g. "the doctor-patient relation," and between institutions and their divisions (see 136, 172). Persons are also exchanged, for example the referral of patients among physicians, and of physicians among institutions.

(c) *Semiotics* may be applied to the Biomedical theory of "signs," "symptoms," and diagnostics, thus to the human body and person as a complex symbolic system; the sources and consequences of the construction of this symbolic system should be explored (13). Semiotic analysis may also be applied more broadly to the communicational exchanges among the participants of Biomedical settings, e.g. physician and patient, and physician and physician or other collaborator [see (161) for examples of application to Biomedicine's psychiatric domain].

Symbolic analyses of the differential cultural construction of disease within the pluralistic Biomedicine strikes us as a particularly useful way to disclose its distinctive and divergent orientations (78).

(d) *Discourse analysis,* stemming from both sociolinguistics and linguistic anthropology, ties the study of doctor-patient and doctor-doctor talk to some of the more interesting issues in social theory. For example, Beeman (7) has analyzed the interpersonal, cognitive treatment of depresssion from the standpoint of pragmatics and rhetoric, and offers a rhetorical model of psychotherapies (149; see also 102). Mishler and colleagues (128a) have pioneered microscopic analyses of medical talk and silence. While the model of the text has been applied principally to psychiatry (144), the mainstream of Biomedicine would also be fruitful for such analyses (155).

(*e*) Heretofore the *comparative study of medical systems* has largely limited itself to a macrolevel of analysis. We are now seeing studies of Biomedicine in distinctive cultural settings which demonstrate the powerful influence of cultural context on Biomedical practice, including microclinical events (87, 119, 184). Cross-cultural comparison between Biomedical practices would seem to be a critical direction for this research to take. There is no reason why Biomedicine should not become a category for the Human Relations Area File and other ethnological samples.

3. We recommend several substantive areas within Biomedicine for research (but do not intend to exclude other areas).

(*a*) The notion of "power" has two prominent senses in the context of ethnomedicine: Efficacy, the capacity of a therapy (or pathogen) to effect some desired (or undesired) end (193, 195), and authority or legitimacy, the social capacity to achieve acceptance and command following. In Biomedicine both efficacy and authority are developed to high degree in unique fashion. Biomedicine thus affords a useful setting for the investigations of power. This is especially so as illness tests replace means tests for access to social resources, and Biomedicine becomes the arbiter of distributive politics (171). Treatment of some pain patients, for example, has been shown to be a negotiation between patient demand for greater control over local work conditions and Biomedical attempts to medicalize a social problem (95, 159). Mishler (128) contends that the discourse on illness between practitioner and patient reveals in exquisite detail the multifaceted techniques of dominance of the voice of medicine over the voice of the life world (see also 139).

(*b*) Medical anthropologists have directed their initial attention to the clinical settings of Biomedicine and to the participants and relations within these settings. This setting is the heart of the Biomedical healing relation, and we recommend the further development of this research throughout the range of Biomedical settings (76). To complement this research we recommend the ethnographic study of different medical institutions as wholes, their interrelations, and their connections with other social institutions of Euro-American, non-Western, and international society, including relations with the popular section of care (30, 100) and commerical interests (52, 114). We recommend attention to processes of "socialization" which include not only formally distinguished "medical education," but the means of Biomedical reproduction and change.

(*c*) We recommend also study of the conditions embraced within Biomedical nosology, etiology, and therapeutics—acute and chronic, deadly and transient, painful and asymptomatic, "organic" and "functional," etc. Such study should consider the disease orientation engendered by these multiple dimensions in practitioners, and the illness careers fostered in the lives of patients. Indeed the ethnography of illness experienced over substantial periods of time (e.g. 1, 47) is in desperate need of analysis as a corrective to the Biomedical focus on discrete disease episodes.

(d) Along similar lines, we recommend exploration of the Durkheimian hypothesis that cultural systems are images and indices of society itself. We suggest examination of the way in which the development and workings of Biomedicine, and the body politic, have left their mark upon the subject of this work, the patient—his person and his body. We suggest also further exploration of the way which social relations and ideologies encourage different experiences of suffering—"psychologization" here, "somatization" there, tension here, backpain there. In this investigation, we will more fully recognize persons and their bodies as sociocultural artifacts. This will complement the extensive medical anthropological emphasis on the Weberian concern with questions of order and meaning in affliction.

4. The anthropology of Biomedicine should be a reflexive enterprise which thus examines itself as a sociocultural process. The study of Biomedicine, like the study of Euro-American science and applied science more generally, invites reflection because the cultural paradigm which informs Biomedicine also informs the discipline of anthropology. While there are sharp divergences, there is commonality as well. In exploring Biomedicine, anthropologists (at least those from Euro-American traditions) cannot help but examine the grounds of their own work.

5. A reflexive anthropology recognizes that the production and distribution of knowledge, including its own, is social action. The question is not whether or not the discipline is to be applied, but how, where, and to what end. We maintain that anthropological research is itself an interactive relation with some community (or several); responsible interaction requires response to that community (8). We recommend that medical anthropologists of Biomedicine embrace that commitment. The commitment need not mean subservience to the given goals of the community; it may mean radical reform.

Properly informed, anthropology is eminently qualified to assess and respond to the problems of Biomedicine, for anthropologists are trained to recognize the interests of and conflicts of interest among community members (for example, the Biomedical community and its patients), to understand their social dynamics, and to see a broader social, ecological, and historical picture. Moreover, we maintain that Biomedicine itself embodies anthropological principles—regarding the forms of suffering, their sources and consequences, and human nature itself; while these anthropological principles are most often implicit (if not explicitly denied), they should be made explicit and more self-consistent, perhaps in collaboration with anthropological participant observers. To this end, anthropologists have proposed and begun to practice a clinically applied medical anthropology (2, 31, 42b).

Medical anthropologists have developed several notions with practical significance in clinical settings. A frequently taken-for-granted skill in anthropology is perspectivism—the ability to move back and forth between viewpoints on the same phenomenon. The introduction of this skill among Biomedical practitioners would be a remedy for the Biomedical tendency to be intolerant of alternative viewpoints, and a particular lack of respect for the patient's point of view (137). Anthropologists have elaborated a distinction between "disease," pathology according to Biomedical practioners, and "illness," pathology as understood by patients [(97); for a revision see (75a, 95)]. Kleinman has developed a notion of "Explanatory Model" which is readily usable in clinical settings. Stein (116) proposes using ethnography to teach the medical relevance of the patient's perspective. Pfifferling (137) has opened up a new path for anthropological intervention in Biomedicine by using cultural analysis to detoxify the effects of Biomedical culture on its practitioners, e.g. the extremely high rates of drug abuse, suicide, and divorce. Katon & Kleinman (90a), Good & Good (70), and others have developed approaches to negotiation between physician and patient (and among physicians) as a means of bridging the disease-illness gap, and promoting healing by this means itself. Weidman (183b; see also 67) has extended the negotiation model to ethnic groups, and Harwood (81) has introduced anthropological reviews of U.S. minority ethnomedicines in summary forms at once culturally sensitive and clinically practical. These conceptual tools of medical anthropology have been well received in at least some fields of medical practice.

In exchange for a testing ground for anthropological theory, anthropologists may provide Biomedicine with social and cross-cultural settings in which to test its theories. Biomedical nosologies, etiologies, and therapies are most often examined in laboratory or clinical settings in which the utmost efforts are made to aseptically remove cultural and psychological influence. Anthropologists would insist first that this goal is impossible, then that cultural and psychological effects should themselves be taken account of, and finally that they should be encompassed within an anthropological medical theory and practice.

Finally, medical anthropology may also serve to provide a more fundamental critique of Biomedicine by insisting upon the cultural roots of this practice. Much of what passes as science in Biomedicine (and in anthropology also) is rather pseudoscience, pretending knowledge by the magical sprinkling of statistical tables and the invocation of shibboleths, devoid of broader theoretical discussion. We propose that the development of anthropological ways of thought in Biomedical settings will enhance the science of Biomedicine and anthropology at the same time as it fosters a common humanity.

Literature Citied

1. Ablon, J. 1981. Stigmatized health conditions. *Soc. Sci. Med.* 15B:5–9
1a. Alexander, L. 1982. Illness maintenance and the new American sick role. See Ref. 31, pp. 351–67
2. Alexander, L. 1979. Clinical anthropology: morals and methods. *Med. Anthropol.* 3(1):61–107
2a. Alland, A. 1970. *Adaptation in Cultural Evolution.* New York: Columbia Univ. Press
3. American Board of Medical Specialists. 1980. *Annual Report and Reference Handbook.* Evanston, Ill.
4. Baer, H. A. 1982. On the political economy of health. *Med. Anthropol. Newsl.* 14(1):1–2, 13–17
5. Balint, M. 1964. *The Doctor, His Patient and the Illness.* London: Pitman
6. Becker, H. S. 1961. *Boys in White: Student Culture in the Medical School.* Chicago: Chicago Univ. Press
7. Beeman, W. 1982. *Dimensions of dysphoria: the view from linguistic anthropology.* Presented at Am. Anthropol. Assoc. Meet.
8. Beiser, M. 1977. Ethics in cross-cultural research. In *Current Perspectives in Cultural Psychiatry,* ed. E. F. Foulks. New York: Spectrum
9. Berger, P. L., Luckmann, T. 1967. *The Social Construction of Reality.* New York: Doubleday
10. Berkowitz, M., Johnson, W., Murphy, E. 1976. *Public Policy Toward Disability.* New York: Praeger
11. Berliner, H. S. 1975. A larger perspective on the Flexner Report. *Int. J. Health Serv.* 5(4):573–92
12. Berliner, H. S., Salmon, J. W. 1979. The holistic health movement and scientific medicine: the naked and the dead. *Socialist Rev.* 9(1):31–52
13. Blacking, J., ed. 1977. *The Anthropology of the Body.* New York: Academic
14. Blau, P. M. 1967. *Exchange and Power in Social Life.* New York: Wiley
15. Bloom, S. W. 1965. The sociology of medical education. *Milbank Mem. Fund. Q.* 43:143–84
16. Blumhagen, D. 1980. Hyper-tension: a folk illness with a medical name. *Cult Med. Psychiatry* 4:197–227
17. Blumhagen, D. 1979. The doctor's white coat. *Ann. Intern. Med.* 91:111–16
17a. Blumhagen, D. 1982. The meaning of hypertension. See Ref. 31, pp. 297–323
18. Bosk, C. 1979. *Forgive and Remember, Managing Medical Failure.* Chicago: Univ. Chicago Press

19. Bosk, C. 1980. Occupational rituals in patient management. *N. Engl. J. Med.* 303:71–76
20. Brody, H. 1977. *Placebos and the Philosophy of Medicine.* Chicago: Univ. Chicago Press
21. Brody, H., Sobel, D. 1979. A systems view of health and disease. In *Ways of Health,* ed. D. Sobel, pp. 87–104. New York: Harcourt, Brace, Jovanovich
22. Brown, E. R. 1979. *Rockefeller Medicine Man; Medicine and Capitalism in America.* Berkeley: Univ. Calif. Press
23. Brown, G., Harris, T. 1978. *The Social Origins of Depression.* London: Tavistock
24. Bucher, R., Stelling, J. 1977. *Becoming Professional.* Beverley Hills: Sage
25. Buckley, W. 1967. *Sociology and Modern Systems Theory.* Englewood Cliffs. NJ: Prentice Hall
26. Cassidy, C. M. 1982. Protein-energy malnutrition as a culture-bound syndrome. *Cult. Med. Psychiatry* 6(4):325–45
27. Chapple, E. D. 1970. *Culture and Biological Man.* New York: Holt, Rinehart & Winston
28. Chase, R. A. 1975. Proliferation of certification in medical specialities: productive or counterproductive. *N. Engl. J. Med.* 294:497
29. Chrisman, N. 1977. The health seeking process: an approach to the natural history of illness. *Cult Med. Psychiatry* 1:351–77
30. Chrisman, N., Kleinman, A. 1983. Popular health care and lay referral networks. In *Handbook of Health, Health Care and Health Professions,* ed. D. Mechanic,. New York: Free Press
31. Chrisman, N., Maretzki, T., eds. 1982. *Clinically Applied Anthropology.* Dordrecht, Holland: Reidel
32. Coleman, J. S., Katz, E., Manzel, H. 1966. *Medical Innovation.* Indianapolis: Bobbs-Merrill
33. Comaroff, J. 1983. The defectiveness of symbols, or the symbols of defectiveness. *Cult. Med. Psychiatry* 7:3–20
34. Coombs, R. H. 1978. *Mastering Medicine: Professional Socialization in Medical School.* New York: Free Press
35. Crane, D. 1975. *The Sanctity of Social Life: Physicians' Treatment of Critically Ill Patients.* New York: Sage Found.
36. Crawford, M. H. 1980. Genetic epidemiology and anthropology. *Med. Anthropol.* 4(3):415–22

37. Croizier, R. 1968. *Traditional Medicine in Modern China*. Cambridge: Harvard Univ. Press

38. Cultural Survival. 1981. Poisons and the peripheral people: hazardous substances in the third world. *Cult. Survival Newsl.* 5(4)

39. Damon, A., ed. 1975. *Physiological Anthropology*. New York: Oxford Univ. Press

40. d'Aquili, E. G., Laughlin, C. D. Jr., McManus, J. 1979. *The Spectrum of Ritual*. New York: Columbia Univ. Press

41. Dreyfus, H. L., Rabinow, P. 1982. *Michael Foucault: Beyond Structuralism and Hermeneutics*. Chicago: Univ. Chicago Press

42. Duffy, J. 1976. *The Healers*. Chicago: Univ. Illinois Press

42a. Dunn, F. 1976. Traditional Asian medicine and cosmopolitan medicine as adaptive systems. See Ref. 105a, pp. 133–58

42b. Eisenberg, L., Kleinman, A. M., eds. 1981. *The Relevance of Social Science for Medicine*. Dordrecht, Holland: Reidel

43. Elstein, A. S. Bordage, G. 1979. The psychology of clinical reasoning: current research approaches. In *Health Psychology*, ed. G. Stone, F. Cohen, N. Adler. San Francisco: Jossey-Bass

44. Engel, G. L. 1980. The clinical application of the biopsychosocial model. *Am. J. Psychiatry* 137(5):535–44

45. Engel, G. L. 1971. Sudden and rapid death. *Ann. Intern. Med.* 74:771–82

46. Engel, G. L. 1977. The need for a new medical model: a challenge for biomedicine. *Science* 196:129–36

47. Estroff, S. G. 1981. *Making It Crazy: An Ethnography of Psychiatric Clients in an American Community*. Berkeley: Univ. Calif. Press

48. Fabrega, H. Jr. 1982. Culture and psychiatric illness: biomedical and ethnomedical aspects. In *Cultural Conceptions of Mental Health and Therapy*, ed. A. J. Marsella, G. M. White, pp. 39–68

49. Fabrega, H. Jr., Silver, D. 1973. *Illness and Shamanistic Curing in Zinacantan*. Stanford: Stanford Univ. Press

50. Feinstein, A. 1967. *Clinical Judgment*. Huntington, NY: Krieger

51. Feinstein, A. 1979. Science, clinical medicine, and the spectrum of disease. In *Cecil's Textbook of Medicine*, ed. P. B. Beeson, W. McDermott, J. Wyngaard. Philadelphia: Saunders

52. Ferguson, A. 1981. Commerical pharmaceutical medicine and medicalization: a case study from El Salvador. *Cult. Med. Psychiatry* 5(2):105–34

53. Flexner, A. 1910. *Medical Education in the United States and Canada*. New York: Carnegie Found. Adv. Teach.

54. Foucault, M. 1973. *The Birth of the Clinic: An Archaeology of Medical Perceptions*. New York: Pantheon

55. Fox, R. C. 1979. *Essays in Medical Sociology: Journeys into the Field*. New York: Wiley

56. Fox, R. C. 1959. *Experiment Perilous*. Philadelphia: Univ. Penn. Press

57. Fox, R. C., Swazey, Jr. 1974. *The Courage to Fail: A Social View of Organ Transplants and Dialysis*. Chicago: Univ. Chicago Press

57a. Fox, R. C., Swazey, J. P. 1982. Critical care at Tianjin's First Central Hospital and the fourth modernization. *Science* 20,21:700–5

58. Frank, J. D. 1961. *Persuasion and Healing*. Baltimore: Johns Hopkins Univ. Press.

59. Frankenberg, R. 1980. Medical anthropology and development: a theoretical perspective. *Soc. Sci. Med.* 14B:197–207

60. Freidson, E., ed. 1963. *The Hospital in Modern Society*. New York: Free Press

61. Freidson, E. 1970. *Profession of Medicine, A Study of the Sociology of Applied Knowledge*. New York: Dodd, Mead

62. Freidman, J. 1974. Marxism, structuralism and vulgar materialism. *Man* 9(3):444–69

63. Gaines, A. D. 1979. Definition and diagnoses. *Cult. Med. Psychiatry* 3(4): 381–417

64. Gaines, A. D. 1982. The twice born: 'Christian psychiatry' and Christian psychiatrists. *Cult. Med. Psychiatry* 6(3):305–24

65. Geertz, C. 1973. *The Interpretation of Cultures*. New York: Basic Books

66. Giddens, A. 1976. *New Rules of Sociological Method*. New York: Basic Books

67. Gilson, B. S., Erickson, D., Chavez, C. T., Bobbitt, R. A., Bergner, M., Carter, W. B. 1980. A Chicano version of the sickness impact profile (SIP). *Cult. Med. Psychiatry* 4:137–50

68. Godelier, M. 1978. Infrastructures, societies, and history. *Curr. Anthropol.* 19(4):763–71

69. Goffman, E. 1959. *The Presentation of Self in Everyday Life*. Garden City, NY: Doubleday

70. Good, B., Good, M.-J. 1981. The meaning of symptoms: a cultural hermeneutic model for clinical practice. See Ref. 42b, pp. 165–96

71. Good, B., Good, M.-J. 1981. The semantics of medical discourse. In

Sciences and Cultures, ed. E. Mendelsohn, Y. Elkana, pp. 177–212. Boston: Reidel

72. Good, B., Good, M.-J. 1982. *The interpretation of Iranian depressive illness and dysphoric affect.* Presented at Am. Anthropol. Assoc. Meet., 81st, panel on Culture and Depression, Washington DC

72a. Good, B., Herrera, H., Good, M.-J., Cooper, J. 1982. Reflexivity and countertransference in a psychiatric cultural consultation clinic. *Cult. Med. Psychiatry* 6:281–304

72b. Goodenough, W. 1964. Cultural anthropology and linguistics. In *Language in Culture and Society,* ed. D. Hymes, pp. 36–39. New York: Harper & Row

73. Goodwin, J. S., Goodwin, J. M., Vogel, A. V. 1979. Knowledge and use of placebos by house officers and nurses. *Ann. Intern. Med.* 91:106–10

74. Hahn, R. A. 1978. Is mental illness cured in traditional societies? Review of paper by N. Waxler. *Transcult. Psychiatr. Res. Rev.* 15:157–62

75. Hahn, R. A. 1982. "Treat the patient, not the lab"; internal medicine and the concept of "person." In *Physicians of Western Medicine: Five Cultural Studies,* ed. A. D. Gaines, R. A. Hahn, Spec. ed. *Cult. Med. Psychiatry* 6:3

75a. Hahn, R. A. 1983. Rethinking "illness" and "disease." In *South Asian Systems of Healing,* ed. V. Daniel, J. Pugh. Spec. vol. *Contrib. Asian Stud.* In press

76. Hahn, R. A., Gaines, A. D., eds. 1984. *Physicians of Western Medicine: Anthropological Approaches to Theory and Practice.* Dordrecht: Reidel. In press

77. Hahn, R. A., Kleinman, A. M. 1983. *Belief as pathogen, belief as medicine: 'Voodoo death' and the 'placebo phenomenon' in anthropological perspective.* Med. Anthropol. Q. In press

78. Hahn, R. A., Kleinman, A. M. 1983. Biomedicine as a cultural system. In *Social History of the Biomedical Sciences,* ed. M. Piattelli-Palmarini. In press

79. Hall, O. 1948. The stages of a medical career. *Am. J. Sociol.* 53(5):327–36

79a. Hall, O. 1949. Types of medical careers. *Am. J. Sociol.* 55(3):243–53

80. Harris, M. 1979. *Cultural Materialism.* New York: Vintage

81. Harwood, A. 1981. *Ethnicity and Medical Care.* Cambridge: Harvard Univ. Press

82. Hauser, S. T. 1981. Physician-patient relationships. See Ref. 128a, pp. 104–40

83. Helman, C. 1978. 'Feed a cold, starve a fever'—folk models of infection in an English suburban community and their

relation to medical treatment. *Cult Med. Psychiatry* 2:107–37

84. Helman, C. 1983. Pseudo angina and magical illness: a case history of pseudo angina. See Ref. 76

85. Henslin, J., Biggs, M. 1971. Dramaturgical desexualization: the sociology of the vaginal exam. In *Studies in the Sociology of Sex,* ed. J. Henslin, pp. 243–72. New York: Appleton-Century-Crofts

86. Hesser, J. E. 1982. Studies of infectious disease in an anthropological context. *Med. Anthropol.* 6(1):1–10

86a. Holzner, B. 1968. *Reality Construction in Society.* Cambridge, Mass: Schenkman

87. Janzen, J. 1978. *The Quest for Therapy in Lower Zaire.* Berkeley: Univ. Calif. Press

88. Johnson, C., Johnson, F. 1983. A microanalysis of senility: the response of the family and the health professionals. *Cult. Med. Psychiatry.* 7(1):77–96

89. Johnson, T. 1983. Consultation-liason psychiatry and the marginality of a psychosocial tradition in the culture of medicine. See Ref. 76.

90. Jordan, B. 1977. The self-diagnosis of early pregnancy: an investigation of lay competence. *Med. Anthropol.* 1(2):1–38

90a. Katon, W., Kleinman, A. M. 1981. Doctor-patient negotiation and other social strategies in patient care. See Ref. 42b, pp. 253–79

91. Katz, P. 1981. Ritual in the operating room. *Ethnology* 20(4)335–50

92. Kelman, S. 1971. Toward the political economy of medical care. *Inquiry* 8(3):30–38

93. Kemper, T. 1981. Social constructionist and positivist approaches to the sociology of emotions. *Am. J. Sociol.* 87(2):336–62

94. Kleinman, A. M. 1980. Cultural, social and political consideration. In *Institute of Medicine, United States Participation in Clinical Research in Developing Countries.* Natl. Acad. Sci., Washington DC

95. Kleinman, A. M. 1982. Neurasthenia and depression. *Cult. Med. Psychiatry* 6(2):117–90

96. Kleinman, A. M. 1980. *Patients and Healers in the Context of Culture.* Berkeley: Univ. Calif. Press

97. Kleinman, A. M., Eisenberg, L., Good, B. 1978. Culture, illness, and care. *Ann. Intern. Med.* 88:251–58

98. Kleinman, A. M., Mendelsohn, E. 1978. Systems of medical knowledge: a comparative approach. *J. Med. Philos.* 3(4):314–30

99. Knafl, K., Burkett, G. 1975. Professional socialization in a surgical specialty: acquiring medical judgment. *Soc. Sci. Med.* 9:397–404

100. Kosa, J., Antonovsky, A., Zola, I. K., eds. 1969. *Poverty and Health*. Cambridge: Harvard Univ. Press

101. Kuhn, T. 1970. *The Structure of Scientific Revolutions*. Chicago: Univ. Chicago Press

102. Labov, W., Fanshel, D. 1977. *Therapeutic discourse, Psychotherapy as Conversation*. New York: Academic

103. Lasker, J. 1977. The role of health services in colonial rule: the case of the Ivory Coast. *Cult. Med. Psychiatry* 1(4):277–97

104. Latour, B., Woolgar, S. 1979. *Laboratory Life: the Social Construction of Scientific Facts*. Beverly Hills: Sage

105. Leslie, C. 1974. The modernization of Asian medical systems. In *Rethinking Modernization: Anthropological Perspectives*, ed. J. Poggie, R. Lynch. Westport, Conn: Greenwood

105a. Leslie, C., ed. 1976. *Asian Medical Systems*. Berkeley: Univ. Calif. Press

106. Leventhal, H., Merenz, D. 1983. Representations of threat and the control of stress. In *Stress Prevention and Management: A Cognitive Behavioral Approach*, ed. D. Meichenbaum, M. Jaremko. New York: Plenum. In press

106a. Levinson, D. 1967. Medical education and the theory of adult socialization. *J. Health. Soc. Behav.* 8(4):253–64

107. Lévi-Strauss, C. 1963. *Structural Anthropology*. New York: Basic Books

108. Lewis, G. 1977. Fear of sorcery and the problem of death by suggestion. See Ref. 13, pp. 111–43

109. Lex, B. 1974. Voodoo death: new thoughts on an old explanation. *Am. Anthropol.* 76(4):818–23

110. Light, D. 1980. *Becoming Psychiatrists*. New York: Norton

111. Lock, M. M. 1982. Models and practice in medicine: menopause as syndrome or life transition. *Cult. Med. Psychiatry* 6(3):261–80

112. Lock, M. M. 1980. *East Asian Medicine in Urban Japan*. Berkeley: Univ. Calif. Press

113. Luce, J. M., Byyny, R. L. 1979. The evolution of medical specialism. *Perspect. Biol. Med.* 22(3):377–89

114. Luft, H. S. 1978. *The Economic Causes and Consequences of Health Problems*. Cambridge, Mass: Ballinger

115. Lumsden, D. P. 1981. Is the concept of stress of any use anymore? In *Contributions to Primary Prevention in Mental Health*, ed. D. Randall. Toronto: Can. Ment. Health Assoc. Natl. Off. Publ.

116. Lutz, C. 1982. *Depression and the translation of emotional worlds*. Presented at Am. Anthropol. Assoc. Meet., 81st, panel on Culture and Depression, Washington DC

117. MacIntyre, A. 1981. *After Virtue*. Notre Dame, Ind: Univ. Notre Dame Press

118. Malinowski, B. 1930. Culture. In *Encyclopedia of the Social Sciences*. New York: Macmillan

118a. Malinowski, B. 1954. *Magic, Science and Religion*. Garden City, NY: Doubleday

119. Manning, P., Fabrega, H. Jr. 1973. The experiences of self and body: health and illness in the Chiapas Highlands. In *Phenomenological Sociology*, ed. G. Psathas. New York: Wiley

120. Manson, S., Shore, J., Bloom, J. 1982. *The depressive experience in American Indian communities*. Presented at Am. Anthropol. Assoc. Meet., 81st, panel on Culture and Depression, Washington DC

121. Mauss, M. 1954. *The Gift*. Glecoe, Ill: Free Press

122. Mayr, E. 1982. *The Growth of Biological Thought*. Cambridge: Harvard Univ. Press

123. McKinlay, J. B. 1981. Social network influences on morbid episodes and the career of help seeking. See Ref. 42b, pp. 77–107

124. Mechanic, D. 1978. *Medical Sociology*. New York: Free Press

125. Mendelsohn, E., Weingart, P., Whitley, R., eds. 1977. *The Social Production of Scientific Knowledge*. Dordrecht: Reidel

126. Merton, R. K., Reader, G. G., Kendall, P. L. 1957. *The Student Physician*. Cambridge: Harvard Univ. Press

127. Miller, S. J. 1970. *Prescription for Leadership: Training for the Medical Elite*. Chicago: Aldine

128. Mishler, E. G. 1982. *The Discourse of Medicine: Dialectics of Medical Interviews*. In press

128a. Mishler, E. G., AmaraSingham, L. R., Hauser, S. T., Liem, R., Osherson, S., Waxler, N. E. 1982. *Social Contexts of Health, Illness and Patient Care*. New York: Cambridge Univ. Press

129. Moerman, D. E. 1979. Anthropology of symbolic healing. *Curr. Anthropol.* 20(1):59–80

130. Mumford, E. 1970. *Interns: From Students to Physicians*. Cambridge: Harvard Univ. Press

131. Murphy, J. 1976. Psychiatric labeling in cross-cultural perspective. *Science* 191: 1019–28

132. Navarro, V. 1976. *Medicine Under Capitalism.* New York: Prodist

133. Ness, R. 1980. The impact of indigenous healing activity. *Soc. Sci. Med.* 14B: 167–80

133a. Osherson, S., AmaraSingham, L, 1981. The machine metaphor in medicine. See Ref. 128a, pp. 218–49

134. Paget, M. 1982. Your son is cured now; you can take him home. See Ref. 76, pp. 237–59

135. Parsons, T. 1951. *The Social System.* Glencoe, Ill: Free Press

135a. Parsons, T. 1975. The sick role and the role of the physician reconsidered. *Milbank Mem. Fund Q.* 53:257–77

136. Parsons, T., Fox, R., Lidz, V. 1972. The gift of life and its reciprocation. *Soc. Res.* 39:367–415

136a. Petersdorf, R. G. Feinstein, A. R. 1981. An informal appraisal of the current status of "medical sociology." See Ref. 42b, pp. 27–48

137. Pfifferling, J-H. 1981. A cultural prescription for medicocentrism. See Ref. 42b, pp. 197–222

138. Pfifferling, J-H. 1980. *The Impaired Physician: An Overview.* Health Sci. Consortium

139. Plough, A. 1981. Medical technology and the crises of experience: the costs of clinical legitimization. *Soc. Sci. Med.* 15F:89–101

140. Porkert, M. 1974. *The Theoretical Foundations of Chinese Medicine.* Cambridge: MIT Press

141. Press, I. 1969. Urban illness: physicians, curers and dual use in Bogota. *J. Health Soc. Behav.* 10:209–18

142. Read, M. 1966. *Culture, Health and Disease.* London: Tavistock

143. Reiser, S. J. 1978. *Medicine and the Reign of Technology.* New York: Cambridge Univ. Press

144. Ricoeur, P. 1970. *Freud and Philosophy: an Essay on Interpretaton.* New Haven: Yale Univ. Press

145. Rieff, P. 1968. *Triumph of the Therapeutic; Uses of Faith after Freud.* New York: Harper & Row

146. Riley, J. N. 1977. Western medicine's attempt to become more scientific: examples from the United States and Thailand. *Soc. Sci. Med.* 11:549–60

147. Rindfuss, R. R., Ladinsky, J. L., Coppock, E., Marshall, V. W., Macpherson, A. S. 1979. Convenience and the occurrence of births. Induction of labor in the United States and Canada. *Int. J. Health Sci.* 9(3):439–60

148. Ritenbaugh, C. 1982. Obesity as a culture-bound syndrome. *Cult. Med. Psychiatry* 6(4):347–61

149. Rittenberg, W., Simons, R. 1983. Gentle interrogation: inquiry and interaction in brief initial psychiatric evaluations. See Ref. 76

150. Robbins, S. L. 1974. *Pathologic Basis of Disease.* Philadelphia: Saunders

151. Rosaldo, M. Z. 1980. *Knowledge and Passion; Ilongot Notions of Self and Social Life.* New York: Cambridge Univ. Press

152. Rothman, D. 1971. *The Discovery of the Asylum.* Boston: Little Brown

153. Rubel, A. 1964. The epidemiology of a folk illness: *Susto* in Hispanic America. *Ethnology* 3:268–83

153a. Sahlins, M. 1976. *Culture and Practical Reason.* Chicago: Univ. Chicago Press

154. Schutz, A. 1973. *Collected Papers.* The Hague: Mouton

155. Scully, D., Bart, P. 1973. A funny thing happened on the way to the orifice: women in gynecology textbooks. *Am. J. Sociol.* 78(4):1045–50

156. Sedgwick, P. 1981. Illness—mental and otherwise In *Concepts of Health and Disease,* ed A. Caplan, H. T. Engelhardt Jr., J. J. McCartney, pp. 119–29. Reading, Mass: Addison-Wesley

157. Seldin, D. W. 1977. The medical model: biomedical sciences as the basis of medicine. In *Beyond Tomorrow: Trends and Propects in Medical Science.* New York: Rockefeller Univ. Press

158. Sheldon, A., Baker, F., McLaughlin, C. P., eds. 1970. *Systems and Medical Care.* Cambridge: MIT Press

159. Shizuko, F., Strauss, A. 1977. *Politics of Pain Management: Staff-Patient Interaction.* Reading, Mass: Addison-Wesley

160. Siegler, M., Osmond, H. 1973. The 'sick role' revisited. Hastings Center Studies. 1(3):41–58

161. Singer, M. 1980. Signs of the self: an exploration in semiotic anthropology. *Am. Anthropol.* 82(3):485–507

162. Sontag, S. 1978. *Illness as Metaphor.* New York: Random

163. Starr, P. 1982. *The Social Transformation of American Medicine.* New York: Basic Books

164. *Stedman's Medical Dictionary.* 1976. Baltimore: Williams & Wilkins

165. Stein, H. 1982. Physician-patient transaction through the analysis of counter transference. *Med. Anthropol.* 6(3):165–87

166. Stein, H. 1982. The ethnographic mode of teaching clinical behavioral science. See Ref. 31, pp. 61–82

167. Sterling, P., Eyer, J. 1981. Biological basis of stress-related mortality. *Soc. Sci. Med.* 15(E1):3–42

168. Stevens, R. 1971. *American Medicine and the Public Interest*. New Haven: Yale Univ. Press
169. Steward, J. H. 1963. *The Theory of Culture Change*. Urbana: Univ. Illinois Press
170. Stone, D. A. 1979. Diagnosis and the dole: the function of illness in American distributive politics. *J. Health Politics, Policy Law* 4(3):570–21
171. Stone, D. A. 1979. Physicians as gatekeepers: illness certification as a rationing device. *Public Policy* 27(2): 227–54
172. Strauss, A., Fagerhau, S., Suczek, B., Wiener, C. 1982. The work of hospitalized patients. *Soc. Sci. Med.* 16(9):977–86
173. Strauss, A., Schatzman, L., Ehrlich, D., Bucher, R., Sabshin, M. 1963. The hospital and its negotiated order. In *The Hospital in Modern Society*, pp. 147–69. New York: Free Press
174. Suchman, E. A. 1967. Stage of illness and medical care. *J. Health Hum. Behav.* 8:197–209
175. Sudnow, D. 1967. *Passing On: The Social Organization of Dying*. Englewood Cliffs, NJ: Prentice-Hall
176. Suppe, F. 1977. Introduction. In *The Structure of Scientific Theories*, ed. F. Suppe, pp. 3–233. Urbana: Univ. Ill. Press. 2nd ed.
177. Titmuss, R. M. 1971. *The Gift Relationship: From Human Blood to Social Policy*. New York: Pantheon
178. Turshen, M. 1977. The political ecology of disease. *Rev. Radical Polit. Econ.* 9(1):45–60
179. Waitzkin, H. 1978. A Marxist view of medical care. *Ann. Intern. Med.* 89:264–78
180. Waitzkin, H. 1979. Medicine, superstructure and micropolitics. *Soc. Sci. Med.* 13A:601–9
180a. Waitzkin, H. 1981. A Marxist analysis of the health care system of advance capitalist societies. See Ref. 42b, pp. 333–69
181. Waitzkin, H., Stoeckle, J. D. 1972. The communication of information about illness. *Adv. Psychosom. Med.* 8:180–215
182. Waxler, N. 1977. Is mental illness cured in traditional societies? A theoretical analysis. *Cult. Med. Psychiatry* 1(1):233–53
183. Waxler, N. 1981. The social labelling perspective on illness and medical practice. See Ref. 42b, pp. 283–306
183a. Waxler, M. 1981. Learning to be a leper: a case study in the social construction of illness. See Ref. 128a. pp. 169–94
183b. Weidman, H. H. 1982. Research strategies, structural alterations, and clinically relevant anthropology. See Ref. 31, pp. 201–41
184. Weisberg, D. H. 1982. Northern Thai health care alternatives. *Soc. Sci. Med.* 16:1507–17
185. Wennberg, J., Gittelson, A. 1982. Variations in medical care among small areas. *Sci. Am.* 246:120–34
186. White, L. 1949. *The Science of Culture*. New York: Grove
187. Willer, D., Anderson, B., eds. 1981. *Networks, Exchange, and Coercion, the Elementary Theory and its Applications*. Westport, Conn: Greenwood
188. Wilcox, R. W. 1920. The field of internal medicine. *Ann. Med.* 1:5–12
189. Wilson, E. O. 1978. *On Human Nature*. New York: Bantam
190. Winch, P. 1958. *The Idea of a Social Science*. New York: Humanities Press
191. Worsley, P. 1982. Non-Western medical systems. *Ann. Rev. Anthropol.* 11:315–48
192. Yelin, E., Nevitt, M., Epstein, W. 1980. Toward an epidemiology of work disability. *Milbank Mem. Fund Q., Health Soc.* 58(3):386–415
193. Young, A. 1976. Some implications of medical beliefs and practices for social anthropology. *Am. Anthropol.* 78(1):5–24
194. Young, A. 1980. The discourse on stress and the reproduction of conventional knowledge. *Soc. Sci. Med.* 14B:133–46
195. Young, A. 1980. An anthropological perspective on medical knowledge. *J. Med. Philos.* 5(2):102–16
196. Young, R. 1973. The historiographic and ideological contexts of the nineteenth century debate on man's place in nature. In *Changing Perspectives in the History of Science*, ed. M. Teich, R. Young, pp. 344–438. Boston: Kluwer
197. Zerubavel, E. 1979. *Patterns of Time in Hospital Life*. Chicago: Univ. Chicago Press

Ann. Rev. Anthropol. 1983. 12:335–54

A SURVEY OF AFRO-AMERICAN ENGLISH

John Baugh

Departments of Linguistics and Anthropology, University of Texas, Austin, Texas 78712; also Center for Applied Linguistics, 3520 Prospect Street NW, Washington, D.C. 20007

INTRODUCTION

The general field of research regarding Afro-American language is substantial, and I will examine a portion of the more productive trends here. This review is divided into four general sections: educational research, theoretical linguistic studies, anthropological research, and emerging topics. Those who are already familiar with the field will appreciate that these divisions are somewhat arbitrary, because several of the same scholars have produced research in more than one of these areas. This has, in actuality, been a source of interdisciplinary strength for Afro-American studies in general, and language related research in particular.

Some additional background is necessary nevertheless, because of the controversial foundation of much of this literature, as well as rapid linguistic changes among Afro-American populations. It is essential to distinguish between Afro-American language, in the hemispheric sense of the term, and the dominance of studies on varieties of black American English, with primary emphasis on usage in the United States. In the first instance we find that Haitain French, dialects of Cuban Spanish, and select dialects of Brazilian Portuguese fall properly within the scope of Afro-American language. In the available space I will concentrate on the English-related studies, since they are the most substantial. The broader topic of Afro-American language is nevertheless quite interesting because the African slave trade has left unmistakable linguistic impressions on several languages and dialects throughout North and South America.

335

The most noteworthy research in this area has been conducted by creole scholars like Bickerton (15), Valdman (72), Hancock (35), Washabaugh (73), and Rickford (57), among others. They have investigated the various sources of linguistic contact among speakers of African ancestry. The corresponding research, including the controversy that still surrounds much of this literature, is outlined in more thorough detail in the writings of Burling (18), Traugott (69), and Baugh (11). Those who are interested in more details regarding the creole foundations of this work should consult the cited works for a more complete scenario.

In this review, then, I will be concentrating on the situation in the United States, where the topic of Afro-American English has been examined through several (inter) disciplinary perspectives. Moreover, because of the growth of black studies as a general field, the corresponding language-related literature is growing and readily available. As might be expected, significant differences of opinion and methodological orientation can be found in these texts.

We will consider the educational literature first, because it was largely due to the concern of both educators and black parents that much of the language-related research emerged. The more technical developments in the related linguistic studies, including the introduction of Labov's (48) variable linguistic rules, will be outlined next. Major emphasis will, of course, be given to the contribution of anthropologists and folklorists who have conducted investigations on this topic. These three branches of analyses will set the stage for examining emerging research trends, containing studies of language acquisition and development among black children, advances in educational research, and studies of black language in the mass media.

This survey of the field is, once again, a limited review, and a more complete bibliography of other related works on this subject can be obtained through publications at the Center for Applied Linguistics. My observations are intended to outline some of the most productive avenues of study in this field. Much of this research continues to be quite controversial in the face of strong attitudes—be they positive or negative—toward vernacular varieties of black American English. As more blacks assimilate into the mainstream culture, more have come to learn and use standard English, with tolerence for regional variation.

Let us therefore begin with a brief examinaton of contemporary black speech patterns in the United States. At this point in history we find that black Americans span a linguistic continuum, as illustrated in Figure 1. The majority of the black population maintains nonstandard vernacular English, although most adults have the ability to shift their speech styles depending on the social situation and their relative linguistic dexterity. It would be inaccurate to suggest that all black Americans speak the vernacular, be it urban or rural. A casual glance at black news broadcasters on television proves the point; these individuals are required to master standard English as part of their qualification for these highly visible positions. In fact, one of the emerging research trends that we will be considering in greater detail later focuses on the image of black speech that has been presented through the mass media. At this point let it suffice to say that the extremes of the linguistic continuum tend to be stressed on television, where the most standard and stereotyped nonstandard varieties typically appear. These linguistic decisions, that is, regarding the type of dialect that is used by blacks on television, are rarely made by blacks themselves, and are worthy of serious investigation in their own right (see Brasch 17).

The actual situation, presented in Figure 1, is far more complicated than the impression given via television, and may be difficult to comprehend for those who have had limited contact with black Americans. Figure 1 also conveys an important social reality, namely, that black Americans are finally "melting into the American cultural pot," although at a much slower rate than white immigrants who, by comparison, are relative newcomers as residents of the United States. This fact has to do with the obvious and overriding influence of racism in the society, and, while I will not dwell on the role of racism on black dialects and related language attitudes in this review, the actual impact on the linguistic behavior of black Americans (as well as other members of nonwhite minority groups) continues to be one of the major social and linguistic borders affecting linguistic behavior and related social isolation (see Keith 44). The impact of racism on this topic has been discussed at considerable length elsewhere, and I have little to add to the available literature [see Baldwin (7) and Smitherman (64)].

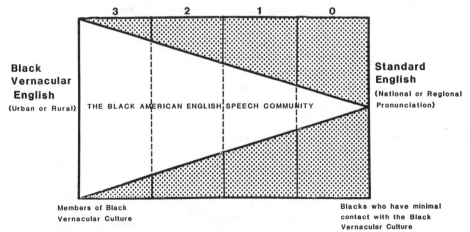

Figure 1 The black American English speech community. The combination of social domains (that is, living, working, and recreational situations) where blacks primarily interact with other members of the Black Vernacular Culture.

Referring again to Figure 1, we find that black Americans, as a racial group, span a linguistic continuum between standard English and nonstandard black vernacular English (henceforth referred to as BVE). Considering the nonstandard position first, we find that urban and rural varieties of BVE are maintained most by those individuals who have limited contact with nonblacks. In other words, those who maintain BVE tend to interact with other blacks, who are primarily members of the working class, in their living, working, and recreational domains. This distincition is critical in any survey of the topic; black Americans—when viewed as a racial group—do not constitute a single speech community. Just because a person is black does not imply that s/he is automatically a member of the vernacular black speech community. In fact, largely because of the stigma that is still borne by BVE in so many social circles, some of the most outspoken critics of nonstandard black speech are black Americans (see Alexander 4).

Based on my own research on this topic (10, 12), which now spans more than a decade of interviews with blacks from all segments of the society, I have found that several diverse opinions thrive regarding dialect attitudes among black Americans. This is not to suggest that one position is right and another wrong; rather, in much the same manner that differences of opinion abound regarding the role of "cockney" in British English, several opinions exist among (black) Americans who simply differ regarding their impression of the role of BVE in the life of Afro-American culture.

As a conceptual point of departure it is best to think of BVE as the nonstandard dialect that exists primarily among those who have limited contact with standard English speakers. At the right end of the spectrum (again see Figure 1) we find those standard black English speakers who have little or no contact with urban or rural varieties of BVE. These standard speakers are a minority within a minority, and often their speech is identical to white Americans of comparable social standing. The children of standard black English speakers tend to learn the standard as their native dialect; depending on their individual experiences and linguistic exposure, they may or may not attempt to learn BVE as a second dialect, say, as they become exposed to a broader population of black speakers in other social settings.

For the most part the research on this topic has concentrated on the nonstandard varieties of black speech which are more different from the standard. This practice has been challenged by black scholars like Taylor (68) and Hoover (38), who have also stressed the preceding point, namely, that some blacks have mastered varieties of standard English. In spite of their observation, the majority of research on black speech focuses on the language of nonstandard speakers.

The bulk of the literature was produced in the wake of the Civil Rights movement of the 1960s. Scholars in several fields have contributed to the general body of knowledge that falls within the general topic of Afro-American language studies. As might be expected with the emergence of new research, some of the early pronouncements were substantially flawed, as reflected by the ludicrous hypotheses by Jensen (43) and others. With the advent of significant advances in social science methodology in general, and linguistic research in particular, we now know that these "genetic" arguments are, quite frankly, absurd and should be dismissed in any serious discussion of black American society.

Here we will be concentrating on the positive contribution of several scholars, many of whom share the goal of producing research that can be applied to the resolution of social problems. For example, Labov's (50) most recent work on this subject focuses specifically on the relationship between sociolinguistic research and language-related educational policies for black school children. Thus, while I will be treating educational, athropological, and linguistic studies separately, this is merely for the sake of organizational convenience. In actuality these diverse topics are spokes on the same wheel, stressing different aspects of a similar topic.

EDUCATIONAL RESEARCH

A combination of historical events gave rise to the vast body of educational literature that concentrates on Afro-American English. The Civil Rights movement, the urban riots of the 1960s, and the financial commitment of the federal government under President Johnson's "Great Society" were all instrumental— each in their own way—to the thrust of research on the educational needs of blacks and other minorities. Here we will be focusing on the nature of the language-related studies.

For the sake of expedience, let us begin with the controversial hypotheses of Bereiter & Engelmann (13), who claimed that black children, that is, those who spoke urban BVE, came to school without a coherent language. Their research has been refuted on several occasions since then, and emphatically so in Labov's (49) well-known paper titled "The logic of nonstandard English." These papers, when considered collectively, illustrate the range of opinions that were available to educators who sought to develop suitable language arts programs for their students who spoke nonstandard English.

In the first instance, Bereiter & Engelmann (13) interviewed many black school children, asking them to perform a variety of linguistic tasks. More specifically, students were asked to describe the activity that was illustrated in several pictures. The students were then asked questions about the pictures and were evaluated based on their oral responses. The limitations of their procedures are amply discussed in Labov's (49) response. Bereiter & Engelmann (13) concluded that BVE students were incapable of expressing certain concepts because their dialect was deficient, that is, when compared to prescriptive standard English. Labov's (49) counter argument runs along the lines of stressing the linguistic differences between standard English and BVE. That is to say, each dialect is simply viewed as an alternative mode of expression, and the implication of linguistic superiority is cast in its proper social context. While some languages or dialects clearly hold greater social status than others, this impression is perpetuated by tradition and has no viable basis in linguistic fact.

Echos of the *difference* versus *deficit* debate continue to surface in some writings on the subject, and Dittmar (27) has provided a detailed explanation between the situation surrounding compensatory education in the United States and the perpetual failure of so many black students who attend public schools.

Several texts have appeared on the general subject of minority education and the education of black children in particular. Much of this literature is quite good, and, while written many years ago, a considerable number of these texts are still pertinent today. The emphasis is usually directed toward the task of teaching black children how to read and write standard English. Those who are interested in more detailed discussion in the area of education should see Baratz & Shuy (8), Abrahams & Troike (3), Cazden et al (19), Labov (47), Cronnell (24), Smitherman (64), and Shuy (60).

In the space that is available I would like to discuss two of the major themes that run throughout this literature. There is generally a consensus among most scholars working in this area that the ultimate goal of education, especially for minority children, is to provide students with the necessary skills that will allow them to compete as productive members of society. However, when dialect differences result in social restrictions, educators are faced with the more complicated task of formulating adequate—and socially sensitive—language policies. Some, like McDavid (54), have called for teaching BVE speakers standard English as if it were a foreign language. Haugen (36) disagrees with this practice, because BVE is not a foreign language; it is another dialect of English. Haugen also made the observation that it is more difficult to master proficiency between two dialects of the same language than to learn an entirely different language, mainly because of the subtle linguistic differences that distinguish one dialect from another.

Sledd (62) has approached this problem from another perspective altogether. He argues that the implications that can be drawn from the unilateral practice of teaching blacks standard English are implicitly racist, because they do not recognize the linguistic legitimacy of BVE. While Sledd's position is controversial, it comes as no surprise that those who are not in positions of social power must ultimately accommodate those who are, that is, in a stable social environment. From a purely egalitarian point of view, however, Sledd's point is well taken; black students are being asked to do more than their standard speaking counterparts. I do not consider this to be a value judgment, but rather a pragmatic recognition of social realities as they are.

The two policy trends that were alluded to previously deal with the best way to teach black children how to read. On the one hand we find some who believe that elementary texts for black children should be written in the vernacular. Others have argued strongly against such a practice, claiming that any effort to isolate black children linguistically is designed to separate the races and slow social assimilation among black American youths. As suggested, no one position represents the views of all black Americans. While black parents categorically agree that they want their children to receive the best possible education, there is still considerable disagreement as to what constitutes "the best."

Because of the tremendous importance of language policies regarding blacks, as well as other groups where the majority of their population does not speak standard English (i.e. standard American English with tolerance for regional variation in pronunciation), I would like to offer some brief observations on this subject. Before turning to these observations, however, I should reinforce the traditional educational goals that most American parents want for their children. They want their children to learn competitive and marketable skills so that they can be financially independent and socially secure.

With this traditional orientation in mind, I believe it is wrong to develop readers in the vernacular for black children, but I do so for reasons that have not been stressed in the literature to date. Figure 1 again illustrates the true complexity of the situation; while black Americans are clearly members of the same race—ultimately tracing their linguistic ancestry to roots in Africa—the social stratification of black America is now such that language policies cannot be formulated on the basis of race alone. Having stated the obvious, let us turn to the more difficult question of why I think BVE readers are untenable.

One of the major distinctions between BVE and standard English, which I have discussed at length elsewhere (see 12), lies in the difference between a language with an oral history and one with a written history. Like many of the standard languages throughout the world, English has a long-standing written tradition, along with strict prescriptive norms. Nonstandard BVE, on the other hand, as an oral language, does not have a comparable documented history, to say nothing of the fact that it was illegal for blacks to learn to read and write throughout most of American history. In other words, someone would be required to determine the "standard" for BVE before black students could receive a comparable education in their native dialect. In order for this to happen, someone would also be required to serve as a grammatical arbitrator in any dispute over the standardization of BVE. To the best of my knowledge, not even linguists who have worked on this topic are in an adequate position to provide sufficient linguistic evidence for such a task. At this stage of our research it would be descriptively premature to produce BVE texts, although some black writers claim that their vernacular style is easier for vernacular speakers to read (see Chennault 21).

Beyond the linguistic realm, where oral traditions and prescriptive norms prevail, lie the genuine concerns of black parents who want to see their children succeed in school. Their concerns are pragmatic, and eloquently expressed by a 51-year-old mother of four and grandmother of nine whom I interviewed in Los Angeles during the summer of 1976:

> J. If you could change the educational system, and do anything you wanted to improve, you know, the education for the black child, . . . uh, what would you do?
>
> K. I'll tell you like this. I ain't had no whole lot of education myself; I come up on the streets and had to learn my lessons the hard way. But the way they be . . . they be doing these childrens today is a shame. I don't want no special I.Q. tests for black kids. I don't want no damn psychiatrist tellin' me my kid can't learn. I want the books that they give to the whites be the same for the blacks. I want the best teachers in black schools too, and I (e)specially don't want no black kids kicked out of school; you gotta keep them kids in the classroom if they ever gonna learn.

This opinion captures the content and passion of the majority of black parents that I have interviewed, particularly those who were active participants in the vernacular black culture. In my opinion, as long as parents are resistent to BVE texts, there is a diminished chance for their success.

Other aspects of this debate over the best educational procedures for black children have been discussed in other recent works by Labov (50), Smitherman (64), and Wolfram (personal communication). Those who are familiar with the broader scope of these educational trends will appreciate that I have simplified the topic greatly here, but we have not seen the last of the controversy over whether or not BVE elementary texts can be useful to some black students.

This issue received national public attention during 1980 when the Ann Arbor school district was sued by black students who claimed their linguitic background, as BVE speakers, restricted their ability to learn how to read standard English. The school district did not make any special arrangements for BVE students, claiming that—as speakers of English—they did not require special attention. Judge Charles Joiner ruled in favor of the children; he determined that their linguistic differences, while part of English grammar in the strictest linguistic sense, were sufficiently different to warrent special educational attention. Labov's (50) discussion of the case, where he, Dillard, and Smitherman provided expert linguistic testimony, is the most thorough account of how this trial intersects with the linguistic research on BVE. Smitherman (64) has also edited a new book containing several papers by scholars, journalists, and others who were familiar with the Ann Arbor case.

At the time educational concerns for black children were at their zenith, during the late 1960s and early 1970s, linguists were called upon to provide some answers and solutions to questions regarding language policy. The Ann Arbor case represents the most recent instance where linguistic theory, practical applications, and the commitment of resources for minority education were examined together, capturing national attention at the same time. However, in the historical context where more linguistis began to examine black speech in greater detail, the opinion gap among scholars widened. Thus, while educators recognized their needs and goals with considerable clarity, the linguistic results—along with competing views in other branches of social science— tended to exaggerate the tradition of disagreement over "what to do about black American English in education."

TECHNICAL LINGUISTIC ANALYSES

As linguists became more involved with analyses of black American dialects, studies emerged within two major foci, including historical investigations and contemporary synchronic studies of black speech. The contribution of anthropology to this endeavor is substantial, having its foundations in the pioneering research of Boas and Sapir among native Americans [see also Hymes (40) and Sapir (59)]. We will concentrate on this orientation in greater detail in the next section. Within the narrower scope of descriptive linguistics, scholars attempted to address the complicated educational and psychological topics that had been raised by educators. Most noteworthy were the linguistic studies that emerged in response to (mis)interpretations of Bernstein's (14) work on elaborated and restricted codes of British English and their relative applicability with respect to black speech in the United States (see Giglioli 32). This educational impetus reinforced linguistic research that attempted to resolve the debate over whether or not black American English was simply different from standard English (i.e. as a legitimate dialect), or linguistically deficient in some way (i.e. it would be lacking significant linguistic structures that would prevent BVE speakers from expressing certain concepts which are available to speakers of standard English). The *difference* versus *deficit* debate has been discussed at length elsewhere and continues to emerge in new writings on this topic (see Smitherman 64).

In the wake of educational concerns, growing black nationalism, and financial support from the federal government, increasing numbers of linguists and psychologists began to seriously debate the point regarding the linguistic legitimacy of BVE. Many social scientists and educators felt, with some justification, that we would be better equipped to address social inequities among the races if we were able to get an "objective" assessment of the social, linguistic, and cultural differences that divided the majority of black and white Americans. For example, many educators called for a survey of the history of black American dialects; they believed that this information would be useful in developing a suitable language policy for black children. Their position is quite understandable, especially in retrospect, because if we had a clear sense of how the various dialects evolved, we should be in a better position to determine the best educational policies.

The historical arguments generally landed into two categories, which are known as the *creolist* and *dialectologist* hypotheses. These historical scenarios are well documented in the literature and have been discussed at considerable length by Burling (18), Dillard (26), Stewart (67), Wolfram (76), Hancock (35), McDavid (55), Rickford (57), Traugott (70), and Baugh (11). The essence of these positions are as follows: the creolists stressed the African foundations of black American English as well as other varieties of Afro-American language throughout North and South America, including dialects of French, Spanish, and Portuguese. The dialectologist orientation, which was prevalent during the 1940s through late 1950s, stressed the English dimensions of BVE.

In the context of growing black nationalism during the late 1960s and early 1970s, the historical debates surrounding black dialects became highly politicized. It was in this period that the creolist position, best expressed in Dillard's (26) book, *Black English,* received its strongest popular support. Since that time we have come to learn that the extreme arguments advocating the creolist or dialectologist viewpoints were considerably overstated. New findings suggest that aspects of both hypotheses represent a more realistic account of the true linguistic evolution (see Baugh 11). There are some unquestionable Africanisms which survive in contemporary BVE. On the other hand, the English dominance of black American dialects is evident and continues to influence ongoing linguistic change processes. As Labov (49) observed, BVE is a dialect of Engligh, and similarities to the standard far outweigh the differences.

We now have a clearer sense of the history of black speech throughout the Americas, although new questions and research have evolved from the pioneering work. It spite of this new evidence, we have made relatively little progress as far as policy suggestions for education are concerned. Most of the early research exaggerated the differences between the dialects and were insensitive to the linguistic diversity of black speakers. Competing linguistic hypotheses also retarded the likelihood that suitable educational policies would be developed. Thus, while the historical studies were important and revealing in their own right, they did little in the way of resolving language policies for the classroom.

While some might argue that linguistic research on this topic was purely scholarly in nature, many of those who studied BVE were completing two agenda simultaneously; one would focus on linguistic analyses, the other would concentrate on social problems and policies. This is an observation and not intended as a criticism, because I too have mixed my technical research with suggestions for educational policy. However, in spite of the admitted limitations that are inherent when we recognize that all of the pertinent linguistic facts are not available, it is possible—perhaps preferable—to develop educational policies based on synchronic usage of BVE.

Wolfram (76) discussed a similar point in his analyses of black and white speech in the South (i.e. southern United States). He observed that his analyses of contemporary speech did not require a complete historical account in order to be understood, at least as far as synchronic usage is concerned. This point is relevant here because so much of the research on BVE has been linked with evolutionary issues, whether explicit or implicit. The fact of the matter is that the documentation that is available on BVE is often unreliable, especially when compared with the tomes that have been used for traditional linguistic reconstruction (i.e. as found with the historical analyses of the Indo-European languages). Given that BVE has an oral tradition, to say nothing of the fact that it evolved from the speech of slaves, it should come as no surprise that our historical analyses require more thorough investigation (see Wolfram & Clarke 77).

There is one final point that we must consider before we move on to the synchronic research, and it has not been stressed in most of the available literature. Black Americans were the only group to migrate to the United States who were not allowed to preserve their native language through transitional bilingual communities. Unlike the European immigrants, who typically left countries with well-established written traditions, black slaves left a homeland where oral histories were common. In addition, slaves were separated from others who shared their language; this practice was instituted to reduce the likelihood of uprisings during the Atlantic crossing (see Dillard 26). The linguistic consequences of this unique history is reflected in the distinctive characteristics that are preserved in modern BVE. Whereas every group that did not speak English upon their arrival in the United States tended to use their native language, say, for an average of three generations, slaves were forced to learn English immediately—without formal education and restricted access to standard English.

Much of the work that grew out of this historical orientation was interdisciplinary by nature, and it has given rise to some important discoveries that have implications beyond black American studies. In the remainder of this section we will consider one such example: namely, the introduction of Labov's (48) variable rules to (socio)linguistic theory. While his early work utilized BVE data as part of the original formulation, variable rules have been employed successfully in several diverse speech communities on an international scale. Those who are interested in more specific details should see Labov's original discussion, along with that of Cedergren & Sankoff (20), Sankoff (58), and Shuy & Fasold (61). For the purpose of this review it is most important to appreciate that this contribution, which grew out of research on BVE, has interdisciplinary foundations and flows out of several productive branches of linguistic theory.

Several other scholars have contributed a great deal to our understanding of contemporary black speech, and a fairly complete bibliography of this work can, once again, be obtained through the Center for Applied Linguistics; the Center has also published many of the more detailed studies on this subject. Fasold's (28, 29) studies of distributive *be* (e.g. They be lazy) and tense marking in BVE are a good example. Wolfram (75) provides complementary research, with detailed phonological and grammatical evidence, based on analyses of black speech in Detroit. Smitherman (63) has synthesized several of these research trends in her book, *Talkin' and Testifyin'*, which is written for more general audiences.

At this point in the development of this field we are beginning to witness a new era, where black scholars—who are relative newcomers to the field—are continuing technical studies of BVE. Rickford (57) has conducted the most detailed studies of stressed uses of *been* in BVE, and his work has historical implications that support aspects of the creole hypothesis. BVE speakers use two forms of the word *been*; one is stressed and the other is unstressed. The unstressed form (e.g. She been working) indicates that a previous state of affairs no longer exists. The stressed form indicates that the prior state is still very much in effect at the time the statement is uttered. Thus, if a BVE speaker says, "She *been* working" (i.e. with the stressed usage), this indicates that she is working now and has been for quite some time. This kind of phonemic stress pattern, where stress alone is sufficient to change the meaning of a word, is not common in English. Such distinctions are nevertheless common in the tone languages of Africa, and probably explain the prevalence of stressed *been* usage among BVE speakers in the United States.

Another recent paper to emerge which continues this tradition is Spears' (65) study of semiauxiliary *come* in BVE, which has a different grammatical function than that of the well-known motion verb. For example, Spears observes sentences where speakers say, "He *come* coming in here like he owned the damn place." The first *come* serves the auxiliary function, while the progressive verb indicates action; these uses of *come* serve different grammatical functions in BVE, yet we had no documented knowledge of this until December 1982.

While auxiliary *come* is common in BVE, it was not recognized sooner because it is a camouflaged form. Spears (65) identifies camouflaged forms as words that are shared by speakers of the same language, yet for some dialects, unique grammatical functions can be found that are not shared by speakers of other dialects of that language. My own research on adult BVE style shifting exposed another camouflaged form; *steady* serves as an aspectual marker in BVE, as in "He be *steady* running" (see 12). When used in this way *steady* indicates that the action of the corresponding verb—which usually appears in progressive form—is completed in an intense and continuous manner.

Stockman & Vaughn-Cooke (67a) have likewise made new discoveries regarding the acquisition and development of BVE as a native dialect. We will have an opportunity to consider their work again under the heading of emerging topics. Most studies of child language development consider the case of standard languages, often under laboratory conditions. Stockman & Vaughn-Cooke (67a) have used video recordings of black children interacting with their parents to provide supplementary evidence to this general field. Their efforts, like those of Labov, Wolfram, and others, will have implications that go far beyond the study of black children.

Up to this point I have said little about the role of anthropology in this field, but it is in the context of the foregoing remarks that we come to appreciate the major role that anthropology, folklore, and the ethnography of speaking play in studies of this kind. By way of transition to the next section, which examines anthropological foundations more directly, we should consider the interdisciplinary work of two of the major pioneering black scholars; Turner (71) and Bailey (6) have produced two of the more important books on black language in the Americas. Turner's book, *Africanisms in the Gullah Dialect,* was influenced greatly by the well-known work of his mentor, Herskovits (37). Bailey's study, *Jamaican Creole Syntax,* was truly innovative, combining aspects of descriptive linguistics with formal rules in transformational-generative grammar (see Chomsky 22).

Both of these black scholars were influenced greatly by the fieldwork orientation of anthropology in their studies, and the tradition of gathering evidence among native BVE informants has been continued by the majority of young black linguists who are conducting new research at the present time.

Recapping the major technical trends, we find that the historical evidence generally emphasizes the English or African foundations of black American dialects. New historical evidence reinforces aspects of both positions, viewing the hypotheses as being complementary rather than in opposition. The synchronic studies continue to provide new insights into the nature and dynamics of contemporary black American dialects, including studies of standard Black English.

While I have drawn special attention to the work of black scholars on this subject, there can be no question that some of the best work has been completed by teams of researchers, where blacks and whites pooled their collective knowledge (see 51). At this point we are in a better position to evaluate the essential role that anthropologists have brought to this research.

ANTHROPOLOGICAL ORIENTIATIONS

Studies of black speech have been more common in anthropology than in other branches of the social sciences, largely because of the research traditions that were established by Boas (16). He recognized, long before many others, that blacks in the United States were worthy of serious anthropological investigation. Willis (74) outlines some of the general research problems that have affected the quality of anthropological work among "colored" third world populations. Much of what he says holds true for linguistic studies of these same groups, including black Americans (see Hymes 41).

Herskovits (37) and Turner (71) played critical roles in redirecting the emphasis of anthropological work on black studies and Afro-American language. Most readers are aware of the broad contributions of Liebow (53), Genovese (31), and Anderson (5); these studies of black American society set the stage for appreciating the unique linguistic rituals that anthropologists have recorded among black Americans. Space restrictions prevent a thorough exposition of work in the anthropological vein. However, based on the strength of this situation, and increased interest on the part of black students, interdisciplinary studies of black language in its cultural capacity should be a productive field of scholarly inquiry for some time.

As a somewhat arbitrary point of departure, Abrahams' (1) book, *Deep Down in the Jungle*, represents one of the first anthropological investigations to emerge during the rapid growth of the Civil Rights movement in the early 1960s. His work is well grounded in folklore as well, and examines linguistic ritual as part of the study. Like others who have worked on black language, Abrahams has been influenced by work in several fields; nevertheless, the anthropological orientation of his work is incontrovertible. This research examined the language of blacks who lived in south Philadelphia. His studies were also among the first to examine the verbal confrontations, like "shuckin," "jivin," and "the dozens," in vernacular contexts. Since that time, several other analyses concentrating on various speech acts that are unique to black Americans have been analyzed.

Mitchell-Kernan (56) carried this work further, and, as a black woman, she gained access to a broader sample of data from other black women. Labov (49) examined the ritual insults of black male teens in Harlem. And Folb (30) has produced the most detailed study of black teen slang that has appeared to date; her work is a longitudinal study, spanning an eight-year period. As a white female, Folb faced considerable obstacles when she began her research. It is largely for this reason that she worked as a participant observer in central Los Angeles, where the majority of the data were collected. Through the years she was able to establish an intimate rapport with several informants, in much the same way that Stack (66) gathered her data on black kinship networks. Anthropologists will find this work useful, because the topics reflect the values of the urban teen culture, and their slang tends to reflect their social values.

In each of the preceding cases, the evidence is based on detailed interviews, generally recorded on audio tape. Some of the data were gathered with the help of black fieldworkers, while others were collected by the analysts themselves. Smitherman's book, mentioned in the preceding section, also contains useful information for anthropologists; not only does she examine values among black Americans, but she reflects on the special problems that she—and other black scholars—face as they enter the academic arena.

Beyond the purely linguistic realm, we find studies of nonverbal communication among black Americans. Cooke (23) and Johnson (43a) have produced the most detailed studies of several significant gestures that convey information between black interactants. I, too, have written a general paper on the nature of handshake usage among young black men (see 9). Studies of nonverbal communication (i.e. kinesics) are clearly beyond the realm of linguistic research in the strictest sense, but these studies are essential to a complete appreciation of the full communicative repertoire of black Americans.

Kochman's (45) edited collection, *Rappin' and Stylin' Out,* which contains Cooke's essay, is one of the best volumes for anthropologists. In this presentation of work by several scholars, their different orientations serve to give this field a sense of scope and depth that cannot be found in the perspectives of sole authors. This is not to suggest that the books by individual scholars are lacking in some vital details; rather, for the reader who wants to consider several opinions in a single text, Kochman's book could be very useful.

Anthropologists will also find Kochman's (46) latest book, *Black and White Styles in Conflict,* particularly helpful in teasing out subtle differences in the ways that blacks and whites view similar speaking situations. For example, when classroom teachers encounter black students who repeatedly raise their voice in class, they often see this as a possible disciplinary problem. In some instances, however, based on the child's experience in vernacular contexts, a raised voice can be a sign of enthusiasm and interest. The potential for confusion is amplified when speakers misinterpret the intentions of other interlocuters. Kochman's (46) most recent work spells out many such sources of conflict in clear and explicit detail; I would recommend this work to anyone who is interested in the nature of black and white communication in the United States.

Readers who are familiar with the more comprehensive role of anthropology to studies of black language will appreciate that I have leapfrogged through different stages of development, leaving large gaps in the actual scenario. The cited works have rather extensive bibliographies, and these should more than serve the needs of fastidious readers who desire to pursue these interdisciplinary foundations in greater detail (see Abrahams 2).

Before we move on to our review of emerging topics, it is important to appreciate the ethnographic orientation of much of this research. In "The Ethnography of Speaking," Hymes' (39) illustrates this point. Many readers are well acquainted with Hymes' (42) concept of *communicative competence,* and the universal aspects of every human speech event (e.g. a sender, receiver, topic, code, etc). Many of the studies that have been cited in this section are sympathetic to the ethnographic goals espoused in Hymes' approach; they try to describe black language as it is perceived and identified by native BVE speakers (see Gumperz & Hymes 33). The universal characteristics that Hymes describes are admittedly more difficult to describe for some cultures than for others; this will depend on the particular group in question and the specific object of investigation. I might add here that the importance of an ethnographic perspective to the study of BVE is stressed in my own writing on this subject (see 12).

EMERGING TOPICS

Several scholars and private entrepreneurs have begun to expand research on black American dialects, along with other minority dialects and languages in the United States. Private publishers, toy manufacturers, and some major computer companies have invested new research and development in creating products that are tailored to the needs of minority students. These products will speak for themselves on the open market; however, for the purpose of this review, it is important to appreciate that investors have attempted to develop new products which will enhance literacy skills.

Nonprofit organizations continue to make contributions in this area, in spite of reduced funding from their traditional sources. The SWRL Educational Research and Development Center has published several books pertaining to the educational needs of minorities, with special attention to literacy needs. The editions by Cronnell (24), Lawlor (52), and Cronnell & Michael (25) are exemplary of this tradition. Some of this work reviews research in progress and the implications of these ongoing studies for future educational policies. Computer-aided instruction is highly touted at the present time, and several software programs are available or being tested in various feasibility studies.

More technical linguistic studies are being conducted at numerous universities across the United States. The continuing research of Stockman & Vaughn-Cooke (67a) in particular shows tremendous promise for the future. As suggested previously, their videotaped analyses of BVE children and their parents will provide new methodologies and results to the already substantial literature on child language acquisition and development. Because so much of linguistic theory rests on assumptions pertaining to language development and the human cognitive capacity to acquire language, their work will have an impact on related studies in several disciplines.

Another area of technical research which is still in the formulative stage focuses on language change among black Americans, as well as members of other minority groups. As the culture changes, so does the distribution of dialects that exist within the broader speech community. Recalling Figure 1, we know that increasing numbers of black Americans have mastered standard English, but we still do not know how this process has taken place, or at what rate of acceleration these changes are progressing. Researchers at several universities are engaged in projects that touch on these topics, and their results should be available in published form within the next 2 to 3 years.

Brasch (17) has opened an important new area of study in this field with his book titled *Black English and the Mass Media*. He uses the term mass media in the broadest and most literal sense, examining different cycles of American history, and how black speech was portrayed to the general American public through print, radio, television, and film. With the growing interest in contemporary mass media, and the increased role of minorities in various media, we can expect interest in this specific topic to grow. Brasch's work is scholarly, although it could be managed by general readers who can appreciate elementary linguistic concepts (e.g. phonetic transcription and grammatical constructions).

A neglected area of research might consider sex-related differences in the distribution of black American English. To the best of my knowledge, there are no published materials on the subject of black women's speech. Judging by previous examinations of socially stratified dialects of English, we typically find women in the forefront of linguistic change, and that change almost always moves in the direction of the standard language. It would be important to learn whether or not similar processes can be observed between black men and women. Social pressures on blacks may be such that new trends might be found, or the pattern of women leading linguistic change may be upheld; at this point in time we simply do not have sufficient data to determine an answer.

Each of these emerging topics reflects two essential facts; BVE is still prevalent among millions of black Americans, and these linguistic differences—between standard English and vernacular black dialects—intersect with the wider society in a multiplicity of ways. Here I have attempted to emphasize some of the more productive trends, yet my observations lack considerable detail when the entire field of black language studies is taken into account. In the limited space that remains, it may be most beneficial to conclude on a philosophical note.

CONCLUSION

I alluded to Hymes' (39) conception of the "ethnography of speaking" as a productive avenue for BVE research. Many of the scholars who have worked on black speech, pidgin and creole languages—as well as Bernstein's (14) formulation of elaborated and restricted codes—have all acknowledged their intellectual debt to Hymes. Most of the scholars who have worked on BVE have approached the topic with a particular research orientation in mind.

Hymes has stressed a combined strategy, which considers language to be the intricate social and behavioral process that it is. His philosophy is best express-ed in his own work with native American texts. Hymes (42a) incorporates aspects of anthropology, folklore, linguistics, and history to arrive at a solution of interpreting native texts. This same kind of interdisciplinary endeavor is needed for BVE research as well if we ever hope to obtain more complete evidence on black American speech patterns.

Few of us will ever serve as President of three different scholarly associa-tions, nor will many of us commit our efforts to such practical matters as the education of culturally diverse children. However, the phiolosphical orienta-tion that will ultimately be required for thorough BVE studies is mirrored in Hymes' work with native American language studies. A multifaceted approach is vital to the success of future black American English research. The urgency of the need becomes clearer in the politicized context that continues to plague this topic and related public policies.

As Hall & Freedle (34) observed, the melting pot myth for American society does not hold when black Americans, and other racial minorities, are taken into account. The best available evidence suggests that the social borders between the races have begun to thaw, but they are far from being melted. It is in this changing social atmosphere that the dynamics of black speech patterns will continue to evolve. This review is intended for those individuals who believe that social science can contribute to the resolution of (some) social problems in general, and language-related issues in particular.

ACKNOWLEDGMENTS

I would like to thank Walt Wolfram, William Labov, Donna Christian, and Fay Vaughn-Cooke for helpful suggestions and guidance. This review was made possible with financial support from the Ford Foundation. Evidence that has been cited from my own research has also been supported by a grant-in-aid from the American Council of Learned Societies.

Literature Cited

1. Abrahams, R. D. 1963. *Deep Down in the Jungle*. Chicago: Aldine
2. Abrahams, R. D. 1976. *Talking Black*. Rowley, Mass: Newbury House
3. Abrahams, R. D., Troike, R. C., eds. 1972. *Language and Cultural Diversity in American Education*. Englewood Cliffs, NJ: Prentice Hall
4. Alexander, G. 1980. Standard English, the hell with anything else. In *Vital Speeches of the Day*, Vol. 46, No. 14
5. Anderson, E. 1978. *A Place on the Cor-ner*. Chicago: Univ. Chicago Press
6. Bailey, B. 1966. *Jamaican Creole Syn-tax*. London: Cambridge Univ. Press
7. Baldwin, J. 1981. Black English: A dishonest argument. See Ref. 64, pp. 53–61
8. Baratz. J., Shuy, R., eds. 1969. *Teaching Black Children to Read*. Washington DC: Cent. Appl. Ling.
9. Baugh, J. 1978. The politics of black power handshakes. In *Natural History* (Oct.), pp. 32–41. New York: Am. Mus. Nat. Hist.
10. Baugh, J. 1979. *Linguistic style shifting*

in Black English. PhD thesis. Univ. Pennsylvania, Philadelphia

11. Baugh, J. 1980. A reexamination of the black English copula. In *Locating Language in Space and Time*, ed. W. Labov, pp. 83–106. New York: Academic

12. Baugh, J. 1983. *Black Street Speech: Its History, Structure, and Survival*. Austin: Univ. Texas Press

13. Bereiter, C., Engelmann, S. 1966. *Teaching Disadvantaged Children in the Pre-School*. Englewood Cliffs, NJ: Prentice-Hall

14. Bernstein, B. 1972. Social class, language and socialization. See Ref. 32, pp. 131–53

15. Bickerton, D. 1973. The nature of a Creole continuum. *Language* 49:640–69

16. Boas, F., ed. 1911. *Handbook of American Indian Languages*, BAE-B 40, Part I, pp. 59–73. Washington DC: Smithsonian Inst. Reprinted in *Language in Culture and Society*, ed. D. Hymes, 1964. New York: Harper & Row

17. Brasch, W. M. 1981. *Black English and the Mass Media*. Amherst: Univ. Mass. Press

18. Burling, R. 1973. *English in Black and White*. New York: Holt, Rinehart & Winston

19. Cazden, C., John, V. P., Hymes, D., eds. 1972. *Functions of Language in the Classroom*. New York: Teacher's Coll., Columbia Univ.

20. Cedergren, H. C., Sankoff, D. 1974. Variable rules: performance as a statistical reflection of competence. *Language* 50:333–55

21. Chennault, S. 1981. *Reliz whut ahm talkin' 'bout*. San Francisco: Angel Press

22. Chomsky, N. 1965. *Aspects of a Theory of Syntax*. Cambridge, Mass: MIT Press

23. Cooke, B. 1972. Nonverbal communication among Afro-Americans: an initial classification. See Ref. 45, pp. 231–45

24. Cronnell, B., ed. 1981. *The Writing Needs of Linguistically Different Students*. Los Alamitos: SWRL Educ. Res. Dev.

25. Cronnell, B., Michael, J., eds. 1982. *Writing: Policies, Problems, and Possibilities*. Los Alamitos: SWRL Educ. Res. Dev.

26. Dillard, J. L. 1972. *Black English*. New York: Random House

27. Dittmar, N. 1976. *A Critical Survey of Sociolinguistics*. New York: St. Martin's Press

28. Fasold, R. 1969. Tense and the form *be* in Black English. *Language* 45:763–76

29. Fasold, R. 1972. *Tense Marking in Black English: A Linguistic and Social Analysis*. Washington DC: Cent. Appl. Ling.

30. Folb, E. 1980. *Runnin' Down Some Lines*. Cambridge: Harvard Univ. Press

31. Genovese, E. D., ed. 1974. *Roll, Jordan, Roll: The World the Slaves Made*. New York: Pantheon

32. Giglioli, P., ed. 1972. *Language in Social Contexts*. Harmondsworth, England: Penguin Books

33. Gumperz, J., Hymes, D., eds. 1972. *Directions in Sociolinguistics*. New York: Holt, Rinehart & Winston

34. Hall, W., Freedle, R. 1975. *Culture and Language: The Black American Experience*. Washington DC: Hemisphere

35. Hancock, I. 1979. Historical insights to Black English. In *Afro-American Studies Working Papers*, No. 2. Austin: Center for African and Afro-American Studies

36. Haugen, E. 1964. Bilingualism and bidialectalism: A response to R. McDavid. See Ref. 60, pp. 10–11

37. Herskovits, M. 1941. *The Myth of the Negro Past*. New York: Harper

38. Hoover, M. 1978. Community attitudes toward Black English. *Lang. Soc.* 8:54–72

39. Hymes, D. 1962. The ethnography of speaking. In *Anthropology and Human Behavior*, ed. T. Gladwin, W. C. Sturtevant, pp. 13–53. Washington DC: Anthropol. Soc. Washington

40. Hymes, D., ed. 1964. *Language in Culture and Society*. New York: Harper & Row

41. Hymes, D., ed. 1972. *Reinventing Anthropology*. New York: Pantheon

42. Hymes, D. 1974. *Foundations in Sociolinguistics*. Philadelphia: Univ. Penn. Press

42a. Hymes, D. 1980. *In vain I tried to tell you*. Philadelphia: Univ. Penn. Press

43. Jensen, A. 1969. How much can we boost IQ and scholastic achievement? In *Harvard Educational Review* No. 39

43a. Johnson, K. 1971. Black kinesics: Some non-verbal communication patterns in the black culture. *Florida FL Reporter* 9:17–20, 57

44. Keith (Ross), J. 1975. Social borders: Definitions of diversity. *Curr. Anthropol.* 16:29–53

45. Kochman, T., ed. 1972. *Rappin' and Stylin' Out: Communication in Urban Black America*. Urbana: Univ. Illinois Press

46. Kochman, T. 1981. *Black and White Styles in Conflict*. Chicago: Univ. Chicago Press

47. Labov, W. 1964. Stages in the acquisition of standard English. See Ref. 60, pp. 77–103

48. Labov, W. 1969. Contraction, deletion,

and inherent variability of the English copula. *Language* 45:715–62

49. Labov, W. 1972. *Language in the Inner City: Studies in the Black English Vernacular*. Philadelphia: Univ. Penn. Press

50. Labov, W. 1982. Objectivity and commitment in linguistic science: The Case of the Black English Trial in Ann Arbor. *Lang. Soc.* 11(2):165–201

51. Labov, W., Cohen, P., Robins, C., Lewis, J. 1968. *A Study of the Non-Standard English of Negro and Puerto Rican Speakers in New York City*. USOE Final Rep., Res. Proj. No. 3288

52. Lawlor, J., ed. 1982. *Computers in Composition Instruction*. Los Alamitos: SWRL Educ. Res. Dev.

53. Liebow, E. 1967. *Tally's Corner: A Study of Negro Street Corner Men*. London: Routlege & Kegan Paul

54. McDavid, R. 1964. Social dialects: Cause or symptom of social maladjustment. See Ref. 60, pp, 2–10

55. McDavid, R., McDavid, V. 1971. Relationship of the speech of American Negroes to the speech of whites. See Ref. 77, pp. 16–40

56. Mitchell-Kernan, C. 1969. *Language Behavior in a Black Urban Community*, Work. pap. no. 23. Berkeley: Lang. Behav. Lab., Univ. Calif.

57. Rickford, J. 1975. Carrying the new wave into syntax: the case of black English *been*. See Ref. 61, pp. 162–83

58. Sankoff, D., ed. 1978. *Linguistic Variation: Models and Methods*. New York: Academic

59. Sapir, E. 1912. Language and environment. *Am. Anthropol.* 15:226–42

60. Shuy, R., ed. 1964. *Social Dialects and Language Learning*. Champaign, Ill: Natl. Counc. Teachers of English

61. Shuy, R., Fasold, R., eds. *Analyzing Variation in Language*. Washington DC: Georgetown Univ. Press

62. Sledd, J. 1969. Bi-Dialectism: The linguistics of white supremacy. *English J.* 58:1307–15

63. Smitherman, G. 1977. *Talkin' and Testifyin'*. Boston: Houghton Mifflin

64. Smithman, G., ed. 1981. *Black English and the Education of Black Children and*

Youth: Proc. Natl. Invitational Symp. King Decision. Detroit: Wayne State Univ., Cent. Black Stud.

65. Spears, A. 1982. The Black English semi-auxiliary *come*. *Language* 58:850–72

66. Stack, C. 1974. *All Our Kin*. New York: Harper & Row

67. Stewart, W. 1967. Sociolinguistic factors in the history of American Negro dialects. In *Florida FL Reporter* 5:11, 22, 24, 26

67a. Stockman, I., Vaughn-Cooke, F. 1982. A re-examination of research on the language of black children; The need for a new framework. *J. Educ.* 14:157–72

68. Taylor, O. 1973. Teachers' attitudes toward black and nonstandard English as measured by the Language Attitude Scale. In *Language Attitudes: Current Trends and Prospects*, ed. R. Shuy, R. Fasold, pp. 174–201. Washington DC: Georgetown Univ. Press

69. Traugott, E. 1972. *A History of English Syntax*. New York: Holt, Rinehart & Winston

70. Traugott, E. 1972. Principles in the history of American English: A reply. *Florida FL Reporter* 10:5–6, 56

71. Turner, L. 1949. *Africanisms in the Gullah Dialect*. Chicago: Univ. Chicago Press

72. Valdman, A., ed. 1977. *Pidgin and Creole Linguistics*. Bloomington: Indiana Univ. Press

73. Washabaugh, W. 1977. Constraining variation in decreolization. *Language* 53:329–52

74. Willis, W. 1972. Skeletons in the anthropological closet. In *Reinventing Anthropology*, ed. D. Hymes, pp. 121–52. New York: Pantheon

75. Wolfram, W. 1971. *A Sociolinguistic Description of Detroit Negro Speech*. Washington DC: Cent. Appl. Ling.

76. Wolfram, W. 1974. The relationship of white southern speech to vernacular black English. *Language* 50:498–527

77. Wolfram, W., Clarke, N., eds. 1971. *Black-White Speech Relationships Revisited*. Washington DC: Cent. Appl. Ling.

Ann. Rev. Anthropol. 1983. 12:355–75
Copyright © 1983 by Annual Reviews Inc. All rights reserved

A DECADE OF MORPHOLOGY
AND WORD FORMATION

Mark Aronoff

Program in Linguistics, State University of New York, Stony Brook, New York 11794

INTRODUCTION

In the last decade there has been a great resurgence of work in morphology, that part of linguistic theory devoted to the internal structure of words. This article will comprise a review of that work. My review pretends neither to completeness nor to impartiality. I have tried instead to take what seem to me to be the important developments and form them into a reasonably coherent picture of the field as it stands. Those I have omitted may enjoy the revenge of history.

Morphology is one of the oldest concerns of linguistics. The term *morphology* was coined in the early nineteenth century to refer generally to any science whose main object is form; the first specifically linguistic use dates from this early period and unlike many other terms its meaning has not changed significantly in the interval since.

Morphology was central to nineteenth century linguistics for two reasons. First, traditional grammar, out of which modern linguistics grew, had been morphologically based, as all of us know too well who have learned their Latin declensions and conjugations. Second, the comparative method of historical linguistics, which provided the most spectacular successes of nineteenth century linguistics, which indeed made linguistics into a respectable modern academic discipline, depends to a great extent on morphology. Morphological investigation therefore flourished along with historical linguistics. The beginning of the twentieth century, however, saw two major changes in the focus of the field, neither one of which was of great benefit to morphology: historical linguistics was supplanted by structural (synchronic) linguistics, and the discovery of the phonemic principle permitted the study of sound systems without reference to other formal aspects of language. Nonetheless, morphology continued to enjoy a respectable though diminished role in structuralist theory-

355

making, both in North America and in Europe, until the advent of *transformational generative grammar*. Excellent samplers of structuralist theory can be
found in (45) and (39), which contain a fair number of articles on morphology.

Early generative grammar (24, 38) presented a comprehensive theory of
grammar with only two main components, syntax and phonology. Semantics
was set aside as being too difficult at that stage of the game, and morphology
was partitioned between syntax and phonology. Though there was some protest
at this partitioning (e.g. 75), and though there were isolated examples of
excellent work on morphology during this period (e.g. 93), the 1960s, when
linguistics flowered, were dark days for morphology.

The classic period of generative grammar ends with two great works,
Chomsky's *Aspects of the Theory of Syntax* (25) and Chomsky & Halle's *The
Sound Pattern of English* (27), known colloquially as *Aspects* and *SPE*. These
works represent what is often called the *standard theory*, *Aspects* for syntax and
SPE for phonology. On actual inspection, though, neither one of these books is
as definitive as one might expect standard works to be. The prefaces to both
emphasize that they represent work in progress, and if both books are truly
classics, it is because they do not present the standard theory as a static
framework, but rather show the framework pushed to its limits. It is therefore to
these works that we should turn if we are to see why it became necessary to
reintroduce a specifically morphological component into linguistic theory.

It is in *Aspects* that questions of morphology are first discussed directly by a
generative theoretician. Prior to *Aspects,* the *lexicon* was viewed as nothing but
an unstructured list of *formatives,* each consisting of a meaning and a form
paired in the manner of the Saussurean sign. In *Aspects,* however, Chomsky
proposed that those formatives which are *members of major lexical categories*
(i.e. nouns, verbs, adjectives, and adverbs) should be regarded as *complex
symbols* made up of various types of *features*. A large portion of the book is
devoted to a discussion of types of syntactic features. However, the last
section, some 30 pages long, entitled "The Structure of the Lexicon," is
concerned specifically with how complex symbols might be used in the analysis of specifically morphological phenomena. This section is admittedly
sketchy, but several years later Chomsky published a paper which elaborated
on some of his earlier proposals. This paper (26) marks the beginning of serious
work on morphological phenomena in generative grammar, for in it Chomsky
explicitly claims that the derivation of certain types of morphologically derived
complex words must be treated outside the syntax in an expanded lexicon of a
type made possible by the complex symbols introduced in *Aspects*. This claim,
though couched in modern formal terms, is in effect a return to the traditional
view, which separates derivational morphology (or word formation) from
syntax.

This separation also permitted a major revision in syntactic theory, for it
reduced rather severely the types of phenomena which are covered by trans-

formations to the point where fairly rigid constraints on transformations might be proposed. Most of the phenomena which were removed from the new syntax were, not coincidentally, just those which most occupied the school of *generative semantics,* Chomsky's main theoretical rival at the time. Newmeyer (70) presents an interesting historical account of this rivalry. It is the latter area of constraints that has most occupied Chomsky's attention in the years since, and one might say that his interest in word formation was largely negative. Nonetheless, the field would not have flourished nearly as well without his initial impetus.

The change in syntactic theory had repercussions for phonology. In the standard theory of *SPE,* the syntax provides the input to the phonology. However, many of the phonological phenomena that *generative phonology* is concerned with arise only in morphologically complex words. For example, in English, changes in stress and vowel quality are almost completely confined to derivationally related sets, as the following examples illustrate: *telegraph, telegraphy, telegraphic; sane, sanity; degrade, degradation; combine* (verb), *combine* (noun). In *SPE,* the morphological structures were provided by the syntax. Chomsky's proposal that morphologically complex words be removed from the syntax therefore set phonology adrift. The syntactician might happily abandon his concern with word derivation and suffer no ill consequences. The phonologist could not, however, rest easy in such a state of benign neglect. Their phonology must rest on some structural base.

Once phonologists realized that the theoretical rug had been pulled out from under them, they sought vigorously for new firm footing. The need to rebuild their morphological foundation also provided phonologists with an opportunity: they could develop a morphological theory more responsive to their own demands than the previous purely syntactic one.

Thus the stage was set for the development of a morphological theory which could be integrated with the rest of the generative enterprise, and though no one can yet claim to have found a definitive theory of morphology, the last decade has seen a good deal of activity and even some progress toward this goal.

Morphology is conventionally divided into two parts. *Inflection* covers those word-internal phenomena which vary with the syntactic role of a given word (e.g. case, agreement, inflection); *word formation* deals with the creation of new nouns, verbs, and adjectives. Word formation itself is usually divided into *derivation* and *compounding*; compounding is restricted to cases where two or more words are joined to form one (e.g. *elevator operator*), while derivation covers those cases where only one word is involved (e.g. *elevation*). The borders of these areas are not entirely clear-cut. For example, it is not clear whether the formation of plurals in nouns is a matter of inflection or derivation. Nonetheless, the division is convenient enough so that little reason has been found to discard it. I will therefore adopt it without necessarily claiming any theoretical significance for it.

Crosscutting this division is the more pervasive one of syntax, semantics, phonology, and the lexicon. The product of these should give us eight distinct subareas. In fact, there are fewer. For example, the phonology of inflection and derivation forms a unit; nor has each remaining subarea received equal attention. I will therefore confine my discussion to the following: 1. the lexicon and word formation; 2. phonology and morphology; 3. the syntax of word formation; 4. the semantics of word formation. I will not discuss inflection separately because that area has received comparatively little attention until very recently (but see 4, 5, 21, 22, 86).

Historically, morphology was the last of the four traditionally recognized subparts of grammar to be granted independent status by generative linguistics. The reason for this tardiness is the difficulty in separating morphology out from the other three—syntax, semantics, and phonology. In fact, as some Europeans have emphasized (33, 46), morphology consists in large part of the interaction of the other three systems where they intersect—at the level of the word. Once this interaction is acknowledged, however, it may be exploited, for it allows one to proceed by triangulation. Every move that is made in one dimension will have consequences for the others. Interaction is accompanied by modularity: each system is independent in theory, but no analysis which treats one in ignorance of the others can ever achieve explanatory adequacy. The best work in morphology recognizes these twin assumptions of modularity and interaction, and it is on work of this sort that I will concentrate my efforts.

THE LEXICON AND WORD FORMATION

Morphology is responsible for describing the internal structure of complex words. Since the lexicon of a language is by and large comprised of such words, morphology is generally assumed to be restricted to a description of the lexicon. In fact, however, this assumption leads inevitably to severe problems, and little progress can be made until it is modified. The problems and their solution are as follows. First, the sole generally recognized criterion for any item being listed in the lexicon of a language is its arbitrariness or irregularity. This criterion was first made explicit by Bloomfield (14), though Saussure had already recognized that even partially motivated complex signs must be listed. All and only those items which are irregular in some way are to be listed in the lexicon. As it happens, and for reasons which are still unknown, the majority of the items found in any lexicon, including traditional dictionaries, are nouns, verbs, and adjectives. These same categories also comprise the domain of morphology, so that it is easy to see why the lexicon was regarded as equal to the domain of morphology. But the lexicon is inherently irregular, and as long as morphology was held responsible for *all* the properties of *all* the members of the major lexical categories, it was doomed to the task of accounting for a highly irregular set of data. The solution to this basic difficulty is to free the morphology from its obligation to handle lexical irregularities directly. Instead the task of morphology should be restricted to describing directly only the possible but nonoccurring words of language, a set which is presumably regular, so that then the regular properties of the actual words in the languge (those which are listed in the lexicon) might be described derivatively. This general solution to the relationship between the lexicon and morphology, first made explicit in (7), has formed the basis of much work since. There are several ways of dealing with the derivative description; the most common is by means of redundancy rules (44), and various ways have been proposed to constrain these rules (78).

More recent work, however, has shown that even this indirect relation between morphology and the lexicon must be taken as fairly abstract. In early treatments, the word formation component was considered to be responsible for the addition of new words to the lexicon, which meant that the morphology had to account for all the properties of *new* words, though it was absolved of complete responsibility for old words. However, the actual use of a new word is conditioned by factors other than word formation rules, as Dressler (33, 34) has demonstrated; nor do all new words become part of a speaker's vocabulary (6). For such reasons, it is best to make a strong distinction between the rules by which words may be formed and the actual coining of words, only some of which may enter the lexicon. If such a distinction is made, then the rules must be viewed as abstract patterns to which potential words should conform to some degree rather than as rules which completely determine the form and meaning of all new words.

Word formation usually involves affixation, though there are cases of *zero derivation,* such as the derivation of English verbs such as *pilot* from the corresponding noun, discussed in (9). Because of this special relation between word formation and affixes and because of the fact that affixes may not stand alone, but always depend on a stem, it was proposed in (7) that all affixes be treated as parts of word formation rules (each affix being assigned to a particular word formation rule), rather than being given a separate lexical entry. That proposal has since been challenged on two fronts. On the one hand, affixes certainly are arbitrary signs, and on this ground alone should be given lexical entries. If so, then having each affix also be part of a rule means that affixes are listed twice, once on their own and once with the rule. The only possible reason for not providing affixes with entries is the desire to restrict all lexical entries to stem or words of the categories noun, verb, and adjective. But such a restriction, though appealing on an intuitive level, is impossible, since higher units, such as irregular inflected forms, phrasal idioms, and even sentential forms such as proverbs and syntactically anomalous fixed express-ions must have lexical entries. The preponderance of nouns, verbs, and adjectives is only a statistical fact. Affixes should therefore be listed in the lexicon. In addition, it has been argued by Slavists (12, 13, 65) that derivation and affixation are distinct phenomena. One type of derivation, say deriving an abstract noun from an adjective, may be represented by more than one affix (e.g. *passiveness, possibility, presence*), while one affix may represent more than one derivational type (e.g. *monetarism* vs *Reaganism*). Affixes, like other formatives, are not reliably unambiguous. It is therefore reasonable to conclude, as many have (56, 78), that affixes are not introduced by word formation rules in the manner described in (7) and that the theory of derivational types must be separated from the theory of affixation, even though the latter instantiates the former.

These theoretical changes, however, though seemingly drastic, have few practical consequences. Most analyses can be expressed either with or without word formation rules interchangeably. Kiparsky (48) has in fact proposed that all lexical entries be regarded as rules, suggesting that the two views are notational variants.

Thus, though there have been changes in the exact mechanisms proposed to account for word formation, the initial observation still remains valid, whether as a theoretical tenet or simply as a heuristic caveat: the study of word formation can be successful only if it is concentrated on potential rather than actual words. Indeed, not even all novel words fall under the domain of the morphology. Beard (13) has demonstrated that there are processes of what he calls "lexemic extension," including such things as *blending* (e.g. *chunnel* derived from *channel tunnel*) and acronyms, which fall outside the realm of morphology proper. The exact relation between word formation and the lexicon is therefore much less direct than one might think.

Word formation, since it interacts with the lexicon, may also tell us something about the structure of the lexicon, an issue which is of great interest to psychologists as well as to linguists. For example, the base (that element to which affixes attach) in almost all types of productive word formation is an uninflected form of a noun, verb, or adjective. Most often it is the bare stem of the word in question; sometimes a stem augment (such as a theme vowel) is present; there are also instances, most typically in Semitic, where a root may be extracted from the stem. Almost without exception, though, a given affix will not attach to more than one particular form of a given word. For the purpose of word formation, therefore, these related word forms can be treated as a single unit or *lexeme*. It is reasonable to conclude from this pervasive pattern that the lexicon is organized in much the same way as a traditional dictionary, with all inflected forms and augmented stems being grouped under the same entry as the bare stem (8, 60). Another example of the interaction of word formation with the lexicon is the well-known phenomenon of *blocking*, whereby a particular potential word which we might expect to occur on other grounds is not found because there already exists another word in the same stem of the same derivational type and meaning. So we do not find *beautifulness* because we already have *beauty*, even though the first is a well-formed word (cf *bountiful-ness,* which is acceptable because *bounty* has a different meaning). In order for blocking to be as pervasive as it is, it must be that speakers, when they form a potential word, are able to scan very quickly all words in the same stem; they will not normally use the potential but nonoccurring word if a blocking word exists. We may therefore assume with some confidence that the lexicon is organized so as to facilitate scanning of just this sort (15). It has been noted (6, 10) that very productive word formation rules tend to be immune to blocking; words formed by productive processes are also the most ephemeral (18); speakers asked to judge novel words are also most likely to confuse actual words and potential words in case they are formed by productive processes. It therefore appears that the output of productive word formation rules is less likely to be even checked against the lexicon before use.

Hypotheses like these are just the sort that should be subject to psycholinguistic experimental verification. There has been some work along these lines (6, 15, 30), but most psycholinguistic studies of the lexicon and lexical access are done without the benefit of a knowledge of morphology. This should change as psycholinguists and morphologists begin to communicate more closely.

PHONOLOGY AND MORPHOLOGY

Morphology and phonology interact in very complex ways. Indeed, much of modern linguistics can be seen as an attempt to separate the two. Nonetheless, the following interdependencies are clear. Most obviously, the structure of phonological representations is determined in large part by morphology. Second, particular phonological processes may make reference to morphological factors. Third, morphemes have phonological forms. The first question is fundamental to phonology. As noted above, the abandonment of word-internal structure by syntacticians was one of the main impetuses for the renewal of interest in morphology. The most important theoretical foundation of phonology to be left unanchored was the *phonological cycle.* Within the theory of *SPE,* phonological rules operate cyclically, starting from the innermost morpheme and working outward, each cycle being triggered by the addition of additional morphophonological material, until the word is exhausted. The word *reorganization,* for example, would be treated as follows: first *organ* is dealt with, then *organize* (unless we treat *organize* as monomorphemic, in which case we skip the cycle on *organ*), then *reorganize,* then *reorganization.* The structure of the word must therefore be [[re[[organ]ize]ation], where each pair of left and right brackets indicates a successively larger domain. But what provides the structure, and why this particular structure rather than another? Chomsky & Halle (27) assumed that the syntax provided the structure, though they never quite spelled out how. Morphological theory provides the answer very simply. The layering results from successive applications of word formation rules, each affix being added by a single rule (7). This observation also extends to other phenomena dealt with by Chomsky and Halle in detail, such as English compound nouns, whose stress pattern depends crucially on layered bracketing of the sort that follows naturally from a word formation rule of compounding which adds a single new word at a time (27, 55). Thus [[high school] principal] and [deputy [school administrator]] have different stress patterns because they have different morphological structures. The morphology automatically provides exactly the type of labeled bracketing which is necessary for the phonology to operate and may therefore be assigned the structure-building role previously assumed by the syntax.

The contribution of morphological theory to phonological structure is so simple and elegant that little has been said about it beyond the initial observation that it works. There is, however, one rather technical issue which has been so hotly debated that it should be discussed here, and that is the question of *levels* or *strata* of affixes. In *SPE* it was noted that there are two types of suffixes in English, those like *-ity* which interact phonologically with the word to which they are attached, and those like *-ness,* which are insulated. Contrast, for example, the pair *pompous/pomposity* with the pair *pompous/pompousness.* In the first pair, there are changes in stress and vowel quality when the affix is added, while in the second pair there is no change. Similarly for *photograph/ photography/photographing* and numerous others. Most of the phonological differences between the two types of affixes, termed *neutral* and *nonneutral* in *SPE,* can be accounted for if, as in *SPE,* each type is attached with a different *boundary symbol,* nonneutral affixes with the *morpheme boundary* for which the symbol + is used, and neutral affixes with the *word boundary* for which the symbol # is used; since cyclic phonological rules do not operate across words, # affixes like #*ness* will be insulated in the desired fashion. On the other hand, + does not block any phonological rules, so that cyclic rules will operate on + affixes like +*ity.*

Within the literature on morphology, there have been a number of attempts to ground this analysis in theory. Siegel (80) first observed that neutral # affixes do not usually appear inside nonneutral + affixes, though the reverse order is common. She proposed that this ordering observation as well as the other peculiarities of the two types were the result of the interaction between the morphology and the phonology. According to Siegel, affixation may apply either before the rules of the phonology are given a chance to operate (as with + affixes) or after the cyclic phonology (as with # affixes). Since the attachment of the former precedes the latter, they will always fall inside, and since the latter are attached after the cyclic phonology has operated, they will be immune to cyclic rules. Since then, various modifications to Siegel's theory have been made (1, 66, 78, 83–85), none of which has unequivocally won the field. In addition, skeptics deride the entire phenomenon, pointing out that Siegel's original observation about the order of types of affixes has many exceptions. It is contradicted in English by such cases as *developmental, vietnamization,* and *derivability,* in all of which a + affix is found outside a # affix, as well as in words like *ungrammaticality* and *reeducation* where a + suffix must be added after a # prefix if the morphological and semantic structures are to be isomorphic (91). Some also claim that the distinction between types is an artifact of the history of English, # affixes being by and large Germanic and traceable to Old English, while + affixes are mostly Latinate, and borrowed either through French or directly from Latin and Greek. Unfortunately, though the historical facts are true, the existence of the two types of affixes is not peculiar to English. The same two types of affixes with the same general phonological and even semantic properties have been found in a totally unrelated language, Kannada (11). The existence of the two classes, though it may be traced to the history of English in some sense, is still principled in another sense and must be explained, even though Siegel's theory and subsequent refinements of it must be false because of the ordering facts noted above. Recently, the two levels of affixes have been related to a fairly old distinction, that between *stem* and *word.* It appears [following (48, 78) with some modification] that the two levels of affixes can be accounted for if we assume that + boundary affixes treat their bases as cyclical stems, while # boundary affixes treat their bases as words. Cyclic rules will operate only within words containing stems, so that in a word like *development,* where #*ment* is a word forming affix, *develop* will be treated as a word, and *ment* will not be processed by any cyclic rules, since it is not a word containing a stem. In *developmental,* on the other hand, +*al* treats #*ment* as a stem, making *mental* eligible for rules of cyclic phonology, which explains why *developmental* has the stress pattern of a two-word compound noun, being constituted formally of two words, *develop* and *mental.* This proposal has two distinct advantages. First, it subsumes the boundary difference under the stem/word difference so that the boundaries may be eliminated (72, 77, 79). Second, it permits the occurrence of + boundary affixes outside # boundary affixes, a phenomenon found in Malayalam (66) as well as in English (91), without relaxing the requirement of strict compositionality (85).

The question of the relation between the rules which add morphemes and the rules of phonology brings us directly to another general topic, the importance of morphological factors in the statement of phonological rules (92). In structuralist theory, phonological phenomena were strictly divided into two types: *allophonic* and *morphophonemic.* Morphophonemic rules spelled out the variant forms of morphemes in terms of phonemes in specific environments.

Allophonic rules spelled out the variant realizations of phonemes in specific purely phonetic environments and were therefore by definition independent of all morphological influence. All morphophonemic rules preceded all allophonic rules. Some modern theorists (42) still subscribe to this clear-cut distinction. However, in one of the earliest and most controversial demonstrations of generative phonology, Halle (38) showed that this division is incorrect and that morphophonemic rules and allophonic rules can be mixed. Nonetheless, the feeling has persisted that rules whose environment is more morphological should in general precede rules whose environment is more phonological.

Various claims have been made about this ordering. In *SPE,* for example, a distinction is drawn between *lexical representations* and *phonological representations.* The term *lexical* refers to the representation of formatives provided in the lexicon. When inserted in utterances, however, lexical formatives acquire syntactically determined features for such things as case and tense. Only after these abstract features are spelled out by a set of rules called *readjustment rules* do we have a phonological representation upon which phonological rules operate to provide a phonetic representation. Note that Chomsky and Halle did not claim that all morphologically sensitive rules precede the phonology, only those which actually spell out syntactic features.

Much energy has been devoted recently to attempting to collapse the two representations, lexical and phonological, of Chomsky and Halle. For the most part, this is done by placing the readjustment rules in the lexicon. A class of rules has been isolated which operates on specific morphemes in the environment of other specific morphemes. For example, in English the Latinate root *vert* appears as *vers* when followed by the suffixes +*ive,* +*ion,* and +*ory,* as in *inversion* or *subversive.* The alternation of *t* and *s* is restricted to this root, as we can see from words like *insertion,* and it does not take place before all + boundary suffixes (cf *convertible*). These rules, called *allomorphy rules,* or analogs to them with other names, are assumed to operate in the lexicon (7, 20, 57). Allomorphy rules also spell out in the lexicon irregular inflections such as *stand/stood, man/men.*

It has further been proposed by Lapointe (49, 50) and others that not only irregular inflection but all inflection be done in the lexicon rather than in the phonology. In a parallel fashion, advocates of this position claim that the interaction of inflection with the rules of the syntax is also highly restricted. However, both these claims have been questioned by Anderson (2, 4, 5), who presents several cases in which the spelling out of inflection seems to be intertwined with both low-level phonological rules and general syntactic rules.

A more radical proposal is that of Mohanan (66) and Kiparsky (48), according to which all phonological rules that operate within the domain of the word are considered to be lexical, largely because they may have exceptions.

Mohanan's lexical representation is in fact very close to certain structuralist phonemic representations, especially that of Sapir (64, 74). A similar position is that of "upside-down phonology" (52), in which cyclic phonological rules operate in a reverse direction from that normally assumed, unraveling the surface rather than constructing it.

As Mohanan points out (66), most of these proposals involve considerable enrichment of the lexicon. They are in fact incompatible with the traditional view of the lexicon as the repository of all and only exceptional items. There is nothing exceptional about most of the inflection that Lapointe regards as lexical, nor is there anything exceptional about an overwhelmingly large proportion of the compounds that Mohanan would assign to the lexicon. The same goes for many lexical rules of syntax. One might reply that by *lexical* we should read *lexicalizable,* but this would still beg many questions. What we need is a good term that refers to linguistic phenomena that have to do with words rather than phrases. In fact, most of these claims boil down to the assertion that morphology is distinct from syntax and phonology. Unfortunately, those who make the claims forget that morphology and the lexicon are two different things.

One consequence of the failure to distinguish lexical and morphological phenomena is that no account can be given of the correlation between semantic lexicalization of complex forms and the weakening of phonological boundaries along Stanley's strength hierarchy (82). It has often been observed that the stronger the phonological boundary between constituents, the less likely it is that the combination will be semantically arbitrary. For example, there are in English many pairs of words which differ phonologically only in that the first has a + boundary where the second has a # boundary. I have discussed these elsewhere (7). Sample pairs are *perceptible/perceivable, comparable/comparable, burnt/burned.* In all such cases, the + boundary word is idiosyncratic semantically, lexicalized. Chambers & Shaw (23) discuss a similar set of data in Dakota, consisting of minimal pairs of compounds. Again, the compound with the stronger boundary has the more predictable semantics. I also have published data from Kannada (11) which exhibits the same characteristics, and Mohanan (66) has a similar set of compounds in Malayalam. There is in fact every reason to suspect that the phenomenon is universal. No "lexical" theory that I know of, with the possible exception of (48), can handle it, simply because they all fail to distinguish between morphological and truly lexical matters. The same goes, by the way, for lexical theories of syntax, as Wasow (88) has pointed out.

I will now turn to recent work in what may be called the foundations of morphology—the question of the phonological form of morphemes. It has long been assumed that at some level of abstraction every morpheme has a single phonological form tied to a single meaning. This assumption has its roots in the philosophical theory of signs, which dates from at least the sixteenth century (29). Much of modern linguistics can be viewed profitably as an attempt to find this level and to define its characteristics. Recent interest in this enterprise has focused on two areas. The first is the question of abstractness—how far can the basic representation of any morpheme differ from its surface manifestations? The second area is exotic morphemes—those morphemes which seem either to have no underlying form or at least peculiar form. The two areas are not really so separate, since a better understanding of unusual morphemes may help to narrow the problem of abstractness.

Abstractness is inevitable. Chomsky & Halle (27) point out that even the level called *phonetic* by earlier phonologists is abstract from a physical point of view. No two instances of any given sound are physically identical, and the goal of phonetics is therefore to isolate the physically abstract qualities which make them sound identical to the listener. Our problem is analogous to that of the phonetician. Most American speakers of English believe that the *t* sound in *write, writes,* and *writer* is the same. Yet we know that they are three different sounds and that their distribution is predictable. We therefore posit a single abstract phoneme *t* of which the three are contextual variants and assume that the speaker "hears" at the level of the phoneme (74). More abstractly, we know that the plural ending has three variants, *s, z,* and *ez,* as in *caps, cabs,* and *caches* respectively, and that the variation is predictable; we therefore assume that there is one underlying abstract representation *z* or which these three are manifestations, so that the plural morpheme is underlyingly phonologically unique, as the doctrine of signs predicts.

Inevitably, difficulties arise in the course of our reductionist enterprise. First, do we allow morphemes with no basic phonological representation? For example, many irregular English plurals contain none of the above variants, yet they are still legitimately plural. Should we then allow a purely semantic morpheme "plural," manifested by *i* in *alumni, im* in *cherubim, odes* in *octopodes,* and so on elsewhere, with the abstract *z* form underlying *s/z/ez* as the default case? Generative grammar says no. "Plural" is not a morpheme but a syntactic feature. It is spelled out differently in different cases, the default case being the *z* plural morpheme. But this means that we either allow many plural morphemes or we give up on the doctrine of the sign in some cases. Nor is this problem confined to grammatical morphemes. Are *sing, sang, sung* three separate morphemes?

A second problem is limiting the extent of our reductive enterprise. If, for example, we wish to handle such related pairs as *telephone/telephonic* or *permit/permissive,* then we must allow particular morphemes to condition phonological variation. But morphological conditioning is a Pandora's box so powerful that it permits us to relate words as far apart as *knee* and *gonad* (58), unless we are able to impose on it conditions of a sort which have yet to be discovered.

Chomsky and Halle were fairly liberal in their treatment of abstractness. They placed few conditions on how far an underlying representation of a morpheme might differ from its surface manifestations or on how legitimate morphological relatedness was to be determined. There were a number of reactions to this attitude. One (42) was to abandon the doctrine of the sign with a vengeance by not attempting to provide single representations for morphemes unless the variation involved was phonetically transparent. This solution is probably too radical (40), but it has had a great influence in phonology. The second (47) was to place limits on the possible relation between surface and underlying forms. In any case, the doctrine of signs and consequent attempts to reduce every morpheme accordingly to a single underlying phonological form had been weakened to the point where it is no longer the central goal of most work in morphology. Within the lexical framework of Kiparksy (48), for example, the problem of abstractness is resolved by effectively making all of + boundary level morphology optional. In this framework, *telephone* and *telephonic* may be related if you are inclined to relate them, but there is nothing to compel you to do so.

Accompanying the movement away from abstraction has been a contradictory willingness to treat at least certain types of morphemes as having much more abstract representations than had previously been countenanced even by Chomsky and Halle. These morphemes are of two types, *base-dependent* and *autosegmental*. Both differ rather strikingly from the usual segmentally specified concatenating morphemes of European languages. The most common base-dependent morphemes are *reduplications* and *infixes*. In reduplication, a part of the base is repeated, while infixes are placed inside the base rather than in front or in back.

Tagalog is a well-studied language which is replete with both reduplication and infixation. My examples of each are drawn from (76). One form of reduplication copies the first consonant and vowel of a base. It appears in many derived word classes, usually preceded by an affix. Accompanied by the prefix *mag-* it produces a class of nouns meaning "vendor of the product designated by the base," as in the following pairs: *baboy* 'pig', *magbababoy* 'pig vendor'; *kandila* 'candle', *magkakandila* 'candle vendor'; *bulaklak* 'flower', *magbubulaklak* 'flower vendor'. This particular class is highly productive, and it is clear that no specific underlying representation can be given to the reduplicated affix. A common infix in Tagalog is *-um-*, which appears after the first consonant of its base, as in the following examples, where the infixed form has "actor focus": *kain* 'eat', *kumain*; *punta* 'go', *pumunta*; *dugo* 'bleed', *dumugo*. The problem with infixes is that they disrupt the integrity of other morphemes.

Both reduplication and infixation gained attention originally because of their importance for the question of the relative ordering of phonological rules and those rules which introduce morphemes (7, 20, 69, 89), though some attention was always paid to matters of form (62, 67, 68). Most recently, it has been suggested that these types of morphemes, which were earlier considered to have no basic phonological form at all, can be treated as regular affixes, albeit with a very abstract form, within a theory that is commonly called *autosegmental*.

This theory arose in connection with work on tone languages. It was discovered that many tonal phenomena could only be described adequately if the tones were treated as constituting a separate morphophonological tier (36, 51, 90). This autosegmental view has since been extended to other classes of phenomena. Most important for morphology, McCarthy (61) has shown how the Semitic verbal system can be analyzed within an autosegmental theory of morphology and has extended this theory to other nonconcatenative morphological phenomena. In Semitic, verb roots consisting exclusively of consonants are matched with tenses and aspects, each consisting of particular vowels in characteristic consonant vowel templates. In Modern Hebrew, the stem *ktv*, meaning 'write', can occur in the past tense as *katav*, in the present as *kotev*, in the future as *yixtov*, and in derived aspects such as causative *hixtiv*, intensive *kitev*, etc. Other verbs will have different consonants but the same vowel patterns. McCarthy shows how the consonantal roots, vocalic patterns, and templates can be matched by principles of autosegmental phonology, much in the same manner as tones are matched to segments in analyses of tone languages. As a consequence, though, he must admit morphemes with rather unorthodox forms. The lexical entries for verbs roots will be purely consonantal, those for different tenses and aspects will consist of particular vowels in templates with completely unspecified consonants. This same approach has also been used to analyze reduplication (59, 63), reduplicative morphemes being treated as segmentally unspecified or partly specified prefixes.

Analyses like these push abstraction to the edge. Not even Chomsky and Halle have morphemes whose underlying representation is so general as CV, as Tagalog reduplication would be in an autosegmental treatment. But it is important to note that with one exception (the Semitic roots, which may be susceptible to a less abstract treatment) all the morphemes for which these highly abstract representations are posited are *grammatical* operators. By limiting abstract representations to these and imposing more stringent conditions on members of major lexical categories (nouns, verbs, and adjectives), as has been suggested by a number of people (8, 25, 48), we may be able to deal with the problem of abstraction in a better fashion. Whether we can impose such limitations is an empirical problem.

SYNTAX AND WORD FORMATION

Two major issues are grouped under this heading. The first concerns the proper division of labor between the syntactic component of a grammar and the word formation component. The question was first raised by Chomsky (26), who pointed out that certain phenomena, hitherto regarded as syntactic, should best be treated in a separate word formation component. Though Chomsky himself has subsequently done little work in this area, his original article spawned an entire enterprise, which generally goes under the name *lexical grammar* and which has several schools, the most prominent being the *lexical functional grammar* school of Bresnan. A representative sample of work within lexical grammar, along with a fine introduction, can be found in (41); (16) and (17) are also recommended. Most of this work deals with phenomena whose status is controversial. For example, a good deal of energy has been expended on discussions of passive constructions, with some arguing that passives are syntactic in origin, while at least one author (87) has claimed that some passives are lexical and some syntactic. Nor will the argument really be settled until there is a better understanding of the distinction.

In view of this uncertainty, I will concentrate my substantive remarks on the second question: the extent to which descriptions of phenomena which lie unquestionably within the domain of word formation must make reference to syntactic notions. The traditional position on this is that word formation rules may make reference only to syntactic categories and not to syntactic operations. Furthermore, only a limited type of syntactic category may be referred to; in particular, not phrasal categories. The first assumption has been questioned by analysts of Eskimo languages (73, 81), which are highly polysynthetic, having entire complex sentences expressed in one word. The jury is still out on this, since the languages are so unusual that it is difficult to agree even on individual analyses. The second assumption, however, has met with more difficulty. Even in such unexotic languages as German, the incorporation of phrases into words is common. Object-incorporating languages such as Mohawk reinforce the conclusion that phrasal categories must be referred to. However, within an *Aspects* theory of major lexical categories, the theoretical boundary between word and phrase is not all that clear-cut. In this theory, each noun, verb, and adjective has specified in its lexical entry a *strict subcategorization frame,* which determines the specific syntactic context within which the item may occur. For example, the frame for a transitive verb is [__NP], meaning that the verb must be followed by a *noun phrase* object, while that for an intransitive verb is [__], meaning that it may not have an object. According to *Aspects,* the subcategorization frame for any major lexical category consists of the phrasal category that immediately contains it. The frame for verbs is therefore *verb phrase,* for nouns *noun phrase,* and for adjectives *adjective phrase*. The frame may contain no information below or above the level of that dominating phrase (see 25, pp. 95–100 for further details). Thus, the lexical entry for any given noun, verb, or adjective already contains phrasal information, though of a restricted kind. It is, incidentally, precisely this property of lexical categories that proponents of lexical grammar take advantage of in their reformulations of syntactic rules as lexical rules. If, therefore, we accept the necessity of subcategorization frames in lexical entries, with their limited reference to phrasal categories, we must also expect word formation rules, even if they make no reference to other syntactic notions, to permit mention of this same limited type of phrasal categories. Word formation rules involving verbs, for example, might refer to direct objects, indirect objects, or manner adverbs, because these are part of the verb phrase, but not to time adverbs or subjects, because they are outside the verb phrase. This prediction is borne out by such phenomena as the above-mentioned object incorporation in Mohawk (note the absence of subject incorporation) and English verbal compounds such as *baby sitter* and *well made* (71). Thus, the restriction against including phrasal material in words must be interpreted so as to exclude only material outside the subcategorization frame of a given word. Further work on Eskimo will tell us whether this must be relaxed further and under what conditions.

In addition to subcategorization, it has been suggested (3) that word formation makes use of thematic relations such as *agent, instrument,* and *patient* (35, 37, 43), rather than or as well as purely syntactic relations such as *subject* and *object*. For example, words containing the suffix *-ee* in English denote the patient of an action, which may be either the syntactic object or indirect object or subject of the base verb: *payee* (indirect object, cf pay the money to the woman), *nominee* (direct object, cf nominate the woman), *standee* (subject). Similarly, the suffix *-er* denotes either the agent or instrument of an action; if a verb has a nonagentive subject, then there is no corresponding noun in *-er*: depress/*depresser (He depresses me/*He is a depresser), but *tongue depressor* is fine, since it is an instrument. Such a finding is not unexpected, if the lexical entry for a verb contains a thematic representation in addition to more strictly syntactic information (17).

A related question is that of the syntactic classes of words to which word formation refers. It is fairly clear that more specific categories than the basic noun, verb, and adjective are involved, as many of the examples already given indicate. Nonetheless, the range of categories to which reference must be made is not known. Furthermore, no present theory of grammar has been able to give a good definition of even the basic categories, and some explicitly reject them, while most treat the basic categories as primitives. There has been almost no good work recently on the problem of dealing with these categories.

It is quite clear on inspection that the range of classes specified by rules of word formation is fairly great. Some rules form wide classes. For example, the rule which forms verbs from nouns in English by zero-derivation (9) forms verbs of all sorts, transitive, intransitive, etc: *blanket, winter, piece together, tee off, feast on,* etc. The rule itself most likely specifies only that the output be a verb. The particular type of verb derived in individual cases is determined by other factors (28). But other rules produce specific subcategories of verbs. Most productive prefixes in English form only transitives: *think/rethink, talk/ outtalk, walk/outwalk.* In these cases, though the base verb is intransitive, the derived verb must be transitive (19). It is therefore reasonable to restrict the rule so that it forms only transitive verbs, regardless of the category of the input. With nouns, there is fairly great variety in English. I know of no rule which simply forms nouns in the way that the zero verb rule forms verbs. In fact, the rule that forms nouns from verbs by zero-derivation forms nouns of a very specific type. Each such noun denotes an instance of the action of the verb: $punch_n$, try_n, $glance_n$, $assault_n$, $rebound_n$. Another quite productive rule which similarly forms a very specific class of nouns is the attachment of the suffix *-ism* usually to (proper) nouns, to form new nouns denoting a system of beliefs: *Platonism, Calvinism, vegetarianism, socialism.* The same suffix can also form nouns denoting a characteristic type of linguistic behavior: *malapropism, Churchillism, Micawberism.* Whether the two uses are related is not clear, but in any case they represent rather narrow classes of nouns. A similar range of cases can be found with adjective suffixes in English. Thus, *-ic(al)* and *-al* simply form adjectives related to the base noun: *philosophical, theological, remedial, exceptional.* However, *-able* is more specific. The derived adjective is passive and potential: something is *readable* if it can be read; it is *repeatable* if it can be repeated, etc.

Nor is English an isolated case. In most languages, we find rules that form very general classes of words and rules that are much more specific. The more general classes recur again and again cross-linguistically, but some of the more specific classes are highly individual. In Kannada, for example, there is a suffix which parallels English suffixes like *-ness* in forming abstract nouns denoting a quality or state. So, /dodda/'big' and /doddatana/'size'; /bada/'poor' and /bada-tana/'poverty'; /kalla/'thief' and /kallatana/'thievery'. On the other hand, the noun suffix -āta has no exact equivalent in any other language I know. Its meaning is demonstrated by the following pairs: /cellu/'to spill' and /cellāta/ 'spilling around'; /huduku/'search' and /hudukāta/'searching all over'; /tikku/ 'rub' and /tikkāta/'skirmish'.

In many of these examples we seem to verge on semantics. These categories are surely not all syntactic in any common sense of the term. The examples therefore show that the categories which word formation deals with must go beyond the strictly syntactic. Whether there is a continuum between such clearly syntactic categories as transitive verbs and the more specific cases discussed above, or whether there is a sharp break at some point is not entirely clear, though it is difficult to find any clean dividing line. Nor can we even say, for some of these cases, whether the categories are semantic rather than pragmatic (cf *-ism*). Having come this far, though, I will turn to semantics.

SEMANTICS AND WORD FORMATION

Modern linguistic semantics has two main branches, *formal semantics* and *descriptive semantics*. Formal semantics has its roots in philosophical logic and is still closely tied to philosophy. There has been a great deal of activity in this area in recent years, especially in the adaptation of notions of formal semantics to the analysis of natural languages. However, most of this activity has been directed at syntax, nor morphology. The most notable exception is Dowty's work on Montague semantics and word formation (32). Descriptive semantics, also known as *lexical semantics,* is a more purely linguistic enterprise, with roots in the nineteenth century. Almost all practitioners of descriptive semantics hold to some version of the thesis of *lexical decomposition,* according to which the meaning of a word can be broken down into component parts, though the exact nature of these components and their relation to one another remains the subject of sometimes heated debate. A related thesis, that of *semantic compositionality,* states that the meaning of any complex form is a function of the meaning of its parts. Within the last decade, there has emerged a fairly coherent view of the descriptive semantics of word formation which, while accepting both these theses, has incorporated them more indirectly than in the past. Though there has been no explicit recognition of any agreement on this point, it seems that most recent work on the semantics of word formation shares the following assumptions: description should be concentrated on potential rather than on lexicalized words, with little attention paid to unproductive patterns; most potential words have a range of meanings rather than a single meaning, and the task of word formation semantics is to delimit this range rather than to predict exact meanings; the choice of a single meaning is determined by linguistic and nonlinguistic context; pragmatics plays a great role in the determination of word meanings, and we must recognize the interaction of pragmatics and semantics in the case of both potential and actual words; the semantics of complex words is compositional, but only once we abstract away from pragmatic and contextual factors. This view is much less ambitious than those of Lees (53) or the generative semanticists (54), who try to derive much more explicitly the meanings of individual words.

One of the earliest and probably still the best example of work along these lines is Downing's (31) analysis of English compounds, which replaces the diverse semantic types into which previous investigators had categorized compounds with the single relation "N_1 is related to N_2" accompanied by independent pragmatic and cognitive conditions and the recognition that words must name (at least momentarily) significant things. Other work has followed this lead in proposing very sparse semantic characterizations for rather complex sets of data (9, 28), and there is always a temptation to reduce as far as possible in semantics, so that one might try to describe all word formation semantics in terms of the interaction of pragmatic factors with very simple semantic rules, as suggested in (9). Unfortunately, it is fairly clear that we need more than this. I have already noted a number of cases where the semantics of a particular class of derived words is fairly specific and not relatable to either syntactic or semantic factors (see the discussion of English -ee, -er, and zero-derived nouns, and Kannada -āta), so that we must assume a more complex semantic representation for the affix involved. Much work quite clearly remains to be done in the area of semantics and word formation, but the questions that must be asked are fairly clear. This alone signals progress.

CONCLUSION

Morphology was once viewed as the key to understanding language. The last decade has seen a renewed interest in this neglected area of investigation, an interest which appears still to be growing. We are not so naive anymore as to believe that one single approach will solve all the mysteries of language, but I hope to have shown that if morphology is indeed a better key, it is precisely because when morphology is done well questions are raised and perhaps even a few answers given which shed light on a variety of aspects of that most complex of human activities.

Literature Cited

1. Allen, M. 1978. *Morphological investigations*. PhD thesis. Univ. Conn., Storrs
2. Anderson, S. R. 1975. On the interaction of phonological rules of various types. *J. Ling.* 11:39–63
3. Anderson, S. R. 1977. Comments on the paper by Wasow. In *Formal Syntax*, ed. P. Culicover, T. Wasow, A. Akmajian, pp. 361–65. New York: Academic. 500 pp.
4. Anderson, S. R. 1977. On the formal description of inflection. *CLS*[1] 13:15–44
5. Anderson, S. R. 1982. Where's morphology? *Ling. Inq.* 13:571–612
6. Anshen, F., Aronoff, M. 1981. Morphological productivity and phonological transparency. *Can. J. Ling.* 26:63–72
7. Aronoff, M. 1976. *Word Formation in Generative Grammar*. Ling. Inq. Monogr. No. 1. Cambridge: MIT Press. 134 pp.
8. Aronoff, M. 1978. Lexical representations. In *Papers from the Parasession on the Lexicon*, pp. 12–25. Chicago: Chicago Ling. Soc.
9. Aronoff, M. 1980. Contextuals. *Language* 56:744–58
10. Aronoff, M. 1982. Potential words, actual words, productivity and frequency. *Preprints of Plenary Session, Int. Congr. Linguists, 13th, Tokyo*, pp. 141–48
11. Aronoff, M., Sridhar, S. N. 1983. *Morphological levels in English and Kannada, or Atarizing Reagan*. Presented at Parasession on the Linguistic Levels, Chicago Linguistic Society, Chicago, Ill. In press
12. Beard, R. 1976. A semantically based model of a generative lexical word-formation rule for Russian adjectives. *Language* 52:108–20
13. Beard, R. 1982. *The Indo-European Lexicon*. Amsterdam: North Holland. 389 pp.

[1]Papers from the annual meeting of the Chicago Linguistics Society, Univ. Chicago.

14. Bloomfield, L. 1933. *Language*. New York: Holt. 564 pp.
15. Bradley, D. 1980. Lexical representation of derivational relation. See Ref. 77, pp. 37–56
16. Brame, M. 1978. *Base Generated Syntax*. Seattle: Noit Amrofer. 127 pp.
17. Bresnan, J. W., ed. 1982. *The Mental Representation of Grammatical Relation*. Cambridge, Mass: MIT Press. 874 pp.
18. Broselow, E. 1977. Language change and theories of the lexicon. *CLS* 13:58–68
19. Carlson, G., Roeper, T. 1980. See Ref. 41, pp. 123–64
20. Carrier, J. 1979. *The interaction of morphological and phonological rules in Tagalog*. PhD thesis. MIT, Cambridge, Mass.
21. Carstairs, A. D. 1981. *Constraints on allomorphy in inflexion*. PhD thesis. Univ. London, London, England. 450 pp.
22. Carstairs, A. D. 1983. Paradigm economy. *J. Ling.* 19:115–28
23. Chambers, J. K., Shaw, P. A. 1980. Systematic obfuscation of morphology in Dakota. *Ling. Inq.* 11:325–56
24. Chomsky, N. 1957. *Syntactic Structures*. The Hague: Mouton. 118 pp.
25. Chomsky, N. 1965. *Aspects of the Theory of Syntax*. Cambridge, Mass: MIT Press. 251 pp.
26. Chomsky, N. 1970. Remarks on nominalization. In *Readings in English Transformational Grammar*, ed. R. Jacobs, P. S. Rosenbaum, pp. 184–221. Waltham, Mass: Ginn. 277 pp.
27. Chomsky, N., Halle, M. 1968. *The Sound Pattern of English*. New York: Harper & Row. 470 pp.
28. Clark, E., Clark, H. 1979. When nouns surface as verbs. *Language* 55:767–811
29. Cohen, M. 1977. *Sensible Words*. Baltimore: Johns Hopkins Univ. Press. 188 pp.
30. Cutler, A. 1980. Productivity in word formation. *CLS* 16:45–51
31. Downing, P. 1977. On the creation and use of English compound nouns. *Language* 53:810–42
32. Dowty, D. 1979. *Word Meaning and Montague Grammar*. Dordrecht: Reidel. 415 pp.
33. Dressler, W. U. 1979. On a polycentristic theory of word formation. *Proc. Int. Congr. Ling., 12th, Vienna*, pp. 426–29
34. Dressler, W. U. 1982. On word formation in natural morphology. See Ref. 10, pp. 149–55
35. Fillmore, C. 1968. The case for case. In *Universals in Linguistic Theory*, ed. E.

Bach, R. T. Harms, pp. 1–90. New York: Holt, Rinehart & Winston. 210 pp.
36. Goldsmith, J. 1976. An overview of autosegmental phonology. *Ling. Anal.* 2:23–68
37. Gruber, J. 1976. *Lexical Structures in Syntax and Semantics*. Amsterdam: North-Holland. 375 pp.
38. Halle, M. 1959. *The Sound Pattern of Russian*. The Hague: Mouton. 206 pp.
39. Hamp, E., Householder, F. N., Austerlitz, R., eds. 1966. *Readings in Linguistics II*. Chicago: Univ. Chicago Press. 395 pp.
40. Harris, J. 1978. Two theories of nonautomatic morphophonological alternations: evidence from Spanish. *Language* 54:41–60
41. Hoekstra, T., van der Hulst, H., Moortgat, M., eds. 1980. *Lexical Grammar*. Dordrecht: Foris. 340 pp.
42. Hooper, J. B. 1976. *An Introduction to Natural Generative Phonology*. New York: Academic. 254 pp.
43. Jackendoff, R. 1972. *Semantic Interpretation in Generative Grammar*. Cambridge, Mass: MIT Press. 400 pp.
44. Jackendoff, R. 1975. Morphological and semantic regularities in the lexicon. *Language* 51:639–71
45. Joos, M., ed. 1966. *Readings in Linguistics I*. Chicago: Univ. Chicago Press. 421 pp. 4th ed.
46. Kastovsky, D. 1977. Word-formation or: at the crossroads of morphology, syntax, semantics, and the lexicon. *Folia Ling.* 1/2:1–33
47. Kiparsky, P. 1973. Abstractness, opacity, and global rules. In *Three Dimensions of Linguistic Theory*, ed. O. Fujimura, pp. 57–76. Tokyo: TEC Co. 376 pp.
48. Kiparsky, P. 1982. From cyclic phonology to lexical phonology. In *The Structure of Phonological Representations* (Part I), ed. H. van der Hulst, N. Smith, pp. 131–76. Dordrecht: Foris. 276 pp.
49. Lapointe, S. 1979. *A theory of grammatical agreement*. PhD thesis. Univ. Mass., Amherst
50. Lapointe, S. 1980. A lexical analysis of the English auxiliary verb system. See Ref. 41, pp. 215–54
51. Leben, W. R. 1980. *Suprasegmental Phonology*. New York: Garland. 198 pp.
52. Leben, W. R., Robinson, O. W. 1977. Upside-down phonology. *Language* 53:1–20
53. Lees, R. B. 1960. *The Grammar of English Nominalizations*. The Hague: Mouton. 204 pp.
54. Levi, J. 1978. *The Syntax and Semantics of Complex Nominals*. New York: Academic. 300 pp.

55. Liberman, M., Prince, A. 1977. On stress and linguistic rhythm. *Ling. Inq.* 8:249–336
56. Lieber, R. 1980. *The Organization of the lexicon.* PhD thesis. MIT, Cambridge, Mass. (Bloomington: Indiana Univ. Ling. Club)
57. Lieber, R. 1982. Allomorphy. *Ling. Anal.* 10:27–52
58. Lightner, T. 1975. The role of derivational morphology in generative grammar. *Language* 51:617–38
59. Marantz, A. 1982. Re reduplication. *Ling. Inq.* 13:435–82
60. Matthews, P. H. 1974. *Morphology: An Introduction to the Theory of Word Structure.* Cambridge: Cambridge Univ. Press. 243 pp.
61. McCarthy, J. 1981. A prosodic theory of nonconcatenative morphology. *Ling. Inq.* 12:373–418
62. McCarthy, J. 1982. Prosodic structure and expletive infixation. *Language* 58:574–90
63. McCarthy, J. 1982. Prosodic templates, morphemic templates, and morphemic tiers. See Ref. 48, pp. 191–224
64. McCawley, J. D. 1967. Sapir's phonological representations. *Int. J. Am. Ling.* 33:106–11
65. Mel'cuk, I. A. 1982. *Towards a Language of Linguistics.* Munich: Fink. 160 pp.
66. Mohanan, K. P. 1982. *Lexical phonology.* PhD thesis. MIT, Cambridge, Mass. (Bloomington: Indiana Univ. Ling. Club)
67. Moravcsik, E. A. 1977. *On Rules of Infixing.* Bloomington: Indiana Univ. Ling. Club. 157 pp.
68. Moravcsik, E. A. 1978. Reduplicative constructions. In *Universals of Human Language,* ed. J. Greenberg, 3:297–334. Stanford: Stanford Univ. Press
69. Munro, P., Benson, P. J. 1973. Reduplication and rule ordering in Luiseno. *Int. J. Am. Ling.* 39:15–21
70. Newmeyer, F. 1980. *Linguistic Theory in America: the First Quarter Century of Transformational Grammar.* New York: Academic. 290 pp.
71. Roeper, T., Siegel, M. 1978. A lexical transformation for verbal compounds. *Ling. Inq.* 9:199–260
72. Rotenberg, J. 1978. *The syntax of phonology.* PhD thesis. MIT, Cambridge, Mass.
73. Sadock, J. 1980. Noun incorporation in Greenlandic. *Language* 56:300–19
74. Sapir, E. 1933. The psychological reality of phonemes. *J. Psychol. Norm. Pathol.* 30:247–65. Reprinted in *Selected Writings of Edward Sapir,* ed. D. Mandelbaum. Berkeley: Univ. Calif. Press
75. Schachter, P. 1962. Review of Lees (1960). *Int. J. Am. Ling.* 28:134–49
76. Schachter, P., Otanes, F. 1972. *Tagalog Reference Grammar.* Berkeley: Univ. Calif. Press
77. Selkirk, E. O. 1980. Prosodic domains in phonology: Sanskrit revisited. In *Juncture,* ed. M. Aronoff, M.-L. Kean, pp. 107–30. Saratoga, Calif: ANMA Libri. 141 pp.
78. Selkirk, E. O. 1982. *The Syntax of Words.* Ling. Inq. Monogr. No. 7. Cambridge, Mass: MIT Press. 136 pp.
79. Selkirk, E. O. 1983. *Phonology and Syntax: The Relation between Sound and Structure.* Cambridge, Mass: MIT Press. In press
80. Siegel, D. 1979. *Topics in English Morphology.* New York: Garland. 195 pp.
81. Smith, L. A. 1982. An analysis of affixal verbal derivation and complementation in Labrador Inuttut. *Ling. Anal.* 10:161–89
82. Stanley, R. 1973. Boundaries in phonology. In *A Festschrift for Morris Halle,* ed. S. R. Anderson, P. Kiparsky, pp. 185–206. New York: Holt, Rinehart & Winston
83. Strauss, S. 1979. Against boundary distinctions in English morphology. *Ling. Anal.* 5:387–419
84. Strauss, S. 1982. *Lexicalist Phonology of English and German.* Dordrecht: Foris. 185 pp.
85. Strauss, S. 1982. On "relatedness paradoxes" and related paradoxes. *Ling. Inq.* 13:694–700
86. Thomas-Flinders, T., ed. 1981. *Inflectional Morphology: Introduction to the Extended Word-and-Paradigm Theory.* UCLA Occas. Pap. 4
87. Wasow, T. 1977. Transformations and the lexicon. See Ref. 3, pp. 327–60
88. Wasow, T. 1980. Major and minor rules in lexical grammar. See Ref. 41, pp. 285–312
89. Wilbur, R. 1973. *The Phonology of Reduplication.* Bloomington: Indiana Univ. Ling. Club
90. Williams, E. 1976. Underlying tone in Margi and Igbo. *Ling. Inq.* 7:463–84
91. Williams, E. 1981. On the notions "lexically related" and "head of a word." *Ling. Inq.* 12:245–74
92. Wurzel, W. U. 1980. Ways of morphologizing phonological rules. In *Historical Morphology,* ed. J. Fisiak, pp. 443–62. The Hague: Mouton. 476 pp.
93. Zimmer, K. 1964. *Affixed Negation in English and other Languages: An Investigation of Restricted Productivity* (Suppl. to *Word,* Monogr. 5). New York. 105 pp.

Ann. Rev. Anthropol. 1983. 12:377–402

ANTHROPOLOGY OF EASTERN EUROPE

Joel Martin Halpern

Department of Anthropology, University of Massachusetts, Amherst,
Massachusetts 01003

David A. Kideckel

Department of Sociology/Anthropology, Central Connecticut State University,
New Britain, CT 06050

INTRODUCTION

Objectives

This essay presents an overview of East Europeanist sociocultural anthropological research concentrating on the work of American anthropogists. Given the relatively late maturation of this field, most work has been published during the past decade. In recent years, the field has been marked by a great diversity in theoretical and methodological approaches.

This survey concentrates on research by Americans and, with few exceptions, materials published in English in Western journals are considered. The contributions of East European ethnologists have been crucial to defining the field, and the works of a few selected scholars form an integral part of this survey.

We define the region surveyed by this article as the Slavic states of Europe outside the U.S.S.R. and the geographically contiguous states of Albania, Hungary, and Romania, excluding East Germany for sociocultural historical reasons. National and even regional boundaries severely restrict work as they frequently tend to be self-conscious entities, often with strong feelings of ethnocentrism. Anthropological research, since it does tend to concentrate on locally defined cultural units, is particularly susceptible to these influences. Aspects of this situation are apparent in certain titles cited. For the most part,

377

books and articles deal with individual states or ethnic groups and lack a comparative perspective.

This is only one of a number of difficulties facing the anthropology of Eastern Europe as it attempts to penetrate into a general anthropological consciousness (31, 32, 69). Though East European data is of great potential significance for anthropology, it has had a limited impact. Therefore, an additional objective of this essay is to develop an understanding of the dimensions of this problem and present some possible solutions.

Confronting East Europe's Marginality Within Socioculturual Anthropology

Marginality develops from the status of both European and peasant studies within anthropology and, from a broader persepective of culture history, the position of Eastern Europe within Europe. Because of its cultural heritage, with a long-standing scholarly tradition, Eastern Europe has been of restricted interest to an anthropology focused on the "other," the non-European world (97, 98).

Though the anthropological literature on the region by Western scholars is significant, it remains relatively sparse when compared to areas of traditional anthropological interest as, for example, Africa and native North America. This situation presents both obstacles and opportunities for East Europeanist anthropologists. It forces researchers to justify their anthropological identity and the legitimacy of some of their research topics. Yet it affords the opportunity for anthropology to become that which it purports: a holistic approach to the human condition.

Marginality and Indigenous Research Traditions

Eastern Europe has long been characterized by its own vigorous social scientific research traditions. This means that American anthropologists working in this region must come to terms not only with a new culture but also with a fully developed system of scholarly investigation. This scholarship is integrated with historically based national identities derived from the dominant peasant cultures (71, 100). The nature of these research traditions and their dominant ideas can differ greatly from Western anthropological thought and practice (17, 48).

As Hofer (97) suggests, in paraphrasing Wallace with analogs from agricultural techniques, the carefully plowed field of studies of European society is uninviting for the "slash-and-burn" oriented (American) anthropologist bent on the cultivation of the new and unexplored. In contrast, East European ethnography demands long-term, painstakingly detailed research to establish the specifics of the interrelationships of specific aspects of local life and national identity. The two approaches often find themselves on different paths.

Criteria of East European Unity

Our definition of this area is based on its peasant nature, peripheral political-economic position to a series of empires, the conflicting ethnic diversity of its populations, and, since World War II, the commonality of its socialist institutions.

Unlike Western Europe with its well-developed urban tradition and Greece with its heritage of Classical civilization, the bases of East European national identities have resided historically with the rural folk. Its relatively small-scale urban centers were principally inhabited by cultural groups from outside the region until well into the nineteenth century. During the period between the two World Wars, politically organized Peasant Parties, based on articulated concepts of cultural heritage, were especially active throughout the region (17, 147).

The incorporation of the peasant societies of Eastern Europe as peripheries to imperial systems (Ottomans, Habsburgs, Russians, Western capital, Soviets) has encouraged a great degree of structural commonality and is reflected in recent research (23, 24, 30, 207–208a). This work has drawn on the earlier writings of both Western (212) and Eastern scholarship (198).

The region is also an ethnic shatter zone marked by a multiplicty of competing groups and overlapping population boundaries both in the past and continuing to the present. To a great extent, East European ethnicity is coterminous with religious identification since church organizations were the chief means by which national identities were maintained while the region was controlled by various imperial powers. The historical dynamics of this region form an analog in terms of cultural processes to Southeast Asia. The latter is also an ethnically diverse marginal area where the cultural traditions of the major world civilizations of India and China have interacted (55, 56).

Since World War II, socialist-communist states with centrally planned industrializing economies have characterized the region. Associated features of socialist political economy also encourage cultural commonality: collective farms, mass cultural institutions, and centralized political parties, among others. In the four decades since these governments have come to power, there have emerged great differences in the ways in which these socialist systems organize their populations and attempt to innovate change.

HISTORICAL TRENDS IN ANTHROPOLOGICAL RESEARCH

Nineteenth and Early Twentieth Centuries

The roots of contemporary anthropological studies go back to the ethnographically oriented travel descriptions or occasional scholarly accounts which were published up to World War II. These accounts, which have some retrospective value, present local cultures as colorful human scenery for the interest of Western readers. There were also books by Westernized politicians and intellectuals who presented their way of life to Western audiences. These people also tended to dwell on the exotic. Doreen Warriner's anthology (212) offers a useful compendium of these writings combined with socioecnomic analyses.

Indigenous research traditions developed early in the nineteenth century. Part of their motivation grew from emerging national consciousness. Resulting research institutions initially concentrated on collecting folklore and oral tradition.

The flowering of national peasant parties in the interwar period provided a base for the development of political economic research interests (17). There are also cases where the folkloric and economic overlap with Western anthropology as in the works of Josef Obrebski, Malinowski's student in London, who carried out field researches in Poland and Yugoslavia during the 1930s (147, 148).

The Formative Period of Western Anthropological Research

Prior to World War II, there were a number of anthropologically oriented researchers who worked in Eastern Europe. Interestingly, Albania, which has been inaccessible for research since the war, was then one of the principal areas studied (33, 96).

The scholar who had the greatest institutional impact was the historian Philip Mosely, a colleague of Margaret Mead (142). He proved instrumental in the development of Soviet and East European area studies at American universities. After training with Malinowski, Mosely hiked through the Balkans, interviewing peasants on socioeconomic aspects of extended family organization, the zadruga, the joint family characteristic of the Balkans. His comparative research in Albania, Bulgaria, Romania, and Yugoslavia was facilitated by the relative openness of pre-World War II frontiers (21).

Mosely's work (21) is important for defining the cultural and ecological sources of regional variation in the zadruga throughout the Balkans. The volume of essays in his honor provides evidence of his scholarly collaboration. On his Balkan travels, he met the Romanians Gusti and Stahl and the Yugoslav Filipovic, whom he helped come to Harvard in 1952 (48, 198).

Parallel to Mosley's work was that of his contemporary Vera Erlich, who published a pre-war survey of Yugoslav family relationships in 1966 after studying at Berkeley (44).

At Columbia, Mosely collaborated with Margaret Mead and Ruth Benedict at the Institute of Contemporary Cultures, where Eastern Europe was a focus within the program. Benedict wrote a paper on Romanian national character (8). Related materials were published in Mead & Metraux's The Study of Culture at a Distance (7). This contribution calls attention to a related unifying theme in East European societies, the impact of distant historical events on contemporary individual identity and behavior. This has also been stressed by Ehrlich (45). Another important work which grew out of the same auspices was Zbrowski and Herzog's treatment of the culture of the East European Jewish shtetl (221). During the same period, Geza Roheim also published on Hungarian values and religious ideology (161, 162) while Irwin Sanders pursued his village study in Bulgaria (176).

Research in the Postwar Period

In the postwar period, the orientation of East European anthropological research has mirrored general trends in sociocultural anthropology. That is, its focus has gradually moved from a concern with cultural description for the purpose of defining national and ethnic traditions to one focusing on the explication of particular questions.

Still, many contemporary themes in East European research were first dealt with by interwar scholars: social structure of domestic groups (21, 48, 176), economic relationships of peasant society (17, 198), function and meanings inherent in religious ritual (9, 147), problems of innovation and migration (147). Today, however, a number of new research foci are apparent: analyzing the historic growth of regional capitalism and the structure, potentials, and problems of contemporary East European socialist societies. Present consciousness of political economy is linked to work associated with peasant parties in the interwar period. Yet the concern with socialism per se represents a significant departure.

CONTEMPORARY PERSPECTIVES

Theoretical Orientations: Contrastive or Complementary?

Since World War II, there have been two overlapping research orientations in the anthropology of the region. These approaches, which for purposes of discussion we distinguish as the "social structural" and "political economic," are (or ought to be) complementary. In many instances they deal with the same topical considerations and share a number of similar theoretical outlooks. We draw a distinction between them here, in part, for heuristic reasons but also because they illustrate some major tendencies in the analysis of Eastern Europe as well as force us to focus on key categories of the East European culture area.

Social structural research, as we define it, is more concerned with East European peasant society as reflected in community, family, related local institutions, symbols, oral traditions, and value systems. This approach emphasizes a notion of cyclical time with its emphasis on recurrent events. Certain aspects of the future then are anticipated only in terms of past developments. It also recognizes the transformations taking place in Eastern Europe and therefore considers the related effects of industrialization, urbanization, and migration on peasant society. Attention is increasingly paid to new social groupings developing from this transformation, such as peasant workers and immigrant communities abroad.

Though modernization is recognized as a potent force of change, most social structural research emphasizes the continuity and adaptability of peasant institutions and values, even as they are encapsulated in the larger socialist political economy. The overriding stress is on the transitory nature of political systems compared to centuries-old cultural patterns. Social structural views more readily encourage us to look at the conditions of individual and community life to understand the historical cultural systems of Eastern Europe.

In contrast to this orientation, political economic research strategies have gained in popularity among American anthropologists over the past decade. They place greater emphasis on the interaction of local cultural units and national or supranational ones for understanding the formation of East European cultural systems. For example, greater weight is given to the influence of capitalist and socialist political economies. Production relations, economic exchange, and class systems are seen as more determinant with emphasis on change rather than continuity. This approach focuses on linear time: present developments can represent qualitative departures from previous patterns and so may not be readily predictable in terms of past events. Socialism and socialist institutions, especially planned social change, are considered to have an enduring effect on East European life.

Despite these differences, political economic research considers many of the same specific topics as the social structural approach. Their different emphases, rather than being diametrically opposed to each other, help unify the field. Combined, they can better address the question of continuity and change in East European cultural systems.   *Bibliographic Surveys*

Contemporary work on Eastern Europe is informed by a series of literature reviews. The most comprehensive multidisciplinary coverage is found in Horecky (104, 105). The works of Sanders and his colleagues specifically concern social science research, but are limited to periodical articles (177, 178). Specifically anthropological are the surveys edited by Salzmann (168) and Maday (136). Included are contributions on the individual countries. A more recent one limited to the Balkans for the 1970s is that of Halpern & Wagner (76). Individual country surveys include Howell (106), Maday (135, 137, 139), and Sozan (196) for Hungary; Kutrzeba-Pojnarowa (121) for Poland; Salzmann (170, 171a) on Czechs and Slovaks in Romania, and Patterson (153) on Romania; Halpern (61) on Yugoslavia; and Wagner (210) on Serbia.

Community Studies

The community study in Eastern Europe takes its impetus from Sander's interwar research, although the orientation was sociological because interaction between social groups was stressed rather than cultural institutions. The works of the Halperns on Serbia [Halpern and Kerewsky-Halpern (54, 59, 73, 112)], Winner (216) on Slovenia, Salzmann & Scheufler (172) on a Czech village, and, to a significant extent, Lockwood's monograph on Bosnia (127) fit this category as they attempt to delineate the culture of a particular people.

These works use history to explain cultural phenomena and exemplify regional patterns as manifested in specific communities. Each of these works, in somewhat different ways, attempts to articulate the compelx net of relationships existing between community, region, and nation. The word attempts is used advisedly because it is not possible to accomplish this task easily. A useful critical article using a Balkan village and a Serbian village delineates some of the problems in community comparison (107).

By contrast, recent community monographs often focus more specifically on how village communities have been transformed by the advent of socialism, particularly via collectivization. Bell (6a) considers how collectivization transforms social hierarchy and individual perception. He contrasts the egalitarian principles of the collective farm with both the hierarcy necessitated by large-scale formal organization and the traditional forms of hierarchy. Hann (95) focuses on the social differentiation growing out of the economic alternatives now available in a formerly isolated tanya settlement. Salzmann & Scheufler (172), however, are more concerned with collectivization as a general vehicle for modernization. Each of these monographs is notable for contrasting the presocialist era with current socialist realities. This framework allows us to gauge more accurately the possibilites and processes of the linear socialist transformation and/or, conversely, the cyclical time dimension of peasant cultural continuity.

Lockwood's monograph (127) is also distinctive in its focus on peasant market relationships among multiethnic populations, taking as his point of departure a Moslem community. Migration, tourism, and associated socioeconomic changes in a community on the Dalmatian coast are dealt with in a monograph and related publications by B. C. Bennett (10–12).

Citing individual volumes does not, of course, exhaust the number of research projects, most of them doctoral dissertations, which have focused on individual rural communities. These investigations have been published as articles focusing on a variety of topics apart from community description (2, 4, 26, 103, 113, 146, 154, 155, 173, 193, 194).

Discussion of East European community studies is incomplete without mention of some significant works by East European scholars available in English translation. In particular, Fel & Hofer's "Proper Peasants: Traditional

Life in a Hungarian Village" (46; see also 47, 99) stands out as a milestone of "thick" cultural description.

Kinship and Social Structure

Although the situation has changed during the last decade with increasing publication on Hungary, Poland, and especially Romania, the predominant role of Yugoslav based research is nowhere more apparent than in the study of family and kinship. Historically, the study of the zadruga has been a main focus of research. Some of the writings of East European ethnologists, notably Yugoslavs, have recently appeared in English. Prominent is an edited post-humous monograph on the work of the Serb Milenko Filipovic (48).

In addition to writing on the zadruga, he also dealt with various forms of lineage organization, symbolic adoption, marriage, divorce, and on property communal to social groups and functions of reciprocity. His objective was to explain in historical terms the social structures that he observed. In describing domestic units, he was particularly interested in nonkinship links and spatially separate residences. One of his most interesting articles deals with women as leaders of kin units (48). A general view of the extended family in Southeast Europe is given by his Croatian colleague Milovan Gavazzi (49). A parallel article by Gunda (52) deals with Hungary. These writings make no specific reference to any of the works enumerated below. Their value may be perceived from an emic perspective unlike the analytically etic articles of Hofer. A unique contribution combines the experience of growing up in a Hercegovinian upland community with the perspective of an American historian (209). Similar autobiographical data is found in Byrnes (21). Unique in its comparative approach to Balkan data is Stahl's article on the household domestic group (199).

Beginning in the 1960s, Hammel and his students Denich, Lockwood, and Simic have worked among Orthodox and Moslem populations in Yugoslavia (80, 81, 86, 88, 89, 92, 93; (40, 123, 124, 192). Taken together with the Halperns' work in Serbia, this has meant that other regions have been studied comparatively little.

Outside Serbia, Baric's writings on Catholic Croatia deal with instrumental uses of village kin ties in the process of modernizations (2, 3). Rheubottom's work on Orthodox Macedonia is concerned with ritual observances, dowry, and the zadruga as they relate to community-based social structures (158–160). Publications on Slovenia (143, 144, 216) emphasize the nuclear family, while Vincze (208b,c) deals with kin terminology among Magyar Romanians.

The sole monograph dealing with kinship is Hammel's (79), analyzing godparenthood as a component of a system of social exchange and detailing the functioning of South Slavic kinship systems, with discussions of household organization, marital patterns, and lineage groups.

Another aspect of Hammel's work is historical demography (85); he takes the social structural typology of the zadruga and transforms it into a methodological framework for understanding process in household cycles, using (Ottoman) census documents in place of field data. Writing on the same topic, Halpern (63), using historic (1863) records from the Serbian community he studied, makes the point that while the extended family was the ideal prototype, many individuals passed at least part of their lives in nuclear or small family households.

The appearance of these articles in a volume also dealing with Western Europe, North America, and Japan is significant in that the East European data is considered analytically in a worldwide comparative context. While the precise categories used in demographic analysis facilitate comparison, it is nevertheless important to stress that the publication of East European anthropological data has seldom been part of an explicit comparative framework, although there is a descriptive comparison for the Balkans (199).

Hammel and Halpern continue to publish results of their historical demographic work. Hammel uses a variety of Yugoslav census records, including medieval data (87, 89–91), while Halpern focuses on records from a Serbian village (65, 67, 70, 77). They have also published jointly, combining the results of field research and computer processing of nineteenth century archival data (72). They find that the zadruga represents a social unit which is flexible and adaptive, suited to rapid geographic expansion and exploitation of land resources but also to quick dispersal and reassembling under trying political situations. Some of these processes were explored previously by Hammel (80, 81, 93, 94). The methodological problems encountered in the use of oral and census data for reconstructing past social structures are set forth by Wagner (211), demonstrating that Serbian oral genealogies only recount males who left descendants, but not others present in archival census lists.

Both the zadruga and lineage are core social structures among the South Slavs. In a joint article, Hammel & Soc (92) develop the concept of lineage density based on demographic, economic, and cultural factors. Simic (182) discusses the role of blood feuds. In an analysis of lineage structure in Albania, Whitaker (213, 214) deals with kin units in prewar politics and the extended family within larger patrilineal units. Grossmith's research on contemporary ethnic Albanian rural households in Macedonia (50) describes units of approximately the same size as those recorded a century ago for Serbia but with a structure corresponding to a culture where fertillity has remained high. Social conflict in an isolated Macedonia village, since abandoned, was dealt with by Balikci (1).

The greatest shift in social relationships has occured as a result of the postwar processes of urbanization and industrialization. Hammel (83), using survey and interview data from modern Belgrade, shows interrelationships between structural alignment of traditional Serbian kinship and the more individualized affective relationships between parents and children. Another monographic study (82) considers a number of variables influencing mobility within the cyclical nature of Yugoslav industrial growth.

The role of corporate kin groups in coping with modernization processes is examined in Simic's volume on Belgrade (184) and in a number of supporting articles (185–187). The relationships between networks of rural-urban kin-linked reciprocity is examined against the development of new urban social networks based on shared interests and experience. Simic's focus on problems of aging is unique, placing it in comparison with similar problems among South Slav migrants in the United States (188, 190).

Sex roles have been studied extensively for Yugoslavia. Hammel (78) points out that the romantic aspects of marriage have not been emphasized, and that spouses are not regarded as kin. Affinal ties in a Moslem setting are dealt with by Lockwood (126), with bride theft a flexible and manipulative mechanism for forming household alliances.

Denich (36, 37, 40) has been concerned with the general role of women in society and less with the specifics of family and kinship relations. She has focused on the ramifying consequences of the concentration of property, residence, and descent in the male line which minimizes the formal structural role of women. However, her research on migrants to an industrializing town in Serbia reveals that there is now an equivalence of parental aspirations for sons and daughters. This is radically different from the past where girls were enculturated in dependence on the economic base provided by male-dominated kin units. Through contemporary employment she sees women gaining an autonomy as individuals.

For Albania, Whitaker notes parallel perceptions about women (215). Doubtless there have been equally dramatic changes here too. These are found fragmentarily in travel accounts, but there are no postwar scholarly studies by Westerners.

A comparative study of changing marital relationships in five different cultural areas of Yugoslavia presents the results of survey research undertaken in the early 1960s. While all regions have changed, the agnatic ideology was still strongly apparent in the southern and eastern regions (74).

Oral Tradition, Ritual, and Symbolism

Research on values and expressive behavior can be complimentary to socioeconomic studies, but these researches can also proceed on separate paths. Both the integration and separation can be seen in the two long-term studies of individual communities by Fels and Hofer in Hungary and Halpern and Kerewsky-Halpern in Serbia.

Much of the literature on these themes has appeared in journals within the last 5 years (19, 42, 108, 109, 111, 144, 166). It should be mentioned, however, that Hungarian scholars have considered related problems (51, 100). To date there are two monographs (117, 143). Kligman's study of the Romanian Whitsuntide ritual goes beyond the description of folklore performance in the context of contemporary secularization in a socialist state. She provides insights into ritual behavior and folk healing in a sociolinguistic framework in which silence and secrecy are potent communicators. In a symbolic analysis of a Macedonian winter solstice ritual, Sachs (166) considers how men are transformed into metaphoric women, reflecting honor/shame polarities. The prewar research of Obrebski (148) approaches sex roles in a Macedonian village in terms of secular and sacred performances.

Using psycholinguistic and sociolinguistic analyses, Kerewsky-Halpern & Foley (111) explicate oral charms in Serbian folk healing. A related article deals with lament as catharsis (109). For Macedonia, Rheubottom (158) writes of the household patron saint, emphasizing the symbols of openness, peace, and community.

Minnich (143, 144) considers the practice of pigsticking in Slovenia for defining local community and regional identity. In contrast to those who employ a political-economic approach, he refers only briefly to the local modern hog farm which provides employment for many villagers. He views identity as based in a peasant society which devolves on assocation with a way of life, grounded in the farmstead, subsistence farming, and the nuclear family. His analysis of ritual provides a link to the community study approach.

Both social structural and political economic approaches are reflected in the volume on Political Rituals and Symbolism in Socialist Eastern Europe. Included are contributions on all countries in the area except Albania and Hungary [Bulgaria (181), Czechoslovakia (164), Poland (22), Romania (116, 118), and Yugoslvaia (43, 206)]. Each article discusses a particular ritual activity or symbolic domain illustrating how presocialist forms have been incorporated into socialist realities or how new, specifically socialist rituals are transformed by the unique cultural features of the communities in which they are practiced.

Oral performance is the theme in the work of Dubinskas (42) and Kerewsky-Halpern (108). The former is concerned with the dynamics of a contemporary folkore performance group, and the latter deals with male recollections of lineages as personal history and as epic (75, 108, 112).

A relatively neglected category is life history and personal narrative. Davis (34) provides a biography of a Slovene laborer, and Y. Lockwood (134) describes a dramatic death as seen through individual narratives. The autobiographical reflections of a young Serbian woman who left her village to seek education in town is given by Halpern (66).

Salzmann's monograph on value orientation among Czechs and Slovaks (167) draws on the work of the Kluckhohns and relates to contemporary studies of ethnicity and nationalism. Emic perspectives on the pan-Mediterranean themes of honor and shame, especially as they apply to male behavior, are considered by Boehm (19). A decade earlier, Simic (183) compared the value patterns of males in the southern regions of Yugoslavia with styles of behavior in Mexico. In both areas there is a shared concern with respect to the role of face presented to the outside world. His concern with this approach has continued (191). A 1978 article explored values in commericalized folk music (189).

An anticipatory integration of these diverse perspectives to provide a view of a civilization was attempted by the social historian Stoianovich (204). Many of his conceptions do not stand close anthropological scrutiny, but the idea of combining perspectives in an integrative approach remains attractive.

World Systems and the Region

CLASS, ETHNICITY, AND EMPIRE   The study of regional ethnicity has long been a prominent feature of anthropological investigation. Until recently such analyses have focused on the symbolic and behavioral content of ethnicity in order to understand the dimensions of particular identities and the processes of boundary maintenance (80, 124, 127–129, 131, 157, 169, 171, 180, 204, 213). These studies have helped explain the historical persistence and intense sentiment associated with East European ethnicity and how these markers of identification developed out of collective religious consciousness. However, content analysis of ethnic identity alone does not provide a total explanation of the intensity of regional interethnic relations.

Recent works consider ethnicity as the medium for structuring political and economic relations. Therefore, ethnicity is considered complementary to class-based action in the East European historical process (5, 6, 28, 163, 205, 207-208a). In this way, the content and symbols of ethnicity, which comprise the universe of previous analyses, now become the means by which conflict over key resources is carried out.

This conception views East European ethnicity as a variable phenomenon, waxing and waning in response to other stimuli. Ethnicity is only one component in the individual's identity; whether it is mobilized depends on its utility compared to other accessible identity components. For example, McArthur's work among Transylvanian Saxons (141) shows, among other things, how Saxon identity is often emphasized as a strategy for emigration, paralleling the stress on Turkish identity among Serbo-Croatian speaking Moslems in Macedonia (64). For multiethnic Yugoslavia, ethnicity is seen as the rationale for regional development (62) and a basis for political struggle (133). Reining (157) writes of the demise of the German minority in Hungary, while Salzmann (171) has studied a Czech village in Romania.

Ethnicity has predominated in the East European cultural landscape at the expense of other markers of identity. It remains a source of conflict because it is often a chief factor in unresolved territorial issues. These grew out of the dissolution of empires and the formation of nation states based on ethnic identities but with spatially mixed multiethnic populations (e.g. Transylvania, Macedonia, Kosmet). The intensity of ethnic sentiment in the region also carries over into scholarship. On occasion, ethnic partisans have taken others to task for failing to support the claims of their particular reference group (163, 195).

A chief concern of current research is to explicate the intensity and persistence of ethnic sentiments as compared to others such as class. World systems theory provides the intellectual framework by which a number of contemporary researchers have addressed these questions. The region's incorporation as the hinterland of contending empires is seen as a primary source of intense ethnic identity and its resulting intergroup conflict (130, 205). Ethnic identity is not so easily neutralized even under the onslaught of socialism's class-based policies.

DEPENDENCY AND UNDERDEVELOPMENT   East Europe's experience as political-economic periphery not only promoted ethnic sentiment but, in corollary fashion, was also a chief factor in the region's underdevelopment. A number of works focus on the debilitating effects of the penetration of capital (23, 24, 119, 198, 212), while Verdery's recent volume (208a) is noteworthy for its linking ethnicity and underdevelopment in a "world systems" perspective. She shows how the differential integration of Transylvania into a shifting field of competing states and their dominant classes not only "underdeveloped" this multiethnic region but fostered particular kinds of interethnic relations and socioeconomic behaviors at the local and regional levels.

Chirot's and Stahl's work, also on Romania, describes how economic dependency sets in motion a chain of events which transform relations among state, peasantry, and nobility. It emasculated the indigenous state and fostered a stratum of dependent nobility living off an impoverished peasantry. Communal lands, their basis of subsistence, were alienated from them in varying degrees, facilitating the differentiation of the peasantry into separate and competitive economic strata.

The effects of economic dependency are not consistent throughout the region but are modified by cultural circumstances. For example, Mouzelis (145) discusses variations in peasant political action in Greece and Bulgaria in the interwar period. Its relative absence in Greece is traced to earlier and more intensive urban development, the growth of an indigenous merchant class, and large-scale overseas migration.

The overwhelming agrarian nature of all the East European nations except for Czechoslovakia, their lack of significant urbanization and industrialization, and the often impoverished circumstances of local peasantries formed the baseline for programs of centrally planned development begun after World War II (17, 27, 114, 115, 147, 154). The desire to overcome dependency-related structural problems thus contributed to the extraordinary comprehensive policies adopted by postwar socialist governments. Viewed from the perspective of the 1980s, the enormous external debt of many East European nations to Western banks is definitive evidence of the revival of economic dependency in the socialist epoch (146). As past dependency undermined the lives of East Europe's peoples, fostering rigid class structures, it threatens to do so today.

The Transformation of Peasant Society

Research on socioeconomic change in Eastern Europe falls into two general categories: the integration of rural communities with regional and national processes, in part through the transformation of peasant agrarian systems, and the complex of behaviors associated with industrialization, urbanization, and related patterns of labor migration.

PLANNED AGRARIAN CHANGE AND COLLECTIVIZATION   The nature of prewar East European peasant society grew directly from its agrarian mode of livelihood. As agriculture was the principal defining characteristic of peasant life, its transformation, represented chiefly by collectivization and state-subsidized farms and cooperatives, has engendered considerable research.

Certain works see state-planned agrarian change as the vehicle for rural economic growth. Class structures have been transformed (95, 178a, 193, 194) and living conditions improved by the economies of scale and the freeing of labor that agrarian modernization introduces (151). Still, the verdict on socialist agrarian systems and their ability to transform rural life is a mixed one.

Greater research effort has been focused on the interrelationships of local communities with processes of socialist agrarian change. Hollos's analysis of two Hungarian collectives (103) attempts to explain variations in the economic performance and degree of local acceptance of these organizations largely by reference to management styles. Kideckel's work in a lowland Transylvanian community details how local class structure and land use patterns force change in the implementation of national collectivization policy (115). He also discusses how the persisting strength of local household organization and attitudes toward technology are manifested in collective farm production organization (113). Bell (6a), Salzmann & Scheufler (172), and Hann (95) also detail the influence of local social and ecological factors on collective farm organization.

Investigation of the agrarian transformation is also directed to understanding its mutually influential relationship with peasant families and local social networks in Hungary (103a), in Romania (4, 26, 29, 155, 200), and in Poland

(146, 154). This work considers the implications of changing agrarian practices on family structure and division of labor. Collectivization and other features of socialist modernization are seen to provide a range of economic opportunites, access to which is assured by the elaboration of suitable domestic strategies. Although family structures may remain the same throughout the socialist transformation, their functions change in accordance with the availability of resources.

Further work on the socialist agrarian transformation is necessary. None of the studies currently available is cross-culturally comparative, though Maday & Hollos (140) offer such a perspective within Hungary itself. Comparative research would be particularly fruitful for analyzing the sources of similarity and variation in East European socialism, especially since agriculture in Poland and Yugoslavia has remained largely private.

INDUSTRIALIZATION, URBANIZATION AND THE PEASANT WORKER   As the agrarian transformation rationalized agricultural labor, workers were freed for participation in urban-industrial employment networks. Both ends of this process have been analyzed: changing occupational patterns and cultural styles in the rural communities (4, 60, 125), as well as rural migration to cities, urbanization, and the cultural circumstances of workers (34, 37, 39, 41, 58, 82, 84, 120, 120a, 138, 173–175, 184–187, 197). A related body of work specifically considers the migration patterns engendered by this transformation (12, 35, 64, 125).

Research on peasant workers is crucial for this region since the massive industrialization of the postwar period has made this a pervasive social category. Certain research centers on the behavioral variations between peasant workers and their more agriculturally oriented co-villagers (73). The consumption ethic of the peasant-worker is frequently noted (95), while Lockwood (125) points to the interesting anomaly that industrially oriented rural folk, generally the poorer segment of a village community, are often those with greater access to prestige goods.

Other researchers discuss the contradictory roles of the peasant-worker associated with their simultaneous participation in agrarian and industrial work. A chief drawback of this situation is that the excessive demands on such individuals may result in poor labor performance in both spheres of activity (57). Cole (29) stresses the benefits derived by industrializing states, such as those of Eastern Europe, when much of the industrial labor force continues to reside in rural areas and remains connected to the resources of an agrarian based network.

There is a reciprocal effect connected with these processes. Not only do urban influences change rural life, but peasant migrants have historically transformed urban life, resulting in the simultaneous urbanization of the village and peasantization of the town (37, 58, 101, 120a, 122, 185). Subsequent research has also analyzed the strategies adopted by rural migrants in urban areas. Simic's monograph (184) is notable for its analysis of the adaptiveness of peasant behaviors and institutions to cities through rural-urban networks.

A subsequent and different approach to urbanization is Sampson's work on Romania, focusing on the specifically socialist nature of the urbanization process by examining it as an aspect of centralized planning. While Simic and others tend to emphasize continuity in urbanization, Sampson stresses contradictions. Examining both a village as it develops into a small regional town (173, 175) and a major urban industrial center (174), Sampson depicts the conflicting nature of urbanization growing from the often divergent needs and interests of state planners, long-term residents, and recent in-migrants. Spangler (197), in his review of the literature on Yugoslav urbanization, also finds the process more stressful than previous researchers. The writings in the recent volume compiled by the Winners (220) probe the historical dimensions of East European urbanization.

Despite the sizable research effort on peasant-workers and urbanization, there are no systematic discussions of socialist industry from an anthropological perspective. This is a significant gap given the growth of industrial enterprises in the area. There are, however, certain topics on which there is useful initial research. The role of education in socialist society is faced with dual expectations: to provide the model of collective behavior necessary for the creation of socially conscious individuals (102), and to serve as the vehicle for the homogenization of class structure. Thus far educational results are ambiguous. In Romania we see the persistence of differences in educational access for various population segments and a definite process of tracking, albeit into socialist institutions (156).

Another lack in area research concerns elites, leadership, and sources of political legitimacy. One work available is Denich's analysis of local leadership in the Yugoslav civil war and socialist revolution (38). Recognizing the inability of the peasantry to organize a revolution by themselves, she analyzes the characteristics of a revolutionary urban elite which enabled them to attract and keep a sizable peasant following.

East European Communities Abroad

A recent focus in East Europeanist anthropology is on communities outside the region. As in cultural anthropology in general, this interest can be traced partially to the uncertainties of fieldwork abroad. This research does, however, provide an important comparative perspective on ethnic identities and their transformation in new cultural settings. Winner & Susel, in their edited volume (219), provide a variety of perspectives with a special focus on America. The contribution by Kutrzeba-Pojnarowa considers the rural exodus from Poland, providing a newer perspective on the interwar situation analyzed by Obrebski (147).

Degh's view of a Hungarian-Canadian community finds regional identities derived from the Old World stronger than a common Hungarian identification. Schuchat (179) describes pressures for assimilation in an urban setting, while Patterson has written on Romanian communities in Canada (152), considering processes of adaptation over four generations. Studies of Slovene communities in Cleveland (217–219) conclude that future Slovene ethnic persistence in the United States will be in a progressively more truncated form. L. Bennett (13–16) focuses on the ritual associated with the feast day of the family's patron saint among Serbian Americans as a form of continuing ethnic identification supplemented by association with Orthodox church parishes. Halley (53) writes about her Croatian and Serbian maternal kin from the Chicago area and considers the similarities between Old and New world structures, and the survival of ethnic values in visibly assimilated individuals. Padgett (149, 150) researched the Serbian community of Milwaukee and found it culturally homogeneous yet factionalized and facing a future of reduced and more permeable group boundaries; she found that the core values are religious orthodoxy, kinship, and nationalism.

Kerewsky-Halpern (110) examines continuity and change in Bulgarian-American oral traditions, giving examples of new forms for older speech events. Halpern (68) writes about the changing forms of identification among Bulgarian-Americans and correlates these changes with cycles of ethnic community development. Stein is concerned with kinship, life cycle, and ritual among Slovak Americans (201–203). Bloch (18) ties the experience of two worlds together, considering the changes in the role of women as they move from a village in Poland to an American community. *The Harvard Encyclopedia of American Ethnic Groups* (1980), utilizing anthropological perspectives, contains articles on all of the East European ethnic groups.

Research on the East European Hasidic religious community, survivors of the Holocaust, is summarized in a bibliographical survey by Burack (20). In addition to citing studies using semiotic, symbolic, and structural analyses, she discusses the role of photography as a research tool. Despite anthropologists' interest in ethnic conflict, the Holocaust has not been a topic for anthropological research.

Writing about the geographically contiguous community of Burgenland Croats in Austria, Lockwood (132) finds an increasing ethnic assertiveness reinforced by a growing sense of identification with the Croats of Yugoslavia. At the same time, he finds that eventual assimilation may be inevitable, occurring at about the same rate among socialist workers and conservative peasants.

Unlike research on Eastern Europe proper, studies of its immigrant populations deemphasize the political aspects of ethnic identity, concentrating on
processes of boundary maintenance, assimilation, variations in generational
behavior, and the interpenetration of cultural systems. This seems a natural
response to widely differing cultural conditions.

ON THE RELEVANCE OF EAST EUROPEANIST ANTHROPOLOGY

In this review of the literature we have tried to comprehensively view the
diverse interests of the increasingly numerous researchers in the field. We are
encouraged by the expansion of interest in the region and the growing delineation of Eastern Europe as a legitimate category of anthropological inquiry. In
addition, the quality of methods and the range of themes expressed in the
literature are significant both for the understanding of East European cultural
systems and for a general sociocultural anthropology.

Methodologically, the exchange of views with indigenous scholars (e.g. 25)
and publication by East European scholars in Western journals (Bicanic,
Filipovic, Gavazzi, Gunda, Hofer, Kutrzeba-Pojnarowa, Markus, and H.
Stahl) tends to distinguish East Europeanist anthropology from studies of other
culture areas where anthropology sets itself apart from those people studied.
The existence of journals such as *Collegium Antropologicum,* published in
English in Zagreb, while focusing on physical anthropology does contain
articles of sociocultural interest. Some are colloborative between Eastern
European and Western researchers (165).

Thematically, the transformation of East European society has provided a
laboratory for the study of rapid and directed social change succeeding conditions of extreme underdevelopment. These circumstances are being duplicated
in the developing world.

Despite the growing body of literature, we are nonetheless concerned about
the limited impact of East European materials on general anthropology. This is
not without reason. As stated earlier, the relative absence of regionally and
cross-culturally comparative analyses is particularly inhibiting. The field also
lacks general theoretical perspectives and integrative works.

While the political economic perspective has proved useful, local, regional,
and national foci still dominate, as do the research agendas of particular
scholars. One of us has been working in this field for over 30 years. During this
time it has been possible to see a universe of cultural problems within the
confines of a single village community (112). But the needs of the field of East
European studies clearly are not identical with individual research priorities.

Groups of scholars share theoretical and methodological approaches. There
are growing numbers of edited volumes of collections on particular topics,

including contributions by East European scholars, but articulated sets of questions for the region as a whole remain to be developed. If there is to be a viable East Europeanist anthropology, there needs to be integrating perspectives consistently addressed on multinational, regional, and cross-culturally comparative levels. Perhaps the pressure of regional identities is too strong for East Europeanist anthropologists who have gone native and become Balkanized in the process.

ACKNOWLEDGMENTS

This essay has benefited from the cooperation of many East Europeanists. We wish to thank especially Linda Bennett, Barbara Kerewsky-Halpern, William Lockwood, Bela Maday, Steven Sampson, Andrei Simic, and Richard A. Wagner.

Literature Cited

1. Balikci, A. 1962. Quarrels in a Balkan village. *Am. Anthropol.* 64:328–39
2. Baric, L. 1967. Traditional groups and new economic opportunities in rural Yugoslavia. In *Themes in Anthropology,* ed. R. Firth, pp. 253–78. A.S.A. Monogr. No. 6. London: Tavistock
3. Baric, L. 1967. Levels of change in Yugoslav kinship. In *Social Organization: Essays Presented to Raymond Firth,* ed. M. Freeman, pp. 1–24. Chicago: Aldine
4. Beck, S. 1976. The emergence of the peasant worker in a Transylvanian mountain community. *Dialect. Anthropol.* 1(4):365–75
5. Beck, S., Cole, J. W., eds. 1981. Ethnicity and nationalism in Southeastern Europe. *Papers on European and Mediterranean Societies, No, 14.* Amsterdam: Univ. Amsterdam, Antropol.-Sociol. Cent.
6. Beck, S., McArthur, M. 1981. Romania: Ethnicity, nationalism, and development. See Ref. 5, pp. 29–69
6a. Bell, P. D. 1983. *Peasants in Socialist Transition: Life in a Collectivized Hungarian Village.* Berkeley: Univ. Calif. Press. In press
7. Benedict, R. 1953. History as it appears to Rumanians. In *The Study of Culture at a Distance,* ed. M. Mead, R. Metraux, pp. 415–15. Chicago: Univ. Chicago Press
8. Benedict, R. 1972. Rumanian culture and behavior (Nov. 1943). Reissued by Anthropology Club, *Occas. Pap. Anthropol. No. 1.* Fort Collins: Colo. State Univ.
9. Benet, S. 1952. *Song, Dance and Customs of Peasant Poland.* New York: Roy
10. Bennett, B. C. 1974. *Sutivan: A Dalmatian Village in Social and Economic Transition.* San Francisco: R & E Res. Assoc.
11. Bennett, B. C. 1979. Peasants, businessmen, and directions for socioeconomic change in rural coastal Dalmatia, Yugoslavia. *Balkanistica* 5:181–94
12. Bennett, B. C. 1979. Migration and rural community viability in Central Dalmatia (Croatia) Yugoslavia. *Pap. Anthropol. Univ. Okla. 20 (1)*
13. Bennett, L. A. 1978. Incentives and constraints on ethnic language maintenance. In *Anthropology at American, Essays in Honor of Katherine Spencer Halpern.* Occas. Pap. No. 1, Anthropol. Dept., American Univ., pp. 5–13
14. Bennett, L. A. 1978. *Personal Choice in Ethnic Identity Maintenance: Serbs, Croats, and Slovenes in Washington, D.C.* Palo Alto, Calif: Ragusan
15. Bennett, L. A. 1981. Nationality and religion in Serbian-American ethnicity. In *Anthropological Careers: Perspectives on Research, Employment, and Training,* ed. R. Landman, pp. 99–109. Washington DC: Anthropol. Soc. Washington
16. Bennett, L. A. 1981. Washington and its Serbian emigres: A distinctive blend. *Anthropol. Q.* 54:82–88
17. Bicanic, R. 1981. How the people live: Peasant life in Southwestern Croatia, Bosnia, and Hercegovina; Yugoslavia in 1935, ed. J. M. Halpern, E. M. Despala-

tovic. *Res. Rep. 21, Dep. Anthropol.* Amherst: Univ. Mass.

18. Bloch, H. 1976. Changing domestic roles among Polish immigrant women. *Anthropol. Q.* 49(1):3–10

19. Boehm, C. 1980. Exposing the moral self in Montenegro: The use of natural definitions to keep ethnography descriptive. *Am. Ethnol.* 7(1):1–26

20. Burack, L. 1979. Hasidism: A selected annotated bibliography of articles of ethnographic interest (1966–1975). *Jew. Folklore Ethnol. Newsl.* 2(2–3):13–21

21. Byrnes, R. F., ed. 1976. *Communal Families in the Balkans: The Zadruga. Essays by Philip E. Mosley and Essays in His Honor.* Notre Dame, Ind: Univ. Notre Dame Press

22. Chase, C. 1983. Food shortage symbolism in socialist Poland. *Anthropol. Q.* 56(2):76–82

23. Chirot, D. 1976. *Social Change in a Peripheral Society: The Making of a Balkan Colony, Wallachia,* New York: Academic

24. Chirot, D. 1980. The corporatist model and socialism: Notes on Romanian development. *Theory Soc.* 9:363–81

25. Cobianu-Bacanu, M. 1977. A Romanian-American dialogue. *Dialect. Anthropol.* 2(4):301–8

26. Cole, J. W. 1976. Fieldwork in Romania: Introduction. *Dialect. Anthropol.* 1(3): 239–50

27. Cole, J. W. 1976. Familial dynamics in a Romanian worker village. *Dialect. Anthropol.* 1(3):251–66

28. Cole, J. W. 1981. Ethnicity and the rise of Nationalism. See Ref. 5, pp. 105–34

29. Cole, J. W. 1981. Family, farm and factory: Rural workers in contemporary Romania. In *Romania in the 1980's,* ed. D. N. Nelson, pp. 71–116. Boulder, Colo: Westview

30. Cole, J. W. 1981. Studies in the political economy of peripheral Europe. *Dialect. Anthropol.* 6(1):81–101

31. Cole, J. W. 1982. East European anthropology as "Anthropology." *Newsl. East. Eur. Anthropol. Group* 1(2):1–2

32. Cole, J. W. 1982. East European anthropology as area studies. *Newsl. East Eur. Anthropol. Group* 2(1):2–4

33. Coon, C. 1950. Mountains of giants: A racial and cultural study of the North Albian Mountain Ghegs. *Pap. Peabody Mus. Am. Archaeol. Ethnol., Harvard Univ.* Vol. 23, No. 3

34. Davis, J. C. 1976. A Slovene laborer and his experience of industrialization. *East Eur. Q.* 10(1):2–20

35. Denich, B. 1970. Migration and network manipulation in Yugoslavia. In *Migra-*

tion and Anthropology,* ed. R. Spencer, pp. 133–48. Seattle: Univ. Wash. Press

36. Denich, B. 1974. Sex and power in the Balkans. In *Women, Culture, and Society,* ed. M. Rosaldo, L. Lamphere, pp. 243–62. Stanford: Stanford Univ. Press

37. Denich, B. 1974. Why do peasants urbanize? A Yugoslav case study. In *City and Peasant: A Study in Socio-Cultural Dynamics,* ed. A. L. LaRuffa et al, pp. 546–59. New York: NY Acad. Sci.

38. Denich, B. 1976. Sources of leadership in the Yugoslav Revolution: A local level study. *Comp. Stud. Soc. Hist.* 18:64–84

39. Denich, B. 1976. Urbanization and women's roles in Yugoslavia. *Anthropol. Q.* 49(1):11–19

40. Denich, B. 1977. Women, work and power in modern Yugoslavia. In *Sexual Stratification: A Cross-Cultural View,* ed. A. Schlegal. New York: Columbia Univ. Press

41. Denich, B. 1978. Yugoslavia: The social side of Socialism. *Hum. Nature* 1(5):30–39

42. Dubinskas, F. A. 1981. Ritual on stage: Folkloric performance as symbolic action. In *Folklore and Oral Communication,* ed. J. Bezic et al. Special issue of Narodna Umjetnost. Zagreb: Inst. Folklore Res.

43. Dubinskas, F. A. 1983. Leaders and followers: Cultural pattern and political symbolism in Yugoslavia. *Anthropol. Q.* 56(2):95–99

44. Ehrlich, V. S. 1966. *The Family in Transition: A Study of 300 Yugoslav Villages.* Princeton: Princeton Univ. Press

45. Ehrlich, V. S. 1983. Historical awareness and the peasant. In *The Peasant and the City in Eastern Europe,* ed. I. P. Winner, T. G. Winner, pp. 99–109. Cambridge: Schenkman

46. Fel, E., Hofer, T. 1969. Proper peasants: Traditional life in a Hungarian village. *Viking Fund Publ. Anthropol.* 46

47. Fel, E., Hofer, T. 1973. Tanyakert-s, patron-client relations and political factions in Atany. *Am. Anthropol.* 75:787–801

48. Filipovic, M. 1982. *Among the People, Selected Writings,* ed. E. A. Hammel et al. Papers in Slavic Philology 3, Dep. Slavic Lang. Ann Arbor: Univ. Mich.

48a. Gaffney, C. C. 1979. Kisker: The economic success of a peasant village in Yugoslavia. *Ethnology* 18:135–51

49. Gavazzi, M. 1982. The extended family in southeastern Europe. *J. Fam. Hist.* 7(2):89–102

50. Grossmith, C. J. 1976. The cultural ecology of Albanian extended family house-

holds in Yugoslav Macedonia. See Ref. 21, pp. 232–43

51. Gunda, B. 1947. Work and cult among the Hungarian peasants. *Southwest. J. Anthropol.* 3(1):147–63

52. Gunda, B. 1982. The ethno-sociological structure of the Hungarian extended family. *J. Fam. Hist.* 7(1):40–51

53. Halley, L. 1980. Old country survivals in the new: An essay on some aspects of Yugoslav family structure and dynamics. *J. Psychol. Anthropol.* 3:119–41

54. Halpern, J. M. 1956. *Social and Cultural Change in a Serbian Village.* New Haven: Hum. Relat. Area Files

55. Halpern, J. M. 1961. Culture change in Laos and Serbia: Possible tendencies toward universal organizational patterns. *Hum. Organ.* 20(3):11–14

56. Halpern, J. M. 1961. The economies of Lao and Serb peasants: A contrast in cultural values. *Southwest. J. Anthropol.* 17(2):165–77

57. Halpern, J. M. 1963. Yugoslav peasant society in transition—stability in change. *Anthropol. Q.* 36(3):136–82

58. Halpern, J. M. 1965. Peasant culture and urbanization in Yugoslavia. *Hum. Organ.* 24:162–74

59. Halpern, J. M. 1967. *A Serbian Village.* New York: Harper & Row

60. Halpern, J. M. 1967. Farming as a way of life: Yugoslav peasant attitudes. In *Soviet and East European Agriculture,* ed. J. Karcz, pp. 356–81. Berkeley, Univ. Calif. Press

61. Halpern, J. M. 1969. Bibliography of English language sources on Yugoslavia. *Res. Rep. No. 3.* Amherst: Univ. Mass. Dep. Anthropol.

62. Halpern, J. M. 1969. Yugoslavia: Modernization in an ethnically diverse state. In *Contemporary Yugoslavia,* ed. W. S. Vucinich, pp. 316–50. Berkeley: Univ. Calif. Press

63. Halpern, J. M. 1972. Town and countryside in Serbia in the nineteenth century; social and household structure as reflected in the census of 1863. In *Household and Family in Past Time,* ed. P. Laslett, R. Wall, pp. 401–27. Cambridge Univ. Press

64. Halpern, J. M. 1975. Some perspectives on Balkan migration patterns (with particular reference to Yugoslavia). In *Migration and Urbanization, Modes and Adaptive Strategies,* ed. B. du Toit, H. Safa, pp. 77–115. Chicago: Aldine

65. Halpern, J. M. 1977. Individual life cycles and family cycles. In *The Family Life Cycle in European Societies,* ed. J. Cuisenier, pp. 353–80. The Hague: Mouton

66. Halpern, J. M. 1980. Memories of recent change: Some East European perspectives. In *The Process of Rural Transformation: Eastern Europe, Latin American and Australia,* ed. I. Volgyes et al, pp. 242–68. White Plains: Pergamon

67. Halpern, J. M. 1981. Demographic and social change in the village of Orasac: A perspective over two centuries. *Serbian Stud.* 1(3):51–70

68. Halpern, J. M. 1982. The Bulgarian-Americans, retrospect and prospect. In *Culture and History of the Bulgarian People, Their Bulgarian and American Parallels,* ed. W. W. Kolar, pp. 121–37. Pittsburgh: Duquesne Univ. Tamburitzans, Inst. Folk Arts

69. Halpern, J. M. 1982. A past in our future—some reflections. *East Eur. Anthropol. Group Newsl.* 1(2):4–7

70. Halpern, J. M., Anderson, D. 1970. The Zadruga, a century of change. *Anthropologica* (NS) 12(1):83–97

71. Halpern, J. M., Hammel, E. A. 1969. Observations on the intellectual history of ethnology and other social sciences in Yugoslavia. *Comp. Stud. Soc. Hist.* 11(1):17–26

72. Halpern, J. M., Hammel, E. A. 1977. Serbian society in Karadjordje's Serbia. *Univ. Mass. Pap. Anthropol.* 17:1–36

73. Halpern, J. M., Halpern, B. K. 1972. *A Serbian Village in Historical Perspective.* New York: Holt, Rinehart & Winston

74. Halpern, J. M., Halpern, B. K. 1979. Changing perceptions of roles as husbands and wives in five Yugoslav villages. In *Europe as a Culture Area,* ed. J. Cuisenier, pp. 159–72. Chicago: Aldine

75. Halpern, J. M., Halpern, B. K. 1980. *Yugoslav Oral Genealogies and Offical Records: An Approach to their Combined Use,* Vol. 7, Ser. 526, pp. 175–204. Salt Lake City: World Conf. Records

76. Halpern, J. M., Wagner, R. A. 1980. Anthropological and sociological research on the Balkans during the past decade. *Balkanistica* 4 (1988–78):13–62

77. Halpern, J. M., Wagner, R. A. 1982. Microstudies in Yugoslav (Serbian) social structure and demography. *Program Sov. East Eur. Stud. Occas. Pap. No. 8.* Amherst: Univ. Mass.

78. Hammel, E. A. 1967. The Jewish mother in Serbia, or les structures alimentaires de la parente. See Ref. 123, pp. 55–62

79. Hammel, E. A. 1968. *Alternative Social Structures and Ritual Relations in the Balkans.* Englewood Cliffs: Prentice Hall

80. Hammel, E. A. 1969. The "Balkan" peasant: A view from Serbia. In *Peasants in the Modern World,* ed. P. K. Bock, pp.

75–98. Albuquerque: Univ. N. Mex. Press

81. Hammel, E. A. 1969. Economic change, social mobility and kinship in Serbia. *Southwest. J. Anthropol.* 25:188–97

82. Hammel, E. A. 1969. *The Pink Yo-Yo: Occupational Mobility in Belgrade, ca. 1915–1965.* Berkeley: Univ. Calif. Inst. Int. Stud.

83. Hammel, E. A. 1969. Structure and sentiment in Serbian cousinship. *Am. Anthropol.* 71:285–93

84. Hammel, E. A. 1970. The ethnographer's dilemma: Alternative models of occupational prestige in Belgrade. *Man* 5:265–70

85. Hammel, E. A. 1972. The Zadruga as process. See Ref. 63, pp. 335–73

86. Hammel, E. A. 1974. Preference and recall in Serbian cousinship: Power and kinship ideology. *J. Anthropol. Res.* 30:95–115

87. Hammel, E. A. 1976. Some medieval evidence on the Serbian Zadruga: A preliminary analysis of the Chrysobulls of Decani. *Rev. Etudes Sud-Est Eur.* 14: 449–63

88. Hammel, E. A. 1977. The influence of social and geographic mobility on the stability of kinship systems: The Serbian case. In *Internal Migration, A Comparative Perspective,* ed. A. Brown, E. Neuberger, pp. 401–15. New York: Academic

89. Hammel, E. A. 1977. Reflections on the Zadruga. *Ethnol. Slav.* 8:141–51

90. Hammel, E. A. 1978. The income of Hilandar: A statistical explanation. In *Statistical Studies of Historical Social Structure,* ed. K. Wachter, P. Laslett, E. Hammel, pp. 449–63. New York: Academic

91. Hammel, E. A. 1980. Household structure in 14th century Macedonia. *J. Fam. Hist.* 5:242–73

92. Hammel, E. A., Soc, D. 1973. The lineage cycle in southern and eastern Yugoslavia. *Am. Anthropol* 75:802–13

93. Hammel, E. A., Yarbrough, C. 1973. Social mobility and the durability of family ties. *J. Anthropol. Res.* 29:145–63

94. Hammel, E. A., Yarbrough, C. 1974. Preference and recall in Serbian cousinship: Power and kinship ideology. *J. Anthropol. Res.* 30:95–115

95. Hann, C. M. 1980. *Tazlar: A Village in Hungary.* Cambridge: Cambridge Univ. Press

96. Hasluck, M. M. 1954. *The Unwritten Law in Albania.* Cambridge: Cambridge Univ. Press

97. Hofer, T. 1968. Anthropologists and native ethnographers in central European villages: Comparative notes on the professional personality of two disciplines. *Curr. Anthropol.* 9(4):311–15

98. Hofer, T. 1970. Anthropologists and native ethnographers at work in central European villages. *Anthropologica* 7(1):5–22

99. Hofer, T. 1979. Hungarian ethnographers in a Hungarian village. In *Long-Term Field Research in Social Anthropology,* ed. G. M. Foster, pp. 85–101. New York: Academic

100. Hofer, T. 1980. The creation of ethnic symbols from the elements of peasant culture. In *Ethnic Diversity and Conflict in Eastern Europe,* ed. P. Sugar, pp. 101–45. Santa Barbara: ABC-Clio Press

101. Hofer, T. 1983. Peasant culture and urban culture in the period of modernization: Delineation of a problem area based on data from Hungary. See Ref. 220, pp. 111–28

102. Hollos, M. 1980. Collective education in Hungary: The development of competitive, cooperative and role taking behavior. *Ethos* 8(1):3–24

103. Hollos, M. 1982. Ideology and economics: Cooperative organization and attitudes toward collectivization in two Hungarian communities. *Dialect. Anthropol.* 7(2):165–83

103a. Hollos, M. 1983. The effect of collectivization on village social organization in Hungary. *East Eur. Q.* 17(1):57–65

104. Horecky, P. L. 1969. *East Central Europe, A Guide to Basic Publications.* Chicago: Univ. Chicago Press

105. Horecky, P. L. 1969. *Southeast Europe, A Guide to Basic Publications.* Chicago: Univ. Chicago Press

106. Howell, D. R. 1975. *Hungarian Ethnography: A Bibliography of English Language Sources.* Hungarian Ref. Shelf, Vol. 1, Hungarian Res. Cent., Am. Hungarian Found.

107. Jensen, J. H. 1968. The changing Balkan family. *Natl. Arch. Ethnogr.* (Leiden) 51:20–48

108. Kerewsky-Halpern, B. 1981. Genealogy as genre in rural Serbia. In *Oral Traditional Literatures (Festschrift in Honor of Albert B. Lord),* ed. J. Foley, pp. 301–21. Columbus: Slavica Publ.

109. Kerewsky-Halpern, B. 1981. Text and context in ritual lament. *Can.-Am. Slavic Stud.* 15(1):52–60

110. Kerewsky-Halpern, B. 1982. Bulgarian oral tradition: Context, continuity and change. In *Culture History of the Bulgarian People, Their Bulgarian and American Parallels,* ed. W. W. Kolar, pp.

511–61. Pittsburgh: Duquesne Univ. Tamburitzan Inst. Folk Arts

111. Kerewsky-Halpern, B., Foley, J. M. 1978. The power of the word: Healing charms as an oral genre. *J. Am. Folklore* 91(362):903–24

112. Kerewsky-Halpern, B., Halpern, J. M., eds. 1977. Selected papers on a Serbian village: Social structure as reflected by history, demography, and oral tradition. *Univ. Mass. Dep. Anthropol. Res. Rep. 17*

113. Kideckel, D. A. 1976. The social organization of production on a Romanian cooperative farm. *Dialect. Anthropol.* 1(3):267–76

114. Kideckel, D. A. 1977. The dialectic of rural development: Cooperative farm goals and family strategies in a Romanian commune. *J. Rural Coop.* 5(1):43–62

115. Kideckel, D. A. 1982. The socialist transformation of agriculture in a Romanian commune, 1945–62. *Am. Ethnol.* 9(2):320–40

116. Kideckel, D. A. 1983. Secular ritual and social change: A Romanian case. *Anthropol. Q.* 56(2):69–75

117. Kligman, G. 1981. *Calus, Symbolic Transformation in Romanian Ritual.* Chicago: Univ. Chicago Press

118. Kligman, G. 1983. Poetry as politics in a Transylvania village. *Anthropol. Q.* 56(2):83–89

119. Krader, L. 1960. Transition from serf to peasant in Eastern Europe. *Anthropol. Q.* 33(1):76–90

120. Kremensek, S. 1979. Suburban villagers—A Slovenian case study, ed. J. M. Halpern. *Program Sov. East Eur. Stud. Occas. Pap. No. 2.* Amherst: Univ. Mass.

120a. Kremensek, S. 1983. On the fringe of the town. In *Urban Life in Mediterranean Europe: Anthropological Perspectives,* ed. M. Kenny, D. Kertzer, pp. 282–98. Urbana: Univ. Ill. Press

121. Kutrzeba-Pojnarowa, A. 1982. The traditions, present state, and tasks of ethnographic science in the Polish Peoples Republic. *Sov. Anthropol. Archeol.,* pp. 3–40

122. Kutrzeba-Pojnarowa, A. 1983. The influence of the history of peasantry on the model of the traditional peasant culture and its transformations. See Ref. 220, pp. 85–98

123. Lockwood, W. G., ed. 1967. *Essays in Balkan Ethnology. Kroeber Soc. Spec. Publ. No. 1.* Berkeley: Univ. Calif. Dep. Anthropol.

124. Lockwood, W. G. 1972. Converts and consanguinity: The social organization of Moslem Slavs in western Bosnia. *Ethnology* 11:55–79

125. Lockwood, W. G. 1973. The peasant-worker in Yugoslavia. *Stud. Eur. Soc.* 1:91–110

126. Lockwood, W. G. 1974. Bride theft and social maneuverability in western Bosnia. *Anthropol. Q.* 47:253–69

127. Lockwood, W. G. 1975. *European Moslems: Ethnicity and Economy in Western Bosnia.* New York: Academic

128. Lockwood, W. G. 1975. Social status and cultural change in a Bosnian Moslem village. *East Eur. Q.* 9:123–24

129. Lockwood, W. G. 1978. Albanian, Bosnian, Gypsies. In *Muslim Peoples: A World Ethnographic Survey,* ed. R. V. Weekes, pp. 19–22, 111–14, 147–50. Westport, CT: Greenwood

130. Lockwood, W. G. 1979. Living legacy of the Ottoman Empire: the Serbo-Croatian speaking Moslems of Bosnia-Hercegovina. In *The Mutual Effects of the Islamic and Judeo-Christian Worlds: The East European Pattern,* ed. A. Ascher, T. Halasi-Kun, B. K. Kiraly, pp. 209–25. New York: Columbia Univ. Press

131. Lockwood, W. G. 1981. Religion and language as critieria of ethnic identity: An exploratory comparison. See Ref. 5, pp. 71–82

132. Lockwood, W. G. 1983. The economic, political and cultural integration of an Eastern Eueropean minority in Western Europe: The Burgenland Croats. In *East European Ethnicity Outside of Eastern Europe,* ed. I. P. Winner, R. Susel. Cambridge: Schenkman

133. Lockwood, W. G., Donia, R. 1978. The Bosnian Muslims: Class, ethnicity, and political behavior in a European state. In *Muslim-Christian Conflicts: Economic, Political, and Social Origins,* ed. S. Joseph, B. L. K. Pilsbury, pp. 185–207. Boulder, Colo: Westview

134. Lockwood, Y. R. 1977. Death of a priest: The folk history of a local event as told in personal experience narratives. *J. Folklore Inst.* 14(1–2):97–113

135. Maday, B. C. 1968. Hungarian anthropology: The problem of communication. *Curr. Anthropol.* 9(2–3):180–84

136. Maday, B. C. 1970. Foreward. Anthropology in East-Central and Southeast Europe. *East Eur. Q.* 4(3):237–41

137. Maday, B. C. 1970. Hungarian anthropology. *Curr. Anthropol.* 11(1):61–65

138. Maday, B. C. 1974. Peasant culture and urbanization in Hungary. In *City and Peasant: A Study in Sociocultural Dynamics,* ed. A. L. La Ruffa et al. *Ann. NY Acad. Sci.* 220:560–68

139. Maday, B. C. 1980. Hungarian ethnography, American anthropology. In *The Folk Arts of Hungary*, ed. W. W. Kolar, pp. 162–70. Pittsburgh: Duquesne Univ. Tamburitzans, Inst. Folk Arts

140. Maday, B. C., Hollos, M. 1983. *New Hungarian Peasants: An East Central European Experience with Collectivization*. New York: Columbia Univ. Press

141. McArthur, M. 1976. The Saxon Germans: Political fate of an ethnic identity. *Dialect. Anthropol.* 1(4):349–64

142. Mead, M. 1976. Introduction. In *Communal Families in the Balkans*, ed. R. Byrnes, pp. xvii-xxvii. Notre Dame: Univ. Notre Dame Press

143. Minnich, R. G. 1979. *The Homemade World of Zagaj: An Interpretation of the 'Practical Life' Among Traditional Peasant Farmers in West Haloze Slovenia, Yugoslavia*. Bergen: Univ. Bergen

144. Minnich, R. G. 1982. The symbolic dimension of West Haloze peasant technology. *Slovene Stud.* 4(1):21–27

145. Mouzelis, N. 1973. Greek and Bulgarian peasants: Aspects of their sociopolitical situation during the interwar period. *Comp. Stud. Soc. Hist.* 18:85–103

146. Nagengast, M. C. 1982. Polish peasants and the state. *Dialect Anthropol.* 7(1): 47–66

147. Obrebski, J. 1976. *The Changing Peasantry of Eastern Europe*, ed. B. K. Halpern, J. M. Halpern. Cambridge: Schenkman

148. Obrebski, J. 1977. Ritual and social structure in a Macedonian village, ed. B. K. Halpern, J. M. Halpern. *Program Sov. East Eur. Stud. Occas.* Pap. No. 1. Amherst: Univ. Mass.

149. Padgett, D. 1980. Symbolic ethnicity and patterns of ethnic identity assertion in American-born Serbs. *Ethnic Groups* 3:55–77

150. Padgett, D. 1981. An adaptive approach to the study of ethnicity: Serbian-Americans in Milwaukee, Wisconsin. *Nationalities Pap.* 9(1):117–30

151. Patterson, G. J. 1976. Modernization in rural Oltenia: A preliminary discussion. *East Eur. Q.* 10:247–54

152. Patterson, G. J. 1977. *The Romanians of Saskatchewan: Four generations of adaptation*. Ottawa, Mercury Ser., Natl. Mus. Man

153. Patterson, G. J. 1980. National styles in the development of the profession of anthropology: The case of Romania. *East. Eur. Q.* 14(2):207–18

154. Pine, F. T., Bogdanowicz, P. T. 1982. Policy responses and alternative strategy: The process of change in a Polish highland village. *Dialect. Anthropol.* 7(1): 67–80

155. Randall, S. 1976. The family estate in an upland Carpathian village. *Dialect. Anthropol.* 1(3):277–86

156. Ratner, M. 1982. Careers, jobs, and young people in Romania. In *Careers in Anthropology: Perspectives on Research, Training, and Employment*, ed. R. Landmann. Washington DC: Anthropol. Soc. Washington

157. Reining, C. 1978. The rise and demise of the German minority in Hungary. In *Sociolinguistic Problems in Czechoslovakia, Hungary, Romania and Yugoslavia*, ed. T. F. Magner, pp. 456–68. Columbus: Slavica

158. Rheubottom, D. B. 1976. The Saint's Feast and Skopska Crna Goran social structure. *Man* 11:18–34

159. Rheubottom, D. B. 1976. Time and form: Contemporary Macedonian households and the Zadruga controversy. See Ref. 21, pp. 215–31

160. Rheubottom, D. B. 1980. Dowry and wedding celebrations in Yugoslav Macedonia. In *The Meaning of Marriage Payments*, J. L. Comaroff, pp. 221–49. New York: Academic

161. Roheim, G. 1951. Hungarian shamanism. In *Psychoanalysis and the Social Sciences*, Vol. 3, ed. G. Roheim et al. New York: Int. Univ. Press

162. Roheim, G. 1954. Hungarian and Vogul mythology. *Am. Ethnol. Soc. Monogr. No. 23*. New York: Augustin

163. Romanian Research Group. 1977. Transylvanian ethnicity: A reply to "Ethnocide in Romania." *Curr. Anthropol.* 20(1):135–40

164. Rotenberg, R. 1983. May Day parades in Prague and Vienna: A comparison of Socialist ritual. *Anthropol. Q.* 56(2):62–68

165. Rudan, P. D., et al. 1982. Strategy of anthropological research on the island of Hvar. *Coll. Antropol.* 6(1):39–46

166. Sachs, N. 1979. Chants that do not wound: Concept and sensation in Koleda. In *Essays in Humanistic Anthropology: A Festschrift in Honor of David Bidney*, ed. B. T. Grindal, D. M. Warren, pp. 253–76. Washington DC: Univ. Press of Am.

167. Salzmann, Z., ed. 1970. A contribution to the study of value orientations among the Czechs and Slovaks. *Univ. Mass. Dep. Anthropol. Res. Rep. 4*

168. Salzmann, Z. 1970. A symposium on East European ethnography. *Univ. Mass. Dep. Anthropol. Res. Rep. 6*

169. Salzmann, Z. 1971. Some sociolinguistic observations on the relationship between Czech and Slovak. In *The Limits of In-*

tegration: Ethnicity and Nationalism in Modern Europe. Univ. Mass. Dep. Anthropol. Res. Rep. 9

170. Salzmann, Z. 1979. A bibliography of sources concerning the Czechs and Slovaks in Romania. East Eur. Q. 13(4):465–88

171. Salzmann, Z. 1982. Naming persons in Bigar, a Czech-speaking village in the southern Romanian Banat. Work. Pap. Sociolog. 39. Austin: Southwest Educ. Dev. Lab.

171a. Salzmann, Z. 1983. Two contributions to the study of Czechs and Slovaks in Romania. Sov. East Eur. Stud. Occas. Pap. Ser. No. 9. Amherst: Univ. Mass. Int. Area Stud. Program

172. Salzmann, Z., Scheufler, V. 1974. Komarov: A Czech Farming Village. New York: Holt, Rinehart & Winston

173. Sampson, S. 1976. Feldioara: The city comes to the peasant. Dialect. Anthropol. 1(4):321–48

174. Sampson, S. 1979. Urbanization—planned and unplanned: A case study of Brasov, Romania. In The Socialist City, ed. A. French, E. I. Hamilton, pp. 507–24. New York: Wiley

175. Sampson, S. 1982. The planners and the peasants: An anthropological study of urban development in Romania. Esbjerg, Denmark: Univ. Center South Jutland

176. Sanders, I. T. 1949. Balkan Village. Lexington: Univ. Kentucky Press

177. Sanders, I. T. 1976. The peasant community and the national society in southeastern Europe: An interpretive essay. Balkanistica 3:23–41

178. Sanders, I. T., Whitaker, R., Cheatham, T. 1981. East European Peasantries. Social Relations: An Annotated Bibliography of Periodical Articles. Boston: Hall

178a. Sárkány, M. 1979. Transformation of peasant economy: A Hungarian example. In Anthropology and Social Change in Rural Areas, ed. B. Berdichewsky, pp. 245–52. The Hague: Mouton

179. Schuchat, M. G. 1981. Hungarian-Americans in the nation's capital. Anthropol. Q. 54(2):89–93

180. Silverman, C. 1982. Pomaks of the Balkans. In Muslim Peoples: A World Ethnographic Survey, ed. R. V. Weekes. Westport, CT: Greenwood. In press

181. Silverman, C. 1983. The politics of folklore in Bulgaria. Anthropol. Q. 56(2): 55–61

182. Simic, A. 1967. The blood feud in Montenegro. Essays in Balkan Ethnology, ed. G. W. Lockwood. Kroeber Soc. Spec. Publ. No. 1, pp. 83–94

183. Simic, A. 1969. Management of the male image in Yugoslavia. Anthropol. Q. 43(2):89–101

184. Simic, A. 1972. The Peasant Urbanites: A Study of Rural-Urban Mobility in Serbia. New York: Seminar Press

185. Simic, A. 1973. Kinship reciprocity and rural-urban integration in Serbia. Urban Anthropol. 2(2):205–13

186. Simic, A. 1974. Urbanization and cultural process in Yugoslavia. Anthropol. Q. 47(2):211–27

187. Simic, A. 1976. Acculturation to urban life in Serbia. In The Social Structure of Eastern Europe, ed. B. L. Faber, pp. 331–52. New York: Praeger

188. Simic, A. 1977. Aging in the United States and Yugoslavia: Contrasting models of intergenerational relationships. Anthropol. Q. 50(2):53–64

189. Simic, A. 1978. Commercial folk music in Yugoslavia: Idealization and reality. J. Assoc. Grad. Dance Ethnol. 2:25–37

190. Simic, A. 1978. Winners and losers: Aging Yugolsavs in a changing world. In Cultural Variations on Growing Old, ed. B. Meyerhoff, A. Simic, pp. 77–105. Beverly Hills: Sage

191. Simic, A. 1979. Sevdah: The ritual containment of machismo in the Balkans. J. Assoc. Grad. Dance Ethnol. 3:26–36

192. Simic, A. 1983. Adaptive and maladaptive aspects of traditional culture in Yugoslav modernization. In Urban Life in Mediterranean Europe, ed. M. Kenny, D. Kertzer, pp. 203–24. Urbana: Univ. Ill. Press

193. Skalnik, P. 1979. Modernization of the Slovak peasantry: Two Carpathian highland communities. In Anthropology and Social Change in Rural Areas, ed. B. Berdichewsky, pp. 253–61. The Hague: Mouton

194. Smollett, E. W. 1980. Implications of the multicommunity production cooperative (agro-industrial complex) for rural life in Bulgaria or the demise of Kara Stoyanka. Bulg. J. Sociol. 3:422–56

195. Sozan, M. 1977. Ethnocide in Rumania. Curr. Anthropol. 18(4):781–82

196. Sozan, M. 1978. The History of Hungarian Ethnography. Washington DC: Univ. Press of Am.

197. Spangler, M. 1983. Urban research in Yugoslavia: Regional variation in urbanization. See Ref. 120a

198. Stahl, H. H. 1980. Traditional Romanian Village Communities: The Transition from the Communal to the Captialist Model of Production in the Danube Region. Cambridge: Cambridge Univ. Press

199. Stahl, P. H. 1978. The domestic group in the traditional Balkan societies. *Z. Balkanol.* 14:194–201
200. Stahl, P. H. 1979. The Rumanian farm household and the village community. In *Anthropology and Social Change in Rural Areas,* ed. B. Berdichewsky, pp. 233–44. The Hague: Mouton
201. Stein, H. F. 1974. Envy and the evil eye among Slovak-Americans: An essay in the psychological ontogeny of belief and ritual. *Ethos* 2:15–46
202. Stein, H. F. 1975. Structural change in Slovak kinship: An ethnohistoric inquiry. *Ethnology* 14:99–108
203. Stein, H. F. 1978. Aging and death among Slovak-Americans: A study in the thematic unity of the life cycle. *J. Psychol. Anthropol.* 1:297–320
204. Stoianovich, T. 1967. *A Study in Balkan Civilization.* New York: Knopf
205. Sugar, P. F., ed. 1980. *Ethnic Diversity and Conflict in Eastern Europe.* Santa Barbara: ABC-Clio
206. Supek, O. 1983. The meaning of carnival in Croatia. *Anthropol. Q.* 56(2):90–94
207. Verdery, K. 1979. Internal colonialism in Austria-Hungary. *Ethnic Racial Stud.* 2(3):378–99
208. Verdery, K. 1981. Ethnic relations and hierarchies of dependency in the late Hapsburg empire: Austria, Hungary and Transylvania. See Ref. 5, pp. 1–28
208a. Verdery, K. 1983. *Transylvanian Villagers: Three Centuries of Political, Economic and Ethnic Change.* Berkeley: Univ. Calif. Press
208b. Vincze, L. 1974. Organization of work in herding teams of the Great Hungarian Plain. *Ethnology* 13:159–69
208c. Vincze, L. 1978. Kinship terms and address in a Hungarian speaking peasant community in Rumania. *Ethnology* 17:101–17
209. Vucinich, W. S. 1975. A study in social survival: Katun in Bileca Rudine. *Monogr. Ser. World Affairs, No. 13.* Denver: Univ. Denver
210. Wagner, R. A. 1981. English language anthropological sources on Serbia. *Serbian Stud.* 1(2):93–101
211. Wagner, R. A. 1983. Different views of historical reality: Oral and written recollection in a Serbian village. *Southeast. Eur.* 10(1). In press
212. Warriner, D., ed. 1965. *Contrasts in Emerging Societies: Readings in the Social and Economic History of South-Eastern Europe in the Nineteenth Century.* Bloomington: Indiana Univ. Press
213. Whitaker, I. 1968. Tribal structure and national politics in Albania, 1910–1950. In *History and Social Anthropology,* ed. I. M. Lewis, pp. 253–93. London: Tavistock
214. Whitaker, I. 1976. Familial roles in the extended patrilineal kin group in northern Albania. In *Mediterranean Family Structures,* ed. J. G. Peristiany, pp. 196–203. Cambridge: Univ. Press
215. Whitaker, I. 1981. "A Sack for Carrying Things": The traditional role of women in northern Albanian society. *Anthropol. Q.* 54(3):146–56
216. Winner, I. P. 1972. *A Slovenian Village: Zerovnica.* Providence: Brown Univ. Press.
217. Winner, I. P. 1977. Ethnicity among urban Slovene villagers in Cleveland, Ohio. *Pap. Slovene Stud.* 51–63
218. Winner, I. P. 1977. The question of cultural point of view in determining the boundaries of ethnic units: Slovene villagers in the Cleveland, Ohio, area. *Pap. Slovene Stud.* 73–82
219. Winner, I. P., Susel, R., eds. 1983. *The Dynamics of East European Ethnicity Outside of Eastern Europe.* Cambridge, Mass: Schenkman. In press
220. Winner, I. P., Winner, T. G., eds. 1983. *The Peasant and the City in Eastern Europe, Interpenetrating Structures.* Cambridge, Mass: Schenkman. In press
221. Zbrowski, M., Herzog, E. 1952. *Life Is With People: The Culture of the Shtetl.* New York: Int. Univ. Press

Ann. Rev. Anthropol. 1983. 12:403–28
Copyright © 1983 by Annual Reviews Inc. All rights reserved

THEORETICAL ISSUES IN CONTEMPORARY SOVIET PALEOLITHIC ARCHAEOLOGY

Richard S. Davis

Department of Anthropology, Bryn Mawr College, Bryn Mawr, Pennsylvania 19010

INTRODUCTION

Descriptions of the Union of Soviet Socialist Republics are often filled with superlatives; from the enormity of hydroelectric projects, the vastness of boreal forests, to the multiplicity of ethnic groups and languages. Archaeologists can only imagine that the more than eight and a half million square miles of territory of the USSR covers a colossal archaeological resource. In proportion to the task, the Soviet Union has assembled the largest centralized archaeological apparatus in the world for the investigation of her prehistory and protohistory. More than 500 expeditions each year are sent out for archaeological reconnaissance and excavation, and the ensuing stream of publications is large and impressive. The latest in the comprehensive series of Soviet bibliographies of archaeological publications lists 14,812 separate publications covering all phases of archaeology in the USSR for the years 1968–1972 (97). Somewhat less than 10% of this outpouring was specifically oriented toward Paleolithic and Mesolithic studies.

The question soon arises, what has been the impact of all this activity on prehistorians living outside of the USSR? Superlatives in this case are not so appropriate. The impact has been uneven, but clearly since World War II it has been growing. In several areas such as the peopling of the New World, the analysis of settlements and dwelling structures, use-wear (traceological) analysis of artifacts, Paleolithic art, Pleistocene environmental sequences, and the investigation of the initial adaptation to northern and arctic environments, Soviet researchers have produced extensive and high quality data of interest to virtually all students of the Paleolithic. Nevertheless, these Soviet data

403

0066–4294/83/1015–0403$02.00

remain considerably under-utilized by Western archaeologists for a variety of reasons. Chief among those reasons is unfamiliarity with the Russian language and the lack of translation resources. In other areas, such as periodization and chronology of the Paleolithic, the evolution of social economic formations, faunal analysis, typology, quantitative data analysis, ethnographic analogy (ethnoarchaeology), paleoecology, or radiometric dating techniques, there has not been much work carried over to the West. This is because the work is regarded as either insufficiently developed or not germaine to Western interests and objectives. The main point here is that although there are many areas of mutual interest between Soviet and Western Paleolithic scholars, there are several large areas of nonoverlap. These latter areas exist mainly because of the developmental histories of the disciplines and the differential expectations for the use of archaeological data.

In this review I will focus on some recent developments in Soviet Paleolithic archaeology, particularly in regard to theoretical orientation. My hope is that this line of approach will be useful to those who would like to use Soviet archaeological data. It seems to me that in order to increase the flow of information and use of data, it is necessary first to recognize what basic goals and problem areas Soviet prehistorians are pursuing and then areas of commonality can be identified. The first part of this review will present some of the major reference publications in English and Russian and will then give a brief look at some major characteristics of the Soviet research apparatus. The aim of this initial part is to provide access to some of the materials and background necessary to understand contemporary Soviet Paleolithic archaeology.

PUBLISHED SOURCES ON SOVIET PALEOLITHIC ARCHAEOLOGY

English Language Publications

There are a number of English language reviews and interpretations of Soviet work, many of which are recent and up to date. The vast majority of these either synthesize regional data or examine particular well-known sites in detail. Most of these papers are constructive evaluations and often convey the desire for further contact and cooperation. A few, however, are decidedly critical (73, 88).

One of the earliest articles reviewing Soviet work was by Golomshtok in 1938 (31). He provided a review of Paleolithic from the European part of the USSR as well as an overview of current theory. Golomshtok's material was compiled just after the turbulent period of the Sovietization of Paleolithic archaeology, and hence his review reflects a significant time in Soviet Paleolithic studies. Henry Field has had a long-standing interest in Soviet archaeology and has produced several papers and bibliographical summaries beginning in the late 1930s (23, 24). V. Gordon Childe was well acquainted with a wide range of Soviet work and was clearly influenced by this exposure (15, 93). Hallam Movius, Jr. became well known for his analysis of the Soviet Central Asian Paleolithic (74) and the famous site of Teshik Tash in Uzbekistan (75).

By the middle of the 1960s, Richard Klein began a long series of extremely valuable and informative publications on Soviet Paleolithic archaeology, including studies on the Lower Paleolithic (48), the Mousterian (49), the Kostanki-Borshevo site complexes on the Don River (50), the Siberian Paleolithic (51), the Middle and Upper Paleolithic of the Ukraine (52), and early migrations into the New World (53). General treatments of the Northeast Asian Stone Age have been presented by Powers (78) and Chard (13). McBurney presented a wide-ranging essay on the issue of initial population movements into Soviet territory and the Middle/Upper Paleolithic transition (72). One of the very few cooperative field projects between Soviet and American archaeologists was organized by Laughlin and Okladnikov, and it was focused on late prehistoric archaeology in the western arctic (60).

More recent works have been on traceological research by Levitt (62), a summary and review of papers on hunters, gatherers, and fishermen which took place in Leningrad (40), Upper Paleolithic symbolic systems (68), and a summary and evaluation of the Central Asian Paleolithic (17, 81). Howe's dissertation, *Soviet Theories of Primitive History,* is a very useful and in-depth treatment of the development of the theoretical underpinnings of Soviet archaeology. He gives an extended evaluation of the theoretical work of Semenov which is particularly relevant to modern work (41). Shimkin has recently published a survey of Upper Paleolithic archaeology in the European and Siberian USSR (84). Olga Soffer-Bobyshev recently presented a paper on the structure of Paleolithic research in the USSR, and her forthcoming dissertation on Upper Paleolithic faunal exploitation and social organization will bring a large amount of previously unpublished data to light (86). Finally, Henry Michael, a long-time observer of the Soviet archaeological scene, has just completed a major review of Paleolithic archaeology in Siberia which will be forthcoming soon.

The above list is by no means exhaustive, but it does give a reasonable representation of the major works by non-Soviet authors. The papers were not, of course, planned to present a balanced or composite view of the whole Soviet Paleolithic, but rather to reflect particular interests of various scholars. Thus significant areas are not represented, for example recent work in Lower Paleolithic archaeology and a wide variety of Middle Paleolithic studies. Although there are some papers forthcoming in these areas, there is a real need for more summary works.

English Translations

Translations from Russian sources have not been plentiful, and there is little current activity in this area. The Harvard University Peabody Museum of Archaeology and Ethnology Russian Translation Series produced several volumes between 1959 and 1970, and the Arctic Institute of North America, Anthropology of the North, Translations from Russian Sources series produced six volumes between 1961 and 1966. The majority of these works, however, were not directly oriented toward Paleolithic archaeology. An extremely valuable current series is *Soviet Anthropology and Ethnology,* edited by S. and E. Dunn. Over the years it has carried many articles which were directly relevant to the theory and method of Soviet archaeology. Some journals, notably *Current Anthropology* and *Arctic Anthropology,* have made a real effort to include articles and comments by Soviet authors and have featured Soviet Paleolithic topics.

Major Russian Language Sources

Despite all of the papers and translations cited above, the researcher interested in pursuing any specific problem in depth will quickly have to turn to Russian language sources published in the Soviet Union. Fortunately for Russian language readers, there are a number of comprehensive guides and encyclopedic works which allow fairly easy access to Soviet research. First there are the complete bibliographies of Soviet archaeological literature covering the periods 1918–1940, 1941–1957, 1958–1962, 1963–1967, and 1968–1972 (97). They are well organized, indexed, and cross-referenced. Second, every year the Institute of Archaeology publishes *Arkheologicheskiye Otkritiya* (Archaeological Discoveries), which contains entries chronicling the field research activities of most of the branches, departments, and detachments of the Institutes of the Academy of Sciences of the USSR as well as the universities and museums. The brief notes authored by the field directors of the various projects give an excellent indication of the scope and focus of archaeological work throughout the USSR year by year. Unfortunately, however, *AO* contains no bibliographical citations. Third, there is the quarterly *Kratkiye Soobscheniya Instituta Arkeologii (Brief Communications of the Institute of Archaeology),* which includes collections of topically organized brief articles and also various notes chronicling developments in Soviet archaeology. Fourth, Beregovaya has published a complete list of Paleolithic sites with location maps and bibliographical references for the period of all Russian and Soviet work up until 1955 (3) and a supplement covering sites found between 1958–1968 (4). A concise review of Paleolithic archaeology from the Soviet point of view has recently been published by Liubin (67). Another brief but informative review is Masson's treatment of the development of Soviet archaeological theory (70).

In addition to the above reference works, there are some major publications which deal specifically with the Paleolithic. In 1970 the Institute of Archaeology published *The Stone Age Within the Territory of the USSR* under the general editorship of A. A. Formozov (25). It contains authoritative reviews by leading Soviet scholars, and at this time it still remains the single basic reference work on the Soviet Paleolithic. A new 16-volume work, *Archaeology of the USSR,* is now being prepared and it will be published over the next several years. In addition to other periods, it will summarize in some detail all major Paleolithic work, region by region, for the entire USSR. To complete this list of summary works, mention must be made of the new series *Paleolithic of the World.* Two volumes, *Africa* and *The Near and Middle East* (10, 11), have already appeared and several more volumes will follow. The series has been organized by P. I. Boriskovsky, an eminent figure in Soviet Paleolithic archaeology, and the reviews will be written for the most part by well-known archaeologists from the Institute of Archaeology in Leningrad. It is a highly significant publication because it will present for the first time a Soviet world view of the Paleolithic. Further, it will be "sharply against burgeoise racism and idealism, against reactionary conceptions of a 'chosen' people leaving the rest to perpetual backwardness" (9, p. 19).

The above list of comprehensive works is impressive, and it well illustrates the monumentality and centrally organized character of the Soviet archaeological enterprise. These works reflect a definite uniformity of approach, and their publication is an integral part of the 5-year plans developed by the Institute of Archeology, Academy of Sciences of the USSR, and its branches.

SOME GENERAL CHARACTERISTICS OF SOVIET PALEOLITHIC ARCHAEOLOGY

There are a number of aspects peculiar to Soviet archaeology which are important to bear in mind when evaluating almost any work since the 1930s. They tend to shape both theoretical and data-oriented papers in a way noticeably distinct from those which appear in the West.

First, Paleolithic archaeology in the Soviet Union is uniformly conceptualized as a part of historical science. Basically this means that all phenomena of social life are placed in specific historical contexts with the aim of understanding their origin, development, and causal determination (76). Thus archaeologists are to use their data to discover and illustrate the laws and regularity ("zakonomernost") of historical processes. This orientation was emphatically introduced in the early 1930s at the expense of other approaches, and in some ways it is fair to say that the Soviets experienced a "New Archaeology" 30 years in advance of what happened in North America during the 1960s. There are important differences, however. Soviet historical science proceeds within the framework of historical and dialectical materialism based on the classic Marxist works. As such, primary attention is focused on the study of the transformation of one social economic formation to another. In the 1930s several archaeologists worked out the social economic formations of the Paleolithic based on Engel's *Origins of the Family, Private Property and the State* (22). According to that analysis, the Paleolithic period falls entirely within the era of Pre-Class Societies. This era is divided into the following series of successive stages: Pre-Clan Society (Primitive horde and Primitive commune), Era of Clan Organization (Matriarchal and Patriarchal), and the Stage of the Decomposition of the Clan and the Emergence of Class Society. Within this rubric, Paleolithic archaeology's major role was to study the transitions between the earlier stages. Social progress, i.e. progress measurable in the development of productive forces, can be traced both within and between the stages. Ultimately, the foundations of this entire stadial approach are grounded in philosophical realism, the notion that abstract entities, in this case the inner essence of social economic formations, exist independently of the mind. Gellner elaborates on this crucial but subtle point and provides excellent insight into the philosophical basis of Soviet theory in a recently published essay (27).

Although it is quite true that in the post-Stalin era the application of the above scheme (often referred to in the literature as the "Theory of Stages") to archaeological data has become increasingly restricted, nevertheless it has not withered away entirely. It is simply too integral a part of the classical Marxist doctrine to be painted out of the picture completely. As will be made clear in a later portion of this review, the current emphasis is on cultures rather than stages as the unit of analysis, but many of the strands of stadial theory remain embedded in contemporary thought.

A second general feature of Soviet Paleolithic archaeology is its centralized organizational structure. Headquartered in Leningrad, the Paleolithic Sector of the Institute of Archaeology (a branch of the Academy of Sciences of the USSR) has a controlling influence on the organization of all union conferences, allotment of publication space in the major journals and monographs, the nature and extent of foreign contacts, and the setting of basic objectives for 5-year plans. The Leningrad sector has also granted a large number of higher degrees (kandidat and doctor).

One indication of the centralized nature of Soviet research is that there are clearly stated goals and objectives. As reported by the Institute of Archaeology to the 25th Congress of the Communist Party in 1976, the central problems for study should be 1. The Origins of Man; 2. The Origins of Human Society; 3. The Study of the Most Ancient (i.e. prehistoric and protohistoric) peoples of the USSR; 4. The Formation of Productive Society (42). Paleolithic archaeologists are particularly concerned with the second and third objectives.

There are signs that the degree of centralization may be lessening somewhat. According to a recent study, in the 1940s about one-half of all field research projects originated from the Institutes in Moscow and Leningrad, but by the 1970s it was down to one-fourth (63). In the past several years new centers of the Institute of Archaeology have been established in Novosibirsk, Irkutsk, Chila, Kemerovo, Magadan, Dushanbe, and Samarkand (89). Eventually the increased number of regional archaeological centers and the number of degree holders granted by regional institutions will create a more diverse, even parochial, archaeological complex. For the forseeable future, however, it seems unlikely that the centralized character of Soviet archaeology will be much changed.

A third important aspect to Soviet Paleolithic research which must be recognized from the outset is that research is primarily oriented toward sites and problems within the territory of the USSR. Soviet archaeological expeditions of any kind abroad are relatively few; in recent years there have been expeditions sent to Mongolia, Iraq, Bulgaria, Afghanistan, Svalbard (Norway), Hungary, and Nepal. For the most part these foreign projects have not involved much Paleolithic research. Of the 707 separate reports of archaeological investigations of all kinds found in *Arkheologichoskiye Otkritiya* for 1978, only 9 (1.3%) are about investigations outside of the USSR.

This is not to suggest, however, that Soviet archaeologists tend to be uninformed or uninterested in a more global archaeology. Indeed, bibliographical citations of foreign work are quite numerous in most monographs and review articles. There is no question that Soviet Paleolithic archaeologists are much more familiar with major Western works and investigators than is the reverse case. Their focus within the USSR is largely due to the difficulty and expense of arranging foreign travel and the stated goal of developing the prehistory of the USSR. This orientation does, however, reduce the potential for international contact and exchange of ideas, and it also tends to limit the number of foreigners working within the USSR.

A fourth major aspect of Soviet Paleolithic archaeology to emphasize here is that its practitioners are usually full-time researchers without teaching duties in the various institutes and branches of the Academy of Sciences. It is quite common for senior scholars to lead at least two field expeditions per year. Budgets for research projects are designed for relatively long periods (e.g. 5 years) which allows for concentrated as well as extended research programs.

There are a number of long-standing expeditions which have accumulated data for several decades. The most famous is the Kostenki-Borshevo Expedition, the flagship of Soviet Paleolithic research. In 1979 a century of investigation at Kostenki was celebrated. More than 50 seasons of excavation have revealed approximately 60 sites of Middle and Upper Paleolithic age and have exposed approximately 7000 square meters of surface area (37, 96). The expedition has been led by the major figures of Soviet Paleolithic archaeology: S. N. Zamyatnin, P. P. Efimenko. P. I. Boriskovsky, and A. N. Rogachev. S. A. Semenov began his traceological studies on Kostenki materials. N. D. Praslov, the current leader of the expedition, and A. N. Rogachev have just edited a summary of all the research from the Kostenki expeditions, a volume which will stand as a landmark in Soviet Paleolithic literature for a long time to come (79). In sum, the centralized and specialized nature of Soviet Paleolithic research allows for large-scale, sustained efforts which most Western archaeological projects can never approach.

THEORETICAL ISSUES IN CONTEMPORARY SOVIET PALEOLITHIC ARCHAEOLOGY

Archaeologists of any country have at least three major problems in common. First is the interpretation of synchronic data from particular archaeological sites in technological, economic, social, and ideological terms. Second is the explanation of variability exhibited between a series of roughly contemporaneous sites. Third is the explanation of observed change manifested through a diachronic sequence of sites. In the 1930s, Soviet archaeologists tended to believe that the third problem was well under control through the application of Marxist principles and the Theory of Stages, and they concentrated their work on the first problem. The second problem, synchronic variability, was either ignored or said not to exist.

Thus Efimenko and Zamyatnin, among others working on the Russian Plain in the 1930s, opened a series of Upper Paleolithic settlement sites in large horizontal exposures in order to reveal evidence of particular social economic formations which could be used in effect to illustrate the accepted stadial theory. Indeed, Soviet Paleolithic archaeology has long been social archaeology, and that is why large-scale horizontal excavations have always been emphasized.

When Rogachev began to lead the Kostenki expedition in the 1950s, he recognized and convincingly documented for the first time that there was marked synchronic variability in Upper Pleistocene industries (82). He soon began to define cultures in more or less the sense of Childe. Eventually this variability demanded explanation. On the other side of the globe, American archaeologists since the beginning of the twentieth century had recognized synchronic variability, but were not embarrassed to explain it in ideological terms; the genius of a culture, diffusion, independent invention, and so on. After World War II, Western archaeologists explored more materialist (but mechanical) explanations. For Soviet scholars steeped in the uniform stadial approach to history and an obligatory dialectical materialist orientation, the problem of synchronic variability was much more perplexing. It is especially problematical because archaeological studies of cultural variability tend to gravitate rapidly toward examination of variables outside the cultural system (e.g. characteristics of environmental setting, subsistence resources, influences of other cultures, etc). In turn this leads to the position that there are significant forces shaping individual cultures external to their systems. Dialectical materialism, however, has traditionally focused on conflicts and contradictions within the system to account for change and variation, and therein lies the dilemma. I submit it is a pivotal issue of contemporary Soviet Paleolithic archaeology.

As several observers have pointed out, the stadial theory has been strongly challenged and even discredited in most quarters since the 1950s (8, 41, 54, 86). However, nothing comparable in scope has been advanced to replace it. Many Soviet archaeologists seemingly avoid the entire issue and publish basically descriptive, data-oriented excavation reports. That is why when one initially peruses the Soviet archaeological literature an impression may be gained that there are no more important theoretical issues left to discuss. But that is not the case! Instead there is a complicated and often cumbersome overlay of theoretical concepts which have accumulated over the past several decades. From that background have emerged some clearly identifiable orientations and debates, as have been outlined recently by a group of archaeologists from Leningrad University (12). Thus Soviet Paleolithic archaeologists, like their counterparts everywhere, face the continual challenge of testing, reworking, and discarding if necessary their theoretical instruments in order for their discipline to thrive and to be productive.

The remainder of this review will discuss three major areas central to contemporary Soviet Paleolithic theory: periodization, the concept of archaeological culture, and the environmental/ecological approach. An examination of these areas should help develop and illustrate some of the arguments just raised.

Periodization

Periodization is the term used in the Soviet Union to describe the process of partitioning history into meaningful units. The problems of periodization are complex and subtle, and they are closely connected to a series of important issues as will soon be seen. The term "periodization" clearly has chronological meaning. Beyond that, however, a scheme for segmenting the Paleolithic must encompass more than time, because a central goal of Soviet archaeology is to discover and to elucidate the regularities and laws of history as it passes from stage to stage. For Soviet archaeologists today the problem is to work out a set of archaeologically recognizable criteria for subdividing the Stone Age in a way compatible with their overall goals. "Archaeologically recognizable" is the key aspect, because the traditional markers of stadial evolution were social organizational features, but the methodology for recognizing social organizations of the past from archaeological data was and is weakly developed and has been an easy target for criticism.

Perhaps the easiest way to begin this discussion is to present the periodization of Boriskovsky, an archaeologist well known since the 1930s and still quite influential today. In the first volume of *Paleolithic of the World,* a publication intended to have wide distribution, Boriskovsky presents the following scheme (10, p. 16):

AGE (× 1000)	PALEOLITHIC EPOCH
10	
	I. Late Paleolithic ("Pozdniy Paleolit")
35	
	II. Ancient Paleolithic ("Drevniy Paleolit") Mousterian
100	
	Late and Middle Acheulean
	Ancient Acheulean (Abbevillian, Chelles)
	Oldowan (also Pre-Chelles)
2600	

The salient feature of this scheme is that the Paleolithic is divided into two parts, unlike in many other regions of the world where a tripartite division is used. According to Kraynov (59), the practice of subdividing into two parts is relatively recent, dating from the 1951 publication of Zamyatnin (98), and rests on the contention of physical anthropologists of the time who held that pre-*sapiens* forms of man, "archanthropus" (now including *Homo habilis* and *Homo erectus*), and "paleoanthropic man" (*Homo sapiens neanderthalensis*), were ape men, biologically organized in a fundamentally different way than "Neanthropus" (*Homo sapiens sapiens*).

The mixing of cultural and biological data points can be observed along Boriskovsky's dividing lines of the Paleolithic. At the base of the Paleolithic, he follows cultural criteria in differentiating the earliest ape-like man ("obez'y-anopodobnye liudi"—*Homo habilis*) from man-like ape ("chelovekoobraznaya obez'yan"—*Australopithecus* sp.). The cultural feature at this point is the appearance of stone tools, or as Engels would have it, the origin of labor ("trud"). The mechanism behind the leap from animal to man, however, is patently Lamarkian. Boriskovsky's citation of a number of Engels' classic observations in the *Dialectics of Nature* regarding the use of the hand, the origin of speech, and the importance of meat-eating make this clear (10, p. 37). The transition occurs as behaviors arising from felt needs repeated countless times from generation to generation gradually become acquired and physically mainfested in the organism.

The boundary between the Ancient and Late Paleolithic in the past in the Soviet Union traditionally has been marked by both biological and cultural features. Since the discovery by Chernysh (14) in the late 1950s of Mousterian dwelling remains and other relatively advanced features, however, the cultural contrasts between the Mousterian and the Late Paleolithic have been increasingly less apparent. Grigor'ev (32) and Liubin (66) have also drawn attention to this cultural continuity. Recognizing this, Boriskovsky now emphasizes the biological distinctiveness between the two epochs:

> . . . only in the course of the Ancient Paleolithic, in distinction from all subsequent epochs, occurred significant changes in the structure of man, and this in the opinion of the author speaks in favor of the decipherment of the Ancient Paleolithic as a special, *qualitatively distinctive* epoch of primitive history (10, p. 40; emphasis added).

The upper boundary of the Paleolithic (i.e. the Late Paleolithic/Mesolithic) is, according to Timofeev (91), held by the majority of Soviet archaeologists to be largely chronological, and it is placed at about 10,000 B.P. This time also marks the conventional end of the Pleistocene and the beginning of the Holocene. Some investigators understand the boundary to mark the adaptation of a preexisting social system to a restructured ecological system (19), and others recognize the difficulty in defining a universal, precise boundary to cover large continental areas (90).

It is fair to say that the major boundaries of the Paleolithic as viewed today in the Soviet Union are a combination of cultural, biological, and chronological factors. Soviet archaeologists are, of course, not alone in lacking a highly systematized periodization. It is a perennial, but perhaps not quite so pressing, issue in the Western countries.

The traditional periodization that Boriskovksy's scheme represents is clearly not accepted by all Soviet investigators, perhaps not even any longer by the majority. Disquiet with the two-part division has been especially evident since the widely attended symposium in Moscow in 1968, The Emergence of Humankind and Human Society (54, 59). The main source of dissatisfaction has been that the bipartite division is closely associated with the theory of stages of social economic formations and the theory of "two leaps." During the 1930s a number of Soviet archaeologists held the idea that the period corresponding to the Lower and Middle Paleolithic of the European terminology, that is, the Ancient Paleolithic, was the time of the primitive horde ("stado"), a social entity characterized by amorphousness, undifferentiated social relations, and the absence of a communal domestic economy. Boriskovsky advanced for the first time the theory that the matriarchal clan society originated with the Late Paleolithic, wherein the role and status of women were highly elevated in the domestic communal economy (7). The source for these ideas was, of course, the classic Marxist works, and Boriskovsky and his colleagues during the

1930s attempted to vindicate this scheme with archaeological data. Thus observations of late Paleolithic female statuettes ("Venus figurines"), what appeared to be large long-house remains, and permanent settlements etc were assigned the meaning of matrilineal clan society.

It is exactly at this point where the debate has become most intense. The younger generation of Soviet archaeological scholars held at the symposium in Moscow that on the basis of archaeological data alone it was not possible to demonstrate an abrupt transition in social economic formation between Mousterian and Late Paleolithic times. Grigor'ev, in fact, has held that no major difference in the communal organization of late Acheulean, Mousterian, or Late Paleolithic times can be detected (34). From analyses of dwelling size and distribution within settlements, Grigor'ev has concluded that the "paring family" (nuclear family) most probably existed back in Lower Paleolithic times, but in any case he can find no really compelling evidence for clan organization in Upper Paleolithic times. (According to classic Marxist thought, the paring family was not supposed to come into existence at all during the Era of Pre-Class Societies.)

It is important to note that one aspect of Grigor'ev's form of argumentation was the use of ethnographic data, which until recently had not been frequently utilized by archaeologists. He noted, for example, that among contemporary societies the presence of female figurines is not highly correlated with matrilinial clans, nor is clan organization a necessary feature of advanced hunters and gatherers (34, p. 23).

Kabo (45), in the Symposium on Hunters, Gatherers, Fishermen held in Leningrad, also explored the use of ethnographic analogy in reconstructing the past, and he concluded that specific, concrete forms such as whether an ancient society had a matrilineal or patrilineal clan may be indeterminate because "the function of the clan is not tied so closely with production as it is with the commune, and the clan consists chiefly in the organization of the family-marriage relations." In fact, Kabo maintains, it cannot be confirmed with confidence if a given prehistoric hunting and gathering society was clan organized at all.

The discussion of periodization has led from basic chronological divisions to the theory of stages, the archaeological visibility of social economic formations, and the use of ethnographic data, in rapid succesion. The crux of the matter is that the traditional approach followed by Soviet archaeologists focuses specifically on transitions from one stage to another, and the archaeological periodizaton is supposed to identify and highlight the points of transition. At the moment, however, available theory provides no universally accepted transition points to look for within the Paleolithic.

By the late 1960s and early 1970s, the leading edge of Soviet Paleolithic archaeology had passed the point where it became generally recognized that artifacts and their stratigraphic coordinates could not be directly interpreted in sociohistorical terms (5). That major change was closely connected with the reappraisal of Soviet periodization schemes.

The Concept of Archaeological Culture

DEVELOPMENT OF THE CONCEPT   During the revamping of archaeological conceptualizations in the 1930s, there was a pronounced tendency for minimizing synchronic variability. Consequently, there was little need of an archaeological culture concept. That is, under the influence of the theory of stages, the social, economic, and technological context of a particular stage tended to be regarded as uniform and widespread. The major turnabout in this outlook came as a result of the detailed work on the Upper Paleolithic sites of the Russian Plain. Particularly influential in this case was the work of Rogachev, a leader of the Kostenki expedition during the 1950s (82). Rogachev not only shortened the prevailing chronology of the Upper Paleolithic in the Soviet Union, thus bringing it more in line with its European counterparts, but he also identified a series of archaeological cultures on the basis of specifics of artifact form and territorial distribution. It was not until the 1950s, therefore, that discrete synchronic variants within specific geographic zones became generally recognized in the Soviet Union. The cultures Rogachev deliniated were intended to reflect actual bounded ethnic groups who traditionally made their stone tools in distinctive ways.

One important result of Rogachev's work was that variability in stone tool assemblages could now be understood in terms other than chronology and progress. Tradition and style were recognized as real contributing factors. Another result was that throughout the Soviet Union, Paleolithic archaeologists in the 1960s and on into the 1970s began to examine their regions for local variants of cultures and began to search for explanations of whatever variability eventually was observed. This tendency has continued to increase in strength and is clearly one of the major challenges faced in contemporary Soviet Paleolithic archaeology today. A third result of the recognition of synchronic and local variability was that archaeological cultures rapidly became the major focal point or unit of study instead of stadials. It is clear from an examination of the Soviet literature of the last 15 years that there is no consensus for an operational definition of archaeological culture, or a uniform means for using archaeological cultures for cultural historical or processual purposes. This point is well recognized by many Soviet investigators (2, 69).

HISTORIC-ETHNOGRAPHIC COMMUNITIES AND ECONOMIC-CULTURAL TYPES   In recent years, however, one major analytical division of culture has taken hold and is discussed frequently. It is the distinction between "historic-ethnographic communities" and "economic-culture types" (20, 30). These terms were originally developed by Soviet ethnographers (61), and have been increasingly adopted by archaeologists. The former concept refers to specific social groups while the latter describes a collection of several possibly different ethnic groups who have similar economic and technical levels of development and live in similar environmental zones.

A basic question for Soviet archaeologists is how do archaeological assemblages reflect this division, and how can it be perceived? Gladkik (30) suggests that local assemblages should be examined for both kinds of information. He contends that stone tools of production reflect economic-cultural types when they show little variation and are widely distributed within a particular environmental zone. Ethnohistoric groups, on the other hand, may be recognized when a specific tool category (e.g. projectile point) shows several variant forms within the same environmental zone. In practice, however, Gladkik notes that the discrimination is difficult to achieve because the degree of contemporaneity and absolute chronology of the majority of Upper Paleolithic sites is not well established.

It appears that the majority of Soviet Paleolithic archaeologists tend to define their archaeological cultures as economic cultural types rather than as historic-ethnographic communities. The reasons are fairly clear. First, the economic cultural type is a broader category and is easier to operationalize. Second, it is frequently recognized that the available evidence in most cases consists mainly of stone tools, but stone tools do not readily reflect distinctive ethnic groups (71). On this point, however, there is considerable discussion.

For example, Grigor'ev relies almost exclusively on stone tools to define archaeological cultures: " . . . archaeological cultures are first and foremost typological characteristics of stone tools" (33, p. 44). Furthermore, he contends that the particular mode of manufacture, retouch, and shape of stone tools are specific categories traditionally transmitted within an ethnic group. In a similar vein, Liubin (66) contends that social isolation of discrete ethnic groups during the Mousterian and Upper Paleolithic times led to the development of specific ethnic norms for each group. The toolmakers believed, Liubin holds, that the effectiveness of a tool was inseparably tied to its form, that the form of a tool was imbued with magical qualities, and hence there was an extremely strong tendency for toolmakers to perpetuate their craft with little variation for generation after generation (66, p. 203). For Liubin, stone tools are the most traditional layer of culture; they are the main carriers of the informational code of the ancient Paleolithic. Thus Liubin uses archaeological data in a way consistent with identifying specific "ethnoses." Ethnos is a term drawn from Soviet ethnography which has been defined by Bromly as:

. . . a firm aggregate of people, historically established on a given territory, possessing in common relatively stable particularities of language and culture, and also recognizing their unity and difference from other similar formations (self awareness) and expressing this in a self appointed name (ethnonym) (quoted in 21, p. 163).

A number of Paleolithic archaeologists, however, do not agree with Liubin or Grigor'ev in their assessment of stone tools and archaeological cultures. Matyukhin (71) follows Bromley's definition of ethnos and understands it to be a complex of many integrated factors, and with stone tools constituting only one element, it could hardly be the basic indicator for ethnic differentiation. Matyukhin would relegate a series of similar stone tool collections from various sites to a "type complex," i.e. a lower order interpretive level than archaeological culture. For Matyukhin, inclusion into archaeological culture would require at least a demonstration that the stone tool collections were produced by similar manufacturing techniques and that they were used for similar functions. A similar lack of enthusiasm for identifying ethnic indicators from material culture is held by Pioro (77), who argues that archaeological cultures are basically in the domain of economic-cultural types. Most recently, some investigators have begun to emphasize that archaeological cultures are multivariate phenomena, and have begun to develop quantitative approaches to investigate a number of factors which contribute to archaeological culture variability. A very recent example is the monograph by Kholyushkin, *Problems of Correlation of the Late Paleolithic Industries of Siberia and Middle Asia* (47). Kholyushkin views artifacts as products of the interaction of a variety of factors: raw material, manufacturing technique, function, culture tradition, experience of the artisan, and site behavior.

The spatial dimensions of archaeological cultures and cultural zones have received considerable attention from Soviet investigators. It has long been the practice to identify a few large, basically natural regions of the USSR as centers for various traditions. Thus Formozov for many years has regarded the European portion of the USSR as divided into two "large scale ethno cultural oblasts" (26). They are the Caucauses-Black Sea area and the Central Russian Plain. Formozov considers the former area to have been dominated by peoples originating from the south (i.e. the Near East) who utilized a unifacial technology of stone working during the Mousterian and Upper Paleolithic. The Central Russian Plain, on the other hand, was populated from the west by peoples of Central and Eastern Europe who used a bifacial technology. In addition, Formozov hints that there may be some correlation between the great longevity of these ethnocultural oblasts and human physical types known from skeletal evidence (26, p. 34).

It would be a great mistake, however, to interpret this as any kind of tendency toward racial determinism. Since the 1930s Soviet archaeology has strived to distinguish itself from "bourgeois archaeology," which they frequently maintain has been characterized by often confusing race with culture and by granting the superiority of one race over another (9, 31).

Formozov's conception of long-standing ethnocultural oblasts maintaining their integrity over tens of thousands of years is giving way to investigators such as Liubin whose data analyses show pronounced variability in restricted areas. In fact, Grigor'ev in his important work, *The Beginnings of the Upper Paleolithic and the Origin of Homo sapiens* (32), has concluded that the areal extent of Upper Paleolithic cultures ranged from 50 to 200 km in diameter.

There has been at least one recent attempt to arrive at a uniform definition of archaeological culture which could be used throughout the USSR. At the 1972 conference in Tashkent on the Stone Age of Middle Asia and Kazakhstan, Masson, now head of the Leningrad Division of the Institute of Archaeology, presented an operational definition of archaeological culture as part of a hierarchical scheme of nomenclature (69). Masson attempted to arrive at a consensus position acceptable to the majority of archaeologists. According to this scheme, an archaeological culture is constructed from a series of sites which share a series of artifact types. Artifact types in turn are built on the basis of shared attributes. Artifact types made from similar raw materials may be clustered into "compounds." For the areal component of culture, Masson uses terms familiar to all Soviet archaeologists: local varient, archaeological culture, and "obshnost" (community). Masson suggested on a preliminary basis that local variants should be defined as those with 100–70% coincidence of types, archaeological cultures 70–30%, and communities 30–20%. The concept behind this classificatory scheme is explicitly recognized to be similar to the approach of the late D. L. Clarke in *Analytical Archaeology* (16). As is well known, Clarke developed a hierarchical scheme of subculture-culture-culture group, and Masson's conceptualization is very close to that. It is appropriate to point out here that in classificatory discussions, Clarke is frequently cited in Soviet literature, and his conception of the systemic nature of culture appears to be widely accepted in the Soviet Union.

Masson's scheme was adopted at the Tashkent conference and was reported as a resolution of the All-Union Conference (38). Although officially sanctioned, this operational definition of culture has not appeared to make a very large impression in the recent literature. Kholushkin has attempted to develop a consensus definition he believes would be acceptable to the majority of Soviet archaeologists: an archaeological culture would consist of "past patterns of behavior fixed in the past by the material activities of primitive collectives, a kin based nature, and a large number of equal reflections of each other in various combinations of archaeological sources." In addition, he sets limited but unidimensioned space and time boundaries for archaeological cultures.

In sum, the prevailing outlook appears to be that archaeological cultures are spatial-temporal entities which may reflect some actual social group, and cultures are recognized on the basis of degree of similarity of artifacts and features. This view, however, is not uniformly expressed. There seems to be the expectation that increased theoretical work should result in a more quantifiable definition of culture. In turn, this definition should fit into a broad historical scheme. In the meantime, there is considerable disparity as to which course to follow.

ORIGINS OF ETHNICITY   The second aspect concerning archaeological cultures considered here is: how far back in time can they be recognized? In essence this is the question of when did ethnically differentiated groups originate? For a long time the answer to this question was the beginning of the Late Paleolithic when clan organization replaced the horde. Distinct archaeological cultures could not be recognized for the Ancient Paleolithic because they did not exist.

The first significant departure from the classic picture was the announcement by Liubin in 1965 that there were archaeological cultures in the Caucasus during Mousterian times. Ten years later in a more emphatic fashion he wrote: "In the Mousterian epoch the surface of the Caucasus was not only a physical or zoogeographic map, but an ethnographic one as well" (66, p. 45). He has identified Typical, Denticulate, and Charentian variants of the Mousterian more or less in the sense of Bordes, and he has been successful in overturning some of the conceptions held by Formozov, who has maintained for a long time that the Mousterian of the Caucasus was relatively uniform.

Liubin's contention that his archaeologically defined entities reflect ethnic divisions of peoples has been challenged by Korobkov (57) and Korobkov & Mansurov (58). They proposed that functional differences in site behavior may well explain lithic variability, particularly with respect to Liubin's Denticulate Mousterian variant. This exchange between Korobkov, Mansurov, and Liubin, of course, shares many elements with the "Bordes-Binford" debate, but has received considerably less attention and limelight.

Grigor'ev has maintained that tribal or ethnic differentiation extends back into the Mousterian and even into Late Acheulean times (32). He uses the term "pre-tribes" ("predplemena") to designate these pre-Upper Paleolithic groups. He envisions these pre-tribes for most of the Mousterian to have been very closed systems without significant contact with other pretribes. Hence innovations were not widely propagated, and several pre-tribes could maintain their identity and live more or less side by side within the same region for long periods of time without much change.

Classification and Typology

In the West, archaeological cultures are generally constructed on the basis of established artifact typologies. In most of Europe, the Lower and Middle Paleolithic typological system of Bordes (6) is widely adopted, and it is used as the basic observational framework for the measurement of assemblage similarities and differences. In the Soviet Union, there is no analogous widely accepted typological system, and the lack of such an instrument clearly creates difficulties for those archaeologists who wish to construct higher order entities such as archaeological cultures and lines of development.

A few archaeologists do use Bordes's system, notably Liubin (64) and Ranov (80), although with reservations and modifications. Liubin has reviewed Bordes's method and feels that the absence of detailed technological information concerning cores, primary flaking, striking platforms, type of secondary flaking (retouch), and unretouched pieces makes it difficult to identify clearly local archaeological cultures. "It can serve, nevertheless, as a basis for treatment of Lower Paleolithic materials in the limits of the whole Acheulo-Mousterian okuminea" (64, p. 74). Ranov emphasizes the pragmatic advantages of using Bordes's system in that it can convey a great amount of standardized information to a wide audience without a great deal of ambiguity. He is one of the very few Soviet archaeologists who have presented lithic data using Bordes's style of cumulative graphs.

Soviet archaeologists are clearly concerned with developing better typological frameworks and with linking them to general questions of Paleolithic dynamics (67). Conferences on particular typological topics are sometimes held, and they allow a forum for the dissemination of new ideas and the creation of new terminological systems. In 1974, for example, the Institute of Archaeology in Leningrad held a conference on denticulate-notched tools and their significance in the Lower and Middle Paleolithic (1).

Most recently, some Soviet Paleolithic archaeologists have consciously "passed beyond the period of enthusiasm with Bordes" and are analyzing collections by using attribute analysis and more complex mathematical- statistical procedures. The beginning of this trend perhaps goes back to the publication of Suleymanov's *The Statistical Study of the Culture of Obi-Rakhmat Cave* (87). Suleymanov's work was one of the first major applications of statistical attribute analysis to a substantial Paleolithic data base, in this case a deeply stratified cave in Uzbekistan with several Mousterian layers. Suleymanov's judicious and clear utilization of chi-square, Student's t, and other measures did a great deal to gain acceptance for quantitative methods by Soviet Paleolithic archaeologists who were at that time a quite skeptical audience. His analysis was oriented toward the identification and deliniation of Middle Paleolithic culture variants.

Also in the beginning of the 1970s, some works advocating the application of quantitative methods appeared, but they were not specifically oriented toward Paleolithic studies (e.g. 55). The most recent trend is the multivariate approach toward artifact analysis mentioned above, wherein artifacts are recognized as a result of several cultural system variables. Increasingly, artifacts may be regarded not as univariate phenomena reflecting some cultural tradition or norm, but by means of attribute analysis, they may be treated as the product of several processes. Full-scale attribute analysis, however, is greatly facilitated by the use of computers, but computer facilities are not easily available to most Soviet archaeologists.

Some typological discussions in the literature have been extensive. One issue that has been given a fair amount of attention is the definition of Levallois technique and its meaning. Liubin (64), Grigor'ev (35), Gladilin (29), and Smirnov (85) have presented various analyses. From their works it is clear that there is not any consensus as to the definition of the Levallois technique, particularly in regard to Levallois/non-Levallois blade cores, and to the significance of Levallois technique as a marker of culture evolution. Liubin presents the importance of Levallois technique in clear cultural historical terms: it is an intermediate and necessary step between discoidal cores and prismatic blade cores. Thus it represents a great technological achievement. Gladilin and Grigor'ev do not agree, and Grigor'ev specifically rejects the notion that prismatic blade cores necessarily must develop from Levallois cores. Grigor'ev does tie the use of Levallois technique to a "culture line of development," but champions the notion that several lines of development existed, all of which had more or less equal likelihood of crossing the evolutionary boundary to an Upper Paleolithic level with prismatic blade core technology. Thus for Grigor'ev, Levallois technique is not necessarily "progressive."

Environment, Ecology, and Culture Change

The ecological systems approach is widely adopted by Western archaeologists, and it is generally regarded as a productive avenue toward the understanding of prehistoric culture change. The approach consists in the measurement of specified cultural and environmental variables and the study of their interactions. Through modeling and simulation, expectations of the archaeological record can be produced, and they can be matched against the actual archaeological record. Jochim (44) and Keene (46) have produced works of this kind. Are there parallel lines of development in the USSR, and is the ecological approach widely accepted there?

Soviet Paleolithic archaeology has had a strong environmental and geological emphasis for a long time. Multidisciplinary studies bringing together Quaternary sciences and prehistorians go back to the 1930s (31). In the post-World War II period particularly, major expeditions had the services of various environmental specialists. Today there are even some Pleistocene geologists who hold postitions designated for the study of archaeological deposits (e.g. 43, 94). This activity is reflected in the final monographs of the vast majority of expeditions wherein many sections will be devoted to describing stratigraphy, depositional history, pollen diagrams, and other related topics.

Certainly one of the major aims of this activity is to build a large and reliable data base that will contain accurate information of the relative and absolute chronology of Pleistocene cultural and environmental events. This has been, I maintain, one of the major successes of modern Soviet Paleolithic archaeology.

The question comes, however, how do Soviet scholars assess the relationship between environment and culture? A landmark conference in this regard was *Primitive Man, His Material Culture, and the Environment in the Pleistocene and Holocene*. This All-Union Symposium, organized by the Institute of Geography and the USSR INQUA Commission, was held in Moscow in 1973. The Soviet participants included a large number of the best-known specialists, and their papers reflect much of the modern thought concerning man-land relationships. As Grigor'ev points out (36), there is a basic division among Soviet archaeologists as to the significance of environmental conditions and oscillations for cultural evolution.

The first view is similar to that held by Leslie White. It holds that culture is man's extrasomatic means of adaptation to the environment. It is a connecting link between man and his natural surroundings. Accordingly, many items of material culture should be sensitive and responsive to environmental changes. The second view is that environment and culture are structural parts of a system tending toward equilibrium, and that "insofar as culture has subsystems, then inside it must exist its own objectives, its internal lawfulness, its internal goals" (36, p. 65).

The two views focus attention on the degree to which cultural variables are dependent or independent of the environment. In more concrete terms, the question becomes: what does the variability observed in Paleolithic stone tool kits mean with respect to the environment?

Velichko (95) has maintained that climatic oscillations will influence the character and the function of stone tool industries. He would predict that environmental influences should be observable on stone tool assemblages and human skeletal remains. The majority view is that these influences will not have such an effect. Liubin (65, p. 174), for example, concedes that environmental factors "regulate the possibilities and limits of settlement of early man, show strong influence on the particularities of economy and mode of life, the character of dwellings and clothing, but in far less degree influence the appearance of stone tools." He makes the point that some Mousterian cultures of the Caucasus maintained their similar character throughout warm to cold oscillations of the Würm and also that several different industries can be found under the same environmental conditions. His main conclusion is that the form of stone tool industries is not directly controlled by climatic or faunal conditions, but by social factors. It would seem, therefore, Liubin approaches the problem of environmental-cultural relationships along the dichotomy of possibilism vs determinism and comes out strongly on the side of possibilism. It is on this level that much of the debate about the role of environment and culture takes place.

The option of an ecological systems approach remains for the most part unexplored. One major exception is the recent work of Dolukhanov (20). Ultimately, when pressed, most investigators will maintain that "social factors" are responsible for some particular change under consideration. These factors are independent, superorganic variables, and they develop according to their own laws.

> It is obvious . . . that nature cannot exert the determining influence on the processes of social development, and moreover, on relations of production which make up the main factors and moving force upon the development of the social structure of human society. Irregardless of the enormous variety of environmental conditions on the earth, the general laws of social development established by Marxism are universal (28, p. 8).

Another approach toward the study of the relation of stone tool industries to the natural environment was made by Gvozdover (39). He examined artifact inventories and faunal collections from nine Upper Paleolithic sites in the Soviet Union. He found that irregardless of whether the fauna consisted largely of mammoth or of northern deer and bison, the artifact categories were the same and no specific projectile type could be correlated with a particular game animal. He concluded that there is no lawful regularity between hunting orientation and the character of stone tool collections. Like Liubin, he looks for the explanation of stone tool variability in social factors: "the origin and growth of cultures and their distribution, i.e. in the concrete historical processes of the Upper Paleolithic epoch" (39, p. 51).

The majority of the papers from the Moscow symposium tend toward similar conclusions. Basically, environmental determinism is rejected, but few workers appear ready to pursue a more encompassing ecological systems approach which has been one of the main components of Western Paleolithic archaeology in recent years.

CONCLUSIONS

It should be clear from the above discussion that because of many factors the conceptual basis of Soviet Paleolithic archaeology developed in a way distinct from the West. It is important to understand what these theoretical differences mean when interpreting some particular discussion going on in Soviet circles. For example, the discussion about the number, size, and shape of dwellings in the Kostenki-Borshevo Upper Paleolithic region summarized by Klein (50) must be seen in the context of the Theory of Stages and its attendant socioeconomic formations. Otherwise the Western archaeologist might believe this exchange has to do simply with the technological proficiency of Upper Paleolithic peoples.

On another level, Western archaeologists should realize that the positivist philosophy which underlies almost all of their archaeological work runs counter to the formal education of virtually all contemporary Soviet archaeologists. That is, positivism and neo-positivism are rejected as bourgeois thought in official textbooks (56) because they are not found to be compatible with Marxist dialectical materialism. Hence the deductive-nomological Hempelian approach familiar to most Western archaeologists cannot be fully accepted by Soviet scientists (83). On the other hand, systems approaches which focus on mechanisms of internal regulation and change are seen in a much more favorable light. Conversely, there are many aspects of the Marxist-Leninist philosophical background which come through in Soviet work that are not acceptable to most Western scholars. For example, Soviet archaeologists frequently use the term "progressive" when describing some culture or technology, and this use is clearly within the tradition of looking at history in stadial terms, an approach which positivists must ultimately reject. Deep-seated conceptual orientations are not always easy to recognize, but if Western and Soviet archaeologists wish to cooperate on more than the empiricist level, much more discussion in this area is warranted.

One of the major aspects of contemporary Soviet Paleolithic archaeological theory is that it is quite diverse and richly interwoven with old and new lines of thought. Although rejected by almost all contemporary Soviet workers, many aspects of the Theory of Stages are still in evidence: the concepts of progress, leaps, unilinial change, matrilineal clans succeeding patrilineal ones (e.g. 18) still frequent the literature. As both Klejn (54) and Trigger (92) have pointed out, there is a need for the development of middle-level theory to bridge high-level abstractions with low-level empirical data. This need has also been recognized recently in the West.

This review may at times have been more critical than laudatory in tone, but it is not my intention to minimize the enormous contributions of Soviet Paleolithic archaeology. Rather, I believe Soviet and Western scholars should engage in as full and frank exchanges as possible. Such interchanges will help scholars recognize not only their counterpart's objectives and methods, but will inevitably subject their own conceptions to closer scrutiny. In any case, Soviet Paleolithic archaeology has achieved great success in its organizational structure, the collection of high quality data, and in focusing on broad questions of historical development. Increasingly it will play a larger role in worldwide archaeology, and Western scholars can no longer afford to remain uninformed about Soviet contributions to their field.

ACKNOWLEDGMENTS

I am grateful to the National Science Foundation Anthropology Program which provided support for the study of Soviet Paleolithic archaeology under grant BNS 78–24945. Also, I would like to thank Olga Soffer for many discussions concerning contemporary Soviet archaeology. Finally, I would like to express my deep appreciation to all my Soviet colleagues who have generously provided me with copies of recent publications.

Literature Cited

1. Anikovich, M. V. 1978. Conference on the question of the classification and nomenclature of denticulated and notched tools of the Lower Paleolithic. *Sov. Arkheol.* No. 3: 303–6 (In Russian)
2. Anisyutkin, N. K. 1981. Concerning the development of Mousterian industries. Abstracts of a conference. *Continuity and Innovation in the Development of Ancient Cultures,* pp. 52–55. Leningrad: Nauka (In Russian)
3. Beregovaya, N. A. 1960. Paleolithic Localities of the USSR. *M.I.A.*[1] 81:1–216 (In Russian)
4. Beregovaya, N. A. 1972. Paleolithic discoveries in the USSR (1958–1968). *M.I.A.* 185:227–43 (In Russian)
5. Bochkarev, V. S. 1973. Toward the question of the structure of archaeological investigations. *Abstracts of the Results of Archaeological Investigations in 1972 in the USSR,* pp. 56–60 (In Russian)
6. Bordes, F. 1961. *Typologie du Paleolithique Ancien et Moyen.* Memoire No. 1. Bordeaux: Delmas. 85 pp.
7. Boriskovsky, P. I. 1935. Historical preconditions for the formation of "Homo sapiens," *Problemi Istorii Dokapitalistcheskikh Obshchestvo* 1–2 (Pt. I); 5–6 (Pt.II) (In Russian)
8. Boriskovsky, P. I. 1970. Problems in the origins of human society and archaeological discoveries of the last ten years. In *Lenin's Ideas in the Study of the History of Primitive Society, Slavery, and Feudalism,* ed. P. O. Zasurcev, pp. 58–75, Moscow: Nauka (In Russian)
9. Boriskovsky, P. I. 1973. Some results of work on "Paleolithic of the World."

Abstracts of a conference, *Results of Archaeological Field Work in 1972 in the USSR,* pp. 18–20. Tashkent: Fan
10. Boriskovsky, P. I. 1977. The origin of human society. In *The Origin of Human Society/The Paleolithic of Africa,* ed. P. I. Boriskovsky, Z. A. Abramova, G. P. Grigor'ev, pp. 11–42. Leningrad: Nauka, 212 pp. (In Russian)
11. Boriskovsky, P. I., Abramova, Z. A. Grigor'ev, G. P., eds. 1978. *The Paleolithic of the Near and Middle East.* Leningrad: Nauka. 264 pp. (In Russian)
12. Bulkin, V. A., Klejn, L. S., Lebedev, G. S. 1982. Attainments and problems of Soviet Archaeology. *World Archaeol.* 13:272–95
13. Chard, C. 1974. *Northeast Asia in Prehistory.* Madison: Univ. Wisconsin Press. 214 pp.
14. Chernysh, A. P. 1960. Remains of dwellings of Mousterian times on the Dnestr. *Sov. Etnogr.* No. 1 (In Russian)
15. Childe, V. G. 1940. Archaeology in the USSR. *Nature* 145:110–11
16. Clarke, D. L. 1968. *Analytical Archaeology.* London: Methuen. 684 pp.
17. Davis, R. S., Ranov, V. A., Dodonov, A. E. 1980. Early man in Soviet Central Asia. *Sci. Am.* 243(6):130–37
18. Dikov. N. N. 1979. *Ancient Cultures of Northeast Asia.* Moscow: Nauka. 352 pp. (In Russian)
19. Dolukhanov, P. M. 1977. The Mesolithic: an ecological approach. *K.S.I.A.* 149:13–17 (In Russian)
20. Dolukhanov, P. M. 1978. *Ecology and Economy in Neolithic Eastern Europe.* New York: St. Martin's. 212 pp.

[1]Abbreviations used in bibliography:

M.I.A. *Materialy i Issledovaniya po Arkheologii SSSR*
K.S.I.A. *Kratkiya Soobshcheniya Instituta Arkheologii*
ANSSSR Academy of Sciences of the USSR

21. Dragadze, T. 1980. The place of 'ethnos' theory in Soviet Anthropology. See Ref. 27, pp. 161–70

22. Efimenko, P. P. 1938. *Primitive Society*. Moscow and Leningrad: ANSSSR IIMK. (In Russian) 2nd ed.

23. Field, H., Price, K. 1949. Recent archaeological studies in the Soviet Union. *Southwest. J. Anthropol.* 5:17–27

24. Field, H., Prostov, E. 1937. Archaeology in the Soviet Union. *Am. Anthropol.* 39:457–90

25. Formozov. A. A., ed. 1970. The Stone Age in the Territory of the USSR. *M.I.A.* 166:1–207 (In Russian)

26. Formozov, A. A. 1977. *Problems of Ethnocultural History of the Stone Age in the European Part of the USSR*. Moscow: Nauka. 143 pp. (In Russian)

27. Gellner, E. 1980. A Russian Marxist philosophy of history. In *Soviet and Western Anthropology*, ed. E. Gellner pp. 59–82. New York: Columbia Univ. Press. 285 pp.

28. Gerasimov, I. P., Velichko, A. A. 1974. The problems of the role of natural factors in the development of primitive society. See Ref. 36, pp. 7–16 (In Russian)

29. Gladilin, V. N. 1977. Toward the question of Levallois technique. In *Problems of the Paleolithic*, ed. N. D. Praslov, pp. 29–34. Leningrad: Nauka. 221 pp. (In Russian)

30. Gladkik, M. I. 1977. Toward the problem of identifying economic-cultural types and historico-ethnographic societies of the Late Paleolithic. In *Paleoecology of Ancient Man*, ed. I. K. Ivanova, N. D. Praslov, pp. 112–17. Moscow: Nauka. 238 pp. (In Russian)

31. Golomshtok, E. 1938. The Old Stone Age in European Russia. *Trans. Am. Philos. Soc.* 29 (Pt. 2): 191–468

32. Grigor'ev, G. P. 1968. *The Beginning of the Upper Paleolithic and the Origin of Homo sapiens*. Leningrad: Nauka. 175 pp. (In Russian)

33. Grigor'ev, G. P. 1970. The Upper Paleolithic. *M.I.A.* 166:43–63 (In Russian)

34. Grigor'ev, G. P. 1972. Reconstruction of the social structure of Paleolithic hunters and gatherers. In *Hunters, Gatherers, and Fishers*, ed. Institute of Archaeology, pp. 11–25. Leningrad: Nauka (In Russian)

35. Grigor'ev, G. P. 1972. Problems of Levallois. *M.I.A.* 185:68–74 (In Russian)

36. Grigor'ev, G. P. 1974. The methodological bases for resolving the question of the relationship of environmental surroundings and human cultures. Materials of the All-Union Symposium, *Primitive Man, His Material Culture and Environment during the Pleistocene and Holocene*, 1973, pp. 65–70 (In Russian)

37. Grigor'eva, G. V. 1981. About the work of the Paleolithic Sector in 1978–1979. *K.S.I.A.* 165:126–29 (In Russian)

38. Grigor'eva, G. V., Islamov, U. I. 1974. A conference on the Stone Age of Central Asia and Kazakhstan. *Sov. Arkheol.* No. 2:318–20 (In Russian)

39. Gvozdover, M. D. 1974. Specialization of hunting and the character of the stone inventory of the Upper Paleolithic. See Ref. 36, pp. 48–52 (In Russian)

40. Howe, J. E. 1976. Pre-agricultural society in Soviet theory and method. *Arct. Anthropol.* 13:84–115

41. Howe, J. E. 1980. *The Soviet Theories of Primitive History: Forty Years of Speculation on the Origins and Evolution of People and Society*. PhD thesis. Univ. Washington, Seattle. 524 pp.

42. Institute of Archaeology. 1976. To the 25th Congress of the Communist Party of the Soviet Union. *Sov. Arkheol.* No. 1:5–8 (In Russian)

43. Ivanova, I. K. 1982. Fossil man and his culture. In *Stratigraphy of the USSR, The Quaternary System*, ed E. V. Shantser, 1(1): 382–415 (In Russian)

44. Jochim, M. A. 1976. *Hunter-Gatherer Subsistence and Settlement: A Predictive Model*. New York: Academic

45. Kabo, V. R. 1972. *History of primitive society and ethnography (Toward the problem of reconstructing the past from ethnographic data)*. See Ref. 34, pp. 53–67 (In Russian)

46. Keene, A. S. 1981. *Prehistoric Foraging in a Temperate Forest*. New York: Academic. 274 pp.

47. Kholyushkin, Yu. P. 1981. *Problems of Correlation of Late Paleolithic Industries of Siberia and Middle Asia*. Novosibirsk: Nauka. 120 pp. (In Russian)

48. Klein, R. G. 1966. Chellean and Acheulean on the territory of the Soviet Union: A critical review of the evidence as presented in the literature. *Am. Anthropol.* 68(2), Pt. 2, pp. 1–45

49. Klein, R. G. 1969. Mousterian cultures in European Russia. *Science* 165:257–65

50. Klein, R. G. 1969. *Man and Culture in the Late Pleistocene*. San Francisco: Chandler. 259 pp.

51. Klein, R. G. 1971. The Pleistocene prehistory of Siberia. *Quat. Res.* 1:133–61

52. Klein, R. G. 1973. *Ice-Age Hunters of the Ukraine*. Chicago: Univ. Chicago Press. 140 pp.

53. Klein, R. G. 1975. The relevance of Old World archaeology to the first entry of

man into the New World. *Quat. Res.* 5:391–94

54. Klejn, L. S. 1977. A panorama of theoretical archaeology. *Curr. Anthropol.* 18: 1–42

55. Kolchina, B. A., Shera, Ya. A., eds. 1970. *Statistical Combinatorial Methods in Archaeology*. Moscow: Nauka. 219 pp. (In Russian)

56. Konstantinov, F. V. 1977. *The Bases of Marxist-Leninist Philosophy*. Moscow: Politizdat. 463 pp. (In Russian)

57. Korobkov, I. I. 1971. Toward the problem of studying Lower Paleolithic settlements of open air type with disturbed cultural layers. *M.I.A.* 173:61–99 (In Russian)

58. Korobkov, I. I., Mansurov, M. M. 1972. Toward the problem of the typology of Tayacian-denticulated industries. *M.I.A.* 185:55–67 (In Russian)

59. Kraynov, D. A. 1970. Some questions about the origin of man and human society. See Ref. 8, pp. 76–93 (In Russian)

60. Laughlin, W. S. 1975. Aleuts: ecosystem, Holocene history and Siberian origin. *Science* 189:507–15

61. Leven, N. G., Cheboksarov, N. N. 1955. Economic-cultural types and historico-ethnographic oblasts. *Sov. Ethnogr.* No. 4 (In Russian)

62. Levitt, J. 1979. A review of experimental traceological research in the USSR. In *Lithic Use-Wear Analysis*, pp. 27–38. New York: Academic. 413 pp.

63. Lisitsyna, N. K. 1980. The department of field investigations of the Institute of Archaeology, ANSSR. *K.S.I.A.* 163:55–57 (In Russian)

64. Liubin, V. P. 1965. Toward the question of the method of investigation of Lower Paleolithic stone tools. *M.I.A.* 131:7–75 (In Russian)

65. Liubin, V. P. 1974. Environment and man in the Pleistocene of the Caucasus. See Ref. 36, pp. 169–177 (In Russian)

66. Liubin, V. P. 1977. *Mousterian Cultures of the Caucasus*. Leningrad: Nauka. 223 pp. (In Russian)

67. Liubin, V. P. 1981. The study of the Paleolithic in the USSR. *K.S.I.A.* 165: 3–9 (In Russian)

68. Marshack, A. 1979. Upper Paleolithic symbol systems of the Russian Plain: cognitive and comparative analysis. *Curr. Anthropol.* 20:271–311

69. Masson, V. M. 1972. The understanding of culture in archaeological systematics. Abstracts of a conference, *The Stone Age of Middle Asia and Kazakhstan*, pp. 9–11. Tashkent: Fan. 102 pp.

70. Masson, V. M. 1980. Sources of Soviet archaeological theory. *K.S.I.A.* 163: 18–26 (In Russian)

71. Matyukhin, A. E. 1981. Concerning the specifics of cultural process in the early Paleolithic (relative to pebble tools and bifaces). See Ref. 2, pp. 43–45

72. McBurney, C. B. M. 1975. *Early Man in the Soviet Union: Implications of Some Recent Discoveries*. London: British Acad.

73. Miller, M. O. 1956. *Archaeology in the USSR*. London: Atlantic Press. 232 pp.

74. Movius, H. L. Jr. 1953. Paleolithic and Mesolithic sites in Soviet Central Asia. *Proc. Am. Philos. Soc.* 97:383–421

75. Movius, H. L. Jr. 1953. The Mousterian cave of Teshik-Tash, southeastern Uzbekistan. Central Asia. *Bull. Am. Sch. Prehist. Res.* 17:11–71

76. Petrova-Averkieva, Yu. 1980. Historicism in Soviet ethnographic science. See Ref. 27, pp. 19–27

77. Pioro, I. S. 1973. Ethnos and archaeological culture. See Ref. 9, pp. 62–64 (In Russian)

78. Powers, R. 1973. Paleolithic man in Northeast Asia. *Arct. Anthropol.* 10:1–106

79. Praslov, N. D., Rogachev, A. N. 1982. *The Paleolithic of the Kostenki-Borshevo Rayon on the Don 1879–1979*. Leningrad: Nauka (In Russian)

80. Ranov. V. A. 1976. The Paleolithic industries of the Central Asia: A revision. *9th Congr. UISPP, Colloq.* 7:91–129

81. Ranov, V. A., Davis, R. S. 1979. Toward a new outline of the Central Asian Paleolithic. *Curr. Anthropol* 20:249–70

82. Rogachev, A. N. 1962. Principle results and problems in the study of the Paleolithic of the Russian Plain. *K.S.I.A.* 92:3–11 (In Russian)

83. Semenov, S. A. 1973. Concerning the mathematimization of archaeology. See Ref. 9, pp. 65–67 (In Russian)

84. Shimkin, E. M. 1978. The Upper Paleolithic in North-Central Eurasia: Evidence and Problems. In *Views of the Past: Essays in Old World Prehistory and Paleoanthropology*, ed. L. Freeman, pp. 193–315. The Hague: Mouton. 446 pp.

85. Smirnov, S. V. 1978. The significance of the Levallois technique in the ancient Stone Age. *Sov. Arkheol.* No. 3: 5–15 (In Russian)

86. Soffer-Bobyshev, O. 1982. *Politics of the Paleolithic in the USSR: A case of paradigms lost*. Presented at Ann. Meet. Soc. Am. Archaeol., 47th, Minneapolis

87. Suleymanov, R. Kh. 1972. *The Statistical Study of the Culture of Obi-Rakhmat Cave*. Tashkent: Fan. 171 pp. (In Russian)

88. Tallgren, A. M. 1936. Archaeological studies in Soviet Russia. *Eurasia Septentrionalis Antigua* 10:129–70
89. Teeter, M. H., Sutter, E. B., Ruble, B. A. 1981. *Soviet Research Institutes Project,* Vol. 3: *The Humanities.* Washington DC: Kennan Inst. Adv. Russian Stud. 731 pp.
90. Telegin, D. Ya. 1977. Concerning the criteria for isolating Mesolithic sites in the Southwestern European part of the USSR. *K.S.I.A.* 149:30–34 (In Russian)
91. Timofeev, B. I. 1977. Absolute dates of the European Mesolithic from C-14 data. *K.S.I.A.* 149:6–12 (In Russian)
92. Trigger, B. G. 1978. No longer from another planet. *Antiquity* 52:193–98
93. Trigger, B. G. 1980. *Gordon Childe/ Revolutions in Archaeology.* New York: Columbia Univ. Press. 207 pp.
94. Tseytlin, S. M. 1979. *Geology of the Paleolithic of Northern Asia.* Moscow: Nauka. 286 pp. (In Russian)
95. Velichko, A. A. 1971. Ties of the dynamics of natural changes and the development of primitive man. *Vopr. Antropol.* 37 (In Russian)
96. Velikova, E. A. 1977. Chronicles of the work of the Kostenki Paleolithic expedition (1922–1976). See Ref. 29, pp. 208–17 (In Russian)
97. Zadneprovskaya, T. N., Levina, R. Sh., Vseviov, L. M. 1980. *Soviet Archaeological Literature. Bibliography 1968–1972.* Leningrad: Nauka. 557 pp. (In Russian)
98. Zamyatnin, S. M. 1951. *Concerning the Origin of Local Differences of Culture in the Paleolithic Period.* Moscow (In Russian)

Ann. Rev. Anthropol. 1983. 12:429–62

SCHEMATA IN COGNITIVE ANTHROPOLOGY

Ronald W. Casson

Department of Sociology and Anthropology, Oberlin College, Oberlin, Ohio 44074

The aim of this review is to examine the "schema" concept being developed in cognitive science from the perspective of cognitive anthropology. Cognitive science is the inter-disciplinary field that was originally formed around the joint interests of cognitive psychology and computer science and now includes cognitive anthropology and cognitive linguistics as well. Schemata (the plural), which are knowledge structures that are "the building blocks of cognition," pervade theorizing about cognitive organization and function in cognitive science (173). "Schema" is the most widely used term for these knowledge structures (7, 22, 39–41, 51, 80, 95, 96, 102, 120, 121, 142, 144–149, 151–154, 170–175, 205, 209, 212), but they are also referred to as "frames" (138, 219), "scenes" (69), "scenarios" (69, 159), "scripts" (1, 2, 183–188), "gestalts" (117–119), "active structural networks" (174), and "memory organization packets" (185).

"Schema" and these other terms, although they are conceptualized somewhat differently by different writers, depending on their particular aims and interests, bear a striking family resemblance to each other. The emphasis here will not be on differentiating among these terms and concepts, but rather on assembling a composite conceptualization that incorporates the most important aspects of all these variants. Because "schema" is the most commonly occurring term, it will be used for this composite concept, and the other terms will be reserved for distinguishing types of schemata and some of their interrelationships.

The schema notion and its importance in cognitive research have been described and examined in numerous previous reviews. These have been reviews concerned either with cognitive science as a whole (21, 94, 144) or with work in cognitive psychology (100, 101, 142), cognitive social psycholo-

429

gy (89, 92, 203), or computer science (83, 140, 158). To date there has been no review that examined the importance of the schema notion in cognitive anthropology. Following general discussion of the schema concept in the first part of the review, attention will be focused in the second part on what D'Andrade (57) has termed "the cultural part of cognition."

SCHEMATA

Schemata are conceptual abstractions that mediate between stimuli received by the sense organs and behavioral responses (212). They are abstractions that serve as the basis for all human information processing, e.g. perception and comprehension, categorization and planning, recognition and recall, and problem-solving and decision-making (173). Schemata theory developed in reaction against associationist theories, which posited mental representations that directly reflected the external world (89). As Tyler, among others, has pointed out, "the structure of knowledge cannot consist of a mere picture of the world or even of a set of concepts which refer to or stand in a one-to-one relation with elements of the external world" (209, p. 98). Iconic representations of this sort are simply not rich enough to account for the complexity of human behavior. Much psychological research, however, continues to be conducted on the basis of associationism. See, for example, Wickelgren's recent review of learning and memory research, which adopts a strictly associationist perspective, maintaining that "there is no evidence supporting the hypothesis of unitary schema nodes, although they could exist" (216, p. 37).

Bartlett, who is generally credited with being the first to use the term schema in its contemporary sense [although Kant used the term in much the same sense in his *Critique of Pure Reason* (175)], argued that "the past operates as an organized mass rather than as a group of elements each of which retains its specific character" (7, p. 197). Remembering, Bartlett maintained, is constructive. Not all stimuli are stored in memory; rather, schemata are employed to provide "a general impression of the whole" and to construct (or reconstruct) "probable details" (7, p. 206). Much of the criticism directed at associationism has been concerned with demonstrating that there are significant differences between external stimuli and mental representations, with showing that schemata may omit much detail or include more information than is contained in the stimulus (89).

Basic to these criticisms is the view that schemata occur at differing levels of abstraction. At relatively low levels of abstraction there are schemata for perceiving geometrical figures, colors, faces, etc, while at higher levels there are schemata for comprehending complex activities and events. There are no important differences in kind between schemata for perception and comprehension: "perception is comprehension of sensory input" (175, p. 110). Schemata at particular levels of abstraction are not necessarily sensitive to schemata at other levels. Neisser (142, pp. 21–22) gives a particularly felicitous illustration of this. Observing someone smiling, he says, may involve only the perception of the shapes of teeth or changing positions of lips, or it may involve more abstract comprehension of a meaningful cultural act of "smiling," from which insights into the smiler's mood (e.g. happiness, cheerfulness, polite indifference) may be gained.

Schemata, unlike associations, are organic wholes comprised of parts that are oriented both to the whole and to other parts (209, p. 109; 117, p. 246). As Tyler states, they are indexical representations "founded in holistic simultaneity," whereas rules are symbolic representations "founded in linear sequentiality" (209, p. 100). Schemata are autonomous and automatic—once set in motion they proceed to their conclusion—and they are generally unconscious, nonpurposive, and irreflexive; rules, in contrast, are conscious, purposive, and reflexive, i.e. they have feedback loops that enable self-modification (209, p. 117). Tyler discusses the nature of rules at some length, distinguishing "five major branches of rule concepts": instructions, precepts, regulations, uniformities, and axioms (209, pp. 122–29).

Structures

Probably the most influential discussion of schema theory is Minsky's article, "A Framework for Representing Knowledge" (138). Minsky uses the term "frame" in discussing knowledge representations, but he places frames in the schema tradition stemming from Bartlett. A frame, according to Minsky (138, p. 212), is "a data-structure for representing a stereotyped situation, like being in a certain kind of living room, or going to a child's birthday party" (138, p. 212). This aspect of the schema concept is elaborated by Rumelhart, who states that a schema is "a data structure for representing the generic concepts stored in memory," and that "there are schemata representing our knowledge about all concepts: those underlying objects, situations, events, sequences of events, actions and sequences of actions" (173, p. 34; see also 170, 171, 175). This representation may be thought of as "a network of nodes and relations" (138, p. 212). It is the "network of interrelations that is believed to normally hold among the constituents of the concept in question" (173, p. 34); moreover, it accounts for "any situation that can be considered an instance of the general concept it represents" (171, p. 266).

The highest levels of schemata are fixed and represent invariant aspects of concepts, whereas lower levels have terminals, or "slots," that must be filled by specific instances of data, that is, they have variables that are associated with, or "bound by" elements in the environment in particular instantiations of the schema (138, p. 212; 173, p. 35). "Instantiation," a term used widely in the schema literature, refers to the binding of particular elements to particular variables on particular occasions (173, p. 36). The schema underlying commercial events in our culture may be taken as an example (66, 69, 173). The schema has the variables BUYER, SELLER, MONEY, GOODS, and EXCHANGE (upper case is used to distinguish conceptual units from words). BUYER is a person who possesses MONEY, the medium of exchange, and SELLER is a person who possesses GOODS, the merchandise for sale. EXCHANGE is an interaction in which BUYER gives MONEY and gets GOODS, and SELLER gives GOODS and gets MONEY. An event is understood as a commercial transaction when persons, objects, and subevents in the environmental situation are bound to appropriate schema variables.

Variables, or slots, have associated conditions that restrict the elements that may be bound to them. These conditions, known as "variable constraints," are knowledge about typical values of variables (simple conditions requiring that the bound element be a person, an object, or a subevent), and knowledge about interrelationships among variables (more complex conditions requiring certain relations among elements bound to sets of variables). Variables in the commercial event schema are constrained by knowledge that BUYER and SELLER are normally persons, that MONEY is generally currency, that GOODS are usually inanimate objects, and that EXHANGES involve transfers between participants of objects that they own or possess, as well as by knowledge that the MONEY and GOODS variables are interrelated: the value of MONEY covaries with the value of GOODS (173, p. 35).

Variable constraints not only restrict variable binding but also assign "default values" to variables for which no matching elements are found in the environmental situation. Default values are expectations or "best guesses" determined by the typical or normal values associated with variables. Because they are not specifically justified by the situation, they are only weakly bound to variables and are easily detached if additional information is revealed that makes more accurate value assignment possible (138, pp. 212, 228). In a transaction interpreted as a commercial event, a transfer of money may be inferred even when no money is seen to have changed hands on the basis of the default values associated with the MONEY and EXCHANGE variables in the schema. Note that this illustrates the point made earlier that a schema may contain more information than the stimulus environment with which it is matched. The use of schemata as a basis for making inferences about stimulus situations is a topic that will be taken up below.

Framing

The term "frame" has recently been used by linguists, principally Fillmore (66–70) and Chafe (39–41), in discussing the relationship between structures in language and underlying schemata. Language itself is, of course, a knowledge system—a system of conceptual abstractions, both unconscious, holistic schemata and conscious, reflexive rules (209, pp. 119–21). Although most contemporary linguistic analysis treats language solely as a system of rules, omitting any consideration of the role of schemata in language structure and process, a particularly lucid analysis of both the rules and schemata involved in past tense formation was recently published by Bybee & Slobin (33). The frame concept of Fillmore and Chafe is not concerned with the organization of language itself, but rather with how lexical and grammatical forms both structure and express underlying schematic representations (69, p. 127; 39, p. 46; see also 50, 64, 102, 120, 121).

The basic notion in framing is that lexical items and grammatical categories and rules are associated in memory with schemata and parts of schemata. Frames and schemata "activate" each other: linguistic forms bring schemata to mind and schemata are expressed in "linguistic reflexes" (66, p. 124; 67, p. 25). Lexical and grammatical forms are the means by which schema variables are labeled and verbalized. "Frame" is an appropriate term because what these language structures do is organize schemata for verbalization by focusing attention on certain variables and not on others. For example, a number of lexical items can activate the commercial event schema, e.g. *buy, sell, pay, cost, spend, charge.* Each of these words selects particular aspects of the schema for highlighting or foregrounding, while leaving others in the background unexpressed (66, p. 25; 69, p. 103). *Buy* focuses on the exchange from the buyer's perspective, and *sell* from the seller's perspective; *cost* focuses on the money-goods relationship, and so forth. Further examples of framing have been discussed in two recent articles: Langacker (120) describes how the single word *orphan* frames a "functional assembly" of kin relations and the life cycle, and Quinn (159; see also 160a) discusses how the key word *commitment* frames three polysemous meanings, PROMISE, DEDICATION, and ATTACHMENT, in the cultural scenario (i.e. schema) for American marriage.

The frame concept is generally used in a wider sense, originally formulated by Bateson (12) and later elaborated by Goffman (82). Frake, in his recent discussion of the dangers inherent in plying frames, assumes this Batesonian view in describing frames as the basic units of interpretative context, as the means by which "people organize their conception of what is happening at this time" (74, p. 4). This more general notion of framing may be dubbed "contextual framing" to distinguish it from "conceptual framing," the latter being a special case of the former (67). Contextual framing, like conceptual framing, involves associations between underlying schematic representations and the means of their expression. In contextual framing, the same reflexive relationship holds between schemata and frames, but the framing of contexts is accomplished not only on the basis of linguistic forms but also nonlinguistic communicative means, such as tone of voice, facial expression, appearance, gestures, and body postures and movements (74). Underlying conceptions of events are associated with the verbal and nonverbal devices by which they are expressed, and these devices shape and organize the conceptions they express.

Contextual framing by means of linguistic devices has been most extensively explored in "The Ethnography of Speaking," a tradition of sociolinguistic research originated by Hymes (97), who remains its leading spokesman. In this area of research, which was reviewed not long ago by Bauman & Sherzer (13), speech events and the language used in realizing them are described in their full reflexivity, e.g. poetry in a particular society is found to be expressed in language characterized by such formal devices as rhyme and meter, and these linguistic properties are shown to be what provides for its recognition as poetry. Tannen (201) adopts a more strictly linguistic approach in attempting to answer the question, "What's in a frame?" In analyzing oral narratives told by Greek women in recounting the contents of a film, she discusses 16 types of surface linguistic features in relation to underlying structures of expectation (i.e. schemata).

Fine-grained analysis of contextual framing by nonverbal means has been done by McDermott and his colleagues (135), who examined the body positionings, or postural configurations, assumed by a group of school children and their teacher during a reading lesson. Their analysis shows that the teacher and children, in taking up and leaving positionings, both express the current state of the reading context and provide each other with the means for organizing their interaction in the ongoing lesson. Basso's (10) description of Western Apache portraits of "the Whiteman" represents something of a culmination of this line of research. It is a seriously amusing account of how interactions that are potentially insulting and therefore dangerous are framed through a combination of both verbal and nonverbal devices (e.g. a joking variety of Western Apache English, discourteous repetitions of requests and demands, a loud tone of voice, and repeated handshaking and backslapping) as nonserious "whiteman joking"—as play in which "the Whiteman" is brought to life in vivid, wholly unflattering portraits.

Prototypes

A schema is also a prototype (51, 66–70, 102, 117, 173, 175). It is a stereotypic, or generic, representation of a concept that serves as a standard for evaluating the goodness-of-fit between schema variables and elements in the environment. Variable binding is constrained by typical or average values of schema variables, not by absolute values (175, p. 105). Conditions on variables specifying that a bound element must be, for example, a person or an object of a particular sort define prototypical instantiations, but less typical elements may be bound if they bear a family resemblance to it, i.e. if they are sufficiently similar to it (163–165, 167). Similarity is, of course, a matter of degree: some elements resemble prototypes more closely than others. Default values are prototypical or near prototypical values. In the schema for commercial events, BUYER is prototypically a person, although it may sometimes be bound by a corporation or institution; SELLER is prototypically a person who owns GOODS, although less typically it may be a salesman or middleman; and MONEY is prototypically cash, but it may also be a check, a charge card, or an I.O.U.

This notion of prototype schemata has lent itself to the development of a theory of meaning, recently christened "prototype semantics" by Coleman & Kay (51). A basic tenet of this theory is that the prototype schema (or schemata) underlying a concept corresponds to the meaning of the concept. Lexical meaning "consists in a cognitive prototype to which various real and imagined events may correspond in varying degrees" (51, p. 26). Linguistic forms, as stated in discussing framing, organize and express schematic representations; the point to be added now is that, because the schemata underlying conceptual categories are taken to be prototypes, these categories have analog representations (164). Meanings are determined on the basis of overall resemblance to prototype schemata. Elements that possess some (but not necessarily all) of the properties defining the prototype are instances of the concept. Thus, membership in semantic categories is a "more" or "less" matter and the boundaries of categories are frequently blurred or fuzzy; elements are instances of categories to a degree and instances differ in the degree to which they are members (51, 102, 104, 105, 109, 111, 112, 116, 164, 165). This approach to meaning is often referred to in anthropology as "extensionist semantics."

The prototype theory of meaning contrasts with what Fillmore (66) labels "checklist" theories of meaning. These are theories that posit digital representations of concepts (164), and have in common the view that meanings can be specified in terms of conjunctions of discrete properties, called variously "distinctive features," "semantic components," and "criterial attributes." Elements that display the list of properties defining a concept are instances of the concept. Thus, membership in semantic categories is a "yes" or "no" matter and the boundaries of categories are clear-cut and definite; elements are either instances of categories or they are not and all instances are equivalent as members. "Componential analysis," as practiced in anthropology and linguistics, is an example of a checklist theory (cf 11, 84, 85, 122).

Prototype theory is not new in anthropology, although it recently has been taken up with considerable enthusiasm in other disciplines, most notably psychology, where work by Rosch (163) has triggered a burst of research. This psychological work has been reviewed by Mervis & Rosch (136). Although not always acknowledged, the development of the prototype concept began with Lounsbury's work on kinship semantics (125–127, 190). Lounsbury's seminal articles demonstrated that the primary meaning of kinship terms derives from the genealogically closest of the types of kin (kintypes) that are included as instances of kin categories, and that this focal or prototypical sense is extended to the more distant kintypes also included in kin categories. Shortly after Lounsbury's work, the extensionist approach was employed by Berlin & Kay (20) in their pioneering study of basic color categories and by Berlin and his associates (15–18) in their work on ethnobotanical taxonomies.

Berlin & Kay's book (20) set off an explosion of research on color classification systems, which has shown rather convincingly that color categories are organized around prototypes (91, 164), and that they are nondiscrete or fuzzy categories in which membership is a matter of degree of approximation to prototypes (103). A further particularly important finding of this research, established most thoroughly by Kay and McDaniel, is that color prototypes are "based on panhuman neurophysiological processes in the perception of color" (103, p. 644; see also 220). Rosch (164) argues that color categories are a special type of category. They are prime examples of what she calls "attribute categories," biologically based categories of perceptual sensations that are "general attributes of concrete things" (164, p. 23). Other examples of attribute categories are geometrical shape categories, which have "wired-in" prototypes for circle, square, and equilateral triangle (163), and categories of facial expressions, which have physiologically determined prototypes for happiness, sadness, anger, fear, surprise, and disgust (61).

Rosch (164) contrasts attribute categories with "object categories." These are categories of concrete entities, such as plants, animals, vehicles, furniture, and so forth, that are not assumed to be biologically based but that are nonetheless organized in terms of prototypes and approximations to prototypes. A particularly popular and productive domain for investigating the internal structure of object categories has been the domain of "containers for liquids." Kempton (104, 105), for example, has shown that categories of drinking vessels (cups, mugs, coffee cups) are fuzzy categories organized in terms of focal members and grades of membership (see also 109, 111, 112). The prototype notion has also been applied in studies of social categories. The line of research on kin categories initiated by Lounsbury has been continued in a number of studies (14, 36, 189). Kay (102) has analyzed the prototype semantics of Tahitian race and class categories. Cantor & Mischel (34) have reviewed research on prototype categorization in abstract person categories, such as *extrovert, madman,* and *activist.* And Coleman & Kay (51) have studied prototypical *lies,* speech acts that are wholly abstract entities.

Embedding and Linking

A schema generally includes a number of embedded subschemata as constituent parts, each of which interacts in its own right with elements in the environment (142, p. 23). A schema, in other words, is most often a complex structure in which variables are bound by subschemata (138). Overall, then, schemata are organized as hierarchical structures in which schemata at the higher levels represent the most general concepts, and schemata at successively lower levels represent more and more specific concepts. Schemata at the lowest level are atomic, i.e. primitive concepts that are components of knowledge that do not break down into constituent parts or further subschemata (174, p. 106).

Taxonomies are the type of hierarchical organization formed on the basis of relations of class inclusion. A commercial event can be understood as "buying dinner in a restaurant" or as "buying a Whopper in a fast food restaurant," for example. Other types of hierarchical organization of schemata are formed on the basis of other types of conceptual relations, e.g. part-whole relations, causal relations, Fillmore's case relations, among others (65; see also 37, 209). Understood generally, a commercial event framed as *buying* involves a BUYER who EXCHANGES MONEY with a SELLER for GOODS. EXCHANGE, however, is not a primitive concept; its schematic representation contains subschemata for DO, CAUSE, and TRANSFER. It represents an event in which a BUYER DOES something that CAUSES two TRANSFERS of possession, one of MONEY from BUYER to SELLER and another of GOODS from SELLER to BUYER [this example is simplified from (78), pp. 212–25]. A commercial event, then, may be comprehended either in general in terms of a major schema alone, omitting any consideration of its internal structure, or more deeply in terms of embedded subschemata (175, p. 106).

Schemata are also organized sequentially. Subschemata embedded in a schema may be ordered to represent changes over time or in location, cause-effect relationships, and sequencing of stages or actions in events (138, p. 234). Continuing the commercial event example, the exchange of goods and money involves two states of affairs, the state prior to the exchange and the state after the exchange. The transfer of possession that characterizes exchanges is represented by two temporally ordered subschemata that share the same set of variables but in different arrangements: one represents the earlier state in which the BUYER POSSESSES the MONEY and the SELLER POSSESSES the GOODS, and the other represents the later state in which the BUYER POSSESSES the GOODS and the SELLER POSSESSES the MONEY (138, p. 240).

Schemata are not only organized into complex hierarchical structures, they are also interlinked with other schemata to form still larger structures. In a commercial event, the money one participant gives another may be specified as a *tip, bribe, ransom, tuition, retainer, change, rebate,* etc (69, p. 114). The framing of this money as a *tip,* for instance, serves to characterize it as money given in exchange for services (rather than goods) and, at the same time, to link the commercial event schema with a wider schema, about which numerous inferences can be made, e.g. that the services involved are those of a waiter or waitress in a restaurant (66, p. 28).

Linkage such as this to wider schemata differs from linkage that organizes schemata into ordered sequences or chains. "Eating in a restaurant," to take a widely discussed example, is an event whose representation is comprised of a sequence of linked schemata—ENTERING, ORDERING, EATING, and EX-ITING (183, 188). These schemata, termed "scenes," are in turn comprised of sequences of actions; TIPPING the waitress and PAYING the check are two of the constituent actions in the EXITING scene, for example. The sequence of actions defining scenes and larger-scale events is an elaborate causal chain: each action in the sequence results in conditions that enable the next action and must be completed before the next action can be started (188, p. 45). The term "script," first adopted by Schank and Abelson (1, 2, 183–188), has come to be the standard label for these sequences of schemata. Scripts are considered at greater length in the second part of this review.

Processes

Schemata are not only data structures, they are also data processors. As Neisser puts it, a "schema is not only the plan but also the executor of the plan. It is a pattern *of* action as well as a pattern *for* action (142, p. 56). Schemata are active processes whose primary activity is the construction of interpretations of experience; they are procedures capable of evaluating their own goodness-of-fit to elements in the environment and of thereby accounting for them (173, pp. 37, 39).

As stated, the top levels of schemata are fixed and invariant, whereas the bottom levels contain variables that are bound by elements in the environment. All the schemata interrelated in a complex schema operate individually in processing information at their respective levels, and supply each other with information for processing. More general higher level schemata direct the overall processing of information, motivating and coordinating the activities of lower level embedded subschemata; more specific lower level schemata pass information along to other low level schemata that follow them in sequential order and feed information up to the wider schemata in which they are embedded (142, pp. 56, 124).

There are two basic modes of processing. "Bottom-up processing," also termed "data-driven processing," is processing initiated when data are bound to variables in bottom level subschemata that move upward to activate the higher level schemata in which the subschemata are embedded. "Top-down processing," also called "conceptually driven processing," is processing initiated when top level schemata activate embedded subschemata in the expectation that these subschemata will fit the data (22, p. 140; see also 21, 45, 146–148). Data-driven processing moves from part to whole, and conceptually driven processing moves from whole to part (173). Data-driven processing is subconscious, automatic, and guided by the principle that "all the data must be accounted for," while conceptually driven processing is conscious, purposive, and guided by high level plans and goals (22, p. 148; see also 209, pp. 98–112).

Top-down and bottom-up processing occur simultaneously, and each requires the other. Expectations are combined with data in constructing interpretations of experience, and schemata are judged to account for elements in the environment when there is goodness-of-fit between expectation and data (22). An example liberally amended from Rumelhart (173, pp. 42–43) may make this somewhat abstract discussion of "mixed initiative processing" more concrete. The event in question occurs in a large enclosure in which automobiles are on display. A number of people are milling around, chatting, and examining the automobiles. The setting, people, objects, and activities suggest that the automobile dealership schema may be relevant to achieving an understanding of the event. Thus activated by bottom-up processing, the high-level auto dealership schema in turn sets off top-down processing of its subschemata. Because an expectation associated with this high-level schema is that automobiles will be bought and sold, one of its subschemata is the now familiar commercial event schema. Top-down processing activates this subschemata, initiating searches for data that may be bound to appropriate schema variables. The GOODS variable may potentially be bound by the automobiles, and a well-dressed man engaged in kicking tires and slamming doors is a reasonable candidate for the BUYER variable. The fact that the man is well-dressed suggests wealth, a possible binding for the MONEY variable. And the presence of a broadly smiling man in a checkered sportscoat who approaches the well-dressed man and engages him in jovial conversation suggests a potential binding for the SELLER variable.

The binding of these variables activates new bottom-up processing, which confirms the expectations of the auto dealership schema and eliminates from consideration alternative general schemata that might have been invoked at the outset of processing, e.g. the auto show schema in which the expectation is not that automobiles will be bought or sold but that they simply will be exhibited. This example is a heuristic fiction, oversimplified to the point of artificiality, but it illustrates how top-down and bottom-up processing work in concert to evaluate the success of schemata in providing interpretations of experience. More complex and realistic examples of schematic processing can be found in articles by Rumelhart (170–175) and Bobrow & Norman (22, 144–146).

Memory

There is general agreement that schemata are mental representations located in memory—that they are frameworks selected from memory when new situations are encountered (138). The structure of memory itself, however, has received relatively little attention (151, 185). Discussion of memory has for the most part been conducted in terms of Tulving's (207) distinction between semantic and episodic memory. The basic difference generally recognized between these two types of memory is that schemata in episodic memory represent specific knowledge, i.e. knowledge that is idiosyncratic, particular, and directly reflective of subjectively experienced stimuli, whereas schemata in semantic memory represent general knowledge, i.e. knowledge that is encyclopedic, relatively permanent, and known independently of experience (151, 175).

Researchers have tended to emphasize one or the other of these types of meaning. Some (52, 53) have concentrated on abstract semantic categories linked in hierarchical networks by class inclusion relationships, e.g. *animal, bird, robin.* Theories of semantic memory have recently been reviewed by Smith (195). Others (183, 184, 188) have focused on experiential groupings of concepts linked together by cooccurrence in events and episodes, e.g. *hammer, wood, nail.* Schank, the leading advocate of episodic memory, goes so far as to argue that memory is basically episodic in nature, that very few—perhaps no more than ten—hierarchical supersets actually occur in memory (183, p. 255). In recent work, however, Schank proposes different levels of memory structures for representing different sorts of knowledge; these levels—"event memory," "general event memory," "situational memory" and "intensional memory"—vary in the degree to which they reflect particular experiences (185, pp. 259–61). The semantic/episodic memory issue has not yet been resolved, but it is reasonable to conclude, even if only provisionally, that memory must contain schemata that represent concepts abstracted from particular events and episodes as well as schemata that represent concepts formed on the basis of particular experiences.

CULTURAL SCHEMATA

Schemata differ in their distribution in populations: some are universal, some idiosyncratic, and some cultural. Universal schemata are uniform in the human species because of innate faculties of the mind and/or inherent divisions in the natural world; idiosyncratic schemata are unique to particular individuals as the result of their personal histories and life experiences; cultural schemata are neither unique to individuals nor shared by all humans, but rather shared by members of particular societies (37, pp. 20–21). Cognitive anthropologists are concerned with cultural schemata, with "the cultural part of cognition," as D'Andrade (57) has recently phrased it. Unlike cognitive psychologists, who want to learn how the brain deals with all sorts of information, including cultural information, cognitive anthropologists focus on how systems of cultural knowledge are constrained and shaped by the machinery of the brain. The assumption here is that, as the result of its regular transmission from generation to generation, cultural knowledge comes to be organized in such a way that it "fits" the capacities and constraints of the human mind (57, p. 182). As succinctly stated by D'Andrade, the program for studying cultural cognition is to "search for commonalities in knowledge systems built into language in order to find out basic characteristics of human thought" (56, p. 3).

The anthropological concern with the interface between systems of cultural knowledge and basic psychological factors is clearly illustrated by Lounsbury's work on kinship semantics. Lounsbury, it will be recalled from the "prototype" discussion, demonstrated that categories in systems of kin classification are regularly organized in terms of prototypes (focal kintypes) and extensions (nonfocal kintypes that are equated with focal kintypes). This general finding about kin classification systems points to the existence of underlying psychological mechanisms that interface with the prototypes-with-extensions organization of kin categories (57, p. 182). Lounsbury's pathbreaking work, as already mentioned, has been followed up by a great deal of research in many non-kinship domains. In psychology, Rosch's work (163–168) has been particularly significant in spearheading efforts to elucidate the psychological factors involved in prototype categorization. Lakoff's (117a) most recent work has also contributed importantly to this line of research.

In the following sections, research exploring the organization of complex cultural schemata is reviewed. Attention is first focused on three types of complex schemata found in the organization of cultural content: object schemata, orientation schemata, and event schemata. Then brief surveys are presented of research concerned with the role of these complex schemata in two currently very active areas of cognitive research, metaphor and narrative.

Object Schemata

Recent research has advanced understanding of the complex schemata underlying a wide range of object classification systems. Object categories, as mentioned in discussing prototypes, are categories of concrete entities. Some of the object classification systems that have been studied are classifications of plants (15–20, 26, 28, 90), animals (27, 29, 93), manufactured objects including vehicles, tools, clothing, and furniture (168), containers (104, 105, 109), persons (34), kinsmen (189, 190), occupations (32), ethnic identities (179), personality descriptors (108, 215), illnesses (55), and emotions (128).

Taxonomies, which occur widely in cultures and have been studied extensively by anthropologists, are a familiar type of classification system. In taxonomic classifications, wider, more general and narrower, more specific categories stand to each other in class inclusion, or "kind of," relations (see 37, pp. 75–77). The English ethnobotanical category *tree*, for example, includes the *oak* category, and *oak* is a kind of *tree*. Other categories included in the *tree* category are *maple, pine, elm, spruce,* and *poplar.* The *tree* category is included in the superordinate category *plant*, as are the categories *bush, grass,* and *vine*, and *oak* includes the subordinate categories *white oak, post oak, scrub oak, red oak, jack oak, pin oak*, and *burr oak*.

Ethnobiological taxonomies are the most thoroughly studied object classification system. Thanks largely to the work of Berlin and Brown and their associates (15–19, 26–29), much is now known about their structure, growth, and development. A major finding is that categories in ethnobiological taxonomies are grouped into mutually exclusive hierarchical ranks, which have been labeled "kingdom," "life form," "generic," "specific," and "varietal" (16). The kingdom rank category is the all-inclusive unique beginner; it is the highest level category and delimits the entire domain (e.g. *plant* in English ethnobotany). Life-form rank categories are the next most inclusive categories. They are few in number and are labeled by primary lexemes (e.g. *tree, grass, vine*). Categories of generic rank are next in inclusiveness. By far the most numerous categories in ethnobiological classification systems, generic categories are also generally labeled by primary lexemes (e.g. *oak, maple, pine*). Generic categories that dominate lower level categories (many do not) immediately include specific rank categories, which in turn include categories of varietal rank. Specific categories are few in number and varietal categories are rare. Lexemes for both are generally binomial secondary lexemes (e.g. *white oak, post oak, scrub oak*).

Berlin (16, 17) has shown that generic rank categories comprise the core of ethnobiological classifications in simpler societies. They are not only the most numerous but also the psychologically most salient or basic categories. Basic level categories are those categories in a classification system that are most frequently used in everyday interaction, most easily recalled by informants, and earliest in ontogenetic development (58). Dougherty (58) has revised Berlin's account of basic level categories, demonstrating that while generic rank categories are most salient in the ethnobiological classification systems of people who interact frequently with their biological environment and whose subsistence depends directly on it, categories superordinate to the generic level (i.e. life-form categories) are most salient in the systems of people who do not maintain a high degree of interaction with their biological environment. Which level is basic in a taxonomic classification system is not fixed but rather determined relative to the overall salience, or cultural significance, attached by society members to the objects classified in the system.

Basic level categories have been described for nonbiological classification systems as well. Rosch and her associates (168) have established the existence of a "basic object level" in their studies of classifications of manufactured objects such as vehicles, tools, clothing, and furniture. *Vehicle*, for example, is a superordinate category dominating *car, bus*, and *truck*, which are basic level categories dominating such subordinate categories as *sportscar, city bus*, and *pickup truck* (168). Basic level categories have long been recognized in studies of color classifications, e.g. *red, green, yellow, blue* (20), and kin classifications, e.g. *uncle, aunt, nephew, niece* (190). Cantor & Mischel (34) have described basic level person categories, e.g. *extrovert, madman, joker, activist*.

Another type of classification system that has received attention is the constituent, or partonomic, classification system (6, 25, 31, 62, 134). Higher level and lower level categories in this kind of classification system are connected by part-whole relations. In English ethnoanatomical classification, for instance, *fingernail* is a part of *finger, finger* and *palm* are parts of *hand, hand* and *forearm* are parts of *arm*, and *arm* is a part of *body* (6, pp. 347–48). Like taxonomies, partonomies also have a basic level of abstraction: *hand, foot*, and *eye* are basic level categories that are dominated by superordinate categories *arm, leg*, and *face* and in turn dominate subordinate categories *finger, toe*, and *pupil*. Other constituent classification systems include membership classifications such as *family*, which has among its members *father, son*, and *brother*, and *baseball team*, which has the members *shortstop, pitcher*, and *manager* (176).

Functional classification systems are constructed on the basis of instrumental, or "used for," relations. Superordinate and subordinate categories in this kind of classification system are related functionally. One way in which shoes, for example, are classified in our culture is by function: a *jogging shoe* is a shoe used for jogging, and a *tennis shoe* is a shoe used for playing tennis. Many basic level categories in classification systems that have been treated as taxonomically related to superordinate categories are shown actually to be functionally related (183). Rosch's taxonomies of manufactured objects are, in fact, not strictly taxonomies at all: a *vehicle* is any kind of object that can be used as transportation, and *car, bus*, and *truck* are categories of objects that function as vehicles. While relations of basic level categories to subordinate categories are generally taxonomic, relations to superordinate categories are very often nontaxonomic (183, 218). It may even be the case that superordinate taxonomic categories occur only in ethnobiological classifications (218).

This survey of object classification systems supports two important observations. First, it establishes that the complex schemata underlying conceptual systems are not simply ad hoc collections of simpler schemata, but rather integrated, organic wholes oriented around a basic level of abstraction. Second, it also supports the idea that underlying psychological capacities must be shaped in a way that is consistent with the basic level organization found in object classification systems.

Attributes, as pointed out in discussing prototypes, are properties or qualities of objects, typically features of form, such as color, shape, texture, or size, and features of function, such as use for sitting, for clothing, or for food. What is a category and what is an attribute of a category is determined relative to level of analysis (136). *Red* and *blue,* for example, are at one level subject to analysis as categories, as the large literature on color classification testifies (20, 91, 103, 164, 220). At a higher level RED and BLUE are units in the analysis of categories. They are primitive elements connecting concepts with objects in the world that do not decompose into constituent parts.

Attributes are of two sorts. Absolute attributes are inherent properties of objects (a *ball,* for example, may have the properties RED, ROUND, and SMOOTH). Relative attributes, on the other hand, are not properties of objects themselves. They are properties of relationships between objects and norms for those objects (a person may be OLD or RICH relative to the norms for age and wealth) and between objects and other objects (an *owner* is a person who POSSESSES an object and a *father* is a person who is the male PARENT OF a child). More detailed discussion may be found in Casson (37, pp. 84–86; see also 35, 49, 63, 122, 197, 209, 214).

The basic level in classification systems is the most inclusive level at which perceptual and functional attributes are shared by most members of each of the categories and at which contrasting categories are maximally discontinuous (165, pp. 30–31). The categories *chair* and *car* are examples. Members of superordinate categories share only a small number of attributes: *furniture* includes chairs, tables, and beds, and *vehicle* includes cars, buses, and trucks. In both cases, included objects share few properties. Members of subordinate categories share bundles of common attributes, but these attributes overlap extensively with the attributes of contrasting categories: *kitchen chair, desk chair, easy chair,* and *city bus, school bus, cross-country bus* are sets of contrasting categories that have many overlapping attributes in common.

Orientation Schemata

Orientation schemata are complex schemata that represent knowledge about spatial orientations (110). Particularly in anthropology, schemata of this type are often referred to as "cognitive maps." Their overall organization is hierarchical. A complex schema representing general spatial concepts occurs at the topmost level, and a number of subschemata representing object concepts are embedded at lower levels. Orientation schemata represent knowledge about spatial relations among objects and their relative positions in the physical environment; they always include a representation of the self because "Ego and world are perceptually inseparable" (142, pp. 113–17). Kuipers (110, pp. 132–34), in proposing a formal model of spatial knowledge, argues that cognitive maps contain three classes of representations: representations for knowledge about particular environments, descriptions of the current position of the self (the "You Are Here" pointer), and representations of processes that manipulate the other two kinds of knowledge, i.e. routes, which are procedures for moving the "You Are Here" pointer through the environmental representation.

Cognitive maps range from representations of very small- to very large-scale spaces. Maps of relatively small-scale spaces have been formulated by Neisser (142, pp. 111–13), who describes a cognitive map of an office and its setting, and by Linde & Labov (123), who describe schemata for the spatial layouts of apartments. In *The Image of the City,* Lynch (129, pp. 46–83) describes large-scale maps of portions of cities, showing that they generally contain five types of elements: paths (routes through the city), edges (boundaries, such as rivers or railroad tracks), districts (sections of the city), nodes (junctions where paths meet), and landmarks (outstanding features, such as tall buildings or mountains). Wallace's (211) classic account of "driving to work" illustrates the use of just such a large-scale cognitive map. T. Gladwin (81) and Oakley (150) have described the complex orientation schemata used by native navigators during lengthy sea voyages in Oceania.

Orientation schemata are used not only in traveling through cities and navigating at sea. They are also used in imagining city travel and sea voyages. Cognitive maps can be detached from their original environments and used abstractly to picture the environments they represent (142). Detached in this way from actual environments, they can serve as mnemonic devices. The "Method of Loci" is a well-known device employed widely in performing feats of memory (23). First invented by the ancient Greeks, the method depends on the representation in cognitive maps of a series of locations along a path or route. Items to be memorized are imagined one at a time in association with each of the locations along the path. Recall of the items in the original order, in the reverse order, or individually out of sequence is achieved simply by taking a mental stroll along the path and examining the images associated with the various locations. In an example related by Harwood (88), the holes of a familiar golf course were used as the loci where images of 18 items for memorization could be mentally placed. "A brown (Bron-) slavic (-slaw) skier (-ski) lying sick (Mal-)" could, for example, be mentally located near a sand trap on the third green, so that later, in attempting to recall the third item in a series, the name Bronislaw Malinowski would be brought to mind by envisioning the third green and its associated image (88, p. 783).

Cognitive maps, like classification systems, are organic wholes. They are not just assemblages of object schemata, but rather integrated conceptual systems that include specific object concepts in general representations of spatial knowledge (142). Furthermore, just as basic level organization in object classifications suggests the existence of matching psychological factors, so the spatial organization of object concepts in cognitive maps suggests the existence of correspondingly organized underlying psychological mechanisms (23, 142).

Attributes of orientation concepts are properties of physical space, e.g. up and down, above and below, tall and short, left of and right of, in front of and in back of. UP/DOWN, ABOVE/BELOW, and TALL/SHORT are relative attributes because they are properties of relationships between objects in physical space. An object has the attributes UP or DOWN, for instance, depending on its position on a vertical axis (defined by the force of gravity) relative to a horizontal plane (ground level) (43, pp. 241–42). Attributes like LEFT/RIGHT and FRONT/BACK are defined in terms of spatial relationships to a canonical, or prototypical, person (44, 54, 132, 139). This person, or self, is typically upright, has significant parts (e.g. head, front, back, right side, and left side), and moves and sees in a forward direction (43, 77).

Event Schemata

Event schemata represent a wide range of activities and interactions, varying from simple actions like giving and taking to complex scenes like ordering a meal in a restaurant. In studying event concepts, investigators have devoted considerable attention to determining the elementary units out of which schemata for events are constructed. Researchers in linguistics (38, 65, 98, 115, 133, 169, 217), artificial intelligence (182–184, 188), and psychology (137, 174) have devised numerous systems of primitive elements. The earliest of these theories were proposed by linguists working in Generative Semantics, particularly Lakoff (115), and Case Grammar, particularly Fillmore (65). The principal aim of this linguistic research, which postulated primitive predicates and case relations as elementary units, was to represent the semantic structures underlying lexical items and sentences. Research in artificial intelligence and psychology stemming from this linguistic work adopted the same aim, plus the additional goal of developing computer models of these semantic representations (175, 182–184).

These theories, which are very similar despite notational differences, all posit sets of primitive predicates and recognize a basic distinction between primitive actions and primitive states (see especially 65, 115, 182). Primitive acts are predicates that specify active relationships in propositions. Examples are DO, GO, PROPEL, GRASP, CAUSE, CHANGE. Primitive states are predicates that specify nonactive states of affairs. Examples include BE, TALL, ALIVE, KNOW, POSSESS. Some investigators (e.g. Schank) maintain that while there is a large number of primitive states, there is a limited set of primitive acts, perhaps as few as 11 (183, 188). Others (e.g. Minsky) argue that the collection of primitive concepts is quite large (138).

These theories also propose elementary concepts specifying the ways in which arguments are related to primitive predicates in propositions. In their influential original formulations, Fillmore (65) and Chafe (38) posited sets of "cases" or "roles" to account for relationships between concepts in argument positions and their predicates. These notions have been clarified and refined in more recent research (68, 78, 141, 174). A current list of cases would include AGENT, OBJECT, RECIPIENT, EXPERIENCER, INSTRUMENT, LOCATION, SOURCE, and GOAL.

To illustrate, the GIVE schema is a relatively simple action schema (78; see also 174, 175). It is composed of a predicate and three arguments: an AGENT GIVES an OBJECT to a RECIPIENT. GIVE is not, however, a primitive concept. Its representation breaks down into subschemata for DO, CAUSE, and TRANSFER; that is, it is an event in which an AGENT DOES something to CAUSE an OBJECT to be TRANSFERRED to a RECIPIENT. DO and CAUSE are primitive concepts, but TRANSFER is not. The representation of TRANSFER includes further subschemata for CHANGE and POSSESS, which are primitive elements; it is an event in which POSSESSION of an OBJECT CHANGES from AGENT to RECIPIENT.

Schemata, as described earlier, are linked into ordered sequences or chains. This is accomplished by way of causal, or contingency, relations. Actions and states are conditionally connected: a state is usually or necessarily followed or accompanied by an action, and an action is the usual or necessary consequence or concomitant of a state (see 37, p. 82). Schank (183, 188) very usefully distinguishes five kinds of causal relations that are needed in accounting for linkages between schemata: RESULT causation (action RESULTS IN state change), ENABLE causation (state ENABLES action), DISABLE causation (state DISABLES action), INITIATION causation (state or act INITIATES mental state), and REASON causation (mental state is REASON FOR action). Causal linking may be illustrated by specifying the relations that connect states and actions in a simple event: John, being thirsty, opens a can of beer and takes a drink (188, p. 28–30).

     John is THIRSTY (state)
       INITIATES
     John DESIRES beer (mental state)
       REASON FOR
     John DO something (unspecified action)
       RESULTS IN
     beer can OPEN (state)
       ENABLES
     John INGEST beer (action).

Persons and objects in events stand to states and actions in the various case relationships: John is AGENT of DO and INGEST and EXPERIENCER of THIRST and DESIRE.

Linked schemata of this sort that represent recurrent, conventionalized activities and interactions are known as "scripts." Schank and Abelson (1, 2, 183–188), who originated the script notion, have generally defined a script as a "predetermined, stereotyped sequence of actions that defines a well-known situation" (188, p. 41). Recently, however, Schank has revised this definition, stating that a script is not a data structure that is available in one piece in memory, but rather a structure that is reconstructed from memory as it is needed to interpret experience (185, p. 264; see also 24). Agar's (3) account of *getting off*, or *shooting up* (injecting heroin), a central event in the culture of *street junkies* (urban heroin addicts), can be rephrased as an example of a script. The organization of some of the sequenced actions comprising this event is as follows:

> junkie COOKS (heats) heroin and water mixture (action)
>   RESULTS IN
> heroin DISSOLVED (state change)
>   ENABLES
> junkie DRAW (transfer) heroin into works (action)
>   RESULTS IN
> works PRIMED (state)
>   ENABLES
> junkie HIT (insert) works into vein

Case relations in this event include: junkie is AGENT of COOK, DRAW, and HIT; works is INSTRUMENT of HIT and RECIPIENT of DRAW.

The GETTING OFF script is an example of what Schank & Abelson (188) call an "instrumental script." It is an invariant sequence of actions that is employed, generally by one participant, to accomplish a particular task (188, p. 65). Dougherty & Keller's (59) "taskonomies" can be regarded as further examples of instrumental scripts. The two other types of scripts identified by Schank and Abelson are "personal scripts" and "situational scripts." Personal scripts are idiosyncratic sequences of actions that single actors use to achieve personal goals (e.g. making a date with a waitress in a restaurant), and as such are not of much cultural interest (see 199). Situational scripts have been the principal focus of script research. They pertain to specific situations—characteristically institutionalized public situations—in which several participants assume interconnected roles and, on the basis of shared understandings, cooperate to achieve certain well-defined goals (188, p. 61). ORDERING in a restaurant is a situational script, comprised of a chain of actions and states linked by causal relations, e.g. EXAMINING the menu, CHOOSING food items, SUMMONING the waitress, etc (188, p. 42–43).

The GETTING OFF and ORDERING scripts may be viewed from a wider perspective as constituents of still larger conceptual structures, as subscripts or scenes in wider scripts. GETTING OFF is causally linked in a cyclical chain of events with two other events, COPPING (buying heroin) and HUSTLING (getting money) (4, pp. 44–46):

junkie POSSESS bread (state)
   ENABLES
junkie COP heroin (action)
   RESULTS IN
junkie POSSESS heroin (state)
   ENABLES
junkie GET OFF/SHOOT UP heroin
   RESULTS IN
junkie BE STRAIGHT (i.e. not sick) (state)
   ENABLES
junkie HUSTLE bread (action)
   RESULTS IN
junkie POSSESS bread (state)

ORDERING in a restaurant, as stated earlier in discussing linking, is one of four scenes that comprise the full restaurant script: ENTERING, ORDERING, EATING, and EXITING (188). Several of Frake's important articles (71–73) are accounts of aspects of Subanun and Yakan culture that could be rephrased as scripts.

A final point to note about event schemata is that events represented in scripts are very likely basic level categories. Rosch (165, pp. 43–44) has tentatively concluded on the basis of pilot research that events like "making coffee," "taking a shower," and "going to statistics class" are basic level event categories, as contrasted with such superordinate event categories as "getting out of the house in the morning" or "going to afternoon classes" and such subordinate categories as "picking up the toothpaste," "squeezing the toothpaste," and so on. More research is needed here, but this seems to be another case in which the organization of systems of cultural concepts suggests underlying psychological mechanisms.

Metaphor

Recently, the nature of metaphor has become a topic of considerable interest in anthropology, linguistics, and psychology. A vast topic, metaphor has been approached from a large number of theoretical perspectives (9, 99, 152–156, 177, 181, 206). The strategy here will be to focus on metaphor research employing schema theory.

One line of research has been concerned with showing how schema theory can account for the comprehension of metaphors (152–154, 172). In general terms, a metaphor states an equivalence between two concepts from separate domains. The metaphor, "George is a lion," for example, states an equivalence between a human being, George, and an animal, a lion. *George* is the "tenor" of the metaphor, the concept that is continuous with the topic of discourse, and *lion* is the metaphor's "vehicle," its discontinuous concept (180, p. 7). Placing the two concepts in juxtaposition, the metaphor forms a concept that subsumes both tenor and vehicle (9, pp. 96–97). The Western Apaches, to cite one of Basso's (9) examples, convey the concept "living earth dweller who wastes food" by juxtaposing *carrion beetle* (vehicle) and *whiteman* (tenor) in their "Wise Words" metaphor, "Carrion beetle is a whiteman." In schema theory terms, the comprehension of metaphors like "George is a lion" and "Carrion beetle is a whiteman" depends on similarities and dissimilarities among the values bound to variables in the schemata underlying tenor and vehicle (154, pp. 359–60). General variables that are similar are maintained as variables in the metaphorical concept (George and lions are ANIMATE BEINGS and carrion beetles and whitemen are LIVING EARTH DWEL-LERS); specific variables that are dissimilar are omitted from the metaphor (George does not have PAWS or TAIL and whitemen are not INSECTS); and at least one specific variable (or subschemata embedded in a variable) that is shared is recognized as a crucial variable in the metaphorical concept (George and lions have COURAGE, STRENGTH, and AGRESSIVENESS and white-men and carrion beetles WASTE FOOD) (9, 180).

A second line of metaphor research employing schema theory deals with larger-scale metaphorical processes. This is the research of Lakoff & Johnson (118, 119), which is concerned with demonstrating that much of everyday experience is structured by metaphorical concepts. In essence, Lakoff and Johnson's argument is that basic abstract concepts that are not clearly deline-ated in experience, such as ARGUMENT, TIME, LOVE, and IDEAS, are metaphorically structured in terms of other basic concepts that are more concrete in experience, such as WAR, MONEY, TRAVEL, and FOOD. Metaphorical structuring is not simply a matter of individual concepts but rather of "experiential gestalts"—multidimensional structured wholes (i.e. schemata) that coherently organize experience in terms of natural dimensions of experience, e.g. participants, parts, stages, causes, purposes (119, p. 81).

The metaphorical concept ARGUMENT IS WAR is an example that Lakoff & Johnson (119) treat at some length. Conversation that is seen as argument is understood as such on the basis of the ARGUMENT IS WAR metaphor. ARGUMENT, an abstract, not clearly delineated concept, is "partially struc-tured, understood, performed, and talked about in terms of WAR," which is a more concrete concept that emerges naturally from the experience of physical combat (119, p. 5). The WAR schema specifies an event in which participants are adversaries who attack and defend positions, plan strategies, maneuver, advance, retreat, counterattack, declare truces, surrender, and triumph. The ARGUMENT schema, derived systematically from the WAR schema, repre-sents an event in which participants are adversaries embattled in a conflict of opinions (not actual combat), who struggle over positions, gain ground, win or lose, and so on.

Lakoff & Johnson (119, p. 7) argue that the systematicity of metaphorical concepts illustrated in this example is reflected in the language used in talking about these concepts and that, as a consequence, linguistic expressions are a source of insight into and evidence for the nature of the human conceptual system. Again, the research strategy, as stated in the passage quoted earlier from D'Andrade (56, p. 3), is to look for regularities in knowledge structures that are built into language to discover basic properties of thought. Some everyday speech formulas or fixed-form expressions reflecting the ARGU-MENT IS WAR metaphor are evident in the following sentences (119, p. 4):

> Your claims are *indefensible*. He attacked *every weak point* in my argument. His criticisms were *right on target*. I *demolished* his argument. He *shot down* all my arguments.

Lakoff & Johnson (118, 119) distinguish three types of metaphors: ontological, orientational, and structural. Ontological metaphors are used in comprehending events, actions, activities, and states. Events and actions are metaphorically conceptualized as objects, activities as substances, and states as containers. The metaphor IDEAS ARE FOOD, which entails

IDEAS ARE OBJECTS, is apparent in a great many expressions.

> What he said *left a bad taste in my mouth*. All this paper has in it are *raw facts, half-baked ideas,* and *warmed-over theories*. I *can't swallow* that claim. That's *food for thought* (119, pp. 46–47).

VITALITY IS A SUBSTANCE is evident in

> She's *brimming* with vim and vigor. She's *overflowing* with vitality. He's *devoid of* energy. That *took a lot out of* me. I'm *drained* (119, p. 51).

and LIFE IS A CONTAINER is reflected in

> I've had a *full* life. Life is *empty* for him. Her life is *crammed with* activities. *Get the most out of* life (119, p. 51).

Reddy (161) has analyzed a particularly intriguing and subtle example, the "conduit metaphor," which structures both lay and many linguistic conceptions of language.

Orientational metaphors are used to structure abstract concepts that are not well grounded in experience in terms of concrete concepts arising from experience with spatial relationships. For example, UP-DOWN metaphors include, among many others,

HAPPY IS UP/SAD IS DOWN

> I'm feeling *up*. My spirits *rose*. You're in *high spirits*. I'm feeling *down*. I'm *depressed*. He's really *low* these days.

HEALTH IS UP/SICKNESS IS DOWN

> He's at the *peak* of health. He's in *top* shape. He *fell* ill. He *came down with* flu. His health is *declining*.

CONTROL IS UP/BEING CONTROLLED IS DOWN

> I'm *on top of* the situation. He's in a *superior* position. He's in the *upper* echelon. He's *under* my control. He *fell* from power. He's *low man* on the totem pole (119, p. 15).

Structural metaphors are used in comprehending complex, highly structured concepts. While ontological and orientational metaphors are basic in providing the means of referring to concepts, quantifying them, orienting them, and so on, structural metaphors provide for the use of "one highly structured and clearly delineated concept to structure another" (199, p. 61). In structural metaphors, the constituent structures of complex object, orientation, and event schemata serve as the means of structuring other complex schemata. The ARGUMENT IS WAR metaphor is an example of a metaphor based on a complex event schema. LIFE IS A GAMBLING GAME is another structural metaphor involving a complex event schema. LOVE IS A JOURNEY is a structural metaphor based on an orientation schema:

> Look *how far we've come*. We're *at a crossroads*. We'll just have to *go our separate ways*. I don't think this relationship is *going anywhere* (199, p. 44).

Examples of metaphors based on complex object schemata have also been published: Basso (8) has described how the Western Apache classification of human body parts is used metaphorically in classifying parts of pickup trucks and automobiles, and Casson (36) has shown how a Turkish kin address system is extended metaphorically in addressing nonkin.

Narrative

Narrative is another burgeoning area of research in anthropology, linguistics, and psychology. Like metaphor, narrative is a huge topic that has been studied from a variety of perspectives (see 30, 42, 60, 75, 76, 79, 87, 114, 124, 194, 202, 208). Again, the strategy here will be to review only research employing the schema concept.

The three types of complex schemata described in this review have all been shown to provide the underlying organization for narrative discourse. Narratives based on event schemata have been by far the most extensively studied, undoubtedly because they are the most widely occurring, and will, for this reason, receive the most attention here. But interesting accounts of the use of object and orientation schemata in organizing narrative have also been published. In describing "the way of the hot pepper," a Cuna curing chant used against high fever, Sherzer (193) shows how the Cuna "hot pepper" taxonomy is projected onto a parallelistic verse pattern. The chanter inserts names for taxonomic categories into the verse pattern, beginning at the top of the hierarchy and moving down through a series of included subcategories, then returning to the top and moving down through another series of included subcategories, repeating this process through as many as 53 verses (193, pp. 283–84). Linde & Labov (123) describe the use by apartment dwellers of cognitive maps of the layouts of their apartments in producing "imaginary tour" narratives, and Harwood (88) discusses the use by Trobriand narrators of a spatial orientation schema representing locations in the Trobriand Islands as a mnemonic device in recounting particular myths and relating them to other myths in the totality of Trobriand mythology.

Event schemata that are used in producing narratives are generally referred to as story grammars or story schemata. They are global structures that break down into two major constituents: a setting subschema, which is comprised of a series of states specifying the time and place of the story, and an episode subschema, which is comprised of an external event and the protagonist's reaction to it (175). Episodes generally involve a problem-solving motif: something occurs that makes the protagonist set up a goal, which he or she attempts, successfully or unsuccessfully, to attain (171, 175). There have been many formulations of story schemata, which, although they vary in detail, generally incorporate this problem-solving motif (107, 130, 131, 162, 170, 171, 198, 204, 210). The EPISODE schema proposed by Rumelhart (170, 171, 175) is representative. This schema specifies relationships among several variables: an initiating EVENT, a GOAL, and an attempt, or TRY, to accomplish the goal. The TRY variable is a subschemata that specifies the internal structure of the attempt (or attempts) to attain the goal. It takes much the same form as the General Problem Solver proposed in Newell & Simon's (143) theory of problem-solving.

Rumelhart's (171, 175) story about Mary and the icecream truck illustrates this EPISODE schema.

> Mary heard the icecream truck coming down the street. She remembered her birthday money and she rushed into the house.

The major constitutents of this EPISODE are an EVENT (Mary HEARS the icecream truck), which initiates a GOAL (Mary WANTS icecream), which is the reason for a TRY (Mary TRIES to get icecream). The principal constituents of the TRY schema are an ACTION (selecting a problem-solving method, here BUYING) and a GOAL (the icecream). The BUY schema, it will be recalled, requires the BUYER to have MONEY (Mary rushes into the house and gets her birthday money) (171, pp. 271–73; 175, pp. 113–15).

The bulk of the story schema research is culture bound in that it is designed to account only for stories in the general European tradition (106). Though it is hardly news that story-telling traditions are quite different in non-Western societies, only a handful of studies have systematically examined cultural differences in story schemata (46–48, 106, 162). This work has, however, revealed specific differences in the way story schemata affect the comprehension and recall of stories. Particularly impressive is Rice's (162) demonstration that American college students recall American stories more accurately than Eskimo stories because the former fit their American story schema and the latter, which have their own distinctive structure, do not.

Story schemata, as described to this point, are hierarchical structures in which processing is top-down. A second approach to narrative comprehension concentrates on bottom-up processing. Schank (183, 184, 187, 188), the leading proponent of this approach, argues that stories are interpreted not only in terms of high level schemata like SETTING and EPISODE, but more importantly in terms of the stereotyped sequences of actions that comprise scripts. The restaurant script, for example, is invoked in interpreting the following simple story:

> John went to a restaurant. He ordered chicken. He left a large tip. (188, pp. 47–48)

Mention in the story of a *restaurant* and the actions of *ordering* and *tipping* is sufficient environmental input to instantiate the restaurant script. On the basis of this instantiation, the story is understood more fully than it is represented in the three sentences. Actions not mentioned in the story are supplied as default values of script variables, so the story is interpreted as

> John went to a restaurant. He sat down. He read the menu. He ordered chicken. He ate the chicken. He left a large tip. He paid the check. He left the restaurant (188, p. 48).

Gaps in the causal chain linking actions in the event are filled in by inferences made on the basis of knowledge represented in the script. It is explicitly stated in the story that John ENTERED the restaurant and ORDERED chicken, so it may be inferred that in between these actions he SAT down and READ the menu; it is also specified that John, having ORDERED chicken, TIPPED the waitress, so it may be inferred that he ATE the chicken; and because TIPPING precedes PAYING and LEAVING, it may be inferred that John EXITED the restaurant (188, p. 48). "The waitress," "the menu," and "the check," which are not mentioned in the story, are included in the inferred account because knowledge of the roles and props (i.e. agents, recipients, instruments, etc) involved in restaurant events is also contained in the script.

Inference is a major topic in discourse analysis, to which investigators working in several traditions have contributed (5, 86, 87, 113, 114, 157, 176, 178, 191, 192, 196, 200). In addition to Schank's (183–188) pioneering work, schema theory research on inferences and event chains has been done by Warren, et al (213), who have developed an "inference taxonomy," a classification of mutually exclusive categories of inferences, including three major types of inferences and a number of subtypes: logical inferences (motivation, psychological cause, physical cause, and enablement), informational inferences (pronominal, referential, spatiotemporal, world frame, and elaborative), and value inferences (evaluative). In discussing a particularly detailed ethnographic example, Trobriand litigation discourse, Hutchins (95, 96) describes a general schema for possession and transfer of land tenure rights, showing how actions and logical connectives that are only implicit in discourse about land tenure cases are supplied by inferences made on the basis of cultural knowledge represented in the general schema. Quinn (160) provides a detailed critical review of Hutchins' contribution to the continuing development of schema theory in cognitive anthropology.

CONCLUSION

The preceding sections have described schema theory and its wide range of applicability in cognitive anthropological research. Research and results from many seemingly disparate fields of cognitive study have been drawn together and discussed in terms of a single, comprehensive and coherent, explanatory framework. New work in cognitive anthropology specifically guided by schema theory has been considered and familiar work has been reconsidered in light of this perspective. One conclusion suggested by this review is that schema theory offers a broad, unified theoretical framework that has the potential to integrate research in cognitive anthropology and cognitive science generally. Although already evincing some of this enormous promise, schema theory is still in the early stages of its development. At present, it is undoubtedly overly powerful and too general. It is invoked in providing accounts of a great many different kinds of data, often in a way that does not take into consideration the particularity of specific aspects of cognitive organization and processing. The work of the next few years hopefully will fill in the details of a unified schema theory and specify the factors that constrain the structure and function of specific varieties of schemata. A second conclusion, then, is that the development of schema theory offers a very exciting prospect for future research in cognitive anthropology.

ACKNOWLEDGMENTS

A number of people were kind enough to read a draft of this review and offer responses, reactions, criticisms, suggestions, and bibliographic information. I want particularly to thank Michael Agar, Keith Basso, Roy D'Andrade, Charles Frake, Naomi Quinn, and Stephen Tyler. This review has benefited in many ways from advice offered by these individuals, but they are in no way to be blamed for any errors or infelicities of thought or expression committed in the review. These are my fault entirely.

Literature Cited

1. Abelson, R. P. 1975. Concepts for representing mundane reality in plans. See Ref. 21, pp. 273–309
2. Abelson, R. P. 1976. Script processing in attitude formation and decision-making. In *Cognition and Social Behavior,* ed. J. S. Carrol, J. W. Payne, pp. 33–45. Hillsdale, NJ: Erlbaum
3. Agar, M. 1974. Talking about doing: Lexicon and event. *Lang. Soc.* 3:83–89. See Ref. 37, pp. 114–20
4. Agar, M. 1975. Cognition and events. See Ref. 178, pp. 41–56
5. Agar, M. 1980. Stories, background knowledge and themes: Problems in the analysis of life history narrative. *Am. Ethnol.* 7:223–39
6. Andersen, E. S. 1978. Lexical universals of body-part terminology. In *Universals of Human Language.* Vol. 3: *Word Structure,* ed. J. H. Greenberg, C. A. Ferguson, E. A. Moravcsik, pp. 335–68. Stanford, Calif: Stanford Univ. Press
7. Bartlett, F. C. 1932. *Remembering: A Study in Experimental and Social Psychology.* Cambridge: Cambridge Univ. Press
8. Basso, K. H. 1967. Semantic aspects of linguistic acculturation. *Am. Anthropol.* 69:471–77
9. Basso, K. H. 1976. 'Wise Words' of the Western Apache: Metaphor and semantic theory. See Ref. 11, pp. 93–121, Ref. 37, pp. 244–67
10. Basso, K. H. 1979. *Portraits of "the Whiteman": Linguistic Play and Cultural Symbols among the Western Apache.* Cambridge: Cambridge Univ. Press
11. Basso, K. H., Selby, H. A., eds. 1976. *Meaning in Anthropology.* Albuquerque: Univ. New Mexico Press
12. Bateson, G. 1972. A theory of play and fantasy. In *Steps to an Ecology of Mind,* ed. G. Bateson, pp. 177–93. New York: Ballantine
13. Bauman, R., Sherzer, J. 1975. The ethnography of speaking. *Ann. Rev. Anthropol.* 4:95–119
14. Bean, S. S. 1975. Referential and indexical meanings of *amma* in Kannada: Mother, woman, goddess, pox, and help! *Southwest J. Anthropol.* 31:313–30. See Ref. 37, pp. 188–202
15. Berlin, B. 1972. Speculations on the growth of ethnobotanical nomenclature. *Lang. Soc.* 1:51–86
16. Berlin, B. 1976. The concept of rank in ethnobiological classification: Some evidence from Aguaruna folk botany. *Am. Ethnol.* 3:381–99. See Ref. 37, pp. 92–113
17. Berlin, B. 1978. Ethnobiological classification. See Ref. 166, pp. 9–26
18. Berlin, B., Breedlove, D. E., Raven, P. H. 1974. *Principles of Tzeltal Plant Classification: An Introduction to the Botanical Ethnography of a Mayan-Speaking People of Highland Chiapas.* New York: Academic
19. Berlin, B., Boster, J. S., O'Neill, J. P. 1981. The perceptual basis of ethnobiological classification: Evidence from Aguaruna Jivaro ornithology. *J. Ethnobiol.* 1:95–108
20. Berlin, B., Kay, P. 1969. *Basic Color Terms: Their Universality and Evolution.* Berkeley: Univ. Calif. Press
21. Bobrow, D. G., Collins, A., eds. 1975. *Representation and Understanding: Some Studies in Cognitive Science.* New York: Academic
22. Bobrow, D. G., Norman, D. A. 1975. Some principles of memory schemata. See Ref. 21, pp. 131–49
23. Bower, G. H. 1970. Analysis of a mnemonic device. *Am. Sci.* 58:496–510
24. Bower, G. H., Black, J. B., Turner, T. J. 1979. Scripts in memory for texts. *Cogn. Psychol.* 11:177–220
25. Brown, C. H. 1976. General principles of human anatomical partonomy and speculations on the growth of parton-

omic nomenclatures. *Am. Ethnol.* 3: 400–24

26. Brown, C. H. 1977. Folk botanical life-forms: Their universality and growth. *Am. Anthropol.* 79:317–42

27. Brown, C. H. 1979. Folk zoological life-forms: Their universality and growth. *Am. Anthropol.* 81:791–817

28. Brown, C. H. 1979. Growth and development of folk botanical life-forms in the Mayan language family. *Am. Ethnol.* 6:366–85. See Ref. 37, pp. 329–52

29. Brown, C. H., Witkowski, S. R. 1982. Growth and development of folk zoological life-forms in the Mayan language family. *Am. Ethnol.* 9:97–112

30. Bruner, E. M. 1983. Ethnography as narrative. In *The Anthropology of Experience*, ed. V. Turner, E. M. Bruner. In press

31. Burton, M. L., Kirk, L. 1979. Ethno classification of body parts: A three-culture study. *Anthropol. Ling.* 21: 379–99

32. Burton, M. L., Romney, A. K. 1975. A multidimensional representation of role terms. *Am. Ethnol.* 2:397–407

33. Bybee, J. L., Slobin, D. I. 1982. Rules and schemas in the development and use of the English past tense. *Language* 58:265–89

34. Cantor, N., Mischel, W. 1979. Prototypes in person perception. *Adv. Exp. Soc. Psychol.* pp. 3–52

35. Casagrande, J. B., Hale, K. L. 1967. Semantic relations in Papago folk definitions. In *Studies in Southwestern Ethnolinguistics*, ed. D. Hymes, W. E. Bittle, pp. 168–93. The Hague: Mouton

36. Casson, R. W. 1981. The semantics of kin term usage: Transferred and indirect metaphorical meaning. See Ref. 37, pp. 230–44

37. Casson, R. W., ed. 1981. *Language, Culture, and Cognition: Anthropological Persepctives*. New York: Macmillan

38. Chafe, W. L. 1970. *Meaning and the Structure of Language*. Chicago: Univ. Chicago Press

39. Chafe, W. L. 1977. Creativity in verbalization and its implications for the nature of stored knowledge. See Ref. 75, pp. 41–55

40. Chafe, W. L. 1977. The recall and verbalization of past experience. See Ref. 50, pp. 215–46

41. Chafe, W. L. 1979. The flow of thought and the flow of language. See Ref. 79, pp. 151–89

42. Chafe, W. L., ed. 1980. *The Pear Stories: Cognitive, Cultural, and Linguistic Aspects of Narrative Production*. Norwood, NJ: Ablex

43. Clark, E. V., Clark, H. H. 1978. Universals, relativity, and language processing. In *Universals of Human language*, Vol. 1: *Method and Theory*, ed. J. H. Greenberg, C. A. Ferguson, E. A. Moravcsik, pp. 225–77. Stanford, Calif: Stanford Univ. Press

44. Clark, H. H. 1973. Space, time, semantics, and the child. See Ref. 139, pp. 27–63

45. Cofer, C. H., ed. 1976. *The Structure of Human Memory*. San Francisco: Freeman

46. Colby, B. N. 1973. A partial grammar of Eskimo folktales. *Am. Anthropol.* 75:645–62

47. Colby, B. N. 1975. Culture grammars. *Science* 187:913–19

48. Colby, B. N. 1978. Plot component and symbolic component in extended discourse. See Ref. 124, pp. 99–110

49. Colby, B. N., Fernandez, J. W., Kronenfeld, D. B. 1981. Toward a convergence of cognitive and symbolic anthropology. *Am Ethnol.* 8:422–50

50. Cole, R. W., ed. 1977. *Current Issues in Linguistic Theory*. Bloomington: Indiana Univ. Press

51. Coleman, L., Kay, P. 1981. Prototype semantics. *Language* 57:26–44

52. Collins, A. M., Loftus, E. F. 1975. A spreading activation theory of semantic processing. *Psychol. Rev.* 82:407–28

53. Collins, A. M., Quillian, M. R. 1969. Retrieval time from semantic memory. *J. Verb. Learn. Verb. Behav.* 8:240–47

54. Cooper, W. E., Ross, J. R. 1975. World order. In *Papers from the Parasession on Functionalism.* ed. R. E. Grossman, J. San, T. J. Vance, pp. 63–111. Chicago: Chicago Ling. Soc.

55. D'Andrade, R. G. 1976. A propositional analysis of U.S. American beliefs about illness. See Ref. 11, pp. 155–80

56. D'Andrade, R. G. 1979. Culture and cognitive science. Memorandum to Cognitive Science Committee, Sloan Foundation

57. D'Andrade, R. G. 1981. The cultural part of cognition. *Cogn. Sci.* 5:179–95

58. Dougherty, J. W. D. 1978. Salience and relativity in classification. *Am. Ethnol.* 5:66–80. See Ref. 37, pp. 163–80

59. Dougherty, J. W. D., Keller, C. M. 1982. Taskonomy: A practical approach to knowledge structures. *Am. Ethnol.* 9:763–74

60. Dressler, W. U., ed. 1978. *Current Trends in Textlinguistics*. Berlin/New York: de Gruyter

61. Ekman, P., Öster, H. 1979. Facial expression of emotion. *Ann. Rev. Psychol.* 30:527–54

62. Ellen, R. F. 1977. Anatomical classification and the semiotics of the body. In *The Anthropology of the Body*, ed. J. Blacking, pp. 343–73. London: Academic

63. Evens, M. W., Litowitz, B. E., Markowitz, J. A., Smith, R. N., Werner, O. 1980. *Lexical-Semantic Relations: A Comparative Survey*. Carbondale, Ill: Ling. Res.

64. Farkas, D., Jacobsen, W. M., Todrys, K. W., eds. 1978. *Parasession on the Lexicon: Papers from the Chicago Linguistic Society*. Chicago: Chicago Ling. Soc.

65. Fillmore, C. J. 1968. The case for Case. In *Universals in Linguistic Theory*, ed. E. Bach, R. Harms. New York: Holt, Rinehart & Winston

66. Fillmore, C. J. 1975. An alternative to checklist theories of meaning. *Proc. Ann. Meet. Berkeley Ling. Soc.* 1:123–31

67. Fillmore, C. J. 1976. Frame semantics and the nature of language. *Ann. NY Acad. Sci.* 280:20–32

68. Fillmore, C. J. 1977. The case for Case reopened. In *Syntax and Semantics*, Vol. 8: *Grammatical Relations*, ed. P. Cole, J. Sadock, pp. 59–81. New York: Academic

69. Fillmore, C. J. 1977. Topics in lexical semantics. See Ref. 50, pp. 76–138

70. Fillmore, C. J. 1978. The organization of semantic information in the lexicon. See Ref. 64, pp. 148–73

71. Frake, C. O. 1964. A structural description of Subanun "religious behavior." See Ref. 85, pp. 111–29

72. Frake, C. O. 1964. How to ask for a drink in Subanun. *Am. Anthropol.* 66 (2):127–32

73. Frake, C. O. 1975. How to enter a Yakan house. See Ref. 178, pp. 25–40

74. Frake, C. O. 1977. Plying frames can be dangerous: Some reflections on methodology in cognitive anthropology. *Q. Newsl. Inst. Comp. Hum. Dev.* 1(3):1–7. See Ref. 37, pp. 366–77

75. Freedle, R. O., ed. 1977. *Discourse Production and Comprehension*. Norwood, NJ: Ablex

76. Freedle, R. O., ed. 1979. *New Directions in Discourse Processing*. Norwood, NJ: Ablex

77. Friedrich, P. 1970. Shape in grammar. *Language* 46:379–407

78. Gentner, D. 1975. Evidence for the psychological reality of semantic components: The verbs of possession. See Ref. 149, pp. 211–46

79. Givón, T., ed. 1979. *Syntax and Semantics*, Vol. 12: *Discourse and Syntax*. New York: Academic

80. Gladwin, H. 1974. *Semantics, schemata, and kinship*. Presented at Mathematics in Social Sciences Board Conf., Riverside, Calif., 1972

81. Gladwin, T. 1970. *East Is a Big Bird*. Cambridge: Harvard Univ. Press

82. Goffman, E. 1974. *Frame Analysis: An Essay on the Organization of Experience*. Cambridge: Harvard Univ. Press

83. Goldstein, I., Papert, S. 1977. Artificial intelligence, language, and the study of knowledge. *Cogn. Sci.* 1:84–123

84. Goodenough, W. H. 1967. Componential analysis. *Science* 156:1203–9

85. Goodenough, W. H., ed. 1964. *Explorations in Cultural Anthropology*. New York: McGraw-Hill

86. Gumperz, J. J. 1982. The linguistic bases of communicative competence. See Ref. 202, pp. 323–34

87. Gumperz, J. J. 1982. *Discourse Strategies*. New York: Cambridge Univ. Press

88. Harwood, F. 1976. Myth, memory, and the oral tradition: Cicero in the Trobriands. *Am. Anthropol.* 78:783–96

89. Hastie, R. 1981. Schematic principles in human memory. See Ref. 92, pp. 39–88

90. Hays, T. E. 1979. Plant classification and nomenclature in Ndumba, Papua New Guinea Highlands. *Ethnology* 18:253–70

91. Heider, E. R. 1972. Probabilities, sampling, and ethnographic method: The case of Dani color names. *Man* 7:448–66

92. Higgins, E. T., Herman, C. P., Zanna, M. P., eds. 1981. *Social Cognition: The Ontario Symposium*, Vol. 1. Hillsdale, NJ: Erlbaum

93. Hunn, E. S. 1977. *Tzeltal Folk Zoology: The Classification of Discontinuities in Nature*. New York: Academic

94. Hunt, M. 1982. *The Universe Within: A New Science Explores the Human Mind*. New York: Simon & Schuster

95. Hutchins, E. 1979. Reasoning in Trobriand discourse. *Q. Newsl. Lab. Comp. Hum. Cognit.* 1:13–17. See Ref. 37, pp. 481–89

96. Hutchins, E. 1980. *Culture and Inference: A Trobriand Case Study*. Cambridge: Harvard Univ. Press

97. Hymes, D. 1974. *Foundations in Sociolinguistics: An Ethnographic Approach*. Philadelphia: Univ. Penn. Press

98. Jackendoff, R. 1976. Toward an explanatory semantic representation. *Ling. Inq.* 7:89–150

99. Johnson, M., ed. 1981. *Philosophical Perspectives on Metaphor*. Minneapolis: Univ. Minn. Press

100. Johnson-Laird, P. N. 1980. Mental models in cognitive science. *Cogn. Sci.* 4:71–115; see Ref. 145, pp. 147–91

101. Johnson-Laird, P. N., Wason, P. C., eds. 1977. *Thinking: Readings in Cognitive Science*. London: Cambridge Univ. Press

102. Kay, P. 1978. Tahitian words for race and class. *Publ. Soc. Océanistes* 39:81–93

103. Kay, P., McDaniel, C. K. 1978. The linguistic significance of the meanings of basic color terms. *Language* 54:610–46

104. Kempton, W. 1978. Category grading and taxonomic relations: A mug is a sort of a cup. *Am. Ethnol.* 5:44–65. See Ref. 37, pp. 205–30

105. Kempton, W. 1981. *The Folk Classification of Ceramics: A Study of Cognitive Prototypes*. New York: Academic

106. Kintsch, W., Greene, E. 1978. The role of culture specific schemata in the comprehension and recall of stories. *Discourse Processes* 1:1–13

107. Kintsch, W., van Dijk, T. A. 1978. Toward a model of text comprehension and production. *Psychol. Rev.* 85:363–94

108. Kirk, L., Burton, M. L. 1977. Meaning and context: A study of contextual shifts in meaning of Maasai personality descriptors. *Am. Ethnol.* 4:734–61

109. Kronenfeld, D. B., Armstrong, J. D., Wilmoth, S. 1981. *Exploring the Internal Structure of Linguistic Categories: An Extensionist Semantic View*. Unpublished manuscript

110. Kuipers, B. 1978. Modeling spatial knowledge. *Cogn. Sci.* 2:129–53

111. Labov, W. 1973. The boundaries of words and their meanings. In *New Ways of Analyzing Variation in English*, ed. C-J. N. Bailey, R. W. Shuy, pp. 340–73. Washington DC: Georgetown Univ. Press

112. Labov, W. 1978. Denotational structure. See Ref. 64, pp. 220–60

113. Labov, W. 1982. Speech actions and reactions in personal narratives. See Ref. 202, pp. 219–47

114. Labov, W., Fanshel, D. 1977. *Therapeutic Discourse: Psychotherapy as Conversation*. New York: Academic

115. Lakoff, G. 1970. *Irregularity in Syntax*. New York: Holt, Rinehart & Winston

116. Lakoff, G. 1972. Hedges: A study in meaning criteria and the logic of fuzzy concepts. In *Pap. 8th Reg. Meet., Chicago Linguistic Soc.*, ed. P. M. Peranteau, J. N. Levi, G. C. Phares, pp. 183–228. Chicago: Chicago Ling. Soc.

117. Lakoff, G. 1977. Linguistic Gestalts. In *Pap. 13th Reg. Meet., Chicago Linguistic Soc.*, ed. W. A. Beach, S. E. Fox, S. Philosoph, pp. 236–87. Chicago: Chicago Ling. Soc.

117a. Lakoff, G. 1982. *Categories and Cognitive Models*. Berkeley Cogn. Sci. Rep. No. 2. Berkeley: Univ. Calif. Cogn. Sci. Program

118. Lakoff, G., Johnson, M. 1980. The metaphorical structure of the human conceptual system. *Cogn. Sci.* 4:195–208. See Ref. 145, pp. 193–208

119. Lakoff, G., Johnson, M. 1980. *Metaphors We Live By*. Chicago: Univ. Chicago Press

120. Langacker, R. W. 1979. Grammar as image. *Ling. Notes from LaJolla* 6:88–126

121. Langacker, R. W. 1982. Space grammar, analysability, and the English passive. *Language* 58:22–80

122. Leech, G. 1974. *Semantics*. Baltimore: Penguin

123. Linde, C., Labov, W. 1975. Spatial Networks as a site for the study of language and thought. *Language* 51:924–39

124. Loflin, M. D., Silverberg, J., eds. 1978. *Discourse and Inference in Cognitive Anthropology: An Approach to Psychic Unity and Enculturation*. The Hague: Mouton

125. Lounsbury, F. G. 1964. The formal analysis of Crow- and Omaha-type kinship terminologies. See Ref. 85, pp. 351–93

126. Lounsbury, F. G. 1965. Another view of the Trobriand kinship categories. *Am. Anthropol.* 67 (5, Pt. 2):142–85

127. Lounsbury, F. G. 1969. Language and culture. In *Language and Philosophy: A Symposium*, ed. S. Hook, pp. 3–29. New York: New York Univ. Press

128. Lutz, C. 1982. The domain of emotion words on Ifaluk. *Am. Ethnol.* 9:113–28

129. Lynch, K. 1960. *The Image of the City*. Cambridge: MIT Press

130. Mandler, J. M. 1978. A code in the node: The use of a story schema in retrieval. *Discourse Processes* 1:14–35

131. Mandler, J. M., Johnson, N. S. 1977. Remembrance of things parsed: Story structure and recall. *Cogn. Psychol.* 9:111–51

132. Markus, H. 1977. Self-schemata and processing information about the self. *J. Pers. Soc. Psychol.* 35:63–78

133. McCawley, J. D. 1976. *Grammar and Meaning: Papers on Syntactic and Semantic Topics*. New York: Academic

134. McClure, E. 1976. Ethnoanatomy in a multilingual community: An analysis of semantic change. *Am. Ethnol.* 3:525–42

135. McDermott, R. P., Gospodinoff, K., Aron, J. 1978. Criteria for an ethnographically adequate description of concerted activities and their contexts. *Semiotica* 24:245–75. See Ref. 37, pp. 377–99

136. Mervis, C. B., Rosch, E. 1981. Categorization of natural objects. *Ann. Rev. Psychol.* 32:89–115

137. Miller, G. A. 1978. Semantic relations among words. In *Linguistic Theory and Psychological Reality*, ed. M. Halle, J. Bresnan, G. A. Miller, pp. 60–118. Cambridge: MIT Press

138. Minsky, M. 1975. A framework for representing knowledge. In *The Psychology of Computer Vision*, ed. P. H. Winston, pp. 211–77. New York: McGraw-Hill

139. Moore, T. E., ed. *Cognitive Development and the Acquisition of Language.* New York: Academic

140. Moyne, J. A., Kaniklidis, C. 1981. Models of language comprehension. *Cogn. Brain Theory* 4:265–84

141. Munro, A. 1975. Linguistic theory and the LNR structural representation. See Ref. 149, pp. 88–113

142. Neisser, U. 1976. *Cognition and Reality: Principles and Implications of Cognitive Psychology.* San Francisco: Freeman

143. Newell, A., Simon, H. A. 1972. *Human Problem Solving.* Englewood Cliffs, NJ: Prentice-Hall

144. Norman, D. A. 1980. Twelve issues for cognitive science. *Cogn. Sci.* 4:1–32. See Ref. 145, pp. 265–95

145. Norman, D. A., ed. 1981. *Perspectives on Cognitive Science: The LaJolla Conference.* Norwood, NJ: Ablex

146. Norman, D. A., Bobrow, D. G. 1975. On data-limited and resource-limited processing. *Cogn. Psychol.* 7:44–64

147. Norman, D. A., Bobrow, D. G. 1976. On the role of active memory processes in perception and cognition. See Ref. 45, pp. 114–32

148. Norman, D. A., Bobrow, D. G. 1979. Descriptions: An intermediate stage in memory retrieval. *Cogn. Psychol.* 11:107–23

149. Norman, D. A., Rumelhart, D. E., LNR Research Group. 1975. *Explorations in Cognition.* San Francisco: Freeman

150. Oakley, K. 1977. Inference, navigation, and cognitive maps. See Ref. 101, pp. 537–47

151. Ortony, A. 1978. Remembering, understanding, and representation. *Cogn. Sci.* 2:53–69

152. Ortony, A. 1979. Beyond literal similarity. *Psychol. Rev.* 86:161–80

153. Ortony, A. 1979. The role of similarity in similes and metaphors. See Ref. 155, pp. 186–201

154. Ortony, A. 1980. Metaphor. See Ref. 196, pp. 349–65

155. Ortony, A., ed. 1979. *Metaphor and Thought.* Cambridge: Cambridge Univ. Press

156. Ortony, A., Reynolds, R., Arter, J. 1978. Metaphor: Theoretical and empirical research. *Psychol. Bull.* 85:919–43

157. Psathas, G., ed. 1979. *Everyday Language: Studies in Ethnomethodology.* New York: Irvington

158. Pylyshyn, Z. W. 1980. Computation and cognition: Issues in the foundations of cognitive science. *Behav. Brain Sci.* 3:111–69

159. Quinn, N. 1982. "Commitment" in American marriage: A cultural analysis. *Am. Ethnol.* 9:775–98

160. Quinn, N. 1982. Cognitive anthropology comes of age in the Trobriands. *Rev. Anthropol.* 9:299–311

160a. Quinn, N. 1982. Understanding the experience of marriage in our culture. Unpublished manuscript.

161. Reddy, M. J. 1979. The conduit metaphor—A case of frame conflict in our language about language. See Ref. 155, pp. 284–324

162. Rice, G. E. 1980. On cultural schemata. *Am. Ethnol.* 7:152–71

163. Rosch, E. 1973. On the internal structure of perceptual and semantic categories. See Ref. 139, pp. 111–44

164. Rosch, E. 1977. Human categorization. In *Advances in Cross-Cultural Psychology*, ed. N. Warren, 1:1–49. New York: Academic

165. Rosch, E. 1978. Principles of categorization. See Ref. 166, pp. 27–48

166. Rosch, E., Lloyd, B. B., eds. 1978. *Cognition and Categorization.* Hillsdale, NJ: Erlbaum

167. Rosch, E., Mervis, C. B. 1975. Family resemblances: Studies in the internal structure of categories. *Cogn. Psychol.* 7:573–605

168. Rosch, E., Mervis, C. B., Gay, W., Johnson, D., Boyes-Braem, P. 1976. Basic objects in natural categories. *Cogn. Psychol.* 8:382–439

169. Ross, J. R. 1972. Act. In *Semantics of Natural Language*, ed. D. Davidson, G. Harman, pp. 70–126. Dortrecht, Holland: Reidel

170. Rumelhart, D. E. 1975. Notes on a schema for stories. See Ref. 21, pp. 211–36

171. Rumelhart, D. E. 1977. Understanding and summarizing brief stories. In *Basic Processes in Reading: Perception and Comprehension*, ed. D. LaBerge, S. J. Samuels, pp. 265–303. Hillsdale, NJ: Erlbaum

172. Rumelhart, D. E. 1979. Some problems with the notion of literal meanings. See Ref. 155, pp. 78–90

173. Rumelhart, D. E. 1980. Schemata: The building blocks of cognition. See Ref. 196, pp. 33–58

174. Rumelhart, D. E., Norman, D. A. 1975. The active structural network. See Ref. 149, pp. 35–64

175. Rumelhart, D. E., Ortony, A. 1977. The representation of knowledge in memory. In *Schooling and the Acquisition of Knowledge*, ed. R. C. Anderson, R. J. Spiro, W. E. Montague, pp. 99–135. Hillsdale, NJ: Erlbaum

176. Sacks, H. 1972. An initial investigation of the usability of conversational data for doing sociology. See Ref. 200, pp. 31–74

177. Sacks, S., ed. 1979. *On Metaphor*. Chicago: Univ. Chicago Press

178. Sanches, M., Blount, B., eds. 1975. *Sociocultural Dimensions of Language Use*. New York: Academic

179. Sanjek, R. 1977. Cognitive maps of the ethnic domain in urban Ghana: Reflections on variability and change. *Am. Ethnol.* 4:603–22. See Ref. 37, pp. 305–28

180. Sapir, J. D. 1977. The anatomy of metaphor. See Ref. 181, pp. 3–32

181. Sapir, J. D., Crocker, J. C., eds. 1977. *The Social Use of Metaphor: Essays on the Anthropology of Rhetoric*. Philadelphia: Univ. Penn. Press

182. Schank, R. C. 1972. Conceptual dependency: A theory of natural language understanding. *Cogn. Psychol.* 3:552–631

183. Schank, R. C. 1975. The structure of episodes in memory. See Ref. 21, pp. 237–72

184. Schank, R. C. 1976. The role of memory in language processing. See Ref. 45, pp. 162–89

185. Schank, R. C. 1980. Language and memory. *Cogn. Sci.* 4:243–84. See Ref. 145, pp. 105–46

186. Schank, R. C. 1981. Failure-driven memory. *Cognit. Brain Theory* 4:41–60

187. Schank, R. C., Abelson, R. P. 1975. Scripts, plans, and knowledge. See Ref. 101, pp. 421–32

188. Schank, R. C., Abelson, R. P. 1977. *Scripts, Plans, Goals, and Understanding: An Enquiry into Human Knowledge Structures*. Hillsdale, NJ: Erlbaum

189. Scheffler, H. W. 1982. Theory and method in social anthropology: On the structures of systems of kin classification. *Am. Ethnol.* 9:167–84

190. Scheffler, H. W., Lounsbury, F. G. 1971. *A Study in Structural Semantics: The Siriono Kinship System*. Englewood Cliffs, NJ: Prentice-Hall

191. Schegloff, E. A. 1972. Notes on a conversational practice: Formulating place. See Ref. 200, pp. 75–119

192. Schenkein, J., ed. 1978. *Studies in the Organization of Conversational Interaction*. New York: Academic

193. Sherzer, J. 1977. Semantic systems, discourse structure, and the ecology of language. In *Studies in Language Variation: Semantics, Syntax, Phonology, Pragmatics, Social Situations, Ethnographic Approaches*, ed. R. W. Fasold, R. W. Shuy, pp. 283–93. Washington DC: Georgetown Univ. Press

194. Sherzer, J. 1983. *Kuna Ways of Speaking*. Austin: Univ. Texas Press

195. Smith, E. E. 1978. Theories of semantic memory. In *Handbook of Learning and Cognitive Processes*, Vol. 6: *Linguistic Functions in Cognitive Theory*, ed. W. K. Estes, pp. 1–56. Hillsdale, NJ: Erlbaum

196. Spiro, R. J., Bruce, B. C., Brewer, W. F., eds. 1980. *Theoretical Issues in Reading Comprehension: Perspectives from Cognitive Psychology, Linguistics, Artificial Intelligence, and Education*. Hillsdale, NJ: Erlbaum

197. Spradley, J. P. 1979. *The Ethnographic Interview*. New York: Holt, Rinehart & Winston

198. Stein, N. L., Glenn, C. G. 1979. An analysis of story comprehension in elementary school children. See Ref. 76, pp. 53–120

199. Steiner, C. 1974. *Scripts People Live*. New York: Bantam Books

200. Sudnow, D., ed. 1972. *Studies in Social Interaction*. New York: Free Press

201. Tannen, D. 1979. What's in a frame? Surface evidence for underlying expectations. See Ref. 76, pp. 137–81

202. Tannen, D., ed. 1982. *Analyzing Discourse: Text and Talk*. Washington DC: Georgetown Univ. Press

203. Taylor, S. E., Crocker, J. 1981. Schematic bases of social information processing. See Ref. 92, pp. 89–134

204. Thorndyke, P. W. 1977. Cognitive structures in comprehension and memory of narrative discourse. *Cogn. Psychol.* 9: 77–110

205. Thorndyke, P. W., Hayes-Roth, B. 1979. The use of schemata in the acquisition and transfer of knowledge. *Cogn. Psychol.* 11:82–106

206. Tourangeau, R., Sternberg, R. J. 1982. Understanding and appreciating metaphors. *Cognition* 11:203–44

207. Tulving, E. 1972. Episodic and semantic memory. In *Organization of Memory*, ed. E. Tulving, W. Donaldson, pp. 381–403. New York: Academic

208. Turner, V. 1980. Social dramas and stories about them. *Crit. Inq.* 7:141–68

209. Tyler, S. A. 1978. *The Said and the Un-*

said: Mind, Meaning, and Culture. New York: Academic

210. van Dijk, T. A. 1977. Text and Context: Explorations in the Semantics and Pragmatics of Discourse. London: Longman

211. Wallace, A. F. C. 1965. Driving to work. In Context and Meaning in Cultural Anthropology, ed. M. Spiro, pp. 277–92 New York: Free Press

212. Wallace, A. F. C. 1970. Culture and Personality. New York: Random House. 2nd ed.

213. Warren, W. H., Nicholas, D. W., Trabasso, T. 1979. Event chains and inferences in understanding narratives. See Ref. 76, pp. 23–52

214. Werner, O. 1978. The synthetic informant model on the simulation of large

lexical/semantic fields. See Ref. 124, pp. 45–82

215. White, G. M. 1980. Conceptual universals in interpersonal language. Am. Anthropol. 82:759–81

216. Wickelgren, W. A. 1981. Human learning and memory. Ann. Rev. Psychol. 32:21–52

217. Wierzbicka, A. 1972. Semantic Primitives. Frankfurt: Athenäum

218. Wierzbicka, A. 1980. Lingua Mentalis. Sidney/New York: Academic

219. Winograd, T. 1975. Frame representations and the declarative-procedural controversy. See Ref. 21, pp. 185–210

220. Witkowski, S. R., Brown, C. H. 1977. An explanation of color nomenclature universals. Am. Anthropol. 79:50–57

SUBJECT INDEX

A

Acclimatization
  and heat tolerance, 273–75,
    279
  to high altitude
    and disease, 298–99
Acculturation
  and social change
    among hunter-gatherers,
      209
Acheulean assemblages
  and time concepts, 188
Acheulean industries
  in Southern African prehis-
    tory, 28–32
  in Soviet archaeology, 414,
    419–20
  in West African prehistory,
    225–28
Achievement
  as American value, 53–54, 58
Acoustic sensing
  in archaeology, 119–20
Active structural networks
  see Schemata
Adaptability
  to altitude
    see High altitude
  to heat
    see Biological adaptations;
      Heat tolerance
Adaptive response
  in American ethnic groups,
    66
Adolescence
  and childhood
    high altitude effects on,
      289, 295–98
Adrar Bous site
  in West African prehistory,
    232–35
Aerial remote sensing
  in archaeology, 107–13, 121
Affixation theory
  and word formation, 360,
    362–63
Affluence
  among hunter-gatherers, 197–
    98
Africa
  artifact style studies, 126, 134
  southern
    Stone Age prehistory, 24–
    Soviet archaeology in, 407

West
  see West African prehistory
Afro-American English
  survey of, 335–52
    anthropological orientations,
      347–50
    conclusion, 351–52
    educational research, 339–
      43
    emerging topics, 350–51
    introduction to, 335–39
    linguistic analyses, 343–47
Age
  and heat tolerance, 275–76
  and high altitude effects, 298–
    301
Age profiles
  of animals
    and prehistoric subsistence
      studies, 38–42
Agricultural variation
  in New World
    see Prehistoric agricultural
      systems
Agriculture
  development of
    and labor requirements,
      197–98, 202
  origins of
    and time concepts, 185–86
    in West African prehistory,
      238–40
Albania
  sociocultural studies, 380,
    385–87
Alexandria Urban Archaeology
  Program
    and public responsibility, 159
Alliance networks
  and environmental change,
    180, 183–84, 187
Allophonic rules
  and word formation, 363–64
Altitude
  adaptation to
    see High altitude
American culture, 49–73
  collections and case studies,
    71–73
  consensus and continuity, 58–
    61
  diversity, conflict, and accom-
    modation, 64–67
  individualism and conformity,
    61–64

introduction to, 49–50
  languages, 70–71
  problem of women, 67–
    70
  special contexts, 55–58
  subjects of study, 50–55
American English
  as cultural expression, 71
  see also Afro-American En-
    glish; Black English;
      Black vernacular English
American Indian languages
  social context studies, 71
American Indians
  case studies of, 73
  and public archaeology pro-
    jects, 158
American Indian women
  studies of, 69
American Medical Association
  and growth of biomedicine,
    314
American Southwest
  artifact style studies in, 130–
    32, 136
Amish
  case study of, 72
Andes
  high altitude adaptation in,
    286, 288, 291, 293–96,
    298–300
  prehistoric agriculture in, 93–
    98
    irrigation, 93–96
    raised fields, 89
    sunken fields, 97
    terracing, 97–98
Animal ecology
  models from
    and hunter-gatherer studies,
      198–99
Animals
  classifications of
    and schemata, 441
Ann Arbor School District
  legal suit
    and language policy, 342–
      43
Appalachian community
  case study of, 72
Aqualithic industries
  in tropical Sahara, 230–32,
    234–36
Archaeological culture concept
  in Soviet theory, 415–19

463

CUMULATIVE INDEXES

CONTRIBUTING AUTHORS, VOLUMES 6–12

CHAPTER TITLES, VOLUMES 6–12

CULTURAL-SOCIAL ANTHROPOLOGY